For Stanley Shepherd

STATE, CONFLICT, AND DEMOCRACY IN AFRICA

EDITED BY
RICHARD JOSEPH

DISCARD

LYNNE
RIENNER
PUBLISHERS

BOULDER
LONDON

Published in the United States of America in 1999 by
Lynne Rienner Publishers, Inc.
1800 30th Street, Boulder, Colorado 80301

and in the United Kingdom by
Lynne Rienner Publishers, Inc.
3 Henrietta Street, Covent Garden, London WC2E 8LU

Library of Congress Cataloging-in-Publication Data
State, conflict, and democracy in Africa / edited by Richard Joseph.
    p. cm.
  Includes bibliographical references and index.
  ISBN 1-55587-799-0 (hc : alk. paper)—ISBN 1-55587-533-5 (pbk : alk. paper)
    1. Democracy—Africa. 2. Social conflict—Africa. 3. Africa—
Politics and government—1960– I. Joseph, Richard A.
JQ1879.A15S84 1998
320.96'09'045—dc21   98-6153
                                                                          CIP

British Cataloguing in Publication Data
A Cataloguing in Publication record for this book
is available from the British Library.

Printed and bound in the United States of America

The paper used in this publication meets the requirements
of the American National Standard for Permanence of
Paper for Printed Library Materials Z39.48-1984.

5 4 3 2 1

CONTENTS

Part 6   Conclusion

ACKNOWLEDGMENTS

Acknowledgments for a collaborative work of this nature can never be wholly complete. The span of time considered, and the sources of inspiration and information, can be contracted or extended. Of particular relevance was the resumption of democratic political competition in Nigeria, 1975–1983, which I was able to study closely. A distinct pattern of political behavior eventually eroded the efficacy and legitimacy of the Nigerian state and facilitated the resumption of power by the armed forces. Subsequently, as a program officer for the Ford Foundation, 1986–1988, I was able to observe similar forms of misrule throughout the west African region, and the widespread aspirations for a civil polity based on group accommodation and democratic participation.

The complexity of these processes, and the challenge of analyzing them adequately, required extensive collaboration among students of African politics. The Rockefeller Foundation, the Ford Foundation, and the Carnegie Corporation of New York shared this perspective and provided sustained support for the African Governance Program (AGP) of the Carter Center, which I directed from 1988 to 1994. In addition to officials and colleagues of the Carter Center and of Emory University, successive heads of Emory's Department of Political Science responded positively to the demands on my time necessitated by these investigations.

The twenty-one other scholars who wrote the chapters of this book represent a fraction of the colleagues originally consulted regarding this project. More than twice as many attended the Conference on African Renewal at the Massachusetts Institute of Technology (MIT), March 6–9, 1997, at which the original papers were discussed. The Ford Foundation and the Carnegie Corporation of New York supported my own research and writing from 1995 to 1997, and the United States Institute of Peace provided a research grant for a related project on armed conflict in Africa during this period.

I benefited greatly from the generosity and facilities of the Chr. Michelsen Institute in Bergen, Norway, and of MIT, whose Martin Luther King, Jr. Visiting Professorship provided appropriate sanction for these studies. The Foreign Ministries of the Netherlands and Denmark, the Global Coalition for Africa, and MIT's Offices of the Provost, Dean of Social Science and the Humanities, and head of the Department of Political Science all provided generous support for the Conference on African Renewal, which, in turn, contributed significantly to the realization of this project.

Even more arbitrary than the list of organizations whose assistance can be acknowledged is that of the many individuals who made this work possible. This book is dedicated to Stanley Shepherd, who, during the course of our spirited arguments three decades ago, first sparked my interest in African politics. All of my former associates, staff, and interns of the African Governance Program deserve suitable mention, albeit such a list would be too extensive for inclusion here. I will therefore limit specific acknowledgment to Steve Clinkenbeard, Natoschia Scruggs, Carolyn Logan, Ivan Sigal, Lois Malone, Sara Jane McCaffrey, Jessica Piombo, and Pamela Clements, who directly assisted me in this project at MIT, and to Aimee Lipschutz, Jane Winzer, and Raymond Hicks, who did likewise at Emory. No list would be complete, however, that did not include Willard Johnson, Jennifer Joseph, and Lynne Rienner, whose sustained support is primarily responsible for this book progressing beyond its initial conception.

Whatever its achievements and shortcomings, an important message of this study is that the challenges being confronted daily by the peoples of Africa—in state building, conflict prevention and resolution, and democratization—deserve more systematic analysis than can be accomplished with available resources, both material and human. I have learned enormously from my engagement with all the coauthors during the various stages in which our chapters evolved. I come away from this project with a heightened awareness of the complexities with which we grappled and of the greater effort required to truly master them. If this project provokes such an effort, that could be its most enduring achievement.

Richard Joseph

PART I

Overview

1

State, Conflict, and Democracy in Africa

RICHARD JOSEPH

There have been several false starts in Africa since the 1960s, when most countries on the continent achieved independence from colonial rule.[1] The chapters in this book will contribute to the eventual assessment of whether the 1990s reflect a new beginning or another series of false starts in Africa. The genesis of this project can be traced to the eve of the most recent global transformations. Several months before the upheavals in Eastern Europe that reverberated throughout the globe, a group of scholars met in Atlanta in February 1989 for the inaugural conference of the African Governance Program (AGP) of the Carter Center of Emory University to share their insights on the prospects for political renewal in sub-Saharan Africa.

A comparison of the report of that meeting, *Perestroika Without Glasnost in Africa,* with that of the Conference on African Renewal held at the Massachusetts Institute of Technology eight years later makes instructive reading.[2] At these two meetings, the central theme was the elusive political and economic renaissance in Africa. Hopes for a more democratic Africa were tentatively expressed in 1997, as they were in 1989, reflecting the fact that the euphoria of the early 1990s had ebbed. On the eve of these transformations, there had been little confidence that viable structures of democracy would be installed in Africa in the near future, so students of the continent pinned their hopes on the revitalizing of civil society, speculating that political reconstruction would germinate at the local level. By 1997, however, it was evident that even a vibrant civil society such as Nigeria's, or a nascent one such as Zambia's, could be suppressed by regimes determined to avoid democratization.

As a project, this book was first proposed during the 1989 AGP conference, and it was nurtured in a variety of smaller meetings and two major consultations organized by the AGP in 1990 and 1994.[3] Throughout this

3

period, the bulletin produced by the AGP, *Africa Demos,* monitored the many political openings on the continent and served as a forum for evaluating their progress. Because of the rapidity of political change after 1989, scholars were initially challenged to produce their analyses in the midst of these upheavals.[4] By the middle of the decade, the tempo of change had subsided, and a more measured and comprehensive analysis of these developments could be pursued. This book is a product of that exercise. All of the original papers have undergone several revisions based on a review process established among the scholars involved. Their main arguments were also subjected to further debate at the 1997 conference by a larger group of scholars that included several Africans based in African institutions.

The Reconstituting of Political Orders

How African political orders are constituted and reconstituted was one of the central themes of the 1997 conference. In 1989, Goran Hyden had proposed a conceptualization of governance as involving the "institutionalization of values and rights,"[5] but that formulation was overshadowed by the pace of change during the early 1990s. After several years of fitful attempts to redemocratize, however, the case for establishing the normative foundations for a viable democracy was bolstered by the inadequacy of transition exercises that had been devoted largely to the reintroduction of multiparty elections and the establishment of new legislatures and political parties. Hyden suggests that the diverse peoples of African states must be able to perceive the emerging systems as connected in fundamental ways to their self-conception as communities, in addition to having their basic individual rights restored.

The general dissatisfaction with electoralist approaches to democratic transitions has led to the search for mechanisms that could bind societies together despite the renewal of partisan competition. John Harbeson explores the importance of pact making in such transitions, which has featured prominently in studies of southern Europe and South America. He suggests that the limited adoption of pacts in Africa may be a major deficiency in attempts to democratize. His preliminary analysis will be elaborated and refined during the course of further debate and research. It is widely acknowledged that the South African transition was propelled at each critical turn by agreements that took the form of foundational pacts. Equally apparent is the fact that South Africa's diverse economic and social communities, as well as the organizations that represent their interests in various configurations, have invested much effort in creating a normative foundation for the postapartheid political order. The continued success of that transition, despite the many challenges it faces, contrasts sharply with the contested authority of popularly elected governments in much of sub-Saharan Africa.

The "self-binding qualities" of stable polities, to use Hyden's expression, can be seen in several transitions since 1989. Bruce Magnusson, in his discussion of institutional design in Benin, demonstrates the extent to which that country's transition has benefited from the authority and efficacy of quite novel institutions, including the Constitutional Court. The merging of secular and sacral rites in the new political system reflects a blending of traditional and legal-rational norms. Such observations suggest the need, as Richard Sklar contends, for a broader approach to the study of how political power is validated. Sklar's emphasis on processes of "political invention and exchange," and on the importance of African peoples having considerable input into the design of their political systems, overlaps with Hyden's concerns.

Sklar demurs from the prevailing "democratic discourse" in suggesting that all that is "good in terms of political systems is not definable as democratic." In a parallel vein, Dele Olowu criticizes the overemphasis on urban politics by both democratic activists and students of these processes. He concurs with Sklar about the importance of examining informal as well as formal governing structures, and about the need to consider how chieftaincy and other traditional institutions provide a range of services at the local level and ensure continuity during periods of national political upheavals. Also pertinent is Deborah Brautigam's analysis of the "Mauritius miracle," as she demonstrates how the accommodationist practices devised in Mauritius enabled the different communities and social classes to experience a sense of inclusion and of sharing in the economy's growth, despite vigorous partisan competition and the periodic electoral defeat of incumbent governments.

Not all cases of political inclusion and accommodation are without drawbacks. Linda Beck contends that Senegal's "enlarged presidential majority" (EPM), which has permitted the Socialist Party of President Abdou Diouf to defuse sharp conflicts among political parties by selectively including their leaders in his cabinet, may represent more of a detour than a deepening of democracy. In some respects, the EPM can be regarded as a variation of the widespread African practice of co-opting opposition politicians by allowing them to share in resources controlled by the state. Although promoted as power sharing, the EPM may more accurately be described as "resource sharing." Diouf and the barons of his party have retained control of the main instruments of government, including the capacity to manipulate elections. The Senegalese political order has steered a path through the turmoil after each national election since 1988 by broadening the composition of the government while retaining power and authority firmly in the hands of the Socialist Party. Beck acknowledges, however, that a positive consequence of this detour has been the achievement of greater political peace, which has enhanced the attractiveness of the Senegalese economy to foreign and domestic investors.

Economic Liberalization and Democratization

In his comprehensive overview of democratization in Africa, Crawford Young identifies the analytical challenges that the post-1989 upheavals have provoked. In addition, he examines the advances and retreats during earlier attempts at democratization. While the experiences of the 1990s suggest "a slow, uneven, halting" movement toward democratic reforms, Young considers it unlikely that there will be a "widespread restoration of the unadulterated autocracy of the past." His assessment of the halfway house that many transitions will engender reflects the general consensus of the scholarly community.[6] Political liberalization that makes possible a freer press, greater respect for human rights, and open contestation is likely to yield semidemocracies in which political rules can be manipulated to make alternation in power improbable in most countries.

Young believes that semidemocratization is intimately connected to the pressure applied by the international system, prompting political openings that have consequently become "part of macroeconomic management to earn external approbation." Contemporary Africa, he points out, is "exceptionally tributary to the international system," and it therefore runs the risk of seeing democracy "derailed or trivialized." In a related vein, Thandika Mkandawire identifies a fundamental contradiction between dictation and choice in these transitions. "Choiceless democracies," he argues, are being fostered in Africa as part of a general strategy involving the imposition of neoliberal economic transformations via structural adjustment programs.[7] The implicit encouragement of authoritarian forms of governance is evident in these interactions, which promotes the installation of bureaucratic structures to implement "correct" policies. Eventually, accounting to external agencies takes the place of accountability to legislatures and the electorate, democratic decisionmaking processes are circumvented, and a resulting "cult of secrecy" discourages debate and dialogue. Ultimately, rather than being considered a good in itself, democracy is treated in an instrumentalist manner, and its promotion becomes dependent on shifting perceptions as to whether or not it is good for development.[8]

While Mkandawire considers the linkage of democratization with economic liberalization to be generally harmful in its consequences, Robert Bates views this nexus as fundamental and unavoidable. That democratization is connected to a broader process of economic reform is not, for Bates, an accidental occurrence. The previous patronage systems, in which the state controlled credits, permits, and foreign exchange, greatly distorted and weakened African economies. Externally imposed reforms of these economies devastated patronage networks and made possible a retreat from single-party rule. African regimes, according to Bates, must still negotiate principally with international donors who finance the transition to open markets, not with their citizenry to procure taxes, nor with a middle class that remains stunted in most countries. Both Bates and Mkandawire, while differing in their basic attitudes toward economic liberalization, recognize the limited scope for democracy building under conditions in which African regimes are not accountable to the populace and are not obliged to seek accommodation with domestic socioeconomic forces.

Nicolas van de Walle identifies other complicating features of the linkage among globalization, the promotion of private markets, and democratization. While he concurs with Mkandawire that the capacity of African governments to pursue independent economic policies has been undermined by external agencies, he contends that African countries are minimally involved in contemporary global transformations. The key issue for him remains Africa's marginalization from these dynamics. The enhanced mobility of private capital in the new global system has had a limited impact on Africa, whose relationship with the world economy can be characterized essentially in the same way it was in the nineteenth century, namely, as reflecting a pronounced reliance on commodity exports. Instead of decrying the subordination of Africa to the demands of globalization, the more urgent question for van de Walle is the identification of pathways for Africa's insertion into the world economy to enable it to benefit from major capital flows and international trade. Moreover, he regards the weakness of African states as a continuing impediment to development, as it is the state that must mediate the relationship between domestic and external economic forces.

State Power and Group Conflict

Democratic aspirations in Africa are also held hostage to the challenge confronting many countries to devise ways of accommodating group identities that are being simultaneously exacerbated by political liberalization. Jeffrey Herbst explores the increasing manipulation of citizenship requirements with the return to competitive party politics. Such actions may deprive whole communities of their nationality and, therefore, of the right to vote in elections. Often the target is more specific, as in Côte d'Ivoire and Zambia, where an incumbent regime seeks to block the candidacy of a particular opposition candidate and does so by denationalizing an entire ethnic or other sectional group. Herbst contends that such manipulations destabilize the polity, as they generate uncertainty regarding the future status of all minority groups in society. Citizenship is fundamental to both the legitimacy of the state and the prospects for democratic rule. When citizenship rules are altered for partisan purposes, both state and democracy are undermined.

In the case of Rwanda, which has become symbolic of the ultimate risk posed by heightened group conflict in Africa, Timothy Longman traces the course of the political opening in 1992 and the creation of a government of transition that heralded a shift from authoritarian rule to pluralist democracy. To foil these initiatives, the regime of Juvénal Habyarimana embarked on a campaign to neutralize the transethnic character of many civil society organizations by fomenting ethnic discord, which led inexorably to the genocide of 1994 and the country's continuing traumas. More generally, Marina Ottaway argues, "in much of Africa, ethnicity is not a problem until it is made a problem." Competitive party politics invites divisive tactics by aspirant politicians as well as by incumbent regimes. One of the paradoxes unveiled by democratic openings after 1989 is that they disrupt the practices of group accommodation by which authoritarian regimes had long co-opted elites from various communities without providing appropriate transitional mechanisms.

Traversing the bridge from authoritarian rule to democratic systems that would eventually function on the basis of inclusion, accommodation, and compromise has been rendered hazardous by the plural nature of most African societies and the scarcity of resources to ease the hardships caused by economic restructuring. Processes of regime transformation, as Herbst and Ottaway recognize, heighten ethnic considerations and provoke defensive postures by politically dominant groups. The return to competitive politics encourages parties to take on a sectional coloration that hinders the capacity of transitional governments to reflect and respect the identities of all groups. Where the political system allows for frank dialogue and negotiations, the evidence suggests that these issues should be addressed prior to the unleashing of full party competition. Don Rothchild, in his examination of countries that embarked on democratic transitions, as well as those seeking an exit from armed conflict, identifies alternate routes to be followed. In place of the manipulation of ethnicity by political elites that occurs when electoral outcomes entirely determine the allocation of power, pact making can greatly increase the probability of a peaceful transition. In countries emerging from prolonged authoritarian rule or a bruising civil war, the absence of trust in the institutions of government among large sections of the population should be directly tackled by creative statecraft. These analyses suggest two sequential phases in democratization. In the short run, achieving such trust may depend on the crafting of a modus vivendi among representatives of the nation's constitutive communities prior to, or at least commensurate with, the resumption of partisan electoral competition. In the long run, institutions of a pluralist democracy can be established to provide more formal mechanisms to foster group amity.

Scott Taylor's study of Zimbabwe is a reminder that ethnicity is not the only basis for inclusion and exclusion in African polities. An initially dynamic Indigenous Business Development Centre and black entrepreneurs who could eventually pose a challenge to white domination of the economy were treated by Robert Mugabe's regime as threats to the neopatrimonial state, despite the regime's verbal commitment to black empowerment. Mugabe, Zimbabwe's leader since independence in 1980, has repeatedly neutralized threats to his political dominance and that of his party. The country's democratic prospects have been further curtailed by the regime's unwillingness to permit the establishment of centers of power outside the state. The emergence of a domestic basis for a democratic transition in the form of market-based social forces, suggested by Bates, has therefore been thwarted in Zimbabwe through the use of state power to stifle such groups or keep them dependent on state patronage.

There are few countries that have engaged in as much constitutional engineering to promote the inclusion of diverse peoples as Nigeria since the mid-1970s. Much of that effort has come to naught, however, as the country was dominated by increasingly authoritarian military regimes since the overthrow of the Second Republic in December 1983.[9] Some of the preconditions for a peaceful democratic transition that were identified by Hyden, Ottaway, and Rothchild can be identified in the various experiments to promote political accommodation in Nigeria, such as the painstaking constitution-making exercise of 1975–1978. Since 1983, however, a contradictory project I have called a "multilayered hegemony" has woven together autocracy, sectionalism, privileged access to oil income, and control of the state's coercive instruments. Political scientists have often contended that "the more reinforced and correlated the sources of cleavage, the less the likelihood of political tolerance."[10] Similar observations have also been regularly cited by Nigerian governments during each transitional exercise while being contradicted in practice. As the military has been increasingly molded to reflect the political projects of autocratic leaders since 1983, it has simultaneously been converted into an instrument to defend their sectional interests. The convergence of these multiple processes transformed the Nigerian armed forces into the predominant barrier to the restoration of constitutional democracy.

The Promises and Pitfalls of Electoralism

Elections and democracy have become virtually synonymous in Western political thought and analysis. The most influential formulations of democracy emphasize the opportunities for the electorate to choose periodically among elites competing for political office. The emphasis on electoralism in post-1989 African transitions has also reflected the disproportionate role played by external forces in these developments. As Young points out, the need to satisfy foreign donors was one of the major inducements for African authoritarian regimes to open up their systems. Moreover, the most tangible demonstration that such a change had been initiated was the re-legalization of political parties and the holding of competitive elections.

An additional reason for the election-centric nature of African transitions is the usefulness of elections in helping bring an end to armed conflicts that have eluded resolution by negotiation. Elections provide combatants a way out of the stalemate of warfare. The risks that electoralism poses for countries seeking an exit from autocracy or war are counterbalanced by its indispensability in initiating a new democratic order. Several of the authors already mentioned have advanced perspectives that will be taken into consideration in reassessing the role of elections. Sklar proposes thinking of transition processes as involving elements of both institutional change and continuity, since all political systems possess democratic and nondemocratic features. Harbeson and Rothchild emphasize the need for preelectoral pacts that can play as much of a foundational role as inaugural elections, while Hyden insists on the need for a continuing process of intercommunal accommodation to sustain the new political systems.

The case of Namibia prompts Gretchen Bauer to examine that country's experiences from the perspective of what had been learned earlier in Africa. Namibia achieved independence in March 1990 following the victory of the South West Africa People's Organization (SWAPO) in elections organized and monitored by international organizations. SWAPO's complete dominance of the political system was further enhanced by its capture of more that 70 percent of the vote in national elections in December 1994. Bauer identifies the many signs of increasing authoritarianism in Namibian political life, which contrast with the persistent weakness of civic organizations and opposition parties. Unlike the situation in the rest of Africa during the immediate postcolonial period, however, there are now real international incentives that constrain dominant-party regimes, such as SWAPO's, from converting their de facto dominance into de jure single-party rule.

The chapter on Zambia by Michael Bratton and Dan Posner and that on Ghana by E. Gyimah-Boadi examine two highly contrasting cases. The electoral defeat in Zambia in October 1991 of the United National Independence Party, led by the country's longtime president, Kenneth Kaunda, was perhaps the most influential event in the first phase of the post-1989 transitions. Five years later, a rerun of these elections was marred by a partial opposition boycott, accusations of malfeasance, troubling questions about a foreign company contracted to provide technical assistance, and Kaunda's disqualification as a presidential candidate by the altering of citizenship requirements. The increasingly repressive actions of the ruling Movement for Multiparty Democracy toward its critics in the media and various interest groups have slowed Zambia's progress to a pluralist democracy. Bratton and Posner discuss these developments within the framework of a comparative study of the declining quality of second elections in Africa. Using Samuel Huntington's identification of alternation in government via elections as the critical indicator of democratic consolidation, they contend that the general failure to improve the quality of elections on the continent does not augur well for democracy building.

Gyimah-Boadi examines the Ghanaian elections of November 1996 in comparison to the highly contested elections four years earlier. Although the former military ruler, Jerry Rawlings, had won a decisive victory in the presidential contest in 1992, the opposition insisted that the vote was rigged, and it boycotted the subsequent parliamentary elections. However, in contrast to Zambia and most other African countries, Ghana experienced a significant improvement in the quality of its second election, which can be attributed to several factors: the return to constitutionalism and respect for governmental institutions; the capable leadership of the Electoral Commission by its chairperson, K. Afari-Gyan; the acceptance by the Rawlings government of the commission's autonomy, including decisions with which it disagreed; and the substantial support for electoral reform by overseas donors, especially Denmark and the United States. Despite these gains, Gyimah-Boadi identifies several shortcomings in the wider political process that affect election performance: the highly disproportionate resources available to the government in contrast to the opposition; the persistence of military structures established during the period of nonconstitutional governance; the overlap between the state and the ruling party; the self-dealing by the government in implementing economic reforms; and official distrust of autonomous civil society organizations.

The varying quality of elections in Africa is likely to continue to reflect the uneven democratic character of its political systems. For most countries, the prime purpose of elections will remain the legitimation of whatever regime currently holds governmental power. Africa has made advances in the apparent competitiveness of elections with the renewed participation of opposition parties. In few instances, however, do elections represent real opportunities for the populace to determine who governs. Elections in Africa are therefore far from being autonomous operations: they reflect the character of the political order and especially the degree of risk incumbents are willing to tolerate. Frederick Chiluba's government in Zambia would have been reelected just as that of Rawlings in Ghana without distorting the electoral process, but it chose a more contentious path. And while defeated dictators in Benin and Madagascar have succeeded in using the electoral process to regain power, autocratic regimes in Cameroon and Kenya continue to block election reforms, thereby denying their people any hope of political peace. If, according to Larry Diamond, electoral democracy is a prelude to liberal democracy, crossing that threshold has become more forbidding as Africa's recent wave of democratization recedes.[11]

Political Power and Institution Building

Of the many issues raised in this book, I will conclude this introduction by discussing two particularly critical ones: change and continuity in the exercise of political power; and the design and functioning of governmental institutions. In my chapter on the reconfiguration of power in Africa, I argue that scholars should be more attentive to the sense of direction, forward or backward, implicit in studies of democratization. While the pursuit of pluralist democracy will remain a major political project in Africa, it is not the only one. An adjusted framework of analysis is needed that takes account of the multiplicity of political projects, the multidirectionality of political trends, and change and continuity in how power is actually exercised.

Such a broader approach can enrich the study of democratization. Students of democracy often remind us that democracy is, fundamentally, about the exercise of power. According to Robert Dahl, "at a minimum, it seems to me, democratic theory is concerned with processes by which ordinary citizens exert a relatively high degree of control over leaders."[12] Other scholars have echoed this point: "democracy must, in our view, mean at a minimum a significant share of the many in political decision-making. . . . Our most basic assumption is that democracy is a matter of power and power-sharing."[13] In established Western democracies, democratic institutions have become the legitimate and central instruments in the exercise of political power. However, in Africa, as in many other areas of the world, such institutions may or may not achieve this status, depending on a variety of factors and contingencies.

An important feature of the exercise of power in late twentieth-century Africa that often eludes the "democracy discourse" is the informalization of both economic life and transnational relations. Some of the frustration that Bayo Olukoshi and other African scholars express about the models applied to Africa by their "Africanist" colleagues concerns the gap between the conceptual dichotomies currently in vogue and the flux and indeterminacy of socioeconomic life on the ground. In addition, Olukoshi suggests that the reconstruction or rehabilitation of the state in Africa is a subject deserving closer attention. His contention that private-sector development and sustainable democracies are contingent on the existence of effective and legitimate state structures is echoed in van de Walle's chapter. These views also coincide with the main conclusion of a collaborative study coordinated by Adam Przeworski that "without an effective state, there can be no democracy and no markets."[14] Olukoshi and Przeworski express an almost identical sense of alarm over "the anti-statist bias of current reforms."[15]

The challenge of explaining how a dysfunctional state can be transformed into a developmental one that enjoys authority and legitimacy while facilitating socioeconomic development can prompt exercises in conjecture and advocacy. A more rewarding approach would be to study the actual exercise of power and the crafting of institutions in the course of political struggles, which have resulted in the creation of acknowledged developmental states. An example of such an approach is Brautigam's study of Mauritius. She traces the institutional decisions that were made to resolve particular group conflicts that, over time, contributed to the emergence of a "well-crafted political system" able to "ensure broad representation, while providing incentives for coalition building, moderation, and compromise." Despite Mauritius's ethnic and class diversity, these institutions have continued to "shape political and economic strategies" and to foster civic peace, the deepening of democracy, and high growth with equity. Since 1989, many political experiments have been launched in Africa. Identifying the ones that are likely to combine state building, democracy, and economic growth is a vitally important project that requires similar studies of the actual exercise of power and the building of institutions in a range of countries.

At the Conference on African Renewal, Olukoshi emphasized the need for building bridges between the communities of African scholars based in Africa and their overseas counterparts. Such an effort must begin with an appreciation of the serious efforts being made by scholars both within and outside of Africa to tackle the challenges posed by the contradictory and often confusing political trends on the continent. Young, for example, calls attention to new regime types that have emerged in recent years from guerrilla movements rather than coups, such as in Chad, Eritrea, Ethiopia, Rwanda, and Uganda, and that rest on core support from particular ethnoregional groups. To these may be added other postconflict states that are less ethnically defined, such as Angola, Mozambique, and South Africa, but that share some of the characteristics of the first group. Political institutionalization in late twentieth-century Africa derives from a variety of sources: constitutional premises, as in Benin and Malawi; governmental authority deriving from armed struggle, as in most postconflict states; a combination of the two, as in South Africa and Namibia; and the monopoly of state power behind a democratic facade, as in Burkina Faso, Guinea, and Zimbabwe. Understanding these diverse trends calls for greater communication and collaboration among the various scholarly communities.

The underlying sentiment common to the authors in this book is that African nations should assume a place in world society as assured actors, rather than as perpetual objects of charitable concern. In this regard, they echo the views currently being expressed in Ghana, where the lessons of past false starts are being used to develop more realistic policies. In his keynote address to the Conference on African Renewal, the chair of Ghana's Electoral Commission, K. Afari-Gyan, declared:

> The role that Ghana can play toward the realization of the larger pan-African dream, which formed part of the vision at independence, will obviously depend on the extent and quality of her own renewal. . . . If we can build a clear sense of where we want to go, with concerted and purposeful effort by our people and the goodwill and help of our friends, the prospects of Ghana's renewal as a nation of free and prosperous people looms large on the horizon.[16]

The analyses provided in this book should encourage the scholarly and practical efforts required to bridge the great gap between this recurrent vision and the sobering realities of late twentieth-century Africa.

Notes

1. See Dumont's *False Start in Africa* (initially published with the more dramatic French title *L'Afrique Noire est mal partie*).

2. Joseph, *Perestroika Without Glasnost;* Joseph, ed., *African Renewal.*

3. See the proceedings of those meetings: Joseph, ed., *African Governance in the 1990s* and *Democratic Challenge.*

4. Joseph, "Africa: Rebirth." For reviews of the relevant literature and comprehensive bibliographies, see Buijtenhuijs and Rijnierse, *Democratization in Sub-Saharan Africa, 1989–1992,* and Buijtenhuijs and Thiriot, *Democratization in Sub-Saharan Africa, 1992–1995.*

5. See Hyden, "Governance and the Study of Politics."

6. Nwokedi, *Politics of Democratization;* Diamond, "Prospects for Democratic Development"; and Bratton and van de Walle, *Democratic Experiments.*

7. For the narrowing of choices in economic and political restructuring as a global phenomenon, see Przeworski, *Sustainable Democracy.* Many of the conclusions of this comprehensive review of political developments in Eastern Europe, southern Europe, and South America coincide with those being reached by students of Africa as reflected in the chapters in this book by Mkandawire and Olukoshi.

8. For a relevant general critique, see Ake, *Democracy and Development.*

9. Two recent major contributions to Nigerian and democratic studies are Diamond et al., eds., *Transition Without End,* and Beckett and Young, eds., *Dilemmas of Democracy.*

10. Lipset, "Some Social Requisites of Democracy," p. 97.

11. Diamond, "Is the Third Wave Over?"; Huntington, "After Thirty Years."

12. Dahl, *Preface to Democratic Theory,* p. 3.

13. Huber et al., "Impact of Economic Development," p. 73.

14. Przeworski, *Sustainable Democracy,* p. 11. See also Lipset, "Social Requisites of Democracy Revisited," and Haggard and Kaufman, *Political Economy.*

15. Przeworski, *Sustainable Democracy,* p. 12.

16. The entire address is reprinted in Joseph, ed., *African Renewal,* pp. 26–28.

2

The Third Wave of Democratization in Africa: Ambiguities and Contradictions

CRAWFORD YOUNG

Crosscurrents in African Democratization

When the Huntingtonian "third wave" of democratization washed over Africa beginning in 1989, even the most sanguine observers expected that a transition from patrimonial autocracy as the dominant mode of governance would be strewn with contradictions.[1] Consider the following events in the mid-1990s: astonishing participation in presidential elections in Algeria in the face of violent intimidation by the extreme fringes of the Islamist opposition; a show of elections, with minimal participation, by the integralist Islamic military autocracy in Sudan; publication of yet another Nigerian constitution, with further prolongation of the "permanent transition";[2] military coups in Niger and The Gambia, swiftly followed by an ostensible democratic restoration confirming the coup leader in power; resurrection of Mathieu Kérékou and Didier Ratsiraka through the electoral mechanism in Benin and Madagascar, which had been landmark sites of national conferences that had earlier driven them from power; elections in Sierra Leone in circumstances of such widespread insecurity that balloting was impossible in many regions; and elections in Mauritius in which the ruling coalition lost all 60 of the directly elected seats. The crosscurrents illustrated by these strikingly divergent events, occurring within a few months of one another, underscore the stubborn vitality, yet precarious fragility, of the political liberalization process.

In this chapter, I propose taking inventory of the contradictory outcomes of the democratization processes that began across most of Africa in 1989.[3] By my calculation, initially only Libya and Sudan resolutely held out against the continental (and global) trend. Even Sudan evidently felt constrained to make token gestures of liberalization: the 1996 nonparty

Sudan elections. The other holdout, the contrarian regime in Libya, has made defiance of conventional norms a source of legitimacy for nearly three decades. But elsewhere in Africa, the tides of political opening have almost always brought changes. Transitions have ranged from the aborted (Nigeria) or denatured (Cameroon, Zaire) to the profoundly transformative (South Africa). But even where incumbent regimes have managed and manipulated democratization to preserve their power, some parameters of politics have changed.

Terminal Colonial Democratization and Postindependence Reversal

The initial works appraising political liberalization in Africa tended to focus on transition dynamics.[4] But in a large number of countries, a second set of postliberalization elections were occurring between 1995 and 1997. The fund of experience is thus becoming sufficient to permit shifting our analytical focus away from the initial transitional dynamics and toward weighing the consequences, evaluating the degree of consolidation, and speculating about the sustainability of altered practices of politics.

To place the African version of the contemporary global trend toward political opening in perspective, a brief backward glance is needed. Borrowing Samuel Huntington's imagery of waves of democratization, one might suggest that experiments in democracy in Africa fall in the latter stages of his second (1943–1962) and third (1974–) surges, while the long phase of patrimonial autocracy (from soon after independence until 1989) roughly corresponds to his period of interwave reversal (1958–1975).[5] The array of constitutional provisions modeled on the colonial metropoles, which defined the institutions through which power transfer occurred during the independence era, was for Africa an initial wave. Formally democratic institutions were a part of the decolonization pact everywhere except in those countries where independence was won by armed struggle rather than negotiation (Algeria), where the metropole itself was autocratic (Cape Verde, São Tomé and Príncipe, and Western Sahara), or both (Guinea-Bissau, Mozambique, and Angola). In Africa's version of the second wave, the larger world conjuncture within which it occurred exercised important influence on the nature and short duration of the liberalization tides.

The imprint of the global environment clearly marked terminal colonial democratization. International hostility to colonial rule and anticolonial nationalism swiftly intensified after World War II, putting the colonial powers on the defensive. To fend off the growing pressures for rapid power transfer, the colonizers claimed to open the formerly exclusionary institutions of rule to indigenous participation and to conduct an apprenticeship in democratic self-rule. In terms of metropolitan political cultures (except for then-autocratic Portugal and Spain), if withdrawal was going to be imposed by the combination of international pressures and rising nationalist challenge, then departure with dignity required equipping the colonial territories with constitutional structures replicating their own.[6] In addition, the nationalist successors needed ritual consecration as popular representatives by electoral triumph if the colonial conscience was to be clear as the imperial flags were lowered.

The Western bloc viewed democratization as the natural end point in the transition to self-rule. But even in those parts of the international community where a liberal polity was not a domestic value (the Soviet bloc and much of the emergent third world), democratization in colonial Africa was favored because it opened new political space to challenge the imperial powers. Meanwhile, nationalist forces embraced political liberalization before independence for two basic reasons. First, at the hour of entry into the international realm of sovereign nation-states, anointment by competitive electoral mandate conferred respectability. Second, and more important, the removal of the potent arsenal of repressive restrictions on political organization, which all colonial states had assembled, enormously facilitated the task of mobilizing mass support for independence.

Powerful forces, both international and domestic, thus converged to create the initial African wave. But almost immediately after independence, support for democratic governance evaporated on all fronts. The doctrine of the mass single party as the vanguard of African progress soon took root, embraced by the most charismatic leaders of the independence generation (Habib Bourguiba, Kwame Nkrumah, Sekou Toure, and Julius Nyerere) and backed by persuasive academic observers.[7] There was little public resistance to the elimination of the fragile constitutional structures of the decolonization settlement or, a little later, to the epidemic of military coups.

With independence won, the transcendent doctrinal goals became rapid development and uprooting neocolonial control of the economy. In the reasoning of the time, state developmental energies were finite; whatever resources were diverted to political competition and opposition debate had to be subtracted from the capacities for a united assault on underdevelopment. Consolidation of nationhood required elimination of opportunities for fissiparous tendencies to find expression. Concentration of authority, not its dissipation, was crucial to forced-draft development and the assertion of economic sovereignty. Competitive democracy, argued the leadership, was a luxury that poor countries could not afford.

At this historical moment, the most inspirational examples of swift economic transformation lay in the Soviet bloc and China. Few in the West then challenged the double-digit figures claimed for Soviet growth and industrialization, while the 1958–1960 Chinese "Great Leap Forward" was viewed by many as a stunning achievement. Not until many years later did the realization spread that there were fatal contradictions in the Soviet economic model and that the Great Leap Forward was an appalling cata-strophe, during which as many as 30 million people perished from starva-tion or other policy-related causes. While Afro-Marxism as a developmen-tal pathway did not appear until the end of the 1960s, at the dawn of independence there were exemplary lessons drawn from the Soviet model (although without embracing Soviet ideology), including the importance of central planning, the capacity of the state to organize and direct develop-ment, the urgency of industrialization, and the political and economic attractions of a large state enterprise sector.

Neither state socialism nor radical, anti-imperial third world national-ism attached much value to constitutional democracy after independence. Nor was there vocal objection in the West to the disappearance of democra-tic process. Most development economists of the day were sympathetic to state-led development. Dominant "modernization" theories readily acknowledged that economic development came first and that democratiza-tion would follow later—a perspective easily enlarged to accommodate military rule.[8] Former colonial powers gave priority to preserving their eco-nomic advantage and privileged connections: the *chasse gardée* syndrome. Global strategists wanted reliable clients in the great game of Cold War maneuvering, while the human rights movement was still weak and scat-tered and gave scant attention to Africa. Thus, although the decolonization wave of democratization had drawn important international system support during the terminal colonial period, this backing vanished almost as soon as the independence celebrations were over. Internally, democracy was above all a weapon in the independence struggle; after nationalist triumph, the democracy of terminal colonial arrangements appeared superfluous.

During much of the interwave period in Africa, the tides of authoritari-anism seemed to flow strongly throughout the third world, as well as within the vast realm of state socialism. In characterizing the dominant political trends in what we then knew as "developing nations," in 1976 I wrote: "Although the routes might vary, most political roads carried the polity to an authoritarian destination."[9] Huntington's influential plea for strong states as the best bulwark against political decay carried authority.[10]

Especially during the 1970s and early 1980s, the Soviet Union pursued an active strategy of backing "socialist orientation" in Africa, cresting with the emergence of seven states laying claim to Marxist-Leninist doctrinal commitment, and the radicalization of several populist socialist states (Algeria, Tanzania).[11] Western powers intensified their efforts to bestow favors upon states that were willing to stand against what Soviet global strategists termed "the changing correlation of forces," and no democratic litmus test was applied. Zbigniew Brzezinski warned that "détente was buried in the sands of the Ogaden," implying that counter-Soviet global strategies would define U.S. regional diplomacy in Africa. Overall, the global conjuncture remained largely unfavorable to democratization.

Erosion of the Credibility
of the Patrimonial Autocratic State

There were, however, some straws in the wind suggesting a different direction, as globally, the "third wave" was beginning to surge. In 1974–1975, dictatorships fell in Portugal, Spain, and Greece, the last in Western Europe; constitutional democracy became the universal mode of governance in Western Europe for the first time in history. Although at this very moment, bureaucratic authoritarianism and the national security state seemed ascendant in Latin America, currents of democratization were beginning to flow. Initially, however, these developments had little resonance in Africa.

Nevertheless, within Africa, the credibility of single-party systems was visibly frayed. The system still had many practitioners, but far fewer intellectual defenders; it had provided convenient cover for political monopoly for the ruler, but was a poorly concealed instrument for predatory extraction for the subject. Military rule also lost its charm; more skeptical analyses, such as those of Samuel Decalo, supplanted the worshipful treatments of the early 1960s.[12] In an intriguing episode revelatory of the changing temper of the times, Nigerian military leaders conducted a series of didactic lectures across the country in 1972, drawing upon the earlier "military as modernizers" academic discourse to test the prospects for a long-term legitimation of army rule. The deeply skeptical public response convinced the officers that there was no market for their product.[13]

The pathologies of African autocracy were illustrated by the embarrassing attention attracted by the most extreme cases: Idi Amin in Uganda, Jean-Bedel Bokassa in Central African Republic, and Francisco Macías Nguema in Equatorial Guinea. All three of these sanguinary tyrants were overthrown in 1979. Although the promise of democratic opening went unfulfilled in the short term in these three instances, the destruction of the public realm by unchecked personal tyranny bore witness to the perils of "developmental dictatorship."[14]

During this interwave period, stirrings of circumscribed political liberalization in Africa did bear witness to the acknowledgment by patrimonial autocrats that the ideological formulas used to justify the exclusion and marginalization of the subject population were losing their force. In a number of countries, single parties sought renewed legitimation by borrowing from the Tanzanian model of competitive contests within the single party for parliamentary seats, although rulers themselves were not challenged (e.g., in Zambia, Kenya, Zaire, Côte d'Ivoire, Malawi, Cameroon, Mali, and Sierra Leone). These elections invariably led to the displacement of roughly half of the incumbent parliamentarians and, at low cost, they provided some outlet for the expression of public discontent.[15]

Beyond this device for circulating some second-tier political elites while entrenching the monopoly of power at the summit, there were other significant instances of democratic openings. In 1976, Senegal abandoned the single-party model, initially opening assigned space on either ideological flank of the ruling Parti Socialiste, then by 1983 moving to an integral multipartyism while remaining under dominant-party control.[16] In the late 1970s, Burkina Faso experienced a period of competitive democracy.[17] The Gambia and Botswana remained moderately democratic throughout, though without political alternation.[18] Mauritius, perhaps only ambiguously an African state, was the sole example during the interwave period where greater political opening actually produced a change of rulers; in the 1982 elections, the former ruling party lost all 60 of the directly elected seats.

Three important cases of democratization occurred in the interwave period: Ghana (1969 and 1979), Nigeria (1979), and Sudan (1965 and 1986). Their failure reinforced the conviction both in and out of Africa that democracy was an improbable, if not an impossible, dream for the continent. In the case of Ghana, a well-conducted restoration of democratic rule in 1969 lasted only two years before the duly elected leader, Kofi Busia, fell victim to renewed military intervention. The military regime of General Ignatius Acheampong, which enjoyed a brief moment of apparent reforming zeal after seizing power in 1972, soon degenerated into unrestrained predation. The cocoa price bonanza of the late 1970s became mere booty for the rulers, as nearly a billion dollars went missing from Cocoa Marketing Board accounts.[19] But then pressures for transition again became irresistible. After a failed maneuver to win support for a military-civilian diarchy ("Unigov"), General Acheampong was ousted. His military successor, General Fred Akuffo, conceded to full democratization in 1979, but was overthrown in a coup led by Flight Lieutenant Jerry Rawlings, who permitted the 1979 elections to proceed. A fair measure of the depth of public revulsion at the venal military autocracy was the public execution of three former army rulers just prior to the transition. But once more, only two years passed before Rawlings's second military intervention.

The most visible failed transition of the interwave period was in Nigeria. Promised since the end of the civil war in 1970, the transition began in earnest only in 1975, with the coup that brought General Murtala Muhammed to power. Although he was assassinated within a few months, Muhammed put the transition machinery in place, and the design was faithfully executed by his successor, General Olusegun Obasanjo. As with the first Nigerian transition in the 1950s, the process unfolded in exceptionally favorable economic circumstances. The happy coincidence of swelling production and soaring prices for oil permitted an extraordinary expansion of state outlays. From a mere 214 million pounds at the end of the First Republic in 1966, state expenditures ballooned between 1971 and 1980 from ₦ 997 million (997 million naira) to ₦ 17,513 million.[20]

The extended political debates surrounding the formulation of the

Second Republic institutions stand out as an unusually creative exercise in constitutional engineering. Although the product proved ephemeral, the originality of the broad-based collective reflection that shaped the constitution was significant. The design of the framework for governance in the Second Republic constitution was remarkably innovative, proposing institutions that explicitly acknowledged cultural diversity as a fundamental and ongoing attribute of civil society and abandoning illusions that it could be coercively contained, marginalized by "national integration," or dissipated by "modernization."

Constitutional engineering could manage cultural pluralism, but institutional ingenuity was no match for corruption. The colossal scale of venality, along with the equally stupendous rigging of the 1983 elections, destroyed the legitimacy of the Second Republic. The popular welcome accorded the renewed military intervention at the end of 1983 seemed to serve as a requiem for African democracy.

In Sudan, the first military regime under Ibrahim Abboud was driven to take cover by Khartoum street unrest and southern insurgency in 1964. However, disillusionment with the restored elected regime cleared the path for a new era of military autocracy from 1969 to 1985 under General Jaafar al-Nimeiry. This versatile autocrat experimented with shifting partners—the radical left, the south, Islamists—but he eventually ran out of ruses and was again supplanted by a democratic interlude from 1986 to 1989. A third failure of electoral politics then followed, as measured by the collective shrug of the shoulders that initially greeted the military's return in 1989, before its implacably Islamist intentions were fully clear. In turn, the utter bankruptcy of military dictatorship with an Islamist face was dramatically clear by 1997, as loosely connected armed insurrection simmered around most of the periphery.[21]

On a global scale, however, the third wave was gathering force, particularly in Latin America. In Asia as well, entrenched autocracies in South Korea, Taiwan, Pakistan, and the Philippines gave way to more polyarchical regimes. African patrimonial autocracy began to stand out as a deviant form of politics, rather than a third world norm.

In addition, the terms of engagement between African states and the international community changed radically. This occurred first in the economic field. In dramatic contrast to the aggressive assertion of economic nationalism in the 1970s, a decade peppered with sweeping indigenization programs (in Nigeria, Uganda, Zaire, and Zambia, among others) and widespread nationalizations, the 1980s opened with a confession of developmental impasse, symbolized by the 1980 Organization of African Unity (OAU) Lagos Plan of Action, and the blistering critique of African development performance in the World Bank's 1981 Berg Report.[22] A widespread debt crisis became evident at the same time, placing African states on the defensive, confronted by a phalanx of public and private international creditors. The World Bank ventured into "policy-based lending" for the first time, teaming up with the International Monetary Fund and Western donor countries to propose rigorous economic liberalization programs as the ransom for debt rescheduling and further development aid. "Neoliberalism" and "structural adjustment" entered the lexicon of political economy.

Meanwhile, the alternative of recourse to the "camp of socialism," previously so valuable to African states in providing some political leverage and room for international maneuver, gradually vanished. By the 1980s, the Soviet Union was reconsidering the magnitude of its third world commitments and had begun to scale back its financial obligations. Critical turning points in Africa were the 1981 rejection of Mozambique's application for membership in the Council for Mutual Economic Assistance and the rebuff to a 1982 Ghanaian delegation's plea for backing to permit a radical strategy of response to the economic crisis. By the mid-1980s, a pattern of Soviet disengagement was becoming clear, which developed into full-scale withdrawal by the end of the decade.

In the West, Keynesian economics and the social democratic ethos, which had earlier flavored much of the developmental discourse in the 1960s and 1970s, came under fierce attack by promoters of the doctrinaire tenets of free market policies, symbolized by Reaganism and Thatcherism. The "Washington consensus" with respect to development crystallized, conditioning external assistance to economic liberalization. The progressive discrediting of state socialism during the 1980s, well before the fall of the Berlin Wall, made "economic reform" the only game in town. Africa had little choice but to accept at least the discourse of reform.

The failure of structural adjustment programs to bring an early recovery, initially expected by their sponsors within three to five years, intensified the mood of crisis on the continent.[23] Influential voices both in and out of Africa began to argue that political reform was a necessary concomitant of economic liberalization. The African state itself, as the historical agent of development, came under challenge.[24] The argument ran that the thorough prebendalization of the public realm had created a state that was incapable of effective macroeconomic management.[25] Without a remoralization of public institutions, and minimal accountability and transparency, economic liberalization could never be sustained.

A propitious climate for political change had been created not only by economic buffeting, but also by vanishing state legitimacy. For the citizen in many lands, the state had become a mere predator, even a vampire. Silent disengagement from the state became increasingly evident, while effective patrimonial management of power at the summit encountered increasing obstacles. The resources available for lubricating clientelistic networks shriveled and became more subject to structural adjustment monitoring by the international financial institutions.

The Third Wave of Democratization Reaches Africa

Thus the stage was set for the third wave of democratization to sweep over Africa, beginning in 1989. A concatenation of dramatic events, internal and external, sparked this moment of enthusiasm at the beginning of the 1990s. The serious riots in Algeria in 1988 were an early omen, shredding the revolutionary mystique of the Front de Libération Nationale (FLN) and forcing open the doors of political competition. Although the transition was aborted in 1992, when it seemed that democratic elections would bring the Front Islamique de Salut (FIS) to power, the abandoning of the claim to political monopoly in 1989 resonated.

Also in 1989, the long-term ruler of Benin and sometime Afro-Marxist Mathieu Kérékou was at bay; he was unable to meet the state payroll or obtain external credits, abandoned by his former clientele, and faced with a crescendo of street protests and a barrage of denunciation from intellectuals, teachers, functionaries, unions, and students. There seemed no way out except to accede to their demand for a "national conference" of the "*forces vives*" of the nation. Once assembled, the conference delegates declared themselves sovereign and proceeded to create transitional institutions. Isolated, Kérékou could not resist this "civil society" power seizure. Contagion at once took hold throughout francophone Africa, for whose publics the Benin national conference, in the words of one of its admirers, "had the beauty of something unique, incomparable."[26] National conferences drove incumbents from power in Niger, Congo-Brazzaville, and Madagascar; they failed to achieve this goal in Gabon, Zaire, and Togo, but nonetheless changed the rules of the political game.

In Zambia, the support system sustaining the three-decade monopoly of the United National Independence Party (UNIP) collapsed. Possibly overconfident of his capacity to survive multiparty politics, Kenneth Kaunda permitted an honestly conducted 1991 election that swept him from power.[27] The continental impact of the unexpected release of Nelson Mandela and legalization of the African National Congress in 1990 was even more potent, setting in motion a process that led ineluctably to the end of apartheid and, in 1994, to genuine majority rule. At the same time, the slowly unfolding Nigerian transition, which still appeared credible in 1990, seemed to promise an early return to constitutional rule in Africa's most populous polity. Thus, currents of change appeared to be running strongly throughout the continent; the claims of opposition voices for democratization seemed garbed in the same cloak of inevitability and invincibility that had clad independence movements in the 1950s.

Equally important was the international conjuncture. The completely unexpected demolition of the Berlin Wall, and the collapse of state socialism and of the Soviet Union itself, echoed powerfully throughout the world. U.S. policy, by 1990, aggressively promoted democratization;

unusually outspoken ambassadors in Cameroon, Central African Republic, Zaire, and Kenya shed the veil of quiet diplomacy to make this position clear. Even France—long indulgent with its African partners—warned that the *pré carré* was not exempt from democratization. Paris, suggested President François Mitterand at the 1990 La Baule francophone summit, would become more tepid in its support of countries under French sway that failed to join the trend. Within the World Bank, influential voices called for political reform as a necessary companion to economic liberalization.[28] "Governance" became assimilated into structural adjustment discourse. Although the concept is ostensibly differentiated from democratization, its defining elements are redolent of polyarchical theory: citizen influence and oversight, responsible and responsive leadership, meaningful accountability and transparency, and productive social reciprocities.[29] Political conditionality was far less systematic than the economic variety, but, nonetheless, it was in the air.

Yet another factor driving democratization was the necessity for an electoral process to permit ratification and legitimation of accords designed to settle long-standing crises. In Angola and Mozambique, some mechanism for roughly measuring the relative sizes of the constituencies of both the internationally recognized regimes and their insurgent challengers was indispensable to any settlement. In Namibia, OAU recognition as the official liberation movement did not suffice to simply install the South West African People's Organization in power; the sanction of an internationally supervised election was a critical component of the transition arrangements. In war-torn Sierra Leone and Liberia, elections—however problematic—were promoted as an integral part of any settlement pact; in both countries, they were remarkably successful in restoring the minimal legitimacy needed to underwrite a negotiated end to years of destructive civil war.

These last two instances, along with Somalia and Rwanda, suggest another conjunctural factor of increasing, even frightening, weight: the incubus of the collapsed state, an outcome as unanticipated as the disappearance of state socialism. Until Charles Taylor's band of insurgents sparked a chain reaction of disintegration in Liberia in 1989, and the ouster of Muhammad Siad Barre from Somalia in 1991 triggered a power struggle in which warlords and their clan militia demolished the institutional superstructure of the state, state collapse had never been seriously contemplated as a likely scenario by analysts of African politics.[30] Although the weakness and declining authority of African states had been widely acknowledged, the international system was expected to sustain at least the shell of what Robert Jackson termed the "quasi state" by assuring a flow of sovereignty-sustaining oxygen through diverse external conduits.[31] But the "collapsed state" goes far beyond the quasi state; the international system is not easily capable of bringing the former back to life. One may note as well the closely parallel new category of the "failed state," defined by the shrinking into virtual irrelevance of the state's institutional apparatus and its incapacity to assure the general welfare or protect the security of the citizenry.[32]

The new wave of democratization is now well into its second half decade. However uneven its progress, democratization remains the dominant political discourse in Africa; in this sense, Africa's version of the third wave has already proved more durable than the decolonization form. Nevertheless, the euphoria that accompanied the arrival of the third wave in Africa has long since evaporated; even the most optimistic advocates of political liberalization would join Larry Diamond in conceding that democratization is "bound to be gradual, messy, fitful and slow, with many imperfections along the way."[33] In no other world region has the third wave encountered so hostile an economic and political environment. African economic difficulties are far more debilitating than elsewhere. The underlying societal cleavages of ethnicity, religion, and race have been exacerbated by prolonged state decline and the attendant corrosion of the effectiveness and legitimacy of the public realm. Even in post-Soviet-bloc countries, the closest parallel, where wrenching economic adjustment, limited social capital, and unsupportive political cultures challenge the consolidation of democratic regimes, the handicaps seem less severe.

Democratization: A Balance Sheet

Nonetheless, many countries have moved beyond the initial phase of transition to the more complex processes of consolidation and institutionalization. In a number of other cases, initially promising transitions were sidetracked, but without necessarily being entirely compromised or abandoned. In some instances, incumbents have strung out the transition process in such a manipulative manner that democratization has degenerated into a permanent charade, devoid of its initial credibility.

In only a handful of instances can one speak with reasonable confidence of consolidation, measured by at least a second equitably managed set of competitive elections, reasonably open to opposition parties. Benin, Madagascar, Mauritius, Ghana, São Tomé and Príncipe, Botswana, and Namibia are plausible candidates, although there has been alternation only in the first three of these.[34] In a number of countries, long-standing incumbents were replaced in the first transition elections (Central African Republic, Congo-Brazzaville, Mali, Madagascar, Malawi, Cape Verde, São Tomé and Príncipe, South Africa, and Zambia). The most extensive and careful classification of degrees of democratization, in my judgment, has been provided by *Africa Demos*. As a point of departure, I use their most recent (1995) categorizations, with small amendment to the typology, and then turn to my own reclassification of states as of the beginning of 1997.[35] These categories are open to debate, as are some of the attributes, but the same could be said of any other taxonomy. The resulting classification of states as of 1997 is shown in Table 2.1.

In a substantial number of cases, incumbent rulers found ways—for example by legalizing opposition parties and then encouraging their proliferation, and by fully exploiting the advantages accruing from control of the regional administration (and whatever life remained in the former single party)—to win electoral mandates. Some observers, such as the late and deeply lamented Nigerian intellectual Claude Ake, conclude that such outcomes reveal a deep flaw in the entire third wave: "the crude simplicity of multiparty elections to the benefit of some of the world's most notorious autocrats, such as Daniel arap Moi of Kenya and Paul Biya of Cameroon, who are now able to parade democratic credentials without reforming their repressive regimes." This observation leads to a broader dismissal of the whole process as a form of democracy "whose relevance to Africa is problematic at best and at worst prone to engender contradictions that tend to derail or trivialize democratization in Africa."[36]

There is no doubt that elections such as the 1992 balloting in Kenya reveal the rigid determination of autocratic cliques to cling to power, at considerable cost to the polity. To discredit the very notion of political competition, key individuals in the inner circle of the Moi regime (Nicholas Biwott and George Saitoti), were believed to have fomented Rift Valley ethnic clashes that drove 350,000 from their homes and killed 1,500. The credibility of these beliefs finds reinforcement in the report of a parliamentary commission composed exclusively of ruling-party deputies, which reached the same conclusion. In the aftermath of the elections, a fraudulent scheme was uncovered (the Goldenberg affair) that had generated an alleged $389 million in illicit funds, apparently intended in good part to fund the electoral campaign.[37] Yet even with these flaws, civil society breathes easier after partial liberalization; the political climate is less fear-ridden and closed than in the late 1980s.[38]

Elections thus denatured lose much of their legitimating value. Opposition formations tend to contest their legitimacy and not infrequently boycott the elections or the resulting institutions. Cases that might fit this pattern include Burkina Faso, Cameroon, Egypt, Ethiopia, Equatorial Guinea, Gabon, Guinea, Guinea-Bissau, Côte d'Ivoire, Kenya, Mauritania, Togo, Tunisia, and Zimbabwe. Opposition protest was most vehement in Cameroon and Kenya, while at the other end of the spectrum, claims that the electoral process was invalid were relatively muted in Burkina Faso, Tunisia, and Zimbabwe.

There has undoubtedly been a political learning curve in African presidential palaces that is applicable to the new parameters set by political liberalization. The capacity of rulers to find instruction in observed experience should not be underestimated. In an earlier, postcolonial age, following the epidemic of military coups in 1965–1966, autocrats eventually constructed

Table 2.1 Degrees of Democratization of 53 African States as of Early 1997

Relatively Democratic (16 states)	Directed Democracy (8 states)	Transition with Moderate Democratic Commitment (12 states)	Transition with Ambiguous or Circumscribed Democratic Commitment (5 states)	Transition Promised, not Implemented (5 states)	Contested Sovereignty (5 states)	Authoritarian (2 states)
Benin	Burkina Faso	Comoros	Chad	Algeria	Angola	Libya
Botswana	Cameroon	Côte d'Ivoire	Djibouti	Equatorial	Burundi	Sudan
Cape Verde	Egypt	Ethiopia	The Gambia	Guinea	Liberia	
Central African	Eritrea	Gabon	Niger	Nigeria	Rwanda	
Republic	Guinea	Guinea-Bissau	Tunisia	Swaziland	Somalia	
Congo-Brazzaville	Morocco	Kenya		Congo (Zaire)		
Ghana	Togo	Lesotho				
Madagascar	Uganda	Mauritania				
Malawi		Mozambique				
Mali		Seychelles				
Mauritius		Zambia				
Namibia		Zimbabwe				
São Tomé &						
Príncipe						
Senegal						
Sierra Leone						
South Africa						
Tanzania						

various protective devices to forestall coups, which kept a number of them in power for three decades; these devices included scrambling command lines, creating ethnic security maps, staffing Presidential Guards with foreign mercenaries, and developing multiple security forces.[39] Ben Ali, Omar Bongo, Robert Mugabe, and Hosni Mubarak are still in power, agile enough to retain the initiative under changed rules.

Since the early 1990s, the global conjuncture has evolved in significant ways. The international community is now less united and compelling in its pressures. Domestically, since political liberalization has not produced the "second independence" initially imagined, citizen skepticism concerning the process is several shades stronger.

Internationally, the competing imperatives of neorealist international policy and what one recent commentator stigmatized as "Mother Teresa diplomacy" have become more evident.[40] Within a year, France had retreated from its La Baule commitment, while Britain and Japan were never enthusiastic partisans of placing a high priority on political liberalization. In the case of the United States, contradictions soon became apparent, as pressures for democratization were not applied in situations where security and strategic preoccupations ranked high (e.g., Egypt). Nor did they override the Huntingtonian "clash of civilizations" preoccupations, present in both the Egyptian and Algerian situations.[41] One may recollect the absence of reaction to the Algerian military's cancellation of elections that would have brought the integralist FIS to power in 1992. Insulation from democratization pressure is also available for countries neighboring "rogue states" that have been accused of harboring terrorists (Uganda, Eritrea, and Ethiopia). States that receive high marks for economic liberalization earn discounts in democratization pressures, such as Uganda and Ghana. "Governance" discourse in the international financial institutions is more confined to the institutional requisites for "sound macroeconomic management" and an "enabling environment" for freer markets.

Limits to Democracy: The Ethnic Question

In the evaluative debates about third-wave democratization in Africa, two major arguments have been advanced by those skeptical of its therapeutic value for the African state. First, competitive political parties and open elections necessarily mobilize and politicize regional, ethnic, religious, and racial solidarities, and therefore intensify disintegrative pressures on fragile states, without notably contributing to either stability or legitimacy. Second, the severity of the economic crisis and the intrinsic difficulties of persuading electorates that painful austerity measures are necessary render recovery impossible and assure a further downward spiral. This is the essence of Thomas Callaghy's warning of a "high historical correlation in the contemporary era between authoritarian rule and the ability to engage in major economic restructuring in the Third World."[42] Here, we may note, one encounters a reprise of the core 1960 arguments in the brief for the single-party regime: the overriding urgency of nation building and the imperative of centralized, unchallenged state developmental authority.

Few today would dispute the premise that electoral competition readily flows along societal fault lines defined by ethnicity, religion, or race, both in the world at large and in Africa. Such identities serve as tempting vote banks for party organizers. With the perhaps momentary eclipse of ideological alignments, in an epoch where all forms of socialism remain blighted by the stigma of the failed Soviet version, political challengers have great difficulty in defining an alternative *projet de société*. Electoral discourse is thus limited to vague slogans of change ("*sopi,*" in the Senegalese version) and opposition to incumbents. One finds few cases (Senegal is one example) where political alignments are little affected by communal solidarities.

But of the many transitions in progress, there has been escalating and repeated communal violence in only four cases: Rwanda, Burundi, Algeria, and Congo-Brazzaville. The endemic civil strife following communal lines in polities such as Sudan and Somalia is entirely unrelated to democratic process, which indeed appears to be a necessary ingredient of any accord that restores peace. Of these four cases, only in Congo-Brazzaville did the ethnic violence involve armed factions directly issuing from electoral politics. The ethnic youth militias, bearing the sinister labels of "Zulus," "Ninjas," and "Cobras," terrorized Brazzaville for several months in 1993 and provoked large-scale ethnic cleansing of neighborhoods in the capital, operating under the patronage of President Pascal Lissouba, Brazzaville Mayor Bernard Kolelas, and former ruler Denis Sassou-Nguesso, respectively.[43] The violence temporarily subsided at the end of 1993, when the leaders who had fomented it reverted to more civil forms of rivalry, partly under the patient and persuasive prodding of an OAU mediation commission led by Algerian diplomat Mohammed Sahnoun. The seizure of power by Sassou-Nguesso in October 1997, however, effectively ended this drama of political liberalization.

In Algeria, violence broke out as a consequence of the military intervention in 1992, suspending an election that the FIS would have won. Whether the FIS would have followed the Iranian path of political exclusion of those not sharing its vision of the Islamic state cannot be known. What is certain is that armed uprising by FIS elements, and later by far more extreme factions of the Groupe Islamique Armé (GIA), began soon after and brought the country to the brink of civil war. It is also clear that the successful political opening initiated by General Liamine Zeroual with the November 1995 elections created a window of opportunity for isolating the extremists and reincorporating most of the religious currents within civil society into the political process.[44] The dilemma, however, remains, as a further intensification of GIA terrorist action, together with renewed talk of "eradication" in military circles, brought on a fearsome cycle of brutal violence in late 1996 and early 1997.

In Burundi, after the searing experiences of ethnic massacres in 1965, 1972, and 1988, the Tutsi-dominated military regime of Pierre Buyoya undertook meaningful steps toward national reconciliation. Buyoya clearly expected that his party, the Union pour le Progrès National, would reap the electoral fruits of his reconciliation project, despite its Tutsi associations. Indeed, the main, Hutu-dominated challenger, the Front Démocratique Burundais (FRODEBU), won only 60 percent of the votes, although its potential ethnic constituency was 85 percent of the electorate. Buyoya accepted defeat graciously and ceded power to the FRODEBU presidential candidate, Melchior Ndadaye.

The fatal flaw in these transitional arrangements, and a threat to a number of others, was the ethnic monopoly in the security forces, especially in the command structure, reflecting the previous ethnic security map.[45] A Tutsi faction of the armed forces obliterated hopes for ethnic accommodation through some form of power-sharing liberalization when it assassinated Ndadaye and several other FRODEBU leaders in October 1993.[46] This tragic event unleashed a spiral of ethnic violence that has brought Burundi to the brink of a genocidal dissolution of state and society.

In the Rwanda holocaust, the evidence is even clearer that only some formula for power sharing, accompanied by political opening, could have averted Armageddon.[47] The independence settlement transferred power to a Hutu ethnarchy, recast as a single-party military autocracy by Juvénal Habyarimana when he seized power in 1973. For more than a decade, the regime enjoyed a reasonable quotient of legitimacy with the Hutu majority, fostered by moderately competent developmental management and substantial external assistance. However, by the late 1980s, a clear pattern of decline had set in, due to increasing venality, growing regional favoritism, and decreasing effectiveness.

The 1990 invasion by insurgents of the Front Patriotique Rwandais (FPR), manned primarily by Tutsi exiles long resident in Uganda, was initially contained with French, Belgian, and Zairian military assistance, but it nonetheless triggered a political crisis that was inevitable. The parties that emerged after single-party rule was abandoned in 1991 were far from a full antidote to the deepening civil society disaffection, but they at least offered the possibility of providing the political brokerage that might have helped contain the escalating ethnic and regional tensions. The genocidal massacres that immediately followed the 1994 assassination of Habyarimana, instigated and executed by extremist Hutu bands linked with the former ruling party, sowed devastation across the land: at least 500,000 were killed, mostly Tutsi, and two million Hutu refugees fled to neighboring countries. The FPR successor regime is unlikely to enjoy peace or stability until the country can come to terms with its past through some kind of negotiated formula that provides security to all citizens. Democratic mechanisms seem to be out of the question for a prolonged period in the wake of this deep trauma and the spread of armed conflict to the entire Great Lakes region in late 1996.

Democratization, in wrestling with the ethnic question, can take many institutional forms; the Ethiopian and Ugandan cases are interesting examples. In Ethiopia, the reaction to the Shoan Amharic hegemony, which characterized the exercise of power in both the imperial and the Afro-Marxist regimes, produced a wave of rebellion around the ethnic and regional periphery. The circumstances of the military defeat of the Derg in 1991, particularly at the hands of the best-organized of the ethnoregional formations, the Eritrean People's Liberation Front (EPLF) and the Tigray People's Liberation Front (TPLF), compelled a far-reaching redefinition of the polity itself: Eritrean independence was accepted, and the nationality principle was utilized as the basis for redrawing provincial boundaries. The new Ethiopian constitution goes further than any other in the world today in embedding comprehensive ethnic self-determination, including the right to secession.

The actual exercise of ethnic self-determination, however, is still constrained by the Leninist residues in the political practice of the ruling Ethiopian People's Revolutionary Democratic Front, essentially a creature of the TPLF. Thus far, the center has managed ethnonationality by creating client regional parties; full acceptance of the new political order by the major peripheral ethnic groups, including the Oromo, the Somali, and the formerly dominant Amhara, who have been forced into sullen submission, remains to be demonstrated. Still, many Ethiopians regard the present, limited political opening as an improvement upon the authoritarian rule of the emperor and the Derg.

In Uganda, President Yoweri Museveni maneuvers to preserve the rule by his National Resistance Movement (NRM) under the ostensible constitutional sanction of a nonparty democratic order. This formula enjoys at best temporary and uneasy acquiescence by large sectors of Ugandan opinion. However, Museveni has earned substantial room for maneuver in the remarkable recovery Uganda has enjoyed under his leadership. Enthusiasm for a return to political parties is tempered by the prospect of a return to prominence of the Uganda People's Congress and the Democratic Party, whose sectarian rivalries in the 1960s are blamed for many of the misfortunes that followed. But the 1994 constitution provided only a five-year delay on the issue of multiparty politics, at which point the question must be revisited. There is not a permanent mandate for NRM rule under the disguise of a no-party system.

The evidence to date, in my reading, does not permit the conclusion that identity politics offers an insuperable obstacle to political liberalization. The saliency of cultural diversity in most African states, however, poses clear challenges to sustainable democratization. There is an opportunity for thoughtful statecraft in seeking constitutional formulas that facilitate accommodation of ethnic, religious, or racial differences. Accumulated experience in many world regions suggests that cultural pluralism needs to be acknowledged rather than ignored, through arrangements that induce inclusionary politics and create structural incentives for intercommunal cooperation.[48]

Dilemmas of Simultaneous
Economic and Political Reform

The critical issue of whether a politically liberalized state can muster the will and authority to sustain the kind of rigorous macroeconomic management that is clearly necessary for restoring economic health is more uncertain. One may acknowledge, at the outset, the cautionary conclusion of Henry Bienen and Jeffrey Herbst, that "the simultaneous pursuit of economic and political reform in Africa will be even more difficult than in most other regions of the world."[49] Yet this observation must be juxtaposed with another conclusion, overwhelmingly supported by the evidence of economic performance since 1960: the form of patrimonial autocracy that predominated in African politics until the third wave has utterly failed the test of effective developmental performance. There is little need to review the dismal statistics on African economies through the 1980s; it suffices to recollect that Ghana's per capita national income comfortably exceeded that of South Korea in 1957, while by 1993 the South Korean figure was nearly 18 times as high.[50]

Thus, although a strong theoretical case can be made for sequencing reform based upon the East Asian "tiger" models, with political opening coming only after a sustainable momentum in economic development has been achieved, the applicability of this model to the African context is dubious. Only Tunisia, in the effectiveness and cohesiveness of its state apparatus, remotely resembles the East Asian countries; however, the Tunisian per capita economic expansion was only 1.2 percent per year from 1980 until 1993.[51]

The logic of sequencing operates in reverse in Africa: partial or substantial liberalizing transitions have occurred in most states, and the present international environment is hostile to overt authoritarian restoration. Although large states such as Nigeria and Sudan, and a rentier maverick such as Libya, can withstand external pressures, smaller and weaker African states are far more vulnerable. One may recollect the speed with which forcible coups have been reversed in the last three years in São Tomé and Príncipe, Lesotho, and Comoros; the authors of the January 1996 Niger coup, though more justified than the others by a debilitating institutional impasse and a poorly designed "national conference" constitution, were compelled to accept new elections by September 1996. Nevertheless, the pedagogy of directed, managed political opening had been well learned; the architects of the coup regained a modicum of respectability by securing an apparent electoral mandate.

Relatively effective economic liberalization can also earn some breathing space, as noted earlier. Ghana and Uganda experienced far less international pressure for further political liberalization than did Kenya and Cameroon, due in part to their relative economic success. But the conscious construction of a regime modeled on the Taiwan or South Korea of the 1960s and 1970s is impossible to imagine, even if internal societal and political circumstances permitted.

Also worthy of note is that the most impressive sustained performance in economic development among the 53 African states belongs to two continuously democratic polities, Botswana and Mauritius. Botswana enjoyed average annual growth of 14.5 percent between 1970 and 1980, and 9.6 percent from 1980 until 1993. Over the same quarter century, Mauritius maintained a steady growth rate of over 6 percent annually. A mere large sugar plantation at the time of its independence in 1968, since the mid-1980s Mauritius has doubled its per capita gross domestic product, which now exceeds U.S.$3,000. Its diversified economy registers an unemployment rate of only 2 percent. Yet in 1982, and again in 1995, fairly conducted national elections resulted in ruling parties losing the entirety of the contested seats. Some special factors operate in both cases, but the indisputable success of these two countries cannot be solely ascribed to geological good fortune. Effective, cohesive bureaucracies, relatively high levels of public integrity, and careful economic management play a large part in their success, and an expanding economy in turn doubtless makes democratic governance more sustainable.

Thus, the question remains open. Scrutiny of World Bank tables or other country-level statistical indicators has, to date, yielded no definitive answers regarding the relationship between third-wave regime type and economic performance in Africa. Indeed, it would be naive to expect clearly evident causal pathways; there are far too many intervening variables. Stephan Haggard and Robert Kaufman, in their comprehensive and thoughtful exploration of the political economy of democratic transitions in Latin America and Asia (but not Africa), conclude with several cautionary observations. The challenge of state capacity building in the poorer developing countries is imposing, especially in the face of the burdens of unpayable debts and acute economic distress for many. Winning positive support for economic reform is difficult at best, and it becomes more so when positive results are not tangible to the citizenry, or at least to its most articulate beneficiary segments.[52] In addition, electoral imperatives create potent incentives for profligate spending by incumbents: the political business cycle. The Tanzanian government, for example, borrowed 33 billion Tanzanian shillings in the run-up to the flawed 1995 elections.[53] Ghana also all but abandoned fiscal discipline and its painfully won reputation for economic rectitude in the 1992 (but not the 1996) electoral period.

I find Adam Przeworski and Fernando Limongi's argument that democratization is not contingent in some deterministic sense on the level of economic development compelling.[54] The role of key actors and the strategies they pursue are critical. Democracy in Mali, despite its poverty, has far better prospects for consolidation owing to the crucial role played by General Ahmadou Toumani Touré, the initial military patron of the transition, and the political skills and commitment of Alpha Oumar Konaré. They succeeded in foiling military interventions, pacifying the endemic Tuareg dissidence in the north, at least for the moment, and adjusting to the painful CFA (Communauté Financière Africaine) franc devaluation. In Togo, in contrast, the intransigence of the opposition, which demanded not only transition but vengeance, in the end facilitated the efforts of Gnassingbé Eyadema to effect a virtual autocratic restoration.[55]

However, the constraints of economic poverty operate in shaping the prospects for consolidation. Przeworski and Limongi merit citation here:

> The emergence of democracy is not a by-product of economic development. Democracy is or is not established by political actors pursuing their goals, and it can be initiated at any level of development. Only once it is established do economic constraints play a role: the chances for the survival of democracy are greatest when the country is richer. Yet the current wealth of a country is not decisive. . . . If they succeed in generating development, democracies can survive even in the poorest nations.[56]

Conclusion

Democratization in Africa, comparatively speaking, unfolds in special circumstances. The African state system is strongly—one might say uniquely—intercommunicating political space. Political leaders are in continuous contact, and the contagion of events is unusually strong. Africa is also exceptionally tributary to the international system, the more so as currents of globalization run ever stronger. African economic performance is subject to the continuous monitoring of the international financial institutions. The "Asian values" argument advanced in East and Southeast Asia to contest external evaluation of human rights observation has no African counterpart. African elections, far more than those in any other region, routinely involve international observation and very frequently are contingent upon external financing and organizational assistance. There is thus a comprehensive superstructure of international accountability to which Africa is subject; the continent is compelled by its economic vulnerability to seek the respect of the international community. These factors render any widespread restoration of the unadulterated autocracy of the past unlikely.

The emergence in the 1990s of a distinctive regime type, born of the progressive weakening of many states in the preceding decades, is worthy of note. These ruling formations have come to power by military means, but not by the coup mechanism that was the principal means of displacement of incumbents from the 1960s through the 1980s. They originate in guerrilla movements with an ethnoregional core. The crucible of years of armed struggle nurtured both a populist doctrine quite distinct from the ethos of earlier regimes that originated in military coups and a relative cohesiveness of the inner leadership cadre. Once in power, these regimes— which invariably alter the cultural configuration of political power— espouse democratic principles, asserting that they are embedded in the nature of their struggle. However, there is a discernible allergy to political formations that reflect the *ancien régime*. In addition, the new regimes all face continued armed opposition from dissident fragments, which often find sanctuary and support in neighboring states. Examples of such systems include Eritrea, Ethiopia, Uganda, Rwanda, and—with qualifications— Chad.

The emergence of "semidemocracies" in a number of countries entrench practices associated with liberalization (freer press, better respect for human rights, open contestation), while forcing political rules that make alternation improbable.[57] One might add, in the African case, that semidemocracy is probably sufficient to deflect international system pressures for more complete political opening, particularly if macroeconomic management earns external approbation.

The balance sheet on democratization is thus mixed but, in my reading, mildly positive. Not all experiments will survive. But important changes have taken place in many countries beyond the more visible issue of multiparty elections: a freer and more vocal press, better respect for human rights, some headway toward an *état de droit*. The more visionary forms of integral populist democracy are difficult to imagine. But a slow, halting, uneven, but yet continuing movement toward a more polyarchical form of governance is possible.

In an essay composed at the beginning of the African third wave, I concluded:

> The many forebodings notwithstanding, the political experiment (or gamble) of democratization is as unavoidable as it is indispensable. . . . Integral liberalization, political as well as economic, offers only the possibility of ascent from the abyss. The political forms of the past carry a guarantee of failure. In the face of such stark alternatives, the choice is clear.[58]

I believe this conclusion still stands. The search for appropriate forms, economically as well as politically, will continue. But there is no plausible and preferable alternative on the horizon for this quest.

Notes

1. Huntington, *Third Wave*.
2. Young, "Permanent Transition."
3. An earlier, shortened version of this chapter appeared as Young, "Africa: An Interim Balance Sheet."
4. For example, Widner, ed., *Economic Change;* Hyden and Bratton, eds., *Governance and Politics;* Harbeson et al., eds., *Civil Society;* and Diamond et al., eds., *Politics in Developing Countries.*
5. Huntington, *Third Wave,* p. 16.
6. This point is developed at greater length in Young, "Decolonization" and *African Colonial State,* pp. 182–217.
7. See, for example, the well-reasoned arguments in Government of Tanzania, *Report of the Presidential Commission.* For influential academic briefs in support of the single party, see Morgenthau, *Political Parties;* Wallerstein, *Africa;* and Hodgkin, *African Political Parties.*
8. One may recollect the (in retrospect) surprisingly indulgent appraisals of the military as an institution equipped with the integrity, nation-building commitment, and discipline to direct the early stages of development, in such influential works as Janowitz, *Military in Political Development,* and J. Johnson, ed., *Role of the Military.*
9. Young, *Politics of Cultural Pluralism,* p. 520.
10. Huntington, *Political Order.*
11. Young, *Ideology and Development.*
12. Decalo, *Coups and Army Rule.*
13. Campbell, "Military Withdrawal," p. 318. In 1972, I attended one episode of this military pedagogy, delivered to a University of Ibadan student audience by Brigadier Rotimi in a packed auditorium. Oluwole Rotimi offered a very academic lecture on "the role of the military in developing nations," drawing liberally on political science classics. The audience was entertained but not persuaded.
14. The term comes from the 1982 African Studies Association presidential address of Richard Sklar, reprinted in Chabal, ed., *Political Domination.*
15. See the various contributions in Hayward, ed., *Elections.*
16. Coulon, "Senegal."
17. Boudon, "Burkina Faso."
18. Wiseman, *Democracy in Black Africa.*
19. For further detail, see Young, "The State and the Small Urban Center," pp. 322–323.
20. Kilby, *Industrialization;* Schatz, "Pirate Capitalism," p. 46; Baker, *Economics of Nigerian Federalism;* and Joseph, "Affluence and Underdevelopment." The official designation of the basic unit of Nigerian currency changed from the pound to the naira (₦) shortly after the end of the Nigerian civil war. Throughout this period, the currency held its value, roughly at an exchange relationship of ₦ 1 to U.S.$1.50.
21. On civil strife in Sudan, see the masterful studies by Deng, *War of Visions,* and Hutchinson, *Nuer Dilemmas.*

22. Often referred to as the Berg Report after one of its principal authors, Elliot Berg.

23. See the various contributions in Callaghy and Ravenhill, eds., *Hemmed In,* especially the useful policy history by Green, "The IMF and the World Bank," pp. 54–89.

24. Among many examples, one may cite Sandbrook, *Politics of Africa's Economic Stagnation;* Rothchild and Chazan, eds., *Precarious Balance;* and Ravenhill, ed., *Africa in Economic Crisis.*

25. Joseph, *Democracy and Prebendal Politics.*

26. Boulaga, *Les Conférences Nationales,* p. 14.

27. Bratton, "Economic Crisis."

28. See, for example, the article by World Bank official Landell-Mills, "Governance."

29. Hyden has most systematically advanced and defended this concept; see Hyden, "Governance."

30. Zartman, ed., *Collapsed States.*

31. Jackson, *Quasi-States.*

32. See the seminal article by Widner, "States and Statelessness."

33. *West Africa,* no. 4089 (March 4–10, 1996): 328.

34. São Tomé and Príncipe has had its second posttransition elections, with reelection of the president, Miguel Trovoado, but reversal of the party majority in the National Assembly and a change of prime ministers.

35. I have relabeled the "democratic" category with the more qualified title "relatively democratic," added the qualifier "or circumscribed" to the "ambiguous democratic commitment" type, and introduced a classification labeled "transition promised, not implemented." The countries that have been reclassified are Ghana, from "moderate democratic commitment" to "democratic," based on a fairly conducted 1996 election; Niger, from "democratic" to "circumscribed democratic commitment," following the January 1996 military coup and new constitution, with the military ruler seemingly legitimated by electoral process; Sierra Leone, from "contested sovereignty" to "democratic," on the basis of the 1996 election and subsequent negotiated peace; Tanzania, from "moderate democratic commitment" to "democratic," on the basis of a second competitive election, even though its conduct was contested in Zanzibar and Dar es Salaam; Eritrea, from "moderate democratic commitment" to "directed democracy," on the basis of limited opening to opposition; Uganda, ditto; and Zambia, from "democratic" to "moderate democratic commitment," on the basis of the serious imperfections in the second competitive elections in 1996. Algeria, Nigeria, Equatorial Guinea, Swaziland, and Congo (Zaire) have all been placed in the newly created category "transition promised, not implemented."

36. Ake, *Democracy and Development,* pp. 130–131. Ake proposes in place of the "impoverished liberal democracy which prevails in the industrial countries" (p. 129) a resolutely utopian integral populist version.

37. *Africa Confidential,* vol. 35, no. 24 (December 2, 1994).

38. This was the consensus among Kenyan political figures and observers I interviewed in Nairobi in January 1996.

39. Enloe, *Ethnic Soldiers.*

40. Mandelbaum, "Foreign Policy."

41. Huntington, "Clash of Civilizations."

42. Callaghy and Ravenhill, eds., *Hemmed In,* p. 467. See also the more pessimistic reading in Callaghy, "Africa," pp. 133–145.

43. The Ninjas were a Lari group, the dominant element in Brazzaville; the Zulus were an offshoot of the *mouvance présidentielle,* whose regional base was in

Niari, Bouenza, and Lekoumou, now combined into the ethnoregional acronym Nibolek; the Cobras were mainly remnants of the Sassou-Nguesso Presidential Guard, drawn from the environs of his northern village. See *Africa Confidential,* 17 December 1993; and Friedman and Sundberg, "Ethnic War."

44. *Jeune Afrique,* no. 1280 (November 23–29, 1995): 14–16.

45. In both Kenya and Togo, the respective Kalenjin and Kabre domination of the military command structure is a serious threat to any genuine hopes for alternation as part of the liberalization process.

46. For illuminating background, see Lemarchand, *Burundi,* and Reyntjens, "Proof of the Pudding."

47. See the careful account by Longman, "Rwanda."

48. Here I share the views of Donald Horowitz on the primacy of incentives for cooperation; see Horowitz, *Democratic South Africa?* The alternative perspective, argued by Arend Lijphart, calls for the use of cultural blocs as the basic structural segments of political society, with power sharing on the basis of proportionality and summit diplomacy by communal leaders; see Lijphart, *Power-Sharing* and *Democracy in Plural Societies.*

49. Bienen and Herbst, "Relationship Between Political and Economic Reform," p. 23.

50. World Bank, *World Development Report, 1995,* pp. 162–163.

51. Ibid.

52. Haggard and Kaufman, *Political Economy,* pp. 377–379.

53. *New African,* March 1996, p. 29.

54. Przeworski and Limongi, "Modernization," pp. 155–183.

55. Heilbrunn, "Togo."

56. Przeworski and Limongi, "Modernization," p. 177.

57. For a discussion of "semidemocracies" in Malaysia, Thailand, and Singapore, see William Case, "Can the 'Halfway House' Stand?" p. 439.

58. Young, "Democratization in Africa," p. 248.

3

Rethinking Democratic Transitions: Lessons from Eastern and Southern Africa

John W. Harbeson

The basic argument of this chapter is that the study of democratization still suffers from disproportionate emphasis on the conduct of initial, national-level multiparty elections. The components of this argument are (1) that this overemphasis derives from an inaccurate reading of the most widely accepted definition of "democracy," upon which much of contemporary democratic transitions theory appears to rest; and (2) that a broadened conceptualization of democratization will result in a significantly improved understanding of the status and quality of democracy and the prospects for it, at least in southern and eastern Africa.

Conceptualizing Democratic Transitions

Democracy in Empirical Theory

The argument that the study of democratization continues to overemphasize the electoral dimension is rooted both in the literature on democratic transitions and upon not necessarily accurate readings of the contemporary empirical democratic theory that undergirds that literature. Charles F. Cnudde and Deane E. Neubauer provided a working definition of "empirical theory" some years ago: theories that "are descriptive and explanatory, constructed from observations of the real world."[1] Giovanni Sartori is careful to insist that while different in their focus, normative and empirical conceptions of democracy must remain connected to each other: "What democracy *is* cannot be separated from what democracy *should be*."[2]

A reprise of Robert Dahl's widely accepted, frequently employed conception of democracy will help to elucidate this point. Eschewing a more comprehensive and idealistic formulation, Dahl limits himself to one key characteristic of democracy: governmental responsiveness to citizens on a continuing basis. He believes that the key requisites for achieving this end are citizen opportunity to (1) formulate preferences; (2) "signify their preferences to their fellow citizens and the government by individual and collective action"; and (3) have those preferences "weighed equally in the conduct of government."[3] Philippe Schmitter and Terry Lynn Karl are among those who join Dahl in the emphasis on responsive government as the core component, though they substitute "accountability" for "responsiveness."[4] They agree with Dahl in broadening the Schumpeterian definition, which had centered principally upon contestation.[5]

From these core requisites, Dahl derives the frequently cited eight "institutional guarantees" necessary for the empirical realization of democratic responsiveness: (1) freedom to form and join organizations; (2) freedom of expression; (3) universal adult suffrage; (4) the eligibility, in principle, of any citizen to seek public office; (5) the right of political leaders to compete freely for votes and support; (6) the existence of alternative sources of information; (7) free and fair elections; and (8) electorally accountable governmental policymaking institutions.[6] He adds that these institutional guarantees of realistically achievable democracy, or polyarchy, can be reduced to two basic theoretical dimensions: public contestation and inclusive participation. In a more recent work, however, Dahl restates some of these requisites in a more qualified manner as predominant tendencies; for example, he writes of free and fair elections, "in which coercion is comparatively uncommon," and the right to form "*relatively* independent associations."[7]

Schmitter and Karl have added two key criteria of their own: freedom of elected officials from "overriding" opposition from unelected officials; and a polity that is self-governing, whose decisions do not require approval by extraterritorial actors.[8] Others have also suggested that Dahl's requisites need broadening, but along different lines. Guillermo O'Donnell has suggested the following additions: (1) elected and some appointed officials should not be terminated before the end of their constitutionally mandated terms; (2) elected authorities "should not be constrained, vetoed, or excluded from certain policy domains by other, non-elected actors, especially the armed forces"; (3) the establishment of "uncontested national territory that clearly defines the voting population"; and (4) "an intertemporal expectation: the generalized expectation that a fair electoral process and its surrounding freedoms will continue into an indefinite future."[9] Note, however, that O'Donnell's recommendations continue to focus on elections.

Three critically important, but infrequently considered, elements of Dahl's formulation are his implicit assumption that public contestation and inclusive participation are sufficient in theory to yield governmental responsiveness, his further implicit assumption that they promote "equal weighting" of citizen preferences, and his explicit statement that the "institutions of society" must guarantee the eight requisites.[10] The key point is Dahl's contention that the eight requisites must be guaranteed by the "institutions of society."[11] Institutionalization of these requisites must be treated not just as evaluative criteria or as indicators of democracy, but as an element embodied in Dahl's very *definition* of democracy; that is, this requirement is fulfilled not by any particular set of institutions, but by the *institutionalizing process itself*. Schmitter and Karl consider various forms of institutionalizing democracy, but argue that these should be considered as indicators or evaluative criteria because "to include them as part of the generic definition of democracy itself would be to mistake the American polity for the universal model of democratic governance."[12] To insert *particular* institutional forms into the definition would in fact be to commit such parochialism (though not necessarily with an American slant, given their list). But the *process* of defining and establishing institutions to ordain these requisites *is* generic and not parochial.

Empirical democratic theory rests upon democratic behavior, or democratic agency. Dahl himself said as much years ago in his *Preface to Democratic Theory*: "At a minimum, it seems to me, democratic theory is concerned with processes by which ordinary citizens *exert a relatively high degree of control over leaders*."[13] Indeed, within the framework of empirical democratic theory, the process of institutionalizing these requisites could be treated as temporally, even logically, *prior* to commencing their enjoyment. The requisite for electorally accountable governmental policy-making institutions, in particular, could reasonably be read to imply *prior* citizen action to constitute a democratic state that can provide for such institutions. At least one important corollary follows: since free and fair elections are but one of the requisites, and since citizen action to establish these requisites is implicit in this definition of democracy, empirical democratic theory may assign logical and temporal priority to constitutional reform that enshrines democratic requisites, rather than to holding initial elections.

Variations in the type of antecedent authoritarian regime and in the manner in which opposition to the authoritarian regime develops may influence the merits and prospects of alternative models both for initiating and for continuing democratization processes.[14]

The applicability of empirical democratic theory and the theoretical literature on democratic transitions to Africa are at best problematic, reflecting important circumstantial differences between African transitions and antecedent transitions in Europe and the Americas. The hypothesis that empirical democratic theory intrinsically implies alternative models of democratic transition represents an injunction to students to develop those models based on the experience of all of the world's regions, including Africa. African experience, so incorporated, may then make a new and substantial contribution to empirical democratic theory.

Africa in Democratic Transitions Theory

When is a transition "democratic," and when is it not? Samuel Huntington makes explicit the connection between temporally constrained definitions of "transitions" and democratic elections: "The critical point in the process of democratization is the replacement of a government that was not chosen [freely and fairly] by one that is selected in a free, open, and fair election."[15] With respect to Africa, Michael Bratton, who has been quite critical of the received democratic transitions theory based heavily on Latin American and European experience, has nevertheless accepted the received definition of democratic transitions. He holds that "a country is held to have installed a democratic regime if, in a context of civil liberties, a competitive election is freely and fairly conducted and the election results are accepted by all contestants."[16]

Much of the literature has tended to define the subsequent consolidation phase of democratization more expansively and in a more open-ended fashion. Juan J. Linz and Alfred Stepan, for example, describe the consolidation phase as a period when "the overwhelming majority of the people [come to] believe that any further political change must emerge from within the parameters of democratic procedures . . . when all of the actors [are] habituated to . . . [conflict resolution by] established norms . . . and violations of these norms are likely to be both ineffective and costly."[17] They set forth five key "mutually interconnected and reinforcing conditions" that most students of democratization would probably agree must obtain for democratic consolidation to be achieved: (1) a free and lively civil society; (2) a relatively autonomous political society; (3) prevalent observance of the rule of law; (4) a state bureaucracy "that is usable by the new democratic government"; and (5) an "institutionalized economic society."[18]

A major problem with the existing, temporally constrained, election-centric conception of the "transition" phases lies in the implicit, excessive expectations of this period. These expectations include the presumptions that (1) democratic elections will ipso facto produce regime change from an incumbent authoritarian to a new, democratically inclined regime; (2) initial multiparty elections and/or regime change will ipso facto generate the momentum necessary to produce subsequent, broader patterns of democratization; (3) this momentum will be sufficient to generate the means to fulfillment of this broader array of democratization tasks in the "consolidation" phase, as outlined by Linz and Stepan;[19] (4) the initial multiparty elections taking place at the national level will lead to democratization processes at subnational levels; and (5) the polity itself will remain sufficiently stable to sustain transition and subsequent consolidation phases of democratization.

African Democratization Processes in Practice

What lessons does democratization experience in eastern and southern Africa offer concerning these problems in the transitions literature?[20] I will confine myself to evaluating three specifically *political* variables that evolving African experience indicates should be given more attention.[21] They support a specific hypothesis: African circumstances make it more likely that transitions will result in democratic progress to the extent that they commence with comprehensive multiparty agreements on the fundamental rules of the game, either through constitutional reform or by constitution-like pact making, than if they begin with initial multiparty elections in advance of such rule making.

This hypothesis represents less a departure from existing transitions literature than a change of emphasis and priorities within it as individual country circumstances dictate. Pact making has always featured in transitions literature, but pacts may be broadly or narrowly constructed. For example, they may (1) include only a narrow range of actors, or be formed by constituent assemblies elected on the basis of universal suffrage; (2) cover only the terms for the "exercise of power on the basis of mutual guarantees for the 'vital interests' of those entering into it," or extend more broadly to the terms of electoral *competition* for power and/or the reconstitution of the state as a whole; and (3) be temporary and "contingent upon ongoing consent," or be constructed so as to be enduring and inviolable for a lengthy period of time or even indefinitely.[22] In addition, pacts are by no means a necessary and sufficient condition for sustainable democratic transitions, particularly to the extent that they are narrowly crafted.[23] Thus, the hypothesis advanced here is that African circumstances often dictate that pacts that are broadly constructed in terms of participants, scope, and duration *prior* to the holding of initial multiparty elections are more conducive to enduring democratization than are more narrowly constructed pacts or the absence of any such pact. The distinction between broadly and narrowly constructed pacts is obviously one of degree. The more broadly constructed a pact is in terms of participants, scope, and duration, the more it may resemble a constitutional reform process.

The three specifically political elements that shape the directions of, and prospects for, African democratization include the strength of polyarchal foundations in the predemocratic era; the extent to which the movement(s) pressing for regime change exhibit polyarchal tendencies within their own ranks during their campaigns; and the degree of stateness in the polity itself in the years preceding and during the campaign to install democracy. "Stateness" may be defined, as suggested by Gilbert Khadiagala, as "the acquisition of capacities for the legitimation and exercise of power" or, according to his more rigorous definition, as "the functional ability of institutions to organize constraints and effect compliance to orient human action toward certain expectations and rules of procedure." The process of developing stateness, then, centers on "the mediations that transform the private lives of individuals into shared and collective identities."[24]

The premise of the first variable is that even where gradual pretransition processes of liberalization and the evolutionary building of foundations for polyarchy do not occur, those foundations may still exist, albeit in a weak condition. They may survive in a somewhat dormant condition under authoritarian rule, and they may be an important variable in the course of transitions.[25]

The second variable, the degree of polyarchy practiced within the insurgent movements that force democratic transitions, is especially important on a continent where several authoritarian regimes have been overthrown by military means as an outcome of prolonged civil war. These circumstances are very different from those in countries where civilian-led democratization movements have emerged and civil war has been avoided. To a varying but often significant degree, democratic transitions in Africa have been propelled by armies that have had little time or opportunity to convert themselves into political parties with polyarchal practices before competing for political power in elections or into leading governments. Africa's unique experience in this respect can make a significant contribution to global democratic transitions literature, and perhaps to underlying empirical democracy theory.

The third variable, the degree of stateness present at the outset of a democratic transition, also reflects distinctively African circumstances, where many polities are fragile and are faced with imminent potential disintegration or have already become failed states. The importance of this factor has been understated and underexamined in much of the literature on transitions and on empirical democratic theory, at least in part because fragile polities have been less characteristic of the Latin American and European experiences on which these literatures are principally based.[26]

Three "positive" and three "negative" examples lend support to the hypothesis presented above, and each of these has been significantly influenced by the political variables just identified. The positive examples— South Africa, Mozambique, and Eritrea—are cases in which detailed constitutional negotiations held prior to the initial elections appear to have played a major role in bringing about a promising start to the country's democratization process. These constitutional negotiations have either served to generate, build, and strengthen polyarchal practices in society at large and within contending political factions, or they have compensated for their relative absence. As a result, in each of these cases, initial multi-party elections and their aftermath have helped to consolidate, rather than undermine, embryonic democratization. The negative examples—Zambia, Kenya, and Ethiopia—are cases where an early emphasis on multiparty elections without prior establishment of constitutional ground rules appears to have been a significant factor in derailing democratic progress. The weakness or absence of constitutional negotiations preceding initial multi-party elections caused the elections to exacerbate or deepen the weakness of polyarchal practices and to tear dangerously at the fabric of the state itself.

Positive Cases

South Africa. In South Africa, detailed negotiations on an interim constitution preceded the holding of the first postapartheid multiparty elections. The negotiations also produced an interim "government of national unity" that reinforced the stability of the transition through the first year of African National Congress (ANC) leadership. The interim constitution has since been replaced by a permanent constitution that was ratified by the combined houses of the South African parliament serving as a constituent assembly. The social and economic challenges to stable democratic government in South Africa remain daunting, as do the many negative legacies of the apartheid era.[27] The new government has confronted potential pact-breaking issues, including the continuing tensions between the Inkatha Freedom Party and the ANC government over the issue of decentralization, as well as the writing of a permanent constitution.

South Africa's civil society had gained considerable strength during the later years of the anti-apartheid struggle, when it was aided by extensive external support. But this very strength has posed a significant challenge to both the new ANC government and to civil society itself, as the polity seeks to convert civil society institutions from instruments of opposition to monitors of democratic adherence, to enlist their constructive participation in postapartheid socioeconomic and political development while not compromising their autonomy, and to institutionalize democratic participation as an alternative to violent confrontation. In addition, notwithstanding their democratic commitments, the ANC and the other parties that collaborated with it to end apartheid were impeded by the nature of the struggle itself from nurturing polyarchal practices within their own ranks.[28] However, in comparison with the situation elsewhere in Africa, threats to the viability of the South African polity have been somewhat subdued.[29]

Despite these immediate challenges and long-term problems, participants in the posttransition struggles have not dared, by deed or by word, to oppose or seek to undermine the democratic rules of the game. Neither the ANC government nor any faction within it has tried to resort to extraconstitutional means to sustain its power, nor have they been accused of doing so by the opposition. All parties accepted the results of the 1994 national elections, and democratization has been further extended by the subsequent conduct of local elections in which the ANC government gained still broader political support. To date, there has been no return, or threat of return, to the violent confrontations of the apartheid era.

One cannot assign sole credit for sustaining embryonic democracy in South Africa to the broadly constructed rules of the game that preceded the first national multiparty elections. For example, the stature of Nelson Mandela has also clearly been an important factor in sustaining both political stability and democracy in South Africa. Encouraging early evidence of sustainable democratization also does not preclude the emergence of more serious challenges in the future. Nevertheless, one can argue that both immediate and long-term crisis-generating issues have been addressed within the newly minted democratic framework precisely because broadly constituted rules of the game have been established and recognized as legitimate. More hastily drawn up and less comprehensively and legitimized rules of the game might well have proved less durable and resilient in the early stages, thereby endangering sustainable democracy.

Mozambique. The November 1994 elections in Mozambique were a stunning achievement. They were broadly acknowledged to have been free and fair, and the outcome was accepted by bitterly opposed parties, which a scant two years earlier had still been mired in a military confrontation that had dragged on for years. Particularly exemplary was the manner in which the thousands of election officials took ownership of the balloting process while operating under the most difficult and onerous logistical difficulties. Also notable was the clear absence of support within the ranks of the Mozambique National Resistance Movement (RENAMO) for leader Alfonso Dhlakama's threatened boycott on the eve of the election. The Front for the Liberation of Mozambique (FRELIMO) and RENAMO have—even in each other's eyes—generally operated within a democratic framework. Plans are under way to extend democracy through local elections and possibly through greater decentralization of the government.

Multiparty democracy began to take root in Mozambique under the most difficult and challenging circumstances. One of the world's poorest countries, Mozambique's communications and transportation infrastructure was shattered as a result of the civil war, which had been waged continuously since, or even prior to, independence in 1975. The duration and bitterness of the civil war rendered the very possibility of a unified Mozambican state problematic at best. Neither FRELIMO nor RENAMO had much inclination or opportunity to evolve polyarchal practices internally, making the early stages of the democratic transition, in which they faced the task of extending polyarchal institutions throughout the country, much more difficult. Caught up in and between the warring armies, the people of Mozambique also had few resources or opportunities to evolve polyarchal civil society institutions. Yet as a result of hastily arranged recruitment and training by the parties, and with the benefit of massive international financial and logistical support, thousands of Mozambican citizens staffed polling stations and conducted the election processes with remarkable professionalism and success. Their performance provides support for the hypothesis that democratic instincts and polyarchal propensities may survive dormant within society, silenced, but not extinguished, by oppression and civil war.

No single factor is responsible for Mozambique's democratic progress to date under these difficult circumstances. There was evident exhaustion on the part of all parties after years of inconclusive warfare, which contributed to a popular sense that conducting the election was a way to institutionalize peace. In addition, the extensive, and intensive, involvement of external donors in providing financial, political, and human resources contributed to the success of the elections. Visionary leadership on the part of the heads of several embassies and donor agencies and unusually effective donor coordination also played an important role. Gifted and dedicated Mozambicans in key places helped as well. The creation of a separate fund for RENAMO, the merits of which have been a source of some disagreement, was justified as a means of helping RENAMO match government resources to convert its battlefield legions into civilian political cadres.

Notwithstanding these powerful influences in support of a peaceful electoral launch of Mozambique's democratic transition, there is room to question whether these influences could have been brought to bear effectively had it not been for the prior comprehensive and detailed agreements among the parties. Agreements on the peace and on the electoral rules did not include constitutional reform, which still lies ahead for the country, but these two agreements covered the basic rules of the game for the initial period of Mozambique's democratization in comprehensive detail.[30] These agreements were less broad than those in South Africa, but they did extend to the period of the initial national elections. Further, although they were conducted by party elites, they were covered extensively by the press and even to some extent by the country's embryonic television facilities.

Eritrea. The Eritrean People's Liberation Front (EPLF)—now renamed the People's Front for Democracy and Justice (PFDJ)—completed the military ouster of Mengistu Haile Mariam's armies in 1991, just as Mengistu was about to be overthrown by a coalition of forces led by the Ethiopian People's Revolutionary Democratic Front (EPRDF). The PFDJ agreed to delay its independence referendum until mid-1993, and it sought to mediate between the EPRDF and the Oromo Liberation Front (OLF) in Ethiopia. These were gestures of support for the EPRDF, motivated by concern for Ethiopia's political stability.

After more than three years of independence, Eritrea remains a single-party state and has yet to conduct national-level multiparty elections. While some members of the Eritrean Liberation Front (ELF), the PFDJ's vanquished former rival, have been incorporated into the PFDJ government at all levels, there has been continuing conflict with unreconciled ELF cadres operating from neighboring countries. Skeptical observers cite this evidence to support their doubts about the future of democracy in Eritrea. In addition, Eritrea's economic prospects are bleak, as the country is heavily dependent upon cooperation with Ethiopia for an economic renaissance in both countries.

While understated by African standards, the potential for tension exists among the country's nine major ethnic/linguistic communities. In a country divided almost equally between adherents of Christianity and Islam, the PFDJ government has been greatly concerned that Sudan has been exporting radical Islam to Eritrea via the thousands of refugees returning to the country from exile in Sudan. Eritrea's diplomatic relations with Sudan have been severed since 1995. Finally, the demobilization of the PFDJ's military personnel has been difficult, both because of unemployment problems and because female soldiers who were treated as equals in the armed forces have now returned to face continued discrimination in less liberated, predominantly rural traditional societies.

Against this daunting array of obstacles, what bases are there for counting Eritrea as a potential democratization success story? First, as a newly independent country, Eritrea's reservoir of stateness is limited, yet there is a significant commitment to the preservation and strengthening of the Eritrean state as a consequence of the energy, skill, and dedication exhibited during the war of independence. Anecdotal evidence suggests that the EPLF leadership recognized that fighting a guerrilla war necessitated a greater-than-normal degree of autonomy for field units, and it encouraged initiative and self-reliance, traits that have become significant foundations for democracy after independence.

Second, the PFDJ has issued a policy statement that incorporates some of the clearest and most comprehensive commitments to democracy of any ruling party on the continent. In addition to specific commitments to the recognition and observance of a wide array of basic human rights, the policy adopted at its March 1994 party conference committed the government to the recognition of other political parties and to the practice of multiparty democracy. Further, in an important step overlooked even in much of the academic literature on democratization, the PFDJ articulated and implemented a commitment to separate the ruling party from the government in organizational, financial, and personnel terms.[31] Two senior ministers left the government to assume the leadership of the PFDJ.

Third, the Eritrean government has allowed an independent, representative Constitutional Commission, appointed by its protoparliament, to operate without governmental interference. Moreover, the Constitutional Commission has set an example for similar bodies everywhere by engaging public participation in the formation of the new Eritrean constitution as it is being developed, not simply through a plebiscite after it is drafted. It has created local advisory committees and held deliberations throughout the country, and it has also conducted meetings outside of the country, including Europe and North America, for the benefit of expatriate Eritreans. The commission has produced a draft that was ratified by a constituent assembly in May 1997.[32] During this prolonged process, the PFDJ government, untested by challenges to its continued leadership of the country, has maintained a creditable human rights record. Eritrea will thus be an important test of the hypothesis that, particularly in African circumstances, constitution formation prior to initial multiparty elections may contribute to sustainable democratization.

Negative Cases

The negative cases from eastern and southern Africa all share the experience of having conducted multiparty elections with only limited prior agreements among the rival parties on the fundamental rules of the game. In two cases, Zambia and Kenya, there were no interparty pacts prior to the initial multiparty elections. In the third case, Ethiopia, a hastily arranged pact proved insufficiently comprehensive and detailed given the circumstances. As a result, the validity and efficacy of the first elections were threatened before they even took place, leading to an apparently indefinite continuation of single-party rule.

Zambia. In Zambia, the multiparty elections of 1991 resulted in a stunning victory for the Movement for Multiparty Democracy (MMD) under Frederick Chiluba, which defeated the United National Independence Party (UNIP) of Kenneth Kaunda, the leader of Zambia's nationalist movement and the country's founding president. Only after this transition did Zambia set about revising its constitution along democratic lines. Despite the advantages of a relatively secure state, evidence of vitality in civil society, and at least the potential for polyarchal practice within Chiluba's insurgent party, by early 1997 Zambia's democratic achievements and prospects had been severely eroded. Having won power in acceptable, if flawed, elections, the Chiluba government has since compiled a mixed human rights record, particularly with respect to the private print media. It resisted strong domestic and donor pressure to publish the Constitutional Commission's draft document for public debate prior to editing by the MMD government, and it insisted that the document would be ratified only by the Zambian parliament, in which the MMD has enjoyed a substantial majority. In one of its most serious departures from democratic practice, the MMD insisted that the draft document should restrict eligibility to run for president to third-generation Zambians, and it pressured its representatives on the Constitutional Commission to incorporate such a provision. This stricture explicitly challenged Kaunda's right to a rematch with Chiluba in the fall 1996 elections, since he is partially of recent Malawian ancestry.[33] In response, UNIP boycotted the 1996 elections. Without agreement among the parties on the basic rules of the game *prior* to the initial multiparty elections, no semblance of democratically legitimated constraints existed that could restrain the abuses of democratic practice by the victors. Far from strengthening and creating momentum for democracy, the 1996 elections in Zambia have had the opposite effect.

The damage that this flawed constitution-writing process has caused to the Zambian state is potentially even more serious than that done to democracy. Rodger Chongwe, a distinguished Zambian lawyer and former minister of constitutional affairs, has observed that the constitutional barrier to "immigrant" presidential candidacies has struck at an important foundation of Zambian national political identity; previously the state has been at least moderately successful at melding a large number of ethnic communities into one multiethnic state.[34]

Kenya.   In Kenya, no pact preceded the first multiparty elections to be held in more than a quarter of a century.[35] Instead, angered by Kenya's poor human rights record and indications of its deleterious effects on the country's economy, donors imposed an embargo on further development assistance until the government of President Daniel arap Moi agreed to permit multiparty national elections. Moi eventually acceded to this pressure, enabling a parliament dominated by his ruling Kenya African National Union (KANU) to make the change in one article of the constitution that was necessary to permit multiparty elections. The elections, held in December 1992, were closely watched by a core of donor-funded international observers. A splintered opposition and an apportionment of parliamentary seats unfavorable to the opposition, particularly in the major cities, enabled KANU to prevail with a strong majority in parliament, despite receiving considerably less than a majority of the popular vote.

Whereas most observers and politically active Kenyans agree that Kenya is more democratic than it was before the 1992 elections, the country has marked time in democratization. The KANU government has resisted carrying out much-needed constitutional reform, even though it dominates parliament. Reforms of existing legislation that are necessary to advance democracy have also bogged down. The government's human rights record has been mediocre. It has repeatedly inhibited opposition-party efforts to exercise freedom of association, and opposition politicians have been harassed and even arrested for political activity in their own districts. Serious ethnic clashes, which have resulted in many deaths and tens of thousands of displaced families, are widely believed to have been encouraged or instigated by individuals within the KANU government. President Moi has also explicitly threatened districts that vote for opposition parliamentarians with loss of official development assistance. Finally, the government has periodically harassed private print media and arrested its editors and publishers.

Whereas by-elections have generally been acceptably free and fair *on election day,* the campaigns have been marred by serious abuses. These abuses are attributable principally to KANU, although the opposition parties have also been at fault in many instances. The opposition parties have also been fragmented by factional feuding, rendering their capacity to form a government highly doubtful. Meanwhile, the judiciary and the election commission are not independent of the KANU government. Civil society pressure on the government to allow further democratization has been unremitting and often courageous, particularly on the part of the churches, the NGO (nongovernmental organization) congress, and the Kenya Human Rights Commission.

Kenya thus provides one of the clearest examples in Africa of the precariousness of undertaking multiparty elections as the first step toward democracy before interparty agreement has been forged and the fundamental rules of the game reformed. Lacking such an agreement, opposition parties and civil society have remained futilely dependent upon a manifestly unsympathetic government to initiate further democratization. Donor pressure upon the Kenyan government to permit multiparty elections should, in retrospect, have extended to fashioning broader multiparty agreement on reforming the rules of the game, and perhaps to electing a constituent assembly to draft a new constitution. Whereas the fragmentation and factional strife within and among the opposition parties are largely the responsibility of the parties themselves, government harassment of opposition-party politicians has obviously not encouraged polyarchal development within any of the parties.

Ethiopia. Ethiopia represents a divergent example of a democratization process that has stalled at least in part as a consequence of the sequencing of elections and restructuring of the rules of the game.[36] The armies of the EPRDF led a coalition of military forces in overthrowing the 17-year military dictatorship of Mengistu Haile Mariam in May 1991. Their final takeover was preceded by a hastily assembled peace conference in London, at which the then U.S. assistant secretary of state, Herman Cohen, blessed the EPRDF's capture of the capital, but with the injunction "no democracy, no cooperation." In July 1991, at a conference hastily convened by the EPRDF, all parties subscribed to a Transition Charter intended to guide the ensuing political transition.[37] The charter ordained a transition of 30 months, during which regional, rather than national, elections would be held first and as soon as possible, a constitution would be drafted and ratified, and only then were national elections to be held for the first permanent, posttransition government. The charter upheld basic human rights and mandated the realization of the EPRDF's fundamental vision for a postimperial Ethiopian state that would end more than a century of Amhara-Tigre ethnic domination.[38] The EPRDF proposed to radically decentralize state power to regions configured on an ethnic basis, thereby building a postimperial state founded on ethnic equality. Since then, the All Amhara People's Organization, established subsequent to the Transition Charter conference, has articulated resentment against what it fears is the Balkanization of Ethiopia inherent in the EPRDF's plan. The Oromo Liberation Front (OLF), representing some of the peoples colonized by Menelik II, actively supported the plan, but questioned the sincerity of the EPRDF, a Tigre-based movement, to implement it.

The interparty consensus articulated in the charter did not persist because it did not take into account the most serious immediate problems confronting the victorious parties: the demobilization and reintegration of the soldiers of all armies into the economy and society, plus the need to fashion an integrated, politically neutral army and police force. The charter was unrealistic in setting a timetable for regional elections and allowed insufficient time for these processes to reach fruition. In acting as the surrogate army/police force for the country as a whole, the EPRDF appeared to act contrary to agreements it made to demobilize and encamp all armies. The mutual distrust between the OLF and the EPRDF fed what may have been a preexisting disposition of the EPRDF to establish its military and political hegemony over the country at all costs. Moreover, the EPRDF established auxiliary parties to compete with its erstwhile military allies in the areas where it claimed hegemony.

The result of these tensions was the withdrawal of the OLF and all of the EPRDF's former allies from the regional elections in June 1992. In effect, the 1992 regional elections proved to be a watershed event, shattering the possibility of achieving a multiparty consensus on the foundations of the postimperial state. The OLF then mounted what proved to be a brief, futile military challenge to the EPRDF. Despite efforts to mediate the divide between the EPRDF and the opposition parties, notably by Jimmy Carter, the opposition parties have remained unreconciled, leaving the military and political field to the EPRDF. Subsequent constituent assembly and parliamentary elections in 1994 and 1995, respectively, have essentially been plebiscitary events confirming the de facto single-party Ethiopian state. The new constitution, although democratic in form, is the creation of the EPRDF alone, rather than a multiparty exercise. The incomplete and unrealistic nature of the hastily formulated Transition Charter was thus an inadequate foundation for a democratic transition.

The key factor underlying the demise of multiparty democracy in post-Mengistu Ethiopia has been not only inadequate attention to demobilization of the armed forces, but also the nearly total failure to convert armies into political parties that exhibit polyarchal organization and a commitment to democratic practices. The development of a democratic civil society had been obstructed by years of military dictatorship following an unrelieved history of feudalism and empire. Civil society was thus too weak to assist the conversion of armies to parties. Combined with the inadequacies of the Transition Charter, the result has been a post-Mengistu state that rests on the military and political hegemony of the EPRDF, rather than upon established polyarchal foundations. The EPRDF's vision of a postimperial state founded upon interethnic equality is likely to remain elusive.

Conclusion

Empirical democratic theory, upon which the democratic transitions literature rests, suggests that establishing the fundamental rules of the game is at least as valuable as elections in the early stages of the democratization process. This demonstrates the possibility and desirability of fashioning alternative models of democratic transitions that are attuned to the circumstances of individual countries. Such an approach would facilitate the incorporation of embryonic African democratization experience into theories of democratic transitions, which have previously been based primarily on the experiences of Europe and the Americas.

The election-centric basis of much current democratic transitions theory weakens the theory in several important ways, but this can be corrected by refashioning this body of theory, allowing it to embrace alternative starting points for democratic transitions. This hypothesis represents less an innovation in democratic transitions theory than its modification, placing greater emphasis upon pacts that are broadly defined in terms of the range of participants, their scope, and their intended durability.

Finally, taking into account the continent's particular circumstances, African democratization experience suggests that democratic transitions are more likely to be sustained when the formation of broadly defined pacts precedes, rather than follows, initial multiparty elections. The experiences of Mozambique, postapartheid South Africa, and possibly Eritrea offer positive support for this hypothesis; each of these countries achieved broad preelection agreements on the fundamental rules of the political game. In contrast, the transitions in Ethiopia, Kenya, and Zambia appear to have stalled or regressed, in large part as a consequence of conducting their initial multiparty elections prior to achieving such agreements.

Notes

1. Cnudde and Neubauer, *Empirical Democratic Theory,* p. 3.
2. Sartori, *Democratic Theory, Revisited,* p. 7.
3. Dahl, *Polyarchy,* p. 3.
4. Schmitter and Karl, "What Democracy Is," p. 76.
5. Schumpeter, *Capitalism, Socialism, and Democracy.*
6. Dahl, *Polyarchy,* p. 3. In later work, Dahl reduces these requisites to seven, treating the fifth requisite—the right of leaders to compete freely for votes—as implicit in the requirements of free and fair election and of freedom of political association (Dahl, *Dilemmas of Pluralist Democracy,* p. 11).
7. Dahl, *Dilemmas of Pluralist Democracy,* p. 11.
8. Schmitter and Karl, "What Democracy Is," p. 76.
9. O'Donnell, "Illusions," pp. 34–51.
10. Charles E. Gilbert provides a useful two-by-two accountability matrix: formal/informal and external/internal. External formal accountability implies constitutional or legislative institutions that define patterns of accountability, including elections and checks and balances, while internal formal accountability consists of intraorganizational rules, guidelines, and regulations. Internal informal accountability involves personal accountability to one's own moral and intellectual convictions, while external informal patterns of accountability encompass interest group representation and their nonelectoral forms of citizen pressure on leaders. See Gilbert, "Framework."
11. Gilbert, "Framework," pp. 2–3.
12. Schmitter and Karl, "What Democracy Is," p. 84.
13. Dahl, *Preface to Democratic Theory,* p. 3; emphasis added.
14. Samuel Huntington contributes to the beginnings of such a comparative study of transition models in his *Third Wave.* However, its empirical scope appears to be limited to Latin American and European experience and to be less applicable to African experience, which began subsequent to the publication of his book. Similarly, Michael Bratton and Nicolas van de Walle have advanced this agenda with respect to Africa in "Neopatrimonial Regimes." However, their emphasis is on the antecedent predemocratic regimes, rather than upon the new democratic regimes themselves.
15. Huntington, *Third Wave,* p. 9.
16. Bratton, "Testing Competing Explanations," p. 3.
17. Linz and Stepan, "Toward Consolidated Democracies," p. 15.
18. Ibid., p. 17.
19. Ibid.
20. From this point forward, I will use the term "transition" to apply to the full course of democratization, rather than to the more conventional, narrower definition discussed earlier.
21. I do not by any means exclude the great importance of socioeconomic factors in democratic transitions. I concentrate here on specifically political elements simply in the interests of brevity.
22. O'Donnell and Schmitter, *Transitions,* p. 37.
23. The point is well made by Herbst in "Prospects for Elite-Driven Democracy."

24. In Zartman, ed., *Collapsed States,* p. 34.

25. O'Donnell and Schmitter, *Transitions,* p. 37.

26. I have explored this theme in Harbeson, *Ethiopian Transformation.*

27. These problems are clearly and carefully portrayed in Stedman, ed., *South Africa,* and Sisk, *Democratization.*

28. An incisive account of these stresses is to be fond in Lodge, *Black Politics.*

29. Sisk, *Democratization.*

30. An as-yet-unpublished paper by Michael Turner examines the processes by which the multiparty "pact" on the election law evolved. See Turner, "Multiparty Conference," as well as his *Electoral Law of Mozambique,* Government of Mozambique, 1992. Professor Turner served as democracy and governance adviser to the Mozambique Mission of the United States Agency for International Development during the critical early years of the Mozambican democratic transition, 1992–1995.

31. While an important commitment, it is not without its complexities. How can ruling or opposition parties legitimately raise funds privately in a country as poor as Eritrea? And like parties in democracies everywhere, how can parties keep from being corrupted by the monies they do raise? The PFDJ has yet to arrive at clear answers to these questions.

32. Constitutional Commission of Eritrea, *Draft Constitution.*

33. Chiluba's opponents have alleged that Chiluba himself is of recent Zairian ancestry.

34. A carefully written, useful history of Zambia that generally supports Chongwe's observation is A. Roberts, *History of Zambia.*

35. Recent studies of Kenyan politics include Holmquist and Ford, "Kenya's Authoritarian Continuity"; Barkan, "Divergence and Convergence"; Chege, "Return of Multiparty Politics"; and Holmquist, "Stalling Political Change."

36. Recent work on Ethiopia includes Harbeson, *Elections and Democratization.* Works on the Mengistu years include Clapham, *Transformation and Continuity;* Keller, *Revolutionary Ethiopia;* and Harbeson, *Ethiopian Transformation.*

37. The Amhara, who were the predominant power holders during the regimes of Ethiopia's four modern emperors from 1851 to 1974, were conspicuously unrepresented by any party, although several prominent Amhara attended as individuals. Two Mengistu-era parties, both of which were eventually alienated from his regime but which also fought the EPRDF, were also excluded.

38. While the empire ended in legal terms with the demise of Haile Selassie's regime, in a larger sense it was perpetuated during the Mengistu era, despite that regime's ideological commitments and its proclamations to the contrary. While the quasi-feudal socioeconomic structure, particularly visible in landholding patterns, was liquidated by Mengistu, the authoritarianism of his regime obstructed the creation of a postimperial state. The armies of Haile Selassie's predecessor, Menelik II, subjected two-thirds or more of the country (as it is presently defined) to his rule and that of the essentially Amhara-Tigre ethnic configuration undergirding his regime. Mengistu's dictatorial rule did little or nothing to alter this underlying pattern of ethnic domination.

4

The Reconfiguration of Power in Late Twentieth-Century Africa

RICHARD JOSEPH

A few years after the end of the Cold War and the collapse of the Soviet Union, sub-Saharan Africa appeared to some observers to be a site of increasing anarchy and destitution.[1] Not only writers for the popular media, but also academic scholars, expressed concern about the "sense of profound disorder on the continent."[2] A number of devastating conflicts contributed to these perceptions, notably, those in Liberia, Somalia, and Rwanda. At the same time, many African countries were experiencing the disruptions of the return to competitive party politics and the slow shift from statist to market-oriented economic systems. Despite these seemingly disparate processes, it has gradually become evident that a reconfiguration of power has been taking place. The term "reconfiguration" is used here to convey the tentative nature of these adjustments. This chapter will delineate the general pattern of these transformations as a prelude to the formulation of new frameworks of analysis.

The Dynamics of State Survival

Christopher Clapham, in his 1996 book *Africa and the International System: The Politics of State Survival,* pulls together many of the factors relevant to an understanding of the new pattern of power relations in Africa. Clapham anchors his thesis to the distinction made by Robert Jackson and Carl Rosberg between empirical and juridical statehood in Africa, and to their discussion of the role of international society in sustaining states that lack most attributes of empirical statehood.[3] He contends that postcolonial African regimes have benefited greatly from the prevailing "international mythologies of statehood" and the premise that "for any given territory or group of people there must necessarily be a corresponding state."[4] Following independence from colonial rule, states that originally aimed to become corporate bodies identified with the people, in reality narrowed to the persons currently in the government, and in some cases to a single individual. The ability to procure resources from the international system was critical to both the creation and the maintenance of these increasingly dysfunctional political entities.

As economies atrophied and populations retreated from this "monopoly state," the distance between the claims to juridical statehood and the reality of domestic ineffectiveness widened. "Statelessness" eventually came to describe more accurately the conditions under which many Africans lived. Clapham points out that the end of the Cold War coincided with, rather than provoked, the failure of this conception of the state.[5] During previous decades, international society has sustained these monopoly regimes as Cold War proxies, protectorates of ex-colonial powers, or both. Clapham advances a revised periodization of the postcolonial era by describing the onset of a second cold war in the mid-1970s in which Africa became more important as an arena of international rivalry, as reflected in arms sales that increased significantly. Instead of being strengthened, however, these recipients of military largesse—"Angola, Chad, Ethiopia, Liberia, Mozambique, Somalia, Sudan, Zaire"—represent "a list of its failed and collapsed states."[6]

The relentless search for external resources to secure or maintain internal dominance is a common characteristic of the international politics of African juridical states, as well as of "warlord insurgencies." Applying his framework of patrimonial politics and "dependent clientelism" to domestic arenas within Africa, and to external relationships between African countries and wealthier states and agencies, Clapham shows the parallels between the patterns of governance in several juridical states and in territories controlled by warlords.[7] As the capacity of the former declined, and as Africa came to be regarded as "a source of problems rather than of opportunities," the advantages of juridical statehood over statelessness also declined. While acknowledging the impact on African societies of the imposition of economic liberalization through structural adjustment programs, and the encouragement of political liberalization, Clapham is generally skeptical about these developments, which he refers to derisively as assumed "technologies of universal validity."[8]

Clapham believes that many African countries have failed to negotiate the passage from "quasi-statehood" to "empirical statehood," a passage that would be reflected in "national integration and a set of viable political and economic institutions."[9] Instead, domestic and international actors, whether governmental or nongovernmental, engage in licit or illicit transfers of resources within national territories or across their boundaries, while leaders of monopoly states seek to capture sufficient external resources, including military armaments, to sustain their often predatory rule. Three major consequences of these dynamics have been sharp economic decline in Africa, especially since 1980; the rise of armed insurgencies; and the emergence of large communities of refugees, which Clapham considers the clearest indicator of state failure.

Power, Violence, and Authority

Achille Mbembe's writings are also pertinent to this inquiry. In a series of probing essays, Mbembe provides abundant insights into the multiple uses of power and what he calls the "recomposition" of authority systems in Africa. Central to his outlook is a deep skepticism about the democratic transitions that have been occurring on the continent. The concern he expressed as early as 1990 that democratization is mainly about "presentability" to influence world opinion has since become the consensus opinion of African scholars:

> There is reason to fear that some of the reforms currently underway in several countries may be limited to mere cosmetic changes. Regimes which long relied on modes of authoritarian governance are making an about-turn and verbally espousing democratic ideals. How do we know they are not just trying to guarantee their survival and defend the interests of those in power?[10]

Mbembe identifies continuities between pre- and postcolonial Africa in the exercise of power, the resort to violence, and the nature of political authority. He cites examples from nineteenth-century Africa of the accumulation of wealth via a blending of trading and raiding activities, and the reliance on force to acquire and expand economic networks. He further demonstrates the extent to which the current interweaving of legitimate and illicit activities on the continent is reminiscent of earlier periods in the historical evolution of African societies.[11] In addition, the command nature of the colonial state, its ultimate reliance on brute force, and its highly exploitative practices paved the way for the predatory character of many postcolonial African regimes and the prevailing "culture of impunity."[12] Contemporary transformations in Africa, according to Mbembe, should not be considered "in a teleological manner," as is often the case in studies of democratic transitions. Rather, it should be recognized that "these 'transitions' are only some of the multiple aspects—and perhaps not the most decisive—of the various transformations currently taking place on the continent." Mbembe perceptively concludes that "Africa is heading in several directions simultaneously."[13]

Mbembe's vision of contemporary Africa is a bleak one. He emphasizes the criminalization of the state and the privatization of violence, the material devastation experienced by the masses of the people, and the steady erosion of the capacity of African governments to effect their own policies under the onslaught of externally imposed austerity programs.[14] The social consequences of the "gangsterism" and "warfare" associated with much of economic life are therefore grim and reflect a pervasive "nihilism."[15] Mbembe would substitute for the terminology of "political transitions" the notion of "recompositions" that involve the introduction of new "formulas of domination," the "co-existence, within the same dynamic, of elements belonging to warfare as to the conduct of civil politics," and the establishment of political systems in which the ethnoclientelist distribution of public goods is being replaced by greater austerity, predation, and repression.[16]

From Authoritarianism to Virtual Democracy

The above summaries of Clapham's and Mbembe's arguments provide important insights into the reconfiguration of power in Africa. While I agree with Mbembe that democratization is best understood as one factor in a broad set of transformations since 1989, I do not fully share his sweeping dismissal of these processes.[17] This reconfiguration has undoubtedly included the creation of several viable constitutional democracies, for example, in Ghana and Benin. In most African countries, significant arenas for political assertion, mobilization, and contestation now exist, even though they may also be utilized and manipulated by incumbent regimes to slow democratic progress.

The end of the Cold War provoked what Lucian Pye has appropriately referred to as a "global crisis of authoritarianism."[18] Political systems in Africa before 1990 were overwhelmingly authoritarian, and the disappearance of the Soviet Union exposed these regimes to criticism that they had previously disregarded or stifled. External interventions to formulate, finance, and monitor economic reform strategies during the 1980s were accompanied by an increased willingness to influence, encourage, and in some cases demand political reforms.[19] The intensity of this crisis of authoritarianism varied in different countries. The natural tendency of African regimes was to seek to protect existing political structures and the configuration of social forces that sustained their power and control.[20] Pye predicted that "a wide variety of systems that will become part authoritarian and part free" were likely to emerge.[21] Moreover, some of these intermediate or hybrid systems could reach "relatively lasting equilibrium," and further analysis may be needed to understand the "conditions that will bring about transitions from one state of equilibrium to another."[22] Similarly, in a review of democratization in Africa, I concluded that most countries were adopting what I characterized as "virtual democracy," some features of which include:

- A formal basis in citizen rule, but with key decisionmaking (especially economic) insulated from popular involvement
- Manipulation of democratic transitions by political incumbents, including the use of violence and electoral fraud, to relegitimize their power
- Wider popular participation, but narrow policy choices and outcomes
- External encouragement of multiparty elections on the premise that they will not threaten vested domestic and foreign interests if incumbents act adroitly[23]

The emergence of virtual, rather than "real," democracies in Africa is not just a consequence of the success of incumbent leaders in thwarting demands for more open political systems; it is the outcome of a more complex interplay of interests and motives. In addition to the essentially political crisis of authoritarianism mentioned by Pye, there was also a fiscal crisis in most African states, as well as enhanced fears of conflict and even chaos on the continent. Attempts to introduce market economies have been more sweeping than the adoption of liberal democratic systems; and economic stabilization programs have been heavily influenced by substantial inflows of public capital. Thus the reconfiguration of power on the continent is now determined by a calculus that reflects key external concerns. In particular, building market economies and a concern for order and stability have vaulted above democratization in the priorities of the donor community.

Incumbent regimes, which had long been able to fend off internal and external demands for political reform, were finally obliged to liberalize their systems after 1989. From the standpoint of many of these regimes, far-reaching democratization was likely to mean defeat.[24] Success, on the other hand, required not simply persistence in power, but a more nuanced process of learning to submit without succumbing. There was a sharp learning curve after 1989 as authoritarian regimes mastered the script of contemporary democratization while finding ways to neutralize and disable its transformative mechanisms. With the exception of a very small number of regimes, such as the Islamic fundamentalist government in Sudan, all African regimes were eventually prepared to reconfigure their political institutions to make continued inflows of aid and loans from Western-financed bilateral and multilateral agencies possible. They learned that they did not have to democratize in order to retain such financial flows. What they had to accept, however, was the abandonment of Clapham's "monopoly state" and the adoption of varying degrees of political liberalization, however effectively constrained in practice.

Seven years after the major Western governments encouraged African governments to democratize or risk having external aid and other assistance reduced, what has come to be regarded as satisfactory political progress is in fact the creation of semicompetitive systems. In these systems, opposition political parties are allowed to exist, although they may be hemmed in, as in Ethiopia, or not allowed to compete in elections, as in Uganda. Independent newspapers are permitted to be published, but they may be regularly harassed by administrative and other measures, as in Zambia. Civic groups are allowed to function, although they may be stymied in their efforts to cohere into a robust civil society, as in Ghana. Elections are regularly conducted, but opposition parties may be subjected to destabilizing stratagems, up to and including the falsification of results, as in Cameroon, Niger, and Togo.

Following D. Rueschemeyer, E. H. Stephens, and J. D. Stephens, I contend that political outcomes in Africa after 1989 can be analyzed in terms of a triangular alignment of forces: incumbent regime, domestic opposition, and external actors and agencies.[25] Each of these forces has undergone shifts in composition and priorities as transition periods have lengthened. Particular outcomes have often been determined by the balance of strength among these "power clusters," to use the terminology of Rueschemeyer and colleagues, and the dynamics of their confrontations and compromises. In the case of Africa, the competing and conflicting interests of external powers facilitated the generally low threshold of political liberalization that African regimes had to reach in order to satisfy Mbembe's criterion of "presentability."[26]

Clapham's notion of the extroversion of Africa is also relevant to this discussion. Africa has been highly "extroverted" in the sense that developments on the continent, including the nature and persistence of its component states, have largely been determined by outside factors and forces. Because of the major role that external actors have played in the promotion and even financing of political transitions after 1989, their inability to sustain consistent policies and their shifting priorities have facilitated the establishment of virtual democracies. In particular, three critical factors have rendered it difficult in the 1990s to establish political systems with the capacity to be more than semicompetitive systems: the pervasive fear that the chaotic conflicts in countries such as Liberia, Somalia, and Sudan were not exceptional occurrences, but harbingers of widening disorder; the dominance that neoliberal structural adjustment reforms have attained in the pursuit of economic recovery on the continent; and the interweaving of legal and illegal business activities by state officials.

Using Mbembe's phraseology, since the late 1980s, Africa has experienced both the decomposition and the recomposition of systems of domination and authority. Yet, during the very period when armed conflicts were attracting intensified world attention, several prolonged wars were also ending or shifting to much lower levels of hostilities, for example, in Angola, Chad, Eritrea, Ethiopia, Mozambique, and South Africa. Nevertheless, the dramatic media impact of the Liberian, Somalian, and Rwandan conflicts dulled the fervor with which Western powers were prepared to promote democratization while bolstering the image of reformist autocracies in Ghana, Uganda, and Ethiopia. These developments led to the retrieval of the discarded argument that autocracy is a necessary antidote to social conflict and disorder. If the modal state in the continent before 1989 was one that exhibited the various features of monopoly statehood, by the mid-1990s it was replaced by a virtual democracy that allowed some space for independent civic and political action, while guaranteeing political order and protecting the sway of economically dominant social groups. In the process, demands for "good governance," now universally proclaimed, were tacitly diluted to what can more appropriately be called "acceptable governance."27

The shoring up of the African state system, even at the expense of stalled democratization, became a point of convergence between the self-interest of African regimes and the geopolitical interests of Western powers. The primacy accorded stability and political order by external powers had been a powerful resource for the consolidation of authoritarian systems in postcolonial Africa. The end of the Cold War created a window of opportunity in which the disruptions of political reform and contestation were tolerated and even supported by external powers to hasten the transformation of these systems. That window, however, steadily closed as a consequence of the complex humanitarian emergencies associated with the conflicts in Somalia and Rwanda. In some cases, as in Mobutu's Zaire after 1994, the urgent need of international agencies for access to airport and other cross-border facilities restored the acceptability of working with discredited regimes. Semiauthoritarian governments throughout the continent, which continued to be assailed externally for their resistance to political reforms, began once again to disregard or deflect such criticisms and to pay more attention to other messages, explicit or implicit, regarding the real priorities of foreign powers and international agencies.

Structural Adjustment and African Renewal

There is an urgent need for students of Africa to reconsider the political consequences of structural adjustment programs and the widespread adoption of market-oriented economic strategies. There are several well-mapped positions. Some dismiss economic liberalization as, to use Clapham's expression, "technologies of universal validity" that have been foisted on

Africa. Others, including Thomas Callaghy, argue that most African governments are not prepared to do what is required to make such strategies work. Africa is therefore likely to remain "hemmed in" from the dynamic currents of global capitalism.[28] Virtually all analysts agree that structural adjustment has tended to undermine the clientelistic pattern of resource distribution, thereby weakening the capacity of governments to maintain their support coalitions.[29] Among the strongest critics of these programs, structural adjustment has been regarded as a stratagem to get African countries to meet debt-repayment schedules while subjecting the masses of the people to further immiseration through currency devaluations, retrenchment in public employment, elimination of subsidies on items of mass consumption, and the imposition of fees for many social services.[30]

Structural adjustment and associated economic liberalization strategies, the renewed concern for order and stability, and the availability of resources for corrupt enrichment by state officials have been critical factors in the consolidation of semicompetitive political systems in Africa. Although it initially seemed to threaten entrenched regimes by sapping their patronage capacity, structural adjustment may have hewed a new path for regime consolidation. With the stalling of economic growth in much of Africa by the early 1980s, external public capital became the main source of income for many governments. Foreign bilateral and multilateral agencies were willing to provide substantial funds to finance structural adjustment policies, even though many governments found ways to avoid fully implementing them, and most rescheduled their debts repeatedly.

Eventually, a contradiction emerged. These programs were intended to be precursors of an economy in which the private sector would replace the former state-owned or state-dominated sectors.[31] However, domestic and foreign private capital did not respond as anticipated to the new investment opportunities. A convergence then occurred among three critical developments: the entrenchment of refurbished autocracies now sustained by the provision of aid and loans tied to stabilization measures; the gradual recognition among these leaders that they could govern effectively despite the erosion of the resources for patronage that had previously been available in the form of public-sector jobs, import licenses, and foreign currency; and the conversion of these leaders into advocates for private capitalism and acquiescent partners of the formerly maligned Bretton Woods institutions.

In his study of structural adjustment in Nigeria during the 1980s, Adebayo Olukoshi shows the ways in which the implementation of these policies, in the absence of significant public support, contributed to the highly directed and eventually catastrophic program of transition to civilian rule. Opponents of these economic reforms were systematically excluded from the political process. While promoting "free market, non-interventionist, economic policies," Olukoshi argues, the regime of Ibrahim Babangida (1985–1993) was also acting in highly interventionist ways in a political terrain that had been "narrowed by decree." The lesson he draws is that "authoritarianism rather than democracy has been the flip side of structural adjustment."[32] The Nigerian experience is particularly instructive. After having skillfully maneuvered his country to adopt the key features of structural adjustment, Babangida and his junta fell into the classic trap identified by Samuel Finer, in which the military in power is unable "to stay or go."[33] This indecision contributed to the disarray and eventual collapse of the political transition program and Nigeria's descent into the hard authoritarianism of Sani Abacha's regime. The option not pursued, however, was the one being seized upon by many other African countries after 1992, namely, "soft authoritarianism" or virtual democracy, which represented an implicit compromise between the unwillingness of African autocracies to undergo more than "political decompression" and the wish of bilateral and international aid agencies for greater "presentability" in regimes with which they negotiated aid and loan agreements.[34]

Most students of the impact of structural adjustment emphasize the deleterious social impact of these policies, the limited initial productive response that they provoke, and the challenges they pose to the distributive clientelist systems of the African "monopoly state." What few foresaw was the possibility that these same programs could be utilized by both autocratic and newly democratizing regimes to limit demands on the state apparatus while refurbishing, and in some cases strengthening, their governing capacities. In both Nigeria and Ghana, for example, military governments were able to break the "policy impasse" during the 1980s, to use Thandika Mkandawire's phrase, and get their countries to adopt structural adjustment programs.[35] There is a profound difference, however, in what then followed that can be largely attributed to political choices made by their respective military rulers. In Ghana, the Rawlings regime accepted an incremental transition to constitutional democracy, while its Nigerian counterpart failed to implement any consistent economic or political strategy.

These observations suggest the need for what may be called a "realist" approach in analyzing the governance of many African states in response to economic liberalization. Such a project will differ from the uncompromising approaches usually taken by advocates and opponents of structural adjustment.[36] Lisa Laakso and Olukoshi argue, for example, that these programs have had several dire consequences, including undermining state capacity and legitimacy; reinforcing structures of authoritarianism; prompting the decay of public institutions; weakening the "social contract" between African governments and societies; eroding the social and welfare gains of the postcolonial years; complicating the economic problems of the continent without resolving them; accelerating the informalization of African economies and the adoption of "multiple livelihood" strategies; decimating the bearers of a national perspective in the form of the professional middle class; heightening uneven development and associated regional and ethnic divisions; exacerbating dislocation at the level of communities and households; precluding the formulation of national economic policies through the loss of control to external institutions; and encouraging the stifling of opposition voices and organizations.[37]

Much of the devastation and dislocation described by these scholars cannot be denied, although it is not readily apparent how much of the decay should be attributed to structural adjustment and how much to Africa's longer-term economic contraction. Moreover, it is also necessary to relate such criticisms to certain observable trends. In 1996, the economies of sub-Saharan Africa grew at 4.4 percent annually, a rate not witnessed since the 1970s; a dozen experienced growth of over 5 percent, notably in southern Africa, while Uganda now ranks among the fastest-growing economies in the world, with 8 percent annual growth since 1992.[38] That Ghana and Uganda experienced considerable economic decay before registering sustained recovery in the late 1980s and early 1990s might be taken to reflect the rule that "other things being equal, poorer countries tend to grow faster than richer ones."[39] But there is obviously more to it than that. Despite the harsh experiences of structural adjustment, renewed growth is now seen in countries widely divergent in their resources across the continent. The many indications of resumed growth in Africa suggest caution in assuming that the dire effects of stabilization programs automatically negate the prospects for economic recovery. Moreover, strategies aimed at connecting reforming African economies to the dynamics of trade and investment in the global economy are finally being designed. If pursued vigorously, and accompanied by a reduction in corruption, such initiatives could reverse the socioeconomic devastation that preceded—and was initially aggravated by—structural adjustment.

Reflecting the sense that Africa is once again an arena of economic opportunity, Western governments are encouraging trade and investment to replace the long reliance on overseas aid. As important as development aid is to Africa at $14 billion annually, such aid has been declining globally.[40] Meanwhile, the volume of foreign private investment in developing countries has steadily increased to $170 billion annually in the mid-1990s, of which a mere $3 billion went to Africa.[41] The U.S. government, the World Bank, the International Monetary Fund (IMF), and other bilateral donors are designing measures to encourage an increase in the flow of investment capital to Africa, greater access for African exporters to the markets of industrialized countries, and large reductions in the foreign debt of the most vigorously reforming economies, beginning with Uganda. This approach has significant implications for the transformation and expansion of

African economies if it is accompanied by the necessary resources and facilities.[42]

It is important that students of late twentieth-century Africa do not repeat the mistake that their counterparts made during the mid-1980s when they scoffed at demands for the introduction of institutions and practices associated with pluralist democracy, only to be overtaken by the sweep of events after 1989. They should be alert to opportunities for African countries to become active agents in their own transformation by developing in the only way possible in the modern world, that is, through establishing profitable connections with the global economy.[43] The fact that Uganda has been chosen as the first beneficiary of these market-stimulating policies and massive debt relief is not surprising. Uganda has emerged as the model country in the reconfiguration of power in late twentieth-century Africa. Under the rule of Yoweri Museveni and the National Resistance Movement since 1986, Uganda has enthusiastically adopted structural adjustment reforms, benefited from large inflows of development aid, introduced partial political liberalization, given early emphasis to human rights and popular participation at the local level, used military force to enhance state cohesion and stability without overt repression (despite the endemic conflicts waged in its northern region), and publicly advocated a shift in external assistance to emphasize trade, investment, debt relief, and support for education and health—the exact policies that are now central to the "Washington consensus."

That Uganda has recovered in a decade from being one of Africa's most severely eroded states to the staging ground for political transformations elsewhere in east and central Africa is suggestive of the dynamics that scholars must now closely analyze. Power is being reconfigured not only on the basis of principles advanced by outside forces, but through the forging of new domestic arrangements that combine hegemonic and participatory principles.[44] I therefore differ in my approach to these issues from some of my colleagues, as I have come to believe that the bitter medicine of structural adjustment may have goaded several African governments to seek ways in which the state, market, and society could be reconfigured to transform their nations into new subjects, rather than perpetual dependent objects, in the world system.[45] There have undoubtedly been many cases of adverse reaction to the medicine, although governments found ways to avoid taking it "as directed." Most countries, however, have begun showing economic recovery beyond the superficial and self-reflecting impact of renewed inflows of public capital and consumer goods. Finally, unattractive as it may seem as an intellectual project, students of Africa must begin distinguishing forms of autocracy that, in association with economic liberalization, are contributing to the enhancement of state capacity, coherence, and legitimacy from the repressive political systems that brought many countries to their knees in the 1980s.

From Zaire to Congo, 1996–1997:
A Tectonic Shift in Africa?

In December 1993, I presented a seminar paper titled "Failed States in Africa: From Crisis to Recovery."[46] Aspects of that presentation can now be revisited to provide a provisional assessment of what one commentator has called a "tectonic shift" in the geopolitics of Africa as a result of the cataclysmic developments in Zaire and the Great Lakes area in 1996–1997.[47] Here are two relevant paragraphs:

> There are cases in which something calling itself the "state" still stands but is unable to conduct any of the normal functions of statehood. Zaire is not the only country in which the "state" disappears a short drive outside its capital or the area of residence of its president. Where civil servants are irregularly paid, and funds for normal functions are absent, government offices may exist in various localities but nothing of consequence takes place within them. The governing structures of the state have thus joined the hospitals and infirmaries that lack medicines and equipment and schools that lack books and chairs.
>
> In addition to the "failed or collapsed states," there are many cases in Africa of the advanced erosion or atrophy of the state. In the 1980s, several scholars applauded what was referred to as "the retreat of the state" and the emergence of what was assumed to be elements of a vigorous and self-reliant civil society.[48] However, community groups cannot operate a national health and education system, or maintain road networks and telecommunication systems. The atrophied state may continue to function long after it ceases to do anything positive for its people if it can establish relations with external actors willing to share in predatory economic activities and in the exportation of valuable commodities.[49]

Several further observations in that presentation concerning the erosion of state capacity and legitimacy in Africa seemed to be called into question by the sequence of events that culminated in the overthrow of the Mobutu regime in May 1997. I had argued in 1993 that:

> 1. State erosion in Africa is compounded by the fact that Cold War interventionism has been succeeded by a general retreat from the continent by external powers.
> 2. There are no bold initiatives in Africa on the part of the U.S. government or other western powers at the current time. Where the United States has been prepared to play a secondary role in the past, for example, in various Francophone countries, a search is underway for a further exit.
> 3. The United States has never devised an effective response to French neo-imperialism in Africa.
> 4. Informal multilateral trusteeship is already a fact of life in much of Africa. Under such a regime can be included states that have lost control over policy making because of the multiplicity of external donors, international NGOs [nongovernmental organizations] and domestic NGOs funded externally. There are others that are in virtual receivership to the

World Bank and the IMF. The erosion of state capacity, and the consequent need to cede sovereign authority in key areas of decision-making, is a general phenomenon that should be considered alongside the more dramatic cases of state-collapse such as Liberia and Somalia.

5. The declining force of the sovereign right of states has led scholars to question whether African states are actually needed in their current form. When the state is seen as a predatory force, and as being captured by a section of the country, state erosion or state collapse becomes a problem that may in some cases represent a solution for the many problems experienced by its citizens.

6. The commitment to promote democratization and human rights, the encouragement of market-based strategies, and the need to support regimes able to maintain domestic political order *and* contribute to restoring order in their sub-region, are policy objectives that may not be mutually consistent.

7. There are states in Africa which have lost the capacity to conduct themselves as such in most respects but can remain operational as predatory rumps that are recognized internationally. No force can be mustered to push them over internally and no external power wants to assume that task. What then occurs is the intensification of certain practices such as the development of illicit linkages to support these predatory entities. In several cases in Africa, illicit transactions, shifting from one commodity to the other, are a powerful force in sustaining structures that would otherwise have fully collapsed.

8. The effects of the Somalia backlash may be experienced for many years. The frustrations associated with that exercise have engendered an extreme reluctance within the U.S. government to become engaged in such efforts elsewhere.

9. As the United States enters a period of limited engagement overseas, a key question is who will assume responsibility for the people of collapsed states, or who are governed by predatory rump-states. Regional bodies such as the OAU [Organization of African Unity], or sub-regional groups like ECOWAS [the Economic Community of West African States] in West Africa and IGAD [Intergovernmental Authority on Drought] in Northeast Africa, are severely limited in financial and operational capacity. Faced with the refusal of the United States to play the role of world's, and particularly Africa's, policeman, and in view of the UN's severe limitations, some process of collective security must be devised to bridge the current operational gap.

10. Most of the situations in Africa of collapsed or severely eroded states are being tackled with inadequate financial and other material resources, with insufficient multilateral cooperation, and with inadequate staffing. Michel Camdessus, head of the IMF, has therefore described Africa as a "sinking continent."[50]

In light of more recent events, including upheavals in east and central Africa, several of these assertions should be reexamined. The juxtaposition of these observations illustrates the interweaving of change and continuity in late twentieth-century Africa:

1. The retreat from Africa has been replaced by a selective international reengagement with the continent, especially to support strong eco-

nomic reformers and governments able to contribute to order and stability in their subregions.

2. Western governments, including the United States, are designing important initiatives to encourage enhanced trade and investment for Africa.

3. The debacle of France's policies in the Rwandan and Zairian conflicts provided the United States with an opportunity to challenge French hegemony in Africa, which has prompted the most extensive debate and review within France of its paternalistic relationship with its former African colonies.

4. Informal multilateral trusteeship may coincide with the expansion of state capacity and authority in African countries experiencing renewed economic growth.

5. Instead of African states being seen largely as artificial and precarious constructs, the viability of these states within their postcolonial borders has been reasserted in a broad sweep of countries from the Horn to the Cape.[51]

6. There is now convergence and compromise between the interests of Western powers and African states, as argued above, in the tacit acceptance of virtual democracies as an acceptable form of governance in late twentieth-century Africa.

7. Zaire was the foremost example of a rump state sustained by predatory economic activities, but a force was eventually mustered to push it over based on a realignment of internal, regional, and external powers.

8. The Zairian experience has tempered, though not effaced, the post-Somalia syndrome, the most tragic consequence of which was U.S. and United Nations inaction to prevent genocide in Rwanda.[52]

9. The willingness of several African countries to coordinate their efforts to bring about the overthrow of the Mobutu regime and the creation of the first units of an African intervention force under OAU auspices suggest the possibility of an eventual collective security system.

10. With growth rates approaching 5 percent annually, officials of multinational organizations are unlikely to refer to Africa today as a "sinking continent." Renewed optimism about Africa's economic prospects, despite persistent conflicts in several countries, is prompting the crafting of new packages of assistance tied to private-sector development and targeted investments in education, health, transportation, and communication facilities.

Upheavals in central and east Africa in 1996–1997 induced commentators to begin speaking of "geopolitical mutations" and "the contours of a new African order."[53] The critical event, in retrospect, was the cross-border insurgency of the Rwandan Patriotic Front (RPF) against the long-entrenched regime of Juvénal Habyarimana in Rwanda in October 1990. The death of Habyarimana in April 1994, the ensuing genocide, and the victory of the RPF created a set of linkages and a dynamic that culminated three years later in the toppling of the Mobutu regime by the Alliance of Democratic Forces for the Liberation of Congo-Zaire (ADFL). Several major themes in Africa's postcolonial history were replayed, and new departures intimated, during these upheavals. Among the most critical are militarism, warlordism, the shadow state and economy, regional geopolitics, and post–Cold War geopolitics. Before the shock waves from Mobutu's overthrow had subsided, however, a war in Congo-Brazzaville that resulted in the overthrow of President Pascal Lissouba revealed these dynamics in even starker relief.

Militarism

Although most African states had achieved independence without resorting to armed struggle, an important dimension of these developments of 1996–1997 was the capacity to organize and sustain an armed insurgency. It is possible to trace the consolidation of state power in Zaire after the ADFL's victory in May 1997 back to other insurgencies in the countries that provided tactical, material, and/or diplomatic support for this movement, including Angola, Ethiopia, Rwanda, Uganda, and Zimbabwe.[54] Moreover, the African government that played a key role in facilitating the transfer of power, that of South Africa, had recently emerged from the longest armed struggle on the continent. Although the Tanzanian government, an important moral supporter of the ADFL, was not itself the product of armed struggle, it had hosted many of these movements as the site of the headquarters of the Liberation Committee of the OAU. Furthermore, Tanzania had established the major precedent when it sent troops across its borders, along with Ugandan dissidents, to overthrow Idi Amin's regime in 1979. Thus, in addition to the implications of the arrival of a new government in a country with immense natural resources, there was also a sudden awareness of a new factor in African affairs: states whose power rested on the successful conduct of armed struggle.

Warlordism

Were it not for the seismic events on the Rwanda-Zaire border in 1996, Laurent-Désiré Kabila would most likely have remained one of a number of African warlords who, as described by Mbembe, "are also military entrepreneurs. Entrenched in regional bases, they seek to bring under their control the totality of disposable resources in their fiefs."[55] Having sustained himself for years as a trafficker in gold, Kabila took advantage of the tumult along the borders with Rwanda to knit together the disparate groups of insurgents, with the direct assistance of the Rwandan army, and catapult himself from being a long-term nuisance to the Mobutu regime into the leader of a movement capable of toppling it.

The Shadow State and Economy

William Reno has applied the concept of "shadow state" to political structures based on informal markets, as, in the case of Sierra Leone, on the

illicit mining and export of diamonds.[56] A considerable part of Mobutu's
republic, financed by pilfered resources, also operated in the shadows.[57]
Representatives of major global corporations rushed to sign contracts with
the ADFL as soon as it took control of areas of Zaire containing exploitable
mineral deposits, thereby, in effect, helping finance the final stages of the
insurgency. The degree of "stateness" in Africa hinges critically on whether
these transactions take place in the shadows or in the legal realm.[58] For the
Kabila regime to succeed in the daunting task of implanting itself in the
vast, complex, and structurally inchoate nation of Congo, it will have to
bring much of the country's economy out of the shadows and apply its
ample resources to reconstruction in place of the pharaonic consumption of
the past three decades.

Regional Geopolitics

One legacy of colonial rule in Africa is the patchwork of official languages
and of communication, legal, and other systems. From October 1996 to
May 1997, an impromptu process of coordination took place across a vast
stretch of the continent, from the northeast to the southwest. The governments involved helped supply an armed movement that grew as it fought
across one of the largest African states, which also has one of the most
eroded infrastructures. While the two chief external protagonists, the
United States and France, accused each other of masterminding the insurgency or counterinsurgency, what was mainly overlooked was that several
African governments had decided to coordinate their efforts to rid the continent of a ruler regarded essentially as an instrument of foreign interests
who had laid waste to his country and facilitated numerous nefarious mis-
sions in their own countries. An implicit understanding emerged that an
opportunity had become available for the assertion of African agency in the
reconquest of a vast land with abundant natural riches. As this reconquest
proceeded, analysts were left to wonder if the other states in the region—
Congo-Brazzaville, Chad, Gabon, Cameroon, and Central African
Republic, all under the protective rule of France—would now "find themselves in the eye of a cyclone."[59]

Post–Cold War Geopolitics

For French commentators on Africa, the overthrow of the Mobutu regime
by Kabila's ADFL symbolized a passing of the guard at three levels: from a
highly corrupt regime to an unknown adversary with a questionable background; from the discredited African leaders allied with France to more
dynamic former revolutionaries outside the francophone bloc—Nelson
Mandela, Yoweri Museveni, Isaias Afewerki, Meles Zenawi, Samuel
Nujoma, Paul Kagame, and Eduardo Dos Santos; and from France as "the

gendarme of the West south of the Sahara" to the United States, now ready to "replace France definitively in its multiform role as 'conductor of the orchestra' in Africa."[60]

Many French commentators saw a grand American conspiracy and covert operation at work in Zaire; and Jean-François Bayart emphasized a linkage with an alleged U.S.-supervised effort involving Uganda, Ethiopia, and Eritrea to overthrow the Sudan regime.[61] Less open to dispute is the recognition that the U.S. government, after having tried for several years to get Mobutu to agree to general elections, seized the opportunity to move quickly to prepare for the post-Mobutu era and make itself a central player in the Zaire endgame. A precedent for this action was U.S. engagement with the Ethiopian insurgents on the eve of their displacement of the Mengistu regime in 1991. Such a policy in Zaire from late 1996 contrasted starkly with France's multifarious efforts to help prevent the military overthrow of the Mobutu regime.

For the American public, these events did not appear to have any but marginal implications for their country's interests. During four decades of independent governments in Africa, the continent has been a minor concern of the U.S. government, which had been prepared to allow the ex-colonial powers to predominate, except for specific struggles with Cold War implications such as the Ethiopian and Angolan wars. France, in contrast, had anchored its middle-power status to the privileged relations it enjoyed with many African leaders, the extensive operations of French companies on the continent, and the stationing of French troops in several former colonies.

The loss of Rwanda to the Uganda-allied RPF, and Zaire to the Rwanda- and Uganda-allied ADFL, was widely interpreted as a great setback to France's prestige and influence in Africa. In the process, the United States assumed the role of grand patron of the governments that had emerged from armed struggles to which, ironically, it had usually been opposed. The U.S. Congress, by passing legislation ending American aid to Mobutu in the 1980s, by imposing sanctions on apartheid South Africa after 1986, and by mandating more direct support to the African people and their civic organizations rather than to corrupt and authoritarian governments, had laid the basis for a policy shift in the executive branch in the early 1990s from being a Cold War manipulator to a promoter of democracy in Africa. In 1997, the United States was therefore able to act decisively, in association with the African National Congress government in South Africa, to elbow aside the ex-colonial powers, especially France and its cohort of African client rulers, from any but marginal roles in managing the transition in Zaire.[62]

It was soon being argued that this decisive show of American power, in alliance with several governments in southern and eastern Africa, had sent "powerful signals to all France's clients that the long era of Paris's supremacy on the continent is over."[63] That Jacques Foccart, the man most

responsible for crafting the network of relations between French governments and African leaders for several decades, died on March 19, 1997,
while Mobutu, whom he had helped rehabilitate as a French ally since
1994, was also critically ill were taken to symbolize the moribund character
of France's African policies. Yet France's involvement in the continent was
too extensive, too lucrative, and too vital to its self-image to permit such
severe reverses to go unanswered.

After Mobutu: The War in Congo-Brazzaville

If the conquest of power in Zaire by the ADFL in May 1997 was a tectonic
shift, its aftershock came one month later with the resumption of armed
hostilities in Congo-Brazzaville by the militia of former president Denis
Sassou-Nguesso, against the government forces and the militia of President
Lissouba. Four months later, despite intensive attempts at mediation by UN
and other envoys, the elected Lissouba government was overthrown. This
event demonstrated how armed force could be swiftly and devastatingly
unleashed to defend major external, regional, and domestic interests in late
twentieth-century Africa. The continuities that Mbembe has suggested in
the exercise of power, the resort to violence, and the nature of political
authority between pre- and postcolonial Africa were starkly revealed in this
reenactment of a nineteenth-century drama involving a charter company,
imperial dominance, subimperial animosities, and warfare among local
chieftains.

While the new socialist government of Prime Minister Lionel Jospin in
France since May 1997 was promising to place "liberty, democracy and the
rule of law" at the center of French relations with Africa, the war in the second Congo was demonstrating that the objectives, policies, and tactics of
"Gaullist Africa" still prevailed.[64] The Gulf of Guinea, ringed by oil-
producing states, has become the Persian Gulf of tropical Africa.
Approximately half the total earnings of Elf-Aquitaine, which is France's
largest petroleum company and its largest corporate enterprise, derives
from its operations in these states.[65] The end for Lissouba's government
was signaled in early September 1997, when he was denied meetings with
President Jacques Chirac and all senior French officials on the grounds that
his presidential mandate had expired at the end of August. That the elections scheduled for July 27 could not be held because of the raging battle in
his country, which had led to a withdrawal of French troops, was conveniently overlooked in this delegitimizing and humiliating of Lissouba. He
never could, in fact, overcome French official distrust of him since his
futile attempt, shortly after his election in 1992, to loosen Elf's iron grip on
his country's oil wealth by trying to negotiate a deal with Occidental
Petroleum.

Since Sassou-Nguesso was stripped of his autocratic powers during the sovereign national conference of 1992 and a new government elected, civil government in Congo-Brazzaville has remained hostage to violent periodic conflicts among the militias of the major politicians, including several months of pitched battles in 1993–1994. As the armed clashes between the forces of Lissouba and Sassou-Nguesso intensified after June 1997, their behavior illustrated one of Clapham's key arguments cited above: "The relentless search externally for resources to secure or maintain dominance internally is a characteristic common to the international politics of African juridical as well as 'warlord insurgencies.'" A victory of the juridical state power or the warlord insurgency in Congo-Brazzaville depended on its relative success in mobilizing external resources, especially armaments. When the Angolan government, whose regular troops had taken part in the final battles in Zaire in May 1997, agreed to provide fighter jets and tanks to support Sassou-Nguesso against Lissouba, the balance in firepower shifted decisively in favor of the former. Although Lissouba had hurriedly tried to win support from the Kabila-Kagame-Museveni alliance to counter Sassou-Nguesso, these exertions did not deter Angola from acting independently in its perceived self-interest on behalf of a long-term ally.

Just a week before the final battle in October 1997 for Congo-Brazzaville, the French foreign minister, Hubert Vidrine, announced during his first African tour that France would not intervene anymore in internal African conflicts, that it supported the ongoing mediation efforts in the Congolese war by President Omar Bongo of Gabon and UN Special Envoy Mohammed Sahnoun, and that it would support throughout Africa democracy, good governance, and the rule of law.[66] Many observers, however, had trouble reconciling what was taking place in war-torn Brazzaville with these declarations by the new socialist minister in various African capitals: "When Paris rushed to embrace the victorious Mr. Sassou-Nguesso after months of behind-the-scene support for him, many Africans immediately concluded that the new model for France's relationship with its former empire was not one of withdrawal at all, but merely of carefully picking one's shots."[67] Just as France failed to make a convincing case for an international humanitarian intervention force to protect the refugees in eastern Zaire while actively maneuvering to save Mobutu, its subsequent campaign to present itself as a born-again democratizer in Africa while simultaneously assisting the violent overthrow of an elected government further strains credulity. Moreover, the Jospin government has an uphill task getting its principles to prevail in the determination of French Africa policies as long as these belong to the privileged domain of President Chirac.[68]

*   *   *

The aim of this exploration has been to prompt the creation of new theoretical frameworks to analyze the multiplicity of factors affecting the exercise of power in late twentieth-century Africa. The term "reconfiguration of power" has been adopted to capture the multidirectional nature of these processes, in contrast to alternatives such as "political transitions," which imply a certain sense of direction. The chapter began with a reference to the distinction made by Jackson and Rosberg between juridical and empirical statehood. Clapham noted that passage to "empirical statehood" would involve "national integration and a set of viable political and economic institutions."[69] Although several African countries appear to be crossing this threshold, empirical statehood must contend with the continuing extroversion of Africa, as reflected in the loss of national sovereignty and the upsurge of cross-border conflicts linked to internal struggles for power.

As the majority of African economies are once again experiencing positive growth, and as the major powers shift to emphasizing trade and investment over aid, a powerful impetus is simultaneously being generated for the building of state institutions to superintend and complement an expanding private sector. Such a possibility was first advanced by Goran Hyden in 1983.[70] More recently, Nicolas van de Walle has argued that there is now "greater pressure on Africans to reinforce their *de facto* sovereignty in order to promote stability." Van de Walle optimistically notes that we may be witnessing "the beginning of a phase of state formation and construction in Africa based primarily on indigenous political processes."[71] Such observations challenge scholars to be more attentive to the ways in which state capacity and national cohesion may be enhanced as governments move away from the highly distributionist political model of the state as the "all-provider and the all-doer."[72]

There are also the contradictory developments to be considered, such as Mbembe's insightful observation that the recomposition of power in Africa involves "the co-existence, within the same dynamic, of elements belonging to warfare as to the conduct of civil politics." As the cases of Kabila and Sassou-Nguesso in the two Congos illustrate, there is today a fine line between military leaders referred to as "warlords" and those who become "heads of state" because the fief they command politically and economically has expanded to embrace the whole nation, rather than just a section of it. War making is once again fundamental to state making in late twentieth-century Africa, though rarely by way of overt interstate wars. With the exception of western Africa, which is still characterized by intermittent military coups, it is armed struggle that is now responsible for regime change in several countries that fall within a broad arc from the northeast to the southwest of the continent.[73] Museveni has crafted in Uganda a political system that is a hybrid between his war-making apparatus and the institutions of civil politics without partisanship. Other countries in this arc demonstrate similar amalgams. A further question to be considered is whether these "part authoritarian and part free" systems will reach what Pye has called a "relatively lasting equilibrium."[74] The likelihood is that several of them will, especially as they are rewarded externally for their economic performance and relative stability, as in the case of Ethiopia, despite their shortcomings in the promotion of human rights and in permitting genuine democratic contestation.

In conclusion, no single statement about the reconfiguration of power can as yet be applied to all of late twentieth-century Africa. Formulas of domination based on armed might or democratic institutions, on private-sector economic development or a shadow state and economy, and on the influence of external patrons or internal political processes can be found in varying configurations. The task of scholars who are intrigued by this inquiry is to probe these dynamics further so that the patterns of change can be discerned within the swirl of contradictory developments. Eventually, on the basis of such analyses, we might be able to make reasonable projections about the long-term consequences of this period of flux and uncertainty.

Notes

1. R. Kaplan, "Coming Anarchy."
2. Olukoshi and Laakso, eds., *Challenges to the Nation-State,* p. 8.
3. Jackson and Rosberg, "Africa's Weak States."
4. Clapham, *Africa and the International System,* p. 274.
5. Ibid., p. 159.
6. Ibid., p. 156.
7. Ibid., p. 273.
8. Ibid., p. 193.
9. Ibid., p. 271.
10 Mbembe, "Democratization and Social Movements," p. 4. For relevant commentaries by African scholars, see Joseph, ed., *African Democratic Perspectives.*
11. Mbembe, "Le Prix de la Force."
12. Mbembe, "Right to Dispose."
13. Mbembe, "Complex Transformations," p. 28.
14. See the above-cited works by Mbembe, as well as "Une Economie de Prédation."
15. Mbembe, "Complex Transformations," p. 28.
16. Mbembe, "Le Prix de la Force" and "Right to Dispose." See also "Pouvoir."
17. Mbembe states boldly in "Une Economie de Prédation": "There does not currently exist a democratic regime in Black Africa" (p. 1).
18. Pye, "Political Science."
19. See Joseph, "Democratization in Africa After 1989," and the collection of relevant articles in Ottaway, ed., *Democracy in Africa.*
20. See Nwajiaku, "National Conferences."
21. Pye, "Political Science," p. 4.
22. Ibid.
23. Joseph, "Democratization in Africa," pp. 367–368. For a relevant discussion of the "choiceless" character of these new democracies, see Mkandawire, "Economic Policy-Making." For a parallel formulation with regard to Latin America, see O'Donnell, "Delegative Democracy."

24. A political system is considered democratic, in my understanding, "to the extent that it facilitates citizen self-rule, permits the broadest participation in determining public policy, and constitutionally guarantees all the freedoms necessary for open political competition" (Joseph, "Democratization in Africa").

25. Joseph, "Democratization in Africa"; Rueschemeyer et al., *Capitalist Development.*

26. Mbembe, "Democratization and Social Movements."

27. For an indication of this emerging orientation, see Cohen, "Good Governance," p. 5. Even France's President Jacques Chirac, known for his dismissive attitude toward pluralist democracy in Africa, now championed the tamed notion of "good governance" at the Franco-African summit in Burkina Faso in December 1996.

28. Callaghy and Ravenhill, eds., *Hemmed In.*

29. van de Walle, "Neopatrimonialism and Democracy"; Herbst, "Structural Adjustment."

30. Two important collections of articles that explore the gamut of issues related to structural adjustment policies are Gibbon et al., eds., *Authoritarianism,* and Mkandawire and Olukoshi, eds., *Between Liberalisation and Oppression.*

31. For a summary of the common features of these programs, see Olukoshi and Laakso, "Crisis of the National-State Project," p. 18, and Olukoshi, "Impact of Recent Reform Efforts," p. 49.

32. Olukoshi, "Extending the Frontiers," pp. 182–183. For a nuanced exploration of the relationship between structural adjustment and democracy, see Mkandawire, "Economic Policy-Making."

33. Finer, *Man on Horseback.*

34. For the notion *"décompression autoritaire,"* a process that enabled African autocrats to moderate the inconveniences of the single-party systems, see Bayart, "La Problématique," p. 7.

35. Mkandawire, "Fiscal Structure, State Contraction," p. 45.

36. An impressive series of studies have emerged from the Scandinavian Institute of Africa Studies in Uppsala, Sweden, including Olukoshi and Laakso, eds., *Challenges to the Nation-State;* Gibbon and Olukoshi, eds., *Structural Adjustment;* and Havnevik and van Arkadie, eds., *Domination or Dialogue?*

37. See Olukoshi and Laakso, eds., *Challenges to the Nation-State,* pp. 10–24. The World Bank publications on Africa (1981, 1989, and 1994) lay out the arguments and strategies for the advocates of structural adjustment.

38. *The Economist,* "Emerging Africa," June 14, 1997, p. 13.

39. Sachs, "Limits of Convergence," p. 19.

40. Bimal Ghosh points out that aid to developing countries in 1995 from Organization for Economic Cooperation and Development countries was, at 0.2 percent of their gross national product, the lowest in 45 years ("Just as Effective Aid Gets Easier," p. 10).

41. James Wolfensohn, World Bank president, quoted in the *New York Times,* March 17, 1996, p. 6.

42. For details of these initiatives, see the following articles: Passell, "Economic Scene"; A. Mitchell, "Clinton Proposes Incentives"; and Oliphant, "Economic Boost."

43. It is intriguing, for example, how an assertion by Mkandawire that structural adjustment "is not only about the liberalisation of domestic markets but also a submission to the logic of global markets" ("Economic Policy-Making," p. 35) could begin a discussion that is sharply critical of the reality described, while, for Jeffrey Sachs, the same statement would fit snugly with his observation that "global

capitalism is surely the most promising institutional arrangement for worldwide prosperity that history has ever seen" ("Limits of Convergence," p. 22).

44. In this regard, I consider several of the arguments advanced by Richard Sklar in Chapter 9 of this book particularly perceptive.

45. Among them is Adebayo Olukoshi, who has produced a remarkable series of essays on structural adjustment. Olukoshi contends, for example, that structural adjustment has generally weakened and undermined "state capacity and legitimacy in Africa." In place of such sweeping statements, I would recommend a close examination of where these consequences, or others, can be discerned. See Olukoshi and Laakso, "Crisis of the National-State Project," p. 10, and Olukoshi, "Impact of Recent Reform Efforts," especially pp. 60–66.

46. This presentation was made at the Harvard-MIT Joint Seminar on Political Development.

47. Bayart, "La Problématique."

48. See Azarya and Chazan, "Disengagement from the State," and Chazan, "Patterns of State-Society Incorporation." This perspective was shared by several participants during the inaugural seminar of the African Governance Program of the Carter Center. See Joseph, ed., *Beyond Autocracy.*

49. Joseph, "Failed States."

50. Ibid.

51. For a relevant debate, see Herbst, "Responding to State Failure," and my commentary and his response in *International Security* (fall 1997).

52. Donald Rothchild has stated that the failure of the United States to act decisively to protect the Rwandan refugees in Zaire shows how much the post-Somalia syndrome is still in evidence (personal communication).

53. Bourgi, "Un Yalta Africain."

54. Another significant force was the southern Sudan rebel movements.

55. Mbembe, "Pouvoir," p. 20. For a discussion of the political behavior of warlords, see Chapter 17 of this book by Rothchild; and for a succinct summary of Zaire's evolution, see Schatzberg, "Beyond Mobutu."

56. Reno, *Corruption.*

57. Within the vast literature on this subject, see Young and Turner, *Rise and Decline;* MacGaffey, *Entrepreneurs;* and Schatzberg, *Dialectics of Oppression.*

58. See Widner, "States and Statelessness."

59. Bayart, "Le Fiasco Français."

60. See the following issues of *Jeune Afrique* in 1997: no. 1890 (March 26–April 1): 52; no. 1896 (May 7–13): 8; and no. 1899 (May 28–June 3): 56.

61. Bayart, "Le Fiasco Français" and "Les Américains sont bien plus responsables," *Le Nouvel Quotidien,* May 12, 1997. Most American experts were initially dismissive about the uproar in France regarding purported U.S. covert operations. See U.S. Institute of Peace, "Zaire's Crisis," p. 10. It was subsequently revealed that the United States had been providing military training to Rwandan soldiers since early 1995. While these reports do not prove that the United States was involved in the Rwandan/Congolese military campaign against Mobutu from October 1996, they do suggest a level and form of U.S. engagement not previously acknowledged. See the *Washington Post* (national weekly ed.), "Witnesses to the Revolution" and "More Than Military Advice," July 14, 1997, and August 25, 1997, respectively.

62. A flurry of meetings of heads of state, convened in April and May by francophone leaders in Togo and Gabon as the ADFL stormed across Zaire, with the aim of arranging a face-saving transitional arrangement for Mobutu, were all ineffective. These leaders were also denied any role on board the *Outeniqua* when Mobutu and Kabila finally met, while the resident French ambassador was unceremoniously

confined to the bar of the South African vessel.

63. French, "France Fears Anglo-Saxons."

64. Bourgi, "France-Afrique: Les Raisons." For the essential features of these policies that have endured throughout the postcolonial period, see Joseph, "Gaullist Legacy" and *Gaullist Africa.*

65. Yates, "Oil and the Franco-American Rivalry."

66. Kpatindé, "France-Afrique," p. 10.

67. French, "New Rules."

68. After President François Mitterand announced in June 1990 at a French-African summit in La Baule that France would use democratic progress as a criterion in its aid policies, it was soon observed that French willingness to defend staunch resisters to such progress—for example, the Gnassingbé Eyadema and Paul Biya regimes in Togo and Cameroon, respectively—remained unchanged. For a lucid statement that France should act more decisively to protect "the positions it had acquired on the black continent in this century," see Pigasse, "Cherche Politique Africaine Désespérément," pp. 28–31.

69. Clapham, *Africa and the International System,* p. 271.

70. Hyden, *No Shortcuts.*

71. Discussant report at the MIT Conference on African Renewal.

72. While I agree with many of the values that Olukoshi outlines in the closing remarks of "Impact of Recent Reform Efforts," I would suggest that state construction must be considered from both realistic and idealistic perspectives, especially since the basic currency remains the pursuit and exercise of political power.

73. While regime changes have occurred in countries such as Malawi and Zambia via multiparty elections, in most countries in this arc, elections fall into the category of "demonstration elections," in which the incumbents' control of power is not allowed to be threatened.

74. Pye, "Political Science," p. 4.

PART 2

The Political Economy of Democratization

5

The Economic Bases of Democratization

ROBERT H. BATES

This chapter argues from the top down, as it were. Rather than explore what has happened in Africa, it explores what might have been expected to happen, given our understanding of the economic bases for democratization. It begins by looking at the politics of transition, then examines the political impact of the structure and composition of Africa's economies; it ends by exploring the political role of Africa's middle class.[1]

The End of Tyranny

Even though it addresses the economic foundations of democracy, the point of departure for this essay is a political one. It focuses on the end of tyranny. When tyrannies collapse, the subsequent political transition can result in renewed authoritarianism; such was the case, for example, in Uganda, with the fall of Idi Amin. Alternatively, the transition can result in violence or chaos, as in Somalia. In some fortunate cases, however, the collapse of tyranny results in the flowering of political liberty and the promotion of political restraint. This outcome characterizes southern Africa. A major reason for the relatively democratic outcome in that region is that the new regimes left the former repressors in possession of a political hostage: the private economy.

By definition, tyrants are not friends of liberty. They scorn the rule of law, shun due process, and run roughshod over rights in person and property. But when citizens rebelling in the name of democracy stand on the brink of political victory, then tyrants convert. They seek the protection of the law and the courts, they demand due process, and, hoping to live out their natural lives in comfort and to die peacefully in bed, they propound the inviolability of persons and property. Formerly the most dangerous enemies of liberal government, they now become some of its most fervent champions.

Even at the end of the political struggle, a retreating despot can threaten to bequeath political chaos and physical destruction, rather than a peaceful and prosperous commonwealth. Lacking the legitimacy to govern, he may still possess the power to destroy. This power renders the period of transition a seedtime for liberty, for it is a time when even the tyrant seeks legal restraints, political guarantees, and fundamental rights, and when the insurgents are motivated to provide them to secure a peaceful political surrender.

What conditions will render these guarantees credible? In order to be credible, the terms of surrender must leave the tyrant in control of hostages. He must possess, and be seen to possess, the capacity to retaliate should others subsequently infringe on the constitutional guarantees.

Two kinds of hostages can be offered: military and economic. Only the latter is truly credible, however. Keeping the tyrant's security forces intact would not offer him much comfort; his army may be tempted to trade his person for money or promotions. More credible is economic power. Should the tyrant or his followers own industries or banks, should they control capital, physical or financial, should they, in short, possess economic power, then those seeking their political surrender should respect their rights. For, possessing economic power, the former tyrant could retaliate whenever constitutional guarantees are infringed upon; by triggering economic collapse, he could put the new government in political danger. The new regime is therefore likely to respect and preserve the legal framework of his surrender.

These dynamics characterize historical experience. Robert Dahl, for example, notes the peaceful separation of political from economic power that occurred in the United States.[2] Anglo-Americans once controlled both wealth and power, but over time, the wealthy moved from the statehouse to the boardroom, surrendering political power to the leaders of immigrant communities. The transition was peaceful, and it left in place an enduring structure of civil liberties. The politicians appreciated the benefits of cooperating with, and feared the economic costs of attacking, those who controlled the wealth of the nation. The uneasy alliances of Irish and Brahmin in Boston and of Italian and WASP in New York found their parallels in other metropolitan centers. The separation between public power and private wealth proved productive of political liberty.

While derived from the historical experience of the West, these dynamics appear to have shaped contemporary politics in southern Africa as well. In Zimbabwe, South Africa, and Namibia, whites, when controlling power, denied political rights and civil liberties to the black majority. The blacks, fighting back, toppled the white regimes. While using the language of democracy, the victorious liberation movements initially sought a central-ized state and single-party system, but from such unpromising beginnings, liberal impulses nonetheless emerged. The retreating racial minority sought political protection, and the victorious blacks conceded constitutional guar-antees to forestall economic sabotage by the wealthy minority. Political restraint thus emerged out of economic necessity in the southern parts of the continent.

The argument advanced here provides an interpretation of this transi-tion. The bequest of democracy may have constituted the terms of a politi-cal surrender, shaped by the ability of the wealthy to penalize the powerful.

The Mobility of Factors

The history of Western Europe suggests a second economic and political path to democratization—one that operates through economic "mobility." Even a casual reading of the literature on the origins of parliaments reveals that these institutions arose as arenas in which monarchs bargained with citizens. The monarchs became supplicants when impelled by the need to raise money for wars. While soldiers could be paid with spoils, and some military campaigns could pay for themselves, wars could also be long and costly. For most states, it was impossible to finance them with loot from military campaigns. Monarchs knew that their armies, if unpaid, could leave frontiers undefended and march against their own capitals. Demeaned though they might be by the need to raise money from their subjects, most monarchs nonetheless found it necessary to do so.

In the literature on the origins of parliaments, it becomes clear that the nature of the economy—and, in particular, the revenue base—strongly shaped the terms of this bargain. The more elastic the revenue base, the greater the degree to which the sovereign had to give control over public policy to those whose money he sought to appropriate for public purposes. By "elastic," I mean responsive: the tendency to grow, in the face of posi-tive incentives, and to diminish, in the face of negative ones.

Sydney Knox Mitchell notes, for example, that in England, monarchs first had to bargain with their citizens for revenues when they began to tax "movable property." Movable property—"cows, oxen, grain, household goods, and other possessions . . . that could be transferred from place to place"—could be concealed; it was very elastic.[3] Taxing it therefore required the cooperation of its owners. In order to enhance the incentives for owners to cooperate, the monarch had to give them greater control over the use to which those tax revenues would be put. Increased taxation there-fore implied increased representation, and thus the creation of parliaments.

A major implication of this argument is that democratic institutions are more likely to characterize polities in which the major factors of the economy are mobile and can thus be supplied elastically. Land is, of course, the least mobile factor of production; capital is the most. The advanced industrial states of Europe were once land abundant and capital scarce; when so endowed, they were absolutist and authoritarian.[4] Now capital is abundant and land is scarce, and the European nations have become democratic.

In contrast with other regions of the world, Africa lacks capital, and it is relatively abundantly endowed with land. In the search for public resources, those in control of the state therefore encounter little reason to bargain; they have felt little need to exchange control over public policy for receipts of public revenues.

In the longer run, however, their behavior has proved counterproductive, as those who work the land in Africa have altered their relationship with the state. Withholding productive effort from agriculture, farmers instead retreated into leisure (as argued by Goran Hyden) or into other sectors of the economy (as argued by myself).[5] This response of the rural sector helped to precipitate Africa's economic collapse. The need to restore economic incentives has helped to spark the subsequent calls for good governance.

Endowed abundantly with land but poorly with capital, the economies of Africa offered few incentives, at least in the short run, for governments to exercise restraint when seeking access to economic resources. It was only after Africa's economic decline that governments felt the need to generate positive economic incentives and to build cooperative political relationships with those who controlled the major source of their revenues.

A second and related feature of Africa's economies is the abundance of natural resources, including oil, diamonds, copper, gold, uranium, and timber. The exploitation of such natural resources can be heavily taxed and yet remain economically profitable. Moreover, at least in the short run, governments in resource-rich economies can secure resources by seizing them, rather than bargaining for them. Thus, in comparison with other economic settings, the revenue imperative in Africa provides a weak impetus for democratization. Governments can secure needed revenues simply by taking them.

The arguments advanced in this section thus suggest that, *insofar as the democratic impulse is animated by economic factors,* it might be relatively weak in Africa in comparison with other regions. But the arguments also suggest patterns of variation within Africa itself. They suggest, for example, that African states that are poorly endowed by nature may be comparatively more democratic; the fact that The Gambia (until the mid-1990s), Senegal, and Mauritius hold elections, contested by competing candidates and backed by rival parties, may not be as anomalous as might first appear. They also suggest that wealthier African nations will tend to be more democratic if they hold their wealth in the form of mobile capital.[6]

The implication, then, is that we should see greater levels of democratization in the southern portions of Africa.

In addition to cross-national variations, the analysis suggests variation over time within countries as well. In the long run, economies adjust, even economies based on relatively immobile resources. When governments extract revenues without providing goods, services, or economically favorable policies in return, then private agents withdraw, or they fail to invest, and physical capital depreciates. The economy therefore declines, and governments that sought short-term gains find that they have, in the longer run, made themselves worse off. Having despoiled their tax base, governments become revenue starved and are consequently driven to reform. That economic reconstruction should spawn political reform therefore emerges as a corollary of this analysis.

The argument thus suggests that an economic logic may underlie political change. Political reform will accompany economic reconstruction, representing a response to the fiscal crisis of the state.

The Interstate System

Monarchs, as noted earlier, sought funds in order to fight. The search for security abroad provoked a search for revenues at home. Under the impetus of political insecurity, monarchs adopted policies designed to enhance their tax base: they reformed their financial institutions, the better to borrow;[7] they transformed their agriculture, the better to grow economically;[8] and they altered the structure of protection, the better to enhance the wealth of their nation.[9] In addition, they empowered parliaments, the better to reassure asset holders that they would keep their promises to repay loans, to limit wars, and to control public spending.[10] Political insecurity at the international level thus animated economic policy at home and provoked political reform,[11] even by monarchs who would no doubt have preferred to exercise less economic discipline and less political restraint.

England provides the canonical example. Long engaged in combat with Catholic Spain and France, the English monarchy made extraordinary fiscal demands upon its subjects. The Spanish and French states remained absolutist; they remained "strong." The English monarchy, in contrast, was overthrown. When restored, it was as a constitutional monarchy that, in comparison with its rivals on the continent, appeared "weak," hedged by constitutional limitations on its power to fight and to tax. And yet the "weak" English monarchy gained access to vastly greater amounts of wealth than did its rivals, and at vastly more favorable terms. Bargaining for resources through Parliament, the English monarch was able to mobilize sufficient resources to prevail over his enemies on the field of battle.[12]

In the modern era, also, states locked in military rivalries have learned to regard economic development as essential for political survival. Japan, for example, has historically treated its economy as a political resource, and since its liberation from Japan, Korea has done the same. Faced with the prospect of military extinction, governments champion economic policies that create wealth. After escaping from the mainland, even the Kuomintang changed from a predatory government to a developmental regime in an effort to secure itself against military invasion.

In Africa, few states have faced the prospect of military defeat at the hands of their neighbors. Few, therefore, have been spurred to improve the productivity of their resource base or to create wealth so as to enhance their prospects for survival. Indeed, on the contrary, states that in an earlier era would have been too poor to survive have, in Africa, nonetheless remained intact. By limiting the number and magnitude of interstate wars, the international system may have achieved humanitarian gains, but at the expense of disabling a mechanism that served to promote good governance in other times and places. This system may therefore have weakened the link between the pursuit of international security and enlightened, albeit self-interested, governance.

The international system may have weakened this link in another way as well: by transferring economic resources to poor states though international aid programs. In an earlier era, governments did, of course, borrow abroad. But the major part of their revenues had to be raised domestically.[13] As already recounted, when forced to borrow funds at home, governments had to grant political concessions.

For many modern African governments, however, the productive margin in their search for resources lies not in their own countryside or their harbors or their domestic industries, but rather in Tokyo, Washington, London, or Paris. In an international order that provides resources to cash-starved governments, Africa's political elites now do as well bargaining with other elites abroad as they do bargaining with their own citizens at home. Faced with the choice between making political concessions to domestic asset holders or playing mouse to the World Bank's cat, political elites choose the latter. Transfers from abroad may enable them to delay forging productive arrangements at home, including the extension of political liberties to those whose economic resources they desire.

Some political entities in Africa have been shaped by international forces in ways that resemble the experiences of older states. South Africa, for example, was long at war, and it is one of the few states in Africa that has promoted technical change, investing in its energy systems in ways that call to mind the actions of governments in East Asia. Eritrea is likewise one of the few states to emerge from war, and its government is forging domestic policies designed to create wealth, rather than to seize it from its citizens or to beg it from abroad. As in Kenya, major reforms have taken place when aid programs have been canceled. When a government's political security rests upon its ability to raise resources from its own economy, then it is driven by self-interest to govern in an enlightened fashion.

The Middle Class: Part I

In the advanced industrial economies, the capital that is embodied in human beings is a key factor of production. Education, skills, and the willingness to apply them become the bases of wealth. In an economy based upon human capital, production plans cannot be imposed; their attainment must instead be elicited. A supervisor cannot make someone think faster or more cleverly. Productivity cannot be accelerated by running a faster production line. Rather, those who possess skills and talents must be listened to, their needs ascertained, and their environment then structured so that they will happily do what they do best.

The impact of these considerations is made manifest in the structure of economic organizations. One need only compare a steel mill in the Rust Belt of the United States with a high-tech firm in Silicon Valley. The one is regimented and authoritarian, the other decentralized, with the pace and organization of work largely determined by the employees themselves. The difference is not, it should be emphasized, between heavy industry and research-oriented firms. As automotive production lines require higher levels of human skill, the Japanese mode of management tends to replace that of Detroit. Even within heavy industry, then, the pattern holds: the more critical the element of human skill, the more employee driven the economic structure.

The argument possesses a political analogue, of course. If a government or nation seeks to prosper economically, it may try methods of command and control. When firms that use high proportions of plant and machinery relative to human skill formed the basis of economies, then centrally directed systems tended to work; in midcentury, the Soviet Union competed successfully with capitalist states, as measured by rates of economic growth. But as the economies of nations have moved toward modes of production that require a high level of human capital, these organizational forms have proved increasingly inefficient. Instead, forms of organization in which those who control the most essential factor—human capital—make the key decisions themselves become more appropriate and effective.

In economies that make intensive use of human capital, governments concerned with economic growth may therefore seek to surrender control over decisions to those who control the key resource: the people themselves. And skilled people are in a strong position to bargain for the devolu-

tion of power, for they can refuse to employ their skills, leaving governments that have invested in their education with a declining economy, incapable of competing in global markets.

These dynamics appear to have characterized the behavior of the middle class in the former socialist nations of Eastern Europe. Rather than
attacking their governments, the educated members of the middle class
instead withheld productive effort. By withdrawing from the economy, they
initiated a political—if velvet—revolution. In contrast, Africa's national
economies are not endowed with large numbers of educated personnel. Nor,
for reasons that have been touched upon, do African governments find it in
their interests to develop economically, the better to compete in the international arena. The productive margin of Africa's economies lies not in industries based on human capital, but in the extraction of natural resources. This
path to democratization therefore appears closed to Africa's aspiring
democrats.

The Middle Class: Part II

This is not to argue that Africa lacks an active private sector. Markets and
trading routes in Africa possess long histories, strong institutions, and highly professionalized cadres.[14] These commercial networks thrived even in
the midst of the interventionist policies of the postindependence period.
They provided the framework for the black markets that burgeoned even as
public institutions decayed.[15]

While it is a major force in the economies of Africa, the market economy has nonetheless failed to produce a coherent bourgeoisie and provide
the impetus necessary for sustained political reform. The most notable evidence for this comes from the period before the economic reforms of the
late 1980s. In the face of macroeconomic imbalances, microeconomic
interventions, and the massive distortion of prices in key markets, Africa's
middle class remained largely silent. Many traders profited from that gap.
A major portion of their profits resulted from arbitrage between official and
unofficial markets. Rather than turning to protest, then, marketers returned
to trade. They survived, and indeed prospered, in an informal economy that
was created by—or at least in reaction to—the heavily distorted policy
regime imposed by African governments.

Nor did the managers of firms form a coherent class and organize in
opposition to their government's economic policies. The managers of
African firms, even ones located in the public sector, have formulated
stinging indictments of government policies. But the reformist impulse
articulated by this elite was muted by the governance structure of Africa's
firms. Much of Africa's plant and infrastructure was, and indeed remains,
publicly owned. By hiring and firing managerial personnel, making judi-

cious use of transfers, and rationing access to credit and foreign exchange, public directors stifled the protests of disaffected managers and their opposition to the prevailing ways of "doing business in Africa."

Africa's middle class also failed to form a coherent opposition to governments for an additional reason: it is readily divided along ethnic lines. Elites often exchange their material wealth for social standing in their communities by contributing to local causes, such as building schools, clinics, or other public works. Some also invest in traditional titles, sacrificing major portions of the incomes they gain in the "modern" sector for "traditional" prestige. Politically motivated appeals to ethnic loyalty can thus divide Africa's elite. As a consequence, it has proven easy for governments to divide the bourgeoisie. Led by ministers, lawyers, and other professionals, the middle class of Kenya, for example, organized in opposition to the incumbent regime of Daniel arap Moi. However, regional ties and ethnic loyalties facilitated the division of the opposition, and Moi prevailed. The story of Kenya finds its parallel throughout Africa, where the splintered ranks of the opposition reflect the internal divisions of the bourgeoisie, enabling inept governments to remain in power.

There is a bourgeoisie in Africa, but it forms a weak middle class. One consequence is that with very few exceptions—Zambia being one of them—the recession of the 1980s sparked remarkably little political opposition. The call for free markets, liberalization, and privatization came from international, not domestic, capital. And the impetus for political reform has come from brave individuals, intellectuals, and the losers in the postindependence struggle for power. The economic and political threads of protest find no common origin in a class program.

Thus, while in other eras and places, the bourgeoisie has provided the political impetus for democratic reform, translating economic forces into political ones, in Africa, merchant capital has traded around the government rather than confronting it. Public authorities have silenced the managerial bourgeoisie, and divisive loyalties that are subject to political manipulation have fractionated the ranks of the political opposition.

An African Path?

In 1995, 29 of Africa's 46 executives were selected in elections in which they faced rivals backed by an opposition party; only three had been so chosen in 1975. Similarly, in 1995, 35 of Africa's 46 states possessed legislatures chosen in competitive elections in which candidates faced rivals sponsored by an opposition party; in 1975, 24 of Africa's 46 states lacked any form of legislature.[16] Given the weakness of the economic forces promoting political democratization in Africa, how are we to respond to this evidence of widespread political reform?

One way is by doubting the depth, while acknowledging the breadth, of the movement toward new forms of government. As demonstrated by Kenya and Zaire, rival parties can enter elections without posing a serious threat to autocratic rulers. Evidence from other nations only deepens the level of skepticism about the depth of commitment to democratic governance in Africa.[17] Despite observer testimonies to the contrary, few elections held in Africa are free and fair. Political transitions, therefore, may not represent a turn to democracy, but rather evidence of continued political stability in Africa.

We may also react by reengaging the central theme of this essay. I will close by doing so and by positing a causal path linking economic bases to political superstructures. It is a path that accounts for the characteristic features of Africa's political transitions.

Consider any market. As seen in Figure 5.1, given competition, normally behaving forces of supply and demand generate a market equilibrium: they establish a price (P_0) at which the quantity demanded (Q_D) equals the quantity supplied (Q_S). Governments may, however, seek to overturn the market solution. For social or political purposes, they may, for example, lower the price to a point below that generated by market forces (say, to P_1).

In their attempts at state-led growth, African governments frequently adopted policies that generated such distortions. In agriculture, for example, they sought to lower the price of food for urban consumers, raw materials for urban industries, and inputs for farmers.[18] In industry, they sought to lower the price charged for electricity and petroleum products. For

Figure 5.1   Market Distortion and the Creation of Rents

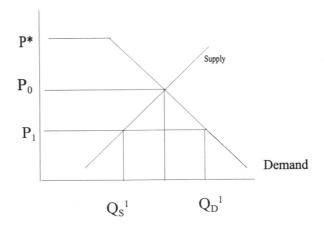

consumers, they subsidized the costs of essential commodities, such as cooking oil, paraffin, processed foods, and clothing.[19] More damaging still, governments have pursued interventionist policies at the macrolevel. In credit markets, they have attempted to lower interest rates, and in markets for foreign exchange, they have sought to lower exchange rates, thereby reducing the costs of importing from abroad.

One result was the creation of characteristic political patterns: clientelistic and patronage politics, corruption, and the privatization of public institutions. Another was the growth of the demand for political reform, as civic-minded leaders grew increasingly disaffected with the political regime. In the economy, as demand exceeded supply at official prices, markets could clear only if the government conferred subsidies and if the nation borrowed resources from abroad. A third result, therefore, was fiscal crisis and foreign debt.

Disequilibria in markets, clientelistic politics, fiscal crisis, foreign debt, and growing political disaffection—these constituted the core characteristics of the African malaise. In the light of this analysis, we can see why these phenomena moved in concert. We can understand why so much of the pressure for economic reform came not from domestic sources, such as the fragmented bourgeoisie, but rather from international capital, which was not subject to the divisive interventions of Africa's governments. And we can also comprehend why changes in economic policies should have accompanied changes in political regimes. The old form of governance was not economically sustainable. The creditors to African governments were no longer willing to underpin their attempts to override market forces. But to alter economic policies in Africa was virtually to alter the political foundations of Africa's governments.

Historically, democracy accompanies economic prosperity; it is the result of growth and rising per capita incomes.[20] But democratic reform occurred at the nadir of Africa's postindependence economic history. We can now understand why.

The argument of this chapter is that the economic determinants of democratization in Africa do not include prosperity, the rise of a coherent middle class, or governmental concessions to the demands of private agents, whose resources they wish to tax. Nor have governments been forced to become enlightened by the economic and political spurs of warfare. Africa's path to democracy is thus not that of the West. Rather, it most closely approximates, perhaps, the path taken by the former socialist regimes of Eastern Europe. The economic foundations for reform in Africa originate from the attempts of revenue-starved fiscs and government creditors to extract political regimes from loss-making policies. They represent, as well, attempts to reenter international markets, especially markets for capital. The economic impetus for political reform originates not from the private economy, but from the needs of the public sector.

Notes

1. This chapter draws heavily from Bates, "Economics of Transition" and "Impulse to Reform."

2. Dahl, *Who Governs?*

3. S. K. Mitchell, *Taxation in Medieval England,* p. 6.

4. This analysis represents an extension of the kind of analysis pioneered by Rogowski, *Commerce and Coalition.*

5. Hyden, *Beyond Ujamaa;* Bates, *Markets and States.*

6. That few of Africa's economies have accumulated capital from sources other than minerals, timber, or oil poses obvious difficulties for this analysis.

7. Root, *Fountain of Privilege.*

8. Hoffman, "Institutions and Agriculture"; Rosenthal, *Fruits of Revolution.*

9. S. L. Kaplan, *Bread, Politics, and Political Economy.*

10. North and Weingast, "Constitutions and Commitment."

11. See Skocpol, *States and Social Revolutions.*

12. The classic remains North and Weingast, "Constitutions and Commitment"; see also Brewer, *Sinews of Power.*

13. Indeed, their ability to do so placed an upper limit on their ability to borrow internationally. See, for example, Root, *Fountain of Privilege.*

14. See, for example, the contributions in Meillassoux, ed., *Development of Indigenous Trade;* Gray and Birmingham, *Pre-Colonial African Trade;* and the superb overview in W. Jones, "Agricultural Trade."

15. Jenkins, ed., *Beyond the Informal Sector.*

16. This data comes from a project being undertaken by Karen Ferree, Smita Singh, and myself, at Harvard University.

17. See, for example, *The Economist.*

18. Bates, *Markets and States.*

19. See Killick, *Development Economics;* Pearson et al., "Incentives and Comparative Advantage"; and Bates and Collier, "The Case of Zambia."

20. The classic analyses remain Deutsch, "Social Mobilization"; Lipset, *Political Man;* and Coleman, "Conclusion."

6

Globalization
and African Democracy

NICOLAS VAN DE WALLE

A number of African countries have recently undertaken transitions to democratic rule and have now begun the arduous task of consolidation.[1] The biggest obstacle they face is the pervasive economic crisis that has gripped most countries in the region. As Adam Przeworski and Fernando Limongi have recently reconfirmed, "what destabilizes regimes are economic crises, and democracies, particularly poor democracies, are extremely vulnerable to bad economic performance."[2] Persistent fiscal crises and balance-of-payment deficits over the last two decades have been associated with stagnant or even negative economic growth and, in some cases, declining welfare for a significant proportion of the population. If democratic regimes cannot overturn the recent pattern of declining real wages, rising levels of poverty, and inadequate public spending on physical infrastructure and social services, they may lose their popular legitimacy and eventually fall prey to political instability.

At its outset, the current wave of democratization was characterized by relative optimism about the economic prospects of the new regimes. Democratization provided a real opportunity to overcome the economic crisis, many observers felt, because the practices of the continent's authoritarian rulers during the first three decades of independence were largely to blame for the severity of the economic crisis. To be sure, the crisis has had multiple causes, including a number of external factors—most notably, the decline and instability of international commodity prices during the last several decades. Nonetheless, it was generally agreed that mismanagement by repressive and nonaccountable governments deserved a good deal of the blame.[3] Thus, the emergence of a more participatory and competitive politics held the possibility of improved management of the economy.[4]

Or so had been assumed at the outset of democratization. As several years have gone by in the fledgling African democracies and economic improvements have been slow and halting at best, the flush of initial optimism has given way to much more circumspect attitudes and even pessimism about the impact of democratization on African economies. There are many causes of the current disenchantment. In this chapter, I will analyze just one set of arguments that has been advanced: the argument that changing global economic forces represent a threat to the viability of Africa's democracies and to the continent's economic welfare.[5] The concept of economic globalization captures the notion that the conjunction of a number of recent, complex changes in the world economy has fundamentally altered the way in which it functions.

In the economic realm, globalization usually refers to the various processes that are promoting increasing integration of the world economy. For the Washington-based international financial institutions (IFIs) such as the World Bank and the International Monetary Fund (IMF), as well as for most mainstream economists, the integration of the international economy has resulted in increased dynamism, which represents opportunities for Africa that have to be aggressively pursued. Jeffrey Sachs and Andrew Warner strike a typically unambiguous note, arguing that the current round of "globalization promises to lead to economic convergence for the [developing] countries that join the system."[6] The survival of current democratic experiments will be assured by the growth that results from policy reforms that promote Africa's integration into the world economy through trade liberalization and the attraction of foreign private capital.[7] For these and other observers, democratization and integration into the world economy are often viewed as mutually reinforcing.[8]

But this optimism is not shared by some Africanist political scientists. While not denying that an export-led growth strategy has the highest probability of long-term success, Henry Bienen and Jeffrey Herbst have argued cogently that pursuing economic and political liberalization simultaneously makes both harder to achieve.[9] For his part, Richard Sandbrook has argued that democracy and "neoliberal" integration into the global economy are not jointly sustainable in the long run.[10] For these and other scholars, the implication is that low-income African economies are too vulnerable to benefit from generalized exposure to international market forces.

Other scholars go further and deny the very compatibility of democracy with a process of economic liberalization that would open African economies to necessarily hostile international forces. As the late Claude Ake recently argued, the current evolution of global economic forces so undermines the sovereignty of African governments over economic matters as to make democracy essentially "irrelevant."[11] He argues that meaningful democracy will be possible only in economies that foster self-reliance, regional integration, and selective links with the economies of the Organization for Economic Cooperation and Development (OECD).[12]

Fantu Cheru goes further, suggesting that globalization will necessarily result in "more hardship and further marginalization for the majority of poor African peasants and the Third World as a whole."[13] In sum, the nature of Africa's integration into the world economy is such as to take away any discretionary decisionmaking from African governments; the democracy that Africans have fought for turns out to be "choiceless"[14]—all of its policy choices having been ordained by international market forces and their privileged agents in Africa, the IMF, and the World Bank. As Thandika Mkandawire argues, the structural adjustment programs "represent not only the liberalization of domestic markets but also a submission to the logic of global markets. This impinges on national sovereignty understood as the ability of the national governments to pursue socially-valued objectives such as growth and equity."[15]

The argument that engagement with the world economy will have nefarious consequences for Africa and its citizens has been a recurrent theme of much scholarly literature about the continent since the appearance of the seminal work of such scholars as Walter Rodney, Immanuel Wallerstein, and Samir Amin.[16] It has also had a profound influence on official attitudes within Africa, both among national decisionmakers and in regional organizations like the Organization for African Unity and the UN Economic Commission for Africa, both of which continue to be lukewarm to calls by the Washington institutions for trade and financial liberalization. Today, these arguments have obtained a new life in the context of debates about globalization.

In this chapter, I assess these arguments about the impact of economic globalization on African democracy. I limit my analysis to the economic dimension of globalization, defined as the process of integration of national economies. I do not analyze the political impact of the new information technologies—or what might be called "cultural globalization"—except insofar as it is captured in trade and financial flows across national borders. The current information and communications revolution may ultimately have an even more significant impact on Africa than economic globalization,[17] but including it would only further complicate what is already a complex story for a short essay.

Instead, I ask: what is economic globalization, and how should we think about its impact on African politics? Does the recent evolution of the world economy really represent a significant historical discontinuity? How will this trend affect the ongoing wave of democratization on the continent? In the next section, I track the recent progress of economic globalization and review the reasons given in the literature for why it might be viewed as undermining democratic rule. In the second section, I argue that the international economy is much less globalized at present than is increasingly being suggested; moreover, in Africa, globalization processes are in fact stagnant, if not in retreat. I argue that the very low levels of private capital flows to Africa serve to distinguish the continent sharply from other regions of the world. Africa's increasing marginalization in the world economy means that the implications of global economic integration are different in Africa than they are in Latin America or Asia. The third section then examines the nature of the challenges that the international economy poses for democratic governments in Africa. I suggest that implementing political and economic transitions at the same time is fraught with difficulty, but that in the long run, greater integration into the world economy holds opportunities, as well as dangers, for African democracies.

Globalization and Its Political Implications

Since the mid-1980s, a large and varied literature has emerged arguing that the integration of national economies has proceeded so far as to change the nature of international economic relations.[18] Observers point to the ever-expanding volume of international trade, the increasing mobility of capital, and the emergence of global private companies with production processes that span nations and continents. The growth of international trade has been particularly rapid, increasing on average at one and one-half times the rate of growth of world gross domestic product (GDP) between 1965 and 1990.[19]

Globalization is particularly striking in the area of finance. Foreign direct investment (FDI) rose at an even faster rate than trade during the 1980s. In 1996, the total stock of FDI exceeded $2,700 billion, roughly double the 1988 level and equal to about 10 percent of world economic output.[20] Overall, total net capital inflows to the developing world in 1995 totaled $193.7 billion according to the IMF, up from $43.5 billion as recently as 1990 and including some $37 billion in portfolio investments.[21] The most awesome growth has come in foreign exchange markets, where the daily transactions recorded by the Bank for International Settlements more than doubled between 1989 and 1995 to reach $1.2 trillion per day in some 150,000 different transactions.[22] Markets for other financial assets such as government bonds and various derivatives have also undergone strong growth and have become seemingly impervious to effective regulation by national governments.

A number of factors appear to be promoting this process of globalization. First, many observers stress the key role of certain technologies. On the one hand, innovations in transportation have lowered costs dramatically, making what were once nontradable goods into products that could be competitive in foreign markets. On the other hand, spectacular advances in information technologies have sharply cut the cost of information and accelerated the speed at which it flows across borders. The role of information technologies is keenly felt in the area of finance, for example, as computerized trading has turned foreign exchange markets into 24-hour-a-day extravaganzas involving eye-popping amounts of capital in interconnected markets all over the globe.

Second, observers stress the role of policymakers in the dominant economies, who have promoted trade through the elimination of tariffs and other national barriers, as well as through economic policy convergence. A host of international organizations, from the IMF to the General Agreement on Tariffs and Trade (GATT), the World Trade Organization, and the Bank for International Settlements, have been established to promote economic integration, which is viewed as the best means to achieve economic efficiency and growth. The recently completed Uruguay Round of GATT and the achievements of such efforts at regional integration as the North American Free Trade Agreement, the Maastricht Treaty of the European Union, the Association of Southeast Asian Nations, and the Southern Cone Common Market in the developing world have all promoted trade growth.[23]

Third, and related to these first two factors, scholars like Gary Gereffi emphasize the growing tendency of business firms to organize themselves across borders in "global commodity chains."[24] A large number of multinational corporations (MNCs) now hold a significant proportion of their productive assets abroad. As a result, a growing proportion of international trade is composed of intrafirm transactions, in which, for example, an MNC's factory in Asia exports electronic components to another of the MNC's factories in the United States for assembly and sale. Intrafirm trade involving American MNCs may account for as much as 30 percent of U.S. exports and 18 percent of imports.[25]

Economic globalization, it is widely agreed, holds two primary implications of political importance for developing countries.[26] First, globalization undermines national sovereignty, in the sense that it lessens the degree of policy discretion available to governments that want to maintain sustainable policies. The international mobility of capital weakens the ability of governments to pursue independent monetary and fiscal policy. Any policy that has a negative effect on the real, risk-adjusted return to holders of financial assets will result in an outflow of capital to other markets that hold the promise of higher returns.

It is thus argued that globalization is resulting in the progressive "convergence" of policies across nations. Governments that try to implement alternative economic policies that are at odds with those of the most powerful economies in the West will see themselves sharply punished by the market. This phenomenon is well illustrated by the dramatic failure of France's go-it-alone reflation of the early 1980s under the first socialist government led by François Mitterand. Although growth was briefly spurred, these policies resulted in a dramatic capital outflow that required three devaluations between 1981 and 1983, and eventually convinced the socialists to adopt the policy of the *"Franc Fort"* and converge on the much more conservative policies set by the German Bundesbank.[27]

Firms that can shift elements of their production processes across borders can more easily evade national regulatory regimes and can engender competition among governments to gain more favorable regulatory environments. This suggests the second, and partly overlapping, political implication of globalization: the relative disempowerment of labor, a less mobile factor of production. As globalization progresses, governments will tend to shift the burden of taxation away from capital—which would only respond by moving to other, more accommodating countries—to labor, which is less mobile and thus less able to evade the burden. Moreover, capital's already relatively higher levels of mobility have been further abetted by recent international negotiations, which have not included efforts to improve labor mobility. On the contrary, the current period of growing international integration has been characterized by a simultaneous movement to curb immigration, particularly, but not only, into the rich economies of the OECD.

Even in the absence of government policy changes, globalization still places a downward pressure on wages, since firms are better able to choose to locate where wages are low and unions weak than workers are able to move to areas where demand for labor is strong and wages are high. A minority of highly skilled labor will retain some leverage by being somewhat more mobile across borders and/or by having skills that are in great demand in the emerging high-tech economy. Thus, the stagnation of real wages in OECD economies, combined with growing disparities between skilled and unskilled labor, is often ascribed to the dynamics of globalization. In sum, heightened capital mobility not only constrains government policymaking; it constrains it in a specific direction that has negative implications for labor. The logic of globalization forces individual governments to accommodate market forces in the name of "national competitiveness," even if it means erosion of wages and labor standards. As a result, in the absence of international cooperation, globalization seems likely to increase social inequalities, an evolution that has already begun, according to a number of observers.[28]

The Limits of Globalization

Even if the trends and dynamics described above are correct, the extent and significance of globalization probably remains much exaggerated. First, the notion that we are witnessing a major historical economic watershed seems overblown. Historians remind us that, at least by certain measures, the international economy is no more integrated today than it had become by the latter half of the nineteenth century.[29] For example, *The Economist* recently pointed out that for many industrialized countries, trade accounts for about the same proportion of GDP as it did a century ago. Similarly, the size of net capital flows among countries is not unprecedented; a century ago, as much as 40 percent of British savings were invested abroad.[30] According to these accounts, the current period is only now overturning the impact of Great Depression protectionism to return to the levels of international openness that had been achieved before World War I.

Second, there remain notable areas in which there is little convergence, suggesting that the process of globalization is less than complete. The one area where recent innovations truly do imply a historical discontinuity is in financial markets. True, high levels of foreign direct investment and international bond issues are far from new, but the sheer *speed* with which these capital markets respond to price signals appears unprecedented. Nonetheless, economists point out that the predicted convergence in interest rates has simply not taken place; national divergences have persisted even in the most integrated economies, such as those in Europe. Robert Wade suggests that real interest rates vary from country to country by up to a factor of five; this is much less than the differential in real wages, perhaps, but is nonetheless larger than would be the case in a completely integrated world economy.[31] Moreover, even if convergence is accelerating, the globalization literature greatly exaggerates its speed and how far along it has progressed.

Third, many of the characteristics ascribed to globalization concern only a minority of mostly developed states. The impressive growth in international trade is almost entirely accounted for by the two dozen states of the OECD and a handful of East Asian economies. Indeed, according to the UN Conference on Trade and Development (UNCTAD), the OECD share of total international trade is above 80 percent, and it has been rising over the last 20 years.[32] Much the same can be said about FDI. True, FDI in the developing world has increased sharply in recent years, but again, most FDI continues to occur among the major OECD economies. Thus, the United States remains the major recipient of FDI, accounting for some 46 percent of world flows between 1985 and 1989, while only 6 percent of FDI flows from the United States went to developing countries between 1989 and 1991.[33] Focusing only on the developing countries reveals that five countries received 53 percent of total net private capital flows in 1996, and 12 countries received 73 percent.[34]

The claims made on behalf of globalization seem particularly suspect in Africa. In 1981, Fred Cooper noted the paradox that Africa's dependence on the world economy was growing even as the continent was becoming increasingly marginal vis-à-vis the outside world.[35] How much Africa was ever integrated into the world economy is open to empirical and conceptual debate; that it is not rapidly becoming more integrated today seems incontrovertible. This is corroborated by a recent World Bank report, which devised an index for the speed of integration into the world economy during the 1980s that incorporates four dimensions: the ratio of real trade to GDP, the ratio of FDI to GDP, the credit ratings of the *Institutional Investor* magazine, and the share of manufactures in exports.[36] According to this definition, only 12 of the 36 African economies rated were considered "fast" or "moderate" integrators, and the African region contained the majority of "weak" and "slow" integrators in the sample. Using several similar indicators, Sachs and Warner's study of the role of trade in development identifies 35 countries that were "closed" at the end of 1994; 23 of them were African.[37]

Trade offers a first example. Africa's integration into world trading markets is long-standing.[38] As early as 1854, western Africa exported some 37,631 tons of palm oil to Great Britain, a total that would reach 50,000 tons by the end of the century and that would be complemented by another 50,000 tons of palm kernels.[39] Groundnut trade between Senegal and France had reached 5,500 tons by 1854.[40] In all, by 1870, on the eve of formal partition and before the diamond and gold boom in southern Africa, the estimated value of sub-Saharan Africa's total maritime trade was some 17 million pounds.[41]

Then, as today, African trade represented an exceedingly small proportion of total world trade. Indeed, sub-Saharan Africa's share of world trade is probably no higher today than at the onset of colonialism. J. Forbes Munro estimates the share in 1880 at between 0.8 and 1.2 percent and shows that the share increased steadily to over 5 percent at the time of independence.[42] Recent World Bank estimates put the proportion at well under 2.0 percent in 1993,[43] a decline that is due to Africa's progressive loss of market share in its traditional markets for cocoa and coffee, combined with the continent's inability to break into new markets, particularly in manufacturing. This decline, it might be noted, cannot be blamed on Western protectionism, but appears to be largely the result of a series of noncompetitive practices and the trade policies of African countries themselves,[44] in contrast to the aggressive pursuit of export markets by other less-developed countries, particularly those in Asia.

The recently completed Uruguay Round of GATT further confirms this marginality.[45] Few African governments were active participants in the negotiations, which focused almost entirely on "North-North" issues. The relatively high official tariff barriers prevailing in the African region were never put on the negotiating table, and no concessions were asked of African governments. Indeed, despite much rhetoric to the contrary, formal protectionist barriers to trade are not significantly lower today in most countries of the region than they were 20 years ago.[46]

The evolution of the importance of international trade to African economies is harder to assess, since we lack adequate estimates of national GDP before the post–World War II era, but there is no reason to believe that the "openness" of African economies has changed appreciably during this period. A standard measure of openness is the proportion of GDP taken up by exports; for sub-Saharan Africa overall, the World Bank estimates that this proportion rose from 20 to 27 percent between 1970 and 1993.[47] This increase seems related in large part to the dramatic upswing in the value of oil during this period, which is exported by only a handful of countries.[48] In 16 countries, or about half of those for which we have acceptable data, the proportion went down during this period.[49] Moreover, the composition of Africa's exports is for the most part almost precisely the same as two and three decades ago, as the same data shows; with a few exceptions, the overwhelming majority of total exports have continued to be primary commodities. The real price of these commodities has on average declined by 50 percent since 1980, so they necessarily have declined in relative importance within Africa's domestic economies.

Overall, trade as a proportion of gross national product (GNP) in Africa does not appear to have changed appreciably during the last 30 years, even allowing for the increasingly poor quality of African trade data.[50] Perhaps more significantly, its *composition* remains essentially unchanged since the dawn of colonialism, with Africa still exporting commodities and minor exotic goods, and importing manufactured goods. There is thus little evidence that African economies are more integrated into the world economy, at least through the conduit of trade, despite the efforts at trade liberalization of economic policy reform programs promoted by the IFIs since the 1970s.[51]

What about capital flows? Private capital in its different guises—equity, portfolio, and foreign direct investment—has barely even noticed Africa in recent years, and there is little reason to believe that the degree to which sub-Saharan Africa is integrated into world capital markets has been increasing. Indeed, the last two decades can probably more accurately be characterized as having witnessed the disengagement of global capital from the continent, with only a few minor exceptions like Botswana and Mauritius, small economies that have exhibited the capacity to attract capital. True, there has been a recent burgeoning of capital flows toward Africa, pushed by the transition to majority rule in the Republic of South Africa and renewed interest in African oil and minerals, but it is not clear yet whether this heralds a lasting trend.

Total foreign capital investment is almost certainly considerably lower in the 1990s than it has been at several past historical junctures in African history. S. H. Frankel estimated total foreign investments in the continent between 1870 and 1913 at some 640 million British pounds, although roughly two-thirds of that amount probably went to southern Africa alone.[52] Then, as today, South Africa was the behemoth that dwarfed the continent's other economies. Belying the recent publicity generated by a small number of high-profile foreign investments in Africa, total FDI to the region is actually quite small once the Republic of South Africa is excluded. The postindependence period has, in fact, witnessed stagnating levels of Western private investment in Africa, and even net disinvestment during the late 1980s. As a result, sub-Saharan Africa accounted for only 5.5 percent of FDI stock in 1995, down from 15 percent in 1980,[53] and between 1990 and 1995, sub-Saharan Africa attracted only 2.9 percent of global FDI flows. These flows have been rising in recent years, with a 50 percent increase since 1990, but they still totaled only $2.1 billion in 1995.[54] Moreover, FDI in manufacturing is minuscule; almost all of it has been focused on the mining and oil sectors, which typically are highly capital intensive and have few multiplier effects on the rest of the domestic economy.[55] This almost exclusive focus on Africa's natural resources also has long historical roots.

Equity flows are even less impressive, though they too have been undergoing recent increases. With much fanfare, new stock markets are opening up across Africa. Eleven stock markets exist today, and another seven are in the works, and there are also plans to transform the Abidjan Bourse into a regional stock exchange. The South African stock exchange boasts capitalization of some $280 billion and is the tenth largest stock market in the world,[56] but all of the other stock markets in Africa together amount to a capitalization of only $10.8 billion, even though they have doubled in size since 1994. Excluding South Africa, portfolio equity investment totaled only $297 million in 1995. In the uncertain investment climate that exists in most African countries, equity investment might be thought to be relatively more appealing to investors, given the fact that it is typically a more liquid investment than FDI. Yet most of these stock markets are small, with no more than a handful of companies being traded, and have extremely low turnover rates. They typically suffer from the weak local demand for stocks, as well as from various regulations that discourage active trading.

Foreign participation has been significant in African stock markets, typically well over the 10 percent or so that characterizes exchanges in the developed countries. In Ghana, for example, foreign participation is well over 60 percent.[57] Given surging investor interest in emerging markets in the West, most African exchanges could probably attract more foreign equity investment, but African governments fear foreign dominance of their exchanges and have thus maintained regulations that restrict foreign participation. Unable to find appropriate equities in Africa, Western investment funds specializing in Africa have typically kept large shares in cash.[58]

In this context, recent claims of an African economic renaissance seem vastly overdrawn. There are tentative signs of sustainable growth today in a dozen countries, with growth levels in 1995 and 1996 in the range of 4 to 6 percent, levels that for too long have been virtually unheard of on the continent. It is increasingly difficult to generalize about African economies, which are today more varied in their performance and prospects than in the past.[59] The larger, richer, and more integrated markets of southern Africa probably hold a fundamentally greater potential for international capital than the balkanized and desperately poor economies of the Sahel. Likewise, countries with mineral wealth will invariably attract greater capital than countries without it, and countries undergoing or at obvious risk of civil strife will not attract significant investment. For some African economies, it is inconceivable that they will begin to attract the attention of private investors and make good on the claims that they represent the "final frontier" for emerging markets.[60] Thus, at present, the verdict must be that Africa has failed to substantially interest private-sector investment during the 1990s.

A number of scholars agree that formal links between Africa and the world economy have weakened, but they advance the thesis that an array of informal links have increasingly integrated Africa into the global economy.[61] These authors point to the growing significance of illegal and unrecorded trade and financial flows that have accompanied the weakening of state structures. They argue that African states are increasingly involved in international criminal activities,[62] which have achieved a preponderant macroeconomic influence on African economies. Béatrice Hibou's recent study of trade reform in the region demonstrates how the recent confusion and uncertainty in trade policy, coupled with the progressive loss of capacity in such state institutions as the customs and national statistics office, have resulted in a generalization of parallel-trade circuits, often with the direct blessing of political elites.[63] William Reno shows how advanced state decay is accompanied by the growing involvement of state, military, and factional elites in various shady economic activities.[64]

It is quite likely that a proper accounting of these unrecorded and fraudulent activities would increase the extent to which Africa is in fact linked to the global economy. But the question is, would this dramatically alter the picture drawn in this chapter so far? I am skeptical. An IMF-sponsored study estimated the upper bound for all illegal international transactions, broadly defined, at no more than 2 percent of global GNP.[65] Even assuming that sub-Saharan Africa's share of global illegal activities is twice that for legal ones,[66] this would still not amount to an impact on the order of magnitude that these scholars appear to have in mind. Moreover, the impact of illegal activities on African economies is tempered by the fact that little of the returns remain on the continent, given its macroeconomic uncertainties and the weakness of local financial institutions.

These activities are surely quite important in a small number of cases. A recent survey in *African Business* estimates that unrecorded African diamond exports totaled somewhere between U.S.$1 and $2 billion a year, with Zaire and Angola leading the way.[67] Even so, this trade is not significant for more than a handful of countries, and it should be noted that few, if any, other tradable goods hold as much potential for fraud as diamonds. In sum, official statistics probably do underestimate the significance of an array of international transactions involving Africa; but in all likelihood, these activities are not significant enough to alter the pattern of progressive delinkage of Africa from the world economy that is suggested by official statistics.

The Advantages of Reinsertion into the World Economy

Adding up these different indicators of integration into the world economy suggests that—for good or ill—it is not happening in Africa. What are the implications of this lack of interest on the part of private capital for Africa? What would be the advantages and disadvantages of reversing the current trends and reintegrating the region into the global economy? Before focusing on the disadvantages (and strategies for overcoming them), three distinct reasons can be adduced for believing that closer integration into the world economy as defined above would have a positive impact on the prospects for democracy on the continent.

Integration Promotes Growth

First, few observers contest that the prospects for democracy are highly improved by the ability of economies to generate growth. Distributional politics are greatly facilitated by an expanding national pie, as it is easier for governments to compensate the victims of economic shocks and redistribute income to the poorest segments. Governments can also increase spending on education and health, which a number of studies have suggested is the best single way to ensure that growth enhances social and economic equality.[68] In turn, improved equity helps sustain democracies. In sum, economic growth can put democratic polities on a virtuous cycle of growth and stability. Other factors will help sustain Africa's young democracies, but there can be little doubt that rapid growth is likely to be part of the successful recipe.

How can these regimes help bring about rapid growth? In the second half of the twentieth century, a strong correlation has existed between long-term sustained economic growth and integration into the world economy, in particular, through trade and investment flows.[69] The economic success stories of East Asia have been built on the aggressive search for export markets and partnerships with multinational technology and/or capital. In sum, the greater the proportion of the economy that is accounted for by the export sector and the greater the amount of FDI, the higher the long-term growth rate.[70] There is, moreover, little evidence that export-led growth strategies have resulted in increasing socioeconomic inequalities.[71]

There are many reasons to believe that East Asia does not represent a viable model for Africa.[72] In particular, African states lack the analytical, administrative, and managerial capacity that East Asian governments put to such effective use. African economies are characterized by considerably lower levels of human capital, as well as poor infrastructure and smaller internal markets. Governments in the region have not proven capable of successfully "picking" winning import-substitution industries in the past, unlike states in Asia, which used targeted export promotion with compelling results.

It is unlikely that in the short to medium run African economies could sustain growth levels on the order of those in East Asia. The World Bank currently forecasts real annual GDP growth for sub-Saharan Africa of 3.8 percent for 1996–2005. Though this level barely keeps up with population growth, it compares favorably with the actual record during the 1980s of 1.7 percent real annual growth and is based on fairly optimistic assumptions about the continued progress of economic reform and the achievement of sustained macroeconomic stability.[73] Higher growth may be possible in the longer term, once the necessary bases have been put in place, but it is probably illusory to expect higher growth in the near future for most of the countries in the region, even with macroeconomic stabilization. First, African economies need to rebuild their infrastructure, improve their international credibility, and demonstrate effective state administrations. Pessimists like Bienen and Herbst or Thomas Callaghy may be right that implementing the necessary reforms may be politically impossible for many African states.[74] Nonetheless, those states that do succeed will greatly promote their long-term prospects for growth, and thus for democratic stability.

Integration Weakens the Leverage of IFIs

Second, integration would change Africa's largely unproductive relations with the international donors. Such a claim requires some justification. The absence of private capital flows to Africa fundamentally alters the relationship between the region and the global economy compared with that prevailing in other regions of the world. Indeed, throughout much of the last two decades, Africa's relationship with the world economy has been almost entirely mediated by official development assistance (ODA) from the main bilateral and multilateral donors of the OECD countries. Strikingly, total private capital flows to the continent amounted to only a small and declining fraction of the nearly $20 billion in annual ODA provided by the donors.[75] Aid resources to Africa have grown steadily, more than doubling during the 1980s, even as private capital was withdrawing from the continent. By the early 1990s, when the growth of aid levels appears to have peaked, African countries were the most aided countries in history, with levels of resource flows averaging the equivalent of over one-tenth of GDP and reaching over 20 percent in 10 African countries.

In much of the academic commentary on globalization in Africa, donor resources have been viewed as abetting the integration of Africa's economies into the global economy. When Africanists complain about the impact of globalization on African economies, they are typically referring to the growing power of public donors on the continent and to the policy conditionality that donors are increasingly willing to attach to their aid. The implication is that the donors are the "handmaidens" of global capital, requiring that African economies open to Western business interests. Indeed, one of the avowed objectives of structural adjustment policies is to make African economies more attractive to foreign (as well as national) investors, although there has been little success in achieving this objective. Recent macroeconomic research even suggests that the high volume of aid to Africa during the 1980s actually slowed down the adjustment process by acting as a substitute for private capital.[76] This analysis suggests that governments have come to rely on aid to avoid facing the discipline of international markets.

Donor conditionality does undermine African democracy. A government's accountability to external donors will inevitably be incompatible with democratic accountability to a national legislature and its elected officials or to the citizenry. Moreover, as the economic crisis has persisted in Africa and the first generation of stabilization and structural adjustment programs (SAPs) has either been only partly implemented or implemented and soon reversed, the IFIs have sought to micromanage the second- and third-generation programs. They have set up teams of Western experts in central ministries to monitor the implementation of increasingly precise policy conditionalities and established a schedule of almost monthly deadlines for reporting and monitoring of progress. As Bjorn Beckman has put it:

> Foreign intervention is open, explicit and humiliating. The general mood of the "development community" is brazenly interventionist. There is "disappointment" and "loss of confidence" in African political leadership, contributing to a decline in respect for national autonomy. . . . They see themselves as trustees for the "common man," the "silent majority." Foreign paternalism reinforces the authoritarian logic of SAP[s].[77]

Notwithstanding the current donor rhetoric about "local ownership" and attempts to forge a less asymmetrical relationship between donor and recipient, there is little reason to believe that real changes are taking place. As a senior government official told *Africa Confidential* about his country's relation with the World Bank, "the only change is that the World Bank tells us we must say it is our policy."[78]

To be sure, the policy impact of conditionality is too often exaggerated, both by the IFIs and by governments. Careful studies of adjustment lending have suggested that most conditions continue not to be fully implemented and sustained over time.[79] Given their own excessive exposure in Africa, the IFIs have been forced into "defensive lending." As a result, the penalties accruing to governments that do not meet the prescribed conditions have not been onerous: there is, for example, little evidence that noncompliance leads to less aid or harsher conditionality. Governments thus lack the incentives to implement reform programs fully that pose substantial political, ideological, and bureaucratic problems for them. For the most part, they have accepted IFI money and have then sought to wheedle out of their implementation promises.

It remains true, however, that donor conditionality is corrosive of democratic practices and values. It empowers international technocrats who are not accountable to the local electorate, and it privileges donor-driven bureaucratic and financial processes such as the Paris Club, the Consultative Group, the Policy Framework Paper, the Letter of Agreement, or the Public Investment Program, while weakening the traditional instruments of national economic decisionmaking such as the national budget, economic planning, and the cabinet. Over time, the corrosive impact of conditionality combines with the cumulative effects of persistent fiscal crisis to undermine state capacity.[80] The decline in working conditions for civil servants, for example, leads to a progressive erosion of skills and planning capacity, while budgetary contractions hit many institutions particularly hard; institutions such as the national statistics office find it increasingly difficult to maintain their publications schedules or provide the government with appropriate economic data to inform decisionmaking.

The government increasingly resorts to a chaotic form of crisis management mediated by donor resources and outside experts. The national budget that is officially passed in the legislature may come to matter less than what has been promised to the donors, and government officials may lack any sense of ownership for agreements that have been more or less authored in Washington or Paris, with little input from the relevant government departments. For example, a recent report noted that the Tanzanian government presented different budget estimates in 1995 to the Consultative Group of creditors and to its own national legislature. In one, it projected a surplus; in the other, a deficit.[81]

There is often little effective communication between the ministerial team that prepares the national budget and the cadre of officials from the presidency that negotiates with donors. As a number of observers have argued, the growing confusion and emasculation of national economic institutions is an invitation for corruption and abuse by powerful interests within the political class. In many countries, an increasing proportion of state expenditures are placed "off-budget" and thus beyond democratic accountability, while revenue collection becomes increasingly haphazard. In Congo-Brazzaville, for example, no budget was even passed in 1993 until most of the fiscal year had expired, and B. Blancq estimates that as much as 30 percent of the budget has been lost or stolen in recent years.[82] Considerable evidence suggests that the government has sold forward several years of oil resources at steep discounts to gain extra revenue, but these operations have not been conducted openly, as they contravene official World Bank and IMF conditionality. Given such circumstances, the country's democratic transition in 1991 cannot be considered to have appreciably increased the popular accountability of the government, and the economy has continued its downward spiral.

In brief, the persistence of economic crisis and the progressive loss of sovereignty to outside public creditors represent a distinct threat to democratic governance in Africa. But this threat does not come from international capital; it comes from the persistence of gaping fiscal and balance-of-payment deficits for most of the last two decades, as well as unproductive economic policies, which compel governments to continue to seek the assistance of international aid. Governments that are able to maintain macroeconomic equilibrium are not so dependent on the goodwill of the IFIs to avert bankruptcy.

The reader may object that I am merely recommending that African governments submit to the IFI agenda. In fact, if they wish to attract and retain international capital, governments can exercise considerable latitude with regard to the details of sectoral policies, even if on matters of broad fiscal and monetary policy there is no viable alternative to the IFI agenda. In what might be called the "nonreform paradox," the IFIs derive their power over day-to-day economic management precisely from the failure of their conditionality. The lesson of the last two decades is that the power of the IFIs in Africa comes from the inability of African governments to meet their capital needs from either the domestic economy or from international private capital. Greater integration into trade and capital markets would directly strengthen the hand of governments in their negotiations with the IFIs, which simply lack leverage in countries whose governments are able to satisfy their capital needs. Surely it cannot be considered a coincidence that the continent's two most successful democracies, Botswana and Mauritius, have fueled their strong development strategies with international private investment and have not had to rely on IFI finances. Such states do not need to give a seat at the decisionmaking table to often imperious local aid representatives.

Integration Weakens Patronage Politics

There should be little doubt that the maintenance of neopatrimonial politics will also undermine the consolidation of democratic rule.[83] On the one hand, neopatrimonialism is profoundly undemocratic in spirit, and it is not compatible with widespread political participation and competition. It weakens civil society relative to the state, and the legislative and judiciary branches relative to the executive. On the other, the systematic resort to patronage, the selective application of laws, the dispensing of favors, and outright corruption engender social inequality and counter popular notions of fairness, serving to erode the public's faith in democratic politics. Over time, the delegitimization of the government facilitates more direct assaults on democratic regimes. Thus, military coups are invariably justified as being motivated by the aim of doing away with corrupt politicians and bringing back efficient government.

Integration into the world economy undermines the old style of neopatrimonial politics for several reasons. First, patronage and rent-seeking politics thrive in closed systems. It is true that evidence from other parts of the world suggests that economic liberalization will never fully eliminate opportunities for corruption; the experiences of countries as varied as Italy, Indonesia, and South Korea should disabuse us of the notion that economic growth cannot coexist with relatively high levels of corruption. But these states are not fully predatory, and they have exhibited the discipline to insulate certain key governmental functions and maintain macroeconomic stability and predictability for long periods of time. The exigencies of international competition will force greater discipline on African governments: central banks will have to pursue cautious monetary policies that maintain low inflation; administrative, police, and military establishments will have to professionalize their staff and respect basic property and political rights; and government spending will need to become more productive than in the past, with more resources devoted to infrastructure and capital investment, and fewer devoted to subsidies or lost to waste and fraud.

Second, attracting and retaining foreign investment requires more transparent, impersonal, and predictable administration of policy and laws.[84] Tariff, tax, and price structures need to be simplified and the state's regulatory framework made less capricious. That certainly does not imply the withering away of the state to a laissez-faire situation, as states will have to provide a host of critical public goods without which investors will not respond. But it does imply a more disciplined and predictable state. In sum, the reforms needed to bring about integration into the world economy weaken the hold of neopatrimonial politics on these regimes.

Third, the reduction of monopoly rents that is achieved by opening up undermines the resource base of traditional politicians and creates incentives for new types of behavior. Rents never fully disappear, but they do shrink, and the old coalitions cemented on patronage and redistribution are more likely to give way to production-oriented coalitions. Some observers have pointed to alleged increases in corruption during the 1980s to argue that economic liberalization actually may increase the amount of rent-seeking behavior that is practiced,[85] but this is surely wrong. The increasing rent seeking in the 1980s resulted from the "partial-reform" syndrome, that is, the fact that the limited reform that did take place was often incomplete, unsustainable, phony, and/or temporary. Rent seeking continued because significant rents continued to be available or were expected to return soon.[86]

Meeting the Challenges of Globalization

Far from accelerating integration, the recent past has witnessed a delinkage of African economies from global production processes. Opening up to international markets will impose a kind of discipline on African democracies that will be constraining and sometimes onerous. Some criticism of structural adjustment programs has implied that more democratic implementation of "homegrown" programs that were the fruit of extensive participatory consultation would prove easier to sustain and thus would be more likely to succeed.[87] I agree, but it must be recognized that even very popular policies may not be sustainable.

Africa's integration into the world economy will thus probably impose limits on the amount of income redistribution that can be attempted by the state in the short run. There is some evidence from other regions that international investors take a broad view of competitiveness and that they value sociopolitical stability, labor skill acquisition and flexibility, and the quality of infrastructure as much as the narrowly defined real cost of labor.[88] Nonetheless, sustaining private investment in Africa will require much greater attention to investments in areas such as education and infrastructure than African governments have demonstrated in the past in order to promote the needed productivity gains.

Integration into the world economy implies, finally, the need to adjust quickly to international shocks even when this is politically difficult and imposes temporary welfare losses. Nonetheless, one should not exaggerate the extent to which this evolution is likely to take away "choices" and force all developing countries into one "neoliberal" mold. In the OECD countries that have proceeded much further along this path than Africa will for the foreseeable future, integration into the world economy has resulted in surprisingly little policy convergence. True, the social democratic model of northern European countries like Sweden and Germany has come under pressure in recent years and imposed a degree of fiscal compression, but there is no reason to believe that the preference of their citizens for a relatively egalitarian income structure and state provision of extensive social and cultural services is not just as viable in the long run as the more laissez-faire approach of the United States.[89] Nor is there any reason to believe that African democracies will not retain some latitude in their policy choices over the size of the state, for example, or the distribution of income.

Are African democracies capable of undertaking such a relinkage? It is important to distinguish among countries and the distinct circumstances in which they find themselves. First, it is easier to be optimistic about countries that have sizable stocks of natural resources, which they can put to good use in developing the needed infrastructure and improving the quality of their labor force. Significant oil and mineral resources provide these countries with an extra margin of security that appeals to investors. Other countries may lack mineral wealth but have the advantage of a significant agricultural export potential. This is the case of Côte d'Ivoire, for example, and Cameroon, which could take advantage of a rich and potentially highly diversified agricultural sector to relink with world markets.

Second, countries in southern Africa have the advantage of a relatively large market integrated by decent road, rail, and communications links and proximity to South Africa. Botswana, for example, has been able to attract FDI in manufacturing by companies explicitly interested in exporting to South Africa. In addition, governments in southern Africa benefit from an "emulation factor." The evident, long-term benefits of virtuous behavior by governments in Botswana and South Africa help their counterparts in countries like Zambia to maintain policy discipline.

Third, it is easier to be optimistic about the handful of countries that have already undertaken significant macroeconomic policy reform. Countries like Ghana and Uganda may well find it difficult to sustain the progress achieved, but the hardest tasks are behind them, and they are poised to reap significant benefits. Uganda, for example, witnessed its FDI jump to $112 million in 1995–1996, following several years of fiscal and monetary discipline.[90] Such countries have a huge advantage over others that have little to show for two decades of "official" commitment to reform.

For many African countries, on the other hand, there is much reason to be pessimistic. They lack resources, have neighbors racked by civil conflict, and have achieved little progress on reform in the past. While competing in international markets may in time promote growth and political stability, there is no clear road map that shows how to get from the current state to a reasonable ability to compete. Two decades of "partial reform" have achieved very little; for example, fiscal deficits often remain unsustainably high, but populations have come to conflate structural adjustment with the underlying economic crisis itself, and a backlash against pro-market policies has set in that complicates future reform efforts. The absence of clear success stories, moreover, provides ammunition for the claims that reform does not work and provides reformers no model to emulate.

Past strategies based on delay and prevarication, combined with a reliance on public aid to manage economic crisis, may not be sustainable much longer as aid levels continue to decline. The challenge for Africa's democracies will be to relink with the world economy in the most productive manner possible. Two requisites for relinkage to the world economy do appear critical. A first requirement will almost certainly be effective state structures. States represent the main mediating set of institutions between the local and global economies. They condition access to the local economy by international capital, and they shape the circumstances in which the local economy confronts global market forces. States provide the key public goods without which no economy can prosper: stable macroeconomic conditions, an effective legal system, a reasonable infrastructure, and an education system that produces a high-quality labor force. Reno's work on Sierra Leone demonstrates that African economies can engage the world economy even in the context of advanced state decay and collapse.[91] But he suggests that in the absence of states that play this role, African economies will increasingly interact only with the seamier sectors of the global economy: international criminal activities and fly-by-night foreign operators and speculators. Sustained, high-quality growth requires effective central state institutions.

A second requirement for relinking productively with global market forces is a much more proactive role by African governments in fostering regional cooperation and economic integration. Enhanced regionalism has too long been a pious wish of public policy discussions in Africa for one to be sanguine about its prospects. The long history of failed attempts and false hopes is particularly daunting. It remains true that African economies are small and vulnerable, with more landlocked countries than on any other continent, and these would benefit from greater regional cooperation. For one thing, the balkanization of African markets has long been a primary obstacle to foreign investment. Improving communications among neighboring countries, lowering tariffs and other trade barriers, and encouraging regulatory policy convergence would make African markets far more attractive. For another, regional agreements bind governments to specific policies, signaling to economic agents that policy reversal is less likely, and thus providing an example of what Paul Collier has called "agencies of restraint."[92]

*   *   *

The central contention of this essay has been that international market forces represent less of a threat to democracy than does the present situation of progressive delinkage from the world economy, which has been driven by two decades of "nonreform," economic crisis, and state decay. Engaging the world economy would be healthier than economic stagnation riddled with neopatrimonial politics, but more or less sustained by international aid. Does globalization take away choices from Africa's young democracies? There can be little doubt that international economic integration lessens the autonomy of all African states. But the progressive delinkage from the world economy that we are witnessing in too many of the region's countries is far more dangerous for the future of African democracy.

Notes

1. Bratton and van de Walle, *Democratic Experiments*.
2. Przeworski and Limongi, "Modernization," p. 169.
3. Callaghy, "State and Development"; Sandbrook, *Politics of Africa's Economic Stagnation*.
4. Lewis, "Economic Reform"; van de Walle, "Political Liberalization."
5. An early version of this chapter was presented at the Thirty-ninth Annual African Studies Association Meeting, in San Francisco, November 23–26, 1996. This revised version has been much improved by comments from Michael Bratton, Richard Joseph, Todd Moss, Alice Sindzingre, and David Stasavage.
6. Sachs and Warner, "Economic Reform," pp. 61–63.
7. See, for example, the last two annual editions of the World Bank's *Global Economic Prospects* (1995, 1996), which directly link economic prosperity with integration into the world economy. For Africa, this was the primary policy implication of an authoritative 1994 report, World Bank, *Adjustment in Africa*.
8. This is the official position of the British and U.S. governments. See, for example, official pronouncements in, respectively, Chalker, *Good Governance,* and USAID, *Democracy Initiative*. This position is also well argued in *The Economist,* "Democracy and Growth."
9. Bienen and Herbst, "Relationship Between Political and Economic Reform"; see also Bienen, "Politics of Trade Liberalization."
10. Sandbrook, *Politics of Africa's Economic Recovery*.
11. Ake, "Globalization."
12. Ake, *Democracy and Development.*
13. Cheru, "New Social Movements," p. 145.
14. Mkandawire, Chapter 7 in this volume, "Crisis Management."
15. Mkandawire, "Economic Policy-Making," p. 35.
16. Rodney, *How Europe Underdeveloped Africa;* Wallerstein, *Capitalist World Economy;* and Amin, *Neo-Colonialism.*
17. Wilson, "Globalization"; Barber, *Jihad vs. McWorld.*
18. McGrew and Lewis, eds., *Global Politics;* Oman, *Globalization and Regionalization;* Schmidt, "New World Order"; and Stallings, ed., *Global Change.*
19. World Bank, *World Development Report, 1992.*
20. Cited in the *Financial Times,* "Foreign Direct Investment." All financial statistics in this essay should be treated cautiously, as even a casual perusal of the different sources reveals highly divergent estimates of overall levels. What is beyond dispute are the general trends suggested by the numbers.
21. IMF, *International Capital Markets,* p. 5.
22. Ibid., p. 34.
23. For a useful review of these efforts as they affect developing countries, see Haggard, *Developing Nations.*
24. See Gereffi, "Global Production Systems." The recent literature has largely updated claims made several decades ago by scholars like Magdoff, *Age of Imperialism,* and Vernon, *Sovereignty at Bay*—another indication that the globalization literature is tapping into long-standing theoretical and substantive claims regarding the world economy.

25. Wade, "Globalization and Its Limits," p. 64.
26. Haggard and Maxfield, "Political Economy"; Frieden, "Invested Interests"; and Marshall, "Understanding Late–Twentieth Century Capitalism."
27. This episode is well described in Hall, *Governing the Economy.*
28. Kapstein, "Workers"; A. Wood, "How Trade Hurt."
29. Maddison, *World Economy.*
30. *The Economist,* "The World Economy."
31. Wade, "Globalization and Its Limits," pp. 73–75.
32. UNCTAD, *Trade and Development.*
33. Wade, "Globalization and Its Limits," p. 71.
34. See World Bank, *Global Development Finance;* these five countries were China, Mexico, Indonesia, Malaysia, and Brazil.
35. Cooper, "Africa and the World Economy"; also Clapham, *Africa and the International System.*
36. World Bank, *Global Economic Prospects* (1996), pp. 20–29.
37. Sachs and Warner, "Economic Reform," p. 24 and passim. Even then, they seem excessively sanguine about several other countries in the region, judging, for example, that implementation of trade reforms in 1993–1994 put Cameroon, Zambia, and Kenya in the "open" camp.
38. Austen, *African Economic History;* Hopkins, *Economic History.*
39. Fieldhouse, *Economy and Empire,* p. 129.
40. Munro, *Africa and the International Economy,* p. 45.
41. Ibid., p. 62.
42. Ibid., p. 15.
43. World Bank, *World Development Report, 1995.*
44. See Yeats et al., "External Barriers." The authors point out that tariffs on sub-Saharan African exports to all OECD countries average 0.63 percent, considerably below the rates faced by other developing countries that do not benefit from as many preferences and exemptions. See also Kappel, "Africa's Marginalisation."
45. Sorsa, "Sub-Saharan African Commitments"; Kappel, "Africa's Marginalisation"; and Davenport et al., "Impact of the GATT."
46. Nash, "Trade Policy Reform."
47. World Bank, *World Development Report, 1995.*
48. In 1993, 18 percent of all of sub-Saharan Africa's exports were accounted for by Nigerian oil exports.
49. See World Bank, *World Development Report, 1995,* table 15, p. 190. Exports of goods and nonfactor services are estimated as a distribution of GDP. For reasons that I do not understand, estimating the same proportion directly from the same publication's data for exports (table 13) and for GDP (table 3) yields somewhat different estimates.
50. Yeats, "Accuracy of Economic Observations"; Ellis and MacGaffey, "Research on Sub-Saharan Africa."
51. On the impact of these reforms on trade, see Hibou, *L'Afrique est-elle protectionniste?* Not the least quality of this work is the compelling evidence offered of how cautiously one must treat trade data, given the growing degree of fraud and misreporting.
52. Frankel, *Capital Investment.*
53. *Financial Times,* "Foreign Direct Investment."
54. IMF, *International Capital Markets,* p. 86.
55. Bearman, "Special Focus," provides a good review of the sector and of the renewal of Western investments.
56. The information in this paragraph is derived from Moss and Kenny, "Africa's Emerging Stock Markets," unless otherwise noted.

57. Moss and Kenny, "Africa's Emerging Stock Markets."

58. Ibid.

59. For evidence of increasing diversity among sub-Saharan Africa's 48 countries, see the World Bank, *Continent in Transition,* pp. 4–8.

60. *Wall Street Journal,* "On the Fringe."

61. Bayart et al., *La Criminalisation;* Ellis and MacGaffey, "Research on Sub-Saharan Africa"; Reno, *Corruption and State Politics;* and Hibou, *L'Afrique est-elle protectionniste?*

62. Bayart et al., *La Criminalisation.*

63. Hibou, *L'Afrique est-elle protectionniste?*

64. Reno, *Corruption.*

65. Quirk, "Macroeconomic Implications."

66. Even if illegal activities are more likely to take place in countries with weak and corrupt states, the structural constraints on economic growth in Africa—for example, the lack of purchasing power and poor infrastructure—in all likelihood inhibit illegal activities as much as legal ones.

67. Misser, "Dirty Dealings."

68. See, for example, Bruno et al., *Equity and Growth.*

69. Maddison, *World Economy;* L. Reynolds, *Economic Growth;* and Sachs and Warner, "Economic Reform."

70. This finding is again confirmed for the 1980s by the World Bank, *Global Economics Prospects* (1996), pp. 25–27.

71. Bruno et al., *Equity and Growth;* Ravallion and Chen, "What Can Survey Data Tell Us."

72. These issues are analyzed in Gyimah-Boadi and van de Walle, "Politics of Economic Renewal," and in Stein, ed., *Asian Industrialization.*

73. World Bank, *Global Economic Prospects* (1996), pp. 6 and 18–19.

74. Bienen and Herbst, "Relationship Between Political and Economic Reform"; Callaghy, "Africa."

75. van de Walle and Johnston, *Improving Aid.*

76. See ibid. for analysis and citations.

77. Beckman, "Empowerment or Repression?" p. 99.

78. *Africa Confidential,* "Nuts to the Bank."

79. Mosley et al., *Aid and Power;* Gwin, ed., *Perspectives on Aid.*

80. Project 2015, *Aid Dependency.*

81. Royal Danish Ministry of Foreign Affairs, *Report,* p. 31.

82. Blancq, "Congo," pp. 191–198; see also Clark, "Oil and Democratization."

83. This point is developed at greater length in Bratton and van de Walle, *Democratic Experiments,* chap. 7.

84. Collier, "Living Down the Past," develops this argument with regard to Nigeria.

85. Hibou, *L'Afrique est-elle protectionniste?*

86. It is also important not to conflate the size of the rents that persist during the reform phase with the degree of rent seeking that is generated. The latter may increase even as the former declines; in fact, it would be logical for competition over declining rents to intensify.

87. Gibbon et al., eds., *Authoritarianism.*

88. See, for example, Rodrik, "Labor Standards."

89. To cite just one example: according to the World Bank (*World Development Report, 1995,* p. 181), in 1993, Sweden ran the largest fiscal deficit of any country in the OECD, at 12.2 percent of GNP. Its total government expenditures that year amounted to 53.9 percent of GDP, compared with 23.8 percent for

the United States. So even if it absorbed its deficit entirely through reductions in expenditures, its relative level of government expenditures would still be almost twice that of the United States.

90. Bhattacharya et al., "How Can Sub-Saharan Africa"; Sharer et al., *Uganda*.

91. Reno, *Corruption*.

92. Collier, "Living Down the Past."

7

Crisis Management and the Making of "Choiceless Democracies"

Thandika Mkandawire

The simultaneous occurrence of globalization and political liberalization in recent history has attracted considerable attention and raised a number of questions among policymakers and researchers. Fundamental among these concerns is whether the exigencies of globalization can be reconciled with the processes of political liberalization and democratization. How can fragile democratic regimes improve their prospects for consolidation at a moment when the distributive impact of concurrent programs of economic liberalization and adjustment may be highly contested? More relevant to the African case, how can the institutional arrangements within which financial support for economic reform by Bretton Woods institutions (BWIs) and bilateral donors are channeled be compatible with democratic governance? This chapter primarily addresses the last question, although it does touch upon the other concerns as well, given the close relationship of the issues.

The pertinence of these questions arises because globalization contains within it two contradictory effects on democratization. On the one hand, the "opening up" of economies and societies, the political conditionalities transmitted through global institutions, and the solidarity from movements encapsulated in the notion of "global civil society" are generally supportive of democratization efforts in many countries. On the other hand, the demands of globalization, especially the erosion of national sovereignty and the uniformalization of what are considered "fundamentals" in economic policy, limit the range of policy options for democratic regimes. Those who hold the first part as the dominant effect of globalization consider democracy and economic liberalization as simply two sides of the same coin—the edification of a liberal order, a natural convergence of processes that marks the triumph of liberal capitalist order and "the end of history,"[1] an end state toward which teleology has dutifully moved us all along. This "good things go together" approach is often derived from first principles, where liberal democracy and free markets always go hand in hand, since both processes entail the dispersion of power and the emergence of a bourgeoisie, both of which are said to be good for democracy.

According to David Held, "liberal democracy was premised on the sovereignty of nation-states and assumed that the state has control over its own fate, subject only to compromises it must make and limits imposed upon it by actors, agencies and forces operating within its territorial boundaries." From this standpoint, therefore, globalization, by eroding national sovereignty, undermines a central tenet of liberal democracy.[2]

For understandable reasons, much of the writing on globalization confines itself to the effects of the "invisible hand" of the market on democratization. However, for developing countries, we have to add the highly visible and not-so-ambidextrous feet of BWIs and bilateral donors, which, especially for African countries, comprise the most immediate force of globalization, since private capital inflows are still insignificant. Although the BWIs have become minor players in the global movements of financial capital and other resources, they are a major force in Africa. In the current wave of massive movements of capital to the "emerging markets," Africa remains marginal. In 1995, of the total U.S.$112 billion lent to the developing countries, only $5 billion went to Africa. More significantly, while private capital dwarfed the contributions of BWIs in most of the developing countries, the reverse was the case in Africa.

This does not, of course, mean that African countries are spared the "silent compulsions of market forces" identified by Karl Marx. On the contrary, because of the relative unattractiveness of African countries to private capital, these silent compulsions may be even stronger as governments preemptively and supinely comply with a whole range of requirements supposedly demanded by "the market," as they introduce "beggar my neighbor" policies in the chase for capital, and as they, in total bewilderment as to what the market wants, simply adopt a waiting stance by ceding decision-making to others. This constitutes what Sylvia Maxfield calls "signaling creditworthiness."[3] Much of this waiting and signaling may be in vain. It has been the contention of the BWIs and the belief of African governments that the stamp of approval of the BWIs would attract private investment. The evidence in Africa has thus far been that the catalytic effect of the stamp of approval of BWIs is extremely weak.[4] Growing theoretical and empirical material suggests that the segmentation in global markets is such that certain regions may not benefit from capital movements, regardless of the improvements in the "fundamentals." In this case, sub-Saharan Africa is invariably cited.[5] Africans will do better by doing such things as stimulating domestic savings and investment than by simply complying and waiting.

This poor catalytic effect of BWI support notwithstanding, the BWIs continue to play a central role in Africa partly because of their own funds and other official donor funds that tend to follow along. The policies that are touted as preparing Africa for a much more rewarding integration into the world system come in the form of stabilization and structural adjustment programs (SAPs). The twinning of these otherwise different processes has led to their being subsumed under the acronym "SAP" in popular parlance; thus I use that umbrella acronym throughout this chapter.

One major question raised in most of these debates about Africa is whether SAPs can be sustained under democratic transitions, whether democratic transitions can survive SAPs, or whether the trade-off is such that one of these must give.

In the dominant non-African literature on the crisis in Africa, it is argued that the current dilemma can be traced to the "unholy alliance" of authoritarian rule and dirigiste economic policies that have "distorted" markets through protectionist trade practices, state monopolies, artificial price fixation (subsidies, price controls), and financial repression (credit rationing, interest rate ceilings). The state's control of the economy has underpinned its political authority and its capacity to use patronage to keep its supporters in line or to buy off potential challengers. It follows from this argument that liberalization of the market is likely to weaken the state's hold on the polity, to undercut its control of "rent-yielding" activities, and to create independent centers of wealth generation within a liberalized market; all this will strengthen civil society and thus democratization processes, especially through facilitating the emergence of a bourgeoisie.[6] For this school, the simultaneous appearance of economic liberalization and liberal democracy is therefore essentially unproblematic. This analysis also posits that the African ruling elites will resist both democratization and liberalization.

In much of African writing, the relationship between structural adjustment programs and democratization is seen as inherently contradictory or, at least, problematic. The African analysis[7] is usually based on the assumption that both democratization and economic policy must address a much larger range of economic issues than merely the efficient allocation of resources. The agenda of most movements in favor of democratization has been broad and inclusive: better economic management, greater equity, respect of human rights, and national sovereignty. SAPs, by sidestepping a whole range of important items on the national agenda, would undermine democracy, which has, perforce, to address these issues. Development, equity, and the much-maligned "nation building" still remain on the agenda, and if there were doubts as to their importance, recent events in Rwanda and Somalia should remove them. If this is the case, then politics (democratic or undemocratic) must allow for the many intricate political compromises that may not always meet the exigencies of economic rationality.[8]

SAPs as currently constructed threaten nation building and democratization by exacerbating social conflict, weakening the capacity of the state to respond in a political way to the many demands on it, and riding roughshod on public opinion without due respect for democratic process. Finally, SAPs have hitherto been essentially an imposition by the international financial institutions (IFIs) on new democracies or by unelected, authoritarian regimes. There is therefore a conflict between economic liberalization and democratization, because democratization is seen by the majority of dissident groups as an instrument for impeding foreign and undemocratically imposed reform programs and for protecting some of the postcolonial gains in public welfare and living standards threatened by reforms.[9]

Supporting these pessimistic views about the relationship between economic reform and democratization are some historical experiences recounted in the literature, which note that the most comprehensive structural adjustment initiatives have generally come under the auspices of authoritarian regimes.[10] However, more recent empirical work casts doubt on a positive correlation between authoritarian rule and adjustment.[11] If anything, it is claimed, the evidence suggests that democracies are more successful in program implementation. And the World Bank, which has been historically associated with a preference for authoritarian regimes such as those of Hastings Banda, Jerry Rawlings, Gnassingbé Eyadema, and Ibrahim Babangida, has now shifted its position, albeit very cautiously, as the following quotation suggests:

> First, the process of political transition may initially slow down the process of economic reform, as the new system settles down, and there is the danger that competing interests may lead to a stalemate in some areas. However, second, the greater political openness will lead to the opening of national dialogue and debate over reforms. This serves both to educate the public and contribute to a national sense of ownership of the reform process. Third, coalitions empowered by political liberalization may contribute lively to the emergence of good governance—that is the practice by political leadership of accountability, transparency, openness, predictability, and the rule of law.[12]

One should, however, note that there is still nervousness among international financial institutions about democratic politics. There remains the lingering belief in the authoritarian advantage in policy formulation as ways and means are sought to circumvent the democratic process or render it ineffective in policymaking. It is to this that I now turn.

Rendering Democracies "Choiceless"

While considerable attention has been paid to the incapacity of SAPs to address the substantive demands of democratic forces, much less attention has been paid to how styles of policymaking and involvement by external donors constrain the formal institutions of democratic rule that are a constituent part of democratization. Globalization and, in the African case, SAPs can influence the competence and reach of democratically elected governments on at least three levels: (1) the level of objectives; (2) the level of instruments; and (3) the level of structural constraints.[13]

Constraining Objectives

The fiscal and foreign exchange crises that led African countries to the doorsteps of BWIs have severely undercut the range of viable objectives African states can pursue. However, the choice set has been further constricted by the particular solutions that the BWIs have imposed in the form of conditionalities.

A modern state must perform a number of tasks with respect to economic policy: (1) it must carry out certain activities that have an obvious "public good" character, such as national defense; (2) it must ensure broad macroeconomic stability; (3) it must introduce measures that increase equity or reduce inequity to levels that are considered politically manageable and socially acceptable; and (4) it must ensure growth either through its own direct involvement in production or, more often, through provision of an environment that encourages private investment. This set of policies addresses two concerns of modern states: the continued growth of economies and material well-being of citizens, and the states' legitimacy. In the case of African countries, legitimacy refers not only to the government in office, but to the legitimacy of the state itself.

For new and fragile democracies, the good performance of these tasks is an important aspect of the consolidation of democracy. However, in current practice, the formulation and implementation of policies is carried out completely oblivious to the demands of good governance and long-term economic development. Indeed, policies are often introduced in isolation from the considerations of political stability or the legitimacy of the authority of elected bodies.

Economic Growth and Development.   SAPs are premised on certain policies that are described as fundamentals that must be respected if economic growth is to be resumed in African countries. As it turns out, these fundamentals have largely been confined to addressing issues of stabilization and the related financial conditions, policy instruments, and objectives. One effect of this approach is that current strategies are focused on macroeconomic stabilization at any cost. Consequently, much less emphasis has been attached to other fundamentals, such as national capacities to initiate and sustain change, dynamic issues of resource mobilization and augmentation, structural reforms, and the social sustainability of policies. The conventional fundamentals of SAPs may perhaps be appropriate for stabilization, but they do not in themselves guarantee the resumption of growth, and they have the distinct danger of producing an Africa that may be stable and efficient, but still poor.

Dealing with "Crises of Legitimacy." The quest for legitimacy was an important feature of postindependence politics, and authoritarian rule did not diminish the centrality of this quest, as power was justified on the ability and willingness of the political authorities to promote public welfare. It is partly this tendency that explains the "distributions" thrust of African state policies and the salience of patronage and patron-client relationships so bemoaned by IFIs. And it is partly these policies that have kneaded together "the nationalist coalition" that underpinned the state's stability in many African countries. SAPs have generally tended to underplay or pour scorn on these objectives (as redistributive, market-distorting, rent-seeking, etc.).

Periods of transition tend to render more transparent challenges to the legitimacy of the state, as hitherto unarticulated or muted claims are openly voiced. Democratization has opened space for self-organization of economic interests and has led to greater pressures on policymakers to meet the demands of the various contending groups. In some of the new democracies, there have been unprecedented waves of strikes.[14] In those states, it was feared that such upheavals would push the state toward the much-dreaded "macropopulism."[15]

So far, for a number of reasons, popular pressures have not led African democracies to engage in macropopulism. None of the newly elected governments has embarked on that policy path. Instead, many countries have adopted orthodox adjustment programs, partly to correct the excessive expenditure and wanton waste by an outgoing authoritarian regime, which may have resorted to populist programs to shore up its sagging fortunes.[16] These adjustment programs are extremely unpopular, and they pose the distinct danger of delegitimizing democratic rule if tangible results are not perceived.

Finally, it should be noted how the choices of the new democracies are constrained by the way that SAPs are packaged and sealed. Both the ideological premises of SAPs and the "strategies" they propose severely limit the domain of competence of democratic governance by foreclosing debates on a wide range of issues of political economy, such as income distribution (intratemporal and intertemporal), taxation, and protection or nonprotection of certain economic activities. Any program of adjustment has trade-offs regarding political choices and decisions. In a democracy, the outcomes of such debates cannot be fixed a priori. They are themselves part of democratic contestation. The rigid prerequisites, the inflexible, built-in positions, and the proliferation of cross-conditionalities of SAPs all force decisionmakers into a take-it-or-leave-it corner, ruling out dialogue or creative political compromises within society at large.

In the current embrace of political liberalization, many believe that free debate will ineluctably lead to a political consensus in favor of orthodox SAPs. The overwhelming ideological and intellectual dominance of neoliberalism and neoclassical interpretations of the nature and performance of African economies have persuaded leading actors in the democratization process that there is no alternative to orthodoxy. Such a view undermines the arduous task of building a democratic political culture by constraining policymakers within a dogmatic straitjacket and encouraging politics of no compromise. As Edward Amadeo and Tariq Banuri note, the failure of the state does not derive from its refusal to adhere to a theoretical dogma. Rather, "it derives, in the short run, from its abandonment of the goal of governance in favor of theoretical certitude; and in the long run, from its inability or unwillingness to create or modify institutions to facilitate the management of conflicts which are forever changing in form and intensity."[17]

Constraints on Instruments:
SAPs and Formal Structures of Democratic Governance

A second set of constraints is often imposed on policy instruments. This can lead to a blunting or even a loss of instruments necessary for democratically elected governments to manage their economies and other national issues.

The Authoritarian Legacy.   Democratic states that are built on the ruins of authoritarian rule often retain some of the previous state's institutions, which linger on due to social inertia and structural rigidities. Authoritarianism established a certain style of policymaking that has left a legacy that complicates democratic policymaking in Africa. In the authoritarian regimes, all power was centralized in the presidency. Ministers usually performed only perfunctory roles, the real business of government being conducted by the president's office and the bureaucrats. Even more significantly, many bureaucrats were not accustomed to preparing documents that may be critically examined at cabinet meetings and be subject to parliamentary or public scrutiny.[18] The cult of secrecy still dominates the conduct of public affairs. This is true in relationships with external actors as well. Aid to Africa has historically existed within essentially authoritarian structures, and a whole tradition of interaction between foreign donors and African governments has been premised on this institutional practice. Aid relationships remained unencumbered by the complexities of national debate or consensus building in the recipient country—in sharp contrast to the situation in donor countries, where aid bills were extensively debated in national parliaments. Traditionally in African authoritarian states, a minister first negotiates and enters into agreement, then announces the result ceremoniously to the nation as an accomplished fact, without debate or scrutiny.

Thus, postauthoritarian governments are confronted with insulated international technocracies ensconced in key economic ministries and wielding enormous influence on policy. This hijacking of key policymaking units has been further facilitated by the cartelization of the donor community, with World Bank officials becoming modern-day "governors." Pronouncements of individual World Bank representatives have acquired Delphic proportions.[19] Such practices undermine the democratic control of state policy. Democratic governance would demand that international treaties entered into by the government are vetted in some form or other by the parliament. And indeed this is beginning to take place,[20] to the chagrin of the donor community, which considers the scrutiny of its contributions an affront, a time-consuming task, and, at times, a downright nuisance.

Technocratic Governance and Democratization.   In a 1989 report, the World Bank extended its analysis of the economic crisis to include political factors. It concluded that "underlying the litany of Africa's development problems is a crisis of governance," defined as the exercise of political power to manage a nation's affairs.[21] It is important to stress that the World Bank view of governance was essentially technocratic in this context, confined to the goals of (1) improving public-sector management; (2) increasing economic and financial accountability; (3) enhancing predictability and the rule of law; and (4) heightening the transparency of public affairs. Such a concept of "governance" made no claims for its association with democracy. It was much later that this view was uneasily extended to include democracy. The Bank's unease with associating governance and democratization is understandable, given the fact that much of its analysis of the politics of policymaking and its historically revealed preferences were for insulated technocracies that could ride roughshod over the clamor of interest groups.[22]

For all the talk about "popular participation," "transparency," and "accountability," it is part of conventional economic wisdom that the general public, including elected political leaders, cannot understand the counterintuitive nature of good economic advice.[23] Consequently, economists tend to believe that seeking consensus and compromise (the essence of democratic politics) is at best a waste of time. On the basis of this lack of faith in the common sense of ordinary people and the efficacy of political institutions, they have urged the insulation of technocrats. Institutions such as the World Bank have found such advice appealing since it is largely an endorsement of what they already do.

At the domestic level, new governments now seem to be leaning on technocrats much more heavily than did their predecessors. The attractiveness of technocrats can be attributed to a number of factors. First, their predecessors, given their highly personalized rule and patrimonial-clientelist politics, had an aversion to technocrats and tended to alienate or marginalize them. This tended to undermine public service by sidestepping bureaucratic demands for meritocratic criteria in promotions and job assignments. The result has been bloated and highly inefficient bureaucracies. The natural response of the new leaders has been to reverse that trend. Second, technocrats who are located in ministries such as finance, which interact most intensively with IFIs, are themselves not averse to "leaking" information that indicates their preferred individuals in key ministries. Third, there is a perception that the devastation created by the economic crises has legitimized calls for "economic doctors." Finally, social movements have had little capacity or interest in building up policy capabilities within their own structures.[24] Few movements, including those in the opposition, have been able to articulate technically sound policy alternatives.

Thus, prior to the wave of democratization, a number of strategies were proposed to overcome the supposedly irrational political choices and the resistance of organized urban interests to rational economic policies and/or the patron-client nexus underpinning state dirigisme. Solutions have included outright authoritarian methods à la Ugarte Pinochet,[25] or stratagems that, by stealth or suddenness, would catch these groups unawares and generate policies that, by the time opposition is able to mobilize, will have become irreversible.[26] Where democratic regimes already exist, the challenge for those who pursue this kind of analysis has been how to circumvent the democratic process by strengthening the "autonomy" of the bureaucracy or by creating what has been referred to as "authoritarian enclaves" within the economy. The Central Bank has been a main candidate for such insulation, as have ministries of finance or teams of technocrats in key ministries. In some cases, nationals on the payroll of international organizations are attached to these ministries—all to ensure their insulation.

This quest for insulated technocracies poses the danger of encouraging technocraticism or "the exclusionary exercise of political influence on the basis of technical knowledge." It is also likely to produce a Janus-faced polity in which politics are democratic but government is not.[27] The role that technocrats can play and their impact on political choices are not unambiguous, there being significant variations in the performance of technocratic roles. Some may facilitate democratic rule by providing the new regimes with a wider range of choice and by serving as the executive and technical arm of elected representatives. Technocrats may be able to identify or elaborate a number of options, each with different political implication. There is, however, the distinct danger that the technocrats' professional instincts may persuade them to seek to circumvent politics and generate solutions that are politically explosive. Technocrats may narrow the choices of politicians either by being part of a transnational technocratic alliance or by identifying themselves with particular international models of crisis management such as the orthodox structural adjustment programs. This is most likely to happen where such technocrats are shielded by international financial institutions and therefore feel more accountable to the institution than to national constituencies. This exclusiveness is enhanced by the transnationalization of key parts of the bureaucracy, which means that, although these groups are autonomous of domestic social forces, they lack autonomy vis-à-vis international financial institutions.[28]

In most cases, the handful of local experts may be so preoccupied with donor demands and schedules, as well as with the complexities of cross-conditionality, that they have little time to engage in dialogues with local social actors and thus build consensus on policy matters. The technocrats also arrogantly and falsely claim that no options exist other than the one they propound, thus severely curtailing national debates on vital issues.

There is little discussion in Africa on the implications of technocratic policymaking during the consolidation of democracy.[29] As I have argued elsewhere, there is a serious contradiction between the ardent quest by IFIs for the insulation of the technocracy and the calls for greater accountability and transparency in economic affairs.[30] The result of such an insulation will be the kind of "hybrid regimes" already emerging in Latin America, in which "an outward democratic form is energized by an inner authoritarian capacity, especially in the realm of economic policy,"[31] or truncated democracies whose area of competence is severely restricted. I do not contest the need to develop and strengthen the technical capacity of the African state. Some technocrats may be politically astute and sensitive and may understand the politics of their countries. Rather, I am suggesting that policy that takes place behind closed doors, insulated from public debate and scrutiny, becomes, in the process, an exercise in technical efficiency from which social groups, unions, parties, parliaments, and even ministers may be excluded.

Instrumentalization of Democracy. While policy instruments wielded by elected governments are blunted or captured by unelected international institutions, there also is the possibility that democracy would also be viewed as one of the instruments of these institutions. In some of the literature on SAPs and democratization, it is assumed that the former as propounded by international financial institutions is either the right thing or simply inevitable; therefore, the latter must either facilitate or accommodate SAPs. In the words of Margaret Thatcher, "There is no alternative." Laurence Summers, in his introduction to the World Bank publication *Voting for Reform,* premises his discussion on the assertion that "policy makers know much more [about] how to design a technically sound adjustment than they do about how to get adequate political support to sustain such a program." The problem, as he sees it, is "how to preserve the benefits of democracy without letting popular forces subvert the economy that supports them."[32] There is, in this view, no consideration of the reverse question: how to carry out the necessary economic reforms without destroying democracy, or how to craft economic policy so as to facilitate the consolidation of the new democracies. We are left with a rather perverse ordering of priorities. Politics is reduced to servicing a technocratically defined "welfare function," instead of technocrats devising the instruments necessary to meet a democratically specified "social welfare function."[33]

Given their broad base of legitimacy, democracies can provide a veneer of equity by seeming to distribute fairly the sacrifices of policy reform. In the absence of economic goods, democracies can distribute political goods, such as freedom of speech and assembly, which are broadly appreciated and may serve as a safety valve. The behavior of the new democratic regimes in Africa would seem to confirm the view that democracy may facilitate adjustment, or at least not hinder it. Ironically, the emphasis on the technocratic aspects of policymaking has the overall effect of undermining the institutionalization of broad consultative mechanisms of both a parliamentary and an ex-parliamentary nature, which cultivate popular understanding and support of national policies. Thus technocratic policymaking undermines one of the instrumental advantages of democratic rule in obtaining support for policies that may be painful in the short term.

Growing Involvement of the BWIs in Internal Matters. Imposing and monitoring an ever-wider range of conditionalities, BWIs find themselves getting deeper into the domestic affairs of recipient countries, extending their control of policy. Earlier research suggested that the World Bank's instruments were flawed and that this accounted for the poor implementation of SAPs.[34] This realization led to a spate of measures, which included capacity building and direct assumption of certain key tasks in policymaking, including country position papers[35] and even the actual soliciting of funds for certain projects.[36] The involvement of these organizations has become a source of embarrassment to the institutions themselves as they furtively beseech Africans to "own" (and not devise) SAPs.

International institutional involvement is not only confined to technical matters and the influencing of policy. It extends to the realm of civil society and includes political mobilization in favor of SAPs. This may take the form of high-profile "safety nets" designed to garner political support for SAPs. The donors can, and often do, contemplate the idea of building political coalitions in support of SAPs. Given the weak intellectual foundations of their political analysis, however, donors are unlikely to constitute meaningful and lasting political coalitions.[37] They will, however, have caused enough confusion as to undercut the "normal" development of democratic politics and cultures in these countries. Even worse, their close identification with a particular government may undermine that government's legitimacy when it is seen as an ally, if not an agent, of foreign interest.[38]

Structural Constraints

Finally, there are the structural constraints that the new democracies face and that SAPs either reinforce or exploit as leverage over governments. Economic crises and adjustment measures have multiplied the number, complexity, and strategic importance of a whole range of constraints within which government authorities can operate. Most new democracies inherited economies that were heavily indebted and with fiscal affairs in a mess. In a number of countries, the outgoing governments had entered into SAP agreements with fixed targets or restrictions on a number of economic instruments that were presented to new governments as immutable and nonnegotiable.

In addition to the policy constraints, there are the exigencies of globalization in general and the peculiar constraints that fiscal and foreign exchange impose on new governments. I have already indicated the form that they assume above.

Policy Trends Under Democracy

It was noted earlier how new democratic regimes have generally pronounced themselves in favor of neoliberal policies. There are many reasons for the acceptance by the new governments of these polices. The first reason is the ideological underpinnings of these movements and their understanding of the roots of the crisis. In the discussion of adjustment and political transformation, little attention has been paid to the platforms of the main political actors. In the absence of a careful reading of the platforms of these movements, there has been a rush to judgment as to whether these movements have kept their promises and stuck to their programs, or whether they have been hoodwinked by the leadership. In most cases, what certain social groups are expected to want has been derived from assumptions about what they will espouse. In a number of these movements, business interests have played a central role in the struggle for democracy, as witnessed by the Movement for Multiparty Democracy in Zambia, the United Democratic Front in Malawi, and the two Forums for the Restoration of Democracy in Kenya. These groups have generally been spawned by the dirigiste strategy that they now so fervently oppose, either as managers of state enterprises who then established their own private industries, or private capitalists who prospered under "indigenization" programs implemented in the postcolonial era. Ideologically, such groups are now attracted to the neoliberal ideologies, although they would still insist that the state somehow protect them or continue to subsidize them while, of course, removing subsidies to other social groups. This partly explains the ambivalence of such groups toward SAPs. Although they wish to roll back the state in a number of areas affecting other social groups, they also want the state to continue being active in those areas in which they need its assistance. They support the removal of food subsidies but call for lowering or subsidization of interest rates or protection of domestic markets.

The second reason might be simply a visceral reaction by the new governments to the policies pursued by their predecessors. Writing on Latin America, Jose Maria Maravall notes that democratic regimes are more prone to "political learning" from past experiences than are authoritarian ones. However,

> such learning was primarily "negative". . . resulting in the adoption of certain policies on the basis of a process of elimination. Indeed, many governments turned to neoliberal blueprints because they seemed to be diametrically opposed to those they had in place at the time. A new "cargo cult" emerged: the policies were widely expected to deliver the goods that had so far eluded those societies.[39]

A similar political learning process seems to have taken place in Africa. To the extent that the crisis is attributed to state dirigisme, which is in turn associated with authoritarian rule and corruption, the new movements are inclined to equate economic liberalization with the demise of dirigisme and authoritarian rule. Not surprisingly, in some cases, the leading lights of these movements, by reaction to the wasteful authoritarian intervention of the past, have been taken in by the simplistic equation of economic liberalization with political democratization. One should add to this the fact that the triumphalism of the West and the ascendancy of neoliberalism do affect political discourse in Africa. The hegemonic political discourse in the post–Cold War era has been strongly neoliberal in both its economics and its politics.

The third and perhaps most important reason is the responses by the democratic governments to the constraints outlined. They come to accept that the "objective conditions" are such that there are simply no alternatives. This is particularly true when economic conditionalities imposed by international financial institutions are indifferent to the political exigencies of the new political dispensation. Perversely, the IFIs have tightened up the conditionalities precisely because the economy has become a central preoccupation of the governments. The willingness of these regimes to gain the international credibility that they believe their predecessors had squandered continues to increase.[40] The newly elected governments are keen to reach agreement with the international institutions or to have funds released that may have been withheld because of earlier failures to meet the demands of the IFIs. These regimes may not have the luxury of protracted negotiations with these institutions enjoyed by the previous regimes. The need for some symbolic demonstration that things are moving on the economic front may be pronounced under transitional democracies.

Finally, there is a misreading by these newly elected governments of the economic consequences of support by the various donors of democratization processes. There seems to be a genuine belief, based on the avowed pronouncements of the donors, that new democracies will definitely receive more financial aid and be awarded more relaxed structural and fiscal restraints than the dictatorships that they replaced. This is particularly the case in countries in which economic sanctions had been used by the donors to help dislodge these regimes. In reality, however, nothing of the sort seems to be happening. Indeed, the downward trend in aid allocation has continued. This has led to pronouncements by African leaders of the dire consequences for democratic transitions caused by a lack of financial support. Frederick Chiluba, Nicéphore Soglo, and Bakili Muluzi have each made warnings to this effect, with Muluzi arguing, rather ominously, that people do not eat democracy, but food.

The fact that democratizing movements have tended to accept and even intensify the implementation of neoliberal policy has been received with a sigh of relief in some circles, or it has been interpreted to reflect the basic compatibility of those policies with democratization. Faced with the immovable reality of a highly competitive international order, the new democracies have had to accept the whole package that accompanies adjustment.

Conclusion

This essay has been written on the premises that current efforts at democratization should be supported and that economic policy and the mechanisms used in making it should be supportive of these endeavors. It highlights one facet of the economic environment within which attempts at democratic consolidation are taking place in Africa. In judging the relationship between democratization and a given set of policies, it is important that such economic policies meet a number of criteria. Aside from the substantive content of policies, they should be supportive or cognizant of the formal decisionmaking structures. If organized social groups are to be convinced that they can meaningfully air their grievances through these formal structures, then they are likely to use these channels and respect the outcomes. If, however, these formal institutions are not receptive to their voices and, worse, if they are empty shells that are bypassed by other institutions or social groups with impunity, then the quest for solutions outside normal democratic channels will be encouraged. In current practice, both form and content are oblivious to the exigencies of the consolidation of democracy and actually run the danger of subverting democratization. Any democracy that appears to withhold significant freedom in economic policymaking for reasons of international pressure could find such a practice rebound on itself: by offering little by way of public choices for parties to compete over, it would encourage precisely those practices it sought to overcome—personalism, factionalism, and clientelism—and would provoke fundamentalist/nationalist attacks on liberal democracy as an alien imposition.[41]

Globalization is a process engulfing the world, and African countries cannot escape it by autarkic policies. African countries must prepare themselves to compete through what has been called "strategic integration" of their economies in a rapidly changing world.[42] This will call for tough choices on intra- and intertemporal distribution of costs and benefits. It will involve individual and collective decisions regarding which activities to invest in. The temptation to circumvent democratic decisionmaking will be enormous, especially when encouraged by BWIs. However, political stability and the credibility of these reforms within democratic structures will demand that such hard decisions be made by elected institutions.

It may be, as neoliberals often remind us, that interstate relationships embodied in aid and conditionality inherently impinge on national sovereignty in a way that markets do not. However, the salient point to recall is that we are talking here of politically constituted economic entities (BWIs and official donor agencies) that are amenable to political influence. Opportunities therefore abound for those genuinely interested in democratization in Africa for political action to change the relationship between the policymaking practice of these institutions and the new democratic governments. We should also recall that current practices are the result of diplomatic and bureaucratic inertia and the absence of serious reflection on the modus operandi of aid-giving compatible with democratic politics. Both research and open debate are needed to address these issues. The implication of this chapter is that we must continue to explore alternatives that can lead to "democracies without tears" and that can allow the new democracies meaningful choices.

Notes

1. Fukuyama, *End of History.*
2. Held, "Democracy and Globalization," p. 141.
3. Maxfield, *Gatekeepers of Growth,* p. 362. Such signaling of creditworthiness is not the exclusive undertaking of developing countries. Only a few days after its election, the British Labour government announced that the Treasury would cede all monetary policymaking functions to the Bank of England, effectively granting the Central Bank autonomy. The main argument cited in the press was that this

would assure financial markets that the "New Labour Party" would be fighting inflation.

4. Tony Killick cites a number of studies suggesting that International Monetary Fund support does not induce any large inflows of capital ("Principals and Agents"). Some studies actually establish a *negative* relationship between IMF support and the new private-sector lending. See Hajivassiliou, "External Debt Repayments."

5. Fernandez-Arias, "New Wave."

6. Diamond, "Beyond Autocracy."

7. This may be a sweeping category, since there are obviously differences among African analysts. However, based on a reading of the available African literature (published and unpublished), it is fair to say there is a predominant African perspective captured in this paragraph. See, for instance, Adesina, "Labour Movements"; Bangura, "Intellectuals, Economic Reform, and Social Change"; Chole and Ibrahim, *Democratisation Processes;* Hutchful, "International Dimensions"; Mkandawire, "Adjustment, Political Conditionality, and Democratization"; and Mkandawire and Olukoshi, eds., *Between Liberalisation and Repression.*

8. This point is well captured by P. Bardhan: "In [the] context of many overwhelming ethnic, class and regional conflicts that threaten nation-building, it is the distributive compromises (in spite of their second best or n-best from the point of view of allocational efficiency) that become primary, and economists, to be of any relevance, should pay more attention to them" ("Alternative Approaches").

9. Bangura, "Intellectuals, Economic Reform, and Social Change."

10. Haggard and Kaufman, "Initiation and Consolidation."

11. See, for instance, Haggard, "Political Economy of Inflation." However, one ought to be wary of statistical exercises used to prove the compatibility of adjustment with democratization. The statistical results seem to depend too heavily on ideological predisposition of the researchers. Prior to 1987, most studies suggested that authoritarian rule was necessary for adjustment. After 1987, analysis of the same data suggested the opposite. See Przeworski and Limongi, "Political Regimes."

12. World Bank, *Adjustment in Africa.*

13. The classification of constraints is drawn from Larda, "Globalisation."

14. Immediately after Frederick Chiluba's victory over Kenneth Kaunda in 1991, Zambia was gripped by an unprecedented wave of strikes. Similarly, Malawi is currently experiencing a wave of strikes, mainly by the civil servants. However, the use of this space for protest against structural adjustment programs or the orthodox policies pursued by the newly elected governments has been more muted than was generally expected.

15. "Macropopulism" is defined by Rudiger Dornbursch and S. Edwards as "an approach to economics that emphasizes growth and income redistribution and de-emphasizes the risks of inflation and deficit financing, external constraints and the reactions of economic agents to aggressive non-market policies" ("Macroeconomics of Populism"). The main ingredients of such a policy often include (1) budget deficits to stimulate domestic demand; (2) nominal wage increases plus price controls to affect income redistribution; and (3) exchange rate control or appreciation to cut inflation and to raise wages and profits in the non-traded-goods sector. Laurence Summers, the current U.S. undersecretary of the Treasury for International Affairs and former senior World Bank official, in a foreword to a World Bank book, *Voting for Reform,* ranks "rampant populism" as the third of the surest ways of destroying an economy, the first and second being communism and bombing, respectively (see Summers, "Foreword").

16. Thus, in its final months, the Malawi Congress Party engaged in what the World Bank regarded as "major over-expenditure" (cited in Venter, "Transition to Democracy"). Similarly, Kaunda abandoned his agreement with the Bretton Woods institutions just before the elections.

17. Amadeo and Banuri, "Policy, Governance, and Conflict."

18. A minister in Malawi told me how his permanent secretary resented his revision of a speech he had drafted for him. He was bewildered by the thought that the documents to be presented by the minister to the cabinet would have to forcefully argue his case to other colleagues. Past practice had been that one argued the case with the president and then drafted the ministerial policy document, which the minister endorsed.

19. The World Bank seems to translate "transparency" in the interaction between donors and recipients to mean the right of World Bank officials to openly state their displeasure with host government policies. In other words, the dictates that were once issued behind closed doors are now aired publicly, not for public scrutiny, but just as a matter of information. In Malawi, the World Bank representative has openly stated that he thought the size of the cabinet of Bakili Muluzi's government was too large.

20. Given the weak positions of the new democratic states, such complaints and oppositions remain highly muted.

21. World Bank, *Sub-Saharan Africa*, p. 60.

22. The governments that the World Bank peddled as strong adjusters—Ghana, Babangida's Nigeria, and Uganda—were essentially military regimes.

23. Rodrik, "Understanding Economic Policy."

24. According to Veronica Montecinos, "probably one of the most serious threats to the consolidation of Latin American democracies stems from the lack of institutionalised forms of communication between the newer, technical and the more traditional political elites" ("Economic Policy Elites," p. 27).

25. Bienen, "Politics of Trade Liberalization"; Callaghy, "Lost Between Market and State."

26. Waterbury, "Political Management."

27. Kohli, "Democracy."

28. The case of Nigeria is enlightening in this respect. The Nigerian government, apparently at the behest of IFIs, simply recruited as minister of finance an economist who had not only been outside the country, but had also been an employee of the World Bank. As economic minister of planning, it appointed a Harvard-trained Nigerian who had spent most of his time in the United States and had weak links with the Nigerian economics profession. See Bangura, "Intellectuals, Economic Reform and Social Change." In a number of countries, nationals have been attached to finance ministries but have been paid international salaries by donor agencies.

29. For one useful exception, see Bangura, "Intellectuals, Economic Reform, and Social Change."

30. Mkandawire, "Political Economy of Privatization."

31. Malloy, "Democracy."

32. Summers, "Foreword," p. xii.

33. The instrumentalization of democracy comes out sharply in some game-theory presentations of the relationship between donors and recipients. National governments are treated as "agents," while the BWIs are the "principals." In extreme formulations, the BWIs seek to maximize the implementation of SAPs and minimize their financial burden. The agent wants the money, but not the SAP. For a presentation of such models, see White and Morissey, "Tailoring Conditionality."

34. See, for example, Harrigan et al., *Aid and Power.*

35. Thus effectively reducing the much-touted "policy dialogues" to something equivalent to the "dialogue" between a ventriloquist and his puppet.

36. The involvement of the World Bank in such activities in Uganda prompted some to describe Uganda as "an international Bantustan" (Himbara and Sultan, "Reconstruction of the Uganda State"). This may be a rather harsh pronouncement, but it does point to the extent of involvement of SAPs in national affairs and the attenuation of national sovereignty that such involvement entails.

37. Sandbrook, "Democratisation."

38. President Nicéphore Soglo of Benin used to pride himself on his close contact with officials of the World Bank, which he had once served. He earned himself the nickname "Monsieur Le Banque m'a dit." This was to be used by the opposition to telling effect.

39. Maravall, "Myth of the Authoritarian Advantage," pp. 22–23.

40. Zambia's self-administration of an overdose of SAPs is a good example of this phenomenon. Faced with a donor community and private sector that had lost faith in the government's commitment to SAPs, Chiluba's newly elected government sought to improve its image by adopting drastic fiscal measures. C. Adam notes that "in the absence of other mechanisms to signal its commitment, the government chose to accelerate the liberalization measures even though this distorted the logical sequence of reform and imposed significant costs on the economy later in the stabilization process" ("Fiscal Adjustment," p. 738). Conventional wisdom is that one should first achieve macroeconomic stabilization before accelerating liberalization measures. The effect of wrong sequencing on the government's discretionary expenditure was dramatic. Increases in interest charges on public debt rose by 285 percent in real terms. The interest charges represented 25 percent of total domestic revenue. The high interest attracted short-term and highly mobile capital inflows, which pushed up the value of the kwacha, undermining the export drive and diversification sought by the government.

41. Woodward, "Democracy and Economy," p. 127.

42. This is an expression used by A. Singh to describe the set of policies adopted by the "Asian tigers" ("Causes of Fast Economic Growth").

8

The "Mauritius Miracle": Democracy, Institutions, and Economic Policy

DEBORAH BRAUTIGAM

The stability of most democratic regimes in Africa remains uncertain, with only a handful having passed the test of peaceful turnover through the ballot box. Mauritius, a multiparty democracy since independence in 1968, is one of the few democracies in Africa to have met Samuel Huntington's two-turnover test of consolidation and Juan Linz and Alfred Stepan's requirement that democracy become universally accepted as "the only game in town."[1] A small, multiethnic island nation colonized first by the French, and later by the British, Mauritius also stands out in Africa for its lively civic culture, relative social harmony, equity, and impressive economic growth. By the mid-1990s, the density of newspapers per capita was twice as high as that of South Africa, which had the highest rate of any continental African country. At $3,380, the gross national product (GNP) per capita was more than six times the average of $509 for sub-Saharan Africa, and unemployment was estimated at 1.6 percent.

In a recent article, Adam Przeworski and Fernando Limongi argue that economic development and democracy are correlated not because economic development leads to democracy (the modernization argument), but because democratic regimes that emerge in comparatively affluent countries are more likely to survive and be consolidated than those emerging in poorer ones, probably because affluence mitigates distributional struggles and eases the impact of economic crises.[2] This might seem to give Africa's new, but still low-income, democracies little hope of survival, yet as the authors also point out, low-income democracies that manage to grow have a better chance of surviving than those that suffer economic decline. Although there is plenty of skepticism about the ability of new democracies to promote growth, there is also encouraging evidence that many of the "third-wave" democracies have managed their economies without being driven back into prolonged recession or the instability of economic populism. This suggests that to understand the possibilities for democratic consolidation in Africa, we need to explore what Przeworski and Limongi admit are the more "interesting questions . . . the mechanisms that mediate between economic development and the dynamics of political regimes."[3]

What are those mechanisms? While the early transitions literature privileged strategic choices and other contingent factors in explaining transitions to democracy, the more recent literature on consolidation emphasizes the interaction between strategic choices and the historically established institutions that frame the range of available options. Research grounded in historical institutionalism emphasizes the importance of early decisions about the *structure* of politics and economic development: intermediate-level institutions such as electoral rules, party systems, labor relations, business interest associations, and the organizations in which economic strategies are embedded (such as state-owned enterprises and economic processing zones).[4] The growing literature in this field suggests that certain kinds of historically contingent choices become the architecture that constrains later decisionmakers. The rules, practices, structures, and institutions established in the first years of a newly democratic regime prove particularly important in shaping the subsequent path of politics in a democracy and the ability to deliver an economic performance that will reinforce, rather than weaken, democracy. Some of these initial choices and conditions are amenable to negotiated change, whereas others are more enduring.

Institutions, Democracy, and Economic Development

What kinds of initial conditions and choices support both economic development and democratic consolidation? How can new democracies frame their development options to generate the stable growth that democratic consolidation requires? These questions are vital for new and emerging democracies in Africa, yet research on these issues has tended to include primarily cases from Asia, Latin America, and the advanced industrial countries. This chapter draws on this research to hypothesize that three initial factors may explain the ability of democratic regimes in Africa and elsewhere to manage their economies to promote broad-based growth while simultaneously reinforcing democracy: (1) an institutional design that promotes coalition building and compromise; (2) an initial set of economic and social policy choices that creates constituencies for broad-based growth; and (3) limits on the power of landed elites and the military.

Institutional Design

Because institutions tend to change slowly, the institutional legacies of previous regimes, as well as the institutional choices made at the time of transition to democracy, tend to structure many of the political options and development strategies of later governments.[5] The design of electoral rules, the choice between presidential and parliamentary systems, the structure of party systems and executive-legislative relations, and the less formal rules and practices of economic policy formation and coalition maintenance all shape opportunities for influence and the ability of different groups to have their interests represented as policies are formed and implemented.[6] Presidential constitutions allow for a stronger executive, but they may also reinforce the neopatrimonial systems of patronage that dominate regime types in Africa.[7] Broadbased, two-party systems and multiparty systems dominated by either center-left or center-right coalitions offer incentives for compromise that may enable political systems to avoid the kinds of polarization and fragmentation that can threaten democracies.[8] Consociational and federal systems aid power sharing and minority representation, easing tensions in multiethnic societies and providing incentives for political entrepreneurs to solicit cross-ethnic support. Multimember districts tend to encourage electoral coalitions and related compromises. Drawing electoral districts that favor certain kinds of voters or interests over others—rural people over urban, for example—can shape politics in the long run, while also affecting the kinds of growth strategies chosen in democratic systems.

This emphasis on formal structures and the incentives that they provide for political action may strike some observers of African politics as misplaced.[9] In most African countries, the informal logic of neopatrimonial politics casts doubt on the utility of a framework that privileges formal rules, since one of the defining characteristics of a neopatrimonial leader is that he or she does not follow formal rules.[10] Two comments are in order here. First, even in neopatrimonial democracies, rules and practices do matter. Michael Bratton and Nicolas van de Walle found that institutions inherited from previous regimes clearly affect the manner of a country's transition to democracy and may also affect the opportunities for consolidation.[11] Second, as internal (and external) demands for better governance rise, neopatrimonial leaders will increasingly be pressured to improve accountability, predictability, and the rule of law.[12] Formal structures are never completely irrelevant, and their importance in shaping democratic governance and economic development should become increasingly important in the African context.

Initial Policy Choices

New policy choices create new politics, as E. E. Schattschneider pointed out in 1935.[13] The initial economic and social development strategies chosen and the expectations created by a new democratic regime can either reinforce or prove problematic for democratic consolidation. Two elements are likely to be important here: a development strategy that will promote broad-based growth (and constituencies in favor of the same), and redistributive social transfer payments, particularly for politically volatile groups such as urban youth and organized workers. To promote sustainable growth that bolsters democratic consolidation, countries need the basics of macroeconomic stability and investment in primary education, and the choice of an economic strategy—whether agriculture-led industrialization for the domestic market or labor-intensive manufacturing for export—that makes best use of a country's resources while creating employment. There are many market-oriented economic packages that might meet these criteria. However, an increasingly strong thread in the democracy literature questions the compatibility of the high degree of economic freedom demanded in neoliberal economic models with democratic consolidation. Although research on this issue is quite preliminary, some evidence suggests that statist intervention in direct support of more equitable growth, including restraints on pure market forces, restrictions on certain property rights, and state-guided, rather than radical, trade liberalization, may be more compatible with democratic consolidation than the minimalist state of the neoliberal model.[14]

The example of trade liberalization may make this more clear. When countries choose an economic strategy that depends on opening up to the international market, they face greater risks, along with the potential for greater gains. Both the price instability of primary commodity exports and the need for flexibility to respond to changing demands for manufactured exports create losers as well as winners, and unhappy losers can threaten an economic program despite net social gains. In the worst instances, losers can threaten a democratic regime. A program of credible, but gradual, state-guided liberalization that lasts several years or even a decade (as was done in East Asia) can ease the transition, allowing less efficient enterprises time to become more competitive. Other interventions, such as transfer payments and broad-based social insurance, can compensate for the lower wages and flexibility required for a country to be competitive in the international market. Research by Robert Bates, Philip Brock, and Jill Tiefenthaler has demonstrated that countries with more social insurance are also more likely to promote free trade.[15] Countries that lack resources for transfer payments to compensate for slower wage growth and temporary employment losses incurred during liberalization are more likely to remain inward oriented, with consequently weaker economic development.

Transfer payments to losers can enable democratic governments to maintain coalitions for growth-promoting reforms, and compensatory social spending has proven critical in the efforts of many developing countries to ameliorate the costs of reforms.[16] Over time, redistributive social policies can improve income equality, and some researchers have argued that equality and growth are positively correlated.[17] Countries with more equal income distribution seem to be able to solve collective action problems associated with reform more easily, thus decreasing the time necessary to adjust to the inevitable crosswinds of the global economy.[18]

Landed Elites and the Military

Outside of Africa, numerous studies point to the intransigence of landed elites and of strong military forces as a critical barrier to democratic consolidation and broad-based economic development.[19] It is similarly clear to observers of Africa that democratic consolidation is likely to be problematic in countries whose militaries have a history of intervention. Without firm civilian control over the military, there is little chance that a democracy will survive for long. Likewise, societies with powerful landed classes that practice labor-repressive agriculture contain significant barriers to both broad-based economic development and sustainable democracy. There is some evidence that countries that have been able to implement effective land reform, or to shift large landowners into commercial and financial pursuits, have fared better in maintaining democracy and in promoting economic development.[20] To date, it is not clear how critical the rural elite is as a barrier to democracy in most African countries, particularly those where rural production is still largely devoted to subsistence agriculture and small-scale commercial activity. Yet Mauritius and a number of other countries already have extensive systems of plantation agriculture, and the privatization and commercialization of communal land is well under way in eastern and southern Africa and many other parts of the subcontinent. As African countries slowly recover from the depression of the 1980s and increase their engagement with the market, the politics of land and the democracy-obstructing role of rural elites may become increasingly salient.

Mauritius, 1968–1995: An Overview

Mauritius became independent on March 12, 1968, under decidedly cloudy skies.[21] The Mauritian government elected in August 1967 as part of the colonial self-government program was forced to call in British troops to help restore order in early 1968 after a series of violent, postelection communal riots that left the country shaken. Socioeconomic indicators were mixed. Unemployment was high, and the multiethnic population—south

Asian Hindus comprised 52 percent of the population, south Asian Muslims 16 percent, Creoles of African ancestry 27 percent, Chinese Mauritians 3 percent, and Mauritians of European (generally French) ancestry 2 percent—had been expanding at approximately 3 percent per annum. Sugar made up almost 100 percent of exports, and the economy fluctuated depending on the weather and the price of sugar; in 1968, the gross domestic product (GDP) fell by 7 percent when sugar export prices dropped, and economic growth averaged only 1.8 percent per annum between 1964 and 1972.[22] However, Mauritius also had some advantages. Cultural values stressing education, combined with government policies offering free primary education, had led to the highest primary enrollment rates in Africa at independence. Life expectancy was also relatively high at 61 years.

Shortly after independence, the economic situation in Mauritius began to improve, largely because of the recovery of sugar prices, but also because the government began promoting labor-intensive manufactured exports as a strategy to create employment and diversify to overcome the country's extreme dependence on sugar. Even with the effects of the first oil shock, the economy grew by 8 percent per annum between 1970 and 1975, and 6.9 percent annually between 1975 and 1979.

Democratic consolidation got off to a less impressive start. The founding election had been won by a coalition of the Mauritius Labour Party (MLP), headed by Seewoosagur Ramgoolam, and several small communal parties. Soon after independence, a radical new party, the Mouvement Militant Mauricien (MMM) rose rapidly to prominence, winning an important by-election. Alarmed, the government moved to postpone elections scheduled for 1972. The MMM responded by organizing a series of general strikes, prompting the government to pass the Public Order Act of 1971, which allowed it to impose a state of emergency, repress the MMM and its supporters, close down critical newspapers, and imprison party leaders.

At this point, the history of Mauritius resembled that of many other African countries that started as democracies after independence. The critical difference in Mauritius was that rather than establishing a one-party state, or moving toward a permanently authoritarian regime, Mauritius eventually resumed its democratic path, much as India had been able to continue normal elections after the end of the emergency period imposed by Indira Gandhi. The MMM leaders were freed, press censorship was lifted, and the 1976 elections were held as scheduled. In these elections, the MMM won more seats (34 out of 70) than any other single party, but the MLP, with 28 seats, was able to form a coalition government with the conservative Parti Mauricien Social Démocrate (PMSD), which had won eight seats.

The MLP-PMSD coalition governed Mauritius until midway through the economic crisis of 1978–1984. This crisis had both international and domestic sources. Balance-of-payment problems were deepened by the oil shock of 1979, and a series of cyclones had damaged sugar production. Domestically, the government had been borrowing on an unsustainable scale in order to pay for electoral-cycle pay increases, public employment expansion, and other benefits. The economic crisis in Mauritius was not dissimilar from the situation in most other African countries at this time: in 1980, total debt service as a percentage of exports in Mauritius was 9.1 percent, and total debt was equivalent to 41.6 percent of GDP, while in sub-Saharan Africa as a whole, debt service averaged 9.7 percent of exports, and total debt averaged 30.6 percent of GDP.[23] Like most other countries in Africa, Mauritius initially had great difficulty complying with International Monetary Fund (IMF) targets. Agreements made in February 1978 and October 1979 were both canceled. However, in 1981—much earlier than in most other African countries—Mauritius was able to successfully complete an IMF stabilization agreement. Two additional IMF agreements were completed in 1982 and 1984, as were several World Bank–financed structural adjustment programs.[24] Growth averaged 2.6 percent during the austerity period from 1980 to 1985.

Political leaders often hesitate to implement austerity policies because they fear the political consequences. In Mauritius, the election called in 1982 during the austerity period vindicated these fears: all 60 seats were won by the opposition, a left-of-center coalition of the now more moderate MMM and the Parti Socialiste Mauricien (PSM). The MMM's Aneerood Jugnauth became prime minister. This was Mauritius's first real turnover, for ousted Prime Minister Ramgoolam had headed every coalition government since independence. Once in office, Finance Minister Paul Bérenger soon realized that Mauritius could not free itself from the IMF without maintaining the austerity policies, but Prime Minister Jugnauth was unconvinced. In March 1983, the MMM split over this and other issues, and Jugnauth formed a new party, the Mouvement Socialist Mauricien (MSM). The inability of either side to form a majority forced new elections, which were held in August. The new government, the "Alliance" coalition formed by the MLP, the PMSD, and the MSM, also won the 1987 elections, as the economy moved through an extended economic boom caused by the recovery of the sugar sector and the sustained expansion of manufactured exports. Even with the economic difficulties of the early 1980s, growth averaged 6.2 percent between 1980 and 1990, and the Gini coefficient of income equality improved to 0.37 from its 1960 level of 0.50.[25]

Rising inflation in the late 1980s and early 1990s pushed the government to tighten monetary policy and reimpose some price controls. The subsequent slowdown in growth may have contributed to the MMM's return to power in the 1991 elections, which were won by a coalition of the MSM and the MMM; Jugnauth remained prime minister. Economic growth again increased, averaging 4.9 percent between 1990 and 1995. The government called early elections in December 1995, but Prime Minister

Jugnauth's MSM party was defeated by a broad-based, left-of-center coalition of the MMM and the MLP, which won almost two-thirds of the vote. In this "second turnover," Navin Ramgoolam, son of the man who had served as prime minister from 1968 to 1982, became prime minister.

Thus, Mauritius has shifted from a highly protected economic regime that relied overwhelmingly on sugar for both employment and revenues to an increasingly liberalized "little tiger" modeled on the East Asian newly industrializing countries. While the country's politics remain contentious and policymakers disagree about the choices necessary to sustain a remarkable record of broad-based economic growth, democracy appears to be quite solidly consolidated, with six national elections and two turnovers since independence.

In a case as unusual as Mauritius in the African context, it is tempting to rely on the "personalities of key political actors" and other contingent variables to explain why the country has been more successful at maintaining policies that support broad-based economic development and democratic consolidation. Political agency does matter. Indeed, Mauritius was fortunate to have leaders who agreed to conduct their political competition within the boundaries of democratic rules and who saw early on that labor-intensive manufacturing for export could provide the employment required by the rapidly growing population. However, once the "defining moment" of independence had passed, the rules of democracy and the other institutions established at that time created the constraints on the existing opportunities for political action, while also shaping the goals and strategies of political actors.[26] The next section of this chapter outlines the initial factors that structured subsequent political and economic policy choices in Mauritius.

Initial Factors

Much of the subsequent development of Mauritius was shaped by institutions put in place during the independence period. Institutions that were particularly important include institutions shaping the electoral system, for these created the incentives that have made coalition formation a major art in Mauritian politics; legislation establishing an export processing zone (EPZ) in 1970, for this became one of the cornerstones of later economic development policy; several Labour and Industrial Relations Acts (1963, 1975), which centralized wage bargaining while weakening the labor movement by dividing it; and the February 1975 signing of the Lomé Convention by the European Economic Community (EEC) and the former European colonies in Africa, the Caribbean, and the Pacific (ACP), whereby Mauritius became a beneficiary of the Sugar Protocol and its generous, above-market prices. The decision *not* to establish a standing army is also likely to have been important. In addition, although landownership remained highly concentrated in Mauritius (at independence, 55 percent of sugar land was held by 21 large estates, while the remaining sugar land was held by 27,569 small and medium-sized planters), it was less concentrated than in many Latin American countries due to the *"grand morcellement."*[27] Between 1880 and 1920, when world sugar prices fell to historic lows, Franco-Mauritian planters sold off or leased about 32 percent of their estate land to their Hindu laborers. The *grand morcellement* created a class of small- and medium-scale rural capitalists who have been an important constituency for an export-oriented agricultural policy in Mauritius.

1966: The Banwell Commission and the Mauritius Electoral System

Democracies are crafted in part by commissions and conferences that seek to establish the rules under which political competition and, ultimately, policy formation will take place. The two major elements of a democratic system are the choice between presidentialism and parliamentarism, and the design of the electoral system.[28] Party systems are structured by electoral rules, which provide incentives for compromise as well as opportunities for representation.

Linz and others have argued that "presidential systems perform poorly . . . in countries with deep cleavages and fragmented party systems."[29] Mauritius is one of only three nonpresidential systems in Africa, and this alone may be significant in explaining the relative success of succeeding generations of politicians in maneuvering through the ethnic cleavages in the country.[30] The succession of debates over various constitutions in Mauritius seem never to have seriously entertained the idea of presidentialism. Much more contentious were the debates over the electoral system, which took more than a decade to shape, after a series of participatory meetings had decided upon the outlines of the rest of the country's independence constitution. The electoral system that was finally established in 1966 provided the structure for political party and distributive competition on the island.[31]

The small amount of political competition that had been allowed under colonialism was generally dominated by Franco-Mauritians, and the majority Hindu and Muslim communities were only gradually allowed to participate in the governing council. The MLP, founded in 1936, was the first true party in Mauritius, and despite efforts to shape the party on a class basis, it was seen by many as a Hindu organization. As political participation and internal self-government expanded in the colony, other political parties were formed. The 1959 Legislative Council elections were dominated by several of the parties that would later play an important role in postindependence politics: the Labour Party; the PMSD, which represented Franco-Mauritians and Creoles; the Comité d'Action Musulman (CAM), which represented many of the Muslims; and several smaller parties formed by Hindu radicals and other, mainly communal, interests.

The importance of the design of the electoral system was not lost on politicians in Mauritius. The Labour Party rejected British proposals for pure proportional representation, partly out of a concern that it would fragment the party system.[32] They pushed instead for 40 single-member districts, which would have ensured MLP domination, since Hindus, their major constituency, were well represented in all of the rural districts and many suburban ones. The PMSD wanted 11 three-member constituencies, since larger districts would improve the chances for Franco-Mauritian and Creole candidates, who enjoyed a majority in urban areas. Rural and urban Muslims demanded reserved seats and separate voter rolls to ensure Muslim representation.

Ultimately, given the impasse, the British decided to bring in a three-person commission from Britain (the Banwell Commission) to meet with Mauritian political elites and propose an electoral system. The system later adopted with minor revisions by the Legislative Council, and still in place in Mauritius, is composed of 20 districts with three members from each, and two additional representatives from the island of Rodriguez. In an effort to ensure representation for all major ethnic groups in each election, the electoral commission can also seat eight of the unsuccessful candidates with the highest numbers of votes as "best losers."[33] Voting is done through a party-list system with simple majority vote. There are very few obstacles to registration of new parties, and there are no vote thresholds for representation. Each voter has three votes, which can be allocated to any three candidates, although voters tend not to split their votes among different parties. The three candidates receiving the most votes in each district are elected, making Mauritius more of a "first three past the post" plurality system than one with proportional representation.[34]

While candidates from a multitude of parties generally stand for election, in most cases only a small number of parties actually win seats. Indeed, in the most recent elections in 1995, although candidates representing 42 different parties stood for election, a coalition of just two parties, the MLP and the MMM, won all of the seats.[35] In addition, since the population of urban districts tends to be larger than that of rural districts, results like those in the 1983 election sometimes occur, where the urban-based MMM won 47 percent of the vote, but only 22 seats, while the opposition Alliance, which has strong rural support, won 46 seats with just 51 percent of the vote.[36]

How has the electoral system influenced democratic consolidation and economic development in Mauritius? The institutional design of the system has had two major effects: there are incentives for political representation of all major communities, and there are relatively strong pressures for moderation in both social and economic policy. First, while smaller, multimember districts should offer more opportunities for minority parties and candidates to be elected than would larger, single-member districts, the experience in Mauritius has been that only three or four parties are ever able to win seats. Instead, parties have strong incentives to offer three-person slates with a diverse ethnic mixture. This has helped to make parties and elections less "communal" than they would otherwise be.[37]

In addition, the best loser system is a democratic consociational compromise that virtually guarantees that groups with strong regional support that fail to win representation through the ballot still have a good chance of having their representatives appointed to the legislature to ensure diversity. This also stimulates the establishment of very small parties, since a single candidate who is a "favorite son" of an ethnic group in a particular area stands a chance of being appointed to a best loser seat even if he or she cannot gain the votes to be elected. While these aspects might seem to increase ethnic awareness and perhaps polarization, by offering strong incentives to work within the system they help ensure that the option of dropping out of the system into violent, antigovernment activities is not taken seriously by any ethnic group. These rules thus tend to build stability, helping the democracy to consolidate.

Second, the design of the electoral system, combined with the ethnic division of the population, forces governments to form coalitions in order to govern. Only the MMM has ever been able to secure a majority of seats by itself, and all of the governments since independence have been coalition governments (see Table 8.1). By making consensus necessary, the electoral rules in Mauritius have steered both the left and the right away from extreme positions on economic policy, which has helped both to manage economic development and to consolidate the democratic system.[38] Finally, the fact that, as in Japan, the districts give slightly more weight to the rural vote means that the urban bias identified in much of Africa by Bates and others has been less strong in Mauritius, and democratic governments have had incentives to design effective agricultural policies and programs.[39]

1970: Export Processing Zones Act

For several centuries before independence, the cultivation and export of agricultural commodities dominated economic development strategies in Mauritius, much as they did in many other colonies. However, almost immediately after independence, the new government passed a major piece of legislation—the 1970 Export Processing Zones Act No. 551—an institution that would reshape economic development in Mauritius in ways that were then very unusual for Africa.

The idea that the densely populated island could choose to use its comparative advantage in low-cost labor to produce labor-intensive manufactured goods was not itself new. A report prepared by Cambridge economist

Table 8.1   Coalition Governments and Leaders, 1968–1995

Period	Major Coalitions	Prime Minister
1967–1969[a]	MLP + IFB[b] + CAM	S. Ramgoolam
1969–1973	MLP + CAM + PMSD	S. Ramgoolam
1974–1976	MLP + CAM	S. Ramgoolam
1976–1982[a]	MLP + PMSD	S. Ramgoolam
1982–1983[a]	MMM + PSM[c]	A. Jugnauth
1983–1987[a]	MSM + MLP + PMSD	A. Jugnauth
1987–1988[a]	MSM + MLP + PMSD	A. Jugnauth
1988–1990	MSM + MLP	A. Jugnauth
1990–1991	MSM + MMM	A. Jugnauth
1991–1995[a]	MSM + PMSD + MMM	A. Jugnauth
1995–[a]	MMM + MLP	N. Ramgoolam

Sources: Ravi Gulhati and Raj Nallari, Successful Stabilization and Recovery in Mauritius, Economic Development Institute Policy Case No. 5 (Washington, DC: World Bank, 1990), p. 34; Colin Legum, ed., African Contemporary Record (London: Africana Publishing, various years); and EIU, Mauritius: Country Report (London: EIU, various years).
Notes: a. Election held during this period.
b. PSM: When Parti Socialiste Mauricien was temporarily split from MLP.
c. IFB = Independence Forward Bloc, a defunct party created during the debate over whether Mauritius should become independent from Britain.

James Meade in 1961 emphasized both export-oriented and import-substituting industrialization (ISI), along with a policy of wage restraint, to absorb the rapidly increasing working-age population.[40] Mauritius began by promoting ISI, as did many other African countries, and established protection and other incentives for production oriented toward the domestic market. However, by the late 1960s, the workforce was still expanding at 3 percent annually. With the realization that ISI was having little impact on the growing unemployment problem, a group of influential Mauritian businesspeople urged the government to begin promoting export-oriented industrialization. Prominent among them was E. Lim Fat, a Sino-Mauritian with extensive contacts with Chinese producers in Hong Kong and elsewhere in East Asia.[41]

Soon after independence, the new government dispatched a team of experts to visit Hong Kong, Taiwan, and other East Asian countries that had begun to attract notice for their initial efforts in export-oriented manufacturing. When the delegation returned, the National Assembly acted on its recommendations; it passed the Export Processing Zones Act in 1970, making Mauritius the first common market country with an EPZ, and one of only 10 countries in the world at that time with such a program. Fat's contacts provided much of the initial foreign investment.

The EPZ was established as a system of decentralized, bonded factories that could be located anywhere on the island. It therefore never became an enclave, and it provided employment opportunities in small towns and

rural areas away from the capital. EPZ firms that exported their entire output were given tax holidays on profits and dividends and duty-free entry of
capital goods and inputs, among other incentives.[42] From the beginning,
half of the investment in EPZ factories has come from Mauritian investors
(especially Franco-Mauritians and sugar interests). Incentives for local capital to invest in the EPZ were increased when the postindependence government imposed capital export controls that stopped local sugar firms from
exporting their profits to invest in sugar plantations in other countries, a
common practice in colonial Mauritius.[43] Profits and dividends from
approved EPZ firms were exempt from the capital export controls.[44] The
EPZ gave the agrarian oligarchy an alternative channel for accumulation,
providing incentives for the country's first industrial producers to support
trade-oriented policies.[45]

Between 1971 and 1975, EPZ exports, mostly from small-scale firms
producing textiles and wigs and assembling simple electronic items, grew
at 31 percent per annum; employment in the EPZ grew by 38 percent. After
the oil price shocks of the mid and late 1970s and the beginnings of world
economic recession, the export-oriented industrialization strategy faltered.
Indeed, a study published in 1982 stated that "the chances of any significant change in the island's dependence on sugar are minimal."[46] By 1990,
however, the net value of exports of manufactured goods (Re 4.1 billion)
was almost equivalent to the gross value of sugar exports (Re 5.2 billion).
At the same time, employment in the EPZ had more than quadrupled, and
unemployment in Mauritius was under 2 percent.[47] Many of the sugar
estates established EPZ factories on their lands, making use of existing
infrastructure.[48]

As an institution, the EPZ initially enabled the government to adopt the
Asian strategy of promoting low-wage, often female employment in electronic assembly, garments, and textiles, while more vocal, longer-standing,
and primarily male constituencies—government workers, ISI employees,
and agricultural workers—received higher wages and benefits. Although
recently, wages have moved closer together, in 1985 sugar industry
workers averaged U.S.$108 per month, whereas EPZ workers averaged
U.S.$74.[49]

The pull of the EPZ and the push of a progressive tax on sugar exports
served to transfer domestic sugar capital into manufacturing, without the
instability that might have accompanied direct expropriation or nationalization of the sugar estates. Given the difficulty democracies have in implementing land reform and the extraordinary circumstances underlying the
few effective land reforms that have been implemented to date (largely in
East Asia), this may have been the only politically feasible way of reducing
the power of the landed elite. Indeed, one of the prices demanded by the
PMSD for its long association with the MLP was a guarantee that nationalization of the sugar industry would never take place.[50]

Labor and Industrial Relations Acts

Labor relations in Mauritius are complicated, but it is important to outline them, for they have affected both the way in which democratic consolidation has proceeded and the opportunities for economic and social development. Unlike the 1966 electoral system and the 1970 Export Processing Zones Act, no single institution has shaped the face of labor relations in Mauritius.

The Mauritius Labour Party was organized in 1936 as the first political party in the country, and as discussed above, it initially drew its support from rural workers. The Industrial Association Ordinance of 1938 allowed the establishment of the first labor union (the Mauritius Agricultural Labourers' Association). The MLP adopted rules in 1957 that allowed trade unions to become affiliated members of the party, but the top-down, state-controlled corporatism common in much of Africa did not take place, and many unions remained independent. In the postindependence period, the major constituency of the MLP remained rural sugar workers and the small Hindu cultivators. Ideology and self-interest have coincided in the MLP's support for improvements in the difficult conditions faced by cane workers.

The 1963 Labour Act and the 1966 Security of Employment (Sugar Industry) Ordinance, pushed through the legislature by the MLP, established a wage council to negotiate minimum wages in the sugar sector and mandated that off-season employment be provided for seasonal sugar workers who had been regularly employed by a sugar estate (growers with fewer than 10 hectares—generally Hindus—were exempt from these regulations). As noted above, average wages for sugar workers in 1985 were almost 50 percent higher than those for workers in EPZ factories. Protections for rural workers mean that plantation agriculture has been considerably less labor repressive in postindependence Mauritius than in many other African countries, a feature that is likely to have been favorable for democracy.[51]

Although they reshaped rural development in Mauritius, the MLP's efforts in the sugar sector were not enough for some workers, and the MLP had made less of an effort in general to develop strong ties with disaffected urban workers, many of whom were Creoles. Thus, when Bérenger founded the radical MMM in 1969, many workers found the party more to their liking than the moderately socialist MLP, particularly after the MLP and its coalition partner, CAM, invited the conservative PMSD to join a "national unity" government in 1969. The MMM quickly won support from 11 unions, including three from the sugar industry, the traditional constituency of the MLP. As noted above, the rise of the MMM alarmed the MLP-PMSD-CAM coalition enough to call off the 1972 elections.

Recognizing that the MMM was drawing much of its support from militant, generally urban unions, the coalition pushed through the Industrial

Relations Act of 1973. This act had some of the corporatist features of similar acts intended to reduce the independence of unions in other parts of Africa. In particular, the act replaced firm- and industry-level wage bargaining with a tripartite National Remuneration Board and made arbitration compulsory. But instead of organizing unions into a state-controlled federation, the act subdued the more threatening unions by dividing them: it lowered barriers to forming new trade unions. The number of registered unions rose from 89 in 1974 to 365 in 1984; by the mid-1980s, three-quarters of the unions in Mauritius had fewer than 100 members.[52] Most of these were not in the sugar sector, where the MLP still had a great deal of support and where seven unions continued to represent about 75 percent of workers.[53]

As structured in the initial years of postindependence Mauritius, labor institutions affected democratic consolidation and economic development in several fundamental ways. First, institutional reforms that improved the situation for rural plantation labor while avoiding outright expropriation and land reform enabled Mauritius to gradually curtail the power of the landed elite, while softening the development- and democracy-debilitating impact of labor-repressive agriculture. By improving equity, these institutions probably made Mauritius's democracy more stable. Second, by partially incorporating labor into the political system through party affiliations and through the tripartite National Remuneration Board, some incentives were created for labor to work within the system, instead of remaining an outside, destabilizing force. At the same time, the Industrial Relations Act served to impede militant activity by dividing the labor movement, increasing the difficulty of collective action. The deleterious effects of the act were offset by the continued commitment of all of the major parties to progressive social and economic policies intended to reduce poverty and improve social welfare for the population as a whole. The ability of successive governments to fund social programs was assisted by a third set of institutional innovations, the Lomé Convention and its various protocols.

The 1975 Lomé Convention

At independence, Mauritius was selling about one-third of its sugar on the world market and the rest to Great Britain at favorable prices negotiated in the Commonwealth Sugar Agreement.[54] When Great Britain joined the EEC, the Commonwealth Sugar Agreement was replaced by the Sugar Protocol to the Lomé Convention, which was signed by the EEC and ACP countries in 1975. In 1974, as negotiations over the Sugar Protocol were being conducted, sugar prices on the world market rose from U.S.$0.15 per pound to U.S.$0.57 per pound, higher than the EEC price of $0.32 per pound being offered to ACP countries through Lomé quotas. Some sugar-producing countries were therefore reluctant to commit large shares of production to the EEC, but Mauritius pressed ahead and was able to gain EEC commitment to sell an amount equivalent to almost 80 percent of local production, a much larger share than other ACP countries, which averaged quotas covering only about 30 percent of local production.

Because quota prices under this arrangement have been based on the high EEC Common Agricultural Policy prices paid to domestic sugar producers in Europe, the Mauritian gamble proved to be a good one. The EEC sugar prices offered under Lomé have generally been higher than world market prices, and a progressive tax first levied in 1973 enabled the government to capture some of these rents. These tax revenues (about U.S.$27.6 million in 1991) help the government in Mauritius to fund some of its redistributive social investments (the cost of food subsidies, an unemployment fund, and a public works employment program was about $25.2 million in 1991), whereas the Lomé proceeds enjoyed by private-sector exporters (U.S.$137.5 million net of the export tax) help ensure their cooperation with the high level of benefits (worth U.S.$59 million in 1991) that they must in turn provide to sugar workers.[55] Some of these rents have funded the active participation of sugar interests in the export-oriented industrialization strategy through the EPZ firms owned by local capitalists. The EPZ also gained from Lomé, since garments made in ACP countries gained duty-free access to European markets, while Asian countries such as Korea and Hong Kong paid duties of some 17 percent. This latter benefit was equally available to other Lomé signatories in Africa, although few of them acted on it.

The Military

This discussion of the initial institutions that structured the choices available to Mauritian actors would be incomplete without mentioning the institution that Mauritius did *not* establish: a standing army. Far from potential enemies, postindependence leaders in Mauritius wisely decided that, like Costa Rica, their democracy would thrive best outside the shadow of the military. Other African island nations in similar positions, such as the Comoros, have made different decisions, while some governments, such as The Gambia's, initially decided against having a standing army, but later (no doubt to their regret) built up their defense forces.[56]

Mauritius established a paramilitary force, the small Special Mobile Force, under the command of the police, to address violent domestic incidents such as riots. Between 1975 and 1979, defense spending in Mauritius amounted to 0.6 percent of total government spending, compared with 5.1 percent in democratic Botswana and over 10 percent in half of the 25 African countries for which data exists.[57] This modest defense spending has had at least two major consequences. First, given the dangers that military intervention has posed for African democracies such as The Gambia, where the government was overthrown in 1994 by the military that it had been building over the past decade, this decision ensured that political conflicts in Mauritius had to be resolved through compromise instead of military force. In addition, low levels of defense spending freed up resources for social spending. In 1992, military expenditure in Mauritius amounted to just 4 percent of combined education and health spending, while in the rest of sub-Saharan Africa, the average was 43 percent (see Table 8.2).[58]

Table 8.2   Military Spending in Africa, 1992 (high and medium human development countries only)

Country	As % of GDP/GNP	Per Capita (1985 U.S.$)	As % of Combined Education & Health Expenditures
Botswana	3.1	48	22
Cameroon	1.6	5	48
Cape Verde	2.0	0.8	n.a.
Congo-Brazaville	3.8	28	37
Gabon	3.7	90	51
Mauritius	**0.4**	**6**	**4**
Namibia	2.9	35	23
Seychelles	4.0	135	n.a.
South Africa	3.0	63	41
Zimbabwe	4.3	20	66
Average for all sub-Saharan African countries	2.8	20	43

Source: United Nations Development Programme, *Human Development Report, 1995* (New York: Oxford University Press, 1995), pp. 182–183.
Note: Absence of data is indicated by "n.a."

In sum, then, the institutions established around the time of independence in Mauritius had important influences on the style and content of the country's governance and economic development. The electoral system, in combination with the particular ethnic balance in Mauritius, ensured that it would be very difficult for any party to win an outright majority of seats. In order to form governments, major parties had to moderate their positions, appeal to more than one ethnic community, and form coalitions with other parties. The early organizational strength of rural labor was reflected in close ties between rural labor and the MLP, and this led to institutional innovations that improved the lot of plantation laborers while making all political parties conscious of the need to maintain trade-friendly economic policies. Passing the Industrial Relations Act after rural laborers were already organized, but before industrial labor had become a major force, meant that the capacity for collective action in industry was weak relative to agriculture; this alleviated the tendencies toward urban bias characteristic of other African countries. The EPZs provided an outlet for domestic capital that created employment and increased family incomes, while also building a new constituency for policies that would support export-oriented manufacturing and trade. The Sugar Protocol of the Lomé Convention and the low level of defense spending enabled the government to pay much of the cost of its social policies. In turn, these social policies gave greater security than was usual in Africa and "bought" the acquiescence of the population in outward-oriented economic policies that entailed greater risks but had greater potential for economic development.

Social Democracy: Politics and Policy

Among developed countries, research has suggested that "better economic performance, less income inequality, and more extensive welfare services are to be found in those developed capitalist countries that combine strong unions with social democratic control of the government."[59] There are very few developing countries that have been both capitalist and social democratic for long enough to develop a track record for analysis, but Mauritius appears to fit this general description: it has strong unions (in the sugar sector), a consistent embrace of social democratic policies, a moderately dirigiste government, and strong economic performance. This combination is counter to much of the neoliberal model that has been prescribed for Africa since the early 1980s, although it does resemble some of the components of East Asian practice.[60]

Economic and Social Policies

In many ways, the initial trajectory of political and economic development in Mauritius did not look unusual in the African context. Mauritius continued to be heavily dependent on a single primary commodity export for many years after independence. The trade regime remained protectionist for local import-substitution industrialists, with extensive controls on capital exports and foreign exchange. Like many other African governments, Mauritius had (and continues to have) parastatals, marketing boards, price controls, and subsidies for the major food staples. However, unlike most other governments, Mauritius never allowed the exchange rate to become grossly overvalued, which would have substantially reduced the domestic value of sugar and manufactured exports.

In addition, the government never established large numbers of state-owned industries, as was common in other African countries; state-owned enterprises made up some 8.7 percent of GDP in the 1970s and 1.8 percent between 1986 and 1991.[61] The promotion of private-sector channels of accumulation meant that the public sector did not become the main channel of accumulation as it did in many African countries. It also appears that the

East Asian–like decision to establish the EPZ and to encourage sugar capital to reinvest in manufactured exports created a balance between constituencies favoring ISI and those in favor of export promotion, whereas the efforts to generate employment while also providing a base of social security enhanced the legitimacy of successive governments.[62] Unlike most countries that have invested heavily in ISI and only belatedly tried to shift toward an outward-oriented strategy, Mauritius had institutions and interests that supported the growth of manufactured exports in place just after independence.

Mauritius resembles the East Asian countries in many of its economic policies; this accounts in part for its successful economic development. However, as an outward-oriented economy vulnerable to changes in the world economy, *and* as a democracy, the government could not ignore the pain incurred by the need to adjust quickly to changes in the world economy to maintain competitiveness. Social policy thus proved to be one of the most important prongs of the country's development model, and the fact that the benefits of this policy were spread widely throughout the society clearly enhanced the legitimacy of successive governments, serving as a "buffer against extremist tendencies," in the words of one Mauritian newspaper editorial.[63]

In many Organization for Economic Cooperation and Development (OECD) countries, social policy has enabled governments to meet the requirements of openness by providing a safety net for those who bear the cost of adjustment. In Mauritius, initial efforts to construct social policies began during the period of self-government before independence. Many of these initial benefits were confined to government workers or to plantation employees, both important MLP constituencies. Education and health spending were higher than average for developing countries: in 1960, the government spent 3 percent of GNP on education (compared with an average of 2.5 percent for all developing countries) and 1.5 percent of GNP on health (compared with 0.9 percent).[64] In 1972, shortly after independence, the government was spending 40 percent of its budget on social services (primary health care, education, water and sanitation, and housing assistance for the poor).[65] These percentages are lower than OECD levels, but higher than East Asian levels, and they appear to be higher than those for other African countries for which data is available.

Aside from the pension schemes and the protective legislation for sugar-sector workers (discussed above), social insurance was also provided through public jobs programs.[66] Public jobs programs may not be the most efficient social insurance scheme, but in a developing-country democracy, such programs have the advantage of creating a highly visible and thus transparent form of insurance that provides valued income while also occupying potentially volatile groups, such as unemployed youth. The *Travail pour Tous* (Work for All) program was providing 19,281 jobs in 1966, two years before independence, and it also proved useful as a form of patronage: a record 32,000 workers were employed in 1967, an election year. The Development Works Corporation (DWC) took over the program in 1971, and the number of jobs provided ranged from 17,000 in 1971, down to 6,000 in 1975. DWC workers received wages that were 20 percent less than the lowest government scale. Together with the other forms of social protection, the DWC provided a safety net for the losers of the economic reforms that were continually necessary in an open economy.

Institutions and Policies in Practice

The distinctiveness of Mauritian politics can be seen in the country's reaction to the economic crisis of the late 1970s and early 1980s, which Mauritius adjusted to much more rapidly than other African countries. The 1976 elections, which narrowly returned a coalition of the MLP and the PMSD to power, were accompanied by increases in social-sector spending, as the MLP-PMSD coalition, which controlled 36 seats in parliament, tried to counter the more radical proposals of the MMM, which held 34 seats. As the budget deficit worsened, and as world recession, higher oil prices, and lower sugar prices took a toll, imports began to outpace exports. Between 1976 and 1979, the current account deficit rose from U.S.$36.3 million to U.S.$148.6 million as the government tried to borrow its way out of the crisis.

Initial efforts to cut government spending led to a spate of illegal strikes, principally among the dockworkers' and sugar workers' unions supported by the MMM. The government reacted by threatening to nationalize stevedoring and import labor to load sugar, neither of which was actually done. When an IMF team visited and appeared reluctant to approve a loan for the government, the media and business interests clamored for action to correct what was in retrospect still a fairly mild disequilibrium. An editorial in the MLP-leaning *Mauritius Times* noted that

> the IMF has been reluctant to lend to any country which is on the brink of precipice and hesitant to take radical action to correct the situation. One of the IMF conditions to lend Rs 730 million is that we must devaluate. Now that it is too late to redress our economy by unpainful measures, Government has no alternative.[67]

Under pressure from the media and from his own party to address the crisis, the MLP prime minister finally joined forces with his finance minister to support a package that included devaluation, price controls, interest rate increases, limits on bank credit, budget deficit reduction, new taxes, a reduction in the rice subsidy, and limits on wage increases.[68]

Although the devaluation and interest rate increase were carried out immediately, most of the rest of the package had to be accomplished through legislation and approval of annual budgets. The resulting political stresses led to changes of government in 1982, and again in 1983, but all three governments were subject to similar constraints. The practices of compromise and consensus building required by the electoral and party system meant that the mix of orthodox and heterodox policies enacted to address the crisis had to spread the costs and benefits of adjustment among various groups. The established institution whereby annual wage adjustments were negotiated through the semicorporatist National Remuneration Board proved useful in limiting annual wage increases to below the level of inflation, and the decision to grant higher-percentage increases to lower-income wage categories helped make this restraint politically palatable to the more numerous low-wage workers.[69]

Devaluing the rupee by about 30 percent in 1979 created immediate gains for the EPZ and sugar exporters, both constituents of the MLP and the PMSD. However, consistent with the pattern of compromise, this windfall gain was offset by a 75 percent surcharge on the sugar export tax, which fell more heavily on the Franco-Mauritian estates due to the progressive nature of the tax. In this way, the bargain allowed the sugar exporters (PMSD supporters) to gain a portion of the windfall, while channeling the rest into maintaining politically important programs such as the (reduced) subsidy on rice and wheat flour.

All parties found it beneficial to support the EPZ. While in opposition in 1980, MMM leader Aneerood Jugnauth agreed that in order to reduce the country's debt, "it has become important for us to export at the maximum," and he said that he would back favorable incentives for EPZ producers. The conservative PMSD also announced that "la Zone Franche" was one of its main priorities.[70] Both of the governments that held office during 1983 supported an "unemployment hardship relief scheme," whereby the Mauritius Development Bank offered loans to unemployed people who wanted to establish small-scale EPZ enterprises. More than 10,000 people were employed in enterprises established through this program, which had a good repayment rate and increased the popularity of the EPZ and the acceptability of trade-oriented policies among ordinary Mauritians.[71] In addition, despite pressure from the World Bank, all three of the 1982–1983 governments were able to resist any substantial trade liberalization during this period, citing concerns about the balance-of-payment pressures that would arise from import liberalization and the likely drop in employment and output from affected ISI firms, which until the mid-1980s still produced a larger share of GDP than did EPZ firms.[72]

Thus, by the mid-1980s, Mauritius looked very different from the rest of Africa. Few African governments had made any sustained effort to adjust by that time, and almost all continued to support ISI to the detriment of exports. In Mauritius, agricultural exporters shared policy interests with EPZ exporters and even with the unions, which, for example, pressured the government to assist the sugar export sector when it ran into financial diffi-culties due to the 75 percent surcharge.[73] This prevented ISI policies (chief among them the overvalued exchange rate) from dominating the policy mix. The social democratic framework ensured that policy formation had to take into account both of the major economic interests, while not placing the entire burden on labor.[74] In addition, because Mauritius had already developed institutions that underpinned a substantial export sector, the "winners" of economic reform were already in place and somewhat orga-nized (plantation owners and workers and EPZ firms and workers) and thus able to offer immediate support for some of the more critical reforms. Throughout, the government was able to maintain a degree of balance in its adjustment, despite pressures from Washington. The finance minister reported to the National Assembly in 1983 that "after arduous negotiations, the IMF and the World Bank have finally accepted our proposal for a more gradual adjustment programme, that makes provision for growth and employment creation."[75]

Conclusion

This chapter has suggested that three initial factors explain a great deal of the ability of Mauritius to combine broad-based economic growth with democratic consolidation: an institutional design that promoted coalition building and compromise; an initial set of economic and social policy choices that created constituencies for broad-based growth; and curbs on the power of landed elites and the military. Although the institutions put in place at the time of independence were established to solve the immediate problem of economic and political instability in an ethnically diverse land, they also created a set of norms, procedures, and constraints that continued to shape political and economic strategies and behavior in the postindepen-dence decades in distinctive ways, making it possible for Mauritius to weather the political and economic storms of the debt crisis, while main-taining the legitimacy of its democratic politics.

What does the case of Mauritius suggest for democratic consolidation and economic development elsewhere in Africa? Some of the early institu-tional decisions made in Mauritius about the role of the military, the Sugar Protocol, and the export processing zone are difficult to replicate else-where, at least with the same degree of success.[76] However, some lessons do have broader application. One is that ethnically diverse societies do not necessarily become more divided in multiparty democracies. A well-crafted political system can ensure broad representation, while providing incen-tives for coalition building, moderation, and compromise.

Another important lesson is that African democracies *can* sustain the kind of difficult economic reforms needed to maintain broad-based growth and that democratic governments may in fact act more quickly than non-democratic governments to adjust to adverse external conditions. Mauritius was one of the earliest African countries to adjust to the economic shocks of the late 1970s. A vigorous media and legislative assembly ensured that political leaders would not be insulated from direct knowledge of the impact their delays were having, as shortages of goods developed, black markets expanded, and exporters received less for their products. The media also served as an effective way for the public to become educated about the costs and benefits of different policy choices. A corollary of this is the finding that democracies can develop effective policies through the legislative process without necessarily depending on a powerful chief executive or insulated "change teams" and autonomous technocracies.

Third, Mauritius succeeded in stabilizing the economy and addressing its growth problems with a mix of orthodox (devaluation, demand reduction, spending cuts) and heterodox (price controls, continued job security for "excess" rural workers, new export taxes, continued import controls) policies. This is not the standard set of remedies, but it does suggest that in order to maintain legitimacy and build coalitions for policy change, policies formulated under democratic conditions may need to contain a mix of heterodox and orthodox elements, as well as sometimes economically irrational side payments that are the incentives necessary to show major actors that they can "process their interests within democratic institutions."[77]

Finally, in Mauritius, the acceptability of temporary economic distress was heightened by the commitment of successive governments to *social* democratic policies, including continued food subsidies on the major imported foods, fertilizer subsidies for small farmers, taxes on the devaluation windfalls enjoyed by reform's "winners," small-enterprise loan programs for the educated unemployed, and continued free primary health care. Although adjustments needed to be made in many of these programs to make them sustainable in view of fiscal limitations, maintaining rather than eliminating them probably helped the government to sustain the legitimacy of the political system in the eyes of the country's citizens. Most countries will not have the advantage of the Sugar Protocol that helped fund these programs, and under the current trade regime, these advantages will also expire for Mauritius in the future. Given their likely importance in maintaining political coalitions that allowed the government to maintain effective economic development policies, the political role of social policies needs additional attention in the African context. As Africa democratizes, African leaders, as well as the IMF and the World Bank (still major actors in African development), will need to become more attuned to the flexible art of crafting policy to meet political as well as economic requirements.

Notes

Many thanks to Steve Arnold, Patrick Barrett, Robert Bates, Larry Bowman, Thomas Callaghy, Michael Carter, Jeffrey Cason, Peter Craig, Anthony Daley, John Echeverri-Gent, Carol Graham, Richard Joseph, Colin Leys, Michael Lofchie, Nicolas van de Walle, and two anonymous reviewers for helpful comments on earlier versions of this chapter. None of them are responsible for any mistakes that may remain.

1. Huntington suggests that "consolidation" be defined as the point when both the first and second parties to lose power through elections have peacefully handed over power to the winners (*Third Wave*, pp. 266–267). See also Linz and Stepan, "Toward Consolidated Democracies," p. 15.

2. Przeworski and Limongi, "Modernization."

3. Ibid., p. 155.

4. Karl, "Dilemmas of Democratization," p. 7; Thelen and Steinmo, "Historical Institutionalism," p. 10. For a good introduction to historical institutionalism, see Steinmo et al., eds., *Structuring Politics*. Haggard and Kaufman raise this issue in *Political Economy*, p. 371: "The links between the initial institutional arrangements agreed at the time of the transition, the policy choices of the new democratic government, and the demand for further institutional change are difficult to trace, but constitute an important avenue for future research."

5. Bratton and van de Walle, "Neopatrimonial Regimes."

6. These elements of democracy are also discussed in Brautigam, "Institutions."

7. Neopatrimonialism in Africa is characterized by "presidentialism." See Bratton and van de Walle, who note that the new constitutions accompanying democratic transitions in Africa have almost always provided for presidential systems (*Democratic Experiments*, chap. 2, p. 2).

8. Haggard and Kaufman, "Economic Adjustment," p. 343.

9. See Bratton and van de Walle, *Democratic Experiments*.

10. Nelson Kasfir, personal communication, March 6–9, 1997.

11. See Bratton and van de Walle, *Democratic Experiments*.

12. Brautigam, "State Capacity."

13. Schattschneider, *Politics, Pressures, and the Tariff*, p. 288.

14. Schmitter and Karl, "What Democracy Is," pp. 86–87; Bresser Pereira et al., *Economic Reforms;* Przeworski, *Democracy and the Market;* and Rock, "Transitional Democracies."

15. Bates et al., "Risk and Trade Regimes." There is, of course, considerable debate about whether freer trade in developing countries promotes growth.

16. See the discussion of India and Costa Rica in Armijo, "Introduction," pp. 25–26; the discussion of Turkey in Waterbury, "Export-Led Growth," p. 141; Graham, *Safety Nets;* and the general discussion in Bresser Pereira et al., *Economic Reforms*, pp. 206 and 213. Note, however, that under democracy, broad-based social spending programs have far more political feasibility than targeted programs. See Gelbach and Pritchett, "More for the Poor."

17. Alesina and Perotti, "Income Distribution."

18. Pastor, "Distributive Effects."

19. See, for example, Rueschemeyer et al., *Capitalist Development;* Karl, "Dilemmas of Democratization"; and Schmitter and Karl, "What Democracy Is."

20. In Venezuela, Japan, Korea, and Taiwan, for example.

21. This historical narrative draws on Bowman, *Mauritius;* Gulhati and Nallari, *Successful Stabilization;* Simmons, *Modern Mauritius;* Wellisz and Saw, "Mauritius"; and World Bank, *Mauritius: Managing Success.*

22. World Bank, *Mauritius: Managing Success,* and pp. 4 and 29–33; Gulhati and Nallari, *Successful Stabilization,* p. 21.

23. World Bank, *World Development Report, 1996,* p. 221.

24. Gulhati and Nallari, *Successful Stabilization,* p. 39.

25. World Bank, *World Development Indicators, 1997,* p. 131; Gini coefficients from Gulhati and Nallari, *Successful Stabilization,* p. 21.

26. Thelen and Steinmo, "Historical Institutionalism," p. 9.

27. Gulhati and Nallari, *Successful Stabilization,* p. 24; Bowman, *Mauritius,* p. 25; and Wellisz and Saw, "Mauritius," p. 223.

28. Sartori, *Comparative Constitutional Engineering.*

29. Cited in ibid., p. 97.

30. Bratton and van de Walle, *Democratic Experiments,* chap. 7, p. 10. The other two are Botswana and Lesotho.

31. This discussion draws on Bowman, *Mauritius,* pp. 31–40, and on Simmons, *Modern Mauritius,* pp. 71–189.

32. Simmons, *Modern Mauritius,* p. 129. The following discussion of the electoral system debate draws on this work by Simmons, pp. 129–143.

33. Best loser seats are not supposed to alter the party balance in the National Assembly.

34. International Parliamentary Union, "Mauritius," p. 1. Although Giovanni Sartori says that "any electoral system in which the voting occurs in two-or-more-member constituencies and produces two-or-more winners elected on a 'highest votes' basis, is a proportional system," he neglects to mention that if voters also have two or more votes, the system becomes in effect majoritarian (*Comparative Constitutional Engineering,* p. 4; see also the discussion on pp. 29–48).

35. Three additional parties were represented in seats appointed under the best loser system. Voters from the island of Rodriguez also elected two representatives.

36. Bowman, *Mauritius,* p. 86.

37. Parties tend to be "loose agglomerations of ethnic and economic interests" (Gulhati and Nallari, *Successful Stabilization,* p. 2).

38. In many ways, Mauritius fits Haggard and Kaufman's hypothesis that consociational and multiparty systems governed by center-left or center-right coalitions are best able to contain the pressures of economic transitions (*Political Economy*).

39. See Bates, *Markets and States.* On the heavier weight for rural districts, see Bowman, *Mauritius,* p. 86.

40. Wellisz and Saw, "Mauritius," pp. 230–231.

41. Bowman, *Mauritius,* p. 127; M. Roberts, *Export Processing Zones,* p. 108.

42. See Mauritius Export Development and Investment Authority, "Fact Sheet No. 4."

43. Wellisz and Saw, "Mauritius," p. 233.

44. Gulhati and Nallari, *Successful Stabilization,* p. 28 n. 11. Only a small percentage of sugar land is owned or controlled by foreign capital (Virashawmy, "State Policies," p. 147).

45. See Lofchie, "New Political Economy," for a discussion of the political implications of varieties of postindependence interest group configurations.

46. Simmons, *Modern Mauritius,* p. 10.

47. World Bank, *Mauritius: Expanding Horizons,* pp. 70 and 132.

48. Virashawmy, "State Policies," p. 156.

49. Bowman, *Mauritius,* p. 129.

50. *Mauritius Times,* "What Price Coalition?"

51. See Rueschemeyer et al., *Capitalist Development.*

52. Gulhati and Nallari, *Successful Stabilization*, p. 35; World Bank, *Mauritius: Managing Success*, p. 64.

53. Bowman, *Mauritius*, p. 111.

54. This section draws on Simmons, *Modern Mauritius*, p. 224 n. 1; World Bank, *Mauritius: Managing Success*, pp. 29–33; Gulhati and Nallari, *Successful Stabilization*, p. 21 n. 8; and United Nations Development Programme and the World Bank, *Mauritius*, pp. 11–22 and 103 n. 48.

55. Figures calculated by author from information in World Bank, *Mauritius: Expanding Horizons*.

56. Defense spending as a percentage of total government spending rose sharply during the 1980s in The Gambia after an attempted coup in 1981 (World Bank, *African Development Indicators*, pp. 205–206).

57. World Bank, ibid., p. 205.

58. United Nations Development Programme, *Human Development Report, 1995*, pp. 182–183.

59. Przeworski, *Democracy and the Market*, p. 131. See also Bruno and Sachs, *Economics;* Lange and Garrett, "Politics of Growth"; and A. Hicks, "Social Democratic Corporatism."

60. For a more extensive treatment of this issue, see Brautigam, "What Can Africa Learn?"

61. Gulhati and Nallari, *Successful Stabilization*, p. 15; World Bank, *World Development Indicators, 1997*, pp. 244–246.

62. Manufactured exports from the EPZs as a percentage of GDP did not overtake the value of other manufacturing in Mauritius until 1986 (World Bank, *Mauritius: Managing Success*, p. 114).

63. *Mauritius Times*, "Social Services."

64. United Nations Development Programme, *Human Development Report, 1995*, pp. 170–171. Unfortunately, there was no breakdown for African countries in this data.

65. Wellisz and Saw, "Mauritius," p. 238. This figure remained at 40.7 percent during the economic crisis of the early 1980s and had risen to 48.6 percent by 1994 (World Bank, *World Development Report, 1996*, pp. 214–215).

66. Information on the public works programs comes from Bowman, *Mauritius*, p. 116; Simmons, *Modern Mauritius*, p. 242 n. 24; Wellisz and Saw, "Mauritius," p. 235; and Gulhati and Nallari, *Successful Stabilization*, p. 21.

67. *Mauritius Times*, "Editorial."

68. *Mauritius Times*, "Black Market."

69. Bowman, *Mauritius*, p. 120.

70. *Mauritius Times*, "Priorités du PMSD" and "L'Île Maurice, Quel Avenir."

71. Bowman, *Mauritius*, p. 128.

72. Gulhati and Nallari, *Successful Stabilization*, pp. 54–55.

73. *Mauritius Times*, "Trade Unions."

74. See Lofchie's illuminating paper, "Cycle of African Governance," for an extensive treatment of this argument.

75. Gulhati and Nallari, *Successful Stabilization*, p. 39.

76. Other African countries can certainly establish an EPZ, and many have. However, there is considerably more competition these days than when Mauritius first caught the crest of the export-led growth wave.

77. Bresser Pereira et al., *Economic Reforms*, p. 5.

PART 3

Political Restructuring and Regime Politics

9

African Polities: The Next Generation

RICHARD L. SKLAR

I think of democracy as an idea about means, not ends. The literal meaning of the Greek word "*democratia*" is "power of the people." Some theorists hold that power is a good thing to have, a desirable end in itself; others believe that power is evil. To my mind, power is neutral between good and evil, a means for the attainment of diverse ends, such as personal freedom, security, happiness, fame, or wealth. Since I do not value popular power as an end in itself, I attach no more than instrumental value to the elementary idea of democracy.

In addition to its foundational meaning, democracy, in its modern form, is widely understood to denote, at the very least, two further conditions of political freedom: (1) governmental protection for the enjoyment and exercise of basic human and political rights and (2) a system of legal limitations to, and restraints on, the exercise of power by governmental authorities or their agents. These requirements signify the complex idea of constitutional, or liberal, democracy, involving the exercise of judicial power by independent courts that are empowered to protect the rights of citizens and restrain the exercise of executive or legislative power when legal limits are exceeded. This is an awesome responsibility, one that is acted upon regularly by judges wherever constitutional democracy prevails, whether or not the power of judicial review is explicitly authorized by the constitution. It is also a prime example of reliance on the principle of oligarchy in modern democracies. The literal meaning and implication of oligarchy, "rule of the few," is diametrically opposed to the classical meaning of democracy. However, judicial review is but one of many oligarchic devices that are routinely incorporated into the structures of modern democratic polities in order to preserve liberty and enhance the overall quality of government.

Scope and Method of Analysis

In comparative political studies, two conceptual issues appear to underlie current debates about the feasibility and consequences of democratic political reforms. The first of these relates to the *scope* of democracy. Is it limited to the institutions of government and those other institutions that affect government directly, particularly political parties and pressure groups? Those who answer this question in the affirmative contend that social justice—a reasonably fair distribution of the means of existence without extremes of poverty and wealth—should not be an issue in the democracy debate. Some of those who hold this view also believe that social justice is a relatively meaningless expression because the only fair judgments of worth and entitlement are those that relate to the conduct of individuals, not groups. Others say, simply, that the variable human condition is not a defining attribute of democracy.

From the standpoint of thinkers who delimit the scope of democracy in this relatively narrow manner, a government controlled by a minority of citizens who are highly educated, or by a pious minority in a confessional polity, can still be democratic despite the privileged position of the minority in question. For example, in African studies, Botswana, a genuinely liberal polity, is often cited as one of the very few examples of genuine democracy in Africa, despite the evidence of political domination by "an educated mandarin class" of elite and prosperous civil servants who have co-opted the traditional authorities of Tswana society and rule in conjunction with the leaders of a dominant political party, while the influence of organized labor is held to a minimum.[1] Similarly, Senegal since 1981, Côte d'Ivoire since 1990, Zambia since 1991, and Malawi since 1994 have been cited regularly as democratic polities without regard to the obvious political dominance of their economic elites.

One point of departure for challenges to this restrictive conception of democracy is the observation that democracy, as a political idea, is about power. The scope of politics and power extends to every societal institution. Hence the existence of oligarchy in any institution is a politically relevant fact, one that bears directly on a society's degree of democracy. That, in brief, is my own viewpoint.

The second basic issue for the study of democratization relates to the matter of *method*, specifically, the widely adopted method of classification. For comparative purposes, it is tempting to classify the political systems of nations into those that qualify as democracies, or for inclusion in one of the various stages of semidemocracy, and those that fall beneath a minimum qualifying standard. Such classifications do not have much, if any, analytical value since all political systems are evidently mixtures of democracy and oligarchy. If my conception of a broad and socially comprehensive scope of analysis is also adopted, the futility of this kind of classification becomes all the more apparent. For example, how can it be alleged that a political system is unambiguously democratic if a wealthy minority enjoys a great political advantage?

In my opinion, the commonplace notion of "transition to democracy" is plainly unscientific. No one has proposed a socially comprehensive scheme of analysis to monitor the course of democratic transitions. Nor have analysts who adopt this approach undertaken to assess the degree of systemic reliance on oligarchic, rather than democratic, practices in particular cases. In African studies, the acceptance of a socially comprehensive scope of political analysis would upset most, if not all, systems of classification. Inevitably, the placement of African countries on a continuum ranging from more to less democratic would be criticized widely for its arbitrariness.

For instance, Botswana, Mauritius, and The Gambia set the standard for liberal democracies in Africa from the mid-1960s until many other countries embraced that form of government in the 1990s. Were those countries really more democratic than semiauthoritarian Tanzania under Julius Nyerere? Everything depends on the criteria; and social democrats continue to respect the humane ideals and practices of Tanzania's experiment with communitarian socialism.[2] Again, shall we believe that either Frederick Chiluba's multiparty Zambia or Robert Mugabe's Zimbabwe is more democratic than Yoweri Museveni's Uganda, which held technically nonpartisan elections for a constituent assembly in 1994, and for president in 1996, and proposes to hold a referendum on the question of no-party elections in the year 2000? A few realistic theories of transition evade this issue by relying heavily on the relatively unambiguous criterion of continuous electoral democracy (free and fair elections at regular intervals with freedom for parties to compete) for reasonably long periods of time. Attempts to broaden the scope of analysis beyond this criterion introduce elements of oligarchy that complicate presumed transitions to democracy until they appear to be dubious.

In South Africa, the celebrated transition from racial oligarchy to constitutional democracy, completed in 1994, involved the creation of a Constitutional Court, consisting of 11 members appointed by the president in consultation with either the cabinet or the judicial service committee. This court is empowered to rule on all matters relating to constitutional interpretation, whether or not they arise from appeals of judgments by other courts, including decisions of the republic's Constitutional Assembly. In 1996, the court ruled that a new constitution, approved by the assembly, failed to satisfy several principles of government that had been established during the course of political bargaining prior to the transition. The assembly was instructed to reconvene and revise the sections concerned, which involved minority and sectional interests, as well as individual rights and protection for the rights of employers vis-à-vis trade unions. South Africa's political democracy is evidently tempered by the restraining authority of its highly principled judicial oligarchy.

In all African countries, traditional hierarchies coexist with the authorities of sovereign states and their subdivisions. In some countries, traditional rulers have been incorporated into the constitutional system of the nation. The establishment of advisory councils of "traditional leaders" at the level of national government, as in Namibia and South Africa, or consultative councils of traditional authorities at provincial or state levels (e.g., South Africa and Nigeria, respectively) is a common practice. In the constitutional monarchy of Lesotho, paramount chiefs, or their designated representatives, occupy two-thirds of the seats in the Senate, an inferior legislative chamber empowered to delay the enactment of bills passed by the National Assembly. In Malawi, chiefs, elected by their peers in local government districts, constitute 30 percent of the Senate.

In South Africa, the 1996 constitution contemplates legislation to provide for a national council of traditional leaders and for both national and provincial houses of traditional leaders. However, these provisions are less generous to traditional authorities than the interim constitution of 1993 had become by the time of President Nelson Mandela's inauguration in 1994. In order to avert a threatened boycott of the country's first nonracial election by the Zulu-based Inkatha Freedom Party, the interim constitution was amended to acknowledge the authority of the "Zulu Monarch" in the province of KwaZulu-Natal. Barring a judicial decision to the contrary, that province will once again create a constitutional monarchy within the framework of a republic. Although "republican monarchy"[3] is a constitutional oxymoron, its use corresponds to a political reality in Africa, one that has been characterized by the present writer as "mixed government."[4]

In the history of political thought, mixed government implies cooperative interaction among distinct and relatively autonomous governmental institutions, each rooted securely in an "estate of the realm" and in functional interest groups associated with that estate. However, this concept had not, in the past, been used to describe the form of government that is emerging in Africa as a result of the coexistence of sovereign and traditional authorities. In Africa, one finds a Janus-like relationship of back-to-back dimensions of authority. The two dimensions are not symmetrical, since all but a few African countries consist of several, or many, separate and distinct traditional polities. In every African country, an overwhelming majority of citizens have dual political identities, but in no case does the second dimension vie with the sovereign dimension for sovereignty. Yet, as a separate source of authority, embedded in tradition, it does help to maintain social stability during the current era of turbulent changes. While the heavens may, and sometimes do, fall on the sovereign states, their hard-pressed citizens derive comfort and reassurance from their inclusion within durable traditional orders.

In most African countries, traditional authorities are restricted to advisory and ceremonial, rather than decisional, roles in the organs of the national government and its subdivisions. Thus, in Nigeria, where literally hundreds of traditional officeholders have been recognized administratively in accordance with the provisions of statutory laws, recent constitutions have withheld from traditional rulers and their councils the right to exercise executive, legislative, or judicial power. In 1996, the Nigerian military government suddenly deposed the sultan of Sokoto, a traditional ruler of immense prestige among Nigeria's largest (Hausa-speaking) linguistic group, in favor of an evidently more popular, and less threatening, rival. In Nigeria, as in nearly all African countries, the powers of the national government vis-à-vis traditional rulers are similar to those of their colonial predecessors. Formal traditional authority is exercised by leave of the sovereign, who may even choose not to recognize it at all, as in the case of Tanzania. However, traditional authorities do not exist as a consequence of their recognition and appointment by the governments of sovereign states. On the contrary, they are recognized and appointed to traditional offices, in accordance with customary rules, because those offices are legitimated by the beliefs of the people, who expect them to exist in practice.

The role of an African traditional ruler in a constitutional democracy was discussed with remarkable clarity by His Majesty, Muteba II, Kabaka of Buganda, Uganda, in a 1996 address delivered at Princeton University.[5] Three years earlier, the government of the Republic of Uganda had restored traditional monarchies, 25 years after they had been formally abolished. The incumbent Kabaka, who does not exercise power under the constitution, envisages the traditional ruler as "part of an effective civil society which countervails and enriches the State." He continued, "If the traditional leader is largely dependent on the State for his survival, he will find it hard to take a neutral position when the State is prompting him to side with it even when he is convinced that the State is wrong." This statement affirms the principle of dual authority in Uganda without derogating the republic's exclusive sovereign authority. It also illuminates the principle of sanctioned oligarchy in Africa's distinctive form of mixed government. That complex system of political authority eludes classification according to schemes that divide countries among the categories of democracy, semidemocracy, and nondemocracy.

On this issue, how might such methods of classification fare if the most obvious of all oligarchic institutions—the use of a foreign language as the official national language—is taken into account? In several countries, official status has been accorded to African languages as well. Yet in all but a few instances, apart from the northern tier of Arabic-speaking countries, the paramount language of government, legal affairs, higher education, and national commerce is a European language—English, French, Portuguese, or Spanish. All of these countries are controlled by linguistic oligarchies that are fluent in the predominant foreign language. But there are side effects of linguistic oligarchy that tend to enhance democratic tendencies in African countries. For one thing, its existence diminishes the degree, or threat, of sectional domination in multilingual countries by unifying their elites on the basis of a common language. For another, it helps to perpetuate the intellectual tradition of constitutional liberalism, which is inseparable from its historical and linguistic origins.

Forms of Government

In Africa, as elsewhere, movements for constitutional democracy have been motivated by yearnings for freedom, during both the colonial era and the relatively brief, but traumatic, era of widespread postcolonial dictatorship.[6] Despite the manifest dedication to political liberty by leaders of opinion in numerous countries, it would be folly to presume that people in general will be disposed to appraise the performance of constitutional forms of government more leniently than they have judged the dictatorships that were displaced. The basis for popular judgment will continue to be a government's demonstrated ability, or inability, to cope with the major problems of society, prominently among them the torments of mass poverty, famine, pestilence, crime, and unemployment. At present, the prime tasks of statecraft, with reference to which governments in Africa will be judged, include both national integration and socioeconomic development.

For decades, dictatorial forms of political organization were justified by their supporters on the grounds that they would accelerate the suppression of ethnic political identities by state-centered national identities. But the residue of evidence supporting that proposition is meager and unpersuasive; during the late 1980s and early 1990s, it crumbled before growing demands for constitutional and democratic freedoms, including the right to organize political parties and other associational interest groups. Several countries have recently completed a second round of electoral competition at the level of national government in a manner adjudged by objective monitors to have been reasonably free and fair. However, the political outcome of democratic elections, based on the pure principle of common citizenship, is troubling. Many thinkers doubt that free elections ameliorate the problem of ethnosectional separatism, which continues to threaten the political stability of multiethnic constitutional democracies. The persistence of ethnosectional divisiveness undermines the national character of governments that have been elected competitively in various countries, prominently among them Kenya, Malawi, Tanzania, and Zambia in eastern Africa;

Angola, Mozambique, Namibia, South Africa, and Zimbabwe in southern Africa; and Benin, Chad, Guinea, Mali, and Senegal in western Africa.[7]

Among current attempts to cope with ethnosectional threats to electoral democracy, two experimental forms of government and one proposal for constitutional change command attention. In Uganda, political parties are not actually illegal, but they are not permitted to participate in electoral campaigns or to raise money for electoral purposes. In Ethiopia, the country is ruled by the leaders of the Democratic Front, which consists of regionalized political parties and is itself effectively controlled by the leaders of one, militarily triumphant region, namely, Tigray. Opposition parties have been marginalized and subjected to routine harassment by the government since their boycott of a parliamentary election in 1995. Despite their diametrically opposite legal postures—unitary government in Uganda, and polyethnic federalism in Ethiopia, whereby each of the 10 regions has the theoretical right to secede—these two countries are governed similarly by their dominant political organizations.

A third attempt to cope with the problem of ethnosectional divisiveness involves Nigeria, a federal republic of 36 states that has been ruled by a military junta since 1984. In 1995, the junta accepted the recommendation of a constitutional conference to introduce "rotational power sharing." This means that each of six top offices, including especially the office of president, shall be rotated among six multistate electoral regions every five years. If this system is put into effect, the political parties that compete in elections will be required to choose their candidates from designated regions according to the rule of rotation. Similar procedures are contemplated for elections at the state level. Although this idea appears to enjoy widespread support in most parts of the country, its flaws from a democratic standpoint are plain enough: it severely restricts the right of voters to choose among candidates for public office; it also appears to reserve the highest offices for members of the largest ethnic group in each of the six electoral regions.

Critics of these attempts to cope with the problem of ethnosectionalism by curtailing freedom for political parties contend that they do not improve upon, but demonstrably debase, regular democratic practices, which involve the formation of parties before an election, followed by coalition building, if need be, to form a government once the election has been held. In this area of political experimentation, no invention of comparable value to that of the South African Constitutional Court has emerged. With regard to federalism, however, the framers of Nigeria's ill-starred constitution of 1989, designed for a prospective Third Republic under civilian rule, proposed the creation of a third tier of government at the local council level that could not be abolished by the states. Stifled by the prolongation of military rule in Nigeria, this idea migrated to South Africa, surfacing there in the form of a three-tier (national-provincial-local) de facto federation, since the African National Congress (ANC) has thus far refused to acknowledge federalism as a legal principle of South African government. Yet the South African example of federalism-in-substance without formal-legal recognition could prove to be influential in several other countries that seek solutions to similar problems of ethnosectional separatism.

Turning to the challenge of socioeconomic development, few countries in Africa cling to the bygone and discredited theories of "developmental dictatorship" or "bureaucratic authoritarianism."[8] Only Libya and Sudan still reject constitutional democracy in principle. Reflection on the wholesale abandonment of authoritarian precepts of government in recent years might heighten the sensitivity of observers to impending, albeit unanticipated, shifts in the overall direction of political change in Africa. Thus a general renewal of the parliamentary form of constitutional government may be in the offing as a reaction to many disagreeable experiences with presidential dictatorship.[9] In this regard, the unmistakable triumph of parliamentary government in South Africa has been obscured by the personal authority of President Mandela. Yet the president is elected by the parliament, which can also vote no-confidence in the chief executive, in which case the incumbent must resign. This form of government may well reflect a deep belief in parliamentary government by leaders of the ANC, an example that might be emulated in other countries with semipresidential political systems.

The invariable consequence of parliamentary government is a pronounced tendency toward party rule, and party-based oligarchy, contrary to the functional specialization of parties as electoral machines in constitutional governments based on the separation of powers. In this, as in other matters of political analysis, scholars have an obligation to assess objectively the strengths, as well as the weaknesses, of both democratic and oligarchic practices.

Another significant manifestation of oligarchy would be the widespread adoption of corporatist forms of political organization. Historically, these involve the transformation of an occupational, or socioeconomic, status into a political status that entails the exercise of a governmental function. This tendency in Africa has been analyzed discerningly by scholars who are, in the main, inclined to doubt its practicability as a major form of government for African states.[10] Corporatism should be differentiated clearly from the far more pervasive practice of market control by large business corporations. Although the latter tendency is virtually universal, there is considerable variation in the degree to which corporate and noncorporate proprietary forms of enterprise are complemented by public and other types of collective ownership. The number of African governments still seeking to impose economic controls that minimize the autonomy of business managers has dwindled to fewer than a handful. Increasingly, liberal forms of democratic government flourish in combination with pronounced inequalities of income and wealth.

The political economy of South Africa exemplifies the strength of corporate liberalism, as opposed to corporatism, in Africa today.[11] With the blessing of government, prominent members of the ANC have entered the ranks of corporate management, aiming to acquire a foothold for Africans in that crucial sector of the economy. Several of the largest South African corporations are actively facilitating the growth of African ownership and management, while trade unions have agreed to participate in the ownership of companies and thereby acquire a stake in their profitability. A pioneering venture has been launched under the leadership of Cyril Ramaphosa, secretary-general of the ANC and chair of the Constitutional Assembly, which completed its two-year task in 1996. Once a militant trade unionist (he had been general secretary of the National Union of Mineworkers) and unequivocal socialist, Ramaphosa announced his timely switch from the "business of politics" to the "politics of business." His conception of partnership between private investment companies and trade unions has been designated "corporate unionism."[12] It signifies self-motivated collaboration between labor organizations and business management, two of the great "developmental estates"[13] of the economic realm in the new political economy of corporate liberalism.

Auxiliary Supports

For the multitude of sovereign states in Africa—53 in all—this is an era of experimental government. Most of these countries have adopted the method of trial, error, and correction to test and improve their new political mechanisms. From time to time during the postcolonial era, leadership in the process of political invention has shifted from one country or region to another. Thus Tanzania's three-decade experiment with one-party communitarian democracy has bequeathed a legacy of valuable experience and thought that was respected widely in its time and will be revisited often in the future as a source of lessons that are not taught as clearly by other comparable experiences. For several years, from 1976 to 1979, intellectual leadership in the pursuit of constitutional government was resplendent in Nigeria's transition to its ill-fated Second Republic. Subsequently, in 1990, Benin inaugurated an extraordinary democratic movement involving the formation of sovereign national conferences in francophone Africa.[14] This authentic African contribution to the theory and practice of democracy continues to inspire political reformers throughout the continent. In 1994, the baton for political invention was passed to South Africa, where it is being carried with extraordinary verve, as the present account indicates. For the time being, South Africa's vision of the next generation of polities is obviously more vivid than other such visions in Africa.

Regardless of their intrinsic qualities, or records of early success, experimental governments are relatively fragile and likely to be upset in heavy political weather. They require an auxiliary architecture to bolster their stability in the short run and for an indefinite future. Traditional authorities can function in this capacity whether or not their offices have been incorporated within the constitutional system of a sovereign government. During the final year of Nigeria's doomed Second Republic, Ladipo Adamolekun, an academic authority on public administration and adviser to the federal government, proposed the creation of a "national consensus assembly," consisting of representatives of "strategic elite groups" and mandated to produce "guidelines for consensus politics." These guidelines would be submitted to an official (constitutional) advisory body for its endorsement and reconsidered by the consensus assembly at five-year intervals.[15] Although this idea was not adopted in Nigeria, it is widely known and might be retrieved there or elsewhere as a potentially effective type of auxiliary support for governments.

However odious it may be, a dictatorial military establishment that clings to power might still be harnessed by reformers to perform a supportive role in the restoration of constitutional government. The Chilean example of 1990, whereby the military was insulated from political control on condition of its reciprocal nonintervention in governmental matters, might be especially relevant to Nigeria's future escape from military rule. Credibly reassured that its internal authority would not be compromised by elected officeholders, the Nigerian military might agree to become part of the auxiliary architecture of a fledgling constitutional democracy, as in the case of Chile.

Perhaps the most dramatic contemporary example of auxiliary support for a newly erected constitutional structure is the Truth and Reconciliation Commission, established in South Africa to reexamine the record of persecution and suffering during the apartheid era. At the commission's inaugural public session in April 1996, its chairman, Archbishop Desmond Tutu, declared that the public disclosure of truths "about our dark past" would help "to lay the ghosts of that past so they will not return to haunt us" and would also "contribute to the healing of a traumatized and wounded people."[16] The commission, which is expected to sit for about two years, does not have criminal jurisdiction. It operates through committees that hold public hearings on alleged abuses, reach conclusions on culpability and intent, grant amnesties in return for full disclosures by individuals, and award compensatory benefits to victims. There is a generic similarity between this confessional procedure and the episodes of public repentance by officials who participated in the sovereign national conferences of the francophone African countries.

Like the forms of government themselves, auxiliary structures, designed to fortify a constitutional order, combine democratic and oligarchic elements of power. Constitutional purists may regret the construction of rude ramparts that deviate from the contours of either democratic or liberal forms of government: for example, an arrangement that would compromise civilian control of the military, or one that might enhance the authority of traditional rulers or provide for the formulation of public policies by the assembled elites of interest groups.

Barricades always impair the beauty of a landscape for the sake of its protection. The constitutional integrity of a liberal-democratic political landscape almost certainly will be marred by the erection of protective barriers against disruptive assaults. However, experimental governments cannot be expected to survive without them. Their construction poses a distinct challenge, one that may not have been perceived as such heretofore, to the architects and students of government in Africa.

Mixed Polities

The sovereign states of Africa exist within boundaries that were delimited by colonial overlords. With relatively few exceptions, the citizens of contemporary African states have dual political identities. They recognize two, coexisting sources of legitimate political authority: the legally sovereign states and traditional orders of both colonial and precolonial origin.[17] These colonial and territorial legacies have been reckoned widely as burdens of African history. Pan-Africanists lament the persistence of colonial-era divisions, while contemporary proponents of a "second liberation" counsel the reconstruction of African governments on political foundations that incorporate indigenous institutions.[18]

The evidence adduced in this analysis indicates a growing propensity in African statecraft to use the troubling legacies of multiple sovereignty and dual political identity for constructive purposes. The existence of a multiplicity of states is conducive to political experimentation, including innovations influenced by custom, while dual authority is compatible with the idea, and practice, of constitutional government. To be sure, the connotations of dual authority in Africa are frequently (but not always) undemocratic because they imply deference by citizens to traditional hierarchies. However, democracies have never been viable without substantial admixtures of oligarchy, which functions to mitigate the less desirable effects of popular power.

Since ancient times, political thinkers have admired Aristotle's idea of a mixed polity, one that combines the elements of democracy and oligarchy in due proportion, depending on a given country's history and circumstance. According to Maxwell Owusu, the principle of mixed government is basic to constitutional thought in postcolonial Ghana. "Chieftaincy," he declares, "is a necessary component of the Ghanaian ideal of a mixed government."[19] Surely, this proposition can be generalized to the practice of statecraft throughout Africa. If, as I suggest, the vast majority of citizens have dual political identities, and if, as I contend, those sentiments are complementary rather than antithetical, then it would be reasonable to conclude that the importance of mixed government in Africa has been seriously underestimated by political scientists.

Other forms and sources of oligarchy also countervail the all-but-irrepressible democratic tendencies of modern times, for both good and ill, as perceptions may vary. Among the mainsprings of oligarchy in modern societies, these practices are familiar: judicial review; the centralization of authority within political parties in parliamentary systems of government; regulation of a nation's money supply by its central bankers; and managerial autonomy for the executives of business corporations. Still another, ineluctable trend toward oligarchy in Africa is the growth of linguistic elitism based on command of an official foreign language.[20] So long as population growth outpaces the provision of adequate instruction at intermediate levels of education, linguistic oligarchy will be manifest at every level of government in the African polities.

Oligarchy, no less than democracy, is a condition of good government and social progress. Recognition of that reality would facilitate effective political communication among citizens of different countries. The conception of a mixed polity, with its oligarchic features, could prove to be an antidote to cultural conceit in the form of one-dimensional images of successful political systems that are frequently recommended for export to countries with unstable governments. It also draws attention to palpable instances of oligarchy in the political systems of stable societies. This idea, derived from ancient political wisdom, fosters cross-cultural respect, rather than condescension, on the part of those who presume to mentor others in the arts of government. Collectively, the experimental African polities might teach as much as they learn through participation in the worldwide exchange of political knowledge.

Notes

An earlier and briefer version of this chapter appeared in *Africa Demos* 3, no. 4 (March 1995): 26–28.

    1. Holm, "Development, Democracy, and Civil Society."
    2. McHenry, *Limited Choices.*
    3. This valuable term was introduced into academic discourse by Takaya, "'Republican Monarchies'?"
    4. R. Sklar, "African Frontier."
    5. "Traditional Leaders and Democracy," *West Africa,* April 15–21, 1996, pp.

557–558. Excerpts from an address delivered by His Majesty, Muteba II, Kabaka of Buganda, Uganda, at Princeton University, New Jersey, on February 5, 1996.

6. Ayittey, *Africa Betrayed.*

7. This enumeration is up-to-date, based on journalistic reports and personal observations. Recent reports in scholarly works that confirm these findings include Kaspin, "Politics of Ethnicity," and Courade and Sindjoun, "Le Cameroun."

8. For a succinct account of the origins of these, and related, concepts, see Perlmutter, *Modern Authoritarianism.*

9. Tordoff, *Government and Politics,* pp. 4–5.

10. Nyang'oro and Shaw, eds., *Corporatism in Africa;* Robinson, "Niger"; and Rothchild, "Structuring State-Society Relations," pp. 221–223.

11. On the origin and evolution of anti-statist "corporate liberalism" in the United States, see M. Sklar, *Corporate Reconstruction* and *United States as a Developing Country.* In the United States, this form of political economy has precluded the creation of corporatist forms of government, which have been associated with dictatorship and traditional oligarchy in Europe, Latin America, and Japan.

12. *Africa Confidential,* vol. 37, no. 9 (April 26, 1996): 4.

13. R. Sklar, "Towards a Theory," pp. 35–39.

14. Heilbrunn, "Social Origins."

15. Adamolekun, *Fall of the Second Republic,* pp. 53–60.

16. *Africa Research Bulletin* (Political, Social, and Cultural Series), vol. 33, no. 4 (May 23, 1996): 12241.

17. The classic study of political dualism in Africa, based on northern Nigeria, is C. S. Whitaker, *Politics of Tradition.*

18. Ayittey, *Africa Betrayed,* pp. 325–334.

19. Owusu, "Chieftaincy and Constitutionalism," p. 36.

20. I am indebted to Dr. Yonusu Rabanza for his elucidation of this idea in a paper on the three-tier hierarchy of languages in Tanzania's system of education, presented at the James S. Coleman African Studies Center, University of California, Los Angeles, December 3, 1996.

10

Governance and the Reconstitution of Political Order

GORAN HYDEN

The political upheavals in Eastern Europe in 1989 that eventually led to the collapse of communism as a global system of power have changed the study not only of international relations, but also of comparative politics. These revolutions are remarkable because they were based on civil disobedience directed against regimes that suffered a serious moral deficit because of decades of adherence to the Marxist notion that there is no morality other than that determined by the existing relations of production. By treating the idea of morality as an independent sphere merely as an expression of bourgeois thinking, communist governments throughout Eastern Europe and the Soviet Union had put a lid on such issues as freedom and justice. A sense of ideological emptiness in combination with access to the legal and constitutional tradition of neighboring Western Europe fueled the emergence of, initially, informal groups of activists working underground and, subsequently, social movements that led to the downfall of the communist regimes.

The demand for reconstituting the political order in accordance with the principles of freedom and justice has since spread to other parts of the world where conditions of authoritarian rule have persisted. In many African countries, similar scenarios were enacted. Activists who had been detained in the past for their opposition to government gained more freedom to speak out. As political groups began to articulate their displeasure with dictatorial methods of rule, they quickly received popular support. African governments capitulated to these popular demands for constitutional reform or did so in response to conditionalities placed upon them by powerful foreign donor governments.

With some years of experience, it is evident that reconstituting the political order in Africa needs to be better understood in its own right. As part of a global reform effort, how does it compare with what is going on elsewhere? What challenges in Africa give the task of reconstituting the political order special significance? This chapter tries to address these questions.

In addition, it also deals with the question of how comparativists might wish to approach this form of "new" politics, which does not easily fit into the categories and concepts applied to the study of political economy. Because we are dealing with politics specifically at the level of the regime, rather than the state, it makes sense to identify a set of concepts that facilitate the analytical distinction between these two levels. Here, I propose "governance" as a concept that can help catalyze the evolution of a sharper focus on the specific issues associated with reconstituting (or constituting) the political order.

This chapter is organized into three sections. The first deals with why policy practitioners and academics focusing on Africa ought to have a stronger focus on governance. The second refines the definition of governance and related concepts. The third examines the challenges to reconstituting the political order in Africa; it also asks what these challenges mean for the research agenda within the emerging field of governance.

The Emergence of a Governance Field

It may seem pretentious to refer to the existence of a field of study called "governance," when there is no consensus about its meaning. It is possible, however, to talk of the emergence of such a field given recent developments in both policy practice and the study of African politics.

The connection between governance and development is relatively recent. It has taken analysts quite some time to accept that development involves more than choice of technique or even policy and is explicitly political. Development became an internationally recognized concept in the 1950s when economic analysts, spurred by the success of Keynesian interventions in the economies of postwar Western Europe—the Marshall Plan being the single most important such measure—began generating a new field within their discipline called "development economics." In the perspective of these economists, development in the emerging states of Africa—as in other parts of what subsequently became known as the "third world"—would be best achieved through transfer of capital and expertise. This philosophy prevailed in the last days of colonial rule and the early years of independence in Africa. Because analysts perceived development as largely a replication of Western experience in compressed time, they treated it as relatively easy and noncontroversial. They were confident that it could be done without changing existing political contexts, hence their inclination to treat development in technocratic terms. For these analysts, the greatest challenge was to design projects in a professional manner, on the assumption that good design was the key to successful implementation. Throughout much of the 1960s, development analysts were ready to treat *projects* as the most important intervention and the most significant level of analysis.

Toward the end of that decade, it became increasingly clear that a narrow focus on projects was rarely good policy. Projects proved to have as many unanticipated as anticipated consequences. The gap between promise and practice could not be bridged by projects alone. Rather, projects had to be seen as part of a more concerted sectoral thrust. A growing number of analysts, therefore, began arguing for a *program* focus. This new orientation translated into integrated development programs, which typically involved devolving authority to field-level administrators to get more action on the ground. Such programs became very popular in Africa in the early 1970s. For example, they were introduced in Ethiopia, Tanzania, and Zambia as part of enhanced rural development strategies. Although this period was characterized by a definite measure of decentralization, government was still expected to play the lead role in development. The challenge to analysts was to make governments work more effectively.

By the end of the 1970s, however, the inability of African governments to realize their development objectives had become painfully evident. Inefficient resource use meant that African states were increasingly living beyond their means. Projects and programs that had been started after independence could not be sustained. This became particularly apparent when energy costs rose in the late 1970s. The "oil shock" in 1979 hit Africa's low-income countries particularly hard. It became necessary, therefore, to return to the drawing board. The challenge was no longer how to manage or administer development, but to discover the incentives needed to facilitate it. Attention shifted to what specific policy conditions could be instrumental in bringing about economic renewal and development. The strategic focus followed, emphasizing *policy*. The World Bank, mandated by its governors, took the lead on this issue and produced a major policy document—the Berg Report (named for its principal author, American economist Elliot Berg)[1]—which was to serve as a guide for the economic reform programs attempted in Africa during the 1980s. Considerable structural adjustment, particularly in the public sector, became necessary in almost all sub-Saharan African countries in order to free resources that could be better utilized by other actors. In combination with the financial stabilization programs drawn up by the International Monetary Fund (IMF), these efforts at reducing embarrassingly high levels of inefficiency became the dominant policy prescriptions for development in the 1980s and into the 1990s.

Throughout the 1990s, it has been increasingly realized that development is not only about projects, programs, and policies, but also about *politics*. For a long time, as suggested above, development and politics were conceived as separate spheres. Although there are still some international organizations that maintain this separation, analysts have increasingly come to accept that politics conditions development. Politics is not only part of the solution, but is itself a problem that needs to be addressed. It is not surprising, therefore, that the 1990s has been characterized by widespread demands for political reform, notably, the introduction of multiparty politics, more respect for human rights, and greater public accountability and transparency in government transactions. Those taking this position assume that these measures will promote faster development. Representatives of the international development community are increasingly demanding that countries reconstitute their political order as a prerequisite for receiving foreign assistance. The quality of political conduct counts as an intermediary variable in the allocation of resources at the global level. Western donors are ready to give quite generously for civic purposes. For example, in the 1996 Ghanaian general elections, the donor community spent approximately $2.50 per voter. This compares, for example, with the $5.00 per capita that is currently being spent on public health in sub-Saharan Africa.

On the academic side, two developments have spurred the shift in interest to governance and regime issues. The first is the limitation inherent in the state focus that emerged in comparative politics in the 1980s.[2] This literature alerted us to such issues as why state capabilities are limited and why people often find ways around state-initiated legislation, but it also had the tendency to juxtapose state and society in ways that implied that all shortcomings were associated with the state, not society. Michael Lofchie noted in 1989 that real authority is not necessarily vested somewhere within the formal-legal institutions of the state.[3] He argued for the need to suspend judgment of the exact relationship between political authority and formal institutions in society. This is especially important in the study of African countries, where informal or unofficial relations often influence political outcomes. Rules that govern political behavior in Africa tend to be unwritten and may overshadow those enshrined in laws and even in the constitution. This has been identified by many scholars as one of the key characteristics of "prebendal" or "neopatrimonialist" politics in Africa.[4] Rules as a subject, then, are problematic in the African context. This emerges very clearly from previous studies of state-society relations.

The issue of rules has also taken on greater significance for those scholars who utilize a rational choice approach. Conventionally, rational choice takes as given the premise that all individuals act in their own self-interest. In this "thin" version of rational choice, there is no room for variables such as rules and institutions with a different moral basis. The guiding question is how rational choice theory may explain a particular phenomenon, rather than the more open-ended question of what explains that phenomenon. This theory-saving impulse has not been common among

Africanists. Instead, the dominant tendency has been to show Africa as exceptional. It is increasingly accepted these days that the more fruitful approach lies somewhere between these two extremes. Strategic calculation is important, but so are a host of other variables ranging from traditions of behavior, norms, and culture, to differences in people's capacities, to the contingencies of historical circumstance. We cannot ignore the possibility that human choice matters, but we also cannot run away from the complexity of the empirical realm. We must be able to theorize in empirically pertinent ways.

Trying to study politics at the regime level poses new challenges that comparativists are still only beginning to appreciate. Since 1990, when democratization began to interest comparativists at large, they have tended to focus on two issues. The first is the study of elections on the premise that they are the initial steps toward democracy. Elections have become the means by which regime transitions are assessed.[5] Following in the footsteps of Joseph Schumpeter,[6] many scholars belonging to this genre operate with a minimalist definition of democracy, in that it stresses the importance only of the institutional mechanisms for acquiring power in a democratic manner. It lacks recognition of such other important principles as the accountability of rulers and of other institutions that are critical to sustaining a democratic system.[7] This criticism of "electoralism" notwithstanding, it is an important line of study that can be further enriched with the help of African data.

The second is the interest that comparativists show in the economic basis of democracy. This follows two separate, but not wholly unrelated, courses. One addresses the classical question of the relationship between capitalism and democracy. This takes on a special significance in the African context, where structural adjustment and democratization are being pursued in tandem.[8] Another focuses on the role that globalization plays in fostering or hindering the political reform process in Africa. For instance, van de Walle concludes his study of this set of issues with the observation that international market forces pose less of a threat to African democracy than a progressive delinkage from the world economy.[9] This is also an empirically pertinent area of study and deserves continued attention by comparativists.

I propose here a third area of study that is both empirically pertinent and methodologically challenging: the politics that surrounds the reconstitution of the political order in Africa. This is a new type of politics that is driven by both domestic and foreign forces. This set of issues transcends the more narrow conception of "regime transition," or the even more specific process of democratization. The latter two concepts imply a linear process, in which countries are measured against a set of purportedly universal principles. From such a perspective, it is easy to underestimate the complexity of regime change and the fact that the politics surrounding the rules of the political game is an ongoing phenomenon. By recognizing this, we are also laying the foundation for a field in which the politics of setting the rules and getting people to abide by them becomes a legitimate and sustained focus among comparativists. The empirical relevance of this kind of research should not be questioned in light of what has been happening both in Africa south of the Sahara and in other regions of the world. A relevant case is Albania, where, in early 1997, the effort to create a new political order on the ruins of the old communist one collapsed, and the country fell into anarchy. Several African cases manifest the same symptoms. For these reasons, attention to governance is warranted among comparativists.

The Concept of Governance

"Governance" has become part of the academic and political vocabulary in recent years, but there is at present no consensus as to its definition. For example, it is frequently used in international development circles, particularly by the international finance institutions (the World Bank and the IMF). These intergovernmental institutions operate under mandates that preempt references to anything specifically political in a partisan sense. Staff of these institutions have to find other words to enable them to engage in a public dialogue about things political. Hence, the frequent use in World Bank publications of such words as "institutions" and "governance."

The language of governance is typically applied by these institutions to serve their own narrow purposes. For example, in its 1989 report on the prospects for development in sub-Saharan Africa, the World Bank defined governance with reference to the exercise of political power to manage a nation's affairs.[10] In a subsequent document three years later, the same institution used governance to refer to the practical exercise of power and authority to conduct public affairs.[11] It is clear that in such terms, governance can refer to just about anything political. It has no other value than allowing the Bank to make reference to things political.

In all fairness to individual World Bank officials, there are some who have tried to give governance a more specific meaning. For example, in a paper presented at a bank-sponsored conference on development economics, E. Boeninger suggests that governance is the same as "good government."[12] Even though he sees the relevance of societal coalitions for development between business and labor as complementary features of good governance, the focus is on the quality of government policy and action, notably, a just exercise of authority, competent problem solving, and efficient implementation of basic functions.

Academic interest in governance has arisen partly in response to the growing popularity of the concept in international development circles.[13] Given the loose meaning the concept has had in the public discourse on governance and development, it is understandable that many scholars have shied away from it, although it must be pointed out that even in academic circles, "governance" has been usually employed without an effort to give it a particular analytical content.[14] There is no reason matters should be left at that, particularly since we are faced with a new type of politics for which we still do not have sufficient and adequate tools. Governance is a strong candidate for helping us to fill the current void.

To fully appreciate the usefulness of the concept, it is necessary to place it in the context of a discussion of some other concepts. The first is regime. The latter is distinct from both state and government. It is typically a more permanent form of political organization than a specific government. Governments, in other words, change more often than do regimes. Sometimes they may change simultaneously, as, for instance, when the resignation or overthrow of a government also implies the end of the very basic rules that had guided political action before. A regime, on the other hand, is typically less permanent than a state. A state is an institutionalized structure of domination and coordination of law and order, as well as development. A state, for example, may remain in place as regimes come and go, something that we have witnessed in many countries in Africa as military regimes have replaced civilian ones and multiparty systems have succeeded one-party systems. Regimes more rarely survive state collapse. Such breakdowns of state functions destabilize regimes as well, as the case of the former Belgian Congo in 1960 and countries such as Liberia and Somalia more recently demonstrate.

A regime is a set of fundamental rules about the organization of the political realm. A regime guides political behavior and also sets the framework within which issues enter the political agenda and policies are made. This is not the everyday politics of making laws and policies. Regimes are not a given, and they are often contested. At a fundamental political level, regimes set the rules of the game. It is to this metapolitical activity that I believe the concept of governance belongs.

Governance, as defined here, refers to that aspect of politics that aims to formulate and manage the rules of the political arena in which state and civil society actors operate and interact to make authoritative decisions. In more operational terms, governance refers to those measures that involve setting the rules for the exercise of power and settling conflicts over such rules. Such rules translate into constitutions, laws, customs, administrative regulations, and international agreements, all of which in one way or the other provide the framework for the formulation and implementation of policy decisions. The actors involved in governance may also be involved in other political arenas, be they in the state or in civil society. The political actors use their power not only to get certain policy preferences enacted, but also to decide on the rules under which such policies are made.

Governance is focused on what we may also wish to call "constitutional politics." "Constitutional" here, however, is used in a generic sense. Thus we recognize that rules are both formal and informal and are set at different levels of political interaction.[15] The notion of constitutional rules in this sense is applicable to local, national, or international levels. They can be studied in the context of a community, an organization, or a nation. For example, in the field of resource conservation, it is not uncommon for local, national, and global regimes to be in conflict. In the case of the Ngorongoro Conservation Area, one of Tanzania's prime tourist sites, it has long been a burning political question as to whose rules should prevail: those of the local Maasai herders, those of the national government, or those of the international conservation community. The emerging governance field is pertinent today because it can offer a system of analysis to examine such conflicts. In a broader sense, it is pertinent because so many countries around the world are attempting political reform and must constantly struggle with questions of regime change, the proper division of power among political levels, and constitutional structure.

Although the concepts of democracy and governance are often used in tandem, as, for example, in the case of programs administered by the U.S. Agency for International Development, the two are different in that it is possible to conceive of governance independently of democracy. Governance, as suggested above, is an aspect of politics that can be found in any system. The question of how rules are handled and regimes established and sustained is an empirical issue of universal validity. Unlike democracy, which has definite normative connotations, governance allows us to examine in a more open-ended fashion the challenges inherent in creating an "enabling environment" that is generally believed to be crucial to human welfare and security, as well as to national development. Governance systematically focuses our attention on issues that in the past have been rather peripheral to students of comparative politics, but that today have acquired new practical relevance. With governance, we no longer look only at the question of "who gets what, when, and how"—that is, distributive politics—but we increasingly examine issues related to the rules of the game, what I call "constitutive politics." Thus defined, governance can contribute to an examination of current political affairs in Africa.

The Governance Challenge in Africa

Few observers of the political scene in Africa in the 1990s would disagree that constitutional or regime issues are in the forefront of African politics today. We have learned in the past few years that what is going on in Africa right now is not really a largely uncontested progress toward democracy, as much of the literature a few years ago implied, but quite a fundamental battle over what kind of political order should prevail. The notion of "reconstituting the political order," therefore, makes more political and intellectual sense than the more limited "regime transition." The latter tends to underestimate the role that regime issues play in today's politics.

While there are many aspects of governance that could be highlighted with the help of African material, I will confine myself to three sets of issues to demonstrate its significance: (1) the tension between domestic and international standards or principles of democracy; (2) the plural character of African society; and (3) the role of international actors.

The Tension Between Domestic and Western Principles

The issue of representation is vital to any political system. History shows us that this principle has always been contested before it is settled in ways that provide political systems a definite measure of stability. It is currently being contested in African countries because the domestic and international—especially Western—actors are bringing quite different perspectives and traditions to this issue. To fully appreciate the significance of this point, it may be helpful to trace the European and African traditions with regard to representation.

Europeans have long abandoned direct democracy, but operate with a concept of indirect democracy, which emerged in response to the challenges of monarchical absolutism. Representatives were originally chosen by electoral colleges drawn from the more important social groups or "estates" in society. This precorporatist system was eventually replaced by "one person, one vote" representation. In this latter situation, competition for power was no longer reserved for particular individuals or limited to specific groups. This served as a guarantee that those who were finally elected would be responsive to the will of the voters. Contemporary Western democracy rests on the rule that representative and accountable democracy is possible only if free choice is guaranteed. Such freedom of choice is important not so much for the *exercise of power* as for the *control of power*. As Giovanni Sartori notes:

> A democracy, then, is a political system in which people exercise power to the extent that they are able to change their governors, but not to the extent of governing themselves. The only way the sovereign people can maintain the degree of power they need and are capable of wielding is not to give their governors unlimited power.[16]

Western democracy, therefore, is more about checks and balances than about avenues to power and influence. These are the principles that Westerners are currently engaged in exporting to other parts of the world. A lot of people in these other regions are sympathetic to this set of principles, but it is being realized in Asia and Latin America, as well as in Africa, that other principles, growing out of indigenous experiences, also count.

In Africa, it is impossible to ignore the fact that most people live in small-scale societies where face-to-face contacts prevail. Even those who now live in urban areas and may be said to form part of a modern large-scale society are not necessarily cut off from that legacy. As manifest in the many studies of local development in Africa, the idea of self-rule is practiced in Africa on a day-to-day basis. It is understandable, therefore, that African political actors bring a different perspective to the question of what kind of democratic order should be instituted. This difference is being illustrated, for example, by their approach to representation. For the majority of Africans faced with a choice to vote, elections are not so much a matter of choosing the persons most capable of ruling the nation as a whole as they are a matter of selecting those who will best promote and protect the interests of a particular community.[17] This is one reason that partisan politics in Africa tend to be nonideological and less focused on national than on local issues.

In the African perception of democracy, the question of who should represent a particular constituency is usually not seen in isolation from the question of which community or communities make up that electoral district. To represent a community, the person interested in seeking election most likely will have to be a member of that community. This insistence on congruence between representative and community grows out of the African tradition of self-rule and means not just that a member of the community can represent the community, but also that only a member of the community can be expected to be accountable to its members. In short, representation is seen within the context of communal, rather than individual, competition. The notion of multipartyism, therefore, in and of itself, is not necessarily as important as access to power that might be secured more effectively by other means. This is one potential reason that broadly based, communal, incumbent parties in African elections tend to be preferred over opposition parties that lack such a basis. It is only in those cases where the opposition has been supported on a multiethnic basis—for example, in Zambia in 1991—that it may succeed. This is also why the Ugandan version of no-party democracy is an acceptable model of representation to many people in that country. It reduces the tendency to make access to government purely partisan and allows individual competition within what constitutes communal realms. A recent doctoral dissertation on perceptions of democracy in Uganda concluded, among other things, that people in that country are inclined to give much higher priority to such principles as freedom of expression than to that of freedom to pursue organized political activities.[18]

What we need at this point are more studies that probe deeper into the politics of governance. African politics is increasingly dominated by divergent perspectives regarding which rules should prevail in countries that strive to realize what some refer to as a "second liberation." These studies need to start from premises that are less instrumentalist than typical studies of democratization. Whether the issue is representation or any other aspect of democracy, African political actors have perspectives of their own that need to be incorporated into studies of how and to what extent the political order in African countries is being reconstituted.

The Plural Character of African Society

There are two aspects of plurality that I find particularly interesting in the current context. The first is the extent to which human rights can be "lateralized" to apply in an operational sense to intergroup relations. Human rights, at least with regard to their civil and political aspects, are typically defined in the context of relations between state and citizen. In plural societies, however, the question of which principles should apply to relations among groups in society also becomes important. This has proven to be the case in many parts of the world, but it has taken on particular significance in Africa because both colonization and, after independence, large-scale development activities have had the effect of displacing aboriginal populations. While this applies very directly to a country like South Africa, the same phenomenon can be found in countries like Ethiopia and Kenya, where some ethnic groups have expanded their control over natural resources at the expense of others. Perhaps the best examples are the Kalenjin and the Maasai in the Rift Valley Province in Kenya, who have claimed that other ethnic groups—notably, the Kikuyu—have acquired their land and marginalized them in what they perceive as their homeland. The political leadership, which has its base in that particular province, has decided, at least so far, to treat this challenge with direct action. Instead of seeking a constitutional or legal solution to the problem by amending the rules of the political game, it has encouraged ethnic clashes in the form of civil violence. This violence is intended to neutralize the economically powerful Kikuyus and satisfy the most immediate demands of the local Kalenjin and Maasai leaders for greater control of the land and natural resources. This crude approach to governance has proven costly to the agricultural sector of Kenya, one of Africa's best in the past, as it has caused disruptions and reductions in agricultural production and productivity.[19]

The South African approach to this issue stands in great contrast to that of the Kenyan government. As part of the constitutional reform process, the South Africans developed a bill of rights that can serve as a statement of democratic aspirations and also as an instrument to be used in judicial settings. Given the apartheid legacy and the suspicion that has naturally prevailed in relations among racial and ethnic groups, this is a bold attempt to ensure that issues of justice in intergroup relations can be handled in both the political and judicial arenas. Black South Africans support such a bill of rights as a safeguard of recently earned rights. White South Africans see it primarily as a safeguard against the tyranny of the majority. It may be too early to say how far expectations among these different groups can be satisfied, but the constitutional move made by the South Africans has at least provided a platform for resolving potential conflicts among groups in society that are regulated by the state's highest possible governance instrument. This and the Kenyan example illustrate that attention to issues of a constitutional character is not only an important practical political concern, but also a subject that scholars may find more significant than is evident from the comparative politics literature.

The second dimension of cultural pluralism that concerns us here is how what appears to locals and foreigners alike as the politics of suspicion and hatred can be turned into a fresh type of politics in which impartial justice has a place. This is again not an exclusively African problem and can be found elsewhere. Nonetheless, it takes on a particular urgency in many African countries because the political manipulation of hatred constitutes a serious threat to political stability and order.

This issue is in part related to the earlier point about the communal dimension of representation, which, among other things, tends to make political leaders not only self-interested in the sense of being able to promote and protect their role as "patrons" of their respective communities. Because African politics tends to follow rules that are generated in face-to-face contexts and thus is characterized by clientelism or patronage, it also tends to be private and centralized.[20] The sense of justice that emerges from this experience is typically based on the principle of mutual advantage, that is, the creation of a modus vivendi between competing forces. The principal significance that competing interests attach to agreements is that they should offer a more effective way of achieving their ends than is provided by the unrestrained pursuit of those ends.

Settlements underwritten by the principle of justice as mutual advantage are, however, often no more than truces, as Brian Barry notes.[21] As soon as either side feels that it can improve its position, there is nothing to restrain it as long as the prospective gains outweigh the anticipated costs. The logic of the social and political order, therefore, is not a notion of justice that is based on a set of "natural laws." The foundation of a system of mutual advantage is fragile because it rests on the structure of the Prisoners' Dilemma.[22] As a subject in a Prisoners' Dilemma, it is in my interest that everybody else cooperates and I defect; in other words, that everybody else adheres to rules that, if followed, are mutually advantageous, but that I break them whenever it is in my interest. This system lacks a sense of the meaning of fairness. It undermines, instead of reinforces, motivation to be fair in dealing with others. One may hypothesize, therefore, that the more competitive the political system, the greater the tendency for such behavior to evolve. In short, the introduction of multiparty politics and the holding of competitive elections do not necessarily make the creation of a new constitutionalized (in the formal sense) political order easier.

Rules in African political systems are usually the result of "hegemonial exchanges,"[23] or opportunistic deals that have little durability because they have been entered into not to abandon the principle of self-interest, but to guard it. There is little scope in such systems for impartial justice, according to which rules are ends in themselves. In theory, fairness and justice are inherent in the rule itself and can be established without any need to predict the outcome at any particular time and place. Rights of individuals are natural. This form of justice calls upon individuals to transcend a narrow, personal conception of the good so as to be able to establish it at a higher level of generality.

Experience in Africa over the past few years indicates that the notion of justice as impartiality is not very broadly embraced in political circles. In such countries as Cameroon, Kenya, and more recently Zambia, constitutional revisions have been tactical retreats, rather than commitments to principles of justice that transcend a very narrow view of political self-interest. This approach needs to be further assessed in the context of the establishment of a new political order. Why do rulers behave this way? What are the implications of these practices for a more formal system of constitutional governance? What incentive do political actors have in this kind of setting to make commitments to rules that are truly self-binding? These are only a few of the interesting questions of governance that may be further pursued by comparativists.

The Role of International Actors

International organizations, particularly multilateral and bilateral donor agencies, have become increasingly entangled in African economies as well as their politics. Their programs of support for activities aimed at strengthening civil society and holding general elections have become significant in terms of overall aid portfolios. It is also clear that many African countries today would be unable to hold general elections were it not for the financial support of the donor community. This kind of intimate involvement in matters that are close to the core of the constitution and distribution of power in society means that donors become involved in national politics. The implications of this direct involvement constitute an interesting research question. Do donors help to provide space for political reform? How much of what they support is being sustained if and when they withdraw? Do they help to instill new democratic values? The time has come to pay greater attention to donors not only as employers of consultants in the field of governance and democratization, but also as agencies with a definite impact on the very process that they support.

There are also a number of questions of strategy that arise in regard to the role of these outside organizations. Thus far, most donors have followed a dual strategy that has focused, on the one hand, on providing financial support for the holding of general elections and, on the other, on the strengthening of civil society. The first has been pursued on the premise that competitive elections constitute a "founding" step toward multiparty democracy. Because they are time-bound events, they lend themselves to project-type support. Even though they have often proved to be quite expensive, and the donors have provided in some instances half or more of the total costs of elections, the commonly held view among the donors has been that elections should be given adequate financial support. The other part of this strategy—support for civil society—has meant financial support of nongovernmental organizations (NGOs) involved in the field of justice and human rights, as well as development. The assumption here is that strengthening such organizations will help lay the foundation for a liberal type of democracy.

This dual strategy has made a lot of sense from the perspective of the needs of African countries that are taking the first halting steps toward democracy. Experience is beginning to show, however, that it also contains shortcomings. One of these is that the funding of NGOs tends to make the most essential component of civil society very dependent on the donor community. Some NGOs are opportunistically established because it is known that external money in the 1990s flows more easily through them than through governments. Even when these NGOs have serious intentions and a good track record, the problem of dependency easily arises, particularly if the donors themselves are not careful in demanding matching contributions as a prerequisite for their support. A more comprehensive assessment of NGO performance in African countries would be welcome. At this point, we have only a series of individual NGO project evaluations.

Perhaps even more pertinent, however, is an assessment of electoral assistance. It is hard to question its justification in the current context of democratization, but some hard governance questions need to be asked in relation to this type of support. Foremost of these is whether it is wise to hold competitive elections before more extensive agreement has been reached about the rules of the new political game. Experience from virtually all competitive elections held in Africa to date shows that there has been cheating or suspicion of cheating during the elections. The perception of impropriety, regardless of actual foul play, is often the element damaging to democracy.[24] As long as justice is perceived as merely a matter of truce among rival parties seeking their own advantages, the threat to fairness is imminent and suspicions of fraud will prevail. In this environment, elections may do more harm than good and represent an immediate threat in societies where justice as impartiality is not institutionalized. This raises the question of the wisdom of holding elections before such an order has been established. A political system in which the principle of impartiality is not yet accepted is like a football game where each team has its own rules and there is no referee.

This is a governance challenge for donors. It is obvious that abandoning support of elections while waiting for a new political order to be established is impractical. It is practical, however, to devote more support to institutions that are capable of promoting a greater degree of impartiality and professionalism, including the judiciary, the Central Bank, and various commissions that act as public bodies but are not captured by a particular political group. Also of growing interest in the African context is the autonomous development fund model, which is meant to channel development finance in ways that preempt the patronage tendencies that occur when such funds are exclusively controlled by the political executive.[25]

Democratization and governance challenges are not always such that donor responses mutually reinforce them. The short-term interest in holding elections to enable societies to qualify as budding democracies may conflict with the more long-term task of reconstituting the political order and laying the normative foundation for a viable democracy.

Conclusion

This chapter is based on the assumption that people in African countries are interested in moving away from authoritarian and capricious rule. Experience with elections and other means to move these countries in a democratic direction, however, indicates that the transition from one regime to another is more complex than analysts and policy practitioners assumed. Reconstituting the political order in African countries is particularly contentious because serious conflicts continue to persist over the most fundamental issues of the shape of the new order. At stake in these countries is not merely the question of redistribution of power and wealth, but the appropriate redistribution of responsibility under conditions where norms are still strongly contested both from within and from outside the country. This is the politics of regime rules to which governance refers.

This type of politics is significant enough not only in the African context but also in many other regions of the world to warrant attention as an emerging field in its own right. It addresses questions that comparativists have largely ignored, but that are empirically very pertinent. As suggested in this chapter, governance deals with issues such as how a polity is constituted or reconstituted, how a system of political rule is legitimized, and how regime rules help transform a multitude of individuals into citizens in a nation where they live under common laws. These issues were part of the academic research agenda in the 1960s, when structural-functionalist ideas made them relevant to the study of politics. Lost or ignored in that approach, however, was the extent to which establishing a political order was imbued with moral and normative issues. These issues were neutralized because the functionalist perspective permitted everything to be seen as serving some purpose. In the 1990s, we are returning to this set of issues largely liberated from the positivist influences that dominated scholarly thinking in comparative politics in the 1950s and 1960s.

Increasingly, we are recognizing that there are politics beyond the state. This does not just mean that there are politics in civil society or that there is an informal type of politics in neopatrimonialist contexts. Equally significant is the politics regarding the rules of the political game. Comparitivists need to capture and incorporate an understanding of this politics into their field. I have suggested that we reserve the concept of governance for this kind of politics. This is distinct from the politics that emanates from competition over how resources should be allocated in society. We have in mind a contest over the most fundamental issues facing a given country: how a political order should be constituted, legitimized, and managed. This is the core of the governance field, and it waits to be fully developed, both at the theoretical and the methodological level.

Notes

1. World Bank, *Accelerated Development.*
2. See, for example, Callaghy, *State-Society Struggle;* Migdal, *Strong Societies;* and Rothchild and Chazan, eds., *Precarious Balance.*
3. Lofchie, "Perestroika Without Glasnost."
4. See, for example, Medard, "Underdeveloped State"; Joseph, *Democracy and Prebendal Politics;* and Bayart, *The State in Africa.*
5. See, for example, Bratton and van de Walle, *Democratic Experiments.*
6. Schumpeter, *Capitalism, Socialism, and Democracy.*
7. Schmitter and Karl, "What Democracy Is."
8. A representative of this approach is Przeworski's *Democracy and the Market;* see also Bates, "Economics of Transition," pp. 24–26.
9. van de Walle, "Globalization and African Democracy."
10. World Bank, *Sub-Saharan Africa.*
11. World Bank, *Governance and Development.*
12. Boeninger, "Governance and Development."
13. In my own case, I began to think about how the concept could be used for analytical purposes as early as 1988, when colleagues of mine in East Africa and at the University of Florida were preparing a project proposal for funding to the Ford Foundation. The main objective at that time was to find a way of thinking about incipient political reforms in East Africa before such concepts as democracy and democratization were on the political agenda in the region. For that reason, "governance" was deliberately defined in rather broad terms, referring to political reform measures aimed at making more effective use of societal resources. Admittedly, this definition came close to how the World Bank defined the concept in 1989. With funding eventually received for this East African Governance Project, I continued to work on the definition of the concept, spurred by both collegial comments and feedback from our project. In 1989, this resulted in a brief presentation at a meeting in

Atlanta organized by Professor Richard Joseph, which resulted in his edited collection *Beyond Autocracy in Africa*. The same year, I prepared another paper for presentation at the American Political Science Association meeting and the following year yet another on governance at the annual meeting of the African Studies Association. Both of these papers were "trial balloons" and never resulted in publication. The first more substantial piece on governance that reflected the evolution of my own thinking about the concept was the introduction to the book that I coedited with Michael Bratton, *Governance and Politics in Africa*. This is where I first tie the concept of governance to the study of regimes and regime politics. The concept has since been in hibernation in my own mind, but this contribution is an attempt to revive it and demonstrate its increasing relevance to the study of comparative politics.

14. For example, the political science journal *Governance* does not attempt to rein in the concept in any particular way. Instead, the net is cast quite widely, and it is clear that the concept has more heuristic than analytical meaning.

15. For a more elaborate explanation of this point, see Kiser and Ostrom, "Three Worlds of Action."

16. Sartori, *Democratic Theory*, p. 66.

17. See, for example, Chabal, *Power in Africa*, pp. 207–208; see also Hayward, ed., *Elections*.

18. Ottemoeller, "Institutionalization."

19. For an illustration of this problem, see, for example, Krugmann et al., "Community Water Management."

20. Jackson, *Plural Societies*.

21. Barry, *Justice as Impartiality*, p. 39.

22. Ibid., p. 51.

23. This concept was first developed by Rothchild in "Middle Africa."

24. It is in this context that the 1996 elections in Ghana must be seen as a great step forward for that country.

25. This project has been promoted by the African Association for Public Administration and Management, headquartered in Nairobi. It has held a series of meetings in Africa, and the model is now in the process of being operationalized in four African countries.

11

Senegal's Enlarged Presidential Majority: Deepening Democracy or Detour?

LINDA J. BECK

Only a decade ago, political observers were praising Leopold Sedar Senghor and Julius Nyerere as two rare examples of African leaders who voluntarily left office. Their orchestrated departures did assure the political tenure of the Senegalese Parti Socialiste (PS) under Senghor's *dauphin*, Abdou Diouf, and the continued role of Nyerere as the leader of Tanzania's ruling party. But in the context of the one-party states and military rule that characterized African politics until the late 1980s, Senghor and Nyerere were exceptional in their commitment to furthering democratization in Africa.

The magnanimity of their final political acts, seen at the time as lessons in democracy for an authoritarian continent, is somewhat dwarfed, however, by the dramatic political changes that have subsequently taken place in Africa. Not only have entrenched authoritarian leaders been ousted from power through international and domestic pressure, but an increasing number of democratically elected leaders are now facing the prospect of being turned out of office by the same electoral processes that brought them to power, as occurred most recently in Benin.

Among the former one-party states of Africa, there are, however, a number of countries that have lagged behind in the democratization process. In countries such as Cameroon, Kenya, and Senegal, the incumbents have been able to manipulate political reforms to remain in power despite the return to a multiparty system. In each case, the electoral process has been tainted by charges of fraud lodged by opposition parties and international observers. Nevertheless, democratizing forces in these dominant-party systems, as Larry Diamond points out, are "pressing out the boundaries of what is politically possible, and may eventually generate breakthroughs in electoral democracy."[1] The timetable for the breakthrough

in these pseudodemocracies would appear, however, to vary among countries.

Given the evidence of the Senegalese government's commitment to
freedom of association and the press, especially when contrasted with the
overt repression of the political opposition and the independent press in
Cameroon and Kenya, the prospects for Senegal to move beyond its current
dominant-party system would appear to be quite good. In addition to the
participation of opposition parties in reforming Senegal's electoral code in
1992, and again in 1996, the PS has been willing to appoint leaders of the
opposition as ministers in its "enlarged presidential majority" (EPM),[2]
including Abdoulaye Wade, the secretary-general of Senegal's largest opposition party, the Parti Démocratique Sénégalais (PDS). The question, however, is whether this development represents a "deepening of democracy,"
as Prime Minister Habib Thiam has asserted, or a detour to forestall the
unseating of the PS.[3]

Since the formation of the first EPM in 1991, the PS has always maintained representatives of the opposition in its government, although the precise membership has changed. Their inclusion has given leaders of the
opposition greater voice in the PS government, as well as access to state
resources to implement their political agendas. Nevertheless, the PS has a
history of co-opting the opposition through the incorporation of its leaders
in the government. In the early 1960s, Senghor combined this strategy with
the repression of resistant opposition leaders such as Cheikh Anta Diop to
establish a de facto one-party state.[4]

In order to assess whether Senegal's experiment with the EPM represents a deepening of or a detour from democracy, we need to examine the
implications of the EPM for the democratization process and for governance in general. To do this, I have chosen to focus on Senegal's electoral
process, political competition, and accountability. After assessing the
impact of the EPM on these three crucial elements of a democracy, I conclude by considering whether Senegal's experience offers a model for
export to other African countries with more repressive dominant-party systems or is a path to be avoided.[5]

Political Reform and the Moving Target of Electoral Fraud

Since the return to a multiparty system in 1975, Senegalese elections have
been plagued by accusations of electoral fraud. While electoral fraud is not
alien to Western democracies—to which democratization in Africa is at
least implicitly compared—the absence of alternation between political
parties makes Senegal's electoral process more suspect. Nevertheless, the
PS, under substantial international and domestic pressure, has taken significant steps over the last decade to reform the electoral code, rectifying some

of the more contentious provisions that assured the political tenure of the ruling party.

After the violent demonstrations surrounding the 1988 national elections, during which the opposition parties claimed that the electoral code permitted the PS to steal the elections, the instability of the Diouf regime was intensified by Senegal's chronic economic crisis, as well as by conflicts with Mauritania, The Gambia, and the separatists of Casamance Province. In the absence of a new electoral code, the opposition parties boycotted the 1990 municipal elections, refusing to participate in what they saw as a flawed electoral process. Domestic pressures to review the code were reinforced by the increasing concern of international donors about the impact of "governance" on economic development. As one World Bank official suggested during an interview following the 1993 elections, if Senegal wanted to maintain its "democracy bonus" as a favored aid recipient, the government needed the cachet of "free and fair" elections in order to keep pace with other African countries that were making great strides in political liberalization.

Besieged by domestic and international criticism, Diouf invited members of the opposition to join a "government of national unity" in March 1991. Although a unified opposition initially rejected the offer, the PDS and the Parti de l'Indépendence et du Travail (PIT), a small Marxist party, reversed their decision when the government agreed to open negotiations on greater access to the state media and reform of the electoral code. Opposition leaders who chose not to join the government, on the other hand, claimed that joining the government was not necessary, since negotiations with the PS to reform the code were already under way when the PDS and the PIT entered the government.[6]

Western political observers applauded the decision to form the first EPM, calling it "responsible politics" on the part of President Diouf and the opposition parties who joined the government. Albert Bourgi of *Jeune Afrique,* for example, asserted that the government of national unity reflected both President Diouf's "willingness to reinforce the democratization process in his country" and the maturity of the opposition, who, considering the socioeconomic crisis the country was facing, chose to abandon their irresponsible *"politique de pire,"* which had culminated in the violence of the 1988 elections.[7] Bourgi and his Senegalese coauthor Elimane Fall quoted Wade as saying, "We were convinced that if one had let things continue as they were, [Senegal] would be heading straight to a national conference!"[8] According to Bourgi and Fall, neither Diouf nor Wade wanted a national conference because it is synonymous with "political decline and settling scores."[9] While Diouf's perspective is understandable given the threat that national conferences posed to the leaders of other African countries, Wade's view on the topic is difficult to understand coming from a member of the opposition.

In fulfillment of the opposition's terms for entering the EPM, a commission to review the electoral code was formed in May 1991. Negotiated by representatives from each political party—both those within and those outside of the government—the new electoral code that was adopted in September 1991 contained a number of fundamental reforms, including bipartisan (ruling and opposition parties') involvement in the various stages of the electoral process, prohibition of the use of public resources for campaign purposes, and equal access to the state telecommunications media. During the months preceding the presidential elections in February 1993, the code was held up by all parties concerned as "the most perfect" electoral code.

By all accounts, the more blatant forms of electoral fraud, including voter intimidation and stuffing ballot boxes, were seriously curtailed during the 1993 elections by the provisions in the new code. Nevertheless, even before the elections, the opposition began charging the PS with various infractions, such as illicit use of the state media (November 1992), illegal registration after the electoral lists were closed (December 1992), and the distribution of blank *ordonnances* signed by justices that permitted individuals to vote without appearing on the electoral list (January 1993).[10] By the time President Abdou Diouf was declared the victor in March 1993, the opposition was calling for new elections or, at the very least, a postponement of the May 1993 legislative elections until the irregularities of the presidential elections could be brought to light and rectified. Nevertheless, the legislative elections went ahead as scheduled, and not surprisingly, the PS won a decisive majority of the seats in the National Assembly.

The experience of the 1993 elections illustrates how electoral fraud has been a moving target for the opposition. While the 1992 electoral code introduced important legal reforms, altering provisions that had formerly protected the incumbency of the ruling party, the electoral process continued to be undermined by the ability of the PS to subvert the intent of the newly negotiated code. Once again, fraud was committed by the patrimonial clients of the PS state, such as justices who signed blank *ordonnances,* government officials who used state resources for campaign purposes, and local party activists involved in illegal registration. Above all others, the opposition parties attributed the ability of the PS to manipulate the electoral process to the role of the minister of the interior, who remained in charge of organizing the elections despite criticisms of his partisan behavior as a Diouf appointee. It is therefore not surprising that, since the 1993 elections, the opposition parties have focused their attention on the need for an independent electoral commission.

In preparation for the 1996 local elections, the current minister of the interior, Abdourahmane Sow, met with 20 political parties to discuss possible improvements in the electoral code. This meeting resulted in important changes to combat fraud, including authorization of the local, bipartisan

Departmental Electoral Census Commissions to review, rectify, and annul the procès-verbal received from each polling station in the department and a ban on illiterate polling station officials, who had been appointed in 1993 by prefects based on their loyalty to the PS state, rather than their competence.[11] The minister of the interior, however, categorically refused to turn over responsibility for the administration of the elections to an independent commission, arguing that the role of the administration in the elections is fundamentally "republican" in character.[12]

When Wade was approached on the subject, he contradicted his colleagues in the opposition, arguing that there was no longer any need for an independent electoral commission. Wade reasoned that, unlike the elections of 1993 when the PDS left the EPM prior to the presidential elections, the PDS would remain in the government during the 1996 local elections and would thus be able to supervise their administration by the PS state.[13] This position may appear naive given that the ministries headed by PDS leaders did not include the Interior Ministry. However, if Wade had acknowledged the need for an independent electoral commission, this would have been tantamount to an admission of the limited influence and power of the PDS in the PS-controlled government. At the time, there were already signs of mounting dissatisfaction within the PDS over the party's decision to rejoin the government in 1995.[14] To admit the need for an independent electoral commission would have strengthened the argument that the PDS had lost more than it had gained by joining the EPM.

Wade's attitude toward an independent electoral commission swung back 180 degrees when the PS swept the November 1996 local elections. The PS won majorities in all of the regional assemblies, 300 out of 320 rural councils, and 56 out of 60 mayoralties. In the capital region of Dakar, where the PDS had won electoral majorities in the 1993 national elections, the PS was able to win 419 of the 523 seats in the regional assembly and 38 of the 43 mayoral positions, even in the poorest areas of Guédiewaye and Pikine that have been hard hit by the recent austerity measures of the PS government.[15]

Immediately after the elections, the familiar pattern of opposition accusations of electoral fraud and calls for the annulment of the elections began. Once again, charges of fraud were made even before the elections. The opposition parties accused the PS of misusing the state media, confiscating and redistributing electoral cards, stockpiling surplus electoral cards for distribution to voters who had been illegally added to the electoral lists, placing PS candidates in charge of polling stations, and the theft and disappearance of the procès-verbal, on which the results and reports of fraud are made, from various polling stations.[16] The reported irregularities were most flagrant in Dakar, where the opposition parties accused the PS of intentionally failing to provide polling stations with the necessary electoral materials in order to keep opposition supporters from voting and thus assure that the ruling party would recapture the capital region.[17] Immediate efforts by the opposition to hold a demonstration for the annulment of the elections were prohibited by the PS state.[18] The opposition parties responded by calling for an international commission to investigate the abuses of the 1996 elections.

In January 1997, 13 opposition parties, including the PDS and the Ligue Démocratique-Mouvement pour le Parti du Travail (LD-MPT), whose leaders are currently ministers in the PS state, signed a public statement requesting "that the international community cease all financial contributions to the Senegalese government under the pretext of organizing elections as long as the conditions for transparent, free, and democratic elections are not in place."[19] The parties went on to claim that the PS had appropriated the monies earmarked for the elections and that the PS had "intentionally disorganized" the elections "with the complicity of the administration to impede the authentic expression of the popular will in order to maintain [the PS] in power." The opposition argued that "the party-state that is the Parti Socialiste, not content with turning the administration, the regional governors, and other prefects into vassals," had transformed the elections through "electoral card grants" (i.e., voter bribery) using foreign aid intended for the organization of the elections.[20] The newly unified opposition also presented its demands for an independent electoral commission to the international donor community, joined now by the defeated PDS.[21] Meanwhile, both the PDS and the LD-MPT began to publicly consider withdrawal from the EPM.[22]

The PS, on the other hand, responded to the opposition's accusations by denouncing them as an attempted *"coup de force."* It decried the statement as an effort to tarnish the reputation of the ruling party and destabilize the government by "an opposition that is largely in the minority and which counts on agitation in the media and political subversion to overturn the wishes of the population to its profit."[23] In addition, the leadership of the ruling party began proceedings for a libel suit against the signatories of the opposition's statement.[24]

President Diouf, apparently attempting a more diplomatic approach, met with Wade immediately after the opposition's statement was published. It was not until the leaders of the opposition began to form delegations to meet with foreign donors in European and North American capitals, however, that President Diouf agreed to consider the question of an independent electoral commission, and he formed a commission to explore the idea.[25] Whether the PS state is willing to retreat from its emphatic refusal to establish independent administration of the electoral process, and precisely what such an electoral commission would look like, remains unclear.

Thus, in terms of the impact of the EPM on the electoral process, the PS state has kept its promise to reform the electoral code in exchange for the "responsible" participation of the opposition in the government.

However, Senegal's electoral experiences since the renegotiation of the code indicate the limited capacity of any code to ensure free and fair elections as long as the PS state retains control of the organization of the elections. As the PDS has now learned, the presence of opposition parties in the government does not permit the opposition to oversee the practices of PS officials in order to prevent the manipulation of the electoral process.

Furthermore, it is still not clear whether it was ever necessary for the opposition to enter the government in order to obtain political reforms as concessions from the PS state. Based on recent experience with the pursuit of an independent electoral commission, the opposition appears to be more effective when it acts in a unified manner, vocally asserting its demands for political reforms from without, rather than pursuing reforms from within the government.

An important question that remains unanswered is why opposition parties have joined the EPM and continue to participate in the government despite the objections of many of their members. In the following section, I examine the motives for participating in the EPM and the impact of this cooperation on Senegal's political opposition.

"Potential Clientelism" and the Opposition's Decision to Join the EPM

Some members of the ruling party—among both the rank and file and the leadership—question the necessity for an EPM. President Diouf's willingness to bring the opposition into the PS government despite this doubt can be attributed to his desire to promote political stability, not only for the sake of a nation in crisis, but also to reinforce the status quo of the dominant-party system. The decision of opposition leaders to join the EPM, on the other hand, is more complex.

While the PDS and the PIT were applauded in 1991 for joining the government during a period of heightened domestic and international tension, the decision by the leaders of the PIT, the LD-MPT, and the Parti Démocratique Sénégalais-Renouvellement (PDS-R)[26] to join the new government that was formed after the 1993 legislative elections can hardly be attributed to the urgent need for political stability in the face of a national crisis. Nevertheless, in 1993, as in 1991, the opposition parties were concerned with gaining access to the centers of decisionmaking in the PS state in order to influence public policy.

The leaders of the LD-MPT, who had refused to join the government in 1991, explained their decision to participate in the 1993 EPM as an opportunity to demonstrate their ability to rule the country. Under the political hegemony of the PS, which extends to the most remote rural councils, opposition parties had been limited to the role of perpetual critics, unable to prove their skills in managing the affairs of state. The leaders of the LD-MPT therefore readily accepted the posts of minister of the environment and deputy minister of literacy, with the hope that the party could demonstrate its capacity for political management and reform in these policy areas.[27] Some PDS members in ministerial positions were also able to pursue a strategy similar to that of the LD-MPT, including the minister of public health and social action, Ousmane Ngom, and the minister of trade, crafts, and industrialization, Idrissa Seck. However, as the minister of state at the presidency, Wade holds no portfolio with which to demonstrate his political prowess. Wade's project to build a second international airport in Dakar, which was unveiled shortly before the 1996 elections, can thus be seen as an attempt to demonstrate his ability to develop Senegal through large infrastructure projects; in so doing, he was behaving much like politicians around the globe, who feel compelled to deliver material benefits, particularly in an election year.

In this sense, joining the government gives the opposition parties access to resources to promote their political agendas. Various PDS supporters would undoubtedly have benefited directly from the airport project through access to employment and state contracts if Ousmane Tanor Dieng, the minister of presidential services and President Diouf's heir apparent, had not squashed the project, notably *before* the 1996 elections.[28] Although no party has publicly admitted it, access to public resources for the distribution of political patronage figures heavily in their calculus for deciding to participate in the government. After decades of failing to gain power through the electoral process, the opposition has experienced the difficulties of mobilizing and sustaining support through "potential clientelism."

Given the persistence of the dominant-party system, opposition parties are no longer able to satisfy the party faithful with their prospects for gaining access through an electoral victory to the resources currently controlled by the PS state. Consequently, the PDS negotiated hard in 1991 for the right to administer several Senegalese embassies, which it staffed with intellectuals who support the PDS, much as the PS has distributed political appointments over the years. There are also reports of struggles by various parties within the current EPM to appoint their associates to the directorships of government parastatals that would provide them with access to financial resources, as well as the opportunity to distribute scarce salaried jobs.[29]

Despite these political advantages for parties that participate in the government, the impact of the EPM on Senegal's opposition has not been wholly positive. One of the major repercussions has been the rift it has caused between those parties that join the government and those that refuse to participate. Most of Senegal's dozen or so opposition parties have not accepted Diouf's invitation to join the PS government, though most of these are microparties with support from less than 2 percent of the population. However, And-Jeff, a former Marxist party now considered to be Senegal's up-and-coming third party after receiving 10 percent of the vote in the 1996 local elections, has also consistently refused to participate in the EPM.[30]

The obvious argument for not joining a PS-led government is the threat of co-optation, which Senegalese opposition parties experienced in the early 1960s. As small parties, the PIT, the LD-MPT, and especially the PDS-R have had to be concerned about being overshadowed, yet thus far, they have been able to avoid absorption into the PS structures. In fact, the PIT minister, Amath Dansoko, was expelled from the government in September 1995 after denouncing poor governance in the country.

Given the bipolar nature of Senegalese politics between the PS and the PDS, absorption would appear to be less of an issue for Senegal's leading opposition party. However, leaders of the PDS are concerned that participation in the EPM may jeopardize the party's identity as an alternative to the PS. Although this concern did not weaken Wade's resolve to participate in the EPM, before reentering the government in 1995 he did propose a "national consultation" (*wakhtane*) among all the political actors in the country. The ostensible aim of the consultation was to define a program of national action in order to conclude a "pact of social peace," but both the PS and opposition parties outside of the government interpreted it as an effort to create an "alibi" that would permit Wade to "enter the government in good conscience."[31] The idea died on the drawing board.

While predictions that PDS participation in the EPM would undermine its support in the 1993 elections proved to be false, the political costs of the party's presence in the government since then appear to have increased, as indicated by the decline in support for the party during the 1996 elections. This decline may be attributed to the fact that while the PDS left the EPM before the 1993 elections after only 18 months in the government, it decided to retain its ministries during the 1996 elections. Consequently, the PDS has confronted the problem faced by all "loyal" opposition parties: the risk of losing the "moral high ground" as a result of becoming a political insider.

The gains of And-Jeff in the 1996 elections, on the other hand, are attributed to the legitimacy of its claim to offer a real political alternative to the PS. Nevertheless, And-Jeff faces an uphill battle in its efforts to establish a sufficient national base of support without access to state resources. All of Senegal's political parties are faced with the problem that only a minority of intellectuals and union activists actually select their party based on an ideological commitment to, or even an awareness of, the party's political program. The majority of the electorate votes on the basis of the access, or potential access, politicians can provide them to public resources. Thus, opposition parties outside of the government, such as And-Jeff, are confronted by the limitations of potential clientelism.

Despite the political alternatives that parties like And-Jeff may offer, the rift that the EPM creates within the opposition circumscribes its critique of the PS state. When opposition parties enter the government, condemnation by those parties outside of the government can be more easily dismissed as the voice of an obstinate minority, while at the same time criticism of the ruling party by members of the EPM is also silenced. The dismissal of the PIT minister is an unusually extreme example; more often, the parties practice self-censorship reflecting their contradictory interests as an opposition party within the government.

In March 1993, for example, Diouf was able to quiet the storm after his reelection by promising that the party that won a majority of the seats in the May legislative elections would be permitted to name the prime minister, who would in turn be given a free hand to form a new government. Certain of their impending victory, opposition leaders focused their energies on the legislative campaign, rather than continuing to protest the electoral fraud that occurred during the presidential elections. When a PS majority was elected to the National Assembly, Diouf once again diverted attention away from flaws in the process by inviting an endless procession of opposition leaders to the presidential palace to discuss their participation in a new EPM. Ironically, the PDS, the opposition party with the broadest support, was not invited to join this government. Allegedly this was because Wade and other members of his party were implicated in the assassination of Babacar Seye, the vice president of the Constitutional Court, which took place just a few days before the court was scheduled to announce the results of the legislative elections. Ultimately, all charges were dropped against PDS officials due to insufficient evidence, thus permitting negotiations for the reentry of the PDS to resume.

When Wade finally rejoined the government in 1995, President Diouf was no longer portrayed as advancing democracy or promoting political stability, but as "neutralizing" Wade.[32] Evidence that this tactic has worked is found in some of Wade's more conciliatory statements after the November 1996 elections. In contrast to his allegations of electoral fraud immediately following the elections, a few weeks later Wade maintained that

> we are building relations for the future. What happened during the electoral campaign is past. . . . That does not change the fact that today we have [returned to] the work of the government. . . . It is necessary for the Senegalese to understand what democracy is, and to teach them that the coalition is an important element of the democracy.[33]

Delegating the contestation of the election results to local candidates, Wade did not exactly acquiesce on the issue of electoral fraud, but he had obviously all but abandoned the fight.

Wade's conciliatory statement seems particularly inconsistent with the emphatic stand, taken together with the other opposition leaders only a month earlier, on the necessity of an independent electoral commission. This apparent paradox, however, reflects the conflicting interests of Wade and his party as members of the opposition who wish to both win power in their own right and yet maintain their position in the current PS government.[34] If the opposition is unable to obtain an independent electoral commission, the contradictory interests arising out of the EPM may create a political pattern in which each electoral campaign is marked by accusations and recriminations yet ends in another PS victory. Charges of fraud by the opposition follow, but they ultimately fade away after the PS offers slots in an EPM government to some, effectively splitting and silencing the opposition.

The opposition parties thus need to assess the costs and benefits of participating in a PS government. Given the toll taken by the EPM in terms of both dividing the opposition and silencing its criticisms, the observations made in *West Africa* when Senegal's first EPM was formed in 1991 now seem prophetic: "For the moment, President Diouf seems to have succeeded in an operation which should cause other African heads of state to meditate, and defuse the bomb of the movement for change."[35] While it might be difficult to sustain a unified front even in the absence of the EPM, as the history of political opposition in Senegal and elsewhere in Africa indicates, it might have been possible for the opposition to join forces on certain commonly held positions. The question, therefore, is whether the influence gained by opposition parties within the government has compensated for the weakening of the opposition's "movement for change."

While I am unaware of any balance sheet kept by opposition ministers to assess their tenure in office, no dramatic claims were made about their accomplishments during the 1996 elections, which would have been an obvious forum for publicizing their contributions. This silence, and the lack of accomplishments that it suggests, may be attributed in part to the PDS's lack of a clearly defined program before joining the EPM, as well as to the fact that the PS retained all of the crucial portfolios in the government. Furthermore, as mentioned above, opposition demands for changes, such as the reform of the electoral code and the adoption of an independent electoral commission, may be at least as effective as when they are made from outside the government, if not more so.

Within the EPM, the opposition parties hold a precarious position that limits their political autonomy. An invitation to join the government is not based on the percentage of seats a party holds in the National Assembly or on its showing in the most recent local elections. Instead, the composition of the EPM reflects the political interests and strategies of the PS leadership; President Diouf determines which parties will be invited to participate and how many and which ministries they will control. Consequently, each opposition minister serves at the discretion of President Diouf, as Dansoko discovered.

The exclusion of the PDS from the government after the 1993 elections illustrates the extremely dependent position of the opposition parties in the EPM. Although Wade and the other leaders of the PDS who had served in the government until the fall of 1992 were excluded because of their alleged implication in the Seye assassination, President Diouf had nonetheless considered their inclusion. He relied on Abdoulaye Bathily of the LD-MPT to serve as his intermediary in an unsuccessful attempt to negotiate the reentry of the PDS into the government. The sticking point was reportedly not the Seye affair, but Wade's demand for a ministry with a more precise domain of competence than his former post as a minister of state without portfolio.[36] When Wade did finally enter the government in 1995, however, he was once again obliged to settle for this ambiguous role.

The decision by the PS leadership to form an EPM, rather than a coalition government, is therefore more than a mere question of semantics. As the senior partner with an electoral majority, the PS does not depend upon the participation of the opposition, other than to enhance the political stability and legitimacy of the PS government. As Dieng pointed out when the tensions between him and Wade came to a head over the airport project, "the PS, the majority party which won the elections, can [decide] the terms under which the parties enter."[37]

In the final analysis, the EPM is a form of political resource sharing, rather than actual power sharing. Given the limitations of potential clientelism in a dominant-party system, the decision of opposition parties to join the PS government can be seen as an attempt to cope with their short-term needs for access to political resources that can be distributed. As junior partners in the EPM, they do not have the same access as the PS. Nevertheless, their alternatives are limited, especially given the importance of patronage in both Senegal's political culture and its economy. They can either join the government to gain political access but lose the moral high ground that they occupy as an alternative to the PS state, or they can refuse to join but face the difficulties of competing in Senegal's patrimonial politics with limited resources. To fully appreciate this dilemma, we now turn to an examination of the centrality of political patronage in Senegal and its impact upon the political accountability of the EPM.

Political Accountability and the Senegalese Electorate: Citizens or Clients?

The arguments for an enlarged presidential majority extend beyond the issue of political stability and the opportunity for opposition leaders to gain a voice in the government. Ideally, by including opposition parties, the broader political base of the EPM would enhance the representative nature of the government and its accountability to the Senegalese electorate, and thereby further the democratization process and improve governance—both economic and political—in general. The nature of political accountability in Senegal, however, makes the logic of this argument less than certain.

As mentioned above, only a handful of Senegalese can be said to support a given political party based on its political platform or ideology. Despite differences in their espoused ideologies—they range from the avowed Marxists of the PIT to the converted liberals of the PDS—there are no significant policy differences among Senegal's political parties.[38] The central issue in each election has been the integrity of the party's leadership: are they honorable men? In Senegal, however, integrity and honor are not synonyms for honesty so much as for generosity. The meaning of being a man of honor, as Christian Coulon has explained, is tied to a culture of clientelism that dates to Senegal's precolonial societies.[39] In this context, concerns about corruption and antidemocratic manipulation of political institutions are overshadowed by the effects of politicians' capacity to distribute patronage.

Popular reaction to two recent political "scandals" illustrates the patrimonial nature of accountability in Senegal. During the 1993 legislative elections, opposition candidates in the department of Mbacke accused the PS deputy, Bassirou Ndao, of skimming large sums of money from the Senegalese lottery, LONASE, during his tenure as its director.[40] Despite the magnitude of the charges, the scandal did not hurt Ndao's popularity among his constituents, who saw themselves as beneficiaries of his largesse and reelected him to office.

When I first learned of the LONASE scandal, I was in a village in the department of Mbacke, listening to the nightly legislative campaign speeches on the radio with a half dozen men and women. They were all aghast. No one was surprised that the deputy who they supported for reelection was accused of embezzlement. But how could the opposition candidate making the accusations talk about such things in public?! The villagers maintained that any transgression by the deputy was justified by the jobs he provided as the director of the lottery commission. However, although Ndao was reelected by a decisive majority, he had become a political embarrassment to the PS and was not reappointed to his ministerial post. Ultimately, it was his lack of access to state resources that eventually led his supporters in Mbacke to dismiss him as the local leader of the PS.[41]

The second scandal was disclosed while I was in a village along the Senegal River valley in the department of Matam. In July 1993, the state radio acknowledged that newly elected deputies from several small opposition parties had revealed a secret pact formed between the PS and the PDS in 1991 to double the salaries of the deputies, at a time when these were the only two parties represented in the National Assembly.[42] This arrangement was allegedly part of the negotiated entry of the PDS into the PS government. Since ministers' salaries were substantially larger than those of deputies, President Diouf sought to placate the PDS, which was to receive significantly fewer ministries than the PS, by raising the deputies' salaries. This pact thus indicated that negotiating their entry into the EPM had diverted opposition parties from the task of keeping the government honest.

Nevertheless, the Matamois with whom I spoke took the revelations about the secret pact in stride and even defended the politicians' decision to double their salaries. As one young educated man explained, the deputies have a lot of expenses; they must, for example, maintain a large home for the people who come to them day and night for money and other favors. Consequently, he argued, the secret funds were necessary to pay for "legitimate" expenses, the benefits of which would ultimately trickle down to the deputies' constituents.[43]

The reaction of Senegalese citizens to these political scandals reflects the patrimonial nature of state-society relations in Senegal, as well as elsewhere in Africa, which subordinates the political rights of citizens to their interests as political clients. Rather than holding politicians accountable for the legislation and implementation of laws that have been negotiated in the public arena, Senegalese are more concerned with the capacity of politicians to gain access to, and distribute public resources through, informal patronage networks.

The "political nomadism" for which Senegalese party politics has become renowned provides further evidence of the patrimonial nature of political accountability, both in the ruling party and in the opposition, especially the PDS.[44] There is essentially a revolving door between these two parties, particularly during an electoral year. PDS supporters join the PS to gain better access to state resources, while PS supporters who have been excluded from access to the resources of the PS state join the opposition, for example, when their faction (*tendance*) has lost an internal party election (*renouvellement*). The PS, of course, has more to offer defectors, which accounts for the large number of PDS supporters who joined the PS during the 1996 electoral campaign.[45] Each defection represents not only greater electoral support for a party, but also a public relations coup against its opponents.

During the 1993 elections, I spoke with various members of the ruling party and the opposition who had chosen to switch parties for precisely these reasons. In one case, an entire village had switched from the PS to the PDS after the defeat of the local PS faction leader had resulted in the village's exclusion from the public resources distributed by the rural council president, including food aid and peanut seeds. A prominent marabout in the area also supported Wade's PDS candidacy in 1993 because Diouf had ignored his requests for a well and a road for one of his villages. However, he switched back to the PS during the legislative elections when he found that the PDS leader was "ungrateful" for the marabout's political support—that is, the PDS had provided no material benefits to the marabout.

Nor are these attitudes restricted to the two major parties. Several months after his party had joined the government, an LD-MPT activist asked me whether he had made the right decision in supporting the party since Bathily refused to use his ministry to distribute patronage to his supporters. Not surprisingly, the results of the 1996 elections suggest that Bathily's emphasis during the campaign on the PS's squandering of public resources on political patronage did not seem to resonate with voters.

As Claude Ake astutely pointed out, "ordinary Africans do not separate political democracy from economic democracy or for that matter from economic wellbeing."[46] Senegalese, however, are less concerned with general economic democracy than with their own economic well-being; their first priority is day-to-day survival in an economy that is perpetually in crisis despite the modest improvements that devaluation has yielded. In this sense, Senegal's political economy has reinforced the country's political culture based on patrimonialism, as well as the dominant-party system. Despite dwindling state resources, the Senegalese state continues to dominate the economy, so who has greater potential for fulfilling their patronage obligations than officials of the PS state?

Given the patrimonial nature of accountability in Senegal, the question remains whether this has an adverse impact on democratization and governance in general. Guillermo O'Donnell has recently written a corrective to his earlier argument that the consolidation of a democratic transition requires institutionalization. He now argues that the issue is not a lack of institutions, but the difference between democracies with formal and informal institutions. Wishing to move away from the teleological and ethnocentric aspects of much writing about consolidation, O'Donnell argues that Robert Dahl's classic definition of polyarchy is exacting in terms of elections, but mute on the precise institutional features of a democracy. Furthermore, O'Donnell claims that Dahl's definition "is silent about important but elusive themes such as if, how, and to what degree governments are responsive or accountable to citizens between elections, and the degree to which the rule of law extends over the country's geographic and social terrain."[47]

Despite the possibility of treating "patrimonial democracy" as another form of "democracy with an adjective," in the absence of free and fair elections, Senegal remains ineligible for categorization as a democracy, whether informally institutionalized or otherwise. Nevertheless, it is important to consider the impact of patrimonialism on the government's performance.

Political patronage is not an absolute evil. Based on asymmetries in social, economic, and/or political power, patronage is a form of political bargaining that exists within all forms of government, including consolidated democracies. In fact, Carl H. Landé argues that patron-client relations may foster an important dimension of trust and commitment that is absent from legal-rational institutions.[48] Furthermore, patrimonialism provides important links between the state and society that assure access, particularly in inclusive patronage networks such as Senegal's that incorporate each ethnoregional and religious group in society. Coulon describes the ambivalence that surrounds Senegal's patronage networks:

> It is true that they are responsible for the corruption, the prevarication, or at the least, the manipulation of institutions for personal aims that are features of modern political life. On the other hand, they are also a way to control power. A "boss" who is unable to furnish the benefits expected will be disowned by his rank and file (his clients) in favor of a rival who appears to be more generous.[49]

Nevertheless, personalized patron-client relationships and private negotiation of political patronage are at odds with the democratic principles of universal rights and political competition in the public sphere.[50] While patronage networks can provide members of peripheral communal groups with access to resources and influence in the implementation—if not the formulation—of legislation, patronage is nonetheless based on inequity and a patron's arbitrary control of the distribution of political resources. Democracy, on the other hand, is predicated on a system of legal rights and equal access to state resources and on competition in a public arena for defining those rights and assuring their implementation.[51]

Therefore, while patrimonialism under an authoritarian regime may assure some form of political access and accountability in an otherwise closed political system, in a fledgling "semidemocracy" such as Senegal, accountability based on the distribution of public resources through personalized patronage networks does not promote democratic institutions or practices. As we have seen in the political scandals involving the director of Senegal's lottery commission and the secret pact on deputies' salaries between the PS and the PDS, unlawful acts by political leaders may be exposed but go unpunished in a political culture based on patrimonialism because the transgressions are not condemned by citizens, whose primary concern is protecting their own clientelist access to public resources.

Elsewhere I have discussed at length how the persistence of electoral fraud is intertwined with the patrimonial nature of the PS state, thus perpetuating the dominant-party system.[52] Given the limited economic opportunities outside the state, it is not surprising that the leaders of the PS state and their clients, in both the institutions of the state and the ruling party, would use their vast resources as political incumbents to ensure their tenure in office by controlling the legislation, administration, and adjudication of the electoral process.

The obvious implications, in terms of both the democratization process and governance in general, are disillusioning. Even if political alternation should occur, the experience of the opposition parties in the EPM suggests that little would change in terms of the patrimonial logic of Senegalese politics. In fact, the EPM appears to have reinforced a system of accountability based on political patronage. Since participation in the government circumscribes an opposition party's claim that it offers a political alternative to the PS state, opposition parties within the EPM have become increasingly reliant upon the distribution of resources to generate and maintain their political support. Consequently, while the EPM has extended political representation and accountability in terms of access by a broader segment of the Senegalese electorate, it has not had the desired effect on democratization and governance.

There are, however, prospects on the horizon for altering Senegal's political culture and thereby advancing the democratization process. Moving beyond a patrimonial form of accountability is not so much a question of educating the Senegalese population about democracy and their rights as citizens as it is a question of restructuring Senegal's political economy. Currently, Senegal's political culture is reinforced by a state-dominated economy in which its citizens are economically reliant upon representatives of the state as their political patrons, who provide access to food aid, development projects, and employment in the dominant public sector. However, the growth of Senegal's remittance economy, based on hundreds of thousands of immigrants living in various African cities and overseas, has increased the potential economic, and therefore political, autonomy of both rural and urban Senegalese from the state. Furthermore, economic reforms such as the devaluation of the CFA (Communauté Financière Africaine) franc and the privatization of various parastatals may also increase autonomy through the development of the private sector and the Senegalese economy in general.

Conclusion

This essay examines the Senegalese experience with the "enlarged presidential majority" since the first "government of national unity" was formed in 1991. It focuses on three crucial elements of a democracy—the electoral process, political competition, and accountability—to analyze the impact of the EPM on Senegal's democratization process and to assess the possible application of the Senegalese model to other African countries that are struggling with repressive dominant-party systems.

The initial motive for the opposition parties to join the first EPM in 1991 was to obtain reforms in the electoral process, but the evidence suggests that entering the government was not actually necessary to negotiate a new electoral code. Furthermore, recent efforts to create an independent electoral commission demonstrate that the opposition parties have more leverage with the PS state when they act as a unified political force outside the government than they do when pursuing reforms from within. The EPM has largely served to divide and silence the opposition. In a semidemocracy such as Senegal, an independent political opposition plays a crucial role in promoting democratic reform and practices. Unfortunately, the EPM has not only circumscribed criticism by the opposition, it has also reinforced a form of political accountability based on political patronage that subordinates a commitment to democratic institutions to clientelist access to public resources.

Despite these limitations, the Senegalese model is regarded in some quarters as conducive to political stability. Representatives of the World Bank and Western donors have promoted the EPM as a means of providing the political stability necessary for the implementation of economic reforms.[53] Ultimately, these reforms may permit economic autonomy from the PS state for both the opposition and the citizenry, thereby enabling Senegal to move beyond its current political culture of patrimonialism. In the short term, however, the EPM should be seen for what it is: not a deepening of democracy, but a detour.

Notes

This chapter draws upon data I collected while doing research in Senegal between October 1992 and January 1994, which was made possible by grants from the Fulbright-Hays Scholarship Board and the Social Science Research Council.

1. Diamond, "Is the Third Wave Over?" p. 25.
2. Although several names have been used to refer to the "enlarged presidential majority," including the initial term "government of national unity," I will use EPM to refer in general to the practice of incorporating opposition parties into the PS-led government.
3. *West Africa*, "Deepening Democracy?" p. 702.
4. Zuccarelli, *La Vie politique*.
5. In defining democracy, I defer to the most widely cited definition, that of Robert Dahl, who identifies eight essential democratic institutions, including free and fair elections, the right to compete for political support, and institutions for making government policies depend upon an electoral mandate and other expressions of political preferences. See Dahl, *Polyarchy*, p. 3.
6. Kpatindé, "Les Tares," pp. 22–23.
7. Bourgi, "Concubinage politique," pp. 20–21.
8. Bourgi and Fall, "Charmes et limites," p. 19.
9. Ibid., p. 20.
10. For a more detailed description of the electoral fraud surrounding the 1993 elections, see Beck, "Senegal's 'Patrimonial Democrats.'"
11. Diawara, "Consensus," p. 3.
12. Mbodje, "Le Code électoral modifié," p. 3.
13. *Soleil*, "Commission électorale indépendante," p. 3.

14. Abdoulaye Wade and two other PDS leaders rejoined the government in February 1995 after the PDS abruptly left the EPM in October 1992, protesting that they had been excluded from the governmental process following Wade's announcement of his candidacy for the 1993 presidential elections.

15. E. Fall, "Sénégal: Le triomphe modeste," p. 24. The official results were published by rural, municipal, and regional districts in *Soleil* between November 30 and December 2, 1996.

16. Diawara, "Bilan des élections: Le PDS exprime," "Bilan des élections locales: La CDP/Garab-gi crie," and "L'Opposition appelle"; Sarr, "Mamadou Ndoye"; *Soleil,* "Idrissa Seck"; and Diouf, "AJ/PADS."

17. E. Fall, "Plus de peur."

18. *Soleil,* "Interdiction."

19. Diawara, "L'Opposition appelle." Although Professor Abdoulaye Bathily, the leader of the LD-MPT, a small former Marxist party, initially opposed participation in the EPM without first negotiating a common platform, Bathily led the LD-MPT into the government after the 1993 legislative elections. See Kpatindé, "Les Tares," p. 22.

20. Diawara, "L'Opposition appelle."

21. Diawara, "Bilan des élections locales: La LD/MPT demande"; Diouf, "Conférence de presse."

22. D. M. Fall, "Le PDS"; Diawara, "Rétrait du gouvernement."

23. *Soleil,* "Bureau politique."

24. D. M. Fall, "Plainte du PS."

25. According to a journalist with the *Sud Quotidien,* an independent Senegalese daily, the commission is to be headed by the vice president of the Constitutional Court, Ibou Dia Diaté. Given Diaté's ties to the PS, however, the opposition demanded that Professor Abdul Kadir Boye, a known critic of the PS state, also be included (personal communication, February 1997).

26. PDS-R, led by Professor Sereigne Diop, is a microparty that splintered from the PDS in the 1980s over a personality conflict with Wade. Although the PDS-R cannot count more than a handful of Dakar intellectuals among its membership, Diop's ministerial appointment may be attributed to his public support for President Diouf during the 1993 elections, thus bolstering the PS candidate's claim to a broad base of support from a coalition of political parties.

27. Personal communications with various leaders of the LD-MPT, 1993.

28. *Soleil,* "Quelques idées-forces."

29. Personal communication with a *Sud Quotidien* journalist, 1997.

30. D. M. Fall, "AJ/PADS: le 3ème parti"; E. Fall, "Sénégal: Le triomphe modeste"; and *Soleil,* "Interdiction." Although accusations of fraud call into question the persistent electoral victories of the PS, both political parties and outside observers accept that the electoral results provide insights into political trends and the relative popularity of Senegal's opposition parties.

31. Faes, "Sénégal," p. 27.

32. Ibid.

33. E. Fall, "Sénégal: Le triomphe modeste," p. 25.

34. Included in Wade's political calculus are his declining prospects of ever becoming head of state as he approaches his eighth decade. My appreciation to Crawford Young for noting my omission of this factor from an earlier draft of this chapter.

35. *West Africa,* "Deepening Democracy?" p. 702.

36. E. Fall, "Sénégal: En attendant Wade."

37. *Soleil,* "Quelques idées-forces."

38. The initial leaders of the PDS, who considered themselves socialists, consented to embrace a liberal agenda in 1975 in order to gain recognition of the party under President Senghor's three-party system.

39. Coulon, "Senegal," p. 60.

40. I. Fall, "Comment la Lonase"; Lom, "Mbacke"; and Talla, "Bassirou Ndao."

41. Bagde, "Commune de Mbacke"; Babou, "Commune de Mbacke: Un budget en souris" and "Commune de Mbacke: Le budget approuvé."

42. *Soleil,* "Salaire"; *Sud Quotidien,* "Salaires."

43. Personal communication, 1993.

44. E. Fall, "Sénégal: Le triomphe modeste."

45. Ameth, "Demission"; Ndiaye, "Défection au PDS"; and *Soleil,* "Un député démissione" and "Un autre député."

46. Ake, "Unique Case," p. 241.

47. O'Donnell, "Illusions," p. 36; Dahl, *Polyarchy.* The teleology that O'Donnell seeks to avoid seems to creep back in, however, when he describes patrimonial deviations from the "full institutional package" of formal rules as antagonistic to polyarchy and "informally institutionalized" democracies as inferior without explaining what makes them substandard. See O'Donnell, "Illusions," pp. 40–41.

48. Landé, "Dyadic Basis of Clientelism."

49. Coulon, "Senegal," p. 160.

50. Clapham, "Clientelism and the State."

51. Roniger, "Comparative Study of Clientelism," p. 9.

52. Beck, "Senegal's 'Patrimonial Democrats.'"

53. Faes, "Senegal," p. 25.

12

Testing Democracy in Benin: Experiments in Institutional Reform

Bruce A. Magnusson

In April 1996, Benin's voters dismissed an incumbent president for the second time in five years. The victor was Mathieu Kérékou, the military-Marxist dictator from 1972 to 1990, now a born-again Christian and newly converted democrat. The election came a year after the second quadrennial National Assembly elections in 1995, which ousted 80 percent of the incumbents elected in 1991. Benin's 1990 National Conference set a continental standard for the nonviolent, civilian toppling of authoritarian rule and the subsequent establishment of a workable democratic regime. By 1996, Benin had become one of the few democratic success stories in Africa in terms of real competitive politics, electorally based alternations of power, respect for human rights, and enforcement of constitutional rules for political behavior.

That it should be Benin that sets such a standard is remarkable. In 1972, Benin (then Dahomey) held the African record for the number of successful coups d'état, all of which came during the first 12 years of its independence. Benin was generally regarded as the "sick man" of Africa. Two years after the putsch that elevated him to power in 1972, Kérékou followed Congo's lead and created the second military-Marxist "people's republic" in France's former African empire.[1] By the end of the 1980s, Benin was one of the 20 most impoverished countries on earth.[2]

The disparity between the political debates of 1990 and those of the 1996 presidential election illustrates the institutional distance Benin has traveled. In 1990, the debates focused on the grand subjects of repression and human rights, the role of the military in the state, the role of the state in the economy, how to fix the moral and financial bankruptcy of the state, and whether the end of the Marxist regime would be peaceful or bloody. By 1996, public attention refocused on "normal" politics such as the implementation of decentralization reforms, the aftermath of the 1994 devaluation, employment and the extent of privatization, crime and security, presidential accountability, nepotism, and minor corruption. Ethnoregional distribution, always a political subtext in Benin, was again a factor in government and alliance formation, but without the high stakes of the 1960s political discourse.

In 1996, human rights are being protected in Benin. The press, despite a few incidents, has been unfettered. Political parties, civic associations, and a spectrum of religious groups are active and growing. The military is back in the barracks. Public finances have been cleaned up substantially, and, although hotly debated, structural adjustment reforms are being implemented. Economic growth rates since 1990 have varied between 3 and 6 percent. Despite residual uneasiness about the durability of democracy, a collective cognitive shift is taking place in Benin from the highly uncertain environment defined by the question "whether democracy?" to one defined by the second-order question "whither democracy?"

In an opinion essay in the *Christian Science Monitor,* former President Nicéphore Soglo characterized the elections that ousted him as a victory for democracy, not because he was defeated, but because of the manner in which he was defeated, rejecting the Afro-pessimist argument that democracy in Africa has peaked, is epiphenomenal, and is destined to fail.[3] Benin, along with a few other African states, serves as a stark antidote to Afro-pessimism. As an African exception to expectations that democracy is unlikely to take root in impoverished countries characterized by communal discord, a lack of civic trust, and a political history of exceptional instability, it is important to examine why and how Benin defies the odds. What is responsible for Benin's apparently successful efforts to establish democratic rules of governance since 1990 amid the failures of its immediate neighbors, Nigeria, Togo, and Niger?

Many factors have contributed to Benin's relative success, including leadership, national will, weariness with authoritarianism, and external support. I will focus on institutional design and testing because they are central to the equation shaping a highly competitive political system in a historical context of perpetual economic crisis and politicized ethnoregionalism. This story has two interrelated parts. The first lies in the design of the new constitution and the explicit lessons its drafters took from the past to address Benin's particular configuration of political, economic, and ethnoregional instability. The second is a saga of crisis and testing of both institutional and democratic boundaries by political leaders, government officials, and society. This is, however, just a small piece of the story of how a constitution in Africa is becoming a normative point of reference for its subjects.

Persistent macropolitical issues transcend the instability of the 1960s, the dictatorship of the 1970s and 1980s, and the civilian rebellion and subsequent democratic regime of the 1990s. First, Benin's colonial history institutionalized a particularly destabilizing, tripartite, ethnoregional competition that, in combination with personal ambitions in a context of economic crisis, resulted in six military coups d'état. Until Kérékou, who first ruled from 1972 to 1990, no regime had ever lasted more than three and one-half years before being toppled by the military. This tripartite division was complicated by important north-south cultural differences and economic disparities.[4] Second, the primary economic contradiction with which Benin has had to cope pits a small-scale agricultural and commercial trading economy, almost entirely bereft of marketable natural resources, against the demands of an oversized and ever-increasing cohort of bureaucratic elites. Economic scarcity intensified the struggle over the definition of institutional arrangements that were meant to distribute power among competing ethnoregional patronage networks. As a result, the country has been in almost perpetual economic crisis since the 1950s.

The intersection of economic scarcity with a struggle over institutional arrangements was the backdrop for an ideological struggle over the appropriate role of the state in the economy and, by extension, over access to state resources. Official corruption generated by state control over much of the economy has been a transcendent theme as well, encouraged by the existence of a one-party state, but intensified by regional, ethnic, and family rivalries. The elimination of official corruption has been one popular expectation of new civilian and military regimes across Africa over the past three decades. However, in the absence of legitimate oppositions with access to effective institutional levers to enforce accountability, attempts to control corruption have failed.

The military-authoritarian solution to political instability became the seedbed of rampant corruption and increasingly untenable repression in the 1980s. The financial restrictions of structural adjustment, the looting of state coffers, and the collapse of the banking system destroyed the regime's ability to finance civil peace. In the years prior to the transition, corruption, lack of paychecks, and broad human rights abuses transformed resentment into more active opposition. Under duress, President Kérékou presided over the dismantling of a bankrupt, patronage-based banking system, as well as the dissolution of the one-party state, the official burial of Marxism-Leninism, dispensations offering freedom of the press and political organization, and a grant of amnesty to political prisoners and exiles. The process Kérékou set in motion led to the National Conference and set the stage for the complete repudiation of the old regime in what he and his supporters bitterly described as a "civilian coup d'état."[5]

The Collapse of Kérékou Authoritarianism

The fall of the Kérékou regime in 1989–1990 and the rise of the successor democratic regime cannot be understood without recognizing the configuration of crisis that had plagued Benin since the 1950s. The solutions

Kérékou imposed to uproot ethnoregional patronage networks and to create jobs by executive fiat were eventually undermined by new patronage networks, insolvent state enterprises, poverty wages (if they were paid at all), and the bankrupting of the state by rampant corruption. This bankruptcy was an important factor in the delegitimation of authoritarianism and the initial legitimation of democracy. It voided any moral authority or pretense of a "higher purpose" that the Kérékou regime could claim.

Kérékou's decision in 1974 to declare Marxism-Leninism as the guiding ideology of the newly named People's Republic of Benin served a variety of purposes. Supported by an anti-neocolonial program of nationalization, he sharply reduced French influence in the commercial and agricultural sectors, while creating over 120 new state-owned enterprises to absorb the ever-growing educated and skilled urban workforce. This vast, new state-controlled system of employment replaced the decentralized economic leverage of the ethnoregional political networks.

Dependent on the twin pillars of the stability of an internationally convertible currency (the French-backed CFA [Communauté Financière Africaine] franc) and the huge Nigerian market on its eastern border, Benin's economy is substantially affected by the health of the Nigerian economy (and of the naira, Nigeria's currency). Nigeria provides enormous informal trade opportunities, which account for much of Benin's "unrecorded" wealth. In the 1970s, increased tax recovery, along with the Nigerian oil-induced spending spree, brought a period of economic growth that was further stimulated by several large industrial projects. By the 1980s, Kérékou had tripled state employment.

However, the combination of an enormous salary bill and the oil price collapse in Nigeria signaled the emergence of a new economic crisis of massive proportions. Early in the 1980s, the International Monetary Fund (IMF), the World Bank, and Benin tentatively began a very slow and cautious dance, negotiating the shape of what many saw as a period of inevitable adjustment, either through economic collapse or by a planned, phased set of reforms. As the 1980s drew to a close and the reform process remained mired in an intractably sclerotic, corrupt, and predatory regime, salary payments stopped, and the commercial trading sector, dependent on a functioning banking system, dried up when the banks collapsed.[6]

The National Conference and Constitutional Design

The 1990 National Conference

In a popular metaphor referring to the expulsion of a sorcerer's malevolence from the body, the people finally "vomited" Kérékou's regime during the 1990 National Conference. Convened on February 19, 1990, and lasting for 10 days, the National Conference brought together representatives of many socioeconomic and professional groups, including teachers, students, the military, government officials, religious authorities, nongovernmental organizations, more than 50 political parties, ex-presidents, labor unions, business interests, farmers, and dozens of local development associations.[7] This kind of national meeting, the representatives of which are chosen based on professional, corporate, and societal affiliations, has been replicated by a series of sectoral *états-généraux* over the past few years. The first was a conference of the education sector in October 1990, aimed at devising a coherent set of policy orientations to reconstruct the country's devastated educational system.[8] The second, the *états-généraux* of territorial administration, met to construct a new system of decentralized national-local relationships. More recently, the *états-généraux* of the judicial system, convened in November 1996, and the December 1996 National Economic Conference have further expanded this unique mechanism for involving civil society in the policymaking process.[9]

On February 20, 1990, the second day of the National Conference, a delegate introduced a motion to declare the National Conference "sovereign." The furor that followed captivated much of west Africa, whose officials and populations were riveted by the unprecedented and unscripted radio broadcast of Benin's second "revolution" and what would become a uniquely African model for changing the way people are governed.[10] The suspense over Kérékou's (and the military's) response to this challenge was heightened by Maurice Kouandété, engineer of several coups in the 1960s, who stormed out of the conference center denouncing the motion as a coup d'état that would be met in kind. Over the next four days, as conference business—including a devastating critique of the regime—continued, fear of a potential military intervention intensified.

On February 25, the sovereignty motion was passed overwhelmingly; this was accompanied first by "a certain frenzy" and then by a spontaneous standing rendition of the national anthem. Only the barons of Kérékou's Parti de la Révolution Populaire du Bénin (PRPB) remained seated. Apparently, only direct intervention with President Kérékou by Archbishop de Souza, the Catholic prelate who had been elected as the chairman of the conference, prevented rupture. The delegates elected Nicéphore Soglo, formerly an executive director for Africa at the World Bank, as prime minister for the transition. Kérékou was not forced to resign as president—his condition for acquiescence—but his powers would be only ceremonial until elections were held. The army, in a written document, reaffirmed its intention to return to the barracks.[11]

The religious dimension of the National Conference cannot be underestimated.[12] Inaugurated with the prayers of Muslims, Catholics, and Protestants, as well as the vodun priests seeking sanction by the ancestors, the election of Archbishop de Souza as the conference chairman sanctified the proceedings. His role in averting the collapse of the conference into a bloody confrontation, and his efforts at displacing vengeance with reconciliation, conferred a sacral authority to decisions of the conference and its constitutional progeny during the transition.

In spite of the sovereignty motion, Kérékou claimed that his resignation would be illegal because the National Conference had not been elected and was therefore not a constituent assembly. Kérékou was still bound by his election under the 1977 constitution (Loi Fondamentale) and his oath of office. He admitted that the Marxist-Leninist option had been a divisive failure, rather than the unifying, developmental ideology that he had envisioned. In local culture, the regurgitation of the sorcerer's wares must be accompanied by an admission of culpability in order for the victim to be freed from its power.[13] Kérékou's admissions, his acceptance of National Conference decisions as binding, and his 1991 acceptance of his electoral defeat proved to be the basis for his national rehabilitation among many people as a heroic figure who had paved the way for African democracy. In return, the new government granted him amnesty for all misdeeds he may have committed as president.

De Souza, the military, Kérékou, Soglo, and the delegates not only managed to prevent a bloody impasse, but they created a semispiritual foundation for a constitutional reconciliation, to which the almost hymnlike qualities of the Final Report of the National Conference, drafted by Albert Tévoèdjrè, are testament. The subsequent normative power of the constitution must in some measure flow from this fusion of legal process with religious authority. The Haut Conseil de la République (HCR), the quasi-legislative arm of the transition state under the leadership of Archbishop de Souza, approved the draft constitution and supervised the 1991 legislative and presidential elections. De Souza's continued involvement enhanced this perception of a fusion of the sacred and secular during the 14-month transition period.

Constitutional Design

The Constitutional Commission appointed by the National Conference had the daunting tasks of designing Benin's seventh constitution in 30 years and creating an electoral system to govern elections for the National Assembly and the presidency. Unlike the situation in neighboring Niger, Togo, and Nigeria, the Constitutional Commission was insulated by the National Conference from manipulation or control by the government and the interests of any dominant ruling party. President Kérékou was not expected to win a competitive election, and Prime Minister Soglo had made a commitment not to run for the presidency. The strategic considerations of the politically ambitious were shaped by the nearly absolute uncertainty about future electoral outcomes, leading to agreement on constitutional checks and balances that would make it difficult for rival parties to control the entire apparatus of the state.

Adam Przeworski's insight that uncertainty of outcome is a defining feature of democracy is crucial.[14] What would follow the transitional government in Benin was indeed uncertain, in terms of which political formations and which political leaders would win or lose. This uncertainty was central to the ways in which both the constitutional institutions of the state and the electoral system were designed.

The Constitutional Commission had two imperatives within the broad framework imposed by the National Conference for a multiparty system of separated powers. First, the constitution had to avoid the ethnoregional paralysis of the 1960s with its specter of military intervention. Second, it had to structure a system that would minimize the authoritarian ambitions of a president and discourage the repression of political and economic freedoms that had characterized the Kérékou regime. Benin's six previous constitutions and many national elections had proved inadequate in serving these objectives.

The people of Benin are deeply, if not cynically, aware that constitutions and elections do not necessarily make a democracy. All previous experiments had foundered: single- and double-headed executives, multiple- and single-electoral districts, representation by population as well as by functional social categories, single- and multiparty states, and even a consociational three-member Presidential Council.[15] The challenge was to find an appropriate mix of constitutional institutions, rules for regulating conflict, and an electoral system that would avoid the failures of the past.

In the end, the commission observed Napoleon's admonition that successful and durable constitutions are those that are "short and vague."[16] The "vague" elements of the constitution concern the electoral system and the design and governance of subnational administrative divisions. The national constitutional institutions are more explicitly defined. It is not an unusual constitution, dividing power among the president, the National Assembly, and the Constitutional Court. Despite preferences from some quarters for a parliamentary system, it establishes a strong, but not omnipotent, executive branch, headed by a president elected to no more than two five-year terms. The National Assembly is subject to elections every four years; it is granted the power to vote on the national budget, oversight of the executive branch, and certain mechanisms to check the power of the president over both legislation and the abuse of power. The Constitutional Court, an innovation in Benin's historical experience, is given the absolute power of judicial review to determine the constitutionality of all laws, regulations, and government actions. In addition, it is charged with enforcing the human rights provisions of the constitution, which alone among African constitutions incorporates as law the African Charter on Human and Peoples' Rights, and it is to be accessible to every individual citizen with claims against the government for unconstitutional behavior and human rights abuses.

In the national constitutional referendum of December 1990, voters were given one outstanding issue to resolve. In order to eliminate the reassertion of political ambitions by the regional leaders of the 1960s, the drafters incorporated a controversial age limit of 65 on presidential candidates. Voters were given three options: a "yes" vote on the constitution, including the age limit; a "yes" vote on the constitution, deleting the age limit; and a "no" vote on the constitution. The constitution was overwhelmingly approved, with two-thirds of voters approving the age limit. Prime Minister Soglo, who had by now decided that he would run for president, defeated President Kérékou in a runoff election by a two-to-one margin, even as some minor but disturbing acts of electoral violence occurred in the northern department of Borgou.

Testing the 1990 Constitution

It is one thing to write a constitution and to hold elections; it is quite another for the system to operate as designed. Formal systems do not operate in a vacuum. Multiple interpretations and interests, persistent political and economic conflicts, and a history in which constitutions were essentially irrelevant documents do not augur well for constitutional compliance. In the first years of Benin's new regime, testing, understanding, refining, and complying with the new rules were the focus of much political conflict.

In this section, the three domains of interinstitutional conflict, electoral systems, and decentralization will be examined. Interinstitutional testing at the national level is essentially defined by the constitutional separation of powers and the procedures set forth for how the courts, the executive, and the legislature should interact. Conflict in this domain is about horizontal relations of power, and it is conducted through a discourse of constitutional interpretation. In Benin, the electoral system and the system of territorial administration and decentralization are subconstitutional arenas belonging to the domain of lawmaking. As such, they have been left to the realm of persistent political debate, revision, and reform. Unsettled, they have become periodic nodes of political mobilization and debate. The electoral system regulates relationships between electors and the elected (representation), while having substantial consequences for horizontal relations of power between the executive and the legislature. The system of territorial administration and issues of decentralization are more exclusively a matter of vertical relations of power between the national center and local communities.

The Constitutional Court and Interinstitutional Testing

The appointment process for the seven-member Constitutional Court is crucial to understanding its importance in legitimizing the new constitution in Benin. Only three members are appointed by the president, while four are appointed by the National Assembly. The president of the court is elected by all seven. Because Soglo lacked a political party of his own in the National Assembly, the rapidly shifting coalitions among the 14 parties represented could guarantee him only a tenuous and occasional majority. By 1993, when an organic law organizing the Constitutional Court was finally negotiated, the National Assembly had already emerged as a major independent political force. The court that was finally assembled—composed of eminent lawyers, constitutional scholars, and even Hubert Maga, Dahomey's first president—reflected a diversity of regional and political interests, as well as an almost universally acclaimed integrity and respect. Had a single political party been in control of both the presidency and the National Assembly, it is unlikely that the court, by its very composition, would have asserted the independence that it did or acquired the aura of national legitimacy that became its most important attribute.

Soon after the Constitutional Court was seated in 1993, it confronted a series of constitutional cases in which the legitimacy of the new democratic constitution was at stake. The court's decisions in these cases, in which both the National Assembly and the president were called to account, fundamentally transformed national perceptions about the feasibility of the rules established in the 1990 constitution, while establishing the court as the arbiter of interinstitutional disputes, displacing the usual recourse to military intervention.[17]

The President of the Supreme Court vs. the President of the Republic.[18] Under the 1990 constitution, the president of the Supreme Court, appointed by the president, enjoys a five-year term. In 1993, President Soglo tried to replace Frédéric Houndéton, who had been appointed during the transition, with the minister of justice, Yves Yèhouéssi. The latter was the target of a lawsuit brought by lawyers of the Court of Appeals in connection with a criminal case stemming from corruption scandals that had helped bankrupt the Kérékou state.[19] Because the president of the Supreme Court is a member of the High Court of Justice, a body otherwise appointed by the National Assembly for the purpose of trying a sitting president for crimes, the public perception was that Soglo had lost confidence in Houndéton's loyalty and was protecting himself from trials that might be instigated by an opposition National Assembly.[20] Soglo argued that because Houndéton was appointed prior to the ratification of the constitution, the governing 1966 law limited his term to three years. Houndéton and the Court of Appeals lawyers appealed Houndéton's dismissal to the Constitutional

Court, on the grounds that the constitutional provision for a five-year term superseded the transitional appointment and that Yèhouéssi's appointment would cause undue harm to the seven lawyers involved in the lawsuit against him.

Just hours before Yèhouéssi was scheduled to take the oath of office before a large diplomatic assemblage, the court issued its ruling on the case. Citing Article 158 of the constitution providing for the transition process, the court ruled that the 1990 provision of a five-year term superseded the 1966 law. In addition, it found that the Yèhouéssi appointment would be unconstitutionally harmful to the plaintiffs in the lawsuit by placing Yèhouéssi in the position of both judge and subject of the lawsuit in his capacity as head of the judicial system.[21]

While this ruling would be a matter of great importance in any country, such a challenge to an African head of state was unprecedented. Public unease over the uncertainty of the response was palpable. Referring to the public discomfort and even fear resulting from open political conflict among constitutional institutions, a commentator for the government-owned newspaper reminded readers that the court, the National Assembly, and the president each had to "assert its independence": "Insofar as they lean on the Constitution, our democracy will end up being more consolidated each time."[22] Despite the embarrassment to the government, the president's spokesperson, Théodore Holo, acknowledged that the government would acquiesce, stating, "we are in a State of Law, and the government bows before the Constitutional Court."[23]

The National Assembly vs. the Ministry of Interior.   One of the most important, precedent-setting constitutional challenges and court decisions of 1994 received little publicity. In this case, the legal counsel to the president of the National Assembly challenged the constitutionality of a Ministry of Interior decision on the conditions and methods for registering local associations.[24] The ministry restricted each administrative entity to one development association and required a prior investigation of morality and good conduct. Any association whose applications were denied or rescinded was required to cease all activities and liquidate its assets within one month. Local development associations, authorized originally under the Kérékou regime, had become parallel social service agencies in many communities, with the objective of gathering resources for local development activities, including building and maintaining education, health, transportation, or market facilities. As a patronage-building mechanism under the centralized Kérékou regime, each held a monopoly in its own community.

The court ruled against the government on two grounds. First, the court found that the domain of the contested ministry decision was legal, rather than regulatory, and therefore a joint responsibility of the executive and the National Assembly as specified in Article 98 of the constitution, which includes in the legal domain "citizenship, civil rights and fundamental guarantees accorded to citizens for the exercise of public liberties."[25] Second, and most important, the court declared the ministry decision an unconstitutional violation of the freedom of association and civil rights, including Article 10 of the African Charter of Human and Peoples' Rights.[26]

In what was probably the first time that the African Charter has been enforced by a supreme constitutional authority, albeit as an integral part of Benin's constitution and law, the decision liberated local communities from state-regulated monopolies over associational activities. It effectively opened up local patronage and power to political and economic competition.[27] A casual reading of the section of the *Journal Officiel de la République du Bénin,* which lists the associations registered by the Ministry of Interior, reveals that hundreds of small, new associations of all kinds have formed since 1990.[28] The possibility of associational competition to collect and allocate local community resources for various development activities has not gone unnoticed by competing politicians and associational entrepreneurs since the 1994 decision.

The National Assembly vs. the President of the Republic and *the President of the Republic vs. the National Assembly.* The second half of 1994 produced a constitutional crisis of major proportions between the president and the National Assembly over the 1994 budget. The 50 percent devaluation of the CFA franc in January had angered the population and produced immediate and uncontrolled inflation in the market, as well as low-level but sometimes violent social unrest among urban-based organized labor and student groups. The president's revised 1994 budget incorporated a 10 percent increase in civil service salaries and pensions and a 15 percent increase in student scholarships. During its budget considerations, the National Assembly amended the budget to increase civil service salaries and pensions by 15 percent and student scholarships by 25 percent.

Soglo rejected the assembly's budget, claiming that it had no jurisdiction over salaries, scholarships, and pensions, as these were regulatory, rather than legal, matters. Further, the president claimed that the assembly's budget did not meet constitutional requirements to balance new expenditures with additional revenues. Finally, he warned that such a budget would violate structural adjustment agreements among Benin, the World Bank, and the IMF, which had been ratified by the National Assembly, thereby endangering all donor financial commitments and devastating the economy. He supported his claims with a report from a French aid mission and a letter from the Chief of the Africa Division of the IMF.[29] In an overwhelming repudiation of the president that even included his allies, the National Assembly voted for their amended budget: 54 in favor, five opposed, four abstaining.

Complicated by a number of procedural issues related to the timing of the budget proposals, and by the need to revise budget figures following the January devaluation, the constitutional battle between the president and the National Assembly intensified when Soglo decided to implement his own budget under the special emergency powers stipulated in Article 68 of the constitution. Article 68 grants the president these powers if "the institutions of the Republic, the independence of the Nation, territorial integrity or the execution of international commitments are threatened in a serious and immediate manner, and when the regular functioning of public and constitutional powers are threatened or interrupted."[30]

In addition to the objections the president raised against the assembly's budget, another set of constitutional questions was raised by the use of Article 68. All of these issues would be decided by the Constitutional Court during the increasingly tense period between August and November 1994. The president warned that the crisis could lead to a repetition of the cycle of economic crisis, belt-tightening, and military coups in the 1960s: "The same causes producing the same effects, the decision of the National Assembly risks driving us toward the same difficulties and the same suffering."[31] In addition to calling for a "government of national unity" (a thinly veiled reference to military governments in the 1960s), Tévoèdjrè, a bitter Soglo rival from the southeast and former deputy director of the International Labor Organization, wrote a letter to most of the donor agencies and governments asking them to back off. "The rules and procedures of the IMF and the World Bank are one thing; social and political reality is also a constraint which it would be wise to keep in mind if one hopes to keep this country on its feet."[32]

The government responded with a blistering attack from the president's spokesperson:

> It will be trouble when someone decides to form a government of national unity, or perhaps, once again it will be a coup d'état—because there are those that dream of one and who are making contacts for that—so that they will be named head of state. Is that democratic behavior? When I see these people getting agitated and announce their intentions, which are putschist intentions . . . and when I arrived to head this department, I felt it. . . . One should not desire to be president outside of the expression of popular suffrage, because today in Africa, power comes from the voting urns; power is no longer at the end of a gun. I appeal to our people to prove their vigilance.[33]

A cartoon in *Le Matin,* the independent daily, illustrated the impasse. In it, the leaders of the three branches are each resting on a copy of the constitution. President Soglo defiantly says, "Constitutionally, I order . . ."; Adrien Houngbédji, president of the National Assembly, says, "Constitutionally, I object . . ."; and Elisabeth Pognon, president of the Constitutional Court, says, "Constitutionally, we shall see . . ."[34]

The series of four Constitutional Court decisions required to resolve the impasse began on August 26, with a decision that declared the president's use of Article 68 unconstitutional on the procedural ground that he did not seek the advice of the court prior to invoking Article 68, as required by the court's own organic law. On the other hand, the court also stated that it had no authority over the president's discretion to decide when the appropriate conditions for invoking Article 68 were present. In other words, the president did not seek the court's prior advice, but in any case, that advice would not be binding.[35] On September 9, the court ruled on the president's challenge to the assembly law that limited the president's use of emergency powers to one day. Article 69 requires the assembly to set such a deadline. This time, the court issued a procedural ruling against the National Assembly, which had allowed a second reading of the law during a special session, rather than during an ordinary session as required by Articles 88 and 57.[36] Promptly closing the special session, the assembly opened an ordinary session and issued a new deadline, which the president immediately appealed to the court.

Meanwhile, having now asked for the court's advice on once again using emergency powers, the president ignored the court's admonition that these powers were unnecessary since the assembly's budget law was never implemented.[37] Two weeks later, the court ruled that the assembly's budget was unconstitutional, but only on one of the grounds claimed by the government. It agreed with the government that salaries, pensions, and scholarships were regulatory in nature and therefore not under the purview of the National Assembly. At the same time, though, it ruled that the budget violated neither the balanced budget provisions of the constitution nor any international agreements.[38] In a separate ruling, the court also ruled that the National Assembly had acted constitutionally in setting a limit on the president's use of emergency powers.[39]

By this time, the fiscal year was almost over, and remaining budget conflicts had been resolved through negotiations under the auspices of the "committee" of ex-presidents, including Justin Ahomadégbé, a deputy and former regional leader of Zou Province; Emile-Derlin Zinsou, a deputy and former president from the south; and Kérékou, still a regional power in the north but living in retirement in Cotonou.[40] Hubert Maga, the northern regional leader who was independent Dahomey's first president, was now a member of the Constitutional Court. In contrast to the trauma over the 1994 budget, the National Assembly voted unanimously for the 1995 budget submitted by the government, 25 days before the deadline.

More recently, the Constitutional Court nullified the election results in two districts after the 1995 elections, including that of Rosine Soglo. Earlier, it had even nullified the candidacy of a major northern politician, Aboubakar Baba Moussa, former president of the West African Development Bank, for not fulfilling Beninese residency requirements. New elections were held on May 28, 1995, in these two districts, and Rosine Soglo was able to retain her seat.

President Kérékou, too, had an immediate lesson in the power of the Constitutional Court. At his 1996 inauguration before the National Assembly, he omitted a reference to the "spirit of the ancestors" from the oath of office required by the constitution. Following citizen complaints to the court, the court required him to return to the National Assembly and to retake the oath in its entirety, ruling that it is "sacramental and indivisible," another indication of the almost spiritual dimension the constitution has acquired.[41]

Debating Electoral Systems: Vertical and Horizontal Relationships

Just as the Constitutional Court has been central in holding political institutions accountable to constitutional rules, the electoral system of the National Assembly is critical for establishing formal vertical relations of power and accountability between electors and elected. In addition, the system shapes horizontal political competition between the executive branch and the legislature. Because the electoral system is not constitutionally determined in Benin, it is the subject of periodic political mobilization, debate, and revision. Prior to the 1995 National Assembly elections, issues of fairness and accountability animated debates about the relative merits of proportional representation (PR) and single-member districts (SMD), as well as those about the advisability of establishing an independent electoral commission.

Benin has experimented with a variety of electoral systems since the 1950s. Avoiding political mobilization based on ethnoregionalism has become the major refrain for all postindependence electoral arrangements. Under the guise of preserving national unity, the 1960 National Assembly was comprised entirely from the party list of the winning party. The victorious ethnoregional party alliance between the north and the southeast thus shut out the Fon ethnic group from any participation in governing institutions from 1960 to 1963. All subsequent electoral systems have likewise permitted only single-party victories. Rather than promoting unity, political competition therefore became a zero-sum, tripartite competition for power among regional party networks and leaders, resulting in a succession of military coups in the 1960s.[42] The aborted 1970 presidential elections then ended all multiparty competition for 20 years.

Kérékou's program of nationalist anti-neocolonialism and Marxism-Leninism was explicitly designed to rid the country of ethnoregional politics. Requiring an end to "unnatural" internal divisions created by colonialism, the new unifying enemy was external, French, and imperialist. Like the Leninist solution in the Soviet Union, the Kérékou regime's Loi Fondamentale recognized the "multinational" character of the state and the cultural rights of all "nationalities." The electoral system for the Revolutionary National Assembly was therefore based on corporate and class membership, rather than electoral district. Designed to avoid ethnoregional mobilization, as well as to promote the ideological agenda of the regime, this kind of representation retains some popular support in Benin, especially among such groups as students, women, and traditional medical practitioners who no longer have guaranteed seats in the assembly.

Consistent with the National Conference's instructions for a system of "integral multipartyism," the 1991 electoral code prepared by the HCR formed a modified pure-proportional system, dividing the country into six districts congruent with its six departments and specifying that there would be proportional representation within each. This system was designed to discourage the rebuilding of the three ethnoregional parties that had afflicted Dahomey in the 1960s. Deputies were to be considered representatives of the nation, rather than of narrow, regional interests.[43] By dividing the country into six multimember districts and establishing a low mathematical threshold for representation, the system created structural incentives for the proliferation of political parties.

The loyalties of the 14 political parties and alliances in the new assembly were extremely fluid during the period from 1991 to 1994. Three parliamentary groups (pro-Soglo, opposition, independent) were evenly divided; no real majority emerged until the May 1992 debate on privatizing the country's brewery, La Béninoise. For a time after this debate, Soglo was able to construct a working majority, but it collapsed under the pressures of a ministerial reshuffle in September 1993. Until the 1995 elections, the president could command only 19 of the 64 votes in the assembly, a number that declined even further during the 1994 budget crisis. This fluidity of loyalty brought charges of *la politique politicienne* (politicians' politics) by which support for the government came only at the price of a personal ministerial post.[44]

The 1991 National Assembly was widely criticized for its elitism and its urban bias. Most voters did not know their representatives and were thus unable to confront them or make demands upon them. People commonly complained that candidates arrived in the village making promises about new roads, health facilities, schools, and electricity, but they would never be seen again.[45] In many cases, the locally popular candidates that had been responsible for obtaining a large portion of a party's vote were too far down on the party list to become deputies themselves. Even as preparations for the 1995 assembly elections began toward the end of 1993, the president launched a new debate over the system of representation, advocating single-member districts, as he sought a way in which to guarantee a governing majority in the assembly.

In April 1994, President Soglo increased the temperature of the debate and generated a new constitutional crisis by announcing that he would seek a national referendum on the creation of an SMD system of representation. Although the president has the constitutional power to call for a referendum, the electoral regime is constitutionally a matter of law and is therefore a joint responsibility of the president and the National Assembly. Condemning the president for overreaching his authority, the assembly and even major political parties were nevertheless deeply divided over the relative merits of SMD, PR, and mixed electoral systems.

Because no legal framework yet existed for holding national referenda, the crisis threatened the timely scheduling of the February 1995 National Assembly elections. Time eventually overcame intention, and the president was forced to approve an assembly compromise increasing the number of assembly seats, tripling the number of electoral districts to 18, and maintaining proportional representation within each district.[46] This solution was expected to increase local accountability while preserving minority party participation in the National Assembly. In addition, the president was forced to accept an independent electoral commission, which stripped electoral supervision from the Ministry of Interior.[47]

Over 5,100 candidates representing 31 eligible political formations (49 parties) participated in the March 28, 1995, elections, an enormous level of active political participation for a country of five million people. The voters removed two-thirds of the incumbent deputies, electing new members from 17 political parties. Soglo's party, Renaissance du Bénin, and the party of his rival, Houngbédji, the Parti du Renouveau Démocratique (PRD), each won 20 seats; they were the only parties to win more than 10 percent of the nationwide vote. The remnants of Kérékou's political core in the northern-based FARD-Alafia won 10 seats based on a share of only 6 percent in the nationwide vote. While these parties are overrepresented nationally, the voting in five of the six departments exhibited a substantial increase in single-party dominance, and fewer parties won seats outside of their regional bases.[48] In 1991, nine parties won seats in three or more departments; in 1995, only three parties succeeded in winning outside of their primary regional constituency.[49]

Despite the suspicion and uneasiness generated by ethnic voting, the electoral system guarantees minority representation and, unlike any previous system, guarantees representation in the National Assembly of more than a single party. It has avoided the zero-sum competition of the 1960s, while guaranteeing what are, after all, legitimate desires by the electorate for regional and cultural representation and accountability. A majority for any single party (or president) is structurally difficult under the current system, and a governing majority obtained through alliance making is likely to be tenuous at best. The resulting loss of legislative efficiency may be more than offset by the increased incentives for (or threat of) executive oversight in a National Assembly that has demonstrated the capacity to exert its will. Because it has become an arena open to intense political competition, periodic debates over the merits of electoral systems channel political mobilization into a domain that is not polarized ethnically or regionally, as long as the commitment to multiparty representation remains.

"Kérékou II" and Democratic Prospects. Kérékou's electoral defeat of President Soglo in 1996 ushered in a new stage in Benin's democratic experiment. Kérékou's victory can be attributed to the second-round coalition he built with the regional leaders of the two southern regions of Ouémé and Mono and the power of these leaders to deliver their constituencies. Adrien Houngbédji, former president of the National Assembly and leader of the powerful PRD, and Albert Tévoèdjrè, leader of the party Notre Cause Commune, are now important members of the governing coalition. Kérékou gave Houngbédji, one of his bitter enemies during "Kérékou I," the post of prime minister, an extraconstitutional cabinet position without portfolio. Tévoèdjrè, a regional rival of Houngbédji's, was named minister of planning and employment and was charged with organizing the National Economic Conference. Bruno Amoussou, the regional leader of Mono, was elected president of the National Assembly. It is difficult to predict the durability of this coalition of expediency, but given the pressures imposed by the National Assembly elections of 1999 and the presidential elections in 2001, it is unlikely that it will hold for the duration of Kérékou's five-year term. Because of his age, Tévoèdjrè will not be eligible to run for president in 2001, but Kérékou, Soglo, Amoussou, and Houngbédji will still be eligible. Houngbédji has already predicted that he will, in fact, be elected president, and his party has already tested its independence from the coalition in the assembly.[50]

Kérékou campaigned on promises to increase employment and to limit the further privatization of state enterprises, particularly the gasoline distribution company. He also accused the Soglo forces of appealing to Fon ethnic sentiments during the campaign, a charge guaranteed to win over rival ethnic voters. Whether Kérékou will be able to hold on to a governing coalition in the National Assembly through the 1998 selection process of the second Constitutional Court will be of special importance to perceptions of its impartiality.

Kérékou's victory is also a testament to the respect and appreciation he earned by conceding to the wishes of the National Conference. His public speeches during the campaign and following his victory emphasize, as they always did, national unity and the dangers of ethnic and regional conflict.[51] At the same time, they proclaim a solid commitment not only to the structural adjustment program, but to the virtues of democracy as "the best barrier against intolerance, fundamentalism, racism, totalitarianism, the division of people, fratricidal conflict, and wars between nations. . . . [We] must abandon our old reflexes and concern ourselves permanently with the protection and the security [of our democracy], like parents jealously watching their dear child."[52] He also emphasized that until 1996, he was the only president in Benin's history to voluntarily leave office.[53]

The winners of the first elections in 1991 were not preordained in a transition process controlled either by a dictator seeking to manipulate the outcome, as they had been in Togo, or by a unified and powerful opposition. The rules were designed to permit real competition, as well as real checks on the monopoly of power, without institutionalizing the internally destabilizing problem of a president competing with a prime minister, as in Niger. Few would have predicted in 1991 that Kérékou would be elected president in 1996 as a reformed democrat able to build an electoral coalition with his enemies of the 1980s. The Constitutional Court's insistence that the rules and procedures of the constitution concerning the horizontal relationships among constitutional institutions be strictly respected, an extremely popular position among the public, along with the willingness of the political class to comply with the court's judgments, has been crucial to creating a resilient framework for channeling political debate and contestation. The Constitutional Court met the initial uncertainty over the 1996 presidential vote and Soglo's challenge of the outcome with firm decisions recognizing Kérékou's victory.

The flexibility of the rules governing vertical relations between the central government and the people has been equally important. In the domain of law, these rules remain open to periodic political contestation and reform. Issues of national representation and local administration have thus channeled a great deal of political activity and discontent into refining national rules of participation and accountability, a salutary development for a new democracy.

These positive developments should not obscure major continuing problems. The economic situation in the cities is still precarious, and the government has little maneuvering room within structural adjustment guidelines to address economic discontent. Internal security, rising crime rates, and police corruption are important signals of the fragility of democratic legitimacy.[54] Nevertheless, the process of democratization is still continuing in Benin. Associational life is flourishing, the press is vigilant, and meetings of the *états-généraux* to help define policy continue. The December 1996 National Economic Conference and ongoing debates about decentralization, the role of local government, and representation are all positive signs that the people of Benin are still committed to democracy, despite its antagonisms and inefficiencies. The imperfections are openly debated, and continuing reform is possible. The population is holding its new democratic regime accountable to a democratic, not an authoritarian, ideal. Most encouraging, these debates are, with few exceptions, taking place within the framework of rules established by the National Conference, the transition, and the constitution.

Notes

Research in Benin during 1993 and 1994 was financed by a Fulbright-Hays Dissertation Fellowship. Subsequent work has been supported by the MacArthur Scholars Program and the Department of Political Science at the University of Wisconsin-Madison.

1. Much has been written about Benin (formerly Dahomey until 1974) prior to the Kérékou takeover in 1972. Among the best sources for this period are Cornevin, *La République Populaire;* Decalo, *Coups and Army Rule;* Glélé, *Naissance;* Manning, *Slavery;* and Ronen, *Dahomey.* There have been fewer studies of the Kérékou era. Among them are Allen, "Benin"; the sections on Benin in Young, *Ideology and Development;* and Westebbe, "Structural Adjustment." See also the fine historical chapters in Heilbrunn, "Authority, Property, and Politics."

2. World Bank, *World Development Report, 1988.*

3. *Christian Science Monitor,* "Benin's Ex-President."

4. See Allen, "Benin"; Glélé, *Naissance;* and Ronen, *Dahomey.*

5. On the events leading up to the National Conference, see Decalo's postmortem in "Benin." See also Dossou, "Le Bénin," and Westebbe, "Structural Adjustment." For accounts of the National Conference, see Boulaga, *Les Conférences Nationales;* Dossou, "Le Bénin"; Laloupo, "La Conférence Nationale"; and Heilbrunn, "Authority, Property, and Politics," pp. 650–709, and "Social Origins."

6. See Adjaho, *La Faillite du Contrôle;* Chabi, *Banqueroute;* Heilbrunn, "Social Origins"; Nwajiaku, "National Conferences"; and Westebbe, "Structural Adjustment."

7. This description of the National Conference and its atmosphere is from Fondation Friedrich Naumann, ed., *Les Actes,* and Boulaga, *Les Conférences Nationales.*

8. Benin, *Actes des États Généraux de l'Education.*

9. It was actually Kérékou himself who called the first such meeting in 1979 of the state administration to discuss low levels of Parti de la Révolution Populaire du Bénin (PRPB) membership among the bureaucracy and to hear a wide-ranging critique of the state by its administrators.

10. Kérékou and the general population referred to his 18-year regime as "the revolution." Usually, the period following the National Conference is referred to as *"le renouveau"* (the renewal) or *"le renouveau démocratique"* (the democratic renewal).

11. Fondation Friedrich Naumann, ed., *Les Actes.*

12. Boulaga, *Les Conférences Nationales.*

13. Alapini, "Le Pouvoir."

14. Przeworski, *Democracy and the Market,* pp. 40–50.

15. Benin's only experience with multiparty representation was prior to independence. Although there were periods of multiparty competition following 1960,

the electoral systems gave all seats to the winning party in National Assembly elections.

16. Przeworski refers to this alleged comment in *Democracy and the Market,* p. 36.

17. For more detail on these Constitutional Court decisions, see Magnusson, "Benin."

18. Constitutional Court cases are not named in Benin. This name and the others that follow are my own fabrication.

19. For an examination of the corruption trials involving Mohamed Amadou Cissé and the Banque Commérciale du Bénin, see Chabi, *Banqueroute.* See also, Wilson, "Yves Yèhouéssi."

20. Several deputies in the National Assembly had been threatening the president with a High Court of Justice trial for various unproved allegations about financial corruption, especially one involving a $20,000 medical evacuation of the president's wife to Paris. See Couao-Zotti, "La Cour Constitutionnelle."

21. Bénin, République du (hereafter Benin), Cour Constitutionnelle, Decision DCC 14-94.

22. Assevi, "Conflits entre partis." For additional discussion, see Goudou and Goudou, "La Souveraineté."

23. Holo, "Interview."

24. Benin, Ministère de l'Intérieur, "Arrêté no. 260."

25. Benin, *Constitution,* p. 38.

26. Benin, Cour Constitutionnelle, Decision DCC 16-94.

27. Loko, "Un Autre cas."

28. See the *Journal Officiel de la République du Bénin,* 1990–1994, in which new associations registered with the government are listed.

29. *La Nation* (1994), "Déclaration du Gouvernement"; Soglo, "Au Sujet de l'examen"; *La Nation,* "Aide-mémoire"; *La Nation,* "Compte rendu des Travaux du Conseil des Ministres"; and Sacerdoti, "Letter."

30. Benin, *Constitution,* p. 30.

31. Soglo, speech on Radio Bénin.

32. Tévoèdjrè, "Letter."

33. Brathier, "La Cour Constitutionnelle." On Tévoèdjrè's threats, see Hado, "Pouvons-nous changer?"

34. Folly, cartoon.

35. Benin, Cour Constitutionnelle, Decision DCC 27-94.

36. Ibid., Decision DCC 29-94.

37. Ibid., Avis CC-001/94. See also Houngbédji, "Lettre d'avis."

38. Benin, Cour Constitutionnelle, Decision DCC 30-94.

39. Ibid., Decision DCC 31-94.

40. For more on the social and political climate during this very tense period, see Magnusson, "Benin."

41. Aplogan, "Benin President."

42. The three major political networks were headed by Hubert Maga, representing the northern regions of Atacora and Borgou; Justin Ahomadégbé, representing the central and southern Fon regions; and Sourou Migan Apithy, representing the Porto-Novo region of the southeast. Until the late 1960s, military intervention was instigated primarily by the Fon, and by General Soglo, Nicéphore Soglo's uncle, in particular. From the late 1960s until Kérékou's coup d'état in 1972, the military coalitions were more diffuse but had a substantial northern component. See Decalo, *Coups and Army Rule,* for insight into the personal and corporate motivations for army coups in Dahomey.

43. Dossou, "Le Bénin."

44. For a deeper analysis of parliamentary loyalty, see *La Recade,* April 1994, p. 4.

45. Discussion (April 19, 1994) with a cabinet official in the Ministry of Labor and Social Affairs. She remarked upon the almost universal complaints about political candidates made to the minister during a tour of rural areas of the department of Ouémé.

46. See Benin, Loi no. 94-013.

47. The Commission Electoral Nationale Autonome is made up of 17 members, seven of whom are chosen by the president, seven by the National Assembly, two by the Commission on Human Rights, and one by the National Union of Magistrates. Seven of the members chosen in 1995 were women.

48. For election figures for the 1991 and 1995 National Assembly elections, see Degboe, *Elections et Realites.* See also the 1995 election coverage in *Forum de la Semaine* (Benin), February 8, April 5, 12, and 19, and May 31, 1995; and in *La Nation,* April 18, May 31, and June 6, 1995.

49. For more on the regionalization of political parties in 1995, see Magnusson, "Benin." For a perspective on the local mobilization of regional sentiments in the 1995 elections, see Gbesséméhlan and Riénierse, "Les Élections."

50. Agbanglanon, "Présidentielles de l'an 2001."

51. See Kérékou, *Préparer le Bénin du futur,* a book written for his presidential campaign and published by Tévoèdjrè's Centre Panafricain de Prospective Sociale.

52. Kérékou, "Message du Chef de l'État."

53. This is not strictly accurate. During the triumvirate period, Hubert Maga, as chair of the Presidential Council from 1970 to 1972, transferred authority as planned to Justin Ahomadégbé in 1972, shortly before the Kérékou coup d'état.

54. See Magnusson, "Democratization."

13

Race, Class, and Neopatrimonialism in Zimbabwe

Scott D. Taylor

In an effort to explain post-1989 democratization in Africa, recent studies have focused on the role of civil society, revealing that this often vibrant center can form the basis for transitions to democratic rule.[1] Despite this finding, transitions have not been sustained. We now know that such an exclusive focus on civil society—particularly on voluntary associational groupings—is misplaced; the emergence of strong civic institutions and nonstate actors is but one component of democratic transitions.[2] This chapter suggests that independent development of the middle class, with its potential to weaken undemocratic, neopatrimonial regime structures, has important and often overlooked implications for economic and political liberalization in Africa.[3]

Scholars of African studies initially denied the significance of class in the 1960s, then shifted to an overriding preoccupation with it in the 1970s.[4] In recent years, class has again been relegated to the back burner. We need to consider a return to the fundamental issues of class development, class consciousness, and the role that class plays in sustaining, or frustrating, democratic governance. This analysis endeavors to refocus on the issue of class by drawing on the case of Zimbabwe.

Many scholars have addressed the emergence of class consciousness in Africa.[5] However, the development and growth of classes has frequently been stunted, and the bourgeois classes that have developed are generally "parasitic" in nature; that is, they are dependent on the state and are probably incapable of reproducing themselves as classes.[6] The Zimbabwean case suggests that three variables combine to retard independent middle-class formation: co-optation of key indigenous (i.e., black) economic actors; an alliance between the state and settler (i.e., white) capital; and deliberate suppression of would-be middle-class elements. Although only a few

African states share a history similar to that of Zimbabwe, this analysis posits that the "suppression" of middle classes may be a common experience on the continent that inhibits the development of more democratic modes of governance.

A reexamination of the middle-class strata and its possible suppression offers a partial explanation for the persistence of neopatrimonial rule and the formation of illiberal but nominally democratic regimes in Zimbabwe and elsewhere. Michael Bratton and Nicolas van de Walle define neopatrimonial regimes as those governed by personal patronage, rather than ideology or rule of law, where the achievement of personal wealth and status by "big men" becomes an accepted rationale for public office. In return for patronage, clients mobilize support for officeholders.[7] Neopatrimonial regimes facilitate and strengthen the development of a dependent, state-based capitalist class—a "bureaucratic bourgeoisie"—rather than an independent class. The prevalence of neopatrimonial rule thus has negative implications for the developmental prospects of Zimbabwe and other African states. Transitions to more liberal regimes are put at risk, or they may never occur at all, because "personal rulers are sensitive to threats to their authority. [As a result,] they set about weakening all independent centers of power."[8]

Despite the large number of transitions that have taken place in Africa, many (perhaps most) have failed to inculcate the norms of democracy. Because it is not technically "authoritarian," Zimbabwe is not among those states that have recently experienced a transition, but it nevertheless shares an inability to entrench democratic values. Labeling Zimbabwe's regime as "neopatrimonial" contradicts Bratton and van de Walle's classification of the country as a "multiparty polyarchy" in the sense conveyed by Robert Dahl.[9] Bratton and van de Walle construct a useful model, and they recognize that all regimes have some neopatrimonial characteristics, but based on Dahl's parameters of participation and contestation, it is clear that Zimbabwe is multiparty and polyarchic in name only. Participation by opposition candidates and their supporters and potential supporters is severely proscribed, and the ruling party uses intimidation, harassment, and fraud to restrict participation by "unfriendly" political interests. The government also uses the machinery of the state to minimize and marginalize opposition parties. For example, the ruling party, the Zimbabwe African National Union (Patriotic Front) (ZANU[PF]), has received Z$30 million in campaign funds from public sources that it has refused to make available to opposition groups. Moreover, the party uses the state-owned media to broadcast its partisan message, and it has also resorted to electoral fraud.[10] The absence of real choice has contributed to annual declines in voter participation.[11]

It is therefore necessary to adapt Bratton and van de Walle's model to fit both the post-1989 period in general and the Zimbabwean case in particular. If not, their logic implies that other tenuous but nominally "democratic" regimes, such as Kenya and Zambia, would also have to be characterized as multiparty polyarchies.[12] For these countries, as well as Zimbabwe, such a categorization would be inconsistent with Dahl's usage, as it fails to take account of important contextual variables and the continued prevalence of neopatrimonialism.

The Middle Class and Neopatrimonial Regimes

There has been an ongoing debate in the literature about the properties, characteristics, and capabilities of the middle class and its democratizing role. A number of scholars, including C. Wright Mills and Rueschemeyer, E. H. Stephens, and J. D. Stephens, contend that the pro-democracy role of the bourgeois or middle classes cannot be assumed. Rather, it depends on "will, know-how, objective opportunity, and organization," each of which is constrained by other factors.[13] As Mills observes, the middle class can be a source of Nazi accomplices as easily as it can foster liberal ruling classes.

Rueschemeyer and colleagues express similarly pessimistic views regarding the democratic credentials of the middle class. Using a comparative historical model that focuses on European, Latin American, and Caribbean democratization, the authors build on Moore's well-known treatise, but disagree with his thesis that a bourgeois class is a prerequisite for democratization. They conclude that "the middle classes played an ambiguous role in the installation and consolidation of democracy."[14] The authors instead contend that it is the *working* class that forms the mobilizing force behind democratic transitions, although it may do so in concert with the middle class. In this view, the middle class neither takes the leading role in, nor is necessarily even supportive of, the process of democratization.

In contrast, some other scholars regard the middle class as the bearer of a democratic-rational worldview that encompasses a belief in the rule of law, respect for property rights, a demand for participation and choice, and an interest in limiting political power and tenure.[15] Middle-class elements can thus play an important role in shaping political transitions. However, we need not assign qualities of magnanimity to the capitalist classes in order to explain their possible support for political liberalization. Instead, middle-class elites may be "backed into" democracy. In a study of three Latin American cases, Catherine Conaghan demonstrates that the commitment to democracy among bourgeois elements was abstract and ambivalent: business elites supported democracy because their interests and property rights were more threatened by autocratic regimes.[16] This view is supported by Bratton and van de Walle, who argue that during transitions from neopatrimonial regimes, middle-class elements align with the opposition. . . . The weak national bourgeoisies of Africa are frustrated by state ownership, over-regulation, and official corruption. . . . [Further,] businessmen and professionals often take on political leadership roles in the opposition, drawing in other middle-class groups, like public servants, whose downward economic mobility is a powerful impetus to forge an alternative ruling coalition.[17]

The difficulty that Africanist scholars face in applying the "models" suggested by this diverse literature stems from three factors. First, we cannot always agree on what the "bourgeoisie" (or middle class) is—especially in different international contexts. Second, the policies of many African states have fostered the growth of "state bourgeoisies," rather than independent capitalist classes. Finally, even if such classes emerge, we cannot predict how they will define their role in relation to the state.

As a result of this quandary, we are forced to make several a priori assumptions about the contributions and potential contributions of the middle class in a developing polity. First, an independent middle class will likely be a force for democratization and representation—if it is allowed free expression and political space to emerge. Second, the absence of a middle class tends to preserve the status quo in Africa, allowing the persistence of the neopatrimonial regime model. Third, as has been argued effectively elsewhere, neopatrimonial regimes are an obstacle to liberal democracy, or at least to multiparty polyarchy.[18] This is not to suggest that all countries that possess a middle class will be democratic. Rather, I argue in favor of the far more modest proposition that the middle class has been inhibited in Zimbabwe—in both its emergence and its interest articulation—as it has elsewhere in Africa, and that this, in turn, has implications for the perseverance of entrenched neopatrimonial systems.

Explaining the Failure of
Middle-Class Development in Zimbabwe

Conceptual difficulties notwithstanding, does a middle class even *exist* in Zimbabwe? And if so, what evidence is there to suggest that it might play a pro-democracy role? As Hyden notes, "the existing inequalities in Africa are not crystallizing into class consciousness."[19] However, as the work of both Moore and Rueschemeyer and colleagues demonstrates, the evolution of a bourgeois capitalist class is a long-term prospect, perhaps measured in centuries, not decades.[20] Bourgeois development has been doubly frustrated in Africa by colonialism's restrictions on indigenous capitalists and by the independent governments themselves. Although the contemporary states inherited bourgeois-capitalist structures from the colonial powers, many resisted independent capitalist class development as they either pursued "African socialism" or adhered to neopatrimonial practices.

Zimbabwe is perhaps peculiar among African states owing to the continued presence of a powerful settler minority, its comparatively recent political independence, and its relative ethnic homogeneity.[21] What is not altogether unique, however, is Zimbabwe's inability (or unwillingness) to develop a viable, independent, and indigenous African middle class, and this is a major part of efforts to preserve ZANU(PF)'s one-party rule and continue building a widespread patronage network. Other states in Africa, despite having ostensibly democratic institutions, have also failed to entrench democracy, perhaps for similar reasons. The Zimbabwean case has implications for democratic stability elsewhere, especially in South Africa, a country whose future will be affected in part by its ability to engender the growth of its own African middle class. The case is also relevant in Kenya, which, though no longer home to a large European settler population, also possesses a large, nonindigenous business class. As is the case with white settlers in Zimbabwe, the much-heralded Kenyan capitalism would be moribund without the Indian "national" bourgeoisie.[22]

While there are several indicators of a middle-class presence in Zimbabwe, and while individuals evincing "typical" middle-class values, aspirations, and socioeconomic status are present, they exhibit little *group* consciousness, particularly when it comes to demonstrable political preferences.[23] In order to translate these intangible qualities into a more useful measure, 1992 census data was used to establish a proxy for "middle class" by accounting for education, employment category, and employment status.[24]

According to the 1992 census, there are approximately 314,000 educated (i.e., completed at least primary school), nonwhite adults in Zimbabwe who are owners, managers, or white-collar employees.[25] This represents 11 percent of the "economically active population" of 3.5 million people, out of a total population of 10.4 million.[26] Another means for assessing the size of the bourgeoisie (specifically based on ownership) is industrial concentration.[27] In Zimbabwe, 50 percent of manufactured output is accounted for by just three firms,[28] while within commercial agriculture, the economy's second leading sector, roughly 4,000 white farmers own 27 percent of the country's farmland. These figures suggest that ownership of the means of production is not well distributed.

This data, albeit imperfect, is not indicative of a large societal grouping that could be labeled an indigenous "middle class," and it certainly does not suggest the presence of a true bourgeoisie. In addition, these aggregate figures obscure the so-called state bourgeois, so the number of independent, private-sector actors shrinks still further. Although some authors do argue that there is a middle class, no discernible group exists that might act as a cohesive socioeconomic block outside the influence of the state.[29] Indeed, several African middle and senior managers and industrialists have expressed exasperation at the lack of unity and cooperation among this would-be class.[30] Thus, while some semblance of class formation has occurred in Zimbabwe, the coalescence of ideologies within various social strata and the consequent crystallizing of class identities are lacking.

Three closely interrelated factors explain the failure of middle-class development in Zimbabwe, the inability of this nascent class to dislodge neopatrimonialism, and the consequent limited democratization: (1) co-optation of blacks active in the private sector; (2) the alliance between the state and white settler interests; and (3) active suppression of black middle-class development by the state. Each factor is the result of deliberate action by state leaders that is intended to maximize the gains available to them. Such actions are geared, therefore, toward ensuring the continued hegemony of the ruling party and the maintenance of neopatrimonial rule.[31] Sustaining neopatrimonialism, however, exacts a tremendous cost on society and, eventually, on the regime itself.[32]

Co-optation

Crawford Young's review illustrates that a modifier such as "state" or "bureaucratic" is almost invariably attached to the discussion of the bourgeoisie in Africa, "which highlights the connection to the state."[33] The separation of the state from the economic sphere—a prerequisite for democracy according to some analysts—is lacking in Zimbabwe.[34] Many of the key blacks in Zimbabwe's private sector who could form the core of a genuine middle class have been co-opted by the state through various patronage networks.

Strange Bedfellows

The state has sought to preserve the status quo by protecting the economic interests of the settler bourgeoisie. The suggestion that the state has formed an implicit alliance with settler business and agricultural interests in Zimbabwe is not a new one, however controversial. In fact, this thesis is expounded convincingly by Tom Ostergaard in his analysis of the textile and clothing sectors, and it is also suggested in the work of Brian Raftopoulos and Sam Moyo.[35] What remains unexplored in existing studies, and is inherently difficult to quantify, is the extent to which state corruption benefits the *white* middle-class community.[36] The state and its officials clearly reap certain benefits from this relationship. Similarly, whites, who control much of the country's wealth and productive capital while posing no threat to ZANU's political hegemony, are provided with a measure of stability and insulation from popular (and, ironically, government) pressure for "indigenization" of the economy.[37]

Suppression

The state's alliance with white interests is the point of departure for the third factor explaining the void of middle-class activity in Zimbabwe: a more calculated *suppression* of a black middle class by the ruling party. A critical component of this argument is that the rhetoric emanating from the government advocating a more equitable redistribution of resources is largely empty. This view of the indigenization "movement" contrasts sharply with the one promulgated by the media, both internationally and especially within Zimbabwe, in which president and party alike are portrayed as being strongly committed to indigenization. The vitriol from many leading proponents of "indigenization," both in and out of government, is often so severe that one might easily conclude that whites are an endangered species, at least economically, in Zimbabwe. This is, however, an inaccurate portrayal.

A number of scholars endorse the view that bourgeois/middle-class interests have not gained expression in Zimbabwe, but they attribute this to "benign neglect" by the state, rather than to intentional suppression.[38] However, empirical evidence supports the argument that, concurrent with its role in preserving white, private-sector hegemony, the state has acted in ways that have deliberately inhibited the development of black business interests and enterprises—on both a large (potentially "bourgeois") and a small (petty bourgeois) scale. If such development were encouraged, these individual efforts could form the basis for an emergent middle-class ideology. Instead, the government has co-opted indigenous economic actors and marginalized those that it has been unable to co-opt.

Of these three factors, class suppression appears to be most significant in explaining the retarded development of a black middle class in Zimbabwe and the consequent failure to advance democratization. The co-optation factor is closely related, but it has been addressed thoroughly elsewhere.[39] Thus, class suppression will receive a more systematic treatment throughout the remainder of this analysis. The nature of the alliance between the state and white settlers requires further examination and represents an important and potentially fruitful avenue for further study.

Governance, Class, and Indigenization

ZANU(PF)'s suppression of the middle class can be viewed through a rational choice framework. At least in the short term, the party has tried "to preempt the development of alternative centres of power in the society," and to a considerable extent, it has been successful in this regard.[40] Such actions contribute substantially to the ruling party's ability to maintain its unrivaled hold on power by diluting potential opposition and by maintaining unfettered linkages to its client groups. At the same time, the state enjoys some of the benefits of white economic power, it has co-opted a number of black actors, and it has maintained its appeal to the rural masses (i.e., peasants and small-scale farmers) by holding out the promise of indigenization.

For the state, however, there are definite limitations to this strategy. The effective suppression of an indigenous political and economic middle class has put ZANU(PF) in an increasingly precarious position. Unprecedented urban unrest, increased unemployment, and a historic victory by a political independent in a 1995 parliamentary election demonstrate that ZANU's grip is weakening, if only slightly, in the urban centers.[41] Even among peasant communities, there is a growing (but far from complete) realization that many of the promises that accompanied political independence, particularly that of land redistribution, have thus far been empty ones; fewer than 60,000 peasant farmers have been resettled since 1980.[42] It is unclear whether the proliferation of negative sentiments will lead to agitation and political unrest or merely to increased apathy.

The state-bourgeois elite currently attempts to recycle itself by co-opting key social actors. However, even among these co-opted elements of the "governing group," ZANU(PF)'s support may be threatened by its own shortsighted policies.[43] Economic decline and the conditionality imposed by structural adjustment have reduced the opportunities and the resources available for state patronage. Gross domestic product (GDP) growth averaged only about 2 percent annually in the early 1990s, and government revenues have fallen, largely due to the continued financial losses of parastatals. The government's access to additional resources is further restrained as Zimbabwe enters the second five-year phase of the Economic Structural Adjustment Program (ESAP), with its requisite austerity measures.

The diminishing resources available for "funding" co-optation may compel the state to rely more on class suppression instead. Paradoxically, however, ZANU(PF) can employ this alternative tool only sparingly. As Bratton and van de Walle assert, "the operations of neopatrimonialism tend to create simultaneously a defensively cohesive state elite and a potential pool of alternative leaders outside of the state. The neopatrimonial practice of expelling rather than accommodating dissenters is a primary cause of the emergence of organized opposition."[44] Thus, the more the state is compelled to "expel dissenters" and attempts to marginalize defiant capitalists, rather than redouble its efforts to accommodate them, the more it sows the seeds of its own demise. As neopatrimonial rewards become increasingly exclusionary, a "recipe for social unrest" emerges, and the regime will have difficulty maintaining stability.[45]

Hyden notes that it is only through market-based principles that countries can empower people who "will constitute the core of a local capitalist class and may serve as the pacesetters of development by rising above clan and neopatrimonial politics."[46] Indeed, the promotion of an independent, indigenous capitalist class appears entirely consistent with the adoption of ESAP in 1990 and the concomitant abandoning of African socialism in the same year.[47] However, the market economy in Zimbabwe has instead created pockets of black nouveaux riches tied to the state.

Furthermore, ESAP has contributed to the cementing of inequalities inherent in the status quo, as whites continue to own a disproportionate share of economic resources. Fewer than 4,000 white farmers and white-owned companies control some 11.2 million hectares of agricultural land (nearly 35 percent of Zimbabwe's total), most of which is situated in the most fertile regions of the country.[48] Within the corporate sector, 62.5 percent of senior management is white, although blacks dominate middle and junior management positions.[49]

Precise figures are not available for the racial composition of company ownership, but in the manufacturing sector, "local private individuals" own 60 percent, foreign companies 22.5 percent, and the government 11 percent of the firms.[50] Research indicates that "the Government has not radically altered the ownership pattern of the Zimbabwe economy . . . [and that] foreign and local 'white' capital are still predominant in key sectors of the economy, namely agriculture, mining, manufacturing, construction, distribution, services, finance and commerce."[51]

Despite these contradictory statistics, the rallying cry for ZANU(PF) has remained "black empowerment" since independence, and ironically, the government frequently blames the limited black advancement on whites. In the 1996 presidential elections, in which incumbent Robert Mugabe ultimately ran uncontested, the preelection rhetoric against white domination of the economy, which has come to be an integral part of Zimbabwean elections, was in plentiful supply, becoming most heated when ZANU, by inciting populist, antiwhite resentment, claimed that it was the only party that could deliver black empowerment. Yet, on such issues, ZANU is in fact running against itself, as Mugabe and his party have failed to redistribute white-owned assets, as they occasionally threaten to do. Of greater concern, the government has also failed to create meaningful wealth among blacks outside of a small, state-based elite. In fact, whites have done considerably better, as a whole, under Mugabe's rule. This is perhaps most true in the large-scale commercial farming areas, where initial fears of black rule were greatest.

Jeffrey Herbst notes that settler interest groups, especially farmers, have remained influential since the advent of black rule, and he points out that black interest groups have remained comparatively weak, a finding supported by Tor Skalnes.[52] This influence and the implicit favoritism that it reflects were presumably changed by the passage of the landmark Land Acquisition Act in 1992. The act ostensibly eliminates a number of the protections that had been granted to white commercial farmers by the independence constitution, allowing the government to acquire land and pay for it over a period of up to five years. However, only a handful of white farmers have been subjected to the provisions of the act since its inception.[53]

The regime's challenge is to continue the delicate balancing act among its differing constituencies. It must play the interests of urban coalitions off of rural ones, and of black coalitions off of white ones, in order to maintain power. The promise of indigenization must be made repeatedly, but not kept. Following a line of inquiry developed by Nicos Poulantzas, Ostergaard contends that "the 'governing groups' feared a challenge from the rise of a black industrial bourgeoisie. Had an indigenous black bourgeoisie arisen, however, it might have been able to penetrate the state apparatus and contest the protected position of the governing group [i.e., ZANU(PF)]."[54] The existence of a white industrial bourgeoisie, conversely, is indisputable; this group had been nurtured by the modestly successful import-substitution industrialization policies under the minority rule of Ian Smith.

The black empowerment initiatives of President Mugabe and ZANU(PF) illuminate the failures of indigenization programs in Zimbabwe, which is still immersed in the unfulfilled rhetoric of liberation. Many interview respondents believe that Mugabe himself remains dedicated to genuine indigenization but that he is institutionally constrained by members of the cabinet, who stand to lose a great deal if a legitimate, independent bourgeoisie supplants the state bourgeoisie. Others believe that Mugabe maintains his strong ideological commitment to socialism and is therefore reluctant to see the expansion of an exploitative black capitalist class. Neither conclusion, however, is consistent with the popular image of Mugabe as nearly omnipotent. The alternative explanation is that Mugabe is not actually committed to indigenization on a meaningful scale.

In fact, numerous white-owned firms or historically white-dominated sectors of the economy have been shown considerable favor by ZANU(PF). Ostergaard notes, for example, that when white-owned textile firms faced difficulties, the government, via the Industrial Development Corporation, provided capital injections. On the other hand, the government showed only lukewarm support for the Small Enterprise Development Corporation (SEDCO), the parastatal it established in 1984 to assist the development of small-scale enterprises: "The limited scope of SEDCO's activities, and its severe loan terms, support the assertion that government was not interested in promoting black industrialists."[55]

Ostergaard hints that some form of class suppression has occurred and acknowledges white benefit, but he then asks:

> What difference does it make . . . if such domestic capitalists are not of the same color, religion, language group, or whatever as the dominant elements in control of the state? . . . [B]eing "outsiders" has some positive advantages for capitalists . . . : (1) outsiders *must* make money, not being eligible for power by ascriptive routes, (2) they may do so efficiently, being free from the precapitalist obligations to others in society . . . and (3) their external links may confer technical-economic advantages on them as capitalists.[56]

Such assessments fail to confront the reality of Zimbabwean politics and the implied promise of its liberation struggle. By neglecting to ask, for example, what the *broader* implications of economic participation and equitable distribution of resources in Zimbabwe are, Ostergaard fails to analyze the implications for democracy in Zimbabwe (or Africa in general) of indigenous middle-class marginalization.

The Myth of Indigenization: The Rise and Fall of the IBDC

The Emergence of the IBDC

It has been estimated that, in 1980, 10 percent of national wealth was in the hands of blacks, 70 percent under the control of foreign firms, and 20 percent owned by white Zimbabweans. By 1990, foreign ownership had been reduced. The space created by the exodus of foreign firms following independence, however, was filled not by blacks, but by local whites. Popular perception has it that "whites control 98 percent of Zimbabwe's economy," though this figure appears somewhat exaggerated.[57] In an effort to reverse this trend, an initiative called the Indigenous Business Development Centre was launched in 1990 by a group of Harare-based businesspeople with the endorsement of the government. The IBDC's stated objectives were to reduce unemployment, alter the concentration of business interests and capital in white hands, and improve the rate of GDP growth, which had averaged around 1 percent per year in the latter half of the 1980s. From its inception, the IBDC mission was not to take over large companies; there was little preoccupation with acquiring assets owned by the white community, with or without adequate compensation. Rather, the IBDC's leaders expressed an interest in increasing the absolute size of the economic pie, not in diminishing the relative share thought to be controlled by whites.

The IBDC message emphasized the positive goals of black empowerment and expansion of the Zimbabwean economy. According to a spokesperson, "business can no longer be the preserve of a few. We want to create jobs for our children. We want to also participate in the joint ventures with external investors. In short, indigenous business people want to fully participate in the ownership and creation of wealth."[58] Among the early goals of the IBDC was the desire to equip indigenous businesspeople with resources, primarily by providing them with access to capital, markets, management skills, training, and technology.[59]

Studies on indigenization in Zimbabwe have not examined the role of the IBDC in depth, especially its rapid rise and precipitous decline. In its early days, the IBDC was an example of an attempt by black business elites—the core of a would-be middle class—to establish a niche for themselves, albeit with some cautious state support. When the organization began to flourish and become independent of state influence, however, Mugabe's government moved quickly to weaken its popular appeal and diminish its potential threat.

The IBDC leadership had envisioned an economy that would be predominantly in indigenous hands by the end of the decade. Overall, their approach was well received, and it garnered the ostensible support not only of the government, but of the international community as well, represented by the World Council of Churches, Britain's Office of Overseas Development Assistance, and others. The IBDC's message also had broad appeal among its potential constituents, namely, black Zimbabweans with an inclination toward business or entrepreneurial activities.[60] Though launched in December 1990 by only a handful of individuals, within six months, the IBDC could claim over 3,000 members. By December 1991, that number had grown to 5,300 members. The leadership boasted that it was recruiting 20 new members daily, each paying a subscription fee of Z$100.[61]

From the outset, the IBDC aspired to engage in more than inward-looking, self-help activities, and it also undertook efforts to directly influence government policy. In conjunction with ESAP, for example, the IBDC advocated a coupon system to allow indigenous Zimbabweans to purchase shares in parastatal companies slated for privatization. Black investors lacked capital, connections, and experience, and so had less access to cash than local whites; they would therefore be issued coupons with which to purchase company shares, rather than relying on the open market. Similarly, IBDC-sponsored research conducted in 1992 revealed that 60 percent of Zimbabwe's exports were controlled by four white-run firms. This led the IBDC to pressure the government for legislation governing mergers and monopolies. By breaking up monopolies, black Zimbabweans would be given access to new export market opportunities.

Among the most urgent priorities for indigenous business is access to capital, and this figured prominently among the IBDC's early objectives. In 1991, the IBDC launched an initiative to form the National Economic Recovery Fund (NERF). NERF initially aimed at a capitalization of Z$100 million and was targeted primarily at viable projects among small- and medium-scale enterprises. A number of foreign donors, as well as the Zimbabwe government, pledged large contributions. For purposes of transparency, the IBDC leadership determined that donor funds should be channeled directly to recipients through the commercial banks, and not through the IBDC. However, after the initial fanfare, the implementation of NERF, which was dependent on the release of donor monies, encountered problems. The program was held up by delays in obtaining the necessary government approvals.

The IBDC's intent was to dovetail each of its activities with the government's *stated* goals of indigenization and with the ESAP program. Each of its programs and policy positions should have placed the IBDC not in a radical position, but in the political-economic mainstream, especially as the organization's rise coincided with the government's adoption of ESAP. Given this apparent harmony of interests, the subsequent demise of the IBDC is all the more surprising.

A series of public disputes soon put the IBDC and the government at loggerheads. The first concerned NERF. The government (which was to act as guarantor) insisted that 75 percent of the disbursement should go to new businesses, a constraint that disqualified existing black entrepreneurs, who formed the core of the IBDC membership and who were in need of a capital infusion. In addition, the rate of interest on NERF loans was set at 15 percent. The IBDC and its constituents argued that the conditions placed on the NERF facility were unfair, especially when compared with a similar loan scheme that benefited the white business community. A short time before, predominantly white commercial farmers had been granted lower rates on a loan facility of Z$400 million.[62] The farmers were able to borrow at a rate of 5 percent, well below the market rate. Furthermore, the farmers' facility was disbursed in just two days, whereas NERF took well over a year, although it operated through the same commercial banks.[63] These glaring discrepancies resulted in accusations against private-sector banks, as well as the government, about the preferential treatment accorded to whites.

NERF funds were finally disbursed in February 1993, but this was followed by many allegations—directed at the banks, the government, and the IBDC leadership—about how the monies had been spent. Most of the funds were reportedly used by the banks to pay back existing debts owed to them by some of the would-be recipients. In fact, little or no money was used to fund new or existing businesses, and most IBDC members received nothing at all, despite their great hopes.[64] Members and leaders of the IBDC alike felt that they had been misled by both the government and the banks.

IBDC-Government Discord

In part due to its problems with NERF, the IBDC became more vocal in its criticisms of the government, and this was not well received.[65] When the

IBDC appeared to be an ally of the government and an endorser of ZANU(PF)'s "commitment" to indigenization, the relationship had been harmonious. However, once the leading indigenization body began to criticize the government, ZANU(PF) faced a major challenge to its credibility. The IBDC also ventured into issues of broader national significance, and its leaders began to feel that their organization was a force to be reckoned with. Indeed, it had a burgeoning membership, international support, and, most important, the apparent blessing of President Mugabe, who was the IBDC's official patron.[66] Commenting on ESAP in 1993, IBDC vice president Chemist Siziba stated, "We have already demonstrated that we are fearless when it comes to criticizing shortcomings in the implementation of ESAP. [At first,] we were treated as heretics, but we were vindicated when President Mugabe recently repeated similar concerns about the management of our national economy."[67] Such statements did not endear Siziba or the IBDC to the cabinet. One minister warned the IBDC leadership that "you are a threat to ZANU(PF)."[68]

It is unclear precisely when the relationship with the government turned sour. A number of former IBDC leaders expressed the view that, aside from the president and the pro-liberalization former finance minister, Bernard Chidzero, Mugabe's cabinet was always threatened by the IBDC, possibly for the very reason that the IBDC had grown too much and too quickly. Former and current IBDC leaders agree that the government played a role in undermining the organization, but they disagree over which elements in government were responsible. The IBDC was pilloried in the print and broadcast media, and as a result, public confidence eroded rapidly.

The current leadership claims that a media smear campaign led by the government-owned *Herald* newspaper and the Zimbabwe Broadcasting Company, under the influence of white backers, undermined the relationship. Specifically, they claim that the campaign against the IBDC was backed by foreign interests and local whites, but spearheaded by ministers in the government who benefit from connections to local whites.[69] One former IBDC leader claims that the ministers were threatened by the perception that businesspeople in general, and IBDC leaders in particular, harbored political aspirations. Both the minister of finance and the minister of commerce and industry publicly attacked the IBDC for lack of loyalty to the government.[70] IBDC leaders probably felt that they would be protected under the wing of President Mugabe, but Mugabe's support did not materialize.

Internal Crisis

In April 1994, the IBDC was faced with a leadership crisis as different factions contended for control of the organization. The situation revealed the deep divisions that had developed within both the indigenization movement and the government. One of the two factions was led by Enock Kamushinda, who had been named secretary-general in April 1993, and by Ben Mucheche, the newly elected IBDC president. The other was dominated by outgoing president Siziba and his supporters. In brief, Siziba alleged that the new leadership had taken power without regard to proper procedures for succession. Kamushinda and Mucheche responded that Siziba was unwilling to cede authority and that they had been duly elected. Throughout these debates, widespread accusations of mismanagement of funds persisted, as did speculation that the cause of the leadership wrangle was a dispute over which individuals would control the disbursement of funds.[71] It is widely believed that the government helped to instigate the struggle by backing alternative candidates (namely, the Kamushinda faction) and forcing individuals whom it opposed out of the leadership, and eventually out of the IBDC altogether. One former IBDC official who had supported the Siziba faction pleaded to a reporter: "My friend, I want to live peacefully in this country. Right now my life is at stake and I have been ordered [by a cabinet minister] to stay out of IBDC business."[72] By the end of 1994, the demise of the original IBDC mission and leadership was largely complete.

Revival of the IBDC-Government Relationship

A more radical style characterized the "second generation" of IBDC leadership, which began to emerge when Kamushinda was elected secretary-general and was solidified with the victory of the Kamushinda faction in 1994. The level of racial antagonism emanating from the IBDC increased dramatically. Kamushinda, unlike the more accommodating leadership before him, took a much more aggressive stance toward indigenization, and his pronouncements became increasingly antiwhite. Many suspect that Kamushinda—who by 1996 had been named as one of the leaders of Mugabe's reelection campaign—was the government's preferred choice to lead the association. Certainly, his inflammatory rhetoric was (and remains) consistent with the government's *public* stance against white domination of the economy, and the party needed a private-sector spokesperson who could rail against white racism, while hailing ZANU(PF) as the only party capable of both protecting and furthering black interests. In this way, the second generation of IBDC leaders helped to legitimize the pro-indigenization credentials of ZANU(PF), despite the party's considerable failures in this regard since independence.[73]

Collaboration or Co-optation?

As the IBDC became increasingly antiwhite in its rhetoric, and as the internal crises of the organization became widely publicized, donors shied away from making additional commitments,[74] leaving the IBDC more reliant on government support for project funding, if not staffing.[75] Yet the government made few financial commitments to the IBDC, entirely rejecting the IBDC's request for Z$800 million in concessionary loans from the 1995 budget, for example. Why did the government co-opt the leadership of the IBDC, effectively hijack its agenda, and then leave it starved for funds?

One might argue that the IBDC's destruction was entirely its own doing and that the government played no role in its demise. Indeed, from its inception, the organization was plagued by a number of institutional and administrative problems, including regional concentration, rapid growth, and an overly broad constituency.[76] Yet the question remains: why was there no tangible government support for an organization that so clearly articulated the government's stated goals? It seems more plausible that certain elements in the government deliberately undermined the IBDC's efforts in order to ruin the credibility of the institution and its founding leadership. Having done so, the IBDC could then be appropriately "reconstituted" into a more pliant and ineffectual organization, one that is now widely seen as a vehicle for advancement and accumulation based on neopatrimonial ties to the state.[77] Although the present secretary-general claims a current membership of over 4,000, most interview respondents in the Harare business community, both white and black, were unaware that the IBDC still existed in late 1995 and early 1996.

The IBDC began as a vehicle for the expansion of black business interests through small- and medium-scale enterprises, as well as larger business entities. It was a largely autonomous body that, through its own external connections to sympathetic donors and others, could have provided significant empowerment for black entrepreneurs independently of the state. That potential was the principal reason for its undoing. No one in the ruling party explicitly stated that they were threatened by "middle-class development," but they were clearly threatened by the IBDC. By embracing instead a state-bourgeois elite, the Zimbabwean government effectively stifled a promising vehicle for independent class advancement among blacks.

In its early years, the IBDC appeared to be a credible organization for changing the structure of the Zimbabwean economy. Its educated, technocratic leadership engendered positive reactions from donors, indigenous entrepreneurs, and, arguably, President Mugabe himself. However, the degree of hostility emanating from the government and white capital varied inversely with the IBDC's success and its advance as a possible harbinger of indigenous bourgeois development.

One implication that emerges from this and other studies is that white business interests allied with certain governmental/state interests to undermine the potential of the IBDC to act as the vanguard of an indigenous bourgeois class. The current generation of IBDC leadership has unequivocally condemned what it claims is a sinister, white-led "plot" against the organization. However, evidence of such an alliance, or of any direct influence of white economic actors on the failure of the IBDC's first generation, is extremely limited.

Despite their initial fears, white Zimbabweans have fared well under black rule. Over 80 percent of large-scale commercial farmers are white, and the sector has benefited from favorable pricing (even pre-ESAP) and loan schemes. Moreover, the massive confiscation of land that had been threatened has not taken place. In the manufacturing sector, which is also dominated by white-owned firms, Skalnes's analysis shows that private-sector associations, notably the CZI, had a major influence on the government's decision to adopt ESAP in 1991, which they strongly favored.[78] In addition, Britain, the United States, and the international financial institutions (IFIs) have been putting pressure on the ZANU(PF) government not to engage in any acquisition of white property that would resemble "seizure." Thus, for the most part, ZANU(PF) has only issued threats.[79] However, although the government's decision to protect white interests may be rational in the short term, in the long term it is implausible to expect that white firms alone can provide enough employment, innovation, and economic growth to support a population the size of Zimbabwe's.

The Case of Econet:
Class Suppression and Cellular Phones

The unraveling of the IBDC demonstrates Zimbabwe's questionable commitment to indigenization and the continuation of neopatrimonial influences within both society and the state. The ongoing case of African businessman Strive Masiyiwa is similarly illustrative of the contradictions in Zimbabwe's indigenization program and the state elites' fear of independent centers of economic and political power. Like the IBDC, Masiyiwa exemplifies the crisis of bourgeois/middle-class development in Zimbabwe and the seeming intractability of neopatrimonialism. Because Masiyiwa was viewed as having a political agenda—despite his and others' protestations to the contrary—his experiences have broader implications regarding the intersection of politics and class.

Masiyiwa was one of the principal founders of the IBDC in 1990, and he was its first secretary-general, a post that he held until April 1993, but he resigned from the IBDC entirely in March 1995, citing the organization's loss of direction as his reason. An astute businessman and former employee of the Posts and Telecommunications Corporation (PTC), Masiyiwa had recognized an opportunity to provide a cellular phone network to Zimbabweans who could not rely on the antiquated and geographically limited PTC system. The PTC, like most parastatal organizations in Africa, is notoriously inefficient and incompetent.[80] Although Zimbabwe is relatively more developed than many of its neighbors, its communications infrastructure is among the worst in sub-Saharan Africa, with fewer than 12 telephone main lines per 1,000 people.[81] Individuals requesting phones, even in cosmopolitan Harare, may have to wait up to four years before receiving a line.

Through a new company that he created, Econet, Masiyiwa offered two tremendous advantages for Zimbabwean economic and social development. First, consistent with both the spirit and the letter of ESAP, Econet was an example of a private-sector individual, using privately secured funds, to initiate a business that would provide both employment and vital infrastructure. The estimated total investment by 1998 was expected to exceed Z$500 million, "making it the second largest private-sector investment since independence."[82] Econet would also relieve the overburdened, overtaxed, and inefficient state-run monopoly, perhaps even improving it by introducing market competition. Second, Masiyiwa's proposed cellular network presented a superb opportunity for indigenous advancement in Zimbabwe: the Econet project would create an estimated 2,500 jobs, either directly or through joint ventures. By late 1995, joint venture partnerships were being set up by which black entrepreneurs would form companies to provide support services to Econet, such as billing, marketing, credit, and customer service.[83] As with the IBDC, however, the government viewed Masiyiwa and his project as a threat to the particularistic interests of the ZANU(PF) inner circle.

Quashing the Entrepreneurial Impulse

Masiyiwa was blocked repeatedly from implementing his network by bureaucratic and legal obstacles orchestrated by the PTC and the Ministry of Posts and Telecommunications. In December 1995, Masiyiwa's company (Econet is the cellular company; the holding company has been known since early 1996 as T. S. Masiyiwa Holdings, Ltd.) was compelled to take its case challenging the PTC's monopoly to the Supreme Court for the second time. The court, which remains relatively independent of political influences, judged in favor of Masiyiwa and Econet, concluding that the government monopoly over communications was a barrier to freedom of expression as enshrined in Zimbabwe's constitution.[84]

With that victory, Econet set about final preparations to launch its service in March 1996. The company had a base station in Harare, Z$30 million worth of mobile phones warehoused, and 5,000 subscribers signed up, all of which represented an investment of over Z$250 million. But in February 1996, with Econet on the verge of starting operations, President Mugabe resorted to the Presidential Powers (Temporary Measures) Act (1986) to block the company's launch. The act made it illegal for anyone to operate a cellular phone network without permission, in the form of a license, from the Ministry of Posts and Telecommunications. The penalties are severe: companies or individuals found operating without a license face fines of up to Z$100,000 (currently about U.S.$10,000), up to two years' imprisonment, or both. Econet did not have the newly mandated license, and the firm was told that it could take up to nine months to obtain one; the company risked losing Z$17 million per month while its network sat idle. Immediately after the act was gazetted, Masiyiwa's American partner, Telecel International, which had a 40 percent stake in the project, withdrew, facing threats from the minister of posts and telecommunications, David Karamanzira, that if they continued with the project, the company's executives would face arrest. International contractors involved with the project also stopped work.[85]

In the meantime, the government announced plans to introduce its own cellular network, a system that has since been fraught with problems. Numerous delays in the project's implementation have been caused as much by administrative incompetence and lack of technological capability as by outright corruption. The project lacked the network of Econet, and the tender process conducted by the government was marked by well-publicized irregularities that forced the PTC to solicit bids from potential suppliers for a second time.[86]

The Masiyiwa case has had adverse implications for other aspiring members of the capitalist class, as well as for governance, transparency, and economic revitalization in Zimbabwe. The government was clearly not forced to enter this sector due to an absence of capable private actors who could supply the necessary product or service. Instead, the minister's and ZANU(PF)'s actions represent a deliberate attempt to undermine Masiyiwa. Are these actions a reflection of "middle-class suppression" or merely a case of a personal assault on the interests of a single individual? Elements of both are present.

Personalities arguably did play a role in this conflict. Masiyiwa has a history of defying government attempts at control, and during his tenure as secretary-general of the IBDC, he did not endear himself to the elite within the ruling party. He was seen as the leader of an increasingly influential and potentially political organization. Yet there is no tangible evidence that Masiyiwa aspires to political office; then as now, he has continually denied that he has any political aspirations or any interests besides the successful launch of his business venture. Masiyiwa maintains that "I am a businessman, not a politician; I am not interested in challenging government."[87]

In the Zimbabwean context, however, Masiyiwa's defiance acquired strong political overtones. The state's response reveals that the durability of neopatrimonialism and the centralization of state power have several broader implications for the prospects for middle-class development and democracy in Zimbabwe. The attack on Masiyiwa's business interests was a thinly veiled attempt to reassert the government's hegemony and its monopoly over the communications market. Any obstacle that could delay or derail

Econet would allow the government to "catch up" with its own project. Second, and more important, control of the communications network provides access to additional spoils, such as the opportunity to profiteer via the tender procedure. Indeed, "top government politicians are opposed to Masiyiwa's project for no other reason than that their friends, relatives or bribers were beaten to it," said one commentator.[88] There were suggestions in the press, also reflected in interviews I conducted, that the problems between Econet and the government are attributable, at least in part, to Masiyiwa's unwillingness to buy off certain political interests to ensure that his business launch proceeded smoothly. "I don't pay bribes," Masiyiwa said, asserting also that government "is surrounded by influence-peddlers looking for a cut of any contract."[89]

Third, these events expose the doublespeak of indigenization: although "black empowerment" is a professed goal, with some exceptions, only those whose loyalty to the state is demonstrated by their co-optation into the patronage network are granted the political space in which to operate. The government's treatment of Masiyiwa, in contrast to the rewards it has bestowed upon less ambitious but more "loyal" individuals, has had the effect of suppressing the emergence of other indigenous entrepreneurs with similar productive aspirations. To gain access to the Zimbabwean market, Telecel eventually abandoned Masiyiwa and took on a local partner acceptable to the government. Other than the state bourgeoisie, few Zimbabweans have benefited from such shortsightedness.

Where neopatrimonialism predominates, truly independent businesspeople and business ventures, especially those competing with the state, are not welcome (excluding small-scale enterprises, which may escape notice). In an alarming number of major business deals, it is an open secret that bids will be rigged and that tenders will eventually be awarded to political cronies. This scenario is not limited to the cellular phone industry; it has recently been repeated in the awarding of the contract to build a new international airport in Harare (the initial bid was awarded to a firm owned by Leo Mugabe, the president's nephew), the lease of planes for the national airline, and a pay-television scheme, to name a few. Siziba has lamented that "'people with the right connections are getting [state] tenders ahead of those without. . . . A black person without the capacity to handle the project wins a tender. He does not have the technology or capacity to do it, but just because of his close association with government he gets it."[90] To add to the paradoxical nature of indigenization in Zimbabwe, when the black "favorite son" firms that win these contracts are unable to complete them, they often turn to white firms that possess the technological capacity to finish the project. Alternatively, the entire project flounders.

Zimbabwe's most "successful" black businesspeople are thus notable for their close ties to the state, and these linkages are generally well known. As a recent editorial pointed out, "the lobby to 'indigenise' has become . . .

trivialised by loud-mouthed characters . . . whose rise from ashes to riches is most suspicious."[91] Many such businesspeople are described as "commission agents" and "briefcase businessmen" who do not actually produce anything or create jobs.[92] Since they are already co-opted into the state network, they pose no political threat to the government. Furthermore, as willing participants in state-based patronage, their economic loyalty is ensured. In fact, these people will likely be the heirs of the ZANU(PF) political machine when the torch is eventually passed from the current generation of leaders who rose to power during the liberation struggle.

Conclusion and Prospects

Zimbabwe's proclaimed crusade for black empowerment is a dubious one. Despite 17 years of rhetoric, little has been achieved, and indigenization remains an elusive goal. This professed goal will be unreachable without a major reversal in both policy design and implementation. It has been suggested in this chapter, however, that policies to encourage black empowerment will not be forthcoming because they would facilitate the formation of an indigenous and independent black middle class whose views are seen by the ZANU(PF) elite as antithetical to its own. Strive Masiyiwa's experience is more than just an interesting story. He represents something greater: independent capital, self-sufficiency, and a role model for other similarly oriented and motivated individuals.

There are other variables that must be taken into account when assessing ZANU(PF)'s recalcitrance on the indigenization issue and the fostering of an indigenous middle class. First, many observers of the Zimbabwean scene, and especially ZANU(PF) partisans and sympathizers, have cited the restrictions placed on the country by the Lancaster House Constitution, which emerged out of the British-brokered transfer of power from the Zimbabwe-Rhodesia government to independent rule in 1980. The concessions granted by ZANU and the Zimbabwe African People's Union (ZAPU) negotiators and embodied in Lancaster included protection of the property rights and business interests of the settler minority, as well as other stipulations, which the independent government agreed not to alter for a 10-year period. These provisions were clearly a constraint on efforts to promote "indigenization." Nevertheless, Zimbabwe was able to resettle black peasants on 2.2 million hectares of land within two years of independence. In the 15 years since, however, they have resettled fewer than 1 million additional hectares. Thus, since 1980, only 56,000 families have been resettled on 3 million hectares of land.[93]

The second variable constraining indigenization, ESAP, is more recent. This program has limited the availability of funds to support indigenous projects, social services, and welfare expenditure. A third confounding factor is the lingering commitment to "scientific socialism," once enshrined in ZANU(PF) doctrine, which sees capitalist accumulation as reprehensible. Closer examination of each of these variables, however, reveals that they are of only limited relevance to the current failure of indigenization and middle-class development.

The ZANU(PF) regime can find comfort in its white "constituents" in part because their numbers are meaningless from an electoral standpoint, but more importantly, because the regime enjoys the benefits of a relatively vibrant white economic class. ZANU(PF) is motivated by the Machiavellian impulse to maintain power and preserve the rewards that go with it. The government and the party are apparently willing to subvert the long-term economic and political interests of the country and its 11 million black citizens in pursuit of this short-term goal. But achieving this goal and keeping the economy in motion require certain tools, one of which is the support of the white business community.

ZANU(PF)'s principal tool for maintaining political power, however, is the "ideology" of indigenization and the use of radical rhetoric to portray itself as the champion of the country's seven-million-odd rural dwellers, the vast majority of whom are poor. Indigenization as currently practiced in Zimbabwe is a neopatrimonial game that rewards inefficiency and depresses productivity. Corruption becomes more likely and more prevalent in the absence of political and economic competition; ZANU's monopoly on power allows it to act with virtual impunity.

While it enriches state elites and a handful of clients, in the long term neopatrimonialism is economically debilitating and inherently antidemocratic. The interests of an independent bourgeois/middle class may prompt it to play a role in facilitating a transition to a more democratic system by weakening neopatrimonial structures, although this is not the only element required to facilitate such a transition. How can Zimbabwe and similarly situated polities extricate themselves from the vicious cycle of neopatrimonialism and weak, dependent capitalist classes?

Democratic transitions from neopatrimonial regimes are difficult to initiate and still harder to sustain. The paradox of neopatrimonial rule, however, is that state-based elites inevitably confront diminishing returns as patronage resources dwindle, thus sowing the seeds of conflict.[94] Regimes might allow independent middle-class development as a possible alternative to this conflict. On the other hand, as long as ZANU(PF) tries to contain these societal elements and remains an independent, indigenous bourgeois class, it must also stifle economic interests and political expression in defense of those interests, and this is potentially explosive.

The pervasiveness of neopatrimonialism in Zimbabwe also calls into question Bratton and van de Walle's conclusion that Africa's former settler oligarchies are the most likely to produce strong democratic outcomes. For democracy to flourish, rather than simply extending the franchise to black populations, steps must be taken by the postsettler state to allow the development of middle-class interests among these populations.

The bourgeois revolution need not be a violent one. However, President Mugabe has continued to make largely unfulfilled promises to the masses for more than 17 years. Is he, ironically, fomenting revolutionary impulses among the masses by his very rhetoric? In a very real way, the president is creating a revolution of rising expectations among the rural poor who make up Zimbabwe's majority. It is a greater irony still that political liberalization, achieved in part through middle-class development, could be his safety valve.

Notes

1. See Harbeson et al., eds., *Civil Society;* Bratton, "Beyond the State"; and Chazan, "Engaging the State." A few authors have deviated from the generally hopeful assessments, notably, Callaghy, "Civil Society, Democracy, and Economic Change."

2. There has also been a preoccupation with elections as the culmination of democratization, rather than as a point of departure. This was particularly so in early analyses of transitional elections. More recently, scholars have recognized that elections are, in some respects, the *beginning* of democratization. See Barkan, "Kenya"; Rosenberg, "Beyond Elections"; Klein, "Who's Afraid"; and McMahon, "Lessons Learned."

3. This research was supported by the Institute for the Study of World Politics and Emory University and is based on fieldwork conducted as a visiting research associate, Department of Political and Administrative Studies, at the University of Zimbabwe from September 1995 to April 1996. Helpful comments on an earlier draft were provided by Richard Joseph, Sarah Gill, and three anonymous reviewers.

4. Young, "Ethnicity."

5. Kasfir, *State and Class;* Lubeck, ed., *African Bourgeoisie.*

6. Schatz, "Pirate Capitalism"; Young, "Ethnicity"; and Lubeck, ed., *African Bourgeoisie.*

7. Bratton and van de Walle, "Neopatrimonial Regimes"; Joseph, *Democracy and Prebendal Politics.*

8. Bratton and van de Walle, "Neopatrimonial Regimes," p. 462.

9. Dahl, *Polyarchy.*

10. Sylvester, "Whither Opposition?"; Raftopoulos, "Zimbabwe." Despite this, two opposition candidates managed to defeat ZANU candidates in the 1995 elections. It is likely that these were, however, exceptional cases.

11. The 1996 presidential poll, highlighted by Robert Mugabe's ultimately unopposed candidacy, failed to attract the public to participate in the superfluous act of voting. Turnout was less than 20 percent of eligible voters.

12. Bratton and van de Walle's basic assumption, that prior regime type conditions both the likelihood of initiating a transition and the chances for its success, is borne out by recent trends on the continent.

13. Mills, "New Middle Class," p. 214; Rueschemeyer et al., *Capitalist Development.*

14. Rueschemeyer et al., *Capitalist Development,* p. 6.

15. Glassman, *Middle Class and Democracy;* West, "Middle-Class Formation."

16. Conaghan, "Capitalists, Technocrats, and Politicians." See also Harris, "New Bourgeoisies?"

17. Bratton and van de Walle, "Neopatrimonial Regimes," pp. 467–468.

18. Bratton and van de Walle, "Neopatrimonial Regimes."

19. Hyden, *No Shortcuts,* p. 22.

20. Moore, *Social Origins;* Rueschemeyer et al., *Capitalist Development.*

21. Numerous analyses have concentrated on the role of ethnicity as a barrier to the achievement of a stable democratic polity. The problems of ethnic heterogeneity and ethnic conflict militate against the very formation of alliances based on class. See, for example, Hyden, *No Shortcuts;* Young, "Ethnicity"; and Horowitz, *Ethnic Groups.* With one ethnic group clearly in the majority (the Shona represent roughly 78 percent of the population), one might expect that a major obstacle to class development is absent in Zimbabwe, and this should aid its emergence.

22. Among indigenous businesspeople in Kenya, *state*-bourgeois elements, not independent business classes, predominate. See Himbara, *Kenyan Capitalists,* and the contributions to Lubeck, ed., *African Bourgeoisie.*

23. This finding is consistent with Herbst, *State Politics,* although it is worth noting that historian Michael O. West argues that by 1965, there had emerged in Southern Rhodesia "a self-conscious and corporate African middle class" in opposition to both white settlers and African peasants and workers" (West, "Middle-Class Formation," pp. 2–3).

24. Harris, "New Bourgeoisies?"; Raftopoulos, "Zimbabwe"; and Strachan, "Report on the Impact of Redressive Action."

25. Based on author's calculations. The major categories excluded are agricultural employees, miners, service-sector workers, and blue-collar employees.

26. Government of Zimbabwe, *Census 1992.*

27. Harris, "New Bourgeoisies?"

28. ZCTU, "ZCTU Report."

29. Ranger, *African Voice,* finds a well-developed middle class. West, "Middle-Class Formation," p. 425, argues that its emergence was "signified by the demand for full transfer of state power." However, such unity of purpose and shared consciousness were perhaps more discernible in 1965, the year that West's analysis concludes, given the unifying objective of independence. He states that "black capitalists now claim the government of independent Zimbabwe as their own." Who forms this class? What are its political interests? With the advent of majority rule, the shared consciousness, born of a struggle for independence rather than an ideological class movement, has dissipated. These arguments seem specious without attaching the modifier "bureaucratic." A "fully emerged black middle class" in Zimbabwe seems never to have evolved beyond its formative stages.

30. Interviews by the author, Harare, 1996. Most respondents also criticized the state.

31. The seminal work on the African state as rational actor is Bates, *Markets and States.* He argues that (prestructural adjustment) states made the rational choice to maintain power by subsidizing, and therefore placating, urban populations at the expense of agricultural producers.

32. Bratton and van de Walle, "Neopatrimonial Regimes."

33. Young, "Ethnicity," p. 467.

34. Ronald Glassman argues that the concept of the "power-limited" state— that is, the basic separation of the economic sphere from the "means of violence"— is a basic tenet of democratic systems and is derived chiefly from John Locke, but

also from the writings of Adam Smith, David Ricardo, and Jeremy Bentham (*Middle Class and Democracy,* pp. 11 and 369).

35. Ostergaard, "Role of the National Bourgeoisie"; Raftopoulos, "Zimbabwe"; and Raftopoulos and Moyo, "Politics of Indigenization."

36. Evidence of black state–white society corruption linkages force a revision in our analyses of corruption and patronage in Africa. Such findings fall outside the traditional studies of corruption in Africa, as well as analyses of comprador classes acting in concert with international actors (white Zimbabweans are themselves residents and citizens).

37. It is difficult to determine at what point the Zimbabwean government helps whites, however indirectly, in order to preserve macroeconomic health, and at what point such interaction becomes complicitous. However, if the government publicly conceded the economic imperative of empowering (or at least maintaining) white economic interests, the party would damage itself politically vis-à-vis the rural poor.

38. This was the phrase used by Sam Moyo, personal communication, March 1996. See also Nicholas, "State and Development." See Ostergaard, "Role of the National Bourgeoisie," for a less benign interpretation.

39. Notably in Bratton, "Micro-Democracy?" Although one might suggest that co-optation is really a *tool* of middle-class suppression (in which case there would be only *two* principal factors), the argument can be made that co-optation/corruption can be separated from "class suppression." Bratton and van de Walle suggest that the cleavage between "insiders" and "outsiders" is a significant one. Those who dissent and are accommodated (co-opted) remain part of the neopatrimonial clique; those dissenters who are "expelled" become outsiders and may form the basis of an organized opposition ("Neopatrimonial Regimes," p. 464).

40. Mandaza, "State and Politics," cited in Sylvester, "Whither Opposition?" p. 409.

41. Thus far, this is an urban phenomenon. Former ZANU(PF) party member Margaret Dongo ran as an independent candidate and won the parliamentary election for Harare South in March 1995 against the ZANU candidate, Vivian Mwashita. See Sylvester, "Whither Opposition?" In the city of Mutare, another independent, Lawrence Mudehwe, won a heated race for mayor against the ZANU candidate in 1995.

42. In the rural areas, indigenization of the economy is equated generally with the issue of land reform, that is, redistribution of the large landholdings of white commercial farmers for subdivision by black peasant and/or small-scale farmers. Meaningful land reform has been a major failing of the ZANU government. See Moyo, *Land Question,* and Skalnes, *Politics of Economic Adjustment.*

43. Ostergaard, "Role of the National Bourgeoisie."

44. Bratton and van de Walle, "Neopatrimonial Regimes," p. 464.

45. Bratton and van de Walle, "Neopatrimonial Regimes."

46. Hyden, *No Shortcuts,* p. 53.

47. A number of authors have argued that "socialism" was an ideology of the liberation struggle, and not a coherent set of policies to be implemented once blacks gained control of the state. See, for example, Herbst, *State Politics;* Nyangoni, *African Nationalism;* Skalnes, *Politics of Economic Adjustment;* Ostergaard, "Role of the National Bourgeoisie"; and Sithole, "Zimbabwe." The president, however, frequently called upon the ethos of the liberation struggle, namely, the achievement of a socialist state. This position could be put forward as a bulwark against the expansion of an indigenous middle class, as well as to explain away ZANU's failure to develop independent black wealth. In fact, many Zimbabwean observers believe

that Mugabe himself still maintains his commitment to socialism despite the market-oriented changes over which he is presiding (author interviews). Nevertheless, given the acceptance of ESAP, that rationalization for the denial of capitalist class development no longer exists.

48. Raftopoulos and Moyo, "Politics of Indigenization."

49. Strachan, "Report on the Impact of Redressive Action" and "Report for the Confederation."

50. CZI, "Update."

51. Strachan, "Report on the Impact of Redressive Action," pp. 60–61.

52. Herbst, *State Politics;* Skalnes, *Politics of Economic Adjustment.*

53. See Skalnes, *Politics of Economic Adjustment,* esp. pp. 150–182, and Moyo, *Land Question.*

54. Ostergaard, "Role of the National Bourgeoisie," p. 17.

55. Ibid., pp. 127–129.

56. Ibid., p. 133.

57. These figures were reflected in Kapata, "Black Empowerment." Omitting the contribution to the economy from international firms and from the state, whose ownership is 22.5 percent and 11 percent, respectively (CZI, "Update"), a substantial share of the economy is controlled by whites. However, although white business interests dominate across the three leading sectors—large-scale commercial agriculture, manufacturing, and mining—no data is available to assess the validity of the 98 percent figure. For their part, white business interests have been reluctant to conduct studies that would bear out such findings (interviews by the author, Harare).

58. *Herald* (Harare), March 22, 1991.

59. The IBDC also set up the Business Extension and Advisory Services (BESA) in 1992 to provide skills training for indigenous small- and medium-scale enterprises.

60. The IBDC was actually made the umbrella organization for all of the indigenous lobbying associations, including those representing black farmers, transport operators, and others, whose leaders compose the IBDC board.

61. *Herald,* May 30, 1991.

62. *Financial Gazette* (Harare), October 22, 1992.

63. *Sunday Gazette* (Harare), February 7, 1993.

64. *Daily Gazette* (Harare), March 15, 1993.

65. For example, in December 1992, Strive Masiyiwa, who was then secretary-general of the IBDC, publicly accused the government of having a negative attitude toward the informal sector, the intended beneficiaries of the BESA program that the IBDC had set up to provide skills training for small- and medium-scale enterprises (*Herald,* November 12, 1992).

66. Note that it is unclear whether Mugabe himself, or only key members of his cabinet, was ever threatened by the IBDC. Indeed, former IBDC leadership takes great pains to point out that it was certain cabinet ministers, and not the president, who later targeted the organization.

67. Quoted in the *Sunday Gazette,* March 14, 1993.

68. Quoted during an interview with a former IBDC officer, Harare, February 22, 1996.

69. Interview, Harare, February 22, 1996.

70. Raftopoulos and Moyo, "Politics of Indigenization."

71. Ethnic rivalry has been cited as another contributing factor. A number of independent observers, though not Siziba himself, assert that Siziba's leadership was never accepted because he is Ndebele. Whether or not Siziba was challenged

because of his ethnicity, the wrangle was increasingly perceived in that light, especially after Vice President Joshua Nkomo, also an Ndebele, lent support to Siziba's faction, though to no avail.

72. Quoted in the *Daily Gazette,* December 16, 1994.

73. There are still examples of the IBDC criticizing the government, for example, with respect to the disbursement of funds in a loan provided by the African Development Bank. The facility, which totaled more than Z$700 million, was distributed to all businesses, regardless of race, based on borrower qualifications (see *Herald,* October 5, 1995). Nevertheless, the IBDC's harshest comments are today reserved for the white establishment: "Whites are happy for us to have only Political Rights, but will appear prepared to fight to the end to ensure that Blacks are denied Economic Rights" (*Herald,* IBDC advertisement, March 14, 1996).

74. Many, including the Irish, Norwegian, and Austrian donor agencies, have, however, maintained ties with the much less political, project-oriented BESA, which has no lobbying function. Although part of the IBDC, BESA maintains a degree of autonomy through its own management.

75. During its heyday, the IBDC had a professional staff of 17, including an executive director to handle administrative tasks, as well as a full-time economist. Today, although BESA has a small headquarters and staff, the IBDC does not even have an office, and the secretariat functions are handled by the secretary-general's own firm.

76. Part of this constituency was the international donor community. Some observers contend that the IBDC was forced to endorse the pet projects of its various donors, even if the projects were too small to be viable for the organization. Because it was donor dependent, the IBDC could not refuse to pursue them (Grierson and Moyo, "Advocacy").

77. The first secretary-general once stated that "in IBDC no one has to be in a leadership position for too long. Our organisation must be democratic and our movements are aimed at strengthening the organisation" (*Financial Gazette,* August 13, 1993). More recently, officeholders have shown some determination to retain their positions. See also *Financial Gazette,* October 4, 1995.

78. Skalnes, *Politics of Economic Adjustment.*

79. The forced acquisition of two white-owned farms was challenged in Zimbabwe's High Court in 1996. It was the first such challenge to the Land Acquisition Act of 1992, which granted the government sweeping powers. It was also the first application of the act once heralded as the antithesis of the Lancaster constitution.

80. Grosh and Mukandala, eds., *State Owned Enterprises.*

81. World Bank, *World Development Report, 1995.*

82. Supplement to *Herald,* January 25, 1996.

83. *Financial Gazette,* December 21, 1995.

84. Zimbabwe boasts a fairly independent judiciary, which not infrequently has handed down decisions unfavorable to the government, including, for example, the reversal of fraudulent elections—paving the way for the victory of independent candidate Margaret Dongo over the ZANU(PF) candidate—and the legal objections to the draft of the Land Reform Bill of 1992.

85. As reported by *The Economist,* April 13, 1996. *Africa Economic Digest* notes that the costs to Masiyiwa personally, his company, and his partners have thus far been exorbitant. In addition to incurring an estimated Z$4 million in legal costs to challenge the PTC in court, by the time of the presidential decree, equipment worth more than Z$87 million had been imported into the country. Econet claims

that the government will have to compensate the company for these imports, as well as for contracts that have been jeopardized (*African Economic Digest,* February 19, 1996, p. 18).

86. The first tender resulted in the contract being awarded to Ericcson Communications of Sweden, which was found to have interfered in the bidding process.

87. BBC Network Africa, July 18, 1996.

88. Quoted in Makamure, "In Search of Sound Leadership," *Sunday Gazette,* February 4, 1996 (Harare, Zimbabwe).

89. Quoted in *The Economist,* March 3, 1996.

90. Interview with Chemist Siziba in *African Economic Digest,* June 10, 1996.

91. *Financial Gazette,* November 2, 1995.

92. *The Guardian,* May 22, 1996.

93. Recall that the roughly 4,000 members of the Commercial Farmers Union, most of whom are white, own approximately 11.2 million hectares in total.

94. Bratton and van de Walle, "Neopatrimonial Regimes," p. 464.

14

The Role of Citizenship Laws in Multiethnic Societies: Evidence from Africa

Jeffrey Herbst

In May 1996, the parliament of Zambia completed work on a new constitution that would prevent Kenneth Kaunda, president of the country from 1964 to 1991, from running for president again because he is now considered to be a foreigner. The bizarre finding that Kaunda (whose parents were migrant Malawian missionaries who settled in what was then Northern Rhodesia in the 1920s, where Kaunda was later born) is not a citizen, when he in fact has an excellent claim to being the father of modern Zambia, points out both the underlying importance and the new contentiousness of laws governing citizenship in multiethnic societies in Africa and elsewhere in the world.

Indeed, the wave of democratization sweeping across Africa and other parts of the world has made citizenship laws even more publicly controversial than in the past, because it suddenly matters a great deal who can and cannot vote. For instance, Kenneth Matiba, a leading member of the Kenyan opposition, has reopened the question of whether Asians, most of whom can trace their ancestry in Kenya back a century, should be considered Kenyan citizens. He wrote, "The issue of citizenship should be addressed more fully so that people do not acquire citizen status only to dominate the locals. Standards should be set so high so that not just anybody becomes a citizen."[1] The question of citizenship in east Africa is particularly important—and this threat, extremely significant—because of Idi Amin's expulsion of 60,000 Asians from neighboring Uganda in 1972. Similarly, Côte d'Ivoire, in many ways a model multiethnic society that long welcomed Africans from neighboring countries, has now reversed its former policy and no longer allows citizens of other countries to vote in its elections. President Henri Konan Bédié defended this change in the law in particularly telling language: "Our electoral law . . . expresses the will of our parliamentarians to ensure and to sustain the nation's unity and independence. This is why, following the example of all democratic countries, they made it a point to ensure that only people holding Ivorian nationality have the right to vote."[2] Zaire had also changed its laws in anticipation of new elections and now requires Tutsis to prove that they had Zairian ancestry dating back to 1850 in order to become citizens, instead of 1960, as had previously been the case.[3]

The Political Impact of Citizenship Laws

Citizenship laws embody the most dramatic changes wrought by colonialism on the African continent. In the precolonial era, when even strong African polities did not exercise much control over defined pieces of territory, there were significant flows of people between territories, and citizenship was an extremely fluid and ill-defined concept. William Shack notes that "there is just enough evidence to suggest that African strangers, and indeed strangers of other racial and ethnic origins, once moved with relative ease between indigenous African polities."[4] In precolonial Africa, land was so abundant and migration so easy that exit to another territory was the preferred form of political protest.[5] The imposition of citizenship on every African, which essentially tied each person on the continent to a specific, territorially defined polity, was thus a revolutionary event.[6] As a result, the conventional wisdom is that "in Africa, ethnic identity runs thicker than national citizenship, reflecting the fact that the continent's national borders were put in place a mere hundred years ago by colonialists who drew lines on maps without reference to the people in them."[7]

However, particularly after independence in the 1960s, citizenship laws did in fact become salient very quickly. For the first time, Africans were asked to permanently define who legitimately lived in their societies and who did not, and this process of community definition and division effectively foreclosed many opportunities to migrate. The creation of the concept of "foreigner," brought about by impending independence, led to riots in the late 1950s and early 1960s in Ghana, Côte d'Ivoire, Sierra Leone, and elsewhere, as new citizens demanded that migrants, who were increasingly resented, be expelled.[8] Closing international borders became an important symbol of sovereignty in what were usually very tenuous states.[9] Indeed, William F. S. Miles and David A. Rochefort report in their careful study that Hausa villagers on the Nigeria-Niger border "do not place their ethnic identity as Hausas above their national one as citizens of Nigeria or Niger and express greater affinity for non-Hausa citizens than foreign Hausas."[10] Thus, citizenship laws seem, as N. J. Small wrote, to "articulate a sense of nationhood in a territory that has political unity but little else."[11]

The political impact of citizenship laws—the formal rules that define the relationship between people and the state—on ethnic conflict, which is one of the greatest threats to the unity of many African countries, is obviously important. It is especially critical to explore the effect of nationality laws in Africa given the newness of the states and the fact that defining who is and who is not a citizen is one of the few unquestioned capabilities of the usually weak states of sub-Saharan Africa.[12] Moreover, citizenship laws are especially important in Africa because of the large number of refugees on the continent. Roughly one-third of the world's 15 million refugees are in Africa. As a result, the question of who is and who is not a citizen of a particular country is tested daily. For example, in Malawi in the early 1990s, 12.5 percent of the population was made up of refugees from Mozambique.[13] Given that the number of failed states that generate these refugees will probably continue to increase,[14] citizenship laws will continue to be critical to the lives of hundreds of thousands, if not millions, of people for the foreseeable future.

As noted above, several countries are currently debating whether stricter nationality laws would promote national unity by more clearly defining who is and is not a citizen. Lower hurdles to citizenship, on the other hand, would allow more people into the polity, but they would obviously dilute the meaning of citizenship to some extent. The initial hypothesis of this chapter is that African countries can best reduce ethnic conflict by following the latter path and allowing as many people as possible to become citizens. This suggests that the current tendency among liberalizing polities in Africa to restrict citizenship is a potentially profound error. Indeed, given the particular circumstances of most African countries, relatively restrictive nationality laws are especially likely to alienate minorities, while failing to promote a greater degree of unity among those who are actually granted citizenship. In addition, whatever a country's initial citizenship laws stipulate, any change that makes naturalization more difficult is probably also a mistake.

Unfortunately, while the importance of citizenship laws is clear, systematic study of the comparative effects of these regulations has been inadequate. Indeed, most of the debates about "constitutional engineering" in new democracies have focused on electoral laws (e.g., proportional representation versus district-based systems) or on the design of national political structures (e.g., prime ministerial versus presidential systems).[15] While these subjects are obviously important, the failure to systematically examine citizenship laws is inexplicable given their particular relevance to multiethnic societies. Indeed, the only area of the world where significant scholarly attention is being devoted to citizenship laws is Western Europe, where the significant influx of migrant labor and the flows of people from former colonies to the metropoles have forced rethinking and reexamination of laws regarding nationality.[16] Scholars thus appear to be ignoring T.

H. Marshall's classic argument that managing citizenship is a critical aspect of the amelioration of conflict among citizens (he was specifically writing about class) because citizenship is the gateway to social rights (trade unionism and collective bargaining).[17] It is peculiar that so much attention has been devoted to laws governing how people can vote, and so little, in comparison, to the regulations that determine who can cast a ballot.

Jus Soli and Jus Sanguinis

Fortunately, there is a rich historic debate about the nature of citizenship laws that can help structure the analysis of nationality laws in new states. When citizenship laws were first developed in England in the early seventeenth century, largely to resolve inheritance disputes, the simple rule was jus soli: those born in the territory were citizens irrespective of the nationality of their parents. However, a counterargument was soon made that tying citizenship to the territory of birth was arbitrary and did not allow for consent. In particular, John Locke argued that since men are born free, "a child is born a subject of no Country or Government."[18] Rather, Locke argued that children should be considered citizens of the country of their fathers until they become adults, at which point they should be able to choose their own citizenship. Similarly, Emmeric de Vattel argued in favor of jus sanguinis—citizenship through descent irrespective of the location of birth—by suggesting that, "in order to be of the country, it is necessary that a person be born of a father who is a citizen; for, if he is born there of a foreigner, it will be only the place of his birth, and not his country."[19] Peter H. Schuck and Rogers M. Smith have similarly questioned the U.S. practice of automatically granting citizenship to all those who happen to be born in the country.[20]

More recently, there has been a tremendous debate in many Western countries about how to cope with significant immigration and guest workers. Many have criticized the current practice in Western countries of maintaining significant guest-worker populations that do not have claims to citizenship rights, an explicit attack on jus sanguinis. For example, while he agrees that countries have the absolute right to draft any immigration policy, Michael Walzer has argued that naturalization must be available to "every new immigrant, every refugee taken in." He claims that excluding people who share the territory from citizenship is "a form of tyranny."[21]

Indeed, citizenship laws based on jus sanguinis are often designed to preserve, at both a factual and a symbolic level, a people or *volk* and to prevent certain groups from becoming citizens even if they were born within the national territory. Thus, Germany does not grant citizenship to Turkish workers, who may have been born in the Federal Republic's territory, but it does allow ethnic Germans who have lived outside the fatherland for generations to become citizens, even if they have no immediate family ties to, and extremely limited knowledge of, modern Germany. Similarly, jus sanguinis is the guiding principle in Indonesia and Malaysia in order to limit the size of the wealthy—but highly resented—Chinese minorities in both countries. Both countries changed their citizenship laws from the colonial practice (by the Dutch and English, respectively), which had recognized the principle of jus soli, in order to limit Chinese influence, particularly due to widespread concern in both countries about the need to uplift the Indonesian and Bumiputra majorities.[22] In part as a result of these policies, there are 220,000 ethnic Chinese who are stateless in Malaysia and 800,000 who have no citizenship in Indonesia.[23] A number of other countries, including Israel, Hungary, and Poland, use jus sanguinis rules to grant citizenship to the people of their diasporas in order to encourage fellow members of their ethnic group to return.[24] However, in Europe, a number of countries (including France, the Netherlands, and Belgium) that largely determined citizenship based on ancestry in the past have now adopted mixed rules, whereby children born in the country with at least one parent who was also born in the country can acquire citizenship.[25]

Citizenship in Africa

As a consequence of the colonial origins of Africa's boundaries, from the dawn of independence there has been a strong attraction to the Pan-African ideal of reducing the salience of the current boundaries. However, interests soon reified around the concept of the modern nation-state as defined by the Europeans, and Africans quickly adopted most of the conventions associated with it. For example, in Nigeria, citizenship for those born after independence is determined by the location of birth. Members of ethnic groups with strong ties to Nigeria dating back to the precolonial period, but who live outside the country's borders, are not considered Nigerian. Thus, a Yoruba born in Benin will not be Nigerian, despite close kinship ties with the Yoruba in neighboring Nigeria, because his or her parents are Beninese.[26] However, in at least some cases (e.g., British-protected persons), people who were not natives of Nigeria could claim citizenship at independence. Only a few African countries extend ancestry-based citizenship laws beyond their borders. For instance, Malawi extends citizenship to Mozambicans north of the Zambezi River,[27] because former President Hastings Banda tenaciously held on to the idea of a greater Malawi that would include substantial parts of its lusophone neighbor. Guinea-Bissau also extends citizenship to all citizens of Cape Verde because of the close ties between the two countries.[28] Similarly, Somalia grants citizenship to all ethnic Somalis living in Kenya and Ethiopia (the so-called unredeemed Somalis).[29]

There are also a few other African innovations to citizenship laws. For example, both Guinea-Bissau and Mozambique grant citizenship to anyone who fought for independence during their wars of national liberation.[30] On the other hand, Eritrea has denied citizenship to Jehovah Witnesses, in part because they did not participate in the country's war for independence from Ethiopia.[31]

Despite J. H. W. Verzijl's claim that it would be "love's labour lost to attempt to collect from the statute books of the present-day sovereign States all the laws relating to the acquisition and loss of their nationality,"[32] I have coded the relevant aspects of citizenship laws for almost all African countries (see Appendix 14.1). In general, African citizenship laws bear a close, but not absolute, connection to the practices of their colonizers. Table 14.1 identifies those countries that retained the citizenship laws of the former colonizer and those that changed practices at independence. In many countries, the colonial inheritance has been exceptionally influential. Of the francophone countries, only Gabon does not fully follow the French practice of relying principally on citizenship through descent.[33] Anglophone countries have also been influenced by the British practice of granting citizenship to anyone born in the territory.[34] However, as with most other things, the colonial connection is less clear in anglophone Africa than among the francophones. Other countries have also been influenced by their own colonial traditions. In Zaire, for example, the old Belgian practice of establishing tiers of citizenship continued long after the former metropole had changed its own citizenship practices.

Of the 40 countries for which information is available, 12 determine citizenship primarily by place of birth, and 28 determine citizenship in the first instance based on ancestry (see Appendix 14.1). However, the dividing line between jus soli and jus sanguinis is, in fact, somewhat ambiguous. Many of the countries that base citizenship on ancestry allow those born within the territory to apply for citizenship after a certain period of time, and all countries that assign citizenship to those born within the borders also provide for citizenship by descent when nationals have children beyond the borders. The critical difference between the two groups, and the deciding factor in the classification, is whether states grant citizenship automatically to those born within the territory (jus soli states), or whether these individuals still have to apply for citizenship (jus sanguinis states). In jus sanguinis states, naturalization usually depends on the approval of government officials, who may deny citizenship on the basis of residency requirements, criminal records, or an inability to demonstrate integration into the community. As noted above, it is precisely during times of political liberalization that politicians will be tempted to use such provisions to exclude certain groups. On the other hand, no country adopts a pure jus soli rule; it would simply be unworkable, as there will always be some citizens who give birth while outside the country. Thus, jus soli countries inevitably

Table 14.1 Patterns of Citizenship Rules Compared with Colonizer at Independence

Retained Colonial Practice	Changed Colonial Practice
Anglophone Countries[a]	
The Gambia	Botswana
Kenya	Ghana
Mauritius	Malawi
Nigeria	Seychelles
Sierra Leone	Sudan
Tanzania	Zambia
Uganda	
Zimbabwe	
Francophone Countries[b]	
Benin	
Burkina Faso	
Cameroon	
Central African Republic	
Chad	
Congo	
Gabon	
Guinea	
Madagascar	
Mali	
Mauritania	
Niger	
Senegal	
Togo	
Lusophone Countries[c]	
Guinea-Bissau	Mozambique
Former Belgian Colonies[d]	
Burundi	
Rwanda	
Congo (Zaire)	

Notes: Angola's laws apparently have not been printed. The available information on Lesotho and Swaziland is inadequate. Ethiopia and Liberia were not colonized. Somalia did not exist until it received independence, at which time Italian-controlled Somalia and British-controlled Somaliland were merged. Somalia's laws resemble Italy's jus sanguinis regulations. Equatorial Guinea received its independence from Spain, and its laws resemble its colonizer's jus soli regulations. Eritrea and Namibia received their independence from Ethiopia and South Africa, respectively.

a. The UK was a jus soli state.
b. France was a jus sanguinis state.
c. Portugal was a jus soli state.
d. Belgium was a jus sanguinis state.

have lower hurdles to citizenship than countries that determine citizenship in the first instance based on ancestry.

For citizenship purposes, ancestry requirements typically require that one is born to a parent who is a citizen, but both jus soli and jus sanguinis countries can be sexist in tracing descent; 19 of the 40 countries trace ancestry, at least in the first instance, only through the father. However, only about one-third (10 of the 28) jus sanguinis countries trace ancestry through the father, whereas three-quarters (nine of 12) jus soli countries have sexist ancestry laws. It is not surprising that countries that trace citizenship primarily by ancestry have more liberal rules regarding parentage, as their primary concern is how well a person is integrated into the society, and birth to a woman who is a citizen is certainly an indication of belonging to the community. Parentage is less of a concern to jus soli states, and they can therefore allow other concerns, including sexist conceptions of how citizenship should be defined, to influence their nationality laws. However, these ancestry provisions are under threat because they are innately biased against women. For example, Botswana initially specified that citizenship should be determined by the father's citizenship, but after protests by feminist groups, this law was recently changed (with retroactive effect back to 1982) to allow citizenship to be passed down from mothers as well.[35]

Both categories of states are about equally liberal when specifying language requirements for citizenship. Five of the 12 states that determine citizenship based at least partially on the place of birth have specific provisions requiring that citizens speak a particular language, while 15 of the 28 jus sanguinis states have such a regulation. Again, the effect of colonial heritage is noticeable; most of the jus sanguinis states are francophone, and France's own laws require that an individual must be assimilated, which includes knowing French, to become a naturalized citizen.[36]

Jus sanguinis states are notably more likely to impose restrictions on citizenship after naturalization. These laws typically prevent new citizens from voting or running for office. Of the 16 states that impose either temporary (five years or less) or permanent (more than five years) incapacities on citizens, 15 are jus sanguinis states. The thrust of the jus sanguinis codes is that citizenship must be based on more than a location; it should also involve a true commitment to the community. It is therefore hardly surprising that countries that trace citizenship primarily by ancestry should be concerned that a person is truly integrated into the community before allowing him or her to vote or to run for office. Likewise, if citizenship is going to be granted at least partially on the basis of where the mother happens to give birth, demanding that new citizens become integrated into the community before allowing them the full panoply of rights makes little sense.

Reflecting the poor status of women in Africa, both types of nations make it relatively difficult for foreign men who marry female nationals to gain citizenship. Only three of the 12 jus soli states, and six of the 28 jus sanguinis states, allow for naturalization of men by marriage. On the other hand, nonnational women who marry male citizens can be naturalized relatively quickly in all of the countries. Despite international calls that date back decades demanding equality for women with respect to naturalization laws, African countries still practice what might be called the "law of Ruth."[37]

It was not possible to establish the extent to which particular laws actually affect naturalization in practice within individual African countries. These countries do not publish statistics on naturalization, reflecting the sensitivity of the issue, the generally opaque workings of many Home Affairs (or equivalent) Ministries, and the weak statistical bases available. Indeed, a thorough review of international statistical sources and publications by individual African countries reveals that no African country appears to publish naturalization data on a regular basis. But studies in Europe have found that the propensity to naturalize is closely connected to citizenship policies.[38]

Citizenship Laws and Ethnic Conflict

Citizenship laws can have several distinct effects on ethnic conflict. In particular, relatively liberal citizenship laws can reduce the number of alienated groups in African societies, as access to the rights of citizenship can alleviate their grievances. In addition, liberal codes can reduce ethnic conflict by allowing a large percentage of the people present in a country to participate in its political life. Indeed, as elections become a more frequent occurrence in African countries, the distinction between citizens and noncitizens becomes more important and more noticeable to all. Finally, relatively liberal citizenship laws can help produce a common identity, which is especially important in poor, multiethnic societies.[39] There is mounting evidence that societies that fail to produce this common identity and instead face increasing divisions are likely to experience lower economic growth, as redistributive politics produce policy gridlock.[40]

The permanent alienation of whole communities due to relatively strict citizenship laws is an especially important problem in Africa, given both the large number of refugees on the continent and the historical repercussions of the establishment of colonial boundaries, which were not necessarily resolved when independence was achieved. For example, members of some Tutsi communities in eastern Zaire, who relocated from Rwanda a century or more ago, have not been able to become Zairian. These communities, estimated to include between 450,000 and 600,000 people, are now engaged in armed conflict with the "original" Zairian inhabitants of the region. In 1993, 40,000 people died in conflicts that were prompted at least partially by discriminatory citizenship laws.[41] The fighting that broke out in eastern Zaire in 1996, leading to the overthrow of Sese Seko Mobutu's regime, was at least partially prompted by Tutsi who wanted above all to be Zairian; having been denied that opportunity, they were forced to form an alliance with the Tutsi government in Rwanda and take up arms.

Similarly, proposed citizenship law changes in Zambia have generated secessionist threats among the Lozi in the western part of the country. During the colonial period, the Lozi lived in what was known as Barotseland, a separate British protectorate under the Northern Rhodesian administration. They believe that the recent changes in the citizenship laws, which affect the legal status of those whose parents were not born in Zambia, will have a profound effect on their political fortunes (a charge denied by Zambian authorities).[42] The permanent designation of these communities as foreign, and therefore as distinctly different from the local populations, would be a sharp departure from precolonial and colonial practices, according to which stranger communities were eventually absorbed, making time of arrival a less salient source of division.

The threat of secession is only the most dramatic threat that might be generated by groups or whole communities that are excluded from the national political community by restrictive citizenship laws. A more routine outcome has been significant levels of political violence that do not directly threaten the design of the state. This political violence may occur either between groups that do and do not have citizenship or between the state and a particular group with significant citizenship grievances. Not surprisingly, as is the case in eastern Zaire, "the issue of nationality has been a recurrent source of contention . . . especially relating to voter eligibility in electoral periods."[43]

The Byzantine nature of many citizenship laws, especially those with relatively restrictive codes, provides many opportunities to increase ethnic hostilities for those so inclined. The experience of Alhaji Shugaba, who brought a famous case against Nigeria regarding citizenship, is instructive. Shugaba's father was a member of the Bagarmi group, born in what is now the Chad Republic, although neither Chad nor Nigeria existed when he was born. Shugaba's father was conscripted into the sultan's army and finally settled in Maiduguri (in what is now Nigeria) in 1911. He married Shugaba's mother, who was from Maiduguri, and this is where their child was born. Shugaba rose to become an important member of the Great Nigeria People's Party and the majority leader of the Borno State House of Assembly (Borno is a Nigerian state that borders Chad and Cameroon). In 1980, in a ploy that would be repeated in other African countries, Shugaba's political foes managed to have him declared an alien and be deported because his father was not Nigerian. In the end, Shugaba managed to convince the courts that he was Nigerian (because of his mother's nationality), but the case is a cautionary tale of how citizenship laws can be manipulated for political purposes.[44] Of course, the more restrictive and complicated citizenship laws are, the greater the potential there is for politicians to use them to their own advantage by expelling or otherwise delegitimizing the leaders of other groups, especially groups that have the kind of complicated history apparent in the Shugaba case.

At the other end of the scale, those countries with less restrictive citizenship laws have experienced less political violence and have scored some notable successes in uniting their populations. For example, Tanzania's relatively good ethnic relations can be attributed, in part, to its fairly liberal citizenship laws. Tanzania has, for instance, extended citizenship to tens of thousands of Rwandan refugees,[45] thereby significantly reducing the likelihood that the refugees will become a separate, alienated population and facilitating their absorption by the already sizable Hutu communities in Tanzania. Similarly, recent efforts by Daniel arap Moi's government to grant citizenship to large communities of Tanzanians that have long been resident in Kenya will remove at least one potential point of ethnic conflict.[46]

The major advantages of relatively restrictive citizenship laws, which have been outlined by many Western theorists, are probably less relevant in poor, multiethnic countries in Africa and the rest of the developing world than they are in more developed polities. Restrictive citizenship laws can create a narrower, but presumably more deeply felt, sense of citizenship. However, African states cannot deliver much to their citizens due to the profound resource and administrative constraints that they face; education and health care services are often minimal, while other social services (e.g., old-age pensions and housing) are often nonexistent, and sometimes the state does not even have an obvious physical presence, especially in rural areas. In addition, since interstate war is all but absent in Africa, states have had little role in providing for the common defense, a role that has been critical to the development of citizenship elsewhere in the world.[47] Thus, all the state can do through citizenship laws is provide a basic, lowest-common-denominator identity; the prospects for creating a narrower but deeper sense of citizenship are severely limited in Africa because the state cannot provide much beyond this. However, this basic identity may still be important to noncitizens, even if the advantages of being a citizen are far fewer than in more developed countries.

Unfortunately, several attempts to establish a statistical relationship between citizenship laws and ethnic violence have failed, in part because the data on political violence in Africa is poor and will only support the most general types of analysis.[48] The best data set on minority political communities was created by Ted Robert Gurr, Barbara Harff, Monty G. Marshall, and James R. Scarritt. However, it examines only those countries with disaffected minorities, so it cannot be used to test the effect of citizenship laws on political violence because it essentially selects on the dependent variable.[49] In addition, the high correlation between the type of citizenship laws and the former colonizer makes it difficult to disentangle effects. For example, francophone countries not only have different citizenship laws from anglophone countries; they are also poorer, they are more prone to military intervention by France, and most are in the franc zone. As a result, in most cases, no direct causality can be established between citizenship laws and violence. In fact, political violence in most countries is due to a combination of demographic, social, and economic factors that are either aggravated or ameliorated by the decisions made by national leaders and the incentives provided by the existing political system. Large-scale political violence in particular usually arises from a combination of structural conditions and counterproductive (at least for the nation as a whole) political strategies that defy simple generalizations regarding causation. However, at the very least, those countries that have, for whatever reason, suffered significant political violence have not availed themselves of a potentially useful mechanism for reducing conflict: relatively liberal citizenship laws.

The Danger of Changing Citizenship Rights

Irrespective of the effects of original citizenship laws on African countries, it seems reasonably clear that changing the rules of the game to make naturalization more difficult or to deny citizenship to current citizens is potentially very dangerous. The importance of citizenship rights to political affairs is analogous to the role of property rights in economic affairs: they define a set of presumably inalienable claims that people have on the state. As with changes in property rights, changes in citizenship rules disrupt individuals' long-term plans and may severely diminish the value of many years of work. Moreover, even those who are not immediately affected by a particular change in citizenship laws become so uncertain about the permanency of the rules of the game that they no longer find it advantageous to make long-term investments that would benefit the nation. Instead, they may embark on other strategies that will enable them to leave the state or enter into conflict with the authorities in order to create a more amenable political order.

Of course, the fact that those threatened by changes in citizenship laws are often among the most economically dynamic in a country (e.g., Asians in Kenya) increases the potential damage that might result if members of those minority groups cease making long-term investments in the country. In fact, for these prosperous minority groups, citizenship rules and property rights are in some ways indistinguishable. Indeed, it is a telling state of affairs that rich countries try to keep poor people from becoming citizens, while poor countries debate whether to make citizenship policies toward the richest of their inhabitants more restrictive. This is one of the reasons that they continue to be poor.

Changing citizenship rules during democratization processes would seem to be especially dangerous because threatened groups, even those not immediately affected by changes in legislation, might perceive that democratization is opening the way to wholesale changes in the political rules of the game. Indeed, the chairman of Zambia's ruling party, Sikota Wina, made exactly this threat during the debate over Kaunda's citizenship: "There is this fallacy of a constitution that stands the test of time. There is no such constitution anywhere in the world. Each generation amends the constitution to suit its environment and they are all free to do so."[50] Precisely because citizenship rules are such a central aspect of the state's relationship with the polity, any measure that legitimizes changes in citizenship laws as an appropriate campaign strategy is probably exceptionally dangerous.

Conclusion

For too long, citizenship laws have been ignored in Africa because it seemed unlikely that regulations affecting naturalization could be consequential in countries with artificial boundaries. However, within individual African countries, citizenship can be important precisely because the state can do little more than indicate who is and is not part of the polity. These designations, in turn, have the potential to affect patterns of ethnic violence. This chapter has provided some preliminary reasoning about why it might be advantageous for African countries to implement relatively liberal citizenship laws. An even stronger case can be made against making existing laws more restrictive. At this point, however, further study of the actual workings of citizenship regulations is still needed.

* * *

Appendix 14.1 Citizenship Laws in Africa

Country	Jus Sanguinis?	Ancestry via Father?	Language Required?	Can Foreigners Gain Citizenship?	Less Than 5 Years to Become Citizen?	Incapacities After Naturalization?
Angola	Yes	Yes	Yes	No	No	Temporary
Benin	Yes	Yes/No[a]	Yes	No	Yes	No
Botswana	Yes	No	Yes	No	No	Temporary
Burkina Faso	Yes	Yes	Yes	No	Yes	Temporary
Burundi	Yes	Yes	No	No	No	Temporary
Cameroon	n.a.	n.a.	n.a.	n.a.	n.a.	n.a.
Cape Verde	Yes	No	No	No	Yes	No
Central African Republic	Yes	No	No	Yes	Yes	Temporary
Chad	n.a.	n.a.	n.a.	n.a.	n.a.	n.a.
Comoros	Yes	No	Yes	No	Yes	Permanent
Congo (Zaire)	Yes	No	Yes	No	Yes	Temporary
Congo-Brazzaville	Yes	No	No	No	No	No
Côte d'Ivoire	No	No	No	No	Yes	No
Equatorial Guinea	Yes	No	Yes	Yes	Yes	No
Eritrea	Yes	No	Yes	No	No	No
Ethiopia	Yes	No	No	No	No	Temporary
Gabon	No	Yes	Yes	No	No	No
The Gambia	Yes	No	Yes	Yes	No	No
Ghana	Yes	Yes	No	No	No	No
Guinea	No	No	No	Yes	Yes	No
Guinea-Bissau	No	Yes	Yes	No	No	No
Kenya	n.a.	n.a.	n.a.	n.a.	n.a.	n.a.
Lesotho	No	Yes	No	No	No	No
Liberia	Yes	No	Yes	No	No	Temporary
Madagascar	Yes	No	Yes	No	Yes	No
Malawi						

Country	Jus Sanguinis?	Ancestry via Father?	Language Required?	Can Foreigners Gain Citizenship?	Less Than 5 Years to Become Citizen?	Incapacities After Naturalization?
Mali	Yes	No	No	No	No	Temporary
Mauritania	Yes	No	No	No	No	Temporary
Mauritius	No	Yes	No	No	n.a.	n.a.
Mozambique	Yes	No	No	No	No	n.a.
Namibia	No	No	No	Yes	No	No
Niger	Yes	Yes	No	No	Yes	Temporary
Nigeria	No	Yes	Yes	No	n.a.	n.a.
Rwanda	Yes	Yes	Yes	n.a.	Yes	Temporary
São Tomé and Príncipe	n.a.	n.a.	n.a.	n.a.	n.a.	n.a.
Senegal	Yes	Yes	No	No	Yes	Temporary
Seychelles	Yes	No	No	Yes	n.a.	n.a.
Sierra Leone	No	Yes	Yes	Yes	Yes	Permanent
Somalia	Yes	Yes	No	Yes	Yes	No
Sudan	Yes	Yes	Yes	No	Yes	No
Swaziland	n.a.	n.a.	n.a.	n.a.	n.a.	n.a.
Tanzania	No	Yes	Yes	No	n.a.	n.a.
Togo	Yes	Yes	No	No	No	Temporary
Uganda	No	Yes	Yes	No	No	No
Zambia	Yes	No	Yes	No: old; yes: new[b]	Unclear	No
Zimbabwe	No	Yes	No	No	n.a.	n.a.

Sources: The primary source for the annex material was United Nations High Commissioner for Refugees (UNHCR) gopher site "REFWORLD," location: gopher://iccuc2.unicc.org:70/11/unhcrcdr/legal.m/refleg.m. The CD-ROM published by the UNHCR under the same name was used to update information. Some material was also taken from the individual country reports in the *International Encyclopedia of Comparative Law* (Tübingen, Germany: J. C. B. Mohr, various years); Melone, ed., *Droit des Personnes et de La Famille*; and United Nations, *Laws Concerning Nationality.*

Individual country information was also derived from Blaise and Mourgeon, *Lois et Décrets*; Vanderlinden, *Droit de L'Éthiopie Moderne*; Jackson, *Law of Kenya*; Nylander, *Nationality and Citizenship Laws of Nigeria*; Noor, *Legal System*; and Brown and Allen, *Law of Uganda.*

Notes: n.a. = data not available.

a. The law was changed in 1995, retroactive to 1982.

b. The provision was changed in the new constitution adopted in 1991. The new constitution can be found at: http://www.uni-wuerzburg.de/law/za00000_html.

Notes

I am grateful to Michael Doyle, Richard Joseph, Carolyn Logan, Donald Rothchild, Nicolas van de Walle, and John Waterbury for helpful comments.

1. In Nduru, "Anti-Asian Sentiment."
2. Radio Côte d'Ivoire, "President Bédié."
3. Human Rights Watch et al., *Zaire*, p. 7.
4. Shack, "Introduction," p. 8.
5. Herbst, "Migration."
6. Elias, "Evolution of Law," p. 189.
7. Crossette, "Citizenship," p. 3.
8. Peil, "Expulsion of West African Aliens," p. 205.
9. Zolberg, "Formation of New States," p. 28.
10. Miles and Rochefort, "Nationalism," p. 401.
11. Small, "Citizenship," p. 18. See also Bendix, *Nation-Building*, p. 74.
12. It is, however, important to note that even in Europe, codification of nationality laws did not generally occur until the nineteenth century (Heldrich et al., "Persons").
13. Adelman and Sorenson, "Introduction," p. ix.
14. Herbst, "Responding to State Failure."
15. See, for example, Barkan, "Elections in Agrarian Societies," and Linz and Stepan, "Presidential or Parliamentary Democracy."
16. See Jacobson, *Rights Across Borders;* Bauböck, ed., *Aliens to Citizens;* Gibney, ed., *Open Borders?;* and Bhabha and Shutter, *Women's Movement.*
17. Marshall, T. H., *Citizenship*, pp. 43–44.
18. Locke, *Second Treatise*. A similar argument was made by Burlamaqui in *Principles*, p. 30.
19. de Vattel, *Law of Nations*, p. 101.
20. Schuck and Smith, *Citizenship Without Consent*, p. 91.
21. Walzer, *Spheres*, p. 62.
22. Sik and Rhadie, "International Law," p. 143; see also, for Malaysia, Sinnadurai, "Nationality and International Law," pp. 314–321.
23. Pacho, "Political Integration," pp. 242–243.
24. Kaldor, "European Institutions," p. 85.
25. de Rham, "Naturalisation," p. 172.
26. Adigun, "Nationality and Citizenship," p. 272.
27. Malawi, *Citizenship Act,* para. 15.
28. Guinea-Bissau, Constitution, May 22, 1976, Article 5, as printed in REFworld.
29. "Any person living beyond the boundaries of the Republic of Somalia but belonging by origin, language, or tradition to the Somali Nation may acquire Somali citizenship by simply establishing his residence in the territory of the Republic" (Noor, *Legal System*, p. 302).
30. Guinea-Bissau, Constitution, Article 1; Mozambique, Constitution, Article 3, as translated in the UNHCR gopher.
31. Reuters, "Eritrea Strips Jehovah's Witnesses of Citizenship," March 10, 1995.
32. Verzijl, *Nationality*, p. 31.
33. Gabon has a system whereby "recognition," a privileged form of nationality, is given to those born in the country of foreign parents (Gabon, *Code de la Nationalité Gabonaise*, 1968).
34. The British, who had been a prime example of jus soli, changed their laws

in 1981 to prevent some born within the United Kingdom from gaining citizenship (de Rham, "Naturalisation," p. 163).

35. Xinhua News Agency, "Botswana Amends Citizenship Act," September 29, 1995.

36. de Rham, "Naturalisation," p. 165.

37. After her husband died, Ruth told her mother-in-law, Naomi, that she would go with her because "your people are my people." An early call for equality of the sexes when considering nationality was the Inter American Commission of Women, *Nationality of Women*. The general issue is discussed by Gaidzanwa, "Citizenship, Nationality, Gender," p. 45.

38. de Rham, "Naturalisation," p. 185.

39. Barrington, "Domestic and International Consequences," p. 742.

40. Easterly and Levine, "Africa's Growth Tragedy."

41. Jean-Baptiste Kayigamba, "Haven for Killers in the Making," Inter Press Service, May 29, 1996.

42. Joe Chilaizya, "Of Appeals, Unrest and Secessionist Threats," Inter Press Service, May 28, 1996.

43. Human Rights Watch et al., *Zaire*, p. 7.

44. The Nigerian law required that those in the country before independence have either a parent or a grandparent who was Nigerian in order to be considered citizens. See Nylander, *Nationality and Citizenship Laws*, p. 112. The Shugaba case is discussed at some length by Adigun, "Nationality and Citizenship," pp. 275–276.

45. Dar es Salaam Radio, "Comment."

46. Kenya Broadcasting Corporation, "Kenyan Citizenship."

47. Herbst, "War and the State."

48. Data on political violence is inherently bad because governments do not want the deaths of their citizens reported and often go to great lengths (e.g., refusing to allow foreign media into the country) to prevent the world from knowing what is happening. Data on African political violence, where the actual size of the population is often not known with any degree of certainty, is particularly difficult. See Morrison et al., *Black Africa*, and Whitten and Bienen, "Political Violence."

49. See Gurr et al., *Minorities at Risk*.

50. Quoted in Joe Chilaizya, "Zambia: Neighbors Ponder Intervention in Crisis," Inter Press Service, May 9, 1996.

15

Local Governance, Democracy, and Development

Dele Olowu

Theoretical Perspectives and Historical Background

Discussions of African governance have tended to concentrate on the national level. Very few scholars or policymakers have addressed the significance of local governance for democracy and development. To be sure, some literature, although very controversial, exists on the relationship among local government, national democracy, and economic growth. There is, however, practically no literature on how these relate to local governance. This is the focus of this chapter.

For many countries of the world, including African countries, local government has been an extension of the central state to the community. It derives its legal existence from the state and, in some cases, all of its human and financial resources as well; it does not possess any independent discretionary authority apart from the state. For most of independent Africa, the promotion of local government as an institution for advancing popular democracy and economic development has been a qualified success at best. Even as an institution for the provision of community services under the control of central government, it has largely been a failure. There are, however, exceptions to this general statement, and I have tried to document these.[1]

The years immediately following independence were often golden years for local governments in Africa. They had access to financial and human resources, and as a legacy of colonial administration, they carried the burden of the provision of most of the basic social and infrastructure services: roads, water supply, agricultural extension, the management of natural resources, and basic health and educational services. However, as African national governments increasingly perceived themselves as the sole modernizing agent in society, they took over the functions and resources of local governments. To be fair, local governments in some countries became a cesspool of political and administrative corruption, but this merely portended what would happen at the national level in several of these countries in later years.[2] Only a few countries—notably, urban Zimbabwe, South Africa, and to some extent, Botswana—were exempt from this withering down of local governments.

Expectations of Local Governments' Impact on Democracy and Development

According to the calculations of the colonial masters, local governments were expected to perform a critical role in the development and democratization of the new states that emerged from the colonial experience. The British and the French had explicit goals for local governments to contribute to democratization and economic development.

Local governments were regarded as critical for training both citizens and the political leadership in democratic life. After all, Alexis de Tocqueville had argued, in agreement with the reasoning of John Stuart Mill, that local governments are to democracy what the primary school is to science. Local governments also promote the accountability of the public administration system because their officials are closer to the public physically, socially, and psychologically. Though few people still argue that local governments can protect a region or locality from the whims of national government, some contend that they can enhance the legitimacy of the government by providing a range of services, as well as by creating a sense of belonging for different social groups within the state.[3] The British were so convinced about these positive roles of the local government system that they became part of the official policy on decolonization in 1947:

> The key to resolving the problems of African administration lay in the development of an efficient and democratic system of local government. I wish to emphasize the words: efficient, democratic and local. *Local* because the system of government must be close to the common people and their problems, *efficient* because it must be capable of managing local services in a way which will help to raise the standard of living, and *democratic* because it must not only find a place for the growing class of educated men, but at the same time command the respect and support of the mass of the people.[4]

It was thus also reasoned that local governments can promote economic growth and development in the new nations. Colonial development plans were based on the expectation that local governments would play an important role in the implementation of these plans, and they actually did in several African countries. For example, local authorities during this period were responsible for building and maintaining the most basic infrastructures, including roads, schools, clinics, bridges, markets, and parks.[5]

The expectation that local government could contribute to economic growth stands on three grounds. First, local governments can enhance allocative efficiency in the production of goods and services. They are the closest to the market and enable each locality to express its preference for the goods and services that it requires. They also make it possible for individuals to vote with their feet by moving away from localities that do not produce what they need to ones that do.[6]

Second, local governments can help to mobilize resources for the provision of needed community services. Their proximity to the people enables them to acquire crucial information on the tax potential of each individual in the community. They can also mobilize members of the community to contribute to the community coffers via donations of time and money. Appeals are usually made to community solidarity and welfare opportunities. In colonial Africa, local governments ensured that the efforts of the state could be linked to those of the local community. This was the thrust of community development programs in French- and English-speaking Africa during the 1950s and 1960s.

Finally, local governments were thought to be critical for the provision of a wide range of social and economic infrastructure because of their proximity to the people and their knowledge of the locality.

The Problems of Local Governments and Explanations of Failure

All of these rationalizations for the benefits of local governments have been vigorously contested, even in the industrialized countries of the world. Georges Langrod, with the strong concurrence of a whole school of thought on the subject, has argued that there was no historical linkage between local government and democracy in Europe. If anything, he submits, local government is contradictory to democracy: "since democracy moves inevitably and by its very essence towards centralisation, local government, by the very division which it creates, constitutes, all things considered, a negation of democracy. . . . Local government and democracy triumphant represent diametrically opposed tendencies."[7]

In Africa, as in other developing countries, the capacity of local governments to enhance local democracy is complicated by a number of factors, both internal and external, including the actions of central governments and multinational corporations, and the state of the economy.[8] Service in local government does not, for example, necessarily create better politicians. Though a number of people who have served in local governments have moved on to national service, this experience has not enabled them to perform more successfully. In addition, local governments have generally been just as corrupt as national governments. This follows from the Weberian logic that the proximity of the local bureaucracy to the people actually compromises the effectiveness of local government, since local officials face great difficulties in being objective and rational. This seems to have been the reality of the African experience.[9]

With respect to their potential to promote economic growth, lack of autonomy has made it impossible for local governments to have a substantial impact. This is true for several reasons. First, under the misguided belief that the largest possible size of a local government unit was necessary to guarantee efficient provision of services, several countries have created very large single-tier units of local government. Unfortunately, because the people living within these jurisdictions could not identify with the artificial boundaries created, local governments have had trouble mobilizing the full potential of local resources. The responsibilities and resources of these local government units have also frequently been handed over to parastatal agencies. Without adequate resources, responsibilities, and legal capabilities, local governments often became mere talking shops. Further, African local governments are often not elected, but are instead frequently appointed by the central government. Even when there are some elected local posts, the central government ensures that it has significant nonelected representation on each council. More conveniently, elected councils have frequently been dissolved and replaced by nominated or appointed councilors. It is therefore not surprising that in a major study of the role of local organizations for rural development, local governments were not regarded as important agents of development.[10]

The Search for Alternative Structures of Local Governance

The failure of the central state and its local counterpart, the local state, has led to the search for alternatives, not necessarily by scholars or state actors, but by ordinary people in practically all African countries. The search for alternative nonstate structures that can respond to the economic and social needs of African people is one of the most important rationales for the new emphasis on local governance. Local governance implies a focus on the totality of structures within the local community that comprise both state and society organizations. It is readily evident that local people in Africa, as elsewhere, have developed alternatives to failed formal structures of local government. These alternatives have been given different labels, including "local development agencies" and "village development organs," but they have the following attributes in common: they are nonstate organs, they are rooted in the indigenous traditions of social order, they are voluntary, and most important, they are active and often successful in the provision of services required by their clientele. In recent times, some of them have become active in the political arena as well.[11]

Even in the cities, it is increasingly evident that traditional authorities and nontraditional organizations such as landlord and tenant associations, professional associations, and town unions are carrying a greater burden of the challenge of managing the cities than the formal structures of local government. The next section describes several cases of successes in local organizational life in Africa and contrasts this success with the failure of formal local government.

Successful Local Community Initiatives in Africa

It would be absurd to suggest that all local community initiatives in Africa have been successful. There are certainly failures. But it is important to focus on the successful cases to enable us to understand how they can succeed with little or no support from the state sector. Fortunately, these success stories have been well documented. I shall focus on three cases, all from west Africa: credit cooperatives in Cameroon, community-based adult education programs in French-speaking western Africa, and village governments in Nigeria.

The Tontines or Njangis of Cameroon

Informal credit and savings associations are almost a universal artifact of the African economic landscape. But they have been more researched and developed in Cameroon. They are referred to as *tontines* in French-speaking parts of the country and *Njangis* in English-speaking sections.[12] The main characteristics of these savings and credit clubs in Cameroon are as follows:

- They are rooted in indigenous culture.
- They are popular and widespread throughout the country; it is estimated that roughly 50 percent of the Cameroonian population participates in *tontines*.
- They render savings and credit services to their members, and they also perform a broad range of social and economic functions in the community.
- They exercise a high degree of autonomy, with members participating in the sharing of benefits, decisionmaking, and management.
- Membership is very homogenous, usually based on ethnic group, language, area of residence, and/or profession. This homogeneity

accounts for a high level of group solidarity, which, together with the strict scrutiny of individual character, ensures that *tontines* can operate as effective institutions based on trust.

- They exist outside of state institutions; they exercise total responsibility for the management of the institution; and they elect their own officers (a maximum of four to five, including a chairman, secretary, treasurer, and in some cases an auditor and/or a chief whip who is responsible for disciplining erring members).
- Generally, *tontines* are organized with either rotational or nonrotational membership. In rotational forms, all members take a turn at receiving savings. In nonrotational forms, the interest charged on loans made to members is shared. Membership in the former is usually small, never exceeding 25. In the latter, membership may be as high as 100. Some *tontines* organize with a combination of rotational and nonrotational forms.

In addition to mobilizing savings and serving as substitute banks, especially in rural communities, the socioeconomic functions of *tontines* include helping to finance the education of members' children, health services, and housing. Most important, they also help finance small- and medium-scale businesses. Some *tontines* invest their funds in transport or in community halls that are rented out. Others give assistance to members to meet emergencies such as births, deaths, marriages, illness, and death. Meetings are also usually accompanied by festivities, providing the community with social opportunities. In rare cases, *tontines* have even provided a platform for articulating political concerns.

The major problem that *tontines* face is the difficulty of managing their own success. Growing memberships often lead to management inefficiencies. However, a number of them have actually transformed themselves into full-fledged banks, including the Banque Unie de Credit and Crédit Mutuel Camerounias.

Adult Education via Community-Based Institutions in French-Speaking West Africa

Whereas state and international development agencies focus on universal primary education as the only means to knowledge acquisition, communities in a number of west African states have pursued a different approach to realize the same goals through community-based adult education initiatives. This approach is premised on the recognition of the many limitations of formal (primary and secondary) education schemes. These limitations include the lack of adult education programs; the lack of participation of the local community in the management and financing of primary schools;

the use of foreign, instead of national or local, tongues as the languages of instruction; and the failure to incorporate productive work into the curricula. Further, there has in recent years been a sharp decline in the motivation of parents to send their children to school because of the increasing rate of joblessness among graduates. Schools have also experienced a financial crisis in recent years, starving them of material and personnel resources. Finally, state institutions have had difficulties paying teachers' salaries, forcing parents to provide more resources on their own.

Several examples of community-based, informal adult learning programs exist in western Africa, including the following.

• *The Nomgana Region of Burkina Faso.* The Nomgana Region is located some 40 kilometers east of Ouagadougou, the capital city. A network of village associations has been created, in part because peasants in the region have recently become literate in More (the local language). A recent report notes that these associations have a capital base of some $42,000, own a number of local enterprises, and are presently experimenting with a course for unschooled children in which just two seasons of instruction in More provides the equivalent of four years of primary school education.[13]

• *The Saye Sabuwa Community of Niger.* In spite of the failure of the nationally directed program of adult literacy run by the National Adult Literacy Agency, this community of 3,044 inhabitants, located 40 kilometers east of Maradi, started adult literacy classes in 1964. The village has successfully established a number of postliteracy activities, the most important being a village library and a newspaper. The village has also been able to attract a lot of donor assistance. The International Labour Office built a cereal bank there in 1990, CARE (the Cooperative for Assistance and Relief Everywhere) International provided a credit facility for female small business entrepreneurs in 1991, and the Cooperatives College of USA gave credit to cooperative members in the community to purchase fertilizers. Finally, the United States Agency for International Development provided funding for the Popular Saving and Credit Bank in 1993. All of these projects are managed by neoliterates or school dropouts and are very successful.

• Other examples exist in Senegal, for example, the Association Communitaire de Fanden, located 30 kilometers from Thiès. This association has created a network of locally managed savings and loans institutions in 10 neighboring villages. It has used proceeds from this activity to fund a local hospital, with contracts for treatment in urban facilities, and technical assistance for poor neighborhoods in adjoining cities. It has also begun developing the training capacity to extend beyond its locality. Again, this association is run mainly by adult literacy program graduates.

Local and Community Governments in Nigeria

The activities of kinship, ethnic, and town unions in Africa are relatively well documented, the best examples being the *harambee* movement in Kenya and the ethnic and town unions of eastern Nigeria. With respect to the latter, Audrey Smock wrote over two decades ago that ethnic unions in the Ibo communities of eastern Nigeria have successfully facilitated accommodation between tradition and modernity by harnessing traditional political culture for the development of the primary community.[14] Similarly, an officer of the British colonial government in Nigeria made the following comment on Ibo town unions:

> By the 1950s, most unions were planning the development of their communities, taxing both themselves and the rest of the community to pay for them while the regional government was stimulating these efforts by agreeing to meet half the costs of major construction works (e.g., pipe-borne water supplies) and to staff any secondary schools or hospitals that were built by the community. *By the 1960s, most progressive unions had become the de facto government of their communities.*[15]

What was not well documented was that this was the means by which development activities were also being carried out in other regions of Nigeria. The mobilization of village community organizations was a main element in the strategy adopted by the Action Group government in the Western Region to promote its "free" primary school program, launched in 1955. It was also used to build roads and health infrastructure in the western, midwestern, and middle-belt sections of the country. The posture of the national government did not, however, help matters, as it took over management of these services from the communities and the state and local governments.[16]

In research conducted between 1988 and 1990, several highly successful community development associations were identified. Two were particularly noteworthy: the Abavo Development Association in the Oredo local government area of former Bendel State, which had built a large amount of rural infrastructure; and the Mbagbden Development Union of Benue State, which has also built a large amount of infrastructure in its community, paid for by membership fees, levies, and, most important, donations received at annual launchings.

It took a structural adjustment program, launched in the mid-1980s, to draw the attention of scholars and Nigerian policymakers to the developmental potential of these community governments. Hometown associations sprang up in most communities in the southwest, organized very much along the lines of the eastern town unions.[17] The hometown association or town union functions as any other form of community government: it is concerned with a defined locality, usually a town or village; it is completely responsible to its membership; and it has a considerable developmental and political impact. Town unions have been influential in mobilizing resources for local-level development, usually by levying on indigenes of the community a tax in an amount that reflects their social status and economic capacity. They also help to resolve conflicts within the political community and influence national and state governments to locate public investment projects such as roads, schools, health clinics, and electricity within the community. In some cases, they lobby for the appointment of indigenes or sons of the soil to important government positions.

An appreciation of the widespread nature of community-based development activities and their ability to raise substantial sums of money for development led to the decision of the Nigerian federal government to establish community banks throughout the country in 1990. A community bank was defined as a "self-sustaining financial institution, owned and managed by a community for the purpose of providing credit, banking and other financial services to its members, largely on the basis of self-recognition and credit-worthiness."[18] A community bank was a unit bank and was not expected to have branch offices. Most important, the primary promoter was the community development association, although other shareholders could include local trade associations, age and social clubs, and individual community members. The government participates by matching the funds of the bank with a loan of ₦ 500,000 (equivalent to U.S.$125,000 at that time) at a concessionary interest rate, to be paid back within five years of the start of the bank's operation. The first community bank was commissioned in December 1990, and by June 1993, there were 645 in Nigeria, located throughout both rural and urban areas.[19]

Toward Building Enduring
Structures of Local-Level Governance in Africa

The examples provided above are confined to west Africa only because of space considerations. Several other documented cases exist for east and southern Africa.[20] Given the importance of local-level structures for enhancing good governance and providing public goods and services, as well as the failure of formal structures of local government based on attempts to extend the state structure to the local community, there are important lessons to be learned from such examples of successful, locally based organizations. There is also an increasing awareness of these institutions internationally.

Recently, the World Health Organization, as part of its effort to promote its program of universal health, undertook a multinational study of institutional infrastructure in the health sector at the district level in eight countries. The results indicate that a number of these informal community structures constitute "hidden resources" waiting to be utilized much more effectively for health development in many developing countries.[21] Similarly, the Africa Technical Division of the World Bank led a multinational study of indigenous institutions and their potential for reinvigorating formal public-sector institutions in African countries. The conclusions of this research, led by Mamadou Dia, point to a need for selective adaptation of traditional or indigenous institutions and values to modern structures.[22]

In other recent research on this subject, Elinor Ostrom documented 12 cases of successful, not-so-successful, and failed cases of community organizations that manage common-pool resources in various countries of the world over extended time periods. She drew up a set of principles to explain relative success or failure. These include clearly defined boundaries, congruence between rules for managing the resources and local conditions, collective choice arrangements, monitoring, graduated sanctions, effective conflict resolution mechanisms, recognition by external bodies (governments) to organize, and nesting among enterprises of various sizes.[23] From the available findings on successful local organizations and governments in Africa, these conditions would also seem to be requirements for robust local governments in Africa.[24]

These principles constitute a rationale for adopting a new approach to building local governments in Africa so that they might become more effective institutions for synchronizing state and societal forces at the local level—what is commonly referred to as "local governance." It is critical that such structures emphasize *locality, popular control,* and *accountability to the community,* as well as the capacity to *mobilize resources,* whereas the national and/or regional government provides financial, personnel, and technical support in such a way that it does not destroy local initiative. The basic community structures necessary for such an approach appear to already exist in most parts of Africa. It remains necessary to recognize them as *community governments* and to provide the legal, financial, and institutional mechanisms for them to take full responsibility for the overall economic, social, and political development of their respective communities.

These principles constitute the social infrastructure necessary for good governance and economic growth in Africa. It is perhaps needless to note that these institutions have continued to function as the basic institutions for governance even in today's most industrialized societies.[25] The fact that there have been several failed attempts to pursue this approach, including the use of indirect rule by some colonial governments, helps to underscore the fact that this is not going to be an easy task.[26] But most close observers of the African scene appreciate that it is best to experiment with these initiatives during the period of economic and political reforms currently under way in many African countries. In some cases, the primordial structures will have to be democratized and given assistance in becoming more effective in processing information and in coexisting with other government institutions.

The usual argument against strong local political and administrative institutions in poor countries is that empowered local government structures may become narrowly based, and more important, they may aggravate regional and local differentiations. But this does not have to be the case if other agencies of governance at regional and/or national levels discharge their own responsibilities for regional and national development. Moreover, central agencies must do more than just generally support the process; they must also create and sustain institutions at the center that will provide needed information, advice, and other technical support to enhance the growth of responsible and effective local governments. Without doubt, a genuine attempt at developing structures of local governance in Africa will not only promote economic development, it will help to defuse much of the ethnically based tensions and restrain recklessness, inefficiency, abuse of power, and corruption by state-based agencies at the center.

Notes

1. Olowu, "Local Institutes"; Olowu and Smoke, "Determinants of Success."
2. Wraith and Simpkins, *Corruption;* Olowu, "Ethical Violations."
3. Smith, *Decentralisation* and "Sustainable Local Democracy"; Gboyega, *Local Government.*
4. Lord Creech-Jones, cited in U. K. Hicks, *Local Government,* p. 4.
5. Olowu, *African Local Governments* and "Local Institutes."
6. Ostrom and Ostrom, "Public Goods."
7. Langrod, "Local Government," pp. 7–8.
8. Smith, "Sustainable Local Democracy."
9. Stren, "Accountability"; Smith, "Sustainable Local Democracy."
10. Esman and Uphoff, *Local Institutions.* For a general description of local government in Africa, see Mawhood, *Local Government.*
11. Olowu et al., *Local Institutions;* Bratton, "Beyond the State."
12. In this article, they will be referred to as *tontines.*
13. Easton et al., "Meeting the Local Skill," p. 10.
14. Smock, *Ibo Politics,* p. 243.
15. G. I. Jones, "Changing Leadership," pp. 60–61; emphasis added.
16. Olowu, *Administration of Social Services;* Oyovbaire, *Federalism.*
17. Barkan et al., "Hometown Associations"; Trager, "Structural Adjustment."
18. Mabogunje, "Capitalization of Money," p. 10.
19. Mabogunje, "Capitalization of Money."
20. See Hyden and Bratton, eds., *Governance and Politics,* chaps. 9–11.
21. Khassay, *District Health Infrastructures.*
22. Dia, "Africa's Management."

23. Ostrom, *Governing the Commons,* p. 90.

24. Olowu et al., *Local Institutions;* Olowu and Smoke, "Determinants of Success"; and Wunsch and Olowu, *Failure of the Centralized State.*

25. See Tocqueville, *Democracy in America;* Seeley, *Local Government;* and Oakerson, "Reciprocity."

26. G. I. Jones, "Changing Leadership"; Sawyer, "Putu Development Association"; and Dia, "Africa's Management."

PART 4

Ethnicity, Conflict, and Insecurity

16

Ethnic Politics in Africa: Change and Continuity

MARINA OTTAWAY

The worldwide increase in the number and violence of open conflicts revolving around ethnic or religious identities during the 1990s provides a strong reminder that communal identities are not a residue of the past, but a live force in today's politics. But most African countries remain reluctant to recognize the inevitability of the ethnic identities that divide the population of the overwhelming majority of states. Instead, they continue to view such identities as the unfortunate residue of a premodern Africa or as the accursed legacy of the divide-and-rule machinations of the colonial powers. In either case, the underlying assumption is that ethnic identities can and should be made to fade away.

This is not a realistic viewpoint. There is no empirical evidence to suggest that ethnic divisions are losing their importance in any part of the world; on the contrary, ethnic identities and ethnic nationalism have gained strength and even a degree of legitimacy in recent years. European institutions are promoting the recognition and protection of ethnic differences and the crafting of legislation and government institutions that give expression to such differences without leading to conflict. In the United States, recognition of cultural diversity has replaced the ideal of the melting pot, although there is little support at this point for the notion that such recognition might require a reform of political institutions.

African governments remain unwilling to confront the implications of this worldwide surge in manifestations of ethnic nationalism. Such an attitude is particularly dangerous at present because the political change under way almost everywhere in Africa—a change optimistically dubbed a "process of democratization"—has made ethnic tensions more acute in many countries by destroying the mechanisms that have regulated ethnic relations and kept conflict in check in the past.

After three decades of independence, ethnicity is more central than ever to the political process of many African countries, as political openings and multiparty elections have led to the formation of innumerable overtly or covertly ethnic political parties. But this is not a sign that a primitive and tribal Africa continues to reassert itself through the thin veneer of modern institutions. In Africa, as elsewhere, the causes of ethnic conflict have to be sought more in the present than in the past, no matter what imagery or myths are used by the participants to defend their stance and explain their enmities.[1] Because ethnic conflict is rooted in the present, its dynamics and the possible solutions change. Ethnic politics in the 1990s is not the same as ethnic politics in the 1960s. In this sense, there is a new ethnicity in Africa today.

This chapter seeks to analyze the changing nature of ethnic politics in Africa and the broader trends of which it is a part. It also argues that an acceptance of the inevitability—and indeed the legitimacy—of ethnic identities is a precondition to finding means of preventing violent conflicts such as the one that devastated Rwanda and those that are threatening similar catastrophes in several other countries.

Ethnicity and Nationalism

The concepts of ethnic group and nation, which are used interchangeably in this essay, belong to that category of familiar notions the meanings of which are perfectly clear until we try to pin them down and define them precisely. The basic idea is simple. Human beings belong to natural groups, which share common culture and language, and sometimes the myth of common ancestry, and which provide their members with a sense of common identity. These natural groups are not political entities, but they often are—and many believe should be—the basis for the formation of one. In nineteenth-century Europe, the natural group called the "nation" was expected to become the basis for the formation of the political "nation-state."[2] The nation-state then came to be regarded as the model of the modern state, to the point that the term is often misused today to refer to countries, including African ones, that are clearly multiethnic, and thus not nation-states in any meaningful sense of the word.

Europeans also applied the nineteenth-century concept to Africa that human beings belong to a natural group before they become part of a modern political entity. Africans also belonged to natural groups, but since their groups were considered to be more primitive, they were thought of not as nations, but as "tribes."[3] Nationalism was seen as a European phenomenon, tribalism as an African one.

In reality, neither the European nation nor the African tribe was a primordial natural grouping. In preindustrial societies, individuals were tied not to large nations or tribes, but to much smaller, localized groups. They belonged to villages, clans, parishes, or small regions. Immigrants coming to the United States at the turn of the century did not identify with a country—that was a bureaucratic classification imposed on immigrants by American authorities. Instead, the emergence of broader national or tribal identities was often the result of deliberate manipulation to help further a particular political project. During the late nineteenth century, for example, the French state relied on publicly provided elementary education and the military draft to develop a French national identity among peasants, whose sense of belonging had previously extended only to a village or a small region.[4] Indeed, in the age of nationalism, all European countries invented myths and rewrote history to prove the long historical roots of their nations, although even the concept of the nation was of recent origin.[5]

In Africa, a combination of socioeconomic change, missionary language policies, anthropological studies, and deliberate attempts by the colonial authorities to establish a workable administrative framework caused Africans to move beyond narrower identification with a lineage or a clan and to see themselves as members of large and newly invented tribes. However, while striving to promote a common national-level identity among their citizens at home, the colonial powers usually sought to keep Africans divided into separate tribes. The white regime in South Africa pushed the idea of strengthening separate tribal identities to an extreme through its apartheid policy, but it was building upon a long colonial tradition of classifying Africans into tribes.[6]

The identities that the colonial powers helped to crystallize were artificial and of recent origin, not natural and primordial. So, of course, were the new national identities that independent African governments sought to promote through their postindependence "nation-building" efforts. The Zambian nation was as artificial a construct as the Zulu tribe, and a more recent one. The epitome of such artificial nation-building efforts is the promotion by the new South African government of the concept of the "rainbow nation." Obviously, the rainbow nation is not a natural, primordial entity, and nobody is trying to argue that it is. But neither are other nations or tribes, although this claim is frequently set forth.

Because they are not primordial, national and ethnic identities are not fixed, but can change a great deal over time. Whether by accident or intent, as the result of manipulation by political authorities, personal decisions, or simply a slow process of social and economic transformation, individuals come to see themselves as part of a particular ethnic group or nation that was not previously a part of their own or anybody else's consciousness. At the beginning of the nineteenth century, there were only a few hundred Zulus in South Africa, the members of a small, obscure clan. By the time the British dismantled the Zulu empire in 1879, most Africans living in the part of KwaZulu-Natal north of the Tugela River considered themselves Zulus, and the young men of the region fought in the defense of the Zulu empire against colonial invasion. Under the apartheid regime, almost all

Africans born in Natal were considered members of the Zulu tribe. The multiplication of the Zulus from a few hundred to seven million in the space of less than two centuries was not the result of a Malthusian nightmare of uncontrolled population growth, but of a political process of ethnic reclassification and identity building. For many Zulus, although by no means all, this ethnic identity has become all-important. In the elections of April 1994, which officially put an end to the apartheid regime, over two million adult South Africans showed that they identified themselves as Zulus by casting their vote for the Inkatha Freedom Party (IFP) and its Zulu nationalist platform.[7]

Not only have national and ethnic identities changed over time, but the character of nationalism has evolved as well. It has at some times been a force for strengthening democracy and popular sovereignty, but at others a means to reinforce the authority of the state. In the course of the nineteenth century in Europe, nationalism challenged the existing empires in the name not only of national self-determination, but also of popular, democratic participation in government. When the major powers convened at Versailles after World War I to decide the fate of the former subjects of the Austro-Hungarian and Ottoman Empires, they still regarded nationalism as a force of progress and democracy.

But there was a darker side to the nationalism that exploded during the 1930s. Having started as the rallying cry of groups caught in the grip of decaying empires and feeling oppressed, nationalism turned into an ideology manipulated by powerful states to impose themselves on others and build new empires. German nationalism in particular turned aggressive toward neighboring countries and excluded all minorities at home. As a result, nationalism came to be regarded not as a force of progress, but as an abomination.

The fear of ethnic nationalism influenced the post–World War II international order. The UN Charter did not assume that the world would be a better place if organized into homogeneous nation-states. Instead, the right to self-determination was narrowly interpreted to mean the right to independence for colonized people, not the right for every nation to have its own state. This approach facilitated the quest for independence in many colonies, but it also provided protection to existing states not only against the ambitions of others, but also against the demands of the national minorities in their midst. The post–World War II international order thus put the state ahead of the nation.

The Early Illusion: From Tribalism to Nation Building

Newly independent African countries were, not surprisingly, influenced by the dominant ideas of the period. They vehemently rejected ethnic nationalism as a threat to the state and the continued modernization of Africa. They preached instead a "civic" nationalism that, in the early period, was liberal, forward looking, and, in retrospect, incredibly optimistic.[8] "In three or four years," Sekou Toure told his compatriots, "no one will remember the tribal, ethnic or religious rivalries which, in the recent past, caused so much damage to our country and its population."[9] This same idea was voiced, in one form or another, by virtually every African leader.

The special conditions of African countries reinforced the rejection of ethnic nationalism. The new states were fragile. In Robert Jackson's terminology, they were "quasi-states" possessing the negative sovereignty granted to them by international recognition, but not necessarily the positive sovereignty that derives from the effective ability to control and govern a country.[10] Outside of the cities, much of the citizenry probably identified more with local areas or groups than with the entire country, much as European peasants had until late in the nineteenth century. The weakness of the state prompted its refusal to acknowledge that ethnic divisions were more than a passing phenomenon.

Another factor that prompted African leaders to reject the legitimacy of ethnic identities—even when relying on them to bolster their power—was the fact that the rest of the world continued to look at ethnic attachments in Africa as primitive tribalism, rather than recognizing them as part of the same phenomenon of nationalism that existed elsewhere. Most European governments acknowledged to some degree that the identity of ethnic minorities within their own borders needed to be recognized, but if Africans did not identify exclusively with the state to which they belonged, they were considered primitive. Many educated Africans shared this point of view and saw themselves as detribalized—modern people who partook in universal cultural values and whose political allegiance was to the new African state of which they were citizens, rather than to the clan or tribe into which they had been born.

Finally, because so many ethnic groups straddled boundaries, subnational ethnic identities were also seen as a complicating factor in the relations among the new states. While it is common throughout the world for population groups to be divided by international boundaries, the problem was more severe in Africa, both because borders had been established by the colonial powers with little knowledge of the situation on the ground and because this had been done so recently that little assimilation had taken place. The decision by the Organization of African Unity (OAU) in 1964 to accept colonial borders as immutable was a reflection of the extent to which all African countries felt vulnerable.

The adoption by the OAU of the principle that colonial borders should be respected was hailed in the world as an act of statesmanship by African leaders, as indeed it was. By renouncing territorial claims, African leaders spared their countries much conflict and contributed to the maintenance of an African state system that remained extraordinarily stable until the 1990s; the only major challenges to the territorial status quo have been the attempted secessions of Katanga and Biafra, Eritrean nationalism, Somali irredentism, and the unresolved issue of Western Sahara.[11] But respect for colonial boundaries had a less-noticed domestic dimension as well, with authoritarian implications: African states were telling their citizens that they had no right to self-determination. Igbos were told not only by the Nigerian government, but also by the overwhelming majority of other African countries, that no matter how bad things might be in Nigeria, they had no choice but to remain part of the country. Respect for colonial borders could thus be seen as either an act of statesmanship or an act of oppression, depending upon the vantage point of those judging the issue.[12]

Ethnic identities and claims did not, however, disappear in Africa simply because they were denied legitimacy. In fact, as all students of the region know, ethnicity has had a pervasive influence on African politics. Even scholars who ideologically upheld the view that politics must be explained in terms of class relations found themselves reluctantly forced to admit that the impact of ethnicity could neither be ignored nor lightly dismissed as false consciousness. Likewise, the same Africans who were quick to denounce Western views of a continent mired in tribalism were compelled to analyze the politics of their countries in ethnic terms.

While officially committed to overcoming tribalism, most African leaders manipulated ethnicity in order to keep themselves in power.[13] Some did so in a rather benign way, forging alliances with leaders of many ethnic groups or co-opting potential ethnic opponents into their governments. This did not make for democracy, but it often made for peace and stability, keeping the country together and preventing open conflict from emerging. The second approach was much more destructive: leaders defended their positions by relying on members of their own ethnic groups, or even their clans, to the exclusion of others. This sharpened divisions and created enmity, particularly when an unpopular leader resorted to strong-arm tactics to control a country, unleashing members of his own ethnic group on the rest of the population. Kenya's experience under President Jomo Kenyatta provides an example of the more benign form of ethnic politics, while Somalia under President Muhammad Siad Barre exemplifies the more destructive approach.

No matter how leaders manipulated ethnicity, they generally maintained the pretense that ethnic groups should not have a role in politics. It is not clear, and it is probably ultimately impossible to determine, whether this official disregard for ethnicity lessened or increased ethnic tensions. Different examples suggest different conclusions. Some countries, particularly those blessed with the absence of a numerically or economically dominant group, such as Tanzania, experienced little ethnic tension. In such a country, a government policy that recognized the legitimacy of ethnic identities might have encouraged ethnic claims, thus creating a more serious problem. On the other hand, Nigeria, where ethnic tensions were high from the beginning, met with limited success in its attempts to neutralize the political impact of ethnicity. Repeated increases in the number of states did make the situation somewhat less explosive and might even have been more effective if oil revenue had not concentrated all financial power at the center. Nevertheless, the ethnic factor continued to lurk as a central issue in Nigerian politics, despite provisions seeking to prevent the formation of ethnic parties. It is possible that a political system that overtly recognized the country's deep divisions and rivalries and that sought to regulate them through open bargaining and power sharing, rather than through underhanded manipulation, might have met with more success in bringing about a viable system of government.

The fact that most African countries did avoid violent ethnic conflict, despite very unfavorable conditions—ethnic diversity on the one hand, and state weakness on the other—suggests that the policy of officially delegitimizing ethnicity, while informally seeking to balance ethnic representation, worked fairly well in most cases. However, in those countries where conflict did arise, this policy left the government helpless in its search to find solutions.

The ethnic politics of the immediate postindependence period can be characterized, on the whole, as remarkably subdued. While both ruling and opposition groups relied on ethnicity as an instrument—even while denouncing it—their goal was generally to control power within existing borders, rather than to form new states. With rare exceptions, ethnic politics did not threaten the integrity of the state. Secession and irredentism were widely condemned, and the persistence of the country within the existing borders was taken for granted by most political rivals. In most cases, ethnicity was used to mobilize support, to allocate favors, to safeguard the power of the incumbent regime, or to mobilize opposition against it, rather than to change state boundaries.

Thus, while ethnic politics was very important in the internal political processes of all African countries, it did not play a major role in their international relations. Internal rivalries among ethnic groups did not translate into external, irredentist wars. While most African countries remained very unstable domestically, the African state system remained remarkably stable.

The New International Context

Attitudes toward ethnic nationalism and ethnicity in the 1990s are quite different from those of the 1960s. Ethnic nationalism has once again become salient, destroying the optimistic assumptions prevalent in the 1960s that it would fade and be replaced by a less threatening civic nationalism. The havoc and destruction brought about by virulent ethnic conflict in countries such as Bosnia and Rwanda have once again raised fears about the problems that nationalism can create. But alongside the revulsion engendered by massacres and ethnic cleansing, there is also greater willingness to accept "cultural pluralism" as a positive phenomenon. European institutions like the Organization for Security and Cooperation in Europe and the Council of Europe have, for example, spent a great deal of time and effort developing guidelines for multiethnic countries on how to protect the rights of minority ethnic groups through special legislation and autonomous local government.[14]

This change in attitudes toward nationalism has evolved slowly, encouraged in recent years by the collapse of the socialist regimes and the accompanying disintegration of the multiethnic states that they controlled. Foremost among the factors that have led to a rethinking of nationalism is the difficulty of manipulating ethnic identities for the purpose of nation building, particularly over the time span relevant to policymakers. There is a paradox here. On the one hand, there is ample evidence that ethnic identities are not primordial, but rather result from often recent political and economic processes. On the other hand, deliberate attempts to manipulate ethnic identities frequently fail, or appear to succeed, only to be reversed at a later date. It is possible to develop ad hoc explanations for specific successes or failures—why immigrants from Europe came to see themselves as Americans, for example, or why Zulus became Zulus—but it is more difficult to reach overall conclusions about what allows a government to successfully manipulate ethnic identities. In general, it is unlikely that a government will succeed in deliberately manipulating identities unless the new identity offers some rewards, if not materially, at least psychologically. Politically and economically weak African countries have not been well placed to provide incentives to their citizens to identify strongly with the new nation, to the exclusion of ethnic allegiances.

Another factor that helps explain the greater acceptance of the permanence of ethnic identities is the fact that processes of assimilation are proving to be reversible. In Yugoslavia, it could be argued that Marshal Tito's "Yugoslavism" was remarkably successful after World War II, bringing decades of peace to a country that had been devastated by conflict between Serbs and Croats during World War II. While ethnic differences were never obliterated, and continued to be politically significant, large numbers of people from different ethnic groups lived side by side and intermarried, despite the atrocities that their fathers and grandfathers had perpetrated on one another in the past. But all of this unraveled quickly. The same has occurred in some African countries. In the days of Haile Selassie, Ethiopia was evolving slowly into a multiethnic "greater Ethiopia." However, in the mid-1970s, large numbers of people started asserting their ethnic, rather than their civic, identities; they ceased thinking of themselves as

Ethiopians, choosing instead to be Oromos or Tigreans, for example.[15] This has led to a period of intense ethnic conflict that shows no signs of abating.

The reversibility of the process of nation building makes it clear that the development of new identities is not simply a matter of time, but also of the political will of distinct groups to assimilate. This political will is lacking in many countries at present. Minorities in former socialist countries are vigorously claiming their right to self-determination, causing considerable instability even in many of the successor states of the USSR, as well as Yugoslavia and Czechoslovakia. The United States is now faced with immigrant communities that refuse to abandon their language and culture in order to become "American," as well as with ethnic minorities that are American, but demand respect for diversity and reject assimilation, while simultaneously pressing both for protection against discrimination and for affirmative action.

The change in attitudes toward ethnic nationalism affects not only domestic politics, but international relations as well. From the end of World War II to the 1990s, international boundaries were extraordinarily stable throughout the world. While many new countries joined the international community during this period, they emerged from the process of decolonization and accepted their colonial boundaries. The separation of Bangladesh from Pakistan was the major example of a country that was not born of decolonization and yet was recognized by the international community.

Since 1990, however, the international community has embraced a score of new countries that were not former colonies, despite the initially strong reluctance to accept a modification of the territorial status quo. The recognition of Croatia and Slovenia by Germany started the process. While this decision was controversial, the criticism was halfhearted; preserving existing borders no longer appeared to be such an important goal. When the Soviet Union itself broke up in 1991, there was even less interest in preserving the status quo. In contrast, only a few years earlier, the United States had been reluctant to provide any encouragement to nationalist movements in the Baltic states, although it had never accepted the legitimacy of their annexation by the Soviet Union.

The disintegration of these former socialist states was brought about, in part, by the opening of their domestic political systems. The collapse of the socialist regimes broadened political participation everywhere and brought new actors into the political arena. In most cases, this political opening was formalized by the holding of multiparty elections. How far any of these particular countries has progressed toward democracy is open to debate, but there is no doubt that almost everywhere, there is now greater popular input into the political process than in the past. With this popular input has come a stronger voice for nationalism. To the extent that "the people" have been consulted, they have made it clear that their ethnic identities remain strong and are possibly growing stronger and that they expect these ethnic identities to be recognized politically. Ethnic nationalism was thus an unexpected by-product of democracy.

The pragmatic decision to recognize these new countries planted the seed for a change in the rules that govern the international community. In the 1990s, the world moved away from fixed borders and nation building within those borders, and it accepted de facto, once again, the legitimacy of self-determination for nations, rather than just for colonized people. Politically, the concept of self-determination is now being interpreted more in the manner of the League of Nations than of the United Nations. It is within this context that the issue of ethnicity is now being played out in Africa.

Implications for Africa

The major developments that have prompted this change in attitudes toward nationalism and self-determination have taken place in the former Soviet bloc, not in Africa. African countries are affected, however, not only because the end of the Cold War has created a different international climate, but also because African political actors have watched these changes with interest and drawn conclusions about their own situations.

The change in the international context came at a time when African countries had reached a political and economic crisis point. By the early 1990s, most were mired in economic decline and political stagnation. Economically, they were paying the price of both the policies embraced at the time of independence and the changes in the international economy. The statist models of development that had been chosen by African countries at independence had been in line with their common wisdom of the time, but not with their resources or management capacities. The assumption that the government had to be the prime motor of economic development had been widely accepted, and the domestic policies of the colonial powers had provided a model of government intervention to control key economic sectors, deliver services, and create a safety net for citizens. But African governments were desperately short of both experienced personnel and resources. There was, in other words, a lack of fit between the chosen policies and the government's capacity to implement them. The oil price increases after 1973 made the situation worse by forcing most African countries to borrow to maintain their level of imports. When sources of borrowing started drying up, interest rates increased, and commodity exports declined. At the end of the 1970s, African countries thus found themselves in deep economic trouble, unable to continue papering over the shortcomings of their economies.

Politically, most African countries had been unable to develop systems that maintained stability while respecting the rights of the citizens and giving them a measure of protection against arbitrary acts by their leaders. Single-party systems and charismatic leaders had long since lost their luster, and socialist experiments had failed. Many countries were caught in endless cycles of military coups and halfhearted attempts to return to civilian rule.

The result of the combined political and economic crisis was that there was very little reason for most Africans to feel an attachment to their governments, or even to their states. The early attempts at nation building had essentially been abandoned. Few governments were still trying to forge a new society and a new national identity by relying on ideological indoctrination and mobilization campaigns; cynicism and fatigue had set in after a few years. The lack of economic progress had also hindered the evolution of a national identity based not on government action, but on a favorable experience in the context of the new state.

The desire for change was great. In fact, "change" was the major slogan used by many opposition parties in the multiparty elections that an increasing number of African states began to hold in the 1990s, for example, in Senegal. But would change mean the reform of political and economic systems in the context of the existing state, or the replacement of the state itself, as had happened in the Soviet Union, Yugoslavia, and Czechoslovakia?

In some African countries, political actors interpreted change to mean the reform of political institutions and the choice of new leaders. In Zambia, for example, change involved holding multiparty elections that brought about the defeat of the party and president that had controlled the country since independence. This was a momentous event, but the character of the state and its boundaries were not called into question.

In other countries, however, political actors did not believe that change was possible unless the state itself was radically altered. Ethiopia has been the most extreme example. The country's transformation was precipitated by the military defeat in 1991 of the regime of Mengistu Haile Mariam, but the winners did not simply set up a new government. First, the two movements that defeated Mengistu—the Eritrean People's Liberation Front (EPLF) and the Tigray People's Liberation Front (TPLF)—agreed to partition the country, and Eritrea became independent in 1993. Second, the TPLF set about to transform the new Ethiopia from a unitary state to a federation of ethnic regions.

All of these events, from the breakup of Ethiopia to the multiparty elections held in most countries, were influenced by the new international climate. In the old context, the multiparty elections in Zambia, and particularly the independence of Eritrea, would have been much less likely. It is not that the decision to hold multiparty elections was merely a copycat gesture on the part of Zambian politicians; the pressure to hold them had come from domestic groups. However, it is doubtful that the incumbent, President Kenneth Kaunda, would have allowed the elections to take place if he had not witnessed the collapse of single-party systems elsewhere in the world. Moreover, the Western countries and international organizations that pressured Kaunda to accept the inevitability of multiparty elections would not have become involved in domestic elections during the Cold War, when the stability of reasonably friendly and predictable regimes was considered much more important than formal democracy.

Similarly, Eritrean nationalists were not inspired to seek independence by the disintegration of Yugoslavia or of any other country—they had been doggedly fighting for this goal since the early 1960s. But the international community had in the past refused to even entertain the possibility of independence for Eritrea, fearing that it would open up the famous Pandora's box of challenges to the colonial boundaries. But in the circumstances of 1993, the international community could not refuse to recognize Eritrea; even African countries accepted the new state without much discussion or hesitation.

It is also improbable that Ethiopia's decision to make ethnicity the organizing principle of its federal system would have won acceptance, much less praise, if the idea that multiethnic countries could forge a new national identity and overcome internal differences had still held as much sway in the world in the 1990s as it had in the 1960s. In the event, the international community accepted the principle of an ethnically organized state in Ethiopia, paradoxically doing so at the same time that it was celebrating the end of the most famous ethnically organized African regime, South African apartheid.

The Renewed Challenge of Ethnicity

Whether fundamentally restructuring the state or democratizing its political institutions, these transitions opened anew the issue of ethnic relations on the continent, issues that had in the past been managed in the context of immutable boundaries and authoritarian forms of government. In the past, the absence of formal democracy had made it possible to rely on solutions that disregarded the numerical importance of ethnic groups. Ethnic minorities could dominate governments in an authoritarian system, but not in a democratic one.

But co-opting ethnic leaders would not necessarily work when people became free to choose their own representatives. Moreover, multiparty elections, particularly when contested by ethnic parties, could potentially disrupt existing arrangements because they changed the balance of power among groups. They therefore necessitated efforts to reach new understandings. As a result, ethnic conflict became much more visible and, in some cases, much more acute and destructive. While the experiences of each country were unique in many respects, it is possible to identify several new patterns of ethnic politics that emerged in the 1990s: the development of ethnic political parties, the emergence of the "ethnic state" organized along ethnic lines, and the collapse of the state.

Ethnic Parties

The most obvious, visible manifestation of politicized ethnicity in new multiparty political systems has been the overt or covert ethnic character of the majority of the emerging political parties. Indeed, recent events have shown that the founding fathers of Africa were absolutely right when they argued that multipartyism would lead their citizens to align themselves based on ethnicity (whether they were therefore right to ban parties is a different matter). The trend toward the formation of ethnic parties was accentuated in the 1990s by the discrediting of socialism. This made it difficult for political parties to define themselves in ideological terms and thus attract multiethnic cross sections of the population on the basis of their programmatic appeal. Only the Islamic parties retained such an ideological foundation in the 1990s, and to some extent, they were able to replace socialist parties by attracting a broad-based vote of discontent. But such organizations did not, and could not, exist in the majority of African countries. The swiftness of the transformation to multipartyism also left new parties with little time to develop their programs; most opposition parties promised little more than change. The absence of ideological and programmatic differences left ethnicity as the major characteristic by which the various parties could differentiate themselves.

Africa's founding fathers had also predicted that the formation of political parties on the basis of ethnicity would exacerbate tensions, destroying the fragile unity of many countries. However, outcomes vary widely, so it is not as clear that this second part of their prophecy has also been proven true. Burundi has been one of the most dramatic cases of increased ethnic violence directly linked to multiparty elections. The country has a history of open ethnic conflict and was dominated since independence by the Tutsi minority. Multiparty democratic elections inevitably handed power to a Hutu party in June 1993. Incumbent Tutsi politicians appeared to accept this defeat, but the Tutsi officers who controlled the army did not. They staged a military coup in October, which ultimately failed, but only after the elected president and many cabinet officers, as well as thousands of civilians, had been killed. Efforts to renegotiate an ethnic pact followed, but they failed to curb violence because neither Hutu nor Tutsi moderate politicians could control the extremists. This leaves the country precariously poised on the verge of a potentially genocidal conflict. Whether Burundi can ever again become a functioning, stable state within the existing borders is not clear, but it is certain that this cannot happen in the absence of formal arrangements that define the relations among ethnic groups and perhaps embody ethnicity in the structure of the political system.

But the open ethnicization of politics resulting from multiparty elections has not always been so dramatic and destructive. Benin is at the other extreme from Burundi. The country has a long history of ethnic rivalries, but it has managed to hold two very successful multiparty elections since 1991. Both led not only to the defeat of the incumbent president, but also to a shift in the ethnic balance of power, yet neither caused ethnic violence. Simple generalizations about the impact of multiparty elections on ethnic conflict are not possible.

In some cases, the openly ethnic nature of political parties may even help the process of democratization in the long run by making these parties more sensitive to the demands of particular constituencies. A case in point is South Africa. Of the three major political parties contesting elections, two are narrowly ethnic: the IFP, which appeals openly to Zulu nationalism; and the mostly white National Party (NP), which has broadened its ethnic identity somewhat since 1994 by winning the vote of the "Coloured" population of the Western Cape. The African National Congress (ANC), on the other hand, has broad appeal among all African ethnic groups, including the Zulus, and it also attracts some Coloured and Indian voters and a sprinkling of whites. These ethnic divisions create a potentially dangerous situation. There was much fear of violence by both Zulu nationalists and white extremists at the time of the 1994 transitional elections, and unfortunately, the Zulu nationalists' fears proved justified.

However, the openness of the ethnic vote also offers opportunities. The NP, for example, has reached the conclusion that its survival as a meaningful political force in South African politics depends on its capacity to attract more African voters and to hold on to its Coloured constituents—in other words, to become a multiethnic party. The party will therefore have to become more sensitive to the demands of different communities and rethink its platform and policies so as to attract those voters. While the party that gave South Africa apartheid will encounter enormous problems in trying to create a new identity for itself, and it may very well fail, the fact that the openly ethnic nature of the vote is forcing the NP to devise a new strategy to attract voters from all groups is promoting a healthy democratic process in the country. The situation is less promising, however, with respect to Inkatha. Since the party's sole support comes from Zulu voters in Natal, it cannot change its nationalist stance without undermining its power base, so the IFP is only likely to survive as a nationalist regional party. Since control of KwaZulu-Natal is the key to its survival, the IFP cannot afford to lose votes there, and this is the source of the continuing tension and violence between IFP and ANC members in the area. The result is neither healthy nor democratic; on the contrary, KwaZulu-Natal is presently divided into tightly controlled IFP or ANC fiefdoms from which the rival party is excluded. It should be noted, however, that the conflict in KwaZulu-Natal is not "ethnic" conflict in the normal sense of the term, because only Zulus are involved. Nevertheless, it is a conflict between groups with different identities, namely, between those who have chosen to define themselves as "Zulu" and those who have chosen to be "South African." In fact, ANC supporters tend to refer to their pro-Inkatha rivals, but not to themselves, as Zulus.

The Ethnic State

Another new pattern of ethnic politics has emerged most clearly in Ethiopia, where the regime that came to power in 1991 restructured the country into a federation of ethnic regions, as mentioned above. While this remains the only example of such a solution to the problem of ethnic diversity in Africa at this point, the tensions existing in other African countries suggest that the Ethiopian case cannot be simply dismissed as an anachronistic imitation of the now-defunct Soviet Union. For better or for worse, it may be a harbinger of things to come elsewhere.

Ethnicity began to dominate Ethiopian politics during the 1970s, when the radical, multiethnic movements that represented the early opposition to the Mengistu military regime were destroyed, and a variety of ethnic liberation movements took their place. The TPLF soon emerged as the most important of these organizations, due largely to the support it received from the Eritrean secessionists in the EPLF. Ideologically, the alliance between the two movements was somewhat paradoxical, because the TPLF was an ethnic organization, but the EPLF rejected the notion of ethnic politics. Indeed, it defended its quest for Eritrean independence by invoking the OAU principle that colonial borders should be respected, claiming that Eritrea, a former Italian colony, had the right to be recognized as a separate state. The alliance made strategic sense, however, since the Mengistu regime was the common enemy of both movements.

The consequences of this alliance were momentous: Mengistu was defeated in 1991, the TPLF came to power, and it paid its debt to the EPLF by recognizing Eritrean independence. But the TPLF, which represented a very small ethnic group, faced the problem of governing a country that was mobilized along ethnic lines. The result was the decision to reorganize Ethiopia into ethnic regions, held together by an umbrella party, the Ethiopian People's Revolutionary Democratic Front (EPRDF), composed of ethnic movements organized by the TPLF to represent the dominant ethnic group in each region. This solution was undoubtedly inspired by the Soviet model of how to manage the "nationalities question." This conclusion is suggested not only by the similarity between the new Ethiopian and the old Soviet systems, but also by the Marxist orientation both of the

TPLF in its early years and of the Tigrean student organization of the late 1960s and early 1970s that had provided many of the party's cadres. By organizing ethnic movements under its own control in each region, and keeping firm control over them through the EPRDF, the Tigrean minority could govern the country. The TPLF was certainly not the first African regime to manipulate ethnicity to keep itself in power. It was, however, the first one, outside of apartheid South Africa, to do so by embedding the separateness of ethnic identities into the structure of the political system.

In a very important way, Ethiopia was going against the African current when it developed these new structures. While in some of the more open political systems of the 1990s—South Africa and Benin, for example—ethnicity had become a legitimate issue for discussion and political strategizing, the trend on the continent was still to play down the importance of ethnicity and to devise institutions that would minimize its impact. Indeed, ethnicity remained a forbidden topic in many arenas. For example, the African Charter on Human and Peoples' Rights (the Banjul Charter), adopted in 1981, stressed the importance of the group in African societies, thus rejecting a purely individualistic notion of human rights as alien to African culture. However, the charter studiously avoided mentioning ethnic groups as a constituent part of the society that could not be ignored, and only mentioned, more safely, the family. The Kampala Document, drafted in 1991 as the founding charter of a proposed Conference for Peace, Stability, Security, Development, and Cooperation in Africa—an African version of the Conference on Security and Cooperation in Europe—was even more explicit in its rejection of ethnicity, stating that political parties based on ethnic identities were not legitimate. The Ethiopian system thus violated the principles that were being advocated for in Africa.

However, at present, an increasing number of African countries appear to be incapable of finding an ethnic modus vivendi and a modicum of stability in unitary systems that ignore ethnic divisions. These countries will probably be forced to turn to political systems that provide a role and a space for ethnic groups. Nigeria, for example, will have to admit at some point that no amount of constitutional engineering can neutralize the ethnic factor. A state that recognizes ethnicity in its institutions does not have to follow the Ethiopian model; variants of consociational democracy have, for example, been suggested for South Africa. Some countries may, however, follow Ethiopia's example, deciding not only that ethnicity cannot be eliminated from politics, but that it must in fact become the organizational principle around which the political system is built.

State Collapse

In a few African countries, the ethnicization of politics has had devastating consequences, leading to the complete collapse of the state. This is a new phenomenon of the 1990s: in the three preceding decades, the survival of existing states, no matter how weak or bankrupt, could be taken for granted; but today, the list of states that have either collapsed or could easily do so is growing. Defining precisely which states have collapsed and which are simply on the verge of collapse is difficult. At the extreme, there are countries like Somalia and Liberia, where no central authority controlled even the capital city. But there is also a gray area, encompassing countries in which a central government still nominally exists, but controls only a limited area and sees its authority and legitimacy challenged even there. Sierra Leone, Burundi, Rwanda, and Zaire (now the Democratic Republic of the Congo) all fall in this category.

The conflicts that have caused these countries to collapse, or to come close to it, are not purely ethnic or "tribal," in the sense of reflecting blind ancestral hatreds that spontaneously burst into violence. Such pure ethnic conflicts do not exist anywhere. But all of these conflicts have, or have acquired, a strong, and in some cases blatant, ethnic dimension that cannot be ignored.

To the extent that these collapsed states can be put back together—and it is by no means certain that this is possible—it will have to be done through a process of negotiation involving all factions and groups, leading to some agreed-upon form of power sharing. The possibility of an authoritarian solution—the reconquest of the country by a single faction able to impose its will—appears remote. Indeed, these states have collapsed precisely because no faction could win a decisive victory.

The political systems of such states, if and when they are reconstituted, are likely to be decentralized, with guaranteed representation for many groups and a large degree of regional or local autonomy. Even if these collapsed states are not reconstituted, power will shift to the local or regional level. In either case, the future of collapsed states is very likely to entail fewer attempts at nation building and a greater recognition of local and regional—often ethnic—groupings.

Conclusion

The ethnic problems that African countries experience today must be understood as a modern phenomenon, a product of colonialism and of contemporary political struggles, not a leftover from a primitive past. Although usually supported by the mythology of the past, these ethnic conflicts are rooted in the present, and they play a major role in modern politics in Africa, as elsewhere.

Economic development, formal education, and all of the other elements of what used to be called "modernization" are not going to make ethnicity disappear, neither in the three or four years that Sekou Toure thought would suffice nor over the course of several decades. But the importance of ethnicity as a political factor waxes and wanes. African countries came to independence at a time when ethnic nationalism was abhorred around the world and when the proclaimed ideal was to overcome such parochial differences. But the power of nationalism has risen again, beginning with the Soviet successor states and Eastern Europe, and spreading elsewhere. The result is a world in which it is becoming possible both to challenge existing power relations among ethnic groups and to rethink the territorial arrangements that put specific populations within current state boundaries.

As they have in the past, the democratic political openings of the post-socialist period have helped give ethnicity and nationalism a new importance. "Government by the people" requires a definition of the people and thus raises issues of identity. From a democratic point of view, the answer that "the people" is the haphazard assemblage of human beings corralled into existing international boundaries by nondemocratic colonial powers is not very satisfactory. Furthermore, democratic elections tend to destroy old arrangements based on raw power or on agreements among elites. They thus have the potential for subverting existing power relations among ethnic groups, causing heightened tension or open conflict.

In this sense, there is a new ethnicity in Africa, as there is elsewhere. The challenge for African countries, as for the rest of the world, is to accept the inevitability, and indeed the legitimacy, of different ethnic identities and to find ways to manage the conflicts that arise, particularly when political movements manipulate these identities for political purposes. Accepting that ethnic identities will not melt away does not, however, mean automatically accepting the inevitable dissolution of existing states. Nevertheless, it is possible that some conflicts cannot be managed within existing state boundaries. African countries may eventually have to face the reality that the colonial boundaries that were once acceptable to their political elites are not acceptable to their populations.

Any increase in the level of popular participation is bound to push the issue of ethnic relations to the fore. Authoritarian systems could more easily repress ethnic tensions, as well as other expressions of discontent, but open regimes cannot do the same. The problem is complicated in the present transitional stage in many countries, in which governments have lost the power, and often the will, to repress expressions of discontent, but the institutions that allow these tensions to be expressed through democratic processes are not yet consolidated.

The rules that successfully contained ethnic conflict in Africa for three decades no longer apply in a world of rampant nationalism, reassertion of cultural pluralism, and democratic pressures. Solutions need to be based on the recognition that ethnic identities are not going to disappear and that they are not bad in themselves, as long as they do not become the basis for violent conflict and discrimination. Africans have little choice but to deal with ethnicity openly; these are global trends from which no part of the world can insulate itself.

Notes

1. On the recent development of national myths, see Anderson, *Imagined Communities;* Hobsbawm and Ranger, *Invention of Tradition;* and, in the African context, Golan, *Inventing Shaka.*

2. On the rise of nationalism, see Hobsbawm, *Nations and Nationalism;* Gellner, *Nations and Nationalism;* and Greenfeld, *Nationalism.*

3. The notion that the tribe is a more primitive entity than the nation is still with us. The revival of ethnonationalism in Eastern Europe, for example, has been dubbed a "new tribalism." See Walzer, "New Tribalism."

4. Weber, *Peasants into Frenchmen.*

5. Hobsbawm and Ranger, *Invention of Tradition;* Anderson, *Imagined Communities.*

6. The evidence now available on the recent origin of the African tribes is overwhelming. Indeed, whenever ethnic conflict erupts in some part of the continent, scholars point out that the ethnic groups fighting one another are of recent origin and often owe their existence to the classifications of colonial authorities. See, for example, Vail, ed., *Creation of Tribalism;* Golan, *Inventing Shaka;* Young, *Politics of Cultural Pluralism;* and Lemarchand, *Burundi.* The list could be expanded to embrace virtually all of the African countries afflicted by ethnic conflict.

7. In the author's experience, political and ethnic identifications among Zulus interact in complex patterns. Supporters of the nationalist IFP readily identify themselves as Zulu. Zulu speakers who do not support Inkatha often refer to Inkatha supporters, but not to themselves, as Zulu, although when questioned, they admit to being Zulu. To outsiders, including other black South Africans, all people coming from a certain area are Zulu, irrespective of political affiliations. Indeed, the opposite phenomenon sometimes occurs, that is, all Zulus are suspected of being Inkatha supporters, particularly in conflict areas.

8. I borrow the concept of civic nationalism from Liah Greenfeld, who distinguished between civic nationalism, which embraces all citizens of a country as members of the nation, and ethnic nationalism, which only accepts the members of an ethnic group as part of the nation (*Nationalism,* pp. 9–12).

9. Cited in Young, *Cultural Pluralism,* p. 6.

10. Jackson, *Quasi-States.*

11. Neither the Eritrean nationalists nor the Polisario party in Western Sahara rejected the OAU principle that colonial borders must be respected. On the contrary, they justified their quest for independence on the grounds that their territories had been separate colonies and thus should have achieved independence within the colonial borders. In the case of Western Sahara, this argument foundered due to power relations. In the case of Eritrea, other African countries refused to accept the nationalists' claims, fearing that the independence of Eritrea would encourage nationalism even on the part of groups that could not claim a separate colonial past.

12. See Neuberger, *National Self-Determination.*

13. See, for example, Young, *Cultural Pluralism,* and Rothchild and Olorunsola, *State Versus Ethnic Claims.*

14. Ottaway, *Democratization and Ethnic Nationalism,* pp. 59ff.

15. Levine, *Greater Ethiopia.*

17

Ethnic Insecurity, Peace Agreements, and State Building

DONALD ROTHCHILD

The return to an orderly system for managing internal conflicts after civil war can be very complicated. Safe landings should not be assumed because peace accords have been signed. In Africa, the list of implementation failures is long, including those in Angola (1975 and 1992), Sudan (1982), Uganda (1985), Rwanda (1994), and Burundi (1994). In 1996, the Liberians negotiated their thirteenth agreement in five years. As such breakdowns continue, it is worth asking what kind of state regime is most likely to discourage the unraveling of carefully negotiated peace agreements. Meticulous planning during the negotiation stage and skillful mediation by third parties in both the negotiation and implementation stages are certainly prerequisites for successful consolidation of agreements.[1]

Two aspects of the implementation process are usually poorly understood by observers of African politics. First, the depth of the security fears of some groups leads to a paralyzing inability to make a credible commitment to the peace accord in question. Second, the range of acceptable regime responses may be too restricted to allow for the development of political rules and institutional arrangements to cope with these security fears. This is especially true in "soft state" circumstances, where the state is unable to apply its regulations throughout territory nominally under its control.

How can parties to a conflict deal more effectively with crippling uncertainty about cultural and physical survival? A better match must be made between group fears, whether rational or irrational, and the proposed conflict management system, emphasizing responsive governance, avoiding state repression, and forestalling state collapse. The challenge of designing an effective state applies to countries the world over: Bosnia, Cyprus, and Sri Lanka, as well as Liberia, Rwanda, Burundi, and Angola.

To meet this challenge and make a safe landing in the postagreement implementation stage, statesmen, academics, and others need to reevaluate their
premises and be more open to new ideas.

This chapter examines some of the grand issues confronted by African
statesmen and third parties as they attempt to reconstruct state structures in
the aftermath of civil wars. We begin by focusing on one of the major causes of state collapse: leaders' manipulation of ethnic ties to produce a spiral-
ing pattern of mutual insecurity and distrust. To rebuild states in the critical
transition following peace agreements, statesmen and third-party actors
must design appropriate structures that will help prevent ethnic-based challenges.

In this discussion, we will limit ourselves to the major choice confronting postagreement state builders: whether a maximalist majoritarian
democracy or a minimalist elite pact is preferable. What factors are responsible for the relative successes and failures of majoritarian democratic
regimes and elite pacts? The answer is determined partly by the prevailing
political, economic, and social circumstances and partly by the short- and
long-term objectives of leaders. At times, we also find that a "satisficing"
(satisfying and sufficing) strategy can seem optimal in light of the circumstances of time and place. This is because elite pacts can be relatively easy
to form, reduce uncertainty for leaders and ethnic minorities, produce a
minimal accord, and then possibly lead, in time, to democracy.

The Challenge of Ethnicity

As long as observers cavalierly dismiss ethnicity as an irrational relic of the
past, they will be unable to recognize its force and attraction in contemporary times. As many social scientists suggest, ethnicity can be dynamic,
changeable, and of very recent origin. In Rwanda, for example, the hatreds
based on claims of ethnic difference that were manifested in the early
months of 1994 were anything but ancient. The Tutsi and Hutu share language and religion, and they are not significantly different from each other
in terms of physical appearance; the formation of these territory-wide identities is relatively recent. Yet, Gérard Prunier calculates that Hutus killed
about 800,000 Tutsi—often crudely hacking them to death with machetes.[2]
The Rwanda massacres can be partly explained as an intense struggle over
scarce economic resources (particularly state positions and landownership);
however, there are clearly also other important parts of the equation. Of
particular relevance is the uncertainty arising from a lack of accurate information regarding the intentions of the adversaries and the profound insecurity that both groups feel about their future.[3] Long political memories
(whether accurate or not) of discrimination, repression, or massacre can

build up or exacerbate the deep-seated anxieties that many ethnic peoples presently experience.

But even these memories may not constitute triggers for violence. Rather, the catalyst is often the willingness of an elite to exploit the ethnic ties of its clients and the collective fears (often promoted through the mass media) of their future exploitation and victimization. As long as members of an ethnic group rank inclusion and individual and collective security among their highest values, militant leaders will be in a strong position to "outbid" the appeals of moderate politicians within their own ethnic community.[4] As a consequence, ethnicity remains a modern and potentially dangerous force in every context where normal group attachments are overlaid by deep fears about the future.

The Range of Choices

Observers mistakenly assume that Africa's ethnic identities will decline in significance over the coming years. For most purposes, they also restrict appropriate regime choices to one—namely, majoritarian democracy. Where societies have been fortunate enough to survive the lengthy transition to full democracy, and where democratic norms and practices have gained widespread public acceptance, as in Mauritius and Namibia, intergroup competition has certainly conformed to the rules of the democratic political game. Under best-case scenarios such as these, strong states will be coextensive with strong civil societies; political leaders will have an incentive to act with moderation and to compete in accordance with regime norms. Leaders can afford to lose an election "because they believe that the institutional framework that organizes the democratic competition will permit them to advance their interests in the future."[5] The possibility of coalition shifts and changes of interest is advantageous for ethnic minorities, because it reduces the likelihood that they will be permanently shut out of office.

Nevertheless, pursuing the single objective of majoritarian democracy can at times prove counterproductive. Some societal factors may undercut a smooth progression to majoritarian democracy, thus creating a pattern of incentives that operates contrary to expectations of moderation and controlled competition. The soft state, lacking both regularized rules for state-society encounters and economic opportunities that foster moderate behavior, may create a political environment that fosters pursuit of ethnic self-interests over community-wide interests. These environments provide a set of incentives that fosters intense competition and conflict and discourages interethnic cooperation. With scarce economic resources, soaring populations, and social education and health infrastructures that are restricted in their reach, the state finds that its ability to respond to legitimate public demands is severely constrained. Group fears about the future may overwhelm moderate politics. Ambitious ethnic leaders may attempt to outflank moderates within their own group through extremist, fear-inflating messages, thus heightening tensions to the point that neutral rules are no longer sufficient to cope with the challenges.

If, for any reason, majoritarian democracy does seem inappropriate, it will then become necessary to think in terms of rebuilding state institutions to establish a new, legitimate, and effective intrastate system of conflict management. Particularly in societies emerging from civil war, rebuilding may require a substantial redesign of state-society relations. At a time when external donors are offering conditional assistance based on the acceptance of democratic principles and practices, and thus narrowing the range of choice, African statesmen have the unenviable task of crafting institutions that reconcile local political imperatives with external guidelines in a context of unremitting scarcity. Unreasonable expectations are not likely to produce effective conflict management systems that stand the test of time. Hence, the time is ripe to consider the question of appropriate regimes for scarcity-prone, multiethnic societies that have recently reached an agreement to end civil war and that seek to rebuild their states. If majoritarian democracy should prove premature in these societies, what other overarching structures or regime types might be appropriate?

Peaceful Interethnic Conflict

In Africa, as elsewhere, diverse ethnic groups often live peacefully side by side, managing to channel their conflicts of interest along predetermined paths. Different groups continuously jockey for favorable opportunities within political systems, competing for preferential allocations of government posts, developmental allocations, school and university scholarships, the location of factories and government facilities in their heartland areas, and so forth. Competition and conflict are ubiquitous, but also, in the best of circumstances, bounded and circumscribed. Although demands for advantageous treatment are ever present, in such environments, they usually remain reasonable and negotiable and can be dealt with by a responsive state elite that operates according to understood rules.[6] In democratic Botswana, for example, a well-entrenched and secure state has an assured base of support among its Bamangwato and Bakwena peoples; its ruling coalition has therefore been able to pursue a relatively equitable policy in its allocation of resources among the country's subregions.[7] By responding in a constructive manner to local claims, the state reassures all groups that it will negotiate with them in good faith and deal pragmatically with their problems.

The cooperation of minority ethnic groups with state elites increases when it is anticipated that the following five conditions will be met: (1) demands are negotiable; (2) the state is responsive to legitimate demands; (3) the perceptions of state elites are pragmatic; (4) authentic representatives of the main ethnic groups are included in the decisionmaking process; and (5) there are no hurtful or antagonistic political memories. When these conditions are expected to persist, ethnic minorities are likely to feel secure in their relationship with the state and with other groups in the society, and it is probable that they will continue to cooperate with those in power to maximize their interests. This sense of security and well-being is furthered when the ruling elite takes steps to include legitimate representatives of minority ethnic groups in the decisionmaking process, to allocate civil service positions and development revenues proportionally (and in the case of highly disadvantaged peoples or units, extraproportionally), and to give local leaders of territorialized groups some autonomous responsibility to handle affairs in their subregion. These measures can prevent troubling suspicions and hostilities from emerging because they foreshadow an ongoing relationship based on equality and reciprocity.

The Collapse of State-Society Connections

When expectations change and ethnic elites can no longer anticipate that these five conflict-alleviating conditions will persist, however, relations built upon interelite reciprocity will be weakened. Demands become less negotiable, state elites fail to respond to valid group claims, perceptions of the intentions of rival groups become increasingly essentialist (or menacing), important ethnic interests are excluded from key decisionmaking activities at the political center, and political memories begin to concentrate attention on the presumed wrongs of the past. As ethnic leaders and their supporters become less certain of the future, they become increasingly defensive and thus take measures aimed at augmenting their security in a threatening political environment. Majoritarian democracy may therefore be a casualty when the networks of trust and reciprocity break down, as ordinary conflicts over resource allocation deepen and become the cause of bitter resentments and demonstrations, state violations of human rights become commonplace, and ethnic militancy and outbidding by elites inflame the passions of resistance. Full democracy, with its reliance on moderation and goodwill, crumbles as interelite connections snap and the stakes of politics rise to unprecedented levels. At times, third-party mediators can step between the polarizing parties and entice them to return from the brink. In the worst-case scenario, the political logic of escalation is followed through to its natural conclusion: destructive civil wars.

Because civil wars can "generate totalistic war aims," peace can be difficult to negotiate.[8] Stephen Stedman, commenting on this observation, notes that "leaders in civil wars can suffer from pathologies that prevent them from changing their preferences."[9] As the word "pathology" is used here, it implies a pervasive sense of anxiety, insecurity, hostility, menace, and estrangement that is projected onto surrounding adversaries.[10] A leader's exaggerated sense of insecurity and threat can lead him or her to adopt an extremely rigid stance regarding compromises on principles or regime practices. However, the threshold of pathology and enmity—the point at which hope for reconciliation must be given up—depends upon individual circumstances. Changes of preferences on the part of elites do occur, as indicated by Sudanese President Jaafar al-Nimeiry's decision to negotiate a political solution with the southern insurgents in the late 1960s, as well as by South African President F. W. de Klerk's dramatic decision in 1990 to lift the ban on the African National Congress (ANC) and other parties opposed to apartheid and to declare his willingness to negotiate with the opposition. However, internal wars have generally contributed to obdurate stances on two or more sides. The effect of this is to make negotiations about power sharing, autonomy, and border rectification difficult and to encourage essentialist perceptions that complicate further bargaining in the postagreement implementation stage.

The Two Transitions from Civil War

As the recent series of civil wars in Africa comes to an end, it becomes important to gain insight into the ways in which these wars were concluded and the impact of these conclusions on subsequent state-society relations. We see two types of transitions occurring following civil war: the *military victory scenario,* in which terms are imposed by the triumphant party, and the *negotiation scenario,* in which the contract between the parties becomes the basis for structuring future interactions. Transitions by means of military victory are clearly the most commonplace. Aggregate data published by Roy Licklider, which largely reconfirms the earlier research of Paul Pillar and Stephen Stedman, indicates that three-fourths of the world's civil wars since 1945 have ended by military victory, with the remaining one-fourth terminated by a negotiated agreement.[11] Although there is only a slightly greater tendency for ethnically and religiously based identity wars to be associated with genocide than their socially and economically based counterparts, Licklider, in line with a thesis put forward by Robert Harrison Wagner, finds that negotiated agreements ending identity wars tend to be less stable than military victories.[12] As we will now see, this finding has important implications for dealing with ethnic demands during the postnegotiation phase.

Military Victory and Implementation

Military victory, especially when it is not followed by guerrilla warfare, greatly reduces the unreasonable expectations of the losing party. The effect is to ease the process of incorporating military cadres, party leaders, civil servants, and others into state institutions. For the time being, the winning party does not encounter intense resistance to political change from defeated ethnic leaders; this allows the party to impose substantial unifying and centralizing measures. The need for ethnic conciliation will not disappear, however. Should regime opponents mobilize at some future time to threaten the government in power, the regime's ability to reshape its society would then weaken considerably.

Ruling elites may act with magnanimity toward the defeated ethnic group or groups (as they did following the Nigerian civil war) or in a heavy-handed manner (as in Rwanda from 1994 to 1996). In either case, the elites are in a favorable position to overwhelm the demands of vanquished ethnic leaders for shared power or autonomous authority.

The experiences of Angola in 1991–1992 demonstrate mixed results in this regard. Angola's armed forces, reequipped with new weaponry and supported by foreign advisers, had held a commanding military position, but their victory was not complete enough to deter Jonas Savimbi's resumption of the guerrilla struggle after his loss in the 1992 election. The government, led by the Popular Movement for the Liberation of Angola (MPLA), was intent on bringing an end to the heavy fighting and destruction of many towns and cities. When a cease-fire was negotiated again in 1994, government leaders insisted that the Lusaka Protocol reaffirm the commitments made in 1991, secure the central government's legitimate authority over the country as a whole, back the holding of a second round of elections, and provide for the unification of the army. In response to concerns about the potential for power sharing based on negotiated pacts, the MPLA did accept the insertion of confidence-building measures into the Lusaka Protocol to promote improved interactions among the adversaries. Provisions were made for the decentralization of certain police functions and for the inclusion of opposition members of the National Union for the Total Independence of Angola (UNITA) at all levels of the government and administration. The willingness of the MPLA leaders to make such concessions reflects their assessment of the best way to achieve administrative efficiency, promote local cooperation and peaceful relations, and acquire international goodwill. Thus, these concessions were motivated less by the stronger party's need to respond to the demands of weaker ones than by its perceptions of the state's interests. Nevertheless, this pact, growing out of the MPLA's military dominance, continues to look shaky, and it still remains to be seen whether both sides will deliver on the bargains struck at Lusaka.

Negotiated Settlements and Implementation

Whereas military victory reveals a distinct asymmetry in power among adversaries, a negotiated agreement indicates a relative equality in power relations. The latter generally reflects the weakness of most African states, which lack the information and capabilities necessary to implement their decrees throughout the territory theoretically under their control. In many instances, insurgent movements have exercised a kind of de facto autonomy in their area of occupation. Soft states negotiate with their opponents out of political necessity, because they are unable to win a military victory over insurgent movements such as the Rwandan Patriotic Front, Angola's UNITA, or the Mozambican National Resistance Movement (RENAMO).

Agreements are most frequently negotiated when a mutually hurting stalemate provides an incentive to search for a political solution. Such a situation exists when two dominant parties in a civil war recognize that a military victory is impossible and that continuing the stalemate will probably be very costly.[13] However, a mutually hurting stalemate becomes more problematic in multifactional, multidimensional conflicts such as those in Somalia and Liberia, because they provide increased incentives for defection.

Hurting stalemates are also difficult to predict because one of the parties can always decide to absorb the pain and continue fighting. Furthermore, one of the parties may negotiate for tactical reasons, with the intention of defecting at an advantageous moment. Genuine negotiations have proven possible when the fear of continued fighting exceeds the fear of reaching an agreement, as was the case in Liberia in late 1996.[14] As peace becomes a real possibility, implementation skills become more critical. Third parties must act deftly to encourage all parties to live up to their agreements and therefore produce an environment that promotes credible commitment.

Because security fears reach their peak during the implementation phase, negotiated agreements are often fragile and difficult to put into effect. The integration of armies is an especially sensitive issue. Rival forces feel exposed and vulnerable as their troops are demobilized and disarmed. They suffer anxieties that their opponent will cheat on its commitments.[15] This problem is exacerbated by the lack of reliable information about the adversary's actions and future intentions. Only a third-party intervenor may be able to resolve these issues at this delicate stage. The cumulative effect of these factors makes the negotiated route necessary but unstable.

Although it is easier to gain a consensus and reach an agreement if the terms remain ambiguous, lack of precision about the organization and powers of state institutions can contribute to a sense of perilous uncertainty for one or more of the parties, ultimately leading to the collapse of the agreement. In Angola, Zairian President Mobutu Sese Seko's hastily mediated Gbadolite Accords of 1989 brought about a cease-fire agreement between bitter enemies. However, no hurting stalemate was evident on either side, and the vaguely worded agreement soon collapsed, and bitter fighting resumed.

On the other hand, agreements may also collapse because the terms specified create new and dangerous anxieties. Rwanda's Arusha Accords, described by two analysts as "a victor's agreement,"[16] created a menacing circle of wounded tigers. Hard-line Hutu associates of President Juvénal Habyarimana, including the Presidential Guard, some senior ministers, high-level army officers, and members of the Coalition for the Defense of the Republic (CDR), felt largely excluded from positions of power under these accords. The accords' power-sharing provisions for the transitional government allocated only five of the 19 ministerial positions to Habyarimana's party, with no post for the CDR in either the cabinet or the transitional assembly. The losers, fearing for their future under the new arrangement, took matters into their own hands and unleashed a terrible genocidal strike against the Tutsi, also killing some Hutu moderates.

In brief, depending upon the circumstances, either ambiguous or highly explicit terms of agreement can result in a breakdown of accords during the implementation stage, with potentially frightening consequences in the loss of lives and destruction of property.

State Building, Democratic Regimes, and Elite Pacts

The collapse of state routines and rules prior to and during a civil war frequently brings about a political situation that lacks behavioral norms. Elites may withdraw to their support bases, their networks of reciprocity undermined, and lacking information about their adversary's intentions. Implementation of agreements in such a postconflict political environment entails starting anew by building institutions that will further interaction between parties, who often continue to be deeply apprehensive about their futures.

Savimbi's lament in March 1996, when his UNITA troops were being disarmed and demobilized, gives some insight into the extent of these uncertainties: "No leader in history that I have known," he told his supporters, "disarmed and stayed in power."[17] In this situation, the military victory scenario seems relatively straightforward: a strong actor (usually a government) imposes its political institutions on the losing side, absorbing its administrators and soldiers into the state's civil service and army to the extent that it deems appropriate. Asymmetrical power—as long as it is maintained—acts to stabilize the society during the transition to a new political system.

The adjustments necessary in the case of negotiated settlements are more complicated. Here, a greater parity of power often causes a protracted war that comes to an end only when the two or more parties involved become fatigued and despairing over the possibility of a military solution. The challenge, in these negotiated settlements, is to pursue state building during the implementation phase, to reduce mutual fears, and to develop an enduring intrastate conflict management system. Assuming that ethnic fears remain intense for all parties, implementation of peace agreements in Africa has generally taken one of two broad routes. The *maximalist route* involves sustained effort and frequent facilitation by external mediators backed by an international peacekeeping and monitoring force, to establish stable institutions leading to a general election. The *minimalist route* emphasizes a political pact among leaders. We will deal with each of these routes to a stable conflict management system.

The Maximalist Route to Implementation

State building by way of elite pacts is an attractive option for ethnomilitia leaders intent on reducing uncertainty for themselves and their supporters, but many Africans concerned with building cohesive states regard elite pacts unfavorably. These state builders recoil from such schemes because they involve an acknowledgment of group differences that may lead to sub-state insularities and prevent the achievement of legitimate, countrywide political and economic goals. In brief, the state builder reluctantly accepts the need for guarantees of group autonomy, but balks when the proposed mechanisms risk impeding unity of purpose and action.

Thus, Kwame Nkrumah and A. Milton Obote dismantled quasi-federal schemes in Ghana and Uganda soon after independence, fearing that entrenched subregional authorities would increase decisional costs and limit the leaders' ability to transform their societies.[18] Some contemporary state leaders may be more skeptical about their ability to transform their societies, but these leaders are likely to be equally concerned about compromise agreements that create pockets of subregional power and resistance during the implementation phase.

Some negotiators and mediators, when implementing peace agreements, have refused to bear the costs of pursuing transitions in a sequence that proceeds from pacts to democracy (as in South Africa). Instead, they are determined to leapfrog over intermediate stages and move straight to majoritarian democracy. During the Zimbabwe independence negotiations, in 1979, British mediators pointedly described elections as the final determinant of legitimate authority in the country's postagreement phase. When he began discussions of a cease-fire, Lord Carrington, the British foreign secretary, emphasized the importance of holding elections to determine which party would rule and to establish the framework of future relations.

As he told the delegates at the thirty-fourth plenary session at Lancaster House in November: "You have agreed to settle your differences in elections under our authority, and we must find a way to bring peace to Rhodesia while those elections are held."[19]

All of the main parties believed that they would fare well in the balloting, so the election process gained general assent. The founding elections were held in February 1980, and they did prove conclusive in the selection of leaders and policies. Robert Mugabe's Zimbabwe African National Union (ZANU) won 63 percent of the votes cast and 57 of 80 common roll seats in the new parliament. From this position of considerable strength, Mugabe was able to centralize a great deal of power in his own hands. Nevertheless, as noted earlier, this concentration of power at the political center did not prevent serious societal challenges, such as that in Matabeleland. In the end, however, Mugabe negotiated a pact with his main rival, Joshua Nkomo, and this pragmatic arrangement fostered a stable form of cooperation under Mugabe's leadership.

In Mozambique, the government of President Joaquim Chissano refused the appeals of Western diplomats for a power-sharing arrangement with RENAMO, and he remained firm in his insistence on majority-party rule after fair elections. Some Western observers drew analogies to the collapse of the Bicesse Accords in Angola and warned against excluding RENAMO, with its base of support among the Shona peoples of central Mozambique, from the political process. In 1993, the U.S. Institute of Peace warned that

> beyond the electoral system it might be advisable to consider a transitional regime or coalition to assure that for an interim period neither of the parties is totally excluded from power. Both Namibia and South Africa provide examples of transitional arrangements which avoid total exclusion. Power sharing can permit both the winners and the losers to remain committed to the system.[20]

As the critically important 1994 elections approached, RENAMO leader Alfonso Dhlakama spoke increasingly of the need to guarantee his party a share of political power in the postelection government. RENAMO spokespeople insisted on more than just symbolic gestures, demanding instead "ministries with teeth." In making these statements, they were encouraged by Western ambassadors and UN officials, who reportedly urged Chissano to form a power-sharing government of national unity.

Chissano's Front for the Liberation of Mozambique won a conclusive victory in the elections, thus strengthening his hand. Chissano therefore resisted Western pressures to appoint RENAMO members as either government ministers or provincial governors. In the end, RENAMO leaders responded favorably to external offers of financial inducements and "grudgingly accepted" the government's preferences on the matter. The country then settled down to what appears to be a relatively peaceful transition to stable, democratic governance.[21]

The Minimalist Route to Implementation

When the state is soft and ethnoregional elites and their supporters are highly insecure about their fate in a unified and democratic society, an elite pact may seem a logical alternative to a political order based on a winner-takes-all election that excludes the losers from the decisionmaking process. As the term is used here, "pacts" reflect the configurations of power in each society, including the major warlords or subregional leaders involved in central government decisionmaking activities. On this basis, the Ethiopian coalition that overthrew Mengistu Haile Mariam and agreed on the Transition Charter in July 1991 cannot be considered sufficiently inclusive to meet the terms of this definition. This coalition of winners, which met under the banner of the Ethiopian People's Revolutionary Democratic Front (EPRDF), failed the test of inclusiveness because Mengistu's supporters, parties that had earlier opposed the Mengistu regime, and the Amhara community officially (apart from one of the EPRDF satellite parties) were not represented.

Timothy D. Sisk writes that pacts "are mutual security agreements in which parties forswear the use of violence to achieve their aims in exchange for protection under agreed-upon rules of the political game."[22] They are a form of negotiated agreement among ethnic and other elites (or militia leaders) who accept a minimal form of elite participation among themselves to achieve political stability and to avoid assaults—violent or nonviolent—on themselves and their supporters. The members of the pact agree to procedural rules that protect their interests during a transitional period. These rules also provide for a balanced distribution of resources among elites and their supporters, and for shared decisionmaking at the political center on certain matters. Meanwhile, ethnoregional leaders are given wide discretion over other issues.[23]

At heart, these arrangements are intended to reduce ethnic and other types of conflict during a transition period before a new regime is established. These elite power-sharing systems are not as open and participatory as full democratic regimes, but they are characterized by a continuing process of bargaining among diverse elites. Such systems therefore build on the logic of the iterated game to achieve a transition to stable societal relations.

In spite of the increasing optimism about the value of elite power-sharing regimes as conflict-regulating mechanisms, these schemes are inevitably rather fragile.[24] Four main elements contribute to this brittleness: elite adherence to inflexible principles on recruitment and resource allocation issues (e.g., in Lebanon and Rwanda); the inability of elites to develop enduring routines and rules of relationship (Marshal Tito's Yugoslavia and Liberia); an extreme imbalance in numbers and power among groups, making it difficult to restrain majoritarian impulses over time (South Africa, Burundi, and Rwanda); and the reluctance of pact members to co-opt new political parties or interests (Liberia). Moreover, where fears about ethnic security are pronounced and the possibility of ethnic defection exists, commitment to a regime based on compromise may prove extremely difficult over an extended time period.[25]

This rigidity may cause some elites to refuse to make a commitment to collaborating with an adversary. Therefore, power-sharing mechanisms are not only fragile but, in a worst-case scenario, can also be a source of intensified conflict. Rwanda's hard-line Hutu leaders, fearing a loss of power from the division of posts called for by the Arusha Accords, unleashed their genocidal assaults in a determined effort to thwart their exclusion from the state's inner circle. Experiences in Liberia further confirm that power-sharing arrangements among personalistic, ethnomilitary rivals are brittle in the extreme, and when they break down, the consequences can be terrifying.

In an African context, the different fates of externally induced and internally negotiated pacts are instructive. When external actors exert pressure on local parties to prompt agreement to a pact, these arrangements are difficult to form and maintain. In an attempt to begin rebuilding the Somali state in March 1993, for example, the UN, with strong support from the United States and Ethiopia, hosted a meeting in Addis Ababa that was attended by the 15 main factional leaders for the purpose of hammering out a cease-fire and an elite power-sharing agreement.[26] Actively using their leverage, the coalition of mediators succeeded in gaining acceptance of a compromise agreement among the clan-based militia leaders and members of civil society. A Transitional National Council was to be composed of representatives of the various clans, plus three elected representatives from each of the country's 18 subregions. This legislative body would have the authority to appoint judges and provide for the election of subregional and local officials.

As might have been expected, this pact among the warlords proved to be a shaky foundation for reorganizing the state. The main militia leaders, General Mohamed Farah Aidid and Ali Mahdi, did not cease engaging in bitter exchanges. Despite further efforts by external actors to promote national reconciliation in the period that followed, the pact remained still-born, and the ethnomilitia leaders, safe in their fiefdoms, continued to carry on low-level skirmishing.

In Liberia, external mediators finally succeeded in promoting a pact among highly personalistic and, in some cases, ethnic-based leaders, only to see the pact shatter during the first major postagreement confrontation. Ethnicity, as noted elsewhere, is a "contingent variable"; it is significant when linked to other variables in the political environment, which in this instance included a history of past conflict, collective fears for the future, and involvement in militia organizations.[27] At Abuja, Nigeria, in August 1995, after years of warfare in Liberia, the five main militias agreed to a collective presidency and cabinet, under pressure from a coalition of African, UN, and other mediators.

Under the rather loose post-Abuja arrangement, Charles Taylor's National Patriotic Front of Liberia (NPFL), which pulled together Gio, Mano, and other ethnic peoples who had a common resentment of the exactions by members of the Krahn community under former President Samuel K. Doe, was the most influential organization. However, because NPFL forces were unable to win an outright victory, they had little choice but to share political power in the Council of State with some of the other major warlords: General Alhaji Kromah, the commander of the Mandingo branch of the United Liberation Movement for Democracy in Liberia (ULIMO-K), and Dr. George Boley, the leader of the largely Krahn Liberia Peace Council (LPC). Also on the council were an academic, who served as chairman, and two other representatives of civil society.

To gain support for the pact from the other main militia chiefs, General Hezekiah Bowen of the predominantly Krahn Armed Forces of Liberia (AFL) and General Roosevelt Johnson of the Krahn branch of ULIMO (ULIMO-J) were both appointed government ministers. Bowen went to the Ministry of Defense and Johnson to the Ministry of Rural Development. In all, ministerial appointments were shared as follows: NPFL, six; ULIMO-K, five; ULIMO-J, three; LPC, three; and AFL, one.[28]

The brittleness of this arrangement would soon become apparent. When Taylor and Kromah tried to arrest Johnson in 1996 on charges of murder, fighting erupted between Johnson's militia forces encamped in the Barclay barracks in Monrovia and the Taylor/Kromah forces (a transethnic alliance of former adversaries). The pact had broken down in less than a year. The foreign ministers of the Economic Community of West African States quickly interceded to reassemble the pieces of the broken pact, and Johnson was reinstated in his position as minister of rural development. However, the fragility of this pact arrangement in the face of its first major challenge was all too plain to see. Well-intentioned external actors had sought to end the militia warfare by building an alliance among the warlords, so the very people most responsible for the chaos were to become the foundation for a future peace. But as long as weaponry remained in the hands of the militias, intense intraelite conflicts were likely to be settled by warfare, not by a negotiated resolution of their differences. Pacts failed to blur the sharp differences of interest among the warlords.

Whereas externally induced pacts have proven difficult to create and seem frail when put into effect, internally negotiated elite power-sharing arrangements have shown greater utility and durability, particularly in short-term transitions to a more stable form of regime. Such compromises

represent credible commitments to interact with others in collectively created executive and legislative branches of government. Two very different
examples of this practical expedient are Zimbabwe's 1987 Unity Accord
and South Africa's interim constitution of 1993.

In Zimbabwe, Mugabe's Shona-based ZANU had a close working
relationship with Nkomo's largely Ndebele Zimbabwe African People's
Union (ZAPU) during the civil war and the independence negotiations.[29]
Following independence, however, the two parties went their separate
ways, and the strained relationship between the two nationalist leaders
came out into the open. Nkomo was eased out of the cabinet in 1982, and
the remaining ZAPU members were removed from the cabinet two years
later. Meanwhile, violent opposition against the Mugabe regime flared up
in Matabeleland, where ZAPU dissidents were ruthlessly suppressed by the
predominately Shona Fifth Brigade. Mugabe, frustrated over continuing
resistance among whites and Ndebele voters in the 1985 election, further
consolidated his control over the country's affairs by creating an executive
presidency, abolishing the second house of the legislature, and terminating
the constitutional provision that called for seats in the legislature to be
reserved for the white community.

While the distance between ZANU and ZAPU appeared to be widening, talks were taking place in an effort to restore unity between them. This
process gained momentum in 1987, when Nkomo agreed to the creation of
a unified party under Mugabe's leadership. From this point forward, tensions between the two leaders eased noticeably, and they went on to negotiate the Unity Accord in December 1987. Under the provisions of this
accord, key ZAPU members were brought into the cabinet and the ZANU
central committee, and Nkomo was appointed one of two party vice presidents. The former ZAPU leaders' inclusion in ZANU provided an important incentive for interethnic cooperation. Although conflicts of interest
remained, they were resolved within the cabinet and other decisionmaking
bodies.

Similarly, in South Africa, local partisan interests succeeded in negotiating a pact among themselves, and the outcome was equally constructive;
it set up stable rules of relations among the adversaries during the transition
to majoritarian democracy. With violence holding out no promise of victory
on any side, white and black elites recoiled from the idea of a costly war of
attrition and came to view a negotiated settlement as the preferred alternative.

The result of negotiated settlement in this context was a series of
preparatory elite pacts in 1990 and 1991—the Groote Schuur Minute, the
Pretoria Minute, the D. F. Malan Accord, and the National Peace Accord—
which dealt with the normalization of political activities, the release of
political prisoners, the problem of violence, and the nature of the negotiating process itself.[30] These initial pacts created a momentum of their own,

building upon one another until 1993, when the parties assembled at the Multiparty Negotiating Forum were able to agree on an interim constitution that combined democratic elections with minority inclusion in the decision-making process. The interim constitution sought to ensure the inclusion of minorities by providing that the party placing second in the elections could nominate a deputy president and that any party that won over 5 percent of the seats in the National Assembly would be included in the cabinet on a proportional basis for a five-year period.

Inevitably, the democratic election process resulted in the emergence of an asymmetrical power relationship among the political parties in South Africa.[31] In the 1994 elections, based on a system of proportional representation that facilitated minority representation, the ANC, led by Nelson Mandela, won 63 percent of the vote—enough for a clear majority, but not enough for the party to change the constitution on its own. The ANC's main opponents, the National Party (NP) and the Inkatha Freedom Party (IFP), won 20 percent and 11 percent of the vote, respectively. The result, based on the constitutional formula for the allocation of cabinet posts, was 18 seats for the ANC, six for the NP, and three for the IFP.

The pact had smoothed the way for a transfer of power to majority African hands by creating confidence within the minority white community that its interests would be protected at the political center. Nevertheless, elite pacts can prove very fragile in the face of majority pressures for decisive political change (particularly concerning redistribution).[32] Consequently, after the formal inclusionary terms of the interim constitution had achieved their confidence-building purposes during the transition period, this constitution was replaced in 1996 with a permanent constitution establishing a majoritarian democracy.

Conclusion

Following the implementation of agreements, safe landings are complicated by the need to establish new institutions, including general elections, a court system, and executive and legislative branches. No challenge is more important for effective implementation than allaying the fears of ethnic minorities about possible abuse at the hands of a dominant state elite. Fears of future insecurity can discourage a group from maintaining its commitment to an agreement, thereby complicating the process of state building. Prudent negotiators must recognize the existence of these uncertainties, whether warranted or not, and must plan to mitigate them by means of institutions that facilitate central initiative while building up minority confidence. Those engaged in state building are likely to agree on the need to establish an intrastate conflict management system that ensures sustained political stability, but they may disagree ardently on the best means to this end.

When the fears of ethnomilitary elites make the application of majoritarian democracy imprudent and possibly hazardous, what institutional arrangements, short of a costly process of partitioning and separating populations, can reconcile—even if only temporarily—state unity and the demands of powerful political actors for autonomy? In the peace that follows civil war, those who would impose majoritarian democracy and those who would negotiate some form of power sharing could both make a strong case. What is appropriate in each context depends on the perceptions of the actors, the power relations among groups, the preparedness of state elites to respond to the legitimate demands of ethnic groups and other societal interests, and the extent of antagonistic political memories. Parity in power relations and the deep suspicions of elites regarding the intentions of their rivals may make elite pacts the only option in some cases, while the absence of such factors in other cases may predispose elites toward more democratic and centralized leadership practices. Being realistic about what constitutes an appropriate regime thus requires careful assessment on a case-by-case basis. Scholars and policymakers have too often generalized about what is best, without taking local preferences and political circumstances into account. Circumspection requires a more open-minded view of what is desirable and acceptable—for Africa and the world at large.

Both majoritarian democracy and elite pacts have their uses and abuses. Either arrangement offers intriguing possibilities for reducing uncertainties and strengthening cooperation in countries with weak states and powerful militia leaders. Elite pacts can reassure the leaders of the main identity groups about their security in a weakly controlled environment, thereby reducing the risks of association to tolerable levels and, in some cases, leading eventually to full democracy. Pacts based on elite consensus, however, can prove very difficult to maintain. Parties cooperate in pacts because the potential costs of defection are high in terms of insecurity and the destruction of property. But pacts require continuing negotiations among the elites involved, a process that is likely to entail a heavy commitment to conflict management over the years. The relative ease of the creation of the pact can thus become the source of administrative difficulties and centrifugal tendencies, creating doubt that these arrangements can act as a foundation for long-term, stable relations.

Majoritarian democracy, whether imposed by a military victor or agreed upon in a negotiated settlement, can (if it survives) become the basis for a stable, long-term relationship between state and society. Even when the power relations of groups are asymmetrical, democratic regimes can build trust among ethnic minorities if the state elite adopts pragmatic perceptions of rival interests and is responsive to reasonable political and economic claims. As has been shown in Mozambique and Zimbabwe, the adoption of majoritarian democracy following a peace agreement can have the effect of legitimizing the exercise of central government power and help to transcend potential challenges by entrenched ethnoregional elites. Africa's democratic regimes can rarely afford to carry the principle of majority rule to its logical conclusion, as this shuts out the political minority from positions of influence. Political stability seems likely to require a retreat from this reasoning and the incorporation of politically inclusive practices instead.

Democracy, the regime type that holds out the greatest promise for sustained legitimacy and for achieving an ongoing balance between state and societal interests, requires certain supporting conditions that may be in short supply, including pragmatic perceptions, negotiable demands, and state willingness to respond to legitimate demands. When these essential conditions are absent, some form of transition sequencing that leads from temporary arrangements such as elite pacts to legitimate, popularly based, democratic governance may be the best option under difficult circumstances.

Notes

1. Rothchild, "On Implementing"; Stedman and Rothchild, "Peace Operations."
2. Prunier, *Rwanda Crisis*, pp. 255–257 and 265.
3. Lake and Rothchild, "Containing Fear."
4. Hardin, *One for All*, p. 23.
5. Przeworski, *Democracy and the Market*, p. 19.
6. Rothchild, "Collective Demands."
7. Holm, "Botswana," p. 191.
8. Stedman, "Negotiation and Mediation," p. 346.
9. Ibid., pp. 346–347.
10. Rothchild and Groth, "Pathological Dimensions," p. 69.
11. Licklider, "Consequences," p. 684; Pillar, *Negotiating Peace*; and Stedman, *Peacemaking*.
12. Licklider, "Consequences," p. 686; Wagner, "Causes of Peace"; and Hartzell and Rothchild, "Political Pacts."
13. Zartman, *Ripe for Resolution*, p. 268.
14. Hobbes, *Leviathan*, p. 109; Stedman, "Negotiation and Mediation," p. 342.
15. Walter, "Domestic Anarchy," p. 9.
16. Adelman and Suhrke, *Early Warning and Conflict Management*, p. 17.
17. Quoted in *Southern Africa Confidential*, "Angola," p. 3.
18. Rothchild and Curry, *Scarcity*, pp. 71–72.
19. Quoted in Rothchild, *Managing Ethnic Conflict*, p. 181.
20. U.S. Institute of Peace, *Achieving Post-Settlement Peace*, p. 5.
21. *Africa Confidential*, vol. 35 (November 4, 1994): 1–2; *Africa Confidential*, vol. 35 (November 18, 1994): 2; and *Africa Confidential*, vol. 36 (January 20, 1995): 4–5.

22. Sisk, *Power Sharing,* p. 81.
23. Hartzell and Rothchild, "Political Pacts," pp. 3–4.
24. Vance and Hamburg, "Avoiding Anarchy," p. 19.
25. Joseph, *Democracy and Prebendal Politics,* p. 25.
26. Rothchild, "Ethnic Bargaining," pp. 67–68.
27. Hill and Rothchild, "Impact of Regime," p. 199.
28. Hartzell and Rothchild, "Political Pacts," p. 160.
29. Sithole, "State Power Consolidation," p. 88.
30. Sisk, *Democratization,* pp. 88–115.
31. Sparks, *Tomorrow Is Another Country,* p. 195.
32. Herbst, "Prospects for Elite-Driven Democracy," p. 27.

18

State, Civil Society, and Genocide in Rwanda

TIMOTHY LONGMAN

In early 1992, Rwanda appeared on the verge of a democratic transition. Just six months earlier, in response to pressure from an increasingly active and organized population, the government had adopted a new constitution that legalized multiparty politics. The main opposition parties that subsequently emerged formed a coalition that demanded of President Juvénal Habyarimana a multiparty government to oversee a transition to democratic rule. Rallies organized by the opposition coalition drew as many as 30,000 people and forced the ruling party into negotiations. Prominent opponents of the regime and democracy activists were confident that power was on the brink of changing hands, and Western scholars who visited the country at the time came back optimistic about Rwanda's democratic prospects.

In the end, Rwanda's history took a much more tragic turn. A multiparty government was indeed formed, but the distribution of power changed very little. Over the next two years, conditions in the country declined sharply as the economy deteriorated and insecurity spread. Allies of the president blamed the problems on the opposition and provoked the population with sharp rhetoric against the minority Tutsi ethnic group. When a plane carrying the presidents of Rwanda and Burundi was shot down on April 6, 1994, probably by the Presidential Guard, supporters of the regime used the accident to justify launching a program to eliminate all opposition. Only hours after the plane went down, the Presidential Guard and other select soldiers swept through Kigali with lists of prominent opposition politicians and critics of the regime to assassinate. In the following days, a plan that had been in preparation for months was set in motion, carrying violence to every corner of the country. In each community, trained civilian militia, directed by local officials and supported by soldiers, attacked and looted the homes of moderate Hutu and members of the Tutsi minority;

then they systematically slaughtered those who sought refuge in churches and other public buildings. By July, as many as one million people were dead, more than two million had fled into exile, and the remnants of the government had escaped into Zaire in advance of a military victory by the largely Tutsi Rwandan Patriotic Front (RPF).

Given the unprecedented extent of the violence and social disruption that engulfed the country in 1994, to speak about civil society in pregenocide Rwanda might, on the surface, seem ludicrous. In a society where so many people, even small children, were brutally raped or murdered by their neighbors or their own families, the answer to Célestin Monga's question "Is civil society civilized?"[1] seems obvious. What better evidence could there be that there are chaotic tendencies inherent in African societies that can lead to what Robert Kaplan has warned is "the coming anarchy" when states collapse in Africa?[2]

In reality, based on field research conducted in Rwanda in 1992–1993 and 1995–1996, I categorically reject any suggestion that the genocide in Rwanda resulted from intractable divisions in Rwandan society that were released by the waning of the state. In fact, I contend that the 1994 genocide reflected the continuing strength of the Rwandan state, at least in coercive terms. Although in Rwanda, as in many African countries, civil and political societies had emerged that sought to force the state to liberalize and democratize, the state remained capable of resisting meaningful reforms. The genocide represented a calculated strategy by those who dominated the state to reassert state control and to eliminate challenges to the existing structures of power being posed by civil and political societies.

Most discussions of state and society in the past decade have posited a zero-sum relationship between the two main spheres of public life. In *Strong Societies and Weak States,* Joel Migdal, based on an evaluation of five cases throughout the third world, concludes that the stronger, more complex, and more autonomous the society is, the less capable the state will be of functioning effectively.[3] The civil society literature that has emerged in reaction to the political transitions that have taken place in Eastern Europe, Asia, and Africa in the late 1980s and early 1990s has, to a great extent, accepted this zero-sum approach to state-society relations.[4] In the African context, authors such as Naomi Chazan and Claude Ake have expressed reservations about the expansion of associational life, fearing that social groups, "far from supporting democratic tendencies, foment particularism, fundamentalism, and ethnic nationalism."[5] The decline of state power and the growth of social strength are to be feared, it is suggested, because the state is needed to contain destructive tendencies in society. The challenge confronting democratization in Africa is to strike a balance whereby social groups can force accountability on the state without undermining state centrality.

Based on the Rwandan case, I dispute the idea that a strong society necessarily means a weak state. In Rwanda, associational life exploded in the 1980s and early 1990s. Associations such as women's groups, rotating credit societies, farmers' cooperatives, and prayer meetings all created for the population alternatives to the patrimonial structures of power that had previously tied people to the state and organized support for the regime. With the legalization of opposition parties in 1992, alternative political alliances, based largely on regional and ethnic loyalties, further challenged the ability of the regime to organize support. However, the growing strength of the society in terms of its independence and capacity was balanced by an increase in the coercive capacity of the state that resulted from a rapid expansion of military personnel and armaments following the RPF's invasion in October 1990. With vastly increased coercive force, the regime was able to secure its position and organize resistance to reformist pressures, ultimately culminating in the 1994 genocide.[6]

The question I wish to explore in this chapter is why civil society in Rwanda was unable to present a more effective challenge to state power if, as I claim, civil society had become increasingly large and strong. The genocide involved a concerted attack on civil society, with leaders of many social and economic groups targeted by death squads. Although most civil society organizations opposed interethnic conflict as a diversion from the serious problems of inequality and national development, many of their Hutu members participated in the anti-Tutsi violence. Following the genocide, many of the organizations have disappeared, while those that remain are generally weak, are poorly organized, and have little popular support.

The Growth of Civil Society in Rwanda

As in many African countries, following independence, Rwanda moved toward single-party rule. The Party of the Movement for the Emancipation of Bahutu/Democratic and Republican Movement (PARMEHUTU/MDR), the political party most associated with the struggle for power for the Hutu majority of the population that had been shut out of political office and other opportunities during colonial rule, won an overwhelming majority in the 1962 independence elections. Once in office, PARMEHUTU/MDR harassed and arrested members of other parties, making Rwanda a de facto one-party state. The role of the party, however, remained relatively limited.[7]

After taking office in a coup in 1973, President Habyarimana initially banned political activity, but in 1975, he organized a single party, the Mouvement Révolutionnaire National pour le Développement (MRND), which, like the Mouvement Populaire de la Révolution in Zaire, was based on the Chinese party model. The MRND, which all Rwandans were required to join, served to organize support for the regime and to extend state control more effectively into the society. The MRND organized *umuganda,* or weekly communal public labor, to build bridges, improve roads, and terrace hillsides, as well as *animation,* regular loyalty rituals to demonstrate support for the state and regime. Habyarimana created parallel state and party structures that reached down to the most local level to facilitate monitoring and control of the population. Social organizations were almost entirely subsumed by the party, which organized women's and youth groups, published its own newspaper, and controlled radio broadcasts. Those few organizations that remained formally independent of the party-state were brought into line through other means. For example, church leaders were invited to participate in national and regional party committees; the archbishop of the Catholic Church was a member of the central committee of the MRND until 1985, when he was forced out by the pope.[8]

During its first decade in power, the Habyarimana regime enjoyed widespread public support. The ethnic conflicts that had plagued the country since 1959 were brought under control, and the government was able to attract substantial international development aid, giving the impression that the economy was expanding. By the mid-1980s, however, the population was becoming increasingly disenchanted. The benefits of economic growth were heavily concentrated in the hands of Habyarimana and his supporters, particularly those from his family and home region, while the growth rate failed to keep pace with population growth. The MRND, once regarded as a unifying and developing force in the country, seemed increasingly to be an instrument for controlling the population and concentrating wealth in the hands of the party elite.

Initially, people did not express their disenchantment with the Habyarimana regime through open protest, but rather through a strategy generally called "disengagement."[9] Realizing that the state and the party were exploiting them rather than providing benefits, people sought to limit their contact with state and party structures and to instead organize other alternatives for social and economic life. In the 1980s, various groups that were outside the auspices of the party and state began to proliferate. Most of the associations, such as women's groups, rotating credit societies, basic Christian communities, and farmers' cooperatives, served both economic and social purposes, seeking to compensate for the declining economic conditions, but also providing a social network of support.[10] Many of the groups emerged out of the churches, and several national organizations were set up to provide networking and support to the local groups. Duterembere, a national women's organization, provided loans and training to women's groups throughout the country, while IWACU (a Kinyarwanda word meaning "Our Place"), a national center for cooperatives, offered support to cooperatives of various sorts.

Research conducted in 1992–1993 suggests that this expansion of social organization, while not overtly political (i.e., not focused on the state), provided the population relief from the totalizing project of the party-state and its attempt to control every aspect of social, political, and economic life. While the organizations were not universally empowering, they did create a greater range of options and offered the space and free-dom necessary to formulate challenges to the existing hegemonic system. What Robert Fatton has observed for Africa generally clearly applies to Rwanda: "aware of civil society's revolutionary potential, Africans are dis-covering or rediscovering ways of keeping private what they wish out of the predatory reach of the state. They are creating a reinvigorated civil soci-ety, space that seeks to resist the intrusion of the state."[11]

Rwandan civil society can be characterized as increasingly "strong" because of the rapidly multiplying number of organizations, through which a substantial portion of the population enjoyed increasing access to resources, and that operated with growing independence from established power structures. Civil society in Rwanda offered possibilities for sectors of the population that had been excluded from and exploited by the party-state system, such as women, farmers, and the urban poor, to defend both their material and ideological interests. I want to be clear in rejecting a romantic image of civil society as the gallant defender of the downtrodden against a rapacious state, since some associations were controlled by the same people who benefited from state power. Nevertheless, civil society in Rwanda represented a more permeable space where, in comparison to the state sphere, a wider range of social sectors and interests could gain access and benefits and eventually formulate political programs.[12]

This research also suggests that many of these economic and social organizations provided support for more overtly political activity and asso-ciations. In 1988, the Catholic newspaper *Kinyamateka* began to flout the rules of state censorship, publishing open discussions about the economic problems of the country and the corruption of state officials. In the next two years, a flurry of new publications appeared, some supportive of the gov-ernment, others critical, but all of them representing a blossoming of inde-pendent public discourse. By late 1989, Rwandans began to openly discuss democratization and political reform. One informal group of intellectuals, which included the leaders of many social organizations, issued a letter in September 1990 demanding a national conference. Several human rights groups were formed in 1990, involving many members of other social orga-nizations. In the following years, a number of groups that had previously focused on social or economic issues took on more clearly political activi-ties. For example, in 1992, IWACU began to provide civic education to prepare the population for a transition to democracy and founded a new publication, *IMABGA,* that discussed political issues affecting farmers.

The increase in social, economic, and political activity outside the aus-pices of the single political party both reflected and, by giving form and direction to previously inchoate sentiments, further inspired public discontent with the Habyarimana regime and, more broadly, with the structures of the state. The alternative support structures and greater personal freedom provided by the expansion of associational life allowed people to challenge exploitation and injustice in ways that would not previously have been possible. Intellectuals and those with the necessary resources often formed explicitly political groups. Most Rwandans, however, expressed dissent through numerous modes of protest—for instance, refusing to pay MRND membership dues, participate in *umuganda* and *animation,* pay taxes, or show deference to officials. These protests were generally spontaneous and unorganized, and some were clearly destructive—such as the burning of communal forests or forests planted by *umuganda,* which were ostensibly intended for public use, but were actually used to benefit government officials. But these protests, as much as the formal organization of opposition groups at the national level, reflected the opening of Rwandan society.

The declining legitimacy of the regime, decreasing compliance with state directives, increasing criticism of state officials and practices, and growing formal and informal protest placed pressures on the Habyarimana regime to consider the possibility of political reform. In July 1990, President Habyarimana announced that he would appoint a commission to propose reforms to the political system, and he encouraged open public discussion of the form these changes should take. These promises fell far short of meeting the demands for a sovereign national conference similar to those held in Benin and Congo, and they were greeted by many community leaders with skepticism and criticism. Nevertheless, Habyarimana appointed a National Commission of Synthesis in September 1990, composed of political, religious, and intellectual leaders. The commission presented its proposals in early 1991, and in June of the same year, a new constitution was adopted that created a post of prime minister, guaranteed increased personal liberties, and ended the MRND's monopoly on power.

Following the adoption of the new constitution and a new party law, a number of political parties emerged. Three of the new parties gained substantial support through a regional or ethnic appeal: the Democratic and Republican Movement (MDR) appealed to independence President Grégoire Kayibanda's base of support among Hutu in the center of the country; the Social Democratic Party (PSD) appealed to both Hutu and Tutsi in the far south of Rwanda; and the Liberal Party (PL) appealed to Tutsi throughout the country. The MRND drew its support from Hutu in the north, Habyarimana's home region. The new parties added their voices to demands for political reform, organizing protests against the formation in late 1991 of a government under an MRND prime minister. In March 1992, in negotiations sponsored by Christian church leaders, Habyarimana accepted the formation of a new "government of transition" with an opposition prime minister and ministries divided between the MRND and opposition parties.

One other important factor that placed pressures on the Habyarimana regime while also creating possibilities for the president and his supporters to solidify their hold on power was the war that had been launched in October 1990 by the RPF, a rebel army composed primarily of Tutsi refugees who had fled political violence in the country in the 1960s and 1970s. While the initial RPF assault was rebuffed fairly quickly, attacks in January 1991, June 1992, and February 1993 reached deep into Rwandan territory and demonstrated the capacities of the RPF. The RPF's two main demands were that refugees be given the right to return to Rwanda and that a democratic government be introduced, thus adding to the reformist pressures on the regime. At the same time, the war was used to justify a massive expansion of the Rwandan army, which was made possible by the assistance of the international community, thus greatly increasing the coercive instruments available to the state.

The combined pressures for reform placed on the state by civil society, the new parties, and the RPF generated considerable optimism that Rwanda could follow the path of Benin, Zambia, and several other African states by pursuing a peaceful democratic transition. Western scholars who visited Rwanda in early 1992 during the period of negotiations for the multiparty government came away hopeful that serious reforms were under way.[13] The population seemed to believe that elections would soon be held and that Habyarimana would be removed from office.

Explaining the Failure of Civil Society

The question that now confronts us is why Rwanda's political evolution followed quite a different trajectory from the optimistic future that seemed possible in early 1992. Why, despite the strengthening of civil society and the opening up of political competition, were elections never held and Habyarimana not forced from office? Why, instead of a democratic transition, did Rwanda experience a terrible bloodbath, arguably one of the greatest human tragedies of the twentieth century? Five primary factors can be identified that frustrated hopes for a peaceful democratic transition.

The Discontinuity Between Civil and Political Societies

Democratic reform efforts failed in Rwanda primarily due to the nature of the state and the regime, but some characteristics of Rwandan civil society also undermined the ability of the supporters of reform to force the government to accept meaningful change. Most important, society's capacity to effectively challenge the state was compromised by the discontinuity that existed between civil society and political society. Although an expanding civil society helped to force the state to legalize political party competition, the new parties that emerged had little connection to civil society. The parties did not attempt to appeal to the sectoral interests that served as the organizing principles of civil society, such as farmers, women, and the urban poor. Instead, they appealed to people largely on the basis of regional and ethnic identities. While it is important to have an independent civil society that is not subsumed within political parties, the nearly complete lack of connection between civil and political societies in Rwanda served to undermine the strength of both vis-à-vis the state. The parties did not represent the interests of civil society organizations, and civil society did not organize support for the parties.

Political society was further limited by the fact that few of the leaders of women's, human rights, farmers', or other organizations in civil society became visibly involved in the new parties. Instead, most of the leaders of the new parties were people who had previously been involved in either the Kayibanda or Habyarimana regimes. (In fact, the MDR took the name of Kayibanda's former party, symbolizing continuity with the First Republic.) As such, the party leaders were tainted by association and were viewed as what Fatton has called "the old guard, the 'dinosaurs'" who "abruptly discover that they are after all good democrats."[14] Many Rwandans suspected that the new parties and opposition politicians offered nothing new and that if they gained office, they would act much like their predecessors, although perhaps favoring a different region or ethnic group. This severely limited both their support and their ability to advocate reform effectively.

The Coalition Government

In retrospect, the greatest strategic mistake that the opposition political parties made was the decision to participate in the coalition government. After the MRND relinquished its political monopoly in July 1991, the three main opposition parties that emerged formed a working coalition. One of their chief demands was that President Habyarimana create a multiparty government with a member of an opposition party in the newly created post of prime minister. The opposition parties believed that placing one of their own in office would force Habyarimana to follow through on his promise to hold presidential and parliamentary elections and would guarantee that the elections would be free and fair. The opposition coalition therefore lobbied hard for inclusion in the government, organizing a number of protest rallies, particularly after Habyarimana named an MRND prime minister in December 1991. In March 1992, Habyarimana acceded to opposition demands and named a "government of transition" under MDR leader Dismas Nsengiyaremye, with cabinet posts evenly split between supporters and opponents of the president.

While naming the transition government initially seemed to be a major concession on the part of President Habyarimana, in fact he was able to exploit the situation. Habyarimana retained strict control of real power, making the opposition ministers little more than figureheads, yet by including the MDR, the PSD, and the PL in the government, he effectively removed their primary grounds for appealing for popular support: their ability to represent an alternative to the regime. The "opposition" parties still lacked real power, but they were now identified with the regime and shared the blame for the government's failures. Habyarimana was able to undermine them by charging them with responsibility for such problems as the continuation of the war, rising crime rates, and declining economic conditions. Thus, rather than providing them with leverage to push for a democratic transition, entering the government proved to be a major miscalculation for the opposition parties.[15]

The Expansion of State Coercive Capabilities

The factors that contributed most significantly to the failure to achieve a democratic transition in Rwanda arose from the continuing strength of the state. Although the expanded civil society empowered the population and undermined the legitimacy of the Habyarimana regime, the War of October led to military expansion, thus creating opportunities for Habyarimana to reconfigure the basis of his authority. In every society, political authority rests on some combination of legitimacy and coercion. Given the declining public support for his regime beginning in the late 1980s, Habyarimana was forced to rely increasingly on coercion to maintain power.

Under ordinary circumstances, the government's ability to rely on coercion to guarantee its power would have been constrained by the expense, its limited access to arms, and the danger of provoking counter-violence. After the RPF's invasion in October 1990, however, Habyarimana was able to appeal to the international community for military assistance. Within six months, the Armed Forces of Rwanda (FAR) had increased from around 6,000 troops to more than 30,000, and both light and heavy arms poured into Rwanda from South Africa, Egypt, and France.[16]

The Rwandan state used this expanded military power not only to defend itself against foreign invasion, but also to control internal dissent. Despite the limited success of the initial RPF assault, the government used the invasion as an excuse to arrest thousands of prominent Tutsi and southern Hutu, the two groups that provided the greatest opposition to the regime. The arrests began after bombs were heard in Kigali on the night of October 4, 1990, in an incident that has since been shown to have been a staged attack by FAR itself that was specifically intended to justify a crackdown on "internal enemies." While most of the prisoners arrested at this time were released within a year, the regime continued to use the military and police to control the population and limit dissent. Roadblocks were established on all major highways, and soldiers were stationed throughout the country. Known opponents of the regime regularly faced harassment, including arrests, threats, and assassination attempts. These sorts of attacks sharply increased following the establishment of the transition government in early 1992, and they continued until the genocide.[17] The Rwandan state lost much of its legitimacy, and the voluntary obedience of the population could no longer be expected, but the expanded coercive capacity of the state limited the degree to which opposition could be organized despite the expansion of civil society.

The effects of increased coercive force were apparent in an incident that occurred in the commune of Bwakira, one of the communities where I conducted my research. In Bwakira, the vast majority of the residents supported the opposition MDR, but the burgomaster (similar to a mayor) was a member of the MRND. In late 1992, an MDR rally in the commune culminated in a march to the burgomaster's office and an attempt to remove him physically from office. The burgomaster was forced to wear an MDR cap and to march with the crowd to the seat of the subprefecture, Birambo. Following this event, the government sent a contingent of troops to provide the burgomaster around-the-clock protection. Wherever he went after this, he was accompanied by three or four soldiers who guaranteed his safety and ensured that he received the respect he demanded. The presence of these soldiers had a chilling effect on the commune, and following their arrival, few incidents of open resistance occurred. Had the expansion of the national military not taken place, troops would certainly not have been available for such a remote and strategically insignificant community. These soldiers later played an important role in supporting the genocide in the commune.

The Organization of Chaos

In addition to their increasing resort to coercion to protect their power, Habyarimana and his supporters sought to undercut the opposition and regain legitimacy through a strategy that I call the "organization of chaos." Beginning with the formation of the multiparty government in 1992, Habyarimana's supporters began to sow disorder in society. The Interahamwe, the youth militia of the MRND, and the Coalition for the Defense of the Republic (CDR), an extreme Hutu ethnonationalist party allied with the MRND, disrupted rallies by the opposition political parties, blocking traffic and starting fights. They also actively harassed opposition politicians and other critics of the government.

In addition to these focused and more obviously political attacks, the Interahamwe, the CDR, and the military were also involved in a growing number of criminal acts. Beginning as early as 1991, Rwanda experienced a substantial increase in crime, particularly robberies and rapes. Though this can in part be attributed to declining respect for the law arising from public alienation from the state, the evidence clearly points to substantial involvement by supporters of the regime. In numerous cases where soldiers were involved in crimes, the authorities made no attempt to find and punish those responsible. In fact, it is clear that authorities not only made no attempt to stop the upsurge in crime despite the expanded police and military forces, but in some cases they actively encouraged it. In addition, following the installation of the transition government, bomb attacks began to occur throughout the country, sometimes in public places such as a nightclub in Kigali and the Butare market. Whereas the government attributed these attacks to the RPF, the opposition parties claimed, with apparent reason, that many of the bombs were actually planted by supporters of the regime who were hoping to create a sense of insecurity.

Another example that illustrates the government's lack of reaction to the declining security situation involved a gang of unemployed youths that had been terrorizing another community I studied, robbing people and harassing women. In one instance, they ambushed a group of merchants returning from market, stole their goods and money, and gang-raped a young woman who had gone to the market to purchase items for her wedding later in the week. The prefectural authorities did not send police to investigate until three days later, and then not in response to the robberies and rape, but rather in response to the killing of three of the gang members by a posse that the community formed because of their frustration with the government's lack of response.

Organizing chaos in this fashion, by tolerating or even actively encouraging criminal activity and political violence, served the interests of the regime in several ways. First, it undercut support for the opposition parties. The expansion of criminal and political violence created a mounting sense of insecurity within the population. Since this occurred after the return to multiparty politics in 1991 and the installation of the transition government, the opposition parties—and multipartyism more generally—were held responsible for the deteriorating situation. Although the MRND retained all of the powerful positions in the government, and the formal powers that opposition ministers should have been able to exercise were in fact stymied by the regime's supporters, many people still attributed the rise in insecurity to the advent of multiparty politics. A few quotes from my interviews in 1992–1993 indicate how the increased insecurity made it more difficult for the opposition parties to gain support:

> Me, I don't like politics, because some profit from it to get revenge or to enrich themselves, without really having a true program. Here it is three years that people have been killing each other, that hatred has been sown between ethnic groups and regions. So if this is democracy, I am against it.

> I am completely against people who sow war between innocents to have
> the means to become governors. They ought to think about our peace if
> they are truly struggling for us as they say in their meetings. We are wait-
> ing for someone who will bring governing back to us. Changes or no
> changes, for us poor peasants, it's the same thing.

> All these changes are just aimed at helping a small group. Multipartyism
> is nothing but criminality, people killing one another. . . . I don't want to
> join any party. The multiparty government is nothing but conflict.

In addition to discrediting the opposition, the increased insecurity also created nostalgia for single-party authoritarian rule. Many of the people interviewed in late 1992 and early 1993 in the center and south of the country,
supposedly the hotbeds of opposition, said that they were afraid of what
was happening in the country and would support Habyarimana if elections
were held.

Ethnicity and Co-optation

Another effective means that the Habyarimana regime used both to attract
support and to undercut the opposition was the encouragement of ethnic
divisions. As political life in Rwanda was liberalized in the early 1990s,
members of the Tutsi ethnic group came to be identified almost entirely
with the opposition to the regime. The Tutsi had been virtually excluded
from administrative posts under Habyarimana, and the ethnic quota system
that Habyarimana implemented shortly after his coup seriously limited
their access to education. While many Hutu credited Habyarimana with
bringing Rwanda's ethnic conflict under control, the Tutsi felt that his policies had relegated them to second-class citizenship.

When the RPF invaded Rwanda in October 1990, it attempted to present itself as a multiethnic coalition seeking to overthrow the autocratic
Habyarimana regime and support a democratic transition. However, since
the overwhelming majority of RPF soldiers were Tutsi exiles, many of
whom had served in Yoweri Museveni's National Resistance Movement in
Uganda, the Rwandan government had little difficulty characterizing the
RPF as a Tutsi movement determined to reestablish the Tutsi hegemony
over social, political, and economic life that had existed during the colonial
period.

The scapegoating of Tutsi began immediately after the invasion. Tutsi
counted disproportionately among those arrested at the beginning of the
war, and in several northern prefectures, where Habyarimana was strongly
supported, ethnic massacres took place in late 1990 and early 1991. Over
the next several years, massacres occurred repeatedly in northern Rwanda
and periodically in other parts of the country. Though these massacres were
made to appear to be spontaneous actions taken by local citizens angry over

the war and driven by hatred of Tutsi, an international human rights commission that conducted investigations in January 1993 found clear evidence that each of the massacres was initiated by government or military officials and, at least in several cases, with the direct permission of the president.[18]

The massacres, combined with increasingly anti-Tutsi rhetoric in government newspapers and on Radio Rwanda (the primary source of news for most of the population), served to augment ethnic tensions. It was clear from the interviews I conducted that most ordinary Hutu in Rwanda in the early 1990s felt no innate hatred of their Tutsi neighbors. They lived together in the same communities, attended the same churches, and frequently intermarried. However, the propaganda promulgated by the regime and its supporters raised fears in people, whose access to other sources of information was limited, that the Tutsi were in fact intent on retaking power, an accusation given credence by the RPF's regular attacks on the country. The use of ethnic rhetoric helped to redirect public attention away from corruption and exploitation by those in power, who were Hutu, and toward the threat of a new Tutsi hegemony. As a result, the Tutsi I interviewed were already extremely worried about their safety by late 1992.

The Habyarimana regime also used ethnicity effectively to undercut the opposition parties. Once negotiations began with the RPF in Arusha in 1992, the MRND promoted itself as the champion of Hutu interests, while characterizing the opposition parties as pro-RPF, ready to sell out the interests of the Hutu masses. The opposition parties involved in the transition government headed the government's negotiation team. While the MRND representatives would sign agreements in Arusha, back in Rwanda, Habyarimana and other MRND leaders would make a great show of rejecting the settlements as unfair to the Hutu.

Building on ethnic arguments, Habyarimana's supporters were eventually able to foment division within each of the opposition parties. In August 1993, the Arusha Accords were signed, setting up a program for transition to a multiparty, democratic government. Several provisions of the Arusha Accords were clearly unacceptable to many Hutu in the country, such as the integration of RPF soldiers into FAR on a one-to-one basis and the granting of sensitive ministries to the RPF. Following the signing of the accords, each of the opposition parties split into two factions, one that supported the accords, such as MDR-Twagirayezu, and one that opposed them, such as MDR-Power. Because of these divisions, the new MDR prime minister, Agathe Uwilingiyimana, was unable to form a government, thus allowing Habyarimana's supporters to roll back the few political gains made by the opposition.

Eventually, the parties opposed to the accords formed a bloc that came to be known as "PAWA," from the English word "power," a reference to Hutu Power. This development greatly expanded Habyarimana's base of support. While some communities in the south and center of the country remained firmly in opposition, many others were divided. In a number of cases, the government was able to maneuver members of PAWA who had substantial local public support into political positions in areas that had formerly been dominated by the opposition; these leaders were then able to use their positions to organize support for the regime. For example, in Nyakizu commune on the Burundi border, the MRND was almost entirely absent by 1993, and political support was divided between the PSD and the MDR. After the emergence of PAWA, the local MDR leader joined the MDR-Power faction, and through intimidation, he managed to win election as burgomaster. He then became a strong ally of Habyarimana and silenced most opposition. In April 1994, he was the chief organizer of the genocide in the area, and among the first persons he targeted were four moderate Hutu public officials, including the local head of the PSD.

Genocide as Resistance to Transition

This strategy of using ethnicity as a wedge to divide the opposition and attract public support ultimately culminated in the genocide that began on April 7, 1994. As early as 1992, the Interahamwe was being transformed into a militia via ideological training and instruction on how to fire guns and throw grenades. After the Arusha Accords, the training of the militia was greatly expanded, and weapons were distributed to the general population. The non-PAWA parties had no comparable militia, and the growth of these pro-government militia severely stifled expressions of dissent. After several years of political opening, in 1993 and early 1994, Rwanda experienced a political closing.

It is not clear exactly when the plan for a genocide was developed, but it appears that it was drawn up by January 1994. While the militias were not initially formed specifically for genocide, they were easily adapted to that purpose. A group of extreme Hutu ethnonationalists formed an independent radio station in late 1993, Radio-Télévision Libre des Milles Collines (RTLM), which broadcast regular anti-Tutsi diatribes and denounced prominent Hutu moderates, such as Monique Mujawamaliya, the founder of the Association Rwandaise pour la Défense de la Personne et des Libertés Publiques, an outspoken human rights group, and André Sibomana, the editor of the Catholic newspaper *Kinyamateka*. By the time Habyarimana's plane was shot down, lists of prominent people to be targeted had already been compiled. These lists included both opposition politicians and leaders of social organizations, like Mujawamaliya and Sibomana (both of whom escaped, though many other human rights activists, moderate priests, and peasant organizers were killed).

Aside from a few small incidents in Gikongoro and Kibuye, the violence was contained in Kigali for the first few days, as soldiers and the

Presidential Guard systematically hunted down the people on their lists. When it became obvious that the international community was not going to intervene, the killing spread outside the capital. The network of PAWA supporters and the militias was put into motion. In each community, the homes of Tutsi and a few Hutu moderates were pillaged and burned, some people were killed, and others fled to churches, schools, and communal offices for sanctuary. The research I conducted in 1995–1996 in Butare, Gikongoro, and Kibuye demonstrated that local officials actively encouraged Tutsi to gather in central locations with promises of protection, even after massacres had already begun to take place in other such "sanctuaries." In Nyakizu, for example, the burgomaster organized a massacre along the Burundi border on April 13, cutting off a route of escape from the country. Then, on April 14, he traveled through the countryside urging Tutsi to come to Cyahinda Catholic parish, where they were systematically slaughtered beginning that afternoon.[19] In many communities, soldiers or police who were ostensibly brought in to protect the refugees in reality helped to organize their massacre. Following the large-scale massacres, communities organized patrols to seek out those Tutsi who had escaped. National and regional officials visited many communities in the following weeks to make certain that the genocide had been carried out completely, since in some places, Tutsi women and children had been spared, especially those from mixed marriages.

Local officials and militias organized their communities to participate in the killings. In many communities, a few moderate Hutu were killed in the early phases of the slaughter, sending a clear message to other Hutu that they should participate or face severe consequences. Even so, many Hutu refused to participate, and many hid Tutsi in their homes or helped them escape. Other Hutu did join in the groups that attacked the churches, motivated in part by fear of reprisal and in part by fear and hatred of the Tutsi.

Meanwhile, with so much attention focused on internal "enemies," the Rwandan army was not capable of responding effectively to renewed attacks by the RPF. The RPF quickly swept through eastern Rwanda and soon laid siege to the capital. By early July, when Kigali fell, FAR had run out of ammunition and was being routed. In mid-July, the government, the army, and more than one million citizens fled into exile in Zaire, while another million fled into Tanzania.

Implications of the Rwandan Case

The genocide in Rwanda did not occur because a decline in state power released primordial divisions within Rwandan society. Instead, the genocide was organized by state officials and their allies and was carried out using the instruments of the state. Genocide was possible both because of the increased coercive capacity of the state and because the bureaucratic mechanisms of the state remained functional. Without an effective and functioning institutional structure, the genocide would never have been possible.[20] The genocide thus reflected state strength, not weakness.

The political parties did prove vulnerable to ethnic divisions, but most of civil society remained largely resistant to these pressures. While most Catholic and Protestant churches were divided between supporters and opponents of the regime, the human rights groups, IWACU, women's groups, and others remained multiethnic and refused to support the anti-Tutsi hysteria. Far from being caught up in the rhetorical and institutional preparations for genocide, many local organizations, including those that, according to Chazan, "do not encourage an interest in matters beyond their own immediate concerns,"[21] continued to champion interethnic cooperation. It is thus my contention that a broad definition of civil society is more appropriate for explaining the reality of changing social, political, and economic structures in Africa.

What made the genocide and the extinguishing of civil society possible in Rwanda was, at the most basic level, the War of October. The RPF's attacks on Rwanda allowed the Habyarimana regime to appeal to the international community (particularly France) for military assistance. With expanded weaponry and military personnel, the regime was able to monitor and control the population more effectively, organize political and criminal violence, and, ultimately, carry out the genocide. The war also provided substantial rhetorical resources for the regime, since claiming that the Tutsi wanted to take over the country was a compelling argument when a predominantly Tutsi army was attacking the country's borders. Though much of the fear encouraged by this pro-regime propaganda was unfounded, my research has indicated that there were, in fact, RPF agents in many communities. Most Tutsi were sympathetic to the RPF, and some young Tutsi men who remained in Rwanda had received training from the RPF. There was just enough truth in the accusations of the RTLM and other state organs to lend credence to their unfounded claims as well. I am convinced that without the war and the opportunities it presented to Habyarimana and his supporters, civil and political society in Rwanda would have been capable of forcing real changes on the state, quite possibly bringing about a democratic transition.

In postgenocide Rwanda, the RPF-dominated government has been careful to prevent an independent civil society from reemerging. The government has actively sought to place its allies in charge of all important social organizations. The government has intervened in the selection of church leaders, in one case using troops to install its candidate as president of the Free Methodist Church. RPF soldiers and others have harassed prominent moderate Hutu, such as Sibomana and Mujawamaliya, accusing them of involvement in the genocide—an ironic accusation since they were themselves targets. The government fears that these moderates, who previously supported a democratic transition, could have substantial appeal among the Hutu masses. Believing that they can count on only Tutsi for support, the new regime feels insecure, since Tutsi comprise only a small portion of the population. As a combined result of the genocide and the attacks by the current regime, civil society in Rwanda has substantially declined, with many organizations having dissolved altogether, slumped into inactivity, or been brought fully under state control.

The Rwandan case should raise serious concerns about the impact of armed conflicts on democratic transitions. The success of rebel movements in Rwanda and, recently, Zaire may inspire other prospective rulers to take up arms and appeal to public support by claiming to struggle for democracy. But the War of October, rather than promoting democracy, strengthened the state and undermined the efforts of civil and political society. The authoritarian behavior of the RPF since taking office also suggests that the claims by its leaders that they are committed to democracy are less than sincere, and that their real goal is attaining power.

Appendix 18.1
Chronology of Rwanda's Recent Political History

1959	Hutu attacks on Tutsi colonial officials drive thousands of Tutsi into exile and lead to a transfer of political control to the Hutu majority.
1962	Rwanda gains independence with an almost entirely Hutu government under President Grégoire Kayibanda, from the central region of the country.
1973	Kayibanda is removed from office in a coup d'état and replaced by military chief Juvénal Habyarimana, from northern Rwanda.
1975	Habyarimana creates the MRND as the sole legal political party in which all Rwandans are members.
July 1990	President Habyarimana announces that he will implement political reforms and welcomes open political debate.
Sept. 1990	A visit to Rwanda by Pope John Paul II bolsters democracy activists. Habyarimana names a National Commission of Synthesis to draft a new constitution.

Oct. 1990	Forces of the RPF invade northeastern Rwanda. Thousands of prominent Tutsi and Hutu dissidents are arrested. The first massacres of Tutsi in 20 years occur in northern Rwanda.
June 1991	A new constitution is implemented, and the MRND cedes its political monopoly. A number of new parties are quickly founded and registered.
Dec. 1991	Habyarimana names a prime minister from the MRND, prompting massive protests from the opposition parties.
March 1992	A multiparty transition government takes power under Prime Minister Dismas Nsengiyaremye from the MDR and is charged with negotiating an end to the war with the RPF and preparing for a democratic transition. Shortly thereafter, security conditions begin to deteriorate as a number of bombings occur throughout the country.
Jan. 1993	Major massacres of Tutsi in the northwest prompt a massive RPF attack, resulting in the RPF's capture of a large area along the Uganda border.
Aug. 1993	The Arusha Accords that officially end the War of October call for a new multiparty government that includes RPF ministers and a one-for-one integration of RPF soldiers into the Rwandan army. Many Hutu activists reject the accords as a negotiated defeat and begin to plot resistance.
Dec. 1993	The Catholic bishop of Nyundo warns that Hutu civilian militia are being given military training and that arms are being distributed to the population.
April 1994	Following the death of President Habyarimana in a mysterious plane crash, his allies launch attacks on their political enemies. This quickly expands into a genocide against Rwanda's Tutsi population, leading to as many as one million deaths and reigniting the war with the RPF.
July 1994	The Rwandan army and government flee into Zaire with more than one million refugees as the RPF takes control of Rwanda.

Notes

This chapter is based substantially upon field research conducted in Rwanda in 1992–1993 under the auspices of the Institut de Recherche Scientifique et Technologique in Butare, with funding from the Graduate School of the University of Wisconsin-Madison and the General Fund of the Board of Higher Education of the Christian Church (Disciples of Christ). Additional field research was conducted under the auspices of Human Rights Watch/Africa and the Féderation Internationale des Ligues de Droits de l'Homme (FIDH) in 1995–1996.

1. Monga, *Anthropology of Anger*, p. 152.

2. R. Kaplan, "Coming Anarchy."

3. Migdal, *Strong Societies.*

4. See, for example, Ake, "Rethinking African Democracy"; Chazan, "Africa's Democratic Challenge"; Pelzynski, "Solidarity"; and Monga, *Anthropology of Anger.*

5. Chazan, "Africa's Democratic Challenge," p. 283.

6. I have made this case more fully in Longman, "Chaos from Above."

7. Lemarchand, *Rwanda and Burundi,* is the best discussion of Rwanda's transition to democracy and early independence years.

8. Reyntjens, *Pouvoir.*

9. Azarya and Chazan, "Disengagement from the State"; Chazan, "Patterns of State-Society Incorporation."

10. For example, one rotating credit society I visited near Ruhengeri on Rwanda's border with Uganda and Zaire held a monthly meeting in a local bar. While the ostensible purpose of the meeting was to distribute funds to that month's recipient, the meeting went on for several hours, and copious amounts of alcohol were consumed. This meeting was an important social event for the 20 or so members.

11. Fatton, *Predatory Rule,* p. 6.

12. I remain intentionally vague in defining "civil society," respecting Monga's claim that "any attempt to define the forces rather hastily grouped together under the label 'civil society' appears problematic and doomed to failure." In leaving the term vague, I am hoping to include a broad range of social action and organization, rejecting the narrow notions of civil society supported by many scholars who seek to limit inclusion in civil society to only those groups that focus on the state and on broad, national issues. From my research, this distinction is an artificial construct that does not represent the complexities and ambiguities of actual social existence.

13. Based on personal conversations in 1992 and 1993.

14. Fatton, *Predatory Rule,* p. 110.

15. See Linda Beck's contribution to this volume (Chapter 11), in which she contends that the effectiveness of opposition parties in Senegal has been compromised by their participation in coalition government.

16. For detailed information regarding this military expansion, see Human Rights Watch Arms Project, "Arming Rwanda."

17. Africa Watch, "Beyond the Rhetoric"; FIDH et al., "Rapport de la Commission Internationale"; and Association Rwandaise pour la Défense de la Personne et des Libertés Publiques, *Rapport sur les Droits de l'Homme.*

18. FIDH et al., "Rapport de la Commission Internationale."

19. The case of Nyakizu, along with several other cases, are discussed in great detail in an extensive report forthcoming from Human Rights Watch/Africa and the FIDH.

20. An extensive paper record to which I gained access in government archives while conducting research in 1995–1996 for Human Rights Watch and the FIDH demonstrates a remarkable degree of bureaucratic efficiency even as the government was being driven out of the country by the RPF. Just days before the flight into Zaire, communal councils continued to meet and minutes of the meetings were

dutifully typed up, letters regarding issues such as distribution of the property of those killed continued to be written in triplicate, and national and regional officials continued to pass written orders to their subordinates.

21. Chazan, "Africa's Democratic Challenge," p. 283.

19

Autocracy, Violence, and Ethnomilitary Rule in Nigeria

RICHARD JOSEPH

Although Nigeria led the way in redemocratization in Africa during the 1970s, two decades later governance was characterized by autocracy, political violence, and ethnomilitary rule.[1] A country that was once a strong voice for the liberation of the continent from colonialism and apartheid became a perennial target of international action to obtain the release of political prisoners, the observance of human rights standards, the reduction of drug trafficking, and the rapid transfer of power to civilians. The military regime of General Sani Abacha was able to withstand these pressures, however, because of Nigeria's strategic importance as the most populous African nation, a major oil exporter, and the possessor of one of the continent's largest armed forces.

Despite its ample resources, the gap between Nigeria's potential and its achievements has steadily widened, as documented by a significant body of literature.[2] Though it had one of the greatest potential among countries that achieved independence in the post–World War II era, Nigeria now exhibits a profound crisis in virtually every dimension of public life.[3] Moreover, the criminalization of state and society in Nigeria has extended to countries to which its people have emigrated. The impressive educational infrastructure constructed at all levels after independence in 1960 has steadily eroded, as have the public transport and health systems.

Nigeria has survived intact as one sovereign nation despite these travails and, in addition, has overcome one of Africa's most devastating wars of secession (1967–1970). Nevertheless, the failure to establish a stable democratic political order since then has deepened Nigeria's predicament as a state and aspirant nation. The political contortions of Nigeria as it has shifted between military and civilian regimes since 1966 are well known.[4] In particular, there are three dates in 1993 that mark the end of the long-held hope that Nigeria would establish a state structure that enjoyed legitimacy and authority and that would, in turn, enhance the sense of nationhood: June 12, June 23, and November 17. On the first date, a presidential election was held in which the unofficial winner, Moshood Abiola, obtained 58.5 percent of the vote and his opponent, Bashir Tofa, 41.5 percent.[5] On the second date, the elections, although adjudged by all independent observers to have been peaceful and fair, were annulled by the military government of Ibrahim Babangida. On the third date, General Sani Abacha, a leading member of several military juntas, pushed aside an interim civilian government and established himself as the most dictatorial ruler Nigeria had ever known.

The traumatic events since these fateful dates have followed inexorably from the victory, against the odds, of Moshood Abiola of the Social Democratic Party, who was elected president on the basis of a different alignment of national forces than had prevailed in each of the previous civilian eras.[6] These events include the cancellation by military fiat of this victory (and the expressed will of the people that it represented), the harsh suppression of all acts of protest against the military regime, and the assumption of power by a ruthless army officer who proceeded to impose yet another "democratic transition" accompanied by extensive human rights abuses and restrictions on civil liberties.[7] The arrest and prolonged detention of numerous journalists, trade unionists, human rights and pro-democracy activists, and former government leaders such as Olusegun Obasanjo; the execution of environmental crusader Ken Saro-Wiwa and his fellow Ogoni militants; and the driving into exile of many prominent citizens including Nobel laureate Wole Soyinka and veteran politician Anthony Enahoro are just some of the more prominent actions of the unprecedented political repression in Nigeria between 1993 and 1998.[8]

A Multilayered Hegemony

There are four tendencies that coalesced to give rise to a multilayered hegemony in late twentieth-century Nigeria: the domination by the military over all civilian political actors and groups; the deepening of the primacy of the northern region in Nigerian politics; the increasingly predatory nature of economic life based on access to and control of state power; and the autocratic nature of military presidentialism.[9] Each of these tendencies will be briefly discussed. Military rule used to be described as an aberration in Nigeria. In fact, it is civilian rule that now merits such a designation, as civilians have governed the country for less than a decade since independence.[10] Moreover, nearly 15 years of unbroken military rule have elapsed since the overthrow of the carefully crafted Second Republic (1979–1983). This long tenure of power already exceeds by two years the 1966–1979 period that began with a devastating war of secession.[11] To retain power, Nigerian military rulers have had to disrupt repeatedly their own transition programs. In the process, the legitimacy crisis of the military-as-government has been superimposed on the many problems of this fragile and now fragmented nation.

In my study of the creation of the Second Republic, I described northern primacy as "a virtual axiom of the country's political life."[12] In 1914, the northern and southern regions were amalgamated by the British, but they continued to be governed separately. As the drive for independence accelerated after World War II, the coexistence of the more populous, Islamic, and educationally disadvantaged northern region in one polity with the more Christianized and educationally advanced southern region was tackled through several constitutional revisions. Following independence in 1960, this issue underlay the turmoil of both civilian and military regimes.[13]

Since 1983, Nigeria has had a succession of northern military leaders: Mohammadu Buhari (1983–1985); Ibrahim Babangida (1985–1993); Sani Abacha (1993–1998); and Abdulsalam Abubaker (since 1998). Because the Nigerian state controls access to the nation's disposable wealth in the form of revenue from petroleum production, the fusion of military and northern hegemony has provoked intense resentment in southern Nigeria toward a system of governance widely viewed as biased, exploitative, and repressive. In April 1990, during an attempted military coup, junior officers put forward the radical proposal that five northern states, dominated by Islamic and traditionalist forces, should simply be excised from the federation. Since 1993, the sentiment that Nigeria should not continue to exist as one entity is no longer an extremist notion, but one that has increasing appeal to southern intellectuals. Rotimi Suberu refers to growing southern paranoia regarding northern political domination reflected in continuing public debates on the revamping of the federation in which regret is openly expressed about the 1914 amalgamation.[14]

The predatory nature of Nigeria's political economy is a subject that has also been extensively examined.[15] The financial scams in which Nigerians have enticed individuals in other countries and the fact that police services in the major industrialized countries have created special units to counter fraudulent behavior by Nigerians are just a few external manifestations of the relentless criminalization of the country's economic life. As Nigeria has become a major transit point in international drug trafficking, the laundering of fortunes from the drug industry and from pilfered public funds generates an immense parallel economy and, with it, the means to finance covert political machinations.[16] When the power accessible to individuals and groups via illicit channels is so extensive, state construction on a legitimate basis becomes highly problematic. In his study of the illegal mining and export of diamonds and other mineral resources in

Sierra Leone, William Reno used the term "shadow state" to refer to the networks and structures that sustain these activities.[17] An indication of the extensive resources available to individuals with access to this shadow state occurred when a commission established by Abacha to try to undermine his predecessor, Babangida, revealed that over U.S.$12 billion of the windfall in petroleum revenues during the 1991 Gulf War could not be accounted for.

The final tendency, the extensive presidentializing of the military system of governance under Babangida, has transformed Nigeria into a more fully patrimonial system, thereby bringing it closer to the mode of governance in other African countries. In my 1987 study, I discussed the "tug" toward patrimonialism in Nigerian politics and argued that prebendalism, based on Max Weber's concept of decentralized patrimonialism, was more helpful in explaining the pursuit of material wealth via the appropriation of state offices. Nestled within various regions of Nigeria, and especially the north, were political units based on loyalty to traditional rulers that more closely corresponded to Weber's idea of patrimonial administration.[18] After two decades of unbroken rule by northern heads of state (beginning with Shehu Shagari, the elected president, in 1979–1983), Nigeria has evolved into more of a neopatrimonial polity in which deference to the authority of the supreme ruler is necessary for gaining appointment to political office and access to wealth-generating opportunities.[19]

Sani Abacha assumed all the powers that Babangida had enjoyed and added to them a more ruthless use of the security services against political opponents and dissidents. It had long been felt by analysts of Nigerian politics that the extreme cultural diversity of the country, the existence of dispersed loci of power in the form of hierarchical traditional institutions, and the vigor of civil society with its modern institutions, professional groups, and an independent press militated against the consolidation of dictatorial rule. Using his considerable political skills, however, Babangida succeeded in constructing a highly personalist and autocratic system in which control was steadily extended over the armed forces, as well as political and civil society. When he was forced to step down in August 1993, waiting in the wings was an individual ready to advance this autocratic project now characterized by military dominance, northern primacy, and privileged access to the nation's oil wealth. To sustain this project, the capacity to use state violence against dissidents was enhanced, and the security services were expanded into more ruthless and reliable instruments of rule.[20]

Authoritarian Renewal: The Regional Dimension

After the Berlin Wall was torn down and a democratic wave swept through Eastern and Central Europe, Africa also experienced a broad drive to demolish political monopolies.[21] That process, however, was paralleled by an equally significant occurrence: the resurgence and renewal of authoritarian systems. These options were anticipated in earlier theoretical formulations: "transitions are delimited, on the one side, by the institution of some form of democracy, the return to some form of authoritarian rule, or the emergence of a revolutionary alternative."[22] In the case of Nigeria, authoritarian renewal and entrenchment have been disguised as redemocratization. Such a distorted process has extended beyond Nigeria's borders and has inspired the country's most sustained diplomatic efforts since the Biafran war.

Before 1990, Nigerian governments had always been reluctant to project the nation's power externally. However, the insurgency in Liberia in December 1989 that led to the removal of the military ruler, Samuel Doe, and the substitution of armed factions for the national state prompted the intervention of regional peacekeeping forces dominated by Nigerian military contingents. After eight years of intermittent conflict and peace negotiations, an elected government was finally established in August 1997 in Liberia under Charles Taylor, who was obliged to accept a strong and continuing Nigerian military presence. The collusion that took place between Nigerian senior officers and leaders of Liberian armed factions for several years in exploiting the country's natural minerals and other spoils of war replicated the economic predation of the Nigerian military at home.[23] The symbiosis of warlordism in Liberia and military dictatorship in Nigeria reached its consummation in an Abacha-Taylor pact reminiscent of the Babangida-Doe alliance of the 1980s.

The emergence of a network of allied military rulers in west Africa has contributed to the containment of democratic forces in the region since the mid-1990s. In March 1996, when Mathieu Kérékou, the former military ruler in Benin, successfully challenged Nicéphore Soglo in a rerun of the 1991 elections in which Kérékou had been defeated, the latter was able to count on direct financial support from his neighbors: Gnassingbé Eyadema in Togo and Sani Abacha in Nigeria. Eyadema overcame a prolonged challenge to his rule and retained power in fraudulent elections in 1993 and 1997. A younger member of this network is General Ibrahim Mainassara Bare of Niger, who overthrew his country's constitutional democracy in January 1996 and then bullied his way to a dubious electoral victory.[24] Bare was able to count on support from Blaise Campaoré in Burkina Faso, who had legitimized his forceful capture of power via boycotted elections in 1991, and on support and advice from Abacha, whom he regularly visited in Abuja, the Nigerian capital.

The convoluted nature of authoritarian renewal in west Africa is also reflected in the political convulsions in The Gambia and Sierra Leone. Nigerian troops had long been stationed in both of these countries prior to the coups that occurred in 1994 and 1997, respectively. By insisting on the restoration of deposed President Ahmad Tejan Kabbah in Sierra Leone, instead of accepting the new military junta (and its subsequent legalization via controlled elections, as in The Gambia), the Abacha regime found itself in the odd position of calling for economic sanctions against the Sierra Leone junta while it was resisting international actions against Nigeria for denying power to an elected president. However hypocritical these external actions may appear, they are consonant with the convoluted logic of military politics within Nigeria and the treatment of democracy in a wholly instrumentalist manner.[25]

Abacha launched a program in October 1995 of transition to civilian rule in Nigeria that was supposed to conclude in 1998 with elected governments at all levels of the federation. However, in local government elections in March 1996, individuals who were critical of the government's strategy found their candidacies peremptorily canceled. The continued arrest of journalists and human rights activists, and the driving into exile of pro-democracy leaders, meant that Nigeria's "democratic transition" was taking place alongside widespread exclusion and intimidation. Even academic seminars on democracy were regularly dispersed by armed soldiers. The five parties that were eventually granted legal status in 1996 sought to outdo one another in their submissiveness to the junta, going so far as to all nominating Abacha as their presidential candidate in 1998. While the Babangida transition program ended in tragedy in 1993, that of Abacha further reduced democracy to pure parody.

In smaller African countries such as Burkina Faso, Cameroon, Togo, and Niger, the head of state can run for office and completely manipulate the process in order to be declared the winner. None of Nigeria's military rulers, however, has ever stood as an electoral candidate, which means that they have always (with the exception of Olusegun Obasanjo in 1979) had to devise reasons to postpone the actual transfer of power. In seeking to manufacture an uncontested electoral victory for himself in 1998, Abacha brought Nigeria to the brink of violent political warfare.[26] However this tragic scenario unfolds, Nigeria will continue to pay a heavy price for the fact that both Abacha and Babangida were never willing to transfer power to a civilian government strong enough, and autonomous enough, to put an end to the hegemonies they represented. Moreover, the people of several west African countries will also continue to have their democratic aspirations thwarted as part of the defensive strategy encouraged by Nigeria's military rulers.[27]

Ethnoregionalism and Military Rule

Students of Nigerian politics must now grapple with the complex ways in which developments since the overthrow of the Second Republic in 1983 have overlaid many unresolved questions about Nigeria's existence as a nation and a state. There have been notable attempts to conceptualize the complex and "unfinished" nature of this polity.[28] In 1973, Ken Post and Michael Vickers described Nigeria as a "conglomerate society" in which "the basic conflict was the mobilization of people not towards some transcending national loyalty but rather towards identification with an intermediate cultural section."[29] They then described the ways in which a "system of rewards" reinforced these political-cultural tendencies.[30] John Paden has continued such explorations in his recent discussion of a "six zone model of political culture in Nigeria": northern emirate states; Borno and its environs in the northeast; middle-belt minorities (between north and south); Yoruba states in the southwest; Igbo states in the southeast; and southern minorities.[31] The comment by a prominent northern intellectual and journalist, Turi Muhammadu, that more fundamental than the political federation is the "cultural federation" of Nigeria is suggestive of the accommodations that are needed to sustain consensual governance among Nigeria's diverse peoples.[32]

The undermining of this cultural federation by the exacerbation of northern hegemony since the collapse of the Second Republic in 1983 has left Nigerians profoundly disoriented regarding the very nature of their country.[33] In an exploration of the overlap between perceptions of political and cultural domination in contemporary Africa, René Lemarchand identifies five types of polities: (1) ethnic or ethnoregional hegemonies; (2) "totalizing" polities; (3) neopatrimonial rulerships; (4) factionalized state systems; and (5) liberalized/transitional polities.[34] Using such a schema, it can be argued that Nigeria's post-1983 military regimes, while avowedly pursuing the creation of type 5 (a liberalized and transitional polity), instead deliberately fostered a combination of 1 and 3: an ethnoregional hegemony and a neopatrimonial autocracy. Yet the Nigerian polity became an even more complicated compound as it included a sixth type missing from Lemarchand's typology: a military system.

The June 12, 1993, election and its aftermath reflect the interplay of these contradictory tendencies: the pursuit of a liberalized polity while strengthening northern hegemony; the development of a civic order alongside military domination; and the construction of a federal state accompanied by autocratic presidentialism. The campaign for a democratic system and civil society in Nigeria, in which universal principles of human rights would be actively fostered, overlapped with resistance to northern political dominance. Southern pro-democracy militants have adopted the expression "the Caliphate" to refer to this multilayered hegemony. The Caliphate of Sokoto was a nineteenth-century theocracy centered in the northwestern state of Sokoto, whose sway over an extensive region via local rulers or emirs covered much of what became the northern region of Nigeria, as well as parts of present-day Benin, Niger, and Cameroon. Although the victorious presidential and vice presidential candidates in the June 12, 1993, elections were both Muslims, and they obtained significant support from all areas of the country including the emirate north, Abiola's ethnic identity as a Yoruba from the southwest was used to portray the election as a contest among cultural sections of the country. The Abacha regime largely succeeded in ethnicizing and regionalizing the pro-democracy struggle, thereby diluting the national significance of Abiola's victory.

A subplot of Nigeria's national political drama has been the political mobilization of the Ogoni people in the southeastern riverine area since 1989 to protest the environmental degradation caused by petroleum production and to demand a greater share by local communities in the wealth generated by this production. This initially localized conflict exploded into a vigorous challenge to the very structure of the Nigerian federation and its prevailing multilayered hegemony.[35] Although the Ogoni numbered only half a million in a country of approximately 100 million citizens, the full force of the military government was mustered against Ogoni dissidents in a brutal campaign of repression. The increasing militancy of the Ogoni movement was also encouraged by the support it attracted externally from the Working Group on Indigenous Peoples in Geneva, from the General Assembly of the Unrepresented Nations and Peoples Organization in The Hague, and from specialized agencies of the United Nations.

The Ogoni demanded self-determination for Nigeria's ethnic communities and the transformation of the highly centralized federation into a confederation in which each constituent group would control the greater part of the revenues generated in its area.[36] During the first half of 1993, a virtual uprising of sections of the Ogoni against the Nigerian state culminated in the appeal by the Movement for the Survival of the Ogoni People for a boycott of the presidential elections of June 1993. Ogoni militancy therefore became a component of the general challenge by southerners who saw "restructuring toward an ethnic confederation or variants of regional autonomy as the answer to present political and economic inequalities."[37] They argued that the structure of the federation, transformed by prolonged military rule into a virtual centralized system, facilitated the appropriation of disproportionate public revenues by a hegemonic regional group.

Ogoni militants perceived the Nigerian state as reflecting a tight circle of causation: oil wealth financed a federal structure, controlled in turn by specific communities, whose representatives were able to determine public policy and allocate national resources to maintain their material advantages and political sway. To end this multilayered hegemony, they contended, the federal structure had to be radically reformed. The execution of nine Ogoni leaders on November 10, 1993, was a grim message from the Abacha regime to all its opponents that such challenges were considered treasonous and would be firmly crushed despite international condemnation. The Ogoni struggle starkly illuminates the interwoven nature of the hegemonic forces in contemporary Nigeria. In addition to the dilapidation of their communal lands from oil production, the Ogoni have paid a huge price for provoking the Abacha regime into displaying how much violence it is prepared to unleash to protect autocracy and ethnomilitary rule.

Derailing Democracy by Threatening Disintegration

Since African countries have widely differing endowments in the cultural composition of their societies, the level of force and the extent of electoral machinations needed to overcome challenges to resurgent authoritarian regimes vary greatly. The essential elements of this scenario, however, appear remarkably consistent across a spectrum of countries: "rulers who resist democratization, whether in Cameroon, Kenya, Togo or Zaire, have a weapon more powerful than all their military armaments, namely tying the fate of their own ethnic group or region to the survival of the regime."[38] It is remarkable how readily political leaders in northern Nigeria, except for a handful of radical and independent thinkers, supported the Babangida government's cancellation of Abiola's electoral victory in 1993. More important to them than adherence to democratic principles, or the turmoil in the country that would result from this decision, was the need to counter what was viewed as a threat to a Nigerian polity that guaranteed northern dominance. The election of a southern president, even one who was a Muslim and a close associate of many northern civic, religious, and military leaders, proved unacceptable. Even when the Nigerian people were prepared, therefore, to take a step outside "the ethnic trap," the social forces in command of the state refused to allow such an evolution to occur.[39]

As disenchantment increased in Nigeria with each postponement of the date for the transfer of power under Babangida, demands mounted for a national conference to revisit a range of constitutional issues, including the structure of the federation. Suberu quotes Bolaji Akinyemi, a former Nigerian minister of external affairs, as saying that if a sovereign national conference had been convened in the mid-1990s, it would have voted "for the dissolution of the Nigerian entity."[40] Eghosa Osaghae concurs: "a national conference appears to be an invitation to a possible dissolution or division of the country."[41] During the remarkable debates that preceded the creation of the Second Republic in 1979, the need to find creative ways to strengthen both national consciousness and state legitimacy was reflected in a number of official documents. In its final report, the Constitution Drafting Committee of 1976 declared: "the State shall foster a feeling of belonging and of involvement among the various sections of the country to the end that loyalty to the nation shall override sectional loyalties." After the republic collapsed seven years later, Sylvester Whitaker acknowledged that little progress had in fact been made in the pursuit of these objectives:

"despite the dreams of dedicated Nigerian nationalists, national institutions and identity today exercise less of a hold on popular sentiment than at any time since the nation's founding."[42]

While discussing the deepening political predicament of Nigeria as a nation-state in 1987, I identified three possible courses of action. Nigeria could

> (1) continue to search for a fully pluralistic democracy, only to find that the vessel of the nation-state cannot sustain the pressures, and that temporary rescue must be provided by the armed forces; or (2) an acknowledgment could be made of the need for a provisional semi-authoritarian governing framework, modified as much as possible by conciliar institutions of representation and by the entrenching of procedures to ensure accountability; or (3) one of the more thoroughgoing authoritarian twentieth-century ideologies, e.g., Leninist or corporatist, could be implemented.[43]

The political predicament of late twentieth-century Nigeria is reflected in the fact that what was advanced as alternative scenarios in 1987 became concurrent strategies of a government under siege. At one level, a program was instituted to create a pluralist democracy with sequential rounds of elections. At another, the regime utilized the mechanisms and structures of semiauthoritarian governance by appointing civilians to ministerial offices, commissions, and councils to deliberate on issues of public concern.[44] An elaborate operation called Vision 2010, for example, was created to bring prominent Nigerians together to share reflections on the major issues confronting the nation. At a third level, Nigerians were subjected to the iron hand of a ruthless dictatorship that penalized opposition by nightly visits from security agents, detention without trial, or executions in broad daylight disguised as armed robbery attempts.[45]

The derailing of democracy in Africa by deliberately heightening fears of national disintegration has had devastating consequences in several African countries. Ethnic hegemonies that relied on highly repressive structures were forced to undertake political openings in the early 1990s, in Rwanda, via power sharing and, in Burundi, via multiparty elections. The brutal halting of these processes catapulted these fragile nations into genocidal conflict. Juvénal Habyarimana, Rwanda's president, was killed on April 6, 1994, to prevent the implementation of the 1993 Arusha agreement that would have ushered in a period of power sharing among representatives of the Hutu and Tutsi peoples. A year earlier, in 1993, Melchior Ndadaye had been elected president of Burundi, and power was transferred to him by Pierre Buyoya, who had headed a military regime since 1987. Buyoya, a Tutsi, had helped stifle an attempted coup in early July against the new, predominantly Hutu government. Three months later, the putschists succeeded, and Ndadaye and other members of the government were killed. Each of these events triggered rounds of bloodletting between

Hutu and Tutsi. With the collapse of a government in Burundi in July 1996 based on power-sharing arrangements between political parties representing both groups, Buyoya returned to head a military (and therefore Tutsi) government while militias of both groups conducted reprisals and counter-reprisals, often against unarmed citizens.

It is suggestive of the depth of the crisis of state and nation in Africa that Rwanda and Burundi, which some treat as pathological cases, cannot in fact be so easily categorized and dismissed. These countries are also governed by multilayered hegemonies that have succeeded one another rather than yielding to political liberalization. In the case of Rwanda, a Hutu-based militarized autocracy has been succeeded by a Tutsi-based reformist version under Paul Kagame. Nigerians, like other Africans, know that the extreme levels of intercommunal distrust and enmity in Rwanda and Burundi are not inconceivable in their own societies, as demonstrated by the chronic eruptions of communal conflicts in Nigeria since the 1970s.[46] There were even unsettling parallels since 1993 in Burundi and Nigeria:

Period	Burundi	Nigeria
June 1993	Election of Ndadaye	Election of Abiola
June–July 1993	Attempted military reversal of electoral victory	Nullification of electoral victory by the military
Oct.–Nov. 1993	Military coup, assassination of Ndadaye, end of democratic transition	Military coup, neutralizing of Abacha, end of transition[47]
1993–1998	Dictatorship and ethnoregional polarization and conflict	Dictatorship and ethnoregional polarization and conflict

In Burundi, the ethnic hegemony of the Tutsi, who represent 15 percent of the population, rests on total control of the armed forces and a level of communal violence that Nigeria has never experienced in a sustained way. Moreover, the greater diversity of Nigeria's population and the multiplicity of sociocultural zones have prevented the emergence of the increasingly sharp ethnic lines of division that now cut across Rwanda and Burundi. Yet Nigeria did not descend into armed conflict after 1993 because of the capacity of the militarized state to stifle all challenges that emerged from the pro-democracy movement. Oil income financed an aggressive policy to co-opt and silence opponents at home and abroad. Nevertheless, ethnoregional polarization since June 1993 was exacerbated by the harsh treatment of dissidents in the southwest and the increasing resort to violence by anti-regime forces. Whether Nigeria will succeed in renewing both its political and cultural federation greatly depends on whether post-Abacha governments are largely civilian in composition, and on their capacity and commitments.

Conclusion

Nigeria is no longer an exception to authoritarian and ethnomilitary systems of governance in Africa, as it was for its first three decades as an independent nation. It instead became a leading example of such a polity from 1983 to 1998. During the late 1970s, it was believed that Nigeria would serve as a model for democratic renewal in Africa. On the eve of the twenty-first century, it is more pertinent to inquire if Nigeria will rediscover such a path. So much effort has been invested by Nigerians in the construction of a polity resting on the willing consent of its diverse peoples, even in the most adverse circumstances, that this aspiration will not be easily extinguished. On June 12, 1993, the Nigerian people surprised the Babangida government by voting peacefully for a party whose support transcended all major regional, ethnic, and religious lines. That vote remains a testament to the freely expressed desire of the Nigerian electorate for a system of pluralist and consensual governance.

A continent that has witnessed the collapse of the apartheid regime and the inauguration of a democratic polity in South Africa is unlikely to abandon hopes for a similar transition in Nigeria. There was little prospect in Nigeria, however, of a repetition of the organized revolutionary violence mounted by the African National Congress and other liberation movements. After the execution of Saro-Wiwa and his fellow Ogoni in November 1995, I wrote that Nigeria under Abacha had become a rogue state that "refuses to abide by prevailing international ethical and legal norms in the conduct of public affairs."[48] This assessment was repeatedly confirmed, as the regime defied every diplomatic effort undertaken to get it to change course. The sudden deaths of Sani Abacha on June 8, 1998, and of Moshood Abiola a month later have created opportunities for reconstruction and reconciliation. If this course is followed, it will require the transformation of many of the entrenched features of governance discussed in this chapter. Having been subjected to so much deception and obfuscation by their leaders, both military and civilian, the Nigerian people must now discover untapped resources to revive the faded dream of a unified, constitutional, and democratic republic.

Notes

1. An earlier version of this chapter was presented at the annual meeting of the American Political Science Association, August 1996, titled, "The Nigerian Nation-State and the Resurgence of Authoritarianism in Africa."

2. T. Forrest, *Politics and Economic Development;* Joseph et al., "Nigeria"; Diamond et al., eds., *Transition Without End;* and Beckett and Young, eds., *Dilemmas of Democracy.*

3. Soyinka, *Open Sore of a Continent.* For my review essay of Wole Soyinka's book, see the *Journal of Democracy* (January 1997). The extent of Nigeria's shortfall is reflected in the fact that its prospects were once considered favorably in comparison with other Asian nations such as Indonesia, Malaysia, and South Korea.

4. For comprehensive discussions, see Diamond, "Nigeria"; Diamond et al., eds., *Transition Without End;* and Beckett and Young, eds., *Dilemmas of Democracy.*

5. The tabulation of the results was completed, but their formal issuance by the election commission was blocked by the military regime. For a discussion of this episode, see Lewis, "Endgame in Nigeria."

6. John Paden discusses the new geographical coalition that supported the victory of Abiola and his vice presidential running mate, Babagana Kingibe, in "Nigerian Unity."

7. Diamond, "Nigeria," pp. 451–460.

8. For details, consult U.S. Government, Human Rights Report of the Department of State, 1996 and 1997.

9. Lewis, "From Prebendalism to Predation."

10. See Joseph, "Nigeria: Inside the Dismal Tunnel," and a more extended version, "Democratization Under Military Rule."

11. When General Babangida reluctantly left government in August 1993, he handed power to an interim national government led by businessman Ernest Shonekan, whom Babangida had earlier brought into his administration. This administration lasted just three months and was never regarded as more than a facade behind which the military continued to rule until Abacha, its defense minister, was ready to dispense with Shonekan's services. For details, see Othman and Williams, "Politics, Power, and Democracy."

12. Joseph, *Democracy and Prebendal Politics,* p. 130.

13. See Diamond, *Class, Ethnicity, and Democracy.*

14. Suberu, "Federalism" and "Religion and Politics."

15. Joseph, *Democracy and Prebendal Politics;* Lewis, "From Prebendalism to Predation" and "Economic Statism."

16. See Bayart et al., *La Criminalisation.*

17. Reno, *Corruption and State Politics.*

18. Joseph, *Democracy and Prebendal Politics,* pp. 63–66. These important subtleties have been obscured by the current tendency to refer to virtually all contemporary African polities as "neopatrimonial."

19. For an indication of how Nigerian academic scholars were co-opted into the patronage structures developed by Babangida, see Ibrahim, "Political Scientists." What he writes about academics is equally true of businesspeople and politicians.

20. For the evolution of these tendencies, see Adekanye, "The Military," and Joseph, "Principles and Practices."

21. Joseph, "Africa"; Nwokedi, *Politics of Democratization;* and Chapter 2 of this book by Crawford Young.

22. O'Donnell and Schmitter, *Transitions,* p. 6.

23. For a discussion of the financial dimensions of the Liberian conflict, see Reno, "Business of War."

24. Using the term "election" to describe what transpired in Niger on July 7 and 8, 1996, would stretch any plausible meaning of the term. The independent

electoral commission was dismissed while the voting was taking place, and the new commission, under the Interior Ministry, reported an increase of Bare's share of the vote from 29 to 72 percent and of voter turnout from 61.6 to 93 percent, to yield a 52.2 percent "victory" for the military leader. The Nigérien experience is reminiscent of a similar fraudulent exercise in Liberia in 1985, when the military dictator, Samuel Doe, had the voting boxes seized and counted by persons he controlled, who then reported him elected by a small margin.

25. I have described Nigerian tyranny as having become decidedly Orwellian and Kafkaesque. See Joseph, "Democratization Under Military Rule."

26. It is generally believed that General Babangida enjoyed such popularity during the early years of his administration (1985–1993) that, as the leader of a political party, he would have stood a reasonable chance of emerging victorious even in an honest election. Instead, Babangida pretended to be preparing to hand over power while preventing the process from culminating in the election of a successor.

27. Also included in these transactions has been the French government, which the Abacha regime has actively courted, since democratization has always meant for France the potential overthrow of allied regimes in Africa.

28. In a special volume of the African Studies Association's *Issue* edited by C. S. Whitaker (vol. 11, nos. 1–2 [1981]), articles by Whitaker, Richard Sklar, John Paden, and myself pull together many of the concerns about ethnicity, religion, democracy, and the nature of the state that are of continuing relevance.

29. Post and Vickers, *Structure and Conflict,* p. 58.

30. Ibid., pp. 58–60.

31. Paden, "Nigerian Unity." Also relevant is Ekeh's "Colonialism" and R. Sklar's discussion of "dual authority" in "African Frontier."

32. Cited in Joseph, *Democracy and Prebendal Politics,* p. 184. Three general studies of continued relevance are Young, *Politics of Cultural Pluralism* and *Rising Tide,* and Rothchild and Olorunsola, *State Versus Ethnic Claims.*

33. See Soyinka's ruminations on the elusive concept of the Nigerian nation, which he refers to as a "nation space," in *Open Sore of a Continent,* pp. 17–36.

34. Lemarchand, "Uncivil States," pp. 184–185.

35. This discussion draws on studies that take up both specific and general issues: Osaghae, "Ogoni Uprising"; Naanen, "Oil Politics" and "Oil-Producing Minorities."

36. For the historical background to these confrontations, see Osaghae, "Ethnic Minorities."

37. Naanen, "Oil-Producing Minorities," p. 49. The demands of the Ogoni also echoed those of a broader movement for national reformation that published blueprints for a confederal republic with eight multistate units. See Suberu, "Federalism."

38. Joseph, "Africa 1994," p. 1.

39. Joseph, "Ethnic Trap." I coined the term "ethnic trap" to capture the ways in which sectional identities determined voting behavior, despite the constitutional and legal mechanisms devised to encourage parties and candidates to make cross-ethnic appeals to the electorate.

40. Suberu, "Federalism," p. 24.

41. Osaghae, "Ogoni Uprising," p. 343.

42. Whitaker, "Unfinished State," p. 6.

43. Joseph, *Democracy and Prebendal Politics,* pp. 184–185.

44. For a discussion of this established mode of governance, see Joseph, "Principles and Practices."

45. No one apparently enjoyed immunity from such actions, as was demonstrated by the assassination of Kudirat Abiola, wife of the detained Moshood Abiola, in broad daylight on June 4, 1996.

46. See Suberu, *Ethnic Minority Conflicts*.

47. When Abiola fled Nigeria in August 1993, he stated that he did so in response to warnings about his likely assassination. After he returned, he was politically neutralized by his arrest and prolonged detention. In June 1996, his wife, Kudirat Abiola, was less fortunate, as she was assassinated in the course of making arrangements to obtain asylum overseas.

48. Joseph, "Nigeria: Inside the Dismal Tunnel," p. 194.

PART 5

Elections and Democratization

20

A First Look at
Second Elections in Africa,
with Illustrations from Zambia

MICHAEL BRATTON AND DANIEL N. POSNER

The early 1990s saw a wave of competitive multiparty elections in Africa. These unprecedented contests can be described as "founding" elections in the sense that, for many countries, they marked a transition from an extended period of authoritarian rule to a new era of fledgling democratic government.[1] By the middle of the 1990s, this wave had crested. Although founding elections continued to be conducted in African countries that were latecomers to the political reform bandwagon, they took place less frequently than before. Meanwhile, in countries that had experienced early regime change, expiring electoral cycles gave rise to a series of second elections. The main purpose of this chapter is to take a first look at this second round of elections to see what they portend for the consolidation of democracy in Africa.

Our objectives are both analytic and interpretive, and our approach is both comparative and idiographic. We begin by staking out our position in the debate about the status of elections in the construction of democracy: are these institutions formalistic or essential? The chapter then analyzes the processes and outcomes of all national elections conducted in Africa in 1995 and 1996. Though the principal focus is on second elections, the record on "late" founding elections during this period is also updated, because useful insights can be gained by comparing general trends over time. The third section of the chapter illustrates emerging electoral issues with a detailed account of Zambia's controversial second election of November 18, 1996. We conclude by drawing together the lessons gleaned from the cross-Africa comparisons and the Zambian case.

To anticipate findings, our survey reveals that second elections reflect a trend of declining electoral quality in Africa. As the Zambian case strikingly illustrates, electoral imperfections are caused mainly by incumbent leaders who openly manipulate constitutional and electoral rules to trip up their competitors. At the same time, African voters continue to judge governments primarily in terms of economic performance, but they now have moderated expectations about quick improvements in living standards. Foreign aid donors play a different role in second elections, at once less critical and more important than in the past; even as donors have reduced their financial assistance for elections, they have become the principal audience at which competitors direct their conflicting claims about the meaning of elections. On balance, second elections in Africa probably helped democracy in Africa survive, not least because these contests began to institutionalize the regularity of competitive elections. Yet wherever the elections did not resolve persistent disagreements among participants about the basic rules of the political game, as in Zambia, second elections did not help to consolidate democracy.

The Role of Elections in the Consolidation of Democracy

The consolidation of democracy involves the institutionalization of rules that fully guarantee political participation and political competition. This approach draws directly on Robert Dahl's formulation of regime types, in which participation and competition are jointly maximized only under "polyarchy," his real-world analogue of the democratic ideal.[2] It also builds on Philippe Schmitter's observation that democracy requires the permanent construction of an array of countervailing political institutions within both state and society.[3] In addition, it adheres to Juan Linz and Alfred Stepan's notion of regime consolidation, in which democratic procedures become, both in law and in elite and mass sentiments, "the only game in town."[4]

Elections—which empower ordinary citizens to choose among contestants for top political office—clearly promote both participation and competition. As Joseph Schumpeter has argued, elections are the defining institution of democracy.[5] Indeed, for most analysts, the convocation of elections for a head of government and a National Assembly (provided that these are free and fair and that the losers accept the results) is sufficient to found a democratic regime. Some analysts have even gone so far as to use electoral criteria to determine whether democratic regimes become consolidated. Samuel Huntington applies a "two-turnover test," according to which consolidation occurs whenever the winners of founding elections are defeated in a subsequent election, and the new winners themselves later accept an electoral turnover.[6] Against this approach, assessments of democratic consolidation based solely on elections have been criticized for risking "the fallacy of electoralism."[7] According to this argument, formal procedures for elections do not a create a democracy because, as Latin American experience has shown, elections can coexist with systematic abuses of human rights and disenfranchisement of large segments of the population.[8]

We hold a view between these two extremes. While seeking to avoid the electoral fallacy, we do not wish to commit its antithesis—what Mitchell Seligson and John Booth call the "anti-electoralist fallacy"[9]—by assuming that elections never matter for democratization. Elections, even if regularly and fairly conducted, do not, in and of themselves, create a consolidated democracy. For democracy to truly take root, civil rights and due process of law must be respected, institutions such as an independent legislature and judiciary and a free press must be present, and military forces must be controlled by civilian decisionmakers. In addition, citizens and politicians must come to accept that this array of democratic institutions is the only legitimate arrangement for governing public life. While elections and democracy are not synonymous, elections nonetheless remain fundamental, not only for the installation of democratic governments, but for broader democratic consolidation. The regularity, openness, and acceptability of elections signal whether basic constitutional, behavioral, and attitudinal foundations are being laid for sustainable democratic rule. It is meaningful to study elections for the simple reason that, while you can have elections without democracy, you cannot have democracy without elections.

If nothing else, convening scheduled multiparty elections serves the minimal function of marking democracy's survival. The most immediate concern for many of Africa's fragile democracies is whether they will endure at all. Recording the occurrence of a second competitive election can at least confirm that democratic gains have not been completely reversed by executive coup or military takeover. Once the survival of a multiparty electoral regime has been established, we will wish to know more about its political trajectory: do the events and processes surrounding the election mark a diminution or a consolidation of the democratic impulse? Are democratic norms and institutions taking root, or are they quickly withering away? The hallmark of competitive elections is that they create uncertainty about who will govern in their aftermath. Precisely because multiparty elections threaten to reallocate power, they generate strong incentives for incumbents to exploit available resources to prevent their replacement by challengers. Analysts must therefore attend to the behavior of ruling elites in Africa's new democracies and to the responses of organized social groups. They must ask, for example, whether elites manipulate political rules (and, if so, whether they target rules that govern participation or rules that govern competition), whether they use state resources unfairly, and whether they break the law in doing so, as well as whether the press criticizes, pressure groups protest, voters withdraw from the political process, or opposition parties call for election boycotts.

Answering questions like these for selected countries and regions can provide the basis for preliminary assessments of whether democracy is likely
to merely survive, to die a slow death, or to gradually consolidate.

The empirical task is straightforward. First are questions of electoral
quantity: are second elections held at all? A positive answer to this question
is required before it becomes meaningful to consider issues of deeper
democratic consolidation. And if elections are held, do they take place on
time? The answer to this question helps to ascertain how strictly officeholders are subjected to the rule of law. Incumbents who accommodate themselves to mandated schedules (rather than illegally altering election timing
to increase their chances of winning) demonstrate a commitment to constitutionalism that bodes well for democratic consolidation.

Second are questions of electoral quality: exactly how free and fair are
elections? Analysts and election observers are learning to distinguish
among different types of electoral malpractice, most notably with regard to
the way the electoral rules are set, the way the campaign is conducted, or
the way the vote and the count are administered. Increasingly, the quality of
elections within any given country can vary considerably across these three
stages. It is not uncommon, for example, for clearly flawed voter registration exercises, outright disqualifications of certain candidates, or highly
unfair campaigns to be followed by relatively open and free balloting on
election day. The assessments of electoral fairness reported in this chapter
are based on considerations of quality with respect to all of these issues: the
rules, the campaign, the vote, and the count. Gross deficiencies in any of
these areas are sufficient to call the integrity of an election into dispute. In
addition, it is necessary to take boycotts by opposition parties into account.
Though the quality of an election held in the face of a boycott is ambiguous—we can never be certain whether the boycott reflects a flawed electoral process or a calculation by opposition parties that they stand no
chance of winning—the absence of a boycott probably indicates that the
electoral process was not impaired by major deficiencies. Whether the boycott was called before, during, or after the polls can also help to clarify its
meaning with respect to the quality of the election.

Because political power involves intangible elements like the perceived legitimacy of the government, elections are contested in symbolic,
as well as empirical, terms. In new democracies where elections are not yet
fully institutionalized, contenders vie to win votes and seats, but they also
struggle to control the interpretation of electoral outcomes. Thus, the third
task is to address questions of electoral meaning. Elections that result in
regime transition or leadership alternation are usually unambiguous, signi-
fying a break with the past and introducing a fresh political era. Those in
which incumbents manage to hold on to power, on the other hand, are more
difficult to interpret, because they involve judgments about whether the
vote enhances or reduces a sitting government's mandate. In part, the legiti-

macy of an election outcome can be determined by objective indicators such as the winner's share of votes or seats. But even these results are subject to interpretation, for example, with respect to voter turnout rates or considerations of campaign context and conduct.

In Africa, disputes about the meaning of multiparty elections are often directed externally at foreign aid donors, especially when funding decisions hinge on judgments of electoral quality. Because the stakes are high—continued balance-of-payment support and project aid is often contingent upon a "free and fair" verdict—disputes over interpretation often come to the fore in postelection discourse. Winners deploy the informational and coercive instruments of the state to reinforce their claim that they have received a mandate, while losers try to undermine this assertion by arguing that the results were rigged or that the electoral process was flawed. This jockeying to assign meaning is further complicated by the fact that it takes place in a context in which various audiences—winning and losing, domestic and international, elite and mass—may apply different standards of judgment. Analysts are thus forced to probe beyond the reported facts in order to evaluate these diverse interpretations, understanding all along that the meaning of elections is a resource manipulated by contending parties to promote their own interests.

Late Founding Elections

Between 1990 and 1996, more than three-quarters of sub-Saharan Africa's independent countries (37 out of 48) held founding elections.[10] These multiparty contests offered voters real choices about who would rule them, often for the first time since independence. By the end of 1996, they had led to the ouster of 18 incumbent heads of government. Founding elections did not, however, always result in leadership alternation; more often than not, sitting presidents found ways to survive. As the 1990s progressed, leaders became more adept at accommodating the emerging global consensus about the desirability of competitive elections, while at the same time learning to manage and manipulate these events to their own ends. In general, the later that founding elections were held, the poorer was the quality of their conduct and the lower was the likelihood that incumbents would be displaced.

Table 20.1 displays a list of the nine countries that convened late founding elections in the two-year period between January 1995 and December 1996. In some respects, these contests resembled the founding elections that were held earlier in Africa's wave of transitions. For example, elections held in 1995 and 1996 reinforced a pattern of relatively high voter turnout: an average of nearly 68 percent of registered voters actually cast ballots, compared with 64 percent for elections held between 1990 and

Table 20.1 Founding Elections in Sub-Saharan Africa, 1995–1996

Country	Date of Election[a]	Type of Election[b]	Opposition Boycott?[c]	Free and Fair?[d]	Leadership Alternation?	Losers Accept?[e]	Voter Turnout (% Reg. Voters)	Winner's Vote Share (Pres. Elec.)	Winner's Seat Share (Leg. Elec.)
Ethiopia	May 7, 1995	Legislative	Yes	No	No	No	67.5 (est.)	–	90.1
Tanzania	Oct. 22, 1995	General	Yes?	No	No	Yes?	76.7	61.8	80.2
Equatorial Guinea	Feb. 25, 1996	Presidential	Yes	No	No	No	86.1	97.9	–
Sierra Leone	Feb. 26, 1996	General	No	No	Yes	No	36.4 (est.)	59.5	39.7
Sudan	Mar. 1, 1996	General	Yes	No	No	No	72.2	75.7	90.0 (est.)
Uganda	May 9, 1996	Presidential	No	Yes?	No	No	73.0	74.2	–
	June 27, 1996	Legislative	Yes	Yes?	No	No	60.7	–	56.5
Chad	July 3, 1996	Presidential	Yes	Yes?	No	No	69.0 (est.)	69.1	–
Niger	July 7, 1996	Presidential	Yes?	No	No	No	82.4	52.2	–
	Nov. 23, 1996	Legislative	Yes	No	No	No	39.2	–	69.9
The Gambia	Sept. 26, 1996	Presidential	No	No	No	No	80.0 (est.)	55.8	–

Sources: Africa Research Bulletin: Political, Social, and Cultural Series (London, monthly); *Election Notes* (http://www.klipsan.com/elecnews.htm); *Parliamentary and Presidential Elections Around the World* (http://www.universal.nl/users/derksen/election/home.html); International Foundation for Electoral Systems, *Elections Today* (Washington, DC, bimonthly); National Democratic Institute, *NDI Reports* (Washington, DC, quarterly); and *Journal of Democracy* (Washington, DC, quarterly).

Notes: a. For elections that lasted more than one day, the date of the election refers to the first day of polling. With reference to two-round elections, the date of the election refers to the first day of the first round.

b. Elections are dubbed "general" if a presidential and legislative election are held concurrently on the same day or days; otherwise, these elections are listed separately.

c. A country scores "Yes" on opposition boycott if any party withdraws from the election. In most cases, boycotts were partial, with some parties and independent candidates participating and others withholding support. A "Yes?" indicates that a boycott occurred in only one round of the elections.

d. A "Yes?" indicates that observer reports were divided or ambiguous about the quality of the election.

e. The acceptance of election results by losers is judged by whether minority parties take up legislative seats won in the election. "Yes?" indicates that they do so only after initially refusing; "No?" indicates that the opposition continues to challenge the legitimacy of the election and the government that it produced.

1994.[11] As in the earlier period, this average concealed a wide variation across countries, from less than 40 percent turnout in Sierra Leone, to more than 75 percent in Tanzania.[12] At the same time, the winners of presidential elections continued to achieve victories by convincing margins, averaging 68 percent of the valid votes in 1995–1996, compared with 63 percent in the earlier period.[13] However, there were again marked differences between countries like Niger, where General Ibrahim Mainassara Bare edged in with 52 percent of the vote, and Equatorial Guinea, where, facing no challengers, Obiang Nguema seized nearly 98 percent.

In other respects, however, late founding elections revealed novel trends. The frequency of opposition boycotts increased to more than two-thirds of all recent founding elections (eight out of 11), suggesting that basic agreement had never been reached on the rules of a democratic game. More important, election observers were unable to endorse any of these elections as fully meeting international standards, calling into question the integrity of the polling, the campaign, or the electoral rules. To be sure, international observers found little fault with polling procedures in Uganda in May and June 1996 (though parties were barred from electioneering), and they disagreed on the quality of the July 1996 presidential election in Chad. But this undistinguished record stands in marked contrast to the record between 1990 and 1994, when more than half of African elections were ruled free and fair by observers.[14] Most strikingly, leadership turnover occurred in only one case after 1994, compared with 14 cases in the preceding period. In Sierra Leone in February 1996, a civilian leader, Ahmad Tejan Kabbah, displaced coup maker Brigadier Julius Maada Bio (who did not run) in an election in which "a military connection was the kiss of death for vote-seekers."[15] In all other cases of late founding elections, the incumbent was returned, and almost invariably, the losers refused to accept the validity of the election results.

The fiasco surrounding the October 1995 general election in Tanzania illustrates these problems well. When the first round of voter registration elicited only a 34 percent response, electoral authorities (to their credit) extended the registration period and succeeded in raising enrollment to 81 percent of eligible voters.[16] Fourteen political parties fielded candidates for the Union elections; the opposition was unable to unite around a single presidential candidate, and four candidates eventually ran. As in many other African elections, opposition parties were able to communicate their messages to urban voters through the print press, but they encountered limited access to the government-controlled electronic media, most notably, Radio Tanzania Dar es Salaam, the only station with national coverage. Voting was first held on Zanzibar, where the opposition claimed that the ruling party engineered a narrow victory by rigging the final compilation of results. The voting that followed on the mainland was therefore marred by an atmosphere of distrust, which was compounded by abysmal election preparations and administration. Polling was so chaotic in the capital city that it had to be rerun, prompting opposition parties either to follow through on their boycott threats or to challenge the results in court. Although most ruling-party candidates were reelected, the country's first multiparty contest since independence dismayed many Tanzanians.

How can the declining quality of founding elections be explained? With the exception of Tanzania, late founding elections were all held in countries whose leaders had come to power either by military coup or, in the cases of Ethiopia and Uganda, by dint of a rebel military victory. In most cases, the person presiding over (as well as competing in) the election was a soldier who had simply doffed his military uniform to run as a civilian. These leaders were usually less committed to democracy than to shoring up their international and domestic standing by acceding to the new expectation that African political leaders should ascend to office via elections. Not surprisingly, the imperfect elections sponsored by such calculating, nondemocratic leaders did little to advance the cause of democratization on the African continent. The trend of declining quality in founding elections was perhaps predictable; because the most reluctant political reformers were the last to concede to demands for elections, they departed furthest from the democratic ideal.

Second Elections in Africa

During the same period, 1995–1996, African countries that had embarked early on political reforms entered a second round of elections. Having completed their transitions by 1992 with varying degrees of success, these countries were due for constitutionally scheduled elections before the end of 1996. A list of 12 such countries and the 16 second elections that took place in them is presented in Table 20.2.

This list excludes countries in which early democratic transitions were reversed by military coups before second elections were scheduled to take place. In Burundi, Melchior Ndadaye's elected government lasted all of four months before being brutally overthrown by the Tutsi-led military. In The Gambia, a long-standing multiparty civilian regime was ousted by soldiers on July 22, 1994. The list does, however, include Niger, which held a second (legislative) election before the military intervened (giving as its reasons the inability of civilian politicians either to break an executive-legislative deadlock or to end a Tuareg rebellion in the north). In several other countries (Lesotho, Comoros, Guinea, São Tomé, and the Central African Republic), attempted coups or military mutinies destabilized the elected governments, but thanks to international military assistance, these events did not actually result in the fall of the regimes. It is notable that even where soldiers did come to power, they hastened to promise citizens

Table 20.2 Second Elections in Sub-Saharan Africa, 1995–1996

Country	Date of Election	Type of Election	Held on Time?[a]	Opposition Boycott?	Free and Fair?	Quality Trend[b]	Leadership Alternation[c]	Losers Accept?
Namibia	Dec. 7, 1994	General	Yes?	No	Yes	Unchanged	No	Yes
Niger	Jan. 12, 1995	Legislative	Yes	No	Yes	Unchanged	Yes?	Yes
Benin	March 28, 1995	Legislative	Yes	No	Yes	Unchanged	Yes?	Yes
	March 4, 1996	Presidential	Yes	No	Yes	Unchanged	Yes	Yes
Côte d'Ivoire	Oct. 22, 1995	Presidential	Yes	Yes	No	Worsened	No	No
	Nov. 26, 1995	Legislative	Yes	No	No	Worsened	No	Yes?
Cape Verde	Dec. 17, 1995	Legislative	Yes	No	Yes	Unchanged	No	Yes
	Feb. 18, 1996	Presidential	Yes	No	Yes	Unchanged	No	Yes
São Tomé	July 21, 1996	Presidential	Yes	No	Yes	Improved	No	Yes?
Mauritania	Oct. 11, 1996	Legislative	Yes	No	Yes?	Unchanged	No	Yes?
Madagascar	Nov. 3, 1996	Presidential	Yes	No	Yes?	Worsened	Yes	No?
Zambia	Nov. 18, 1996	General	Yes?	Yes	No	Worsened	No	No?
Comoros	March 6, 1996	Presidential	Yes	No	Yes	Improved	No	Yes
	Dec. 1, 1996	Legislative	Yes?	Yes	No	Worsened	No	No
Gabon	Dec. 15, 1996	Legislative	No	Yes	No	Unchanged	No	No?
Ghana	Dec 7, 1996	General	Yes?	No	Yes	Improved	No	Yes

Sources: See Table 20.1, ibid.

Notes: See notes to Table 20.1, in addition to notes below.

a. Elections that are called early or held on time according to the electoral timetable are scored as "Yes." If elections are only slightly delayed (i.e., held within three months of the scheduled date), the score is "Yes?"

b. Quality trend is measured by change, if any, in reported judgments by election observers on whether the elections were free and fair between founding and second contests.

c. Leadership alternation refers only to presidential elections. "Yes?" indicates instances in which a new party (or party coalition) took over control of the National Assembly.

and international donors that they would convene competitive elections as soon as possible.

Otherwise, in countries that retained civilian rule, second elections were held as constitutionally required; it appears that only one African country failed to adhere to its electoral cycle, and then only temporarily. President Omar Bongo breached Gabon's 1990 constitution, abandoned a written accord between the ruling and opposition parties, and ignored a Constitutional Court ruling that National Assembly elections should be held before June 8, 1996. Instead, he reappointed the prime minister, whose term had expired, and hinted that he would bring his own family members back into the government. Commentators speculated that Bongo was worried that a loss by the ruling Parti Démocratique Gabonais (PDG) in the legislative elections would force him to appoint a premier from the opposition, and thus cede executive control over the Ministries of Finance, Oil, and Internal Security on which his power was based.[17] In the end, however, he allowed elections to be held six months late, on December 15, 1996. The PDG was returned to power, and Gabon resumed its halting journey in search of democracy.

The remainder of the 12 countries that had completed their election cycles held second elections for president or National Assembly representatives before the end of 1996 essentially as scheduled, although in a few cases, the elections were held several weeks after the original due date (Namibia, Zambia, Comoros, and Ghana; see "Yes?" in Table 20.2, column 4). In Zambia, the government and the opposition could not agree on the starting date for calculating the expiration of the electoral cycle, while in Ghana, the delay was incurred against the wishes of the government in order to facilitate holding the presidential and parliamentary elections on the same day. Even where incumbents exploited their discretion over scheduling to the utmost, elections were ultimately held with sufficient timeliness to at least satisfy the spirit of the law. In four other cases, elections were actually called ahead of schedule (Niger, Cape Verde, Mauritania, and Madagascar). In Niger, parliamentary elections were held prematurely, in January 1995, when the ruling coalition broke up and the National Assembly was dissolved. In Madagascar, the impeachment of President Albert Zafy, a legislative decision that was subsequently upheld by the Constitutional High Court, led to early presidential elections in November 1996. In Mauritania, second elections were brought forward by several months to enable the incoming National Assembly to vote on a government budget for 1997. In the other eligible countries (Benin and Côte d'Ivoire), second presidential and legislative elections were held precisely on schedule.[18]

The same cannot be said for municipal or other local government elections. In perhaps half of Africa's new democracies, elections at the local level were held either late or not at all. Again, Gabon was one of the main offenders. Bongo postponed local government polls, which were first due in December 1993, on five separate occasions, saying in each instance that more time was needed for preparations. While incumbent leaders had self-serving reasons for avoiding exposure at the polls, there was some truth to the claim that logistically demanding local elections were beyond the financial and administrative capacity of poorer African countries (though not of Gabon, which ran a budget surplus in 1996). In Malawi, for example, overdue local government polls had not been convened by the end of 1996, in large part because international donors were unwilling to pay for them. Until elected local governments are established or restored in African countries, however, the task of building democracy will remain seriously incomplete.

Did the quality of second elections decline, like that of the late founding elections that occurred during this same period? The answer depends on the point of comparison. Consider judgments of whether elections were free and fair. Table 20.2 (column 6) indicates that in nine of the 16 cases, monitors ruled second elections in Africa to be acceptable by international standards. If the point of comparison is the late founding elections held in 1995 and 1996—of which not one passed muster (see Table 20.1)—then second elections are clearly much more open than recent founding elections. This assessment is reinforced by the fact that, due to lower levels of international electoral assistance, judgments about second elections were usually made by domestic monitors with intimate knowledge of their countries. The relative openness of second elections compared with late founding elections stands to reason once the nature of the respective political regimes is taken into account. We would expect second elections in new democracies to be freer than founding elections in late-reforming military or one-party regimes for the simple reason that rulers in the latter group are among the most reluctant and weakly committed democratizers.

But elections in nondemocratic regimes are not the best point of comparison for making judgments about democratic survival or consolidation. A new democracy's own immediate past history is more relevant: the key question is whether the quality of its elections improved or worsened the second time around. Here the findings are less encouraging (see Table 20.2, columns 6 and 7). Countries with flawed founding elections (like Côte d'Ivoire, Mauritania, and Gabon) also tended to experience imperfect second polls, as incumbents reinforced and refined their control of electoral processes. A few "democratizers" (such as Madagascar and Zambia) slid back toward autocracy, as indicated by the declining quality of their second elections. Indeed, as a group, Africa's liberalized regimes experienced fewer acceptable elections during 1995–1996 (56 percent) than in their own founding round between 1990 and 1994 (83 percent).[19]

This trend can be illustrated by the experiences of particular countries. In Côte d'Ivoire, President Henri Konan Bédié introduced a new electoral code stipulating that a presidential candidate must be born of Ivorien parents and reside in the country for at least five years, thereby effectively sidelining Alassane Ouattara, his only serious rival. As in Zambia, where similar institutional doctoring took place, the incumbent appeared determined to rig the rules of "an election he would probably have won anyway."[20] Bédié marshaled his main assets—the patronage machine of the ruling Parti Démocratique de Côte d'Ivoire, the paramilitary gendarmerie, and backing from France—to engineer landslide victories in both presidential and legislative polls. In Comoros, where the presidential election of March 1996 went relatively smoothly, the legislative election of December 1996 was a disaster. Voter turnout was reportedly "low" following the arrest of two former prime ministers and a series of arson attacks in the run-up to the election.[21] In a searing symbolization of electoral decline, the central administrative building in Moroni was burned to the ground, destroying ballot boxes and other electoral materials.

Although incumbent parties were returned to power in these cases, the poor quality of the elections called the legitimacy of the resulting governments into question. In Côte d'Ivoire and Comoros, these outcomes represented a measure of institutional continuity, since neither of these countries had strong democratic records in their own founding elections or in the period that followed. Zambia, on the other hand, had held a model founding election in 1991. It provides perhaps the clearest example of the trend of declining quality of second elections in sub-Saharan Africa. Because the Zambian case illustrates so many of the weaknesses apparent in other new African multiparty regimes—such as the lack of internal democracy in ruling parties, the abuse of government resources during the campaign, and the growing hostility of governments to democracy-monitoring nongovernmental organizations (NGOs)—its problematic second election will be analyzed in greater detail below.

This regional trend, however, obscures significant variation at the level of individual countries. In Ghana and São Tomé, the quality of elections improved, as earlier proceedings of questionable quality were superseded by more open and transparent contests. In São Tomé's 1991 founding election, Miguel Travoada won unopposed when his two main rivals pulled out shortly before election day. The second presidential election of July 1996 was thus the first to feature more than one candidate. Observers uniformly praised the conduct of the December 1996 general elections in Ghana, noting the independence and professionalism of the national Electoral Commission and the determination of voters to peacefully exercise their political rights. All seemed to agree that the elections represented "a positive step forward in the strengthening of Ghana's democracy and its electoral process."[22] In both of these cases, the incumbent was returned to office, and the losers accepted the results. While hardly conclusive, this constitutes at least anecdotal evidence that African political actors are beginning to focus less on the removal of individual strongmen and more on procedures to install lasting institutions of political competition.

What, then, was the meaning of second elections? To be sure, these events were perceived differently by sitting governments and their opponents, as indicated by the increased frequency of opposition boycotts. Opposition parties protested electoral procedures by withdrawing from one-quarter of the second elections conducted by the end of 1996 (four out of 16 elections; see Table 20.2, column 5), a higher rate than during founding elections in the same countries. In these cases, boycotts were called to protest the manipulation of constitutional or electoral rules by elected leaders, especially the disqualification of candidates for the presidency. Given the political strength of the incumbent rulers, however, it is uncertain whether the protesters were entirely motivated by issues of principle, or whether they also sought a convenient way to avoid revealing their weaknesses at the polls.

Irrespective of motivations, opposition boycotts were a surefire way to call the integrity of an election into question. Table 20.2 confirms that every case of an election boycott in a second election in Africa was accompanied by unfavorable reports from observers and monitors. Hence, even if opposition parties undertook boycotts partly for self-serving reasons, they succeeded in drawing attention to situations in which incumbents were unfairly bending rules or monopolizing public resources. Not surprisingly, there was also a strong correlation between election boycotts and the refusal of losers to accept the results of elections.

With regard to leadership alternation, Africa's second elections closely resembled late founding elections. By the end of 1996, an unambiguous change of presidents took place in only two cases (see Table 20.2, column 8).[23] In Benin, the most famous case of alternation, Nicéphore Soglo was ejected in March 1996 by the same voters who had swept him to power in one of Africa's landmark democratic transitions just five years earlier. Although reportedly privately bitter about the result, Soglo honorably hailed the principle of multiparty elections: "my greatest consolation comes from the conduct of my fellow countrymen . . . all the people of Benin were the winners."[24] In an equally close but more sharply disputed contest, leadership alternated in Madagascar in a drawn-out electoral process that began in November 1996. After trying to delay the second round of voting, as well as charging malfeasance in vote counting, former President Zafy eventually conceded defeat in early 1997. In both of these cases, second elections restored to power former strongmen who had been ousted in founding elections. But while Mathieu Kérékou of Benin proclaimed that he had been born again as a Christian and a democrat, there was little indication that Didier Ratsiraka of Madagascar had changed his autocratic ways. The fact that his party did not enjoy a majority in Madagascar's parliament did, however, impose some measure of constraint on his powers as president.

Everywhere else in sub-Saharan Africa, sitting leaders weathered second elections and retained their posts. In most cases, voters reaffirmed their support for political reform by reelecting leaders who had first come to office during the regime transitions of the early 1990s (e.g., in Namibia, Cape Verde, São Tomé, and Zambia). In Ghana, on the other hand, a leader who had initially slipped into elected office through a flawed transition managed, through a second election, to enhance his democratic credentials. Provided that voters had not been entirely disillusioned by an incumbent's economic mismanagement, they generally sought continuity in political leadership in the aftermath of the turbulent interludes of regime transition. In addition, voters may have chosen to give incumbents another term in office before passing judgment on whether the government had delivered on its promises; this may, for example, have been the case in Zambia.

Did second elections therefore reflect a deepening or an undermining of democracy in Africa? Table 20.3 shows few clear trends with regard to the institutionalization of political participation and political competition. For example, voter turnout figures are ambiguous. In some second elections, voter turnout increased compared with the levels observed in founding elections (e.g., in Benin, Cape Verde, Ghana, and Zambia; see Table 20.3, column 4); but in others, it declined (e.g., in Namibia, Niger, Madagascar, and Mauritania). Election observers and monitors often commented, however, on the seriousness of purpose displayed by voters, suggesting that African citizens were becoming attached to their political rights and wished to continue exercising them regularly.

Similarly, few consistent patterns emerged with regard to political competition. Both cases of unambiguous leadership alternation (Benin and Madagascar) were associated with close races, suggesting that vigorous contestation was becoming routinized in these countries. But where incumbents were returned, there were no apparent trends in the data on the winners' shares of votes or seats. Presidents were reelected in some African countries with increased majorities (e.g., in Namibia, Côte d'Ivoire, and Cape Verde), but by reduced margins in others (e.g., São Tomé and Zambia).[25] Similarly, legislative elections led to seat gains for ruling parties in some countries, and seat losses in others. Only in Namibia and Comoros did dominant political parties make gains in both presidential votes and legislative seats. It would be premature on the basis of this slender evidence to announce that dominant parties are losing their grip on African electorates.[26] But it is evident that African voters are beginning to depart from the slates of legislative candidates presented by ruling parties in order to pick opposition party and independent candidates on their own.

Finally, what does the increasing rate of opposition boycotts signify about the meaning of Africa's second elections? At a minimum, boycotts express persistent conflicts over electoral processes and outcomes, and they raise the alarm that even elected leaders may resort to political abuse in

Table 20.3   Second Elections in Africa: Comparisons with Founding Elections

Country	Type of Election[a]	Voter Turnout[b] (2nd Elec.)	Change in Turnout (vs. Founding Election)[c]	Winner's Vote Share (Pres. Elec.)	Change in Vote Share (vs. Previous Pres. Elec.)[d]	Winner's Seat Share (Leg. Elec.)	Change in Seat Share (vs. Previous Leg. Elec.)[e]
Namibia	General	76.1	-18.9	74.5	+17.6	73.6	+16.7
Niger	Legislative	35.0	-3.0	–	–	34.9	0.0
Benin	Legislative	75.9	+11.9	–	–	24.1	+6.8
	Presidential	86.8	+22.8	52.5	-15.2	–	–
Côte d'Ivoire	Presidential	56.2	-3.8	95.2	+13.5	–	–
	Legislative	48.9	-11.1	–	–	84.0	-9.1
Cape Verde	Legislative	76.5	+17.5	–	–	69.4	-4.1
	Presidential	43.4	-15.6	80.0 (est.)	+6.5	–	–
Comoros	Presidential	62.0	+2.0	61.2	+6.1	–	–
	Legislative	"Low"	"Lower"	–	–	85.7	+33.3
São Tomé	Presidential	67.5	+7.5	52.2	-29.0	–	–
Mauritania	Legislative	30.0 (est.)	-21.7 (est.)	–	–	88.6	+27.0
Madagascar	Presidential	60.0 (est.)	-20.0 (est.)	50.5 (est.)	-16.2	–	–
Zambia	General	58.7	+15.3	72.6	-2.5	87.3	+4.0
Gabon	Legislative	n.a.	n.a.	–	–	68.4	+13.4
Ghana	General	77.9	+29.6	57.4	-0.7	66.0	-28.5

Sources: See Table 20.1, ibid.

Notes: See notes to Table 20.1, in addition to notes below.

a. For election dates, see Table 20.2.

b. Turnout is measured as total valid votes as a percentage of registered voters.

c. Change in turnout is measured as the difference in turnout percentage between founding and second elections. The values of these entries cannot be compared across countries since these have not been standardized to account for the initial level of turnout in each country. What matters most is the direction of the change (indicated by plus or minus signs), rather than the specific values reported by governments, which, in any event, are undoubtedly less precise than they appear. Data on founding elections is taken from Bratton and van de Walle, *Democratic Experiments*, table 8. For two-round elections, all data refers to second-round results.

d. Change in the winner's share of the vote is measured as the difference in the winning presidential candidate's percentage of votes between founding and second elections (Bratton and van de Walle, ibid.).

e. Change in the winner's share of seats is measured as the difference in the winning party's share of seats between founding and second elections. Data on first elections is taken from the variable LEGSEATS in Bratton et al., *Political Regimes and Regime Transitions*.

order to remain in power. They suggest that the agreements achieved among political actors regarding the rules of political competition for founding elections were tentative and conditional at best. The efforts of political elites to limit the field of contenders thus encountered stiff resistance from both election monitors and opposition political parties. Flawed second elections therefore had contradictory implications for democracy: whereas they stimulated and mobilized civil society, they also undercut consensus on the rules for constituting a legitimate government. In the final analysis, however, the boycotters emphasized electoral flaws and violations; they did not challenge the legitimacy of holding elections in the first place. This serves to underscore the basic agreement that has been emerging among all participants that elections are the only acceptable institutional device for choosing top leaders.

Second Elections in Zambia

When it restored multiparty political competition in October 1991, Zambia was held up as a model for democratization in Africa.[27] Since that date, however, the record of Frederick Chiluba's Movement for Multiparty Democracy (MMD) government has given analysts of Zambian affairs reason to rethink their earlier optimistic assessments. While the MMD has scored some important successes in the area of economic reform, its performance on the political front has been regressive. Although rhetorically committed to openness and transparency, Chiluba's government has proven to be intolerant of criticism, slow to react to allegations of corruption within its ranks, and disturbingly willing to exploit its command over government resources and institutions (including the police and parliament) to undermine the opposition and favor its own party members. All of these undemocratic tendencies were apparent in the country's flawed second elections of November 18, 1996. Because Zambia's experience reflects an emerging continental trend of declining electoral quality, we describe this experience in detail below. In so doing, we hope to illustrate at a deeper level some of the general patterns that are evident in the 11 other countries that have also already experienced second elections.

One of the MMD's key promises during the election campaign of 1991 was that it would rewrite the national constitution to strengthen the protection of civil liberties and to ensure the delinkage of party and government. The process of constitutional reform did not begin in earnest, however, until two years after the transition. In November 1993, a 24-member review commission was appointed to collect views from the general public and provide proposals for the content of a new constitution. The Mwanakatwe Constitutional Review Commission, named for its chairman, John Mwanakatwe, released its report in June 1995. The government responded with a white paper that agreed with many of the commission's proposals, but in a manner reminiscent of the old one-party regime, it unilaterally rejected several positions that did not square with its agenda.[28]

Among several contentious provisions that were both contained in the commission's report and accepted in the government's white paper, a clause requiring that both parents of any presidential candidate must be Zambians by birth evoked particular controversy. This provision effectively disqualified former President Kenneth Kaunda, whose parents were Malawian missionaries, from standing for the presidency on the United National Independence Party (UNIP) ticket in the 1996 elections. An additional provision also barred Kaunda from standing by restricting eligibility for the presidency to those who had not already served two terms as president. Although many petitioners to the Mwanakatwe Commission had made clear their desire that the presidency should be held by a "true Zambian" and that presidents should be limited to two terms in office, the parentage and term-limits clauses were widely—and, we believe, rightly—interpreted as attempts by the MMD government to remove its most powerful potential opponent from the coming electoral campaign.[29] Another provision adopted in the white paper and supported by many petitioners to the commission required that a traditional chief must abdicate his chieftaincy before becoming eligible for elected political office. This provision was included because the government knew that it would disqualify pro-opposition chiefs, including Kaunda's vice presidential running mate, Senior Chief Inyambo Yeta, and prevent them from participating in the elections. As the son of the Lozi paramount chief, Chief Inyambo was almost certain to draw wide support for the Kaunda ticket in Western Province.

In the midst of an ongoing and vigorous public debate about the provisions of the proposed constitution, however, the government and the MMD-controlled parliament decided to go ahead and adopt a constitutional amendment act. This decision, while constitutionally defensible, was a gross violation of the spirit of democratic discourse that President Chiluba claimed to champion, and it prompted a fierce public outcry by opposition parties, civil society groups, and representatives of the donor community. Not only did it fly in the face of repeated promises by the government that the constitution would only be revised following a period of wide public consultations, but it also ignored the recommendation of the Mwanakatwe Commission, as well as the demand of many civil society groups and the recommendation of key Western donors, that any new constitution should be ratified by a national referendum and a constituent assembly, rather than by parliament.

The adoption of the government's constitutional amendment act provoked such heated controversy because so much was at stake. During Kaunda's temporary retirement from politics following his defeat in Zambia's 1991 founding elections, UNIP had foundered badly. His return

to politics in June 1995 had reenergized the party and convinced its organizers (as well as the MMD's political strategists) that UNIP's electoral fortunes depended on having Kaunda as the party's presidential standard-
bearer. Because the ratification of the constitution by the MMD-dominated
parliament ensured that the clauses blocking Kaunda from participating
would be retained, it also meant the elimination of UNIP's only realistic
chance of competing with the MMD at the polls.

In the view of both international donors and domestic civil society
groups, such as the Law Association of Zambia and other human rights and
pro-democracy NGOs, the government's efforts to steamroll the constitutional amendment act through parliament represented a clear violation of
the principle—and the MMD's promise—that major national decisions
would only be made following open dialogue and vigorous public debate.
The government's handling of these issues thus reflected much of what
seemed to be going wrong with democratic rule in Zambia. The debates
about the anti-Kaunda provisions in the amended constitution were not the
first time that the issue of national authenticity had emerged in Zambian
politics. Under Chiluba, NGOs, journalists, and public figures critical of
the government or its leaders had regularly been accused of being
"un-Zambian" or "fronts for foreign interests." Several political opponents
had even been deported or threatened with expulsion by immigration
authorities following the government's allegations that they were not, in
fact, true Zambians.[30] The government's exploitation of its parliamentary
majority to enact the constitutional amendment act echoed the way it had
forced through other pieces of questionably democratic legislation, like the
brief state of emergency declared in 1993 and the Criminal Procedures
Code (Amendment) Act of the same year, which denied bail to individuals
accused of certain crimes. It also reminded critics of how the government
had used the Speaker of the National Assembly, a ruling-party nominee, to
sanction, and in one instance even imprison, journalists or parliamentarians
who criticized government spokespeople in parliament.[31] The MMD government's willingness to curtail public debate on contentious issues was, by
this time, also familiar, as was its tendency to go back on assurances that
were privately made to donor representatives about impending government
decisions.

Another controversial issue in the months leading up to the 1996 general elections involved the revision of the voters' roll. Given that the last
comprehensive voter registration exercise had been carried out in 1987, a
fresh registration of voters was a clear prerequisite for meaningful elections.[32] Following months of delay and a tender procedure that was fraught
with irregularities, the contract for compiling the new voters' register was
awarded and the registration of voters began in December 1995.[33] Three
months and several deadline extensions later, the exercise concluded with
only 2.3 million registrants, out of an estimated population of 3.8 million

eligible voters.[34] This represented a marked decline since 1991, not only in the number of registered voters (there had been 3.0 million in 1991), but also in the number of registered voters as a percentage of those eligible (87 percent in 1991 versus 59 percent in 1996).[35] Opposition parties and democracy-monitoring organizations criticized the suspicious conditions under which the tender had been awarded, the low yield of the registration exercise, and the numerous problems in the registration process itself: thousands of names were omitted from the register at the same time that thousands of other individuals were issued duplicate registration cards. These groups demanded that the entire registration exercise be scrapped and that citizens over the age of 18 be permitted to vote with their national registration cards. The government refused these demands, pointing out that it had extended the registration period several times and that it was not the government's fault if eligible voters were not coming forward to register.[36]

By the time President Chiluba signed the constitutional amendment into law on May 28, 1996, political tensions were high. Opposition parties and civic leaders demanded the immediate repeal or revision of the new legislation and appealed to donors to suspend their economic support for the government until it did so. Protest rallies were watched carefully by armed paramilitary police. Threats by UNIP to disrupt the elections if the government decided to go ahead with the polls under the new constitution coincided with a rash of antigovernment graffiti and a series of bomb attacks in Lusaka and the Copperbelt. Whether the Black Mamba organization that claimed responsibility for these bombings was really a front group for UNIP, as the government alleged, or an MMD-sponsored attempt to justify cancellation of the elections, as opposition leaders insisted, is not clear. Whatever the truth, eight UNIP leaders, including the party's vice president, Chief Inyambo, were arrested on June 3 and charged (wrongly, the High Court later ruled) with treason and the murder of a policeman (who had been killed when trying to dismantle one of the bombs).[37] Days later, tensions between pro-UNIP and pro-MMD students at the University of Zambia erupted into violence. By the end of June, several donor countries announced the review or suspension of bilateral assistance to Zambia, and a Southern African Development Community meeting in Gaborone took the unprecedented step of holding discussions about what it should do about the "Zambian crisis."

As the expected date of Zambia's second elections drew near, another controversy emerged concerning when the contest would actually take place. Although local government elections, which had been due in November 1995, were postponed without significant public comment, the timing of presidential and parliamentary elections was taken much more seriously. Many people assumed that second elections would have to be held on or before October 31 because that was the date in 1991 on which the first elections had taken place. Opposition leaders asserted that the government would be illegally constituted if it remained in power after October 31, and declared that they would refuse to recognize its authority after that date. The government, however, insisted on a very different timetable, claiming that elections did not have to be held until 90 days after the dissolution of parliament, which in turn had to take place within five years of its first sitting on November 29, 1991. This pushed the deadline for the second election to the end of February 1997, well into the rainy season. Quite apart from whether this interpretation was legally valid, the government's position served to heighten the atmosphere of uncertainty surrounding the elections and to reinforce misgivings about the integrity of the election process. Chiluba's eleventh-hour concession to alter the composition of the Electoral Commission in order to give it greater independence did little to increase the confidence of election observers or participants.

In the end, the dispute over the timing of the vote was superseded by others that arose after the start of the electoral campaign. On October 19, President Chiluba announced that the election would be held on November 18, 1996. Four days later, UNIP, along with six other small opposition parties, declared that it would boycott the polls, citing, among other reasons, the government's mismanagement of the voter registration exercise. In addition to withdrawing all of its parliamentary candidates from the race, UNIP promised to mount a campaign to encourage citizens not to participate in the election and began pressing its party organizers to (illegally) confiscate voter cards from party members to ensure that the boycott call would be heeded.

Even with UNIP out of the race, the MMD still faced several challenges. Two of the remaining opposition parties, the National Party (NP) and the Zambia Democratic Congress (ZDC), fielded candidates in most constituencies and enjoyed pockets of strength around the country. Two others, the National Lima Party (NLP) and the Agenda for Zambia (AZ), put up only a handful of candidates, but they posed a real threat in the constituencies that they were contesting. An additional challenge came from 96 independent candidates. Most of these candidates were individuals who had failed to win party nominations, and in many cases, this reflected a lack of grassroots support. However, in some instances, the independent candidates had won constituency-level primary elections as representatives of the MMD, only to be displaced by the party in favor of candidates preferred by the leadership. Given both their demonstrated ability to attract grassroots support and the anger that their supporters felt toward the MMD for failing to adopt their chosen candidate, these independents posed a particularly serious threat.

In the face of these challenges, the MMD took advantage of its control over government resources to bolster its electoral prospects. While the MMD was not the only party to hand out T-shirts, beer, and money to attract supporters, other parties lacked the resources that were available to the MMD by virtue of its position as the ruling party. MMD candidates enjoyed the use of government vehicles (sometimes equipped with false, nongovernment number plates) and Zambia Information Service public-address equipment for campaigning purposes. Fertilizer, maize meal, and development funds were distributed by the government to attract supporters in rural constituencies. In urban areas, the MMD won support by selling council houses at bargain prices. MMD campaigners also threatened to withdraw development funding from constituencies that elected members of the opposition.

Perhaps the most important campaign resource at the MMD's disposal was the media. Two of Zambia's three major newspapers, almost all of its radio stations, and its only television channel are all government owned. Although opposition rallies and speeches did receive coverage in these media outlets, an analysis of their content conducted by the Foundation for Democratic Process, an indigenous NGO, found "glaring disparities in the allocation of air-time and space among the main contenders in the election."[38] In addition, independently owned newspapers that published articles or editorials critical of the way the election exercise was being conducted faced harassment by MMD supporters or the police. Many of these articles and editorials were, in fact, irresponsible, and the criticisms levied at the government by some segments of the independent press often appeared motivated as much by personal vendettas against President Chiluba as by a desire to report objectively on government affairs. Nevertheless, the government's reaction was often disproportional to the offense, and in any case, it was not directed through proper legal channels. According to Human Rights Watch/Africa, the most prominent of these independent newspapers, the *Post*, was the target of 20 separate acts of harassment by the government or its supporters between January 1994 and October 1996.[39]

After all of the tension that developed during the months preceding the elections, election day itself passed peacefully. Despite widespread expectations of violence and confusion, observers across the country reported that voters were orderly and serious as they waited to cast their ballots. Compared with 1991, when Zambians anticipated sweeping change, voters in 1996 came to the polls with more realistic expectations about how quickly their lives would improve. At the same time, and not very far away, tens of thousands of Hutu refugees were being repatriated from Zaire to Rwanda, leading many voters to comment that they viewed voting as a preferable alternative to the ethnic violence that had engulfed their neighbors.[40] The maturity displayed by members of the electorate stood in marked contrast to the immaturity of some opposition leaders, who made unjustifiably inflammatory statements about the government and its leaders, threatened civil unrest, vacillated regarding the validity of the elections, and even called for international sanctions to be levied against their own country.

The results of Zambia's 1996 general elections are displayed in Table 20.4. Facing four other candidates, President Chiluba won reelection by a landslide, with 73 percent of the vote, only three points below his mark in the two-candidate race of 1991. His nearest rival, Dean Mung'omba of the ZDC, won only 13 percent. In the parliamentary elections, the MMD captured 61 percent of the vote and 131 of the 150 available seats. The ZDC, which won 14 percent of the parliamentary vote, managed to win only two seats, while the NP and the AZ took five and two seats, respectively. The NLP and six other minor parties failed to win any seats. Independent candidates won in 10 constituencies, giving them one seat more than all of the opposition parties combined.

The election results revealed a number of interesting trends. First, while voter turnout, at nearly 59 percent of registered voters, was more than 15 points higher than it had been in 1991, it still represented only 33 percent of those eligible. Thus, while President Chiluba may have received 73 percent of the vote, his mandate came from only about 24 percent of the voting-age population. Second, while the MMD's strength was similar in urban and rural areas, it varied considerably across regions. In the parliamentary poll, for example, it ranged from 70 percent in the Copperbelt and Luapula, the president's home region, to a low of 44 percent in Northwestern Province. Twelve of the 19 parliamentary seats won by opposition or independent candidates were located in just two provinces: Western and Northwestern.[41] A third trend was the emergence of ticket splitting. While the MMD's presidential and parliamentary vote tallies were nearly identical in 1991, they showed significant differences in 1996, particularly in constituencies where strong independent candidates were standing. The substantial gap between President Chiluba's overall share of the vote (73 percent) and that of his party's parliamentary candidates (61 percent) suggests that the individual qualities of parliamentary candidates may have been as much a part of voter decisionmaking as party affiliation.

Perhaps the biggest difference in voting patterns between 1991 and 1996 appears in Eastern Province, where UNIP won every constituency in 1991, but lost all 19 seats to the MMD in 1996. A comparison between voter turnout rates in Eastern Province and the rest of the country makes it clear that the opposition boycott was successful in keeping many voters away from the polls in this region. While Eastern Province residents were slightly more likely than other Zambians to register to vote in 1996, their turnout of only 37 percent in the elections was more than 20 points below the national average. Eastern Province was also the only region of the country to record a drop in voter turnout from 1991.[42] Since the call for a stay-away came well after the conclusion of the voter registration exercise,

Table 20.4 Results of Zambia's Second Elections, November 18, 1996

Province	Legislative Election				Presidential Election	
	Voter Turnout 1996 (% registered voters)	Voter Turnout 1991 (% registered voters)	MMD Vote Share (% valid votes)	MMD Seats Won [opposition seats]	Chiluba's Vote Share (% valid votes)	Split Tickets (Pres. minus parl. %)
Central	56.6	35.4	49.8	12 [2]	73.2	23.4
Copperbelt	71.7	49.4	70.5	22 [0]	86.3	15.8
Eastern	37.0	46.0	61.9	19 [0]	64.0	2.1
Luapula	64.8	41.1	70.2	14 [0]	85.5	15.3
Lusaka	57.8	43.8	64.3	10 [2]	74.4	10.1
Northern	64.4	42.4	63.0	18 [3]	80.5	17.5
Northwestern	68.1	40.0	44.4	6 [6]	51.2	6.8
Southern	57.7	42.2	57.0	19 [0]	67.1	10.1
Western	53.5	40.0	49.8	11 [6]	43.1	−6.7
Total	58.7	43.4	61.0	131 [19]	72.6	11.6

Sources: For 1996 results: *Presidential and Parliamentary Elections, 1996: Provisional Results* (Lusaka: Electoral Commission of Zambia, November 25, 1996), For 1991 results: *Summary of Parliamentary Election Results* (Lusaka: Zambia Independent Monitoring Team, 1991).

the comparatively low turnout rate in Eastern Province attests to the effectiveness of the boycott there. In addition, those most likely to heed the embargo were also those most likely to vote against the MMD, so the boycott probably accounts for a large part of the change in the MMD's fortunes in the region.

There is no evidence, however, that the opposition boycott had any demonstrable effect on voting patterns in the rest of the country, where UNIP was much weaker to begin with. UNIP sympathizers outside of Eastern Province seem to have reacted to their party's withdrawal from the election by voting for other opposition parties, or even for the MMD, rather than by boycotting. In the end, the boycott proved to be an enormous tactical, and even strategic, miscalculation for UNIP. Not only did it fail to generate the broad-based compliance that would have been required for UNIP to credibly claim that the election had been illegitimate, but by depriving the party of the parliamentary representation that it otherwise would undoubtedly have won, it effectively removed UNIP from the political arena. Moreover, the boycott's failure served to discredit Kaunda, and it generated deep, and perhaps insurmountable, divisions within the party. It is unclear whether UNIP will be able to recover. UNIP's experience suggests that while boycotts may have worked against colonial regimes or in one-party settings, they are far less effective in democratic contexts where alternative channels are available for citizens to communicate their disagreement with the status quo.

Even if the UNIP boycott had been more effective, it still would not have explained the MMD's broad electoral success in the country as a whole. To do this, we need to look not simply at the enormous advantages in campaign resources that the MMD possessed—UNIP, after all, possessed similar advantages in 1991—but also at the MMD's ability to convince voters that it should be given another five years to finish its program of reforms. The MMD won mass support in 1991 because, after 27 years of Kaunda's increasingly repressive and economically destructive rule, it was viewed as an agent of change. It won mass support again in 1996 because it was able to draw upon its early successes in market liberalization, health care reform, and transport-sector liberalization to convince voters that it was still the party best positioned to raise living standards for average Zambians. The failure of the opposition parties to exploit the MMD's more mixed record in other areas and to persuade voters that they represented a better alternative was also critically important. Although the opposition parties did succeed in winning the sympathy of donors and urban elites due to the government's handling of the constitution and voter registration, these issues failed to resonate with the vast majority of voting Zambians, who seemed to feel that the MMD was doing a reasonable job.[43] In addition, the energy that opposition parties devoted to arguing over these issues deflected their attention away from grassroots mobilization efforts that might have allowed them to capitalize more fully on the MMD's weaknesses. By focusing their energies on the wrong issues (the constitution, rather than jobs and agriculture) and the wrong audiences (the donor community, rather than voters), opposition parties left the field open for an easy MMD victory.

The events that followed November 18, 1996, demonstrated that Zambia's second elections were more than simply a contest for votes and seats. No sooner had the election results been announced than a new competition began to assign a meaning to the process. The ZDC, which was genuinely stunned by its thrashing by the MMD, immediately made allegations that the elections had been rigged, though only slim anecdotal evidence for its claim of widespread electoral fraud was reported in the independent press. Former President Kaunda and his colleagues in the "Opposition Alliance" declared the elections a sham and promised to organize a civic action campaign to make the country ungovernable. Meanwhile, the country's three most prominent election-monitoring NGOs announced that, although the voting itself appeared to have been free of serious rigging, the process that led up to the elections had been so flawed as to call the whole exercise into question.[44] The theme running through all of these charges was that Zambia's democracy was stumbling badly.

The MMD government responded to these allegations by claiming that the peacefulness of the polls and the fact that so many candidates and parties had participated evidenced that Zambia's democracy was fundamentally on course. It stressed that while some groups may have disagreed with particular clauses in the new constitution, those who did so had been free to take the matter to court. The courts had, on several occasions, found both the clauses in question and the government's adoption of the constitution through parliament, rather than through a referendum or an extraordinary constituent assembly, to have been within the boundaries of the law. Moreover, the government pointed to the results of the election itself to argue that, whatever its critics might say, the vast majority of Zambian voters—the audience that matters—were unfazed by allegations of impropriety or unfair play.[45]

In addition to mounting seemingly reasonable defenses of this sort, the MMD also lashed out at its opponents. It accused those who questioned the integrity of the elections of being fronts for foreign interests or puppets acting on the instructions of the government's enemies. When the Zambia Independent Monitoring Team and the Committee for a Clean Campaign called press conferences to announce their opinion that the elections had been flawed, their offices were raided, their bank accounts were frozen, and their chairmen were detained by the police. As a way of further threatening these groups, President Chiluba announced his intention to scrutinize NGOs that receive foreign funds more closely.

The intense struggle over how the elections would be interpreted dominated Zambia's political discourse during the weeks following the vote. Both the MMD and the opposition parties had a great deal at stake in the verdict that would emerge. The MMD, which had been under pressure from the donor community for some time to demonstrate its commitment to democracy (and which had already suffered a significant cutback in donor funding for its failure to do so), stood to lose the balance-of-payment support that it needed to pay government salaries and prevent the economy from slipping back into the stagnation of the Kaunda era. The opposition parties, which had failed to win power at the ballot box, stood to lose the leverage over the government that they had formerly held by virtue of the sympathy they enjoyed in the donor community and among certain segments of the Zambian elite. In press conferences and newspaper editorials, which were aimed as much at the international audience as at Zambian nationals, each side aggressively presented its view of how the November 18 elections should be interpreted. The intensity of the struggle signaled that the elections had failed to resolve the political tensions in the country.

In the end, the most influential view was expressed by the international donors, neighboring countries, opposition parties, and civic organizations, which chose to make Kaunda's exclusion the centerpiece of their objections to the election. They asserted (rightly, in our view) that no election could be fair in which a major opposition candidate was barred from competing. Against this convincing argument by a coalition of domestic and international forces, the government failed to successfully "spin" the interpretation in its own favor. Somewhat overlooked in the discourse, however, were the views of those who voted. By largely ignoring the opposition boycott and granting the MMD a second term, many Zambians indicated that they wished to avoid a return to the "bad old days" of UNIP, instead hoping that the "old man" (Kaunda) would quietly step aside from politics. Many also supported the idea that candidates whose ancestry was not "authentically Zambian" should be barred from contesting for the presidency and saw nothing wrong with altering the constitution to ensure that this principle would be upheld.[46] Thus, different audiences judged the election by different standards. An election that was unquestionably flawed from the standpoint of most foreign—and many domestic—critics was more acceptable from the standpoint of a majority of Zambian voters. This observation poses a challenge to all who are interested in analyzing the meaning of elections in Africa.

What, then, did second elections portend for consolidation of democratic procedures in Zambia? The answer is clear: they set the process back. The 1996 elections in Zambia contrast sharply with the founding elections of 1991, which had signaled an emerging consensus—however temporary and fragile—about the rules and norms of a democratic political game. The second elections five years later reflected the unraveling of that consensus: the government wrote rules to its own advantage, thereby calling into ques-

tion its legitimacy with opinion leaders in international and domestic arenas; the major opposition party opted not to play and, in the process, weakened the presence of the opposition in parliament and other public arenas;
and the main remaining opposition party, which contested the election but
lost overwhelmingly, discredited itself by refusing to accept that its defeat
was genuine. This left civic organizations and independent newspapers as
the most vocal defenders of participatory and competitive politics, but
these groups were beset by problems, including alienation from popular
political opinion, their own growing politicization, and their susceptibility
to the heavy hand of an increasingly intolerant government. The fact that
Zambian voters were more concerned with issues of personal economic
survival than with the constitutionality of electoral rules suggests that ordinary citizens are unlikely to stand up against the gradual erosion of democracy. In this sense, the consolidation of a civic culture in Zambia is still
seriously incomplete. At the end of 1996, democracy was barely surviving
in Zambia, and its future did not look promising.

Conclusion

Sub-Saharan Africa's second elections, of which Zambia's 1996 contest
was a prime example, provide insight into the nature of democratic development in Africa. On the basis of the 16 second elections that we have
studied, several working conclusions can be drawn that can be further tested and refined as electoral cycles continue to unfold.

At a purely formal level, presidential and legislative elections have
thus far taken place in Africa's new multiparty systems with acceptable
punctuality. These elections have been meaningful, in the sense that they
have injected a measure of competitiveness and uncertainty into contests
for top political office, and there is a growing sense among political elites
and masses alike that competitive elections are the only legitimate way to
choose national leaders. The fact that recent electoral boycotts have usually
led their proponents into the political wilderness has only reinforced the
impression that elections are the principal game in town. The intensity of
postelection discourse regarding disputed second elections further underscores the importance that all political actors now attach to the election
exercise.

By the same token, the quality of elections in Africa's multiparty systems is far from perfect, and it is probably declining. Sitting leaders continue to be less than fully transparent about their intentions regarding election
timing, thereby keeping opponents off balance. In addition, incumbents
have not hesitated to use legislative majorities or sheer executive power to
structure the rules of electoral competition to their own advantage. The
more dominant the elected ruling party in relation to other political parties,

and the more secure its majority in the legislative body, the greater its latitude in this regard.

For the most part, leaders have not chosen to tamper with rules of political participation as a means of ensuring their continued hold on power. There is virtual unanimity among civilian (and even some military) leaders in contemporary Africa that all qualified citizens have certain political rights, including the rights to be enfranchised, to vote, and to be consulted in some fashion when making policy. Unreliable voter registers remain a problem in several of Africa's new democracies, but these flaws are just as likely to be due to the state's weak administrative capacity and to voter indifference as to deliberate interference on the part of politicians. Incumbents' efforts to retain political control have instead focused on manipulating the rules of political competition by restricting the eligibility for candidacy. In Africa's personalistic political regimes, such rule changes usually involve disqualifying the principal rivals for the presidency. This finding confirms that the biggest challenge in making the transition to democracy, especially from the mass-mobilizing, one-party systems that were previously so common in Africa, is not so much the expansion of political participation, but the introduction of genuine political competition. Although a normative consensus may be emerging in Africa about the principle of broad popular participation, there is still fundamental disagreement about the rules for open political contests.

With few exceptions, second elections (Zambia's included) also confirm that polling procedures and vote counting are not the principal sources of electoral malpractice in Africa. If "rigging" occurs, it is in the form of vote buying and political intimidation, which happen long before polling day. Indeed, the reports of observers and monitors on second elections increasingly distinguish between the growing efficiency and effectiveness of polling administration, on the one hand, and persistent problems with election rules or campaign conduct, on the other. Incumbents who are intent on retaining office have found "wholesale" rule changes to be a far more efficient and reliable means of controlling election outcomes than seeking to influence votes individually at the "retail" level.

In part because incumbency provides advantages in shaping rules, but also because voters sometimes extend real support to, or are at least unwilling to pass judgment on, new governments until they have completed ambitious reform programs, the winners of founding elections have usually gone on to win second elections as well. Thus, following an interval of turbulent transitions, African politics is returning to a familiar equilibrium in which the electoral alternation of leaders is once again becoming exceptional. However, while this trend is clear in presidential elections, it is less so in legislative contests, where the possibility of increased turnover cannot be excluded. Indeed, democratic transitions have emboldened African voters to demand greater accountability from hometown representatives. Where independent candidates or small, regionally based parties have emerged, they have begun to demonstrate the ability to mount electoral challenges to the legislative representatives of ruling parties.

A fragile form of democracy will survive in some African countries as long as multiparty elections continue to be held in which voters are free to exercise meaningful choices. To further analyze the prospects for surviving democracies, analysts must learn to distinguish between those that are slowly dying (like Zambia by 1996) and those that are gradually consolidating (like Ghana by 1996). Under no circumstances, however, should we underestimate the difficulty of democratic consolidation on the African continent. Among African countries, only Mauritius has thus far satisfied even the most minimal (excessively electoral) conditions for consolidation set by the "two-turnover test." We cannot be at all certain that countries like Benin and Madagascar, which have experienced one post-transition turnover, will also tread this path. After all, the ruling parties in Africa's longest-surviving multiparty systems, Botswana, Senegal, and Zimbabwe, have never been defeated at the polls. The experiences of Zambia may therefore illustrate a much more common trajectory: the dominant party, aided by an election boycott but checked by a barrage of international criticism, manages to imperfectly renew its domestic mandate.

In all political regimes, including democracies, the meaning of incumbent victories is more difficult to interpret than the meaning of historic voter realignments. Especially in Africa, where the influence of "big men" continues to loom large over electoral and other political processes, it is rarely clear whether the reelection of an incumbent constitutes the extension of a leader's mandate or the resignation of the electorate to his inevitable dominance. For these reasons, the meaning of Africa's second elections will necessarily be murkier than the watershed contests of the early 1990s. This round of elections will challenge comparative analysts to cut through the rival rhetorics of winners and losers. When all is said and done, however, the fact that intense political struggles are being waged over the convening, conduct, and meaning of second elections is proof positive that, in Africa, elections as an institution are beginning to matter.

Notes

1. O'Donnell and Schmitter, *Transitions*, p. 57.
2. Dahl, *Polyarchy.*
3. Schmitter, "Consolidation of Democracy."
4. Linz and Stepan, *Problems of Democratic Transition*, p. 5.
5. Schumpeter, *Capitalism, Socialism, and Democracy.* See also Dahl, *Preface to Democratic Theory.* For critiques of such definitions as narrow and elitist, see Pateman, *Participation and Democratic Theory.*
6. Huntington, *Third Wave*, pp. 266–267. The "two-turnover test" may be

something of a misnomer, since its fulfillment actually calls for three elections, which could potentially involve three alternations.

7. Karl, "Imposing Consent."

8. Carothers, *In Search of Democracy;* Herman and Brodhead, *Demonstration Elections.*

9. Seligson and Booth, *Elections and Democracy,* p. 18.

10. This leaves only five sub-Saharan African countries that had not completed competitive elections in the 1990s: Liberia, Nigeria, Somalia, Swaziland, and Congo (Zaire).

11. Bratton and van de Walle, *Democratic Experiments,* table 8.

12. The turnout figure of 86 percent in Equatorial Guinea may be falsely inflated.

13. Bratton and van de Walle, *Democratic Experiments,* table 8.

14. Ibid., table 7.

15. *Africa Confidential,* vol. 37 (1996): 2.

16. Information in this paragraph is drawn from Richey and Ponte, "1995 Tanzania Elections," pp. 80–87.

17. *Africa Confidential,* vol. 37 (1996): 6.

18. In Côte d'Ivoire, elections were postponed in three constituencies, and the results were annulled in three more (out of a total of 185 constituencies).

19. The raw figures are nine out of 16 (for 1995–1996) and 10 out of 12 (for 1990–1994). Data for the earlier period is drawn from Bratton and van de Walle, *Democratic Experiments,* table 7.

20. *Africa Confidential,* vol. 36 (1995): 7.

21. Reuters, "Low Turnout."

22. NDI, "Preliminary Statement." See also Network of Domestic Election Observers, "Interim Report"; OAU, "Statement by the Observer Group"; Commonwealth Observer Group, "Interim Statement"; and IFES, "Supporting the Electoral Process."

23. In Comoros, a new head of government was elected, but under circumstances where the incumbent (Said Mohammed Djohar) did not run again.

24. Quoted in *Christian Science Monitor,* "Benin's Ex-President."

25. Bédié's sweep is in good measure attributable to an opposition boycott.

26. It would be helpful to have not only more electoral cases and a clearer trend before pronouncing definitively on this issue, but also a comprehensive set of data on the winning party's share of votes in legislative elections (rather than the currently available data on seats).

27. See, for example, Joseph, "Zambia," and Bratton, "Zambia Starts Over."

28. An important example involved the insertion, over the recommendations of the commission, of a clause declaring Zambia to be a Christian nation (Government of Zambia, "Summary of Recommendations").

29. Evidence that barring Kaunda's candidacy was, in fact, the purpose of the clause may be adduced from the chants of "We've defeated Kaunda!" by MMD parliamentarians following the adoption of the constitution (*Post,* May 16, 1996).

30. Senior UNIP politician William Banda was deported to Malawi by Zambian immigration authorities in August 1994. UNIP official John Chinula was deported in September 1995. In October 1995, the minister for home affairs publicly threatened to deport former President Kaunda because, he claimed, Kaunda had never officially renounced his Malawian citizenship. The government soon backed down from this position (Human Rights Watch/Africa, "Zambia," pp. 34–36).

31. On February 22, 1996, the Speaker of the National Assembly ruled that a pair of articles that had appeared in the *Post* newspaper contained "libeling . . .

inflammatory and contemptuous remarks" that lowered the dignity of the House. When the authors of the articles, *Post* managing director Fred M'membe, editor Bright Mwape, and columnist Lucy Sichone, twice refused to respond to the Speaker's summons, he declared them in contempt of parliament and directed that they be arrested by the police. They were released three weeks later after the High Court ruled that the Speaker had exceeded his authority (Human Rights Watch/Africa, "Zambia," pp. 19-21).

32. The 1991 elections had been held using a combination of the outdated voters' register from 1987 and a supplementary roll prepared during a three-week registration period in October 1990.

33. Nikuv Computers, Ltd., the company that won the contract, was one of the highest bidders, prompting speculation that it had been awarded the tender either as part of a kickback scheme or as a payoff for rigging the elections in favor of the MMD.

34. The figure of 2.3 million registered voters comes from Electoral Commission of Zambia, "Provisional Results, 1996." The figure of 3.8 million eligible voters was calculated from the 1990 Census of Population and Housing.

35. Both the number and percentage of registered voters in 1991 are probably somewhat inflated due to the inclusion in the rolls of voters who had passed away since 1987.

36. The government's contention that voter apathy, rather than its alleged mishandling of the registration process, was responsible for the poor yield of the exercise is supported by the fact that, by election day, only 1.1 million of the 2.3 million freshly registered voters had picked up their voter cards.

37. Two of the detainees were released soon after their arrest; the remaining six were acquitted on November 1, 1996.

38. *Monitor*, "How Some Monitors Arrived."

39. Human Rights Watch/Africa, "Zambia," pp. 23–24.

40. Authors' discussions with voters on, and after, election day.

41. Along with Central Province, these were the only regions of the country in which MMD candidates won a smaller share of the vote than the combined totals for opposition candidates.

42. Although the turnout of registered voters rose by 15 percent nationally, it dropped by 9 percent in Eastern Province.

43. A United States Agency for International Development–sponsored survey of 1,200 eligible voters, conducted by Michigan State University and the University of Zambia immediately following the 1996 elections, found that 43.2 percent of Zambians assessed the overall performance of the MMD government as good or very good, whereas only 21.7 percent saw it as poor or very poor. The remaining 35.1 percent ranked the MMD's performance as fair. Notably, these figures were virtually unchanged from a survey conducted over three years earlier in June 1993, suggesting that the government's support was holding steady over time.

44. Most international monitoring organizations refused to participate in the monitoring exercise lest their presence be seen to lend legitimacy to what they viewed as an already flawed electoral process.

45. In the same survey (see note 43), 80.9 percent of Zambians said that they thought the 1996 elections had been "fair" and that no candidate had enjoyed "an unfair advantage."

46. Of the 19.1 percent of Zambians who disputed the quality of the 1996 elections (see previous note), just 16.4 percent (i.e., 3.1 percent of the national population) said they did so because of the exclusion of Kaunda from the presidential race. Most cited other reasons.

21

Ghana: The Challenges of Consolidating Democracy

E. GYIMAH-BOADI

The Ghanaian elections of December 7, 1996, raised two sets of questions. The first was narrow but urgent. Would the electoral process be free, fair, and transparent? Would the outcome be broadly accepted or vigorously disputed, as it had been in 1992? Happily, the predominant answer to this line of inquiry was positive. Ghana's presidential and parliamentary polling went ahead peacefully; violence, though widely expected, never materialized. Moreover, the 1996 elections were freer and more transparent than those of 1992.

The second set of questions were broader and more difficult to answer concisely. They concern the longer-term impacts of the elections: whether they will advance, delay, or even reverse democratic progress; whether they will weaken or strengthen governmental accountability; whether the entrenched neopatrimonial "party-state" will flourish or wither; whether the prospects for economic reform and renewal will wax or wane; whether civilians will gain more control over the military; and whether they will foster the growth and development of civil society and its participation in the political process. Responses to these queries will require a look at the four years following the return to constitutional rule in 1992, and even then, only tentative answers can be given.[1]

Democratic Progress in the Fourth Republic

The elections of 1992, though disputed, ushered in Ghana's Fourth Republic, a period of modest but significant gains in democratic governance. These gains included political liberalization, which allowed Ghanaians to enjoy a much wider range of rights and liberties, and they gave vibrant, privately owned media greater scope to emerge. The postelection period also saw a modest boost in governmental transparency and accountability, thanks to the resumed publication of the Auditor General's reports, the institution of parliamentary debate, and the increasing activism of constitutionally established watchdog bodies such as the Commission on Human Rights and Administrative Justice (CHRAJ) and the Media Commission, as well as the crusading spirit of the private media.

Renewed efforts to foster an environment that is conducive to economic growth and private-sector development also bore fruit. Constitutional provisions for the protection of private property were generally respected. With one exception, the state refrained from confiscating private property, and assets that had previously been confiscated by the state were gradually restored to their original owners. Moreover, official commitment to economic renewal remained strong, despite increased popular pressure in favor of reversing some aspects of the reform measures.

Constitutional rule also opened a larger political space for civil society in Ghana, and civic associations proliferated. Many were devoted to the protection of human rights and the promotion of democratic governance. These include the Institute of Economic Affairs (IEA), the Ghana Legal Literacy and Resource Foundation, and the Ghana Committee on Human and People's Rights. Indeed, the years since 1992 have seen many initiatives by Ghanaian society to promote democratic development. Civic groups and public-interest organizations have sought to improve the quality of analysis and deliberations in the National Assembly through preparing memoranda and arranging for expert testimony on topics being taken up by the assembly, and some even attempted to mediate a dispute between President Jerry Rawlings and his vice president, Kow N. Arkaah, after an incident in December 1996 during which Rawlings was reported to have physically attacked Arkaah at a cabinet meeting. These society-based initiatives were not always welcomed by the ruling National Democratic Congress (NDC), but they reflected a new level of independent societal involvement in politics.

Such achievements notwithstanding, the hope that January 7, 1993—the date of the inauguration of the Fourth Republic—would mark a fresh start in democratic governance was frustrated in many respects. In fact, Ghana's latest attempt at democratic governance began on a decidedly inauspicious note, and it faced many critical challenges. In the parliament that emerged from the 1992 elections, Rawlings's NDC held 189 of the 200 seats (and nine more were held by the two smaller parties aligned with the NDC). Presidential nominees for key posts came under only the most casual legislative scrutiny. In addition, the new government attempted to pass illiberal laws, such as the Serious Fraud Bill, which sought to give the proposed Serious Fraud Office sweeping powers to investigate, monitor, and prosecute an unspecified portfolio of frauds and economic crimes, and a nongovernmental organization (NGO) bill, which sought to place these bodies under a government-appointed advisory council.[2]

Relations between the government and the extraparliamentary opposition turned highly acrimonious. Political society was also sharply polarized, with the ruling NDC and its supporters at one end and the older, postcolonial elites at the other. The latter included leaders of the two main pre-Rawlings political traditions—the conservative Kofi Busia/J. B. Danquah camp and the heirs of the left-leaning Nkrumahist movement—as well as former Rawlings supporters who had left the president's camp. Relations between the government and key elements of civil society also reflected mistrust. Consensus regarding such key questions as how best to promote direct investment and fund basic and tertiary education remained elusive.

Ghana's economy began to falter, as economic growth decelerated. Macroeconomic imbalances, caused at least in part by election-related public spending, reemerged.[3] Inflation soared, unemployment remained very high, and the modest gains in poverty reduction in the late 1980s and early 1990s were undermined. The enviable record of prudent fiscal management compiled since the 1980s appeared to be in jeopardy. Paralyzing strikes and violent protests by unions and other organized groups compelled the government to slow the pace of economic reforms, such as public-sector job retrenchments and caps on the growth of salaries and allowances. The newly introduced value-added tax had to be dropped. The Ghanaian economy, many analysts concluded, was headed "back to the intensive care unit."[4]

The Fourth Republic's experiment in democratic governance seemed about to break down as violent ethnic and communal clashes erupted in many parts of the country in 1994 and 1995, especially in the northern regions. In the middle of 1995, antigovernment demonstrations rocked the larger cities, killing at least five people and wounding several others. Meanwhile, the fracas between Rawlings and Vice President Arkaah threatened to provoke a constitutional crisis.

It was against this background of unmet aspirations for democratic and economic renewal that Ghanaians began to prepare themselves for the next multiparty elections, slated for December 1996. These elections became the object of great expectations, especially as regards the revival and consolidation of political reform.

Positive Elements in the December Polls

The December 7 election marked the first time in Ghanaian history that two multiparty elections had occurred under the same constitution. It was also a keenly contested election, at least in comparison with that of 1992. On the surface, Rawlings and the main opposition candidate, John A. Kuffour, appeared to be equally confident of their chances of winning.[5] For a short while, there even appeared to be a slight chance that Rawlings might lose.

The hard-fought campaign produced an instant "democracy dividend." Accountability and transparency got a boost as Rawlings found himself compelled to campaign with utmost seriousness, to defend his record, and to address some of the issues raised by his opponents. For example, he conceded the truth of the widely heard criticism that, at a time of public-sector contraction and general austerity, his cabinet was bloated, and he promised, if reelected, to employ fewer ministers. To dispel the widespread allegations of self-dealing and opacity in the process of state enterprise divestiture, the government published a list of all enterprises that were sold from January 1, 1995, to July 31, 1996, their new investors or owners, the prices charged, and the balances outstanding.[6] Indeed, Rawlings made history of a sort when, in midcampaign, he broke his 15-year record of silence toward the domestic press and gave an interview (including a public phone-in session) to a privately owned radio station.

Most significantly, the official outcome of the elections appears to have been broadly accepted, with the losing candidates conceding defeat and congratulating the victor. Even more impressively, the defeated political parties and their supporters appear to have already started looking to the year 2000, when the next elections are scheduled to take place. This bespeaks both a belief that elections offer at least the possibility of winning political office and a broad (albeit provisional) consensus that the ballot box is, in any case, the sole legitimate instrument for seeking power. Many of the candidates who had complaints about the 1996 results are seeking redress through the Electoral Commission and the judiciary, rather than resorting to colorful but dubious tactics such as marching naked through the streets (as some female supporters of the New Patriotic Party [NPP] reportedly did in 1992).

The great improvements made in the electoral system since the 1992 election, as well as the presence of 60,000 party agents at polling stations on election day, were crucial to the success of the 1996 elections and the instant acceptability of its results. A share of the credit must go to civil society. Having played only a limited role in 1992, it emerged as a major player in the latest round. Determined to avoid the mistakes of 1992 and the bitter disputes that they engendered, and desiring to assume ownership of the electoral process and its outcomes, key elements of civil society mounted programs to support the election. Prominent national organizations such as the Christian Council, the Conference of Catholic Bishops, the Ghana Legal Literacy and Resource Foundation, and others mounted campaigns of voter education, while religious bodies organized prayer-for-peace campaigns to prepare the ground for a peaceful election.

The epitome of societal involvement in the Ghanaian political process was the emergence of society-based, domestic poll-watching bodies, despite strong opposition from the ruling party. The two organizations that adopted this role were Ghanalert, led by veteran journalist Ben Ephson, and the Network of Domestic Election Observers (NEDEO), led by Joseph Kingsley-Nyinah, a retired appeals court judge and former electoral commissioner (1979–1983). NEDEO was composed of 23 prominent national organizations, including the Christian Council, the Catholic Secretariat, the Federation of Muslim Councils, the Ahmadiyya Muslim Mission, the Ghana National Association of Teachers, the National Union of Ghana Students, the Ghana Journalists Association, the Trade Union Congress, the Ghana Union Traders Association, and the Ghana Association of Women Entrepreneurs. These groups helped to mobilize most of the available non-state, human, and material election-monitoring resources in the country. In addition to helping to select suitable personnel from their organizations for training and deployment as election monitors, the member groups of NEDEO placed communications and transport equipment at the network's disposal. For example, the Catholic Secretariat provided a nationwide wireless communication network, and the IEA provided technical support and managed the secretariat of NEDEO.

The domestic poll-watching groups began their preparations as early as July 1996, four months before the election. They were better placed than most international observers to monitor developments before, during, and after the voting. The IEA initiated a program that trained and deployed personnel to 35 key constituencies to observe and report on the preelection environment until three months before the polling day. It also commissioned a team, based at the School of Communications at the University of Ghana, to monitor the coverage of the election in both the private and the state media. But the domestic poll-watching groups' most ambitious efforts involved the training of election monitors at the national, regional, and district levels and their deployment to polling stations across the country on election day. In the end, over 4,200 domestic election monitors—over 4,100 from NEDEO alone and another 100 from Ghanalert—were deployed.

All of this presented a sharp contrast to 1992, when only about 200 domestic monitors took part in the elections. At that time, the government and its agencies dominated the field, while external observers (including the African American Institute, the Carter Center, and the Commonwealth Secretariat) played only a limited watchdog role. In 1996, however, local NGOs and civic organizations were heavily involved. Before the voting, they provided their own independent analyses of the situation to international observers. A sizable share of outside contributions for the support of democracy flowed to local NGOs and civic groups, whereas four years earlier, the government received almost all such funds. This funding shift was a major factor contributing to the growing sense of local ownership of the electoral-cum-democratization process and the leveling of the institutional playing field.

The domestic election-monitoring organizations enjoyed full cooperation from the Electoral Commission and had access to the commission's officials and facilities. The commission's officials participated in all of the training sessions for the domestic observer groups, it provided samples of election material for demonstration and simulation exercises at the training sessions, it worked closely with the groups to develop a code of conduct for election monitors, and it readily provided official accreditation and identification cards to certified, trained observers. The unhindered access to the polling stations enjoyed by the domestic poll-watching groups, as well as their ability to set up their own mechanisms for a simplified parallel vote count to verify claims of fraud, was key not only to deterring fraud and irregularities, but also to boosting public confidence in the voting and its outcome. The full involvement of the independent local monitors enhanced both the commission's credibility and the transparency of the electoral process.

The media also contributed greatly to the quality of the electoral process in 1996. In 1992, the capital city, Accra, did not have a single, privately owned FM station; by the last quarter of 1996, there were about half a dozen. The independent print media had also become stronger. The more active presence of the independent media, which provided a constant stream of election analysis and chatter, in combination with court orders mandating equal opportunity for all political party broadcasts, helped to generate a high degree of public interest in the election and contributed greatly to the unprecedented 78 percent voter turnout. By providing channels of discourse outside of the state's control, and by leading the cheers for the opposition, the independent media was largely responsible for keeping the election somewhat competitive and for saving the opposition candidates from total despair about their chances of winning against the incumbents, who had ample resources and the vocal support of the state-run media.

The campaign also confirmed the presence of a modest consensus regarding at least the broad outlines of economic policy. The NDC ran largely on its economic record, openly embracing neoliberal economic reforms and the search for global markets and investments.[7] The opposition offered few, if any, clear alternatives, contenting itself with throwing jabs at certain aspects of the Rawlings-NDC economic reforms such as the "cash-and-carry system" of health care and cost sharing in education. In fact, the manifesto of the main opposition party, the NPP, hewed fairly closely to the NDC's neoliberal line, though it promised to strengthen the welfare content of reforms, to offer more support for domestic investment, and to restore fiscal discipline.[8] In the heat of the campaign, opposition presidential candidate Kuffour pledged that his government would not discard Rawlings's Vision 2020 economic policy document.[9]

The opposition gained a solid 43 percent of the vote in the presidential race (Kuffour took almost 40 percent, and Dr. Edward H. Mahama of the People's National Convention Party took the remainder), while non-NDC representation in parliament rose from 11 to 66 seats, out of a total of 200 (see Table 21.1). The government still has a controlling majority, but it faces a minority bloc studded with stalwarts like Nana Akuffo Addo (a legal luminary) and J. H. Mensah (an ex–finance minister and veteran politician). At a minimum, this should enliven parliamentary debate and bring future presidential nominations and proposed bills under more than casual scrutiny. The presence of these opposition figures on parliamentary committees should help to improve policymaking. Governmental accountability and transparency, never strong in the previous parliament, should also get a boost.

Danger Signs

A close look, however, at the December 7 polls and the political developments in the four years leading up to them reveals the persistence of a number of formidable obstacles to democratic consolidation. Despite all the money that was spent and the extensive preparations that were made, the 1996 elections were marred by serious lapses.[10] The voter registration figures alone are disturbing. How could 9.2 million voters be enrolled in a country with only about 17 million people, many of whom are under the age of 15? Add to this the episodes of voting by children witnessed by

Table 21.1   1996 Election Results, Ghana

Presidential		
Candidate	Party	% of Votes Received
Jerry Rawlings	Progressive Alliance	57.4
J. A. Kuffour	Great Alliance	39.7
E. A. Mahama	People's National Convention Party	3.0
Parliamentary		
Party	Number of Seats[a]	
National Democratic Congress	133	
New Patriotic Party	60	
People's Convention Party	5	
People's National Convention Party	1	

Source: Electoral Commission, Accra, December 16, 1996.
Note: a. One seat in Afigya Sekyere to be contested later.

domestic monitors, especially in remote areas, and the integrity of voter registration must be seriously questioned. The relatively high incidence of rejected ballot papers, meanwhile, suggests inadequate voter education, while the evidence of polling stations that were poorly lit or left vulnerable to the elements betrays poor preparation. Indeed, the high cost of the elections and the elaborate arrangements put in place to deter rigging and prevent postelection disputes, as well as the deep public anxieties over the delays in releasing the results (despite the fact that the delays were technically defensible), reflect the deep mistrust that still exists between the government and the opposition parties, and the fact that polarization in Ghanaian politics still prevails in a largely unattenuated form in spite of electoral reforms.

The elections of the 1990s have also revealed a troubling pattern of bloc voting by region and ethnic group. For example, the results seem to confirm the return of Ewes to levels of bloc voting not seen since 1969. In that general election, half of the 30 seats in the 140-seat parliament that were won by the National Alliance of Liberals, under the leadership of Ewe politician Komla Gbedema, came from the Volta Region. At the same time, Kofi Busia's victorious Progress Party, which was perceived as an Akan party, won only two seats in the Volta Region. A similar pattern of voting emerged in 1992 (see Table 21.2). The NDC, led by Rawlings, who is Ewe on his mother's side (his father was a Scot), captured 93.2 percent of the presidential vote (his best showing) in the Volta Region. His opponent, the NPP's A. Adu Boahen, won 60.5 percent of the vote in the Ashanti Region, the bastion of NPP support. This pattern repeated itself in 1996, with Rawlings receiving 94.5 percent of the presidential vote in Volta, and Kuffour making his strongest showing (65.8 percent) in his home region of Ashanti (see Table 21.3).

It is likely that there is more than just ordinary communal solidarity at work here. The gradually increasing practice of ethnoregional voting is, at least in part, a reflection of the parties' decision to play the "ethnic card." They have done so in different but disturbing ways. Only a handful of the leading figures in the 1996 opposition coalition known as the Great Alliance could claim Ewe origins, and the party barely campaigned in Volta. The candidates on its presidential ticket, Kuffour and his running mate, Rawlings's estranged Vice President Arkaah, were both Akans. The public use of ethnic taunts and slurs by some young NPP supporters reinforced the impression that the Great Alliance was a vehicle for Akan-Ashanti chauvinism. Non-Akans could hardly feel welcome in the party when one song popular with youthful NPP supporters in Accra and Kumasi suggested that Rawlings did not deserve to marry an Ashanti woman and that being married to one was the main reason for his "unbearable arrogance."

While the NDC sought support in all regions of the country, the most avid mining for votes was done in "migrant" communities or "stranger

Table 21.2   Presidential Vote by Region, 1992 Elections (percentage)

Region	Presidential Candidate[a]		
	A. Adu Boahen	Hilla Limann	Jerry Rawlings
Akan-speaking regions			
Ashanti	60. 5	2.5	32.9
Brong-Ahafo	29.5	5.3	61.9
Central	26.0	1.9	66.5
Eastern	37.7	1.9	57.3
Western	22.8	8.2	60.7
Ewe-speaking regions			
Volta	3.6	0.7	93.2
Mole/Dagbani-speaking regions			
Northern	16.3	11.0	63.0
Upper East	8.9	37.1	51.0
Upper West	10.5	32.5	54.0
Ga/Adangbe-speaking regions			
Greater Accra	37.0	4.3	53.4

Source: Interim National Electoral Commission, Accra, December 14, 1993.
Note: a. Voter shares for two minor candidates, Kwabena Darko of the National Independence Party and General Emmanuel Erskine of the Heritage Party, are not included.

Table 21.3   Presidential Vote by Region, 1996 Elections (percentage)

Region	Presidential Candidate		
	J. A. Kuffour	E. W. Mahama	Jerry Rawlings
Akan-speaking regions			
Ashanti	65.8	1.4	32.8[a]
Brong-Ahafo	36.0	2.3	61.7
Central	43.3	1.5	55.2
Eastern	45.0	1.2	53.8
Western	40.9	1.8	57.3
Ewe-speaking regions			
Volta	4.7	0.7	94.5
Mole/Dagbani-speaking regions			
Northern	33.0	5.9	61.2
Upper East	17.4	13.7	69.0
Upper West	11.2	14.2	74.6
Ga/Adangbe-speaking regions			
Greater Accra	43.3	2.7	54.0

Source: Electoral Commission, Accra, December 16, 1996.
Note: Some rows do not total 100 percent due to rounding.

quarters" in the towns and villages. In urbanized Akan areas, the NDC courted non-Akans; in the countryside, the target of its appeals was migrant farmers. NDC candidates and their operatives engaged in fear mongering among migrant communities, suggesting that if the NPP won power, it would expel them, just as the Busia regime had expelled undocumented aliens several decades earlier. Rawlings may have been joking, but he struck a raw nerve among many Akans when he declared at a campaign rally in Ho, Volta's capital, that the region was his "World Bank" of votes. Whatever the intention behind the president's remark, the lopsided nature of the pro-Rawlings vote in that region is bound to reinforce the widespread perception, especially among Akans, that the Rawlings regime harbors a strong pro-Ewe bias.[11]

Ghanaians of non-Ewe descent, Akans in particular, have been complaining bitterly (though usually in private and among fellow Akans) about the lopsided voting in Volta. Some Ewes have also been voicing embarrassment over the phenomenon, but again, mainly in private. The prevailing atmosphere of national denial regarding a matter that raises great subnational concern can only be described as unhealthy. At best, it is delaying true national reconciliation. At worst, it is creating an environment in which the next election could take an even sharper ethnic cast. Pride in region and ethnic group is not about to disappear from the Ghanaian scene; how to combine this sentiment with competitive, multiparty elections will remain a challenge.

The Advantages and Drawbacks of Continuity

The second Rawlings-NDC victory can be said to have helped the cause of Ghana's democratic transition in two ways. First, it may facilitate a smoother, if rather protracted, transition away from the quasi-militarized authoritarianism of the Provisional National Defense Council (PNDC) on which Rawlings first rode to power. The continuity entailed in a second consecutive electoral triumph for the president and his party creates the opportunity for the gradual (and, therefore, perhaps more politically tenable) negotiation of the trickier passages in this transition. For example, Rawlings and officials of the erstwhile PNDC (and all previous military regimes in Ghana) will be able to fully enjoy the controversial provisions granting complete immunity from prosecution for all acts committed while in power, which had been inserted in Section 34 of the Transitional Provisions of the 1992 constitution at the last minute, just before that constitution was adopted in a referendum. It also allows officials of that regime to keep many of the perks of their previous offices, such as government-provided housing and cars, and thereby enjoy de facto semipermanent but comfortable early retirement at public expense. In addition, members of the revolutionary cadres of the PNDC paramilitary units may be gently resettled into purely "civilian" life.

The second advantage arises from the assurance of continuity in economic reform. The Rawlings administration can continue its infrastructure building and rehabilitation projects, and it can follow up on promising contacts initiated with prospective foreign investors. There remains, however, the problem of promoting domestic private investment in the face of the very poor relations between the Rawlings regime and key elements of the local capitalist class. The president's preferred solution has apparently been to sponsor a new domestic capitalist class that is beholden to the regime, but this approach faces uncertain prospects, not least because the new class of investors is likely to lack experience, but also because it is likely to be ridden with rent-seeking interests.

Unfortunately, the continuities between the elected Rawlings administration and its military-authoritarian predecessor offer no advantages from the standpoint of democratic consolidation. In effect, the election of 1996 was only a second transition election. As such, it did not satisfy the maximalist criterion for democratic consolidation, which requires that democracy "become so broadly and profoundly legitimate, and so habitually practiced and observed, that it is unlikely to break down."[12] Perhaps more important, the election of 1996, like that of four years earlier, involved no change of government. At best, it was a case of an incumbent regime renewing its mandate to govern through the ballot box. Thus, Ghana has yet to take, much less pass, the crucial test of achieving a peaceful and orderly transfer of power if a new government defeats the incumbents in a multiparty election.

It is noteworthy in this regard that the first democratically elected NDC administration was mostly composed of holdovers from the PNDC era; there were few new faces. As many as 13 out of 34 substantive ministerial positions, including the most influential portfolios in the first post-PNDC government, went to people affiliated with the PNDC. In fact, many retained the same ministries that they had run under the PNDC regime, while others took positions as top presidential advisers and staffers or as NDC party bosses.

Moreover, the ability to exploit incumbency and to commandeer state resources was a key factor in the Rawlings-NDC electoral victories in both 1996 and 1992. The electoral playing field was not level for all of the parties, as the ruling party had cornered state resources, including the state print and electronic media,[13] and the opposition parties had only the very weak private sector to rely on for its resources. The NDC campaign was certainly a lavish affair. Its billboards were splashed around the country, and its campaign vehicles vastly outnumbered those of the opposition (by a ratio of five to one, according to some reports). The NDC ran a slick advertising blitz for months, and it reportedly threw plenty of money around. Very little is known about the sources of the NDC's deep pockets, but the money is likely to have come either directly or indirectly from the state, in the form of kickbacks and extortion from state corporations, government contractors, and business interests seeking favors from government. With no reliable mechanisms in place to enforce postelection accountability, the NDC has no reason to abandon these questionable methods of mobilizing resources in future elections. It thus appears that Rawlings and his followers have simply traded their mastery over coup making for mastery over election winning. The danger is that if the NDC becomes a permanent majority party, the opposition will be driven to despair, as the ballot box becomes ineffective as a route to power.

Another concern is the further entrenchment of the undemocratic political culture left over from the PNDC's heyday. It is far from reassuring to note that the newly elected NDC government seems determined to continue celebrating the anniversaries of the "uprising" of June 4, 1979, and the coup of December 31, 1981, as national holidays. This can only heighten the alienation of the government's political opponents and delay the process of national reconciliation. When the Supreme Court upheld an opposition lawsuit seeking to bar the celebration of December 31 as a national holiday, the president responded with an intimidating outburst, claiming that the courts were staging a coup against the other branches of government.

At bottom, the NDC still retains attitudes and practices derived from the authoritarian PNDC era, a time when subversives seemed to lurk in every corner, and several countercoups had to be defeated. There is little intraparty democracy. Rather, the party operates more like a former national liberation movement, akin to Robert Mugabe's Zimbabwe African National Union (Patriotic Front). For example, in about 70 cases in 1996, the results of parliamentary primaries were overturned by NDC leaders. Rawlings remains the "supreme leader," whose word is final in most cases. Loyalty to the leader and the party are esteemed above all, while principled dissent is heavily frowned upon.

The PNDC Legacy

The liberalization of politics since 1992 has not extended to separating the state from the ruling party. Departments in some ministries (such as the Non-Formal Education Division of the Ministry of Education), the National Disaster Relief Committee, the National Service Secretariat, and the state media (especially the *Ghanaian Times*) are heavily influenced by the NDC. Some of these public bureaucracies were established under PNDC rule; their chief executives are holdovers from that period, and nearly all of their mid- to high-ranking officials have ties to the PNDC "revolution." There are reports that resources allocated to government departments for their regular functions have been diverted to NDC political tasks. In addition, editors of the state-owned newspapers, particularly the *Ghanaian Times*, have continued to use their positions to propagandize in favor of the NDC government and to spew venom at its perceived opponents.

There is also a high degree of integration between the NDC regime and key parastatals, such as the Ghana National Petroleum Corporation (GNPC) and the National Mobilization Program, as well as several state-owned banks that are still run by PNDC-era appointees. The officials who manage these bodies know that their tenure depends on the NDC, and they therefore put their support behind the ruling party with varying degrees of openness; some have also served as top political advisers to the regime. Whether by accident or by design, several of these government-aligned parastatals, especially the GNPC, are also among the most active institutional investors in the state companies that are being privatized. The strong relationship among such parastatal agencies, their heads, and the NDC creates possibilities for corruption and confers enormous advantages to the NDC as it builds its election war chest.

In the countryside, the 110 district assemblies and their presidentially appointed district chief executives supposedly have nothing to do with partisan politics, yet they too are tightly fused with NDC political structures. Many "bush governors" hold appointments that date back to the late 1980s and have close ties to the minister of local government (a key NDC political operative), as well as the old authoritarian instruments of mobilization such as Mrs. Rawlings's 31st December Women's Movement, the Association of Committees for the Defense of the Revolution, and the Mobisquads of the National Mobilization Program. Along with the party hierarchy and many traditional rulers, this array of leaders and organizations constitutes the political machine that makes Rawlings and the NDC so strong in the rural areas. This strength, in other words, comes not simply from the regime's record of rural development, but it flows in at least equal measure from the resilience of the clientelist network that the PNDC developed in the late 1980s and nurtured in the 1990s.[14]

The continued fusion of party and state suggests that political liberalization has failed to bring such democratic essentials as the separation of powers or checks and balances into Ghanaian political life. It also underscores the limited possibilities available for governmental accountability and transparency, even under constitutional rule.

That there has been no alternation of power is all the more significant in view of the military antecedents of the incumbent regime. The PNDC regime may have been unconventional as far as military regimes go, but like most others, it was undergirded by an extensive security apparatus, which consisted of the Bureau of National Investigation, Military Intelligence, the Castle Annex, the Forces Reserved Battalion (popularly known as "commandos"), the Civil Defense Organization, and Mobisquads, as well as elements of the Committees for the Defense of the Revolution, who participated through largely informal and personalized channels. Rawlings and retired Captain Kojo Tsikata have been at the helm of this security apparatus, and of course, there has not been any public oversight of these agencies.

The return to constitutional rule has so far done little or nothing to bring Ghana's military and security agencies into conformity with democratic standards. The issue of the proper role of the military and the need for civilian political control over it in a democratic context has been broached indirectly and with great circumspection at seminars held by the Institute of Economic Affairs, which have featured visiting U.S. military personalities and academic experts on civil-military relations.[15] The military command structure—composed of Rawlings as commander in chief, Tsikata (a member of the Council of State) as his unofficial security adviser, and the minister of defense, Alhaji Iddrisu Mahama, who has held the portfolio for more than a decade—has remained largely unchanged since the PNDC era. Moreover, one of the few non-PNDC elements in the new political command structure of the army was a constitutional provision that made the vice president the head of the Armed Forces Council and a member of the National Security Council, but this provision was removed by an amendment to the constitution in the final weeks of the 1992 parliament.

In addition, parliamentary oversight of military and security agencies through the Parliamentary Committee on Defense and Interior has been extremely superficial. The chairman of that committee in the previous parliament, Lieutenant Colonel E. K. D. Anku-Tsede, a retired army officer and a member of the ruling party, was highly accommodating to the Ministry of Defense.[16] In general, the committee has gone along with the claim of the minister of defense that the defense budget is a national security document.

Military and security arrangements that date from the period before competitive elections have also persisted since 1992. In theory, the paramilitary units that existed under the PNDC have been disbanded or integrated into the regular military, but in practice, this has been only partially accomplished; most of the paramilitary units have gone underground, occasionally resurfacing to act against opponents of the government.[17]

The 1996 election campaign saw a number of ominous reminders of the military's disturbing position in contemporary Ghana and of the distance that must be traversed before true civilian control is achieved. Two months before the elections, the veteran head of the Bureau of National Investigation, a dreaded security organ during the PNDC era, was appointed to head the police. In addition, in the military high command, the positions of Ewe officers appear to have been strengthened at the expense of Akan officers.[18] The chief of defense staff ordered the arrest and interrogation of the writer of an editorial opinion in a private newspaper on a charge of "subversive activities leading to a treasonable offense." Meanwhile, a pro-Rawlings group has published newspaper advertisements calling attention to supposedly antimilitary statements made by opposition stalwarts in the past.

Civil Society and Consolidation

While civil society has grown and developed substantially since 1992, it continues to suffer from severe handicaps. Civic groups in Ghana are often enthusiastic, but they are also beset by organizational and financial shortcomings. They are heavily dependent on external agencies for their funding, and sometimes for moral and political support as well. Domestic election-monitoring groups, for example, depended almost completely on foreign donors. NEDEO had a strong human resource base, but little money of its own, slender material resources, and no experience in undertaking the massive and complex task of monitoring an election. This organization could not have trained and deployed its monitors, or collated the reports on the election, without the generous funding it received from the U.S. Agency for International Development and the National Democratic Institute for International Affairs.

The availability of donor funding was a mixed blessing. Competition among these organizations for access to their own donor money seems to have provoked factionalism, turf battles, and one-upmanship among civic organizations. Credibility, efficiency, and democracy building all suffered as a result. NEDEO survived in part because donors preferred to provide resources to a coalition of observers rather than to individual groups.

The negative attitudes of public officials have also inhibited the growth and development of civil society. The NDC government is openly hostile toward organizations not under its control, especially if they are not apolitical. Moreover, officials of both the government and the party shun engagements with civil society groups and independent NGOs, mainly out of fear of being censured by the NDC leadership. While the government was happy to invite in international election observers, it objected vehemently to the presence of domestic observers. Its agents attempted to compromise the domestic monitoring groups, especially NEDEO. It opposed the Electoral Commission's decision to grant accreditation to domestic observer groups and made outrageous demands that NEDEO change its name and drop key members (such as the Christian Council, the Catholic Secretariat, and the Ghana National Association of Teachers) that are thought to oppose the government. The entire domestic observation process was threatened when the government's agents announced plans to form an alternative network of domestic election observers out of NDC-aligned groups (such as the Association of the Committees for the Defense of the Revolution, the 31st December Women's Movement, and the Civil Defense Organization) unless NEDEO agreed to bring such groups under its umbrella.

To be sure, the presence in NEDEO of several civic associations that had long histories of anti-state struggles (such as the Christian Council, the Catholic Secretariat, the Ghana National Association of Teachers, and the Ghana Union Traders Association) reinforced the NDC's erroneous perception that NEDEO was partisan. But the problem derives largely from the prevailing political culture, in which dissent is often viewed as treason, and government officials are unaccustomed to the presence of countervailing domestic forces. NEDEO broadened itself to include Islamic organizations and others that are not normally seen as anti-NDC, and it carefully selected and trained its monitors, but this meant little in the government's eyes. The fact that the regime did tolerate NEDEO's presence and did not order the arrest and detention of any of the domestic election observers (as President Frederick Chiluba did after the November 1996 elections in Zambia) may be due in large part to the generally favorable reports of these domestic observers on the Ghanaian election, not to rising levels of political tolerance. Indeed, the support and encouragement given to the 31st December Women's Movement and other former revolutionary organs, the infiltration of government departments with former cadres of the revolution, and the distance the regime and its officials maintain between themselves and even the most well-meaning elements of civil society betray the present government's hegemony-seeking and corporatist tendencies.

Conclusion

Despite its unpromising beginnings, Ghana's experiment in democratic governance has survived into its fifth year, thus setting a record for Ghana and for many other African countries. The first four years of constitutional rule brought a marked degree of political liberalization and advances in democratic governance, suggesting that even a flawed transition can set the stage for democratic progress. The widely acclaimed success of the recent presidential and parliamentary elections in Ghana shows that even an electoral system (and an Electoral Commission) with suspect origins can produce a credible outcome that meets with broad public acceptance. Finally, the continued, if somewhat diluted, commitment to economic renewal and accelerated investment promotion indicates that democratic reform is not necessarily inimical to economic renewal, although in Ghana, it has proven difficult to combine competitive politics with the promotion of domestic private investment.

Ghana's experience, however, also shows that keeping democratic transitions on track is costly. It takes a considerable amount of donor support to construct a credible electoral system and build an efficacious civil society. Most of all, the Ghanaian experiment underscores the intractable problems of democratic consolidation and deepening that lie beyond successful multiparty elections and mere democratic survival. The modes and orders of authoritarianism may linger despite political liberalization; replacing them with the norms and institutions of democracy is a slow and arduous affair.

Consolidating the gains in democratic governance over the course of Rawlings's second civilian administration will be extremely difficult in spite of the stronger opposition presence in parliament, a resurgent civil society, and a vibrant independent press. The opposition parties, like other key institutions of democratic politics, remain weak. Civil society does not yet present a strong countervailing force to the state. The independent media continue to struggle with an unfriendly legal system, limited resources, and government machinations designed to circumvent constitutional guarantees of free speech. In addition, the Ghanaian judiciary has become increasingly hostile to press freedom. Recent rulings by the courts have expanded the scope of the country's already strict criminal libel laws, and many judges have shown themselves eager to punish journalists who run afoul of the government. Official attitudes toward activist watchdog agencies, such as the CHRAJ and the Media Commission, have ranged from lukewarm to openly hostile.

Clearly, Rawlings and his NDC government are not inclined to enhance transparency and accountability, and there is little in civil society or the constitution that compels a significant degree of governmental openness. Against the background of continuity in the executive branch and the government's controlling majority in parliament, the party-state and its neopatrimonial habits and trappings are likely to persist.

The conclusion is clear: for its democratic progress to continue, Ghana needs stronger opposition parties, a more independent press, and a more vibrant civil society, as well as constitutional bodies (e.g., the courts, the CHRAJ, and the Media Commission) that can restrain undemocratic governmental impulses. Of course, reforms in the electoral system and its administration must continue, but supporting civil society in general, and sustaining organizations like NEDEO, must take priority in any scheme to move Ghana's democratization forward.

Notes

1. A slightly revised version of this essay was published in the *Journal of Democracy* (spring 1997).
2. These bills ran into a storm of protest by civil society and extraparliamentary opposition groups. The version of the Serious Fraud Bill that was eventually passed by parliament was highly watered down to remove the illiberal and anti-

private-sector elements. The NGO bill was shelved after parliament proposed several changes; its official status remains unknown.

3. Sowa, "Adjustment in Africa."

4. Holman and Wrong, "Ghana 1996"; see also Moss and Williams, "Ghana's Economic Reform."

5. The Progressive Alliance comprised the National Democratic Congress and its partners, the Egle Party and the Democratic People's Party, and it put forward Jerry Rawlings as its presidential candidate. The Great Alliance comprised the New Patriotic Party (tracing its heritage to the pro-market, right-wing Busia-Danquah political tradition) and the People's Convention Party (claiming the left-leaning Nkrumahist heritage), and J. A. Kuffour was its flag bearer. The People's National Convention Party, founded by ex-president Hilla Limann, put forward Dr. Edward A. Mahama as its presidential candidate.

6. *Daily Graphic,* September 5, 1996, pp. 10–11.

7. See "NDC Election 1996 Manifesto" and *Ghana: Vision 2020.*

8. See "Manifesto of the Patriotic Party."

9. *Ghana: Vision 2020.*

10. It has not been possible to obtain the full details of funding for the elections and their sources, but my own estimates suggest external funding of between $12 and $15 million for Electoral Commission activities. The commission's sources list the funding received from international donors and the respective activities the funding was used to support as follows: $6.5 million from the United States for the purchase of election materials and equipment, technical assistance for the registration of voters, exhibition of voters' registers, and the payment of some of the election expenses; $3 million from Denmark to purchase 41,000 transparent ballot boxes, to train registration staff, exhibition staff, polling staff, and political party agents, and to conduct voter education programs; $0.8 million from the United Kingdom to provide voter registration forms and equipment for scanning voter personal data on registration forms; $745,000 from Canada to purchase paper used for printing ballots, voting screens, and tamper-evident envelopes for conveying election documents; $500,000 from the European Union for the purchase of 500 electricity generators to offset power outages during printing of voter registers and to fund the printing of educational posters for the exhibition of voters' registers, as well as for training manuals for election staff; $275,000 from the United Nations Development Programme for communications equipment; $185,000 from Germany for 23 two-way radio sets to facilitate communication in remote districts; $164,000 from the Netherlands for printing election materials; and $57,000 from China to provide motorbikes for operation in difficult terrain. For details, see Afriyie and Larvie, *Elections in Ghana,* pp. 75–76.

This must be added to the major financial contributions and technical support provided by donors to support the electoral process through their NGOs, including the Friedrich Ebert Foundation of Germany (which provided $79,000 to support training for media personnel, theater performances, and video productions on electoral rules); the Westminster Foundation of the UK (which funded programs to build the capacity of some of the opposition political parties); and the U.S.-based National Democratic Institute for International Affairs' funding and technical assistance to NEDEO.

11. Boahen, *Ghanaian Sphinx* and "Conflict Reoriented."

12. This maximalist definition is from Diamond, "Introduction," p. 53.

13. There was a clear pro-NDC bias in news coverage and editorial opinion in the state-controlled print and electronic media, though the opposition parties had equal opportunity to hold press conferences and to broadcast on Ghana television.

14. For a recent analysis of the PNDC-NDC rural political machine, see Nugent, *Big Men, Small Boys,* and Gyimah-Boadi, "Economic Recovery."

15. IEA discussion programs on civil-military relations in the context of Ghanaian democratization include "Civil/Military Relations: The American Experience," led by Colonel Dan Henks (June 11, 1996); "Civil-Military Relations in Africa," led by Professor Jendayi Frazer of the Kennedy School at Harvard; and "Changing Military/Civilian Relationships in Argentina," led by the public affairs officer of United States Information Service–Accra (August 8, 1996).

16. He apparently believes that there is sufficient accountability and transparency in the military's internal processes for drawing up budget estimates. See Anku-Tsede, "Defense Budgeting."

17. The Association of Committees for the Defense of the Revolution had reportedly been used to quell antigovernment riots in Accra in May 1995. See *Africa Confidential,* "Kume Preko."

18. *Africa Now,* October 1996, p. D3.

22

Challenges to Democratic Consolidation in Namibia

Gretchen Bauer

Since achieving independence in March 1990, Namibia has been hailed around the world as one of Africa's most promising new democracies. In the intervening years, observers have pointed to a range of indicators as evidence of a successful transition to democracy and of the likelihood of its equally successful consolidation in the not too distant future. Yet, as this chapter will show, the challenges to democratic consolidation in Namibia are persistent and numerous. As in many other recently liberalized polities in Africa, some of the greatest challenges stem from the difficulty of creating viable opposition political parties and building strong and autonomous organizations of civil society. These challenges can, in turn, be traced back to, among other things, the enduring legacy of decades of authoritarian rule and the continuing limitations of weak African economies.[1]

The Transition to Democracy

The transition to democracy in Namibia has differed from other recent transitions on the continent. This has not been a transition from indigenous authoritarian rule to indigenous democratic rule. Rather, it has been a transition from a century of German and South African colonial rule to political independence. Moreover, the formal transfer of power was finally achieved after both a long struggle at the UN, where South Africa's illegal occupation of the country was repeatedly contested, and a prolonged armed struggle between the South West Africa People's Organization (SWAPO) and the South African forces of occupation. It came as the culmination of a one-year transition supervised by the UN and guided by United Nations Security Council Resolution (UNSCR) 435. Ultimately, this transition was the result of a negotiated settlement involving representatives of a number of other countries whose fate had become inextricably linked with that of Namibia.[2]

In many respects, it could be argued that the transition to democracy in Namibia began in the mid-1980s with the Transitional Government of National Unity, the second of two South African–sponsored "interim" governments, which was in power from 1985 until 1989.[3] During this period, political space opened up, allowing a new level of organized activity, and the transitional government was forced to concede a number of reforms. This period contrasted sharply with the late 1970s and early 1980s, when political repression in the territory had been particularly harsh.

While the political repression of the late 1970s and early 1980s initially succeeded in suppressing political activity, by the mid-1980s, relatively large numbers of community-based organizations began to emerge, especially in urban townships. In addition, a national students' organization, the first enduring black trade unions, a regional women's group, a more active church federation, and other territory-wide associations all came to the fore during this same period. Formed in part in response to the harsh conditions in Namibia's townships, many of these groups combined their development goals with more overt political objectives. Indeed, the final years of the transitional government were marked by the heightened mobilization of students and workers (including a two-day stay-away in June 1988) and considerable unrest. As such, Namibia's experience was not unlike other "negotiated and controlled transitions," in which "the stimulus for democratization, and particularly the pressure to complete the process, have typically come from the 'insurrection of civil society,' the restructuring of public space, and the mobilization of all manner of independent groups and grassroots movements."[4]

In the end, the transitional government, aware that a UN-sponsored resolution to the Namibian crisis was imminent, and under pressure due to the upsurge in organized activity, initiated a number of reforms in an attempt to obtain future political support from the Namibian populace. While gradual, piecemeal political reform had been under way since the late 1970s, the process accelerated after the mid-1980s. Even so, the *formal* transition to independence and democracy would only commence in 1989, after a negotiated settlement was delivered by external powers, and after agreement by all sides that the transition would follow the stipulations of UNSCR 435.

Has the transition to democracy in Namibia been accomplished? According to nearly all of the popular conceptualizations of the transition to democracy, the response would be affirmative.[5] As noted, a formal transfer of power from South African to Namibian rule was achieved under UN auspices, essentially without incident, between 1989 and early 1990. Among other things, this transition involved the largely peaceful demobilization of thousands of armed combatants and the repatriation and resettlement of tens of thousands of refugees and exiles. Following "free and fair elections" in November 1989, a Constituent Assembly was convened, and through a relatively consensual process, a new constitution was drafted and adopted. The Constituent Assembly was then transformed into the first National Assembly; Sam Nujoma, leader of the majority SWAPO party, was elected president; and independence was declared on March 21, 1990.

Since independence, the fundamental human rights and freedoms enshrined in Namibia's much-lauded constitution have been carefully monitored. In addition, two more elections have been held, each with universal franchise and secret ballot, and under Namibian direction. The first was for the newly established local and regional authorities in 1992, and the other was the second round of presidential and National Assembly elections, held in 1994. Today, five political parties represent the Namibian people in the National Assembly, and three of those parties hold seats on the National Council. During the last several years, the activities of the new government have largely focused on abolishing old laws and implementing new ones to redress the many grievances of Namibia's disadvantaged majority. On the economic front, the SWAPO government has embraced all the tenets of the currently ascendant model of economic liberalism, proclaiming from the start its commitment to a "mixed economy"—that is, one that clearly privileges the private sector. The challenge ahead is to find a way to consolidate this nascent democracy.

Challenges in Political Society

To date, many external assessments of the consolidation of democracy[6] in Namibia have been cautiously optimistic. During the early 1990s, most of these evaluations praised the country's "promising start." In a 1992 article, Joshua Forrest cites a number of factors that could offset the challenges to democratic consolidation. These include the manner in which democracy was inaugurated (multiparty elections and the Constituent Assembly to draft a constitution); the policies and activities of all political parties, which suggest support for pluralistic freedoms; a functioning National Assembly that provides a forum for the expression of diverse political views; and the promotion of a democratic political culture by the government and the national media. Two years later, however, Forrest is more circumspect, noting that while Namibia has been a functioning multiparty democracy with a political culture "among the most tolerant and free in the Third World" since independence, it will take more time for democratic institutions to become solidly entrenched.[7]

In their assessment of the 1992 local and regional elections, William Lindeke and Winnie Wanzala suggest that both "the procedures and the out-

comes" of the elections "confirm a continuing pattern of democratic participation in national life" in Namibia. They argue that the results of the elections "show gains for Namibian self-governance, majority rule and gender
equality over the prior colonial experience." An exit poll confirmed this,
"as respondents saw voting as an expression of 'freedom and democracy.'"[8]

Yet, as noted earlier, there are indications that the challenges to democratic consolidation in Namibia remain formidable. These can be seen, first
and foremost, within the institutions of political society,[9] where partisan
contestation for state power takes place. In a manner reminiscent of political developments elsewhere in Africa after independence, there has been a
fairly rapid movement toward a one-party-dominant political system, as
demonstrated by a number of developments.

First, just a few years after independence, the ruling party, SWAPO,
already holds a better than two-thirds majority in both chambers of parliament. SWAPO's hegemony has been matched by a corresponding decline in
the number and strength of viable opposition political parties. During the
first elections in 1989 for the Constituent Assembly, 10 political parties out
of a reported total of 40 or more qualified to participate and were listed on
the ballot. Of these 10, seven won enough votes to obtain at least one seat
in the Constituent Assembly (which became the first National Assembly).
SWAPO won a clear majority with 57.3 percent of the vote, followed by the
Democratic Turnhalle Alliance (DTA) with 28.6 percent. Three years later
in the local and regional elections, seven parties fielded candidates, but
only three of them—SWAPO, the DTA, and the United Democratic Front
(UDF)—won seats in the regional councils or local authorities, and thus in
the National Council. In these elections, SWAPO garnered 67.3 percent of
the vote, although when the uncontested (SWAPO) constituencies are
included, SWAPO won well over 70 percent.

Results of the December 1994 presidential and National Assembly
elections reinforced this trend. In the National Assembly elections, in
which eight parties fielded candidates, SWAPO polled 72.3 percent of the
vote (winning 53 of the 72 seats), and the DTA gained 20.4 percent (for 15
seats). The UDF won two seats with 2.7 percent, while the Monitor Action
Group (MAG) and the Democratic Coalition of Namibia (DCN) each won
one seat. Three parties failed to win any seats.[10]

Second, while no one is publicly embracing the notion of a one-party
state, there are constant appeals by the government and party leaders to
promote national reconciliation, build the nation, and foster national unity.
While these appeals are perfectly understandable in the current Namibian
context, they are also the same ones made three decades ago by many new
African leaders seeking to consolidate single-party rule. So far, no attempts
have been made to change the constitution, but as President Nujoma nears
the end of his second term, rumors abound about the possibility of extend-

ing the maximum presidential service from two to three terms. Indeed, at the SWAPO party congress in May 1997, delegates endorsed a central committee proposal that Nujoma be allowed to serve a third term. According to the *Namibian,* "the Central Committee recommended that the Constitution be changed so that the first President of Namibia is able to serve two terms of office 'upon a mandate by direct popular vote'" (the first term having been by vote of the Constituent Assembly). According to the proposal, only President Nujoma will be allowed this third term.[11]

Third, there has been a clear pattern of local, regional, and national leaders, many of whom were formerly among the most ardent foes of SWAPO, joining the ruling party. These have included Barney Barnes, a former DTA member of parliament and strong SWAPO adversary; Hampie Plichta, the former mayor of Keetmanshoop; a number of Ovambo-speaking chiefs and headmen formerly affiliated with the DTA; and many ordinary members of the DTA. Thus, as happened in an earlier era in many African states, political opponents have been induced to join the ruling party, usually attracted by the prospect of preferential access to a range of opportunities.

Fourth, the distinction between the ruling party and the government has steadily blurred; government leaders often justify their actions on the basis of "party discipline,"[12] and party leaders rarely articulate policy positions distinct from those of the government. Moreover, there has been a clear effort by the party to strengthen its grip over its auxiliaries or wings. For example, when the Namibian National Students Organisation (NANSO) voted to disaffiliate from the party in 1991, party leaders promptly repudiated the organization and assisted in the creation of a new, SWAPO-affiliated national student association. Similarly, any hint by members of the National Union of Namibian Workers (NUNW), the major trade union federation, that they might seek disaffiliation or form their own party has resulted in strong rebukes from the SWAPO leadership.[13] In addition, vocal and effective leaders of these and similar groups have increasingly been co-opted, usually by giving them positions in the government.[14]

Finally, the ruling-party apparatus shows signs of atrophy.[15] This tendency has been manifest, at one time or another, in a lack of funds to pay employees, minimal (if any) local-level organization, a failure to attract large numbers of supporters to rallies, and, as noted, a lack of independent party positions distinct from those of the government on most issues. The party's lack of organizational capacity was especially apparent following the 1992 local and regional elections.[16] Similarly, in 1996, according to the *Namibian,* frustrated trade union leaders complained about "the non-functional existence of the SWAPO Party" and charged that the party no longer provided "leadership guidelines" or any "supervisory control."[17]

SWAPO held its first party congress in an independent Namibia in December 1991, and it finally held a second one in May 1997. Among other things, reports from the congress claimed "a complete mess" with respect to voting procedures for new central committee members. The election of Hendrick Witbooi (over Prime Minister Hage Geingob) was widely interpreted as "a vote for the "status quo."[18] Still, speculation remains rife about the possibility of a future split within the party, but only *after* President Nujoma relinquishes power.

Despite SWAPO's domination of party politics, elections have proceeded largely unfettered since independence. At least 70 percent of eligible voters participated in the two national elections held since 1990, and they were considered free and fair by nearly all observers. The main complaint regarding elections at this time concerns the fact that the Directorate of Elections is located in the Office of the Prime Minister, provoking fears about the impartiality of the directorate in the minds of many opposition politicians.[19] In addition, opposition politicians have expressed considerable dismay over ruling-party efforts to maintain the party-list system as the basis for upcoming local authority elections, rather than changing to the ward system, as mandated in the Local Authorities Act of 1992. According to the *Namibian,* "near chaos" erupted in the National Assembly when the minister of regional and local government and housing, Nicky Iyambo, announced in February 1997 that he would soon introduce an amendment to the Local Authorities Act to this effect. For months, SWAPO had been denying that such a change was being contemplated.[20]

Again, despite SWAPO's rapidly emerging dominance, Namibia's national legislative bodies have functioned largely unimpeded since their establishment. As noted, the first National Assembly was formed out of the Constituent Assembly in 1990, and the second was elected in late 1994. The second house of parliament, the National Council, is composed of two members from each of the regional councils, and it was first constituted after the 1992 local and regional elections.[21]

Concerns have been expressed, however, about the ruling party's apparent lack of commitment to the National Council, since it is based on constituencies rather than on political parties, and about the failure to devolve power to the regional councils and local authorities. It is well known that SWAPO initially strongly opposed the establishment of a second chamber of parliament. The party agreed to it only during the constitution-drafting process on condition that the National Council could only review, not veto, legislation passed by the National Assembly.[22] Writing in 1994, Foreign Minister Theo Ben Gurirab charged that "the National Council (second house of our parliament) was—and is—an unworkable idea." He complained that SWAPO "got stuck with this very expensive and powerless house, like an albatross around the neck of the Namibian polity" and concluded that "it goes without saying, as far as I am concerned, that the second house will have to go, eventually."[23] Indeed, it is only quite recently, after a protracted struggle, that the National Council's lower salaries and inferior conditions of service (relative to those of the National Assembly) have been improved.

The position of the regional councils and local authorities remains even more ambiguous. In July 1995, the director of elections and chair of the First Delimitation Commission, Gerhard Toetemeyer, reportedly called the position of the regional councils—their structures and task assignments—too weak to be considered an effective second tier of government.[24] According to Forrest, the regional councils "have been hampered by the reluctance of national officials to accord them a significant degree of decision-making authority or independent revenue-raising powers."[25] In interviews for a democracy and governance assessment in Namibia in 1994, members of the regional councils repeatedly complained about a lack of sufficient authority, training, and financial resources to do their work.[26] Regional governments are still largely dependent upon the central government for their funding, although they are theoretically entitled to 5 percent of property taxes collected by local authorities. As for decisionmaking powers, in a 1995 interview, Prime Minister Geingob reiterated that Namibia is a unitary, not a federal, state: "We must not confuse those powers given to regions in a federal system with those given in a unitary state." But he did concede that the regions must be given more money, and the regional governors "some powers."[27]

Challenges in Civil Society

The organizations of civil society are equally critical to the consolidation of democracy, and like the institutions of political society, they face many challenges and constraints that make the prospects for democratic consolidation appear somewhat problematic. As noted earlier, it was during the 1980s that community-based organizations and regional- and national-level nongovernmental organizations (NGOs) began to appear in large numbers in Namibia. Community activist Andre Strauss reported in 1987 that the formation of community organizations "surged" in 1984. He estimated that 50 to 100 relatively stable organizations, focusing on literacy, legal advice, housing, community media, education, agriculture, handicrafts, sports, community drama, culture, and women's affairs, had been formed in the early to mid-1980s.[28]

Just a decade later, a wealth of organizations exists, despite Namibia's population of only 1.5 million. These include more than 30 national NGOs, 40 religious organizations, approximately 30 agricultural cooperatives, 15 environmental and 15 housing organizations, 130 community-based organizations and cooperatives, two dozen women's groups, many trade unions, employers' organizations, and professional associations.[29] In Namibia, many of these organizations might be considered as constituting a nascent civil society.

But as Colin Leys and John Saul have cautioned: "While a formally democratic system has indeed emerged in Namibia, it seems fair to say that little popular empowerment has been realized."[30] This lack of popular empowerment is manifested most clearly in the weakness of civil society. To some extent, trade unions, the student movement, and women's groups have all been immobilized by the continuing legacy of past divisions, the nagging issue of political party affiliation, the loss of qualified cadres, and inadequate material and organizational resources.

The experiences of Namibian trade unions demonstrate the adverse effects of these phenomena. Just over half of Namibia's small, formal-sector labor force (about 120,000 of 230,000 workers) are members of more than 15 trade unions. These unions, however, are divided into two federations: the National Union of Namibian Workers, which claimed a total membership of 88,000 in 1995, and the Namibian People's Social Movement (NPSM), which claimed a membership of about 33,000 in 1994.[31] The NUNW and its member unions are formally affiliated with the ruling party; the NPSM disavows any political party affiliation, although a number of its member unions emerged from former public service (thus mostly "white" and "Coloured") staff associations or from unions that were encouraged by interim government authorities during the reform period of the 1980s. In general, the two federations organize different sectors, although there are significant exceptions, including the civil service and food and retail workers. Intermittent discussions have taken place between the NUNW and the NPSM to promote trade union unity, and in May 1995, representatives of the two federations conducted formal unity talks, issuing a document that included 20 points of agreement and six of disagreement.[32] However, no further progress has since been made.

The issue of party affiliation has profoundly affected the NUNW. The federation formally confirmed its affiliation with SWAPO at an extraordinary congress in March 1991, noting that, in affiliating with the party, unions would be able to participate more effectively in policymaking and achieve greater support for common goals.[33] The affiliation question was, however, revisited at the NUNW's first ordinary congress in September 1993. While three member unions introduced a resolution calling for the NUNW's disaffiliation from SWAPO, the issue was never brought to a vote following the debate.[34] Those who oppose affiliation charge that it prevents the unions from developing their own programs and identity, as many workers fail to distinguish between the two organizations. They further argue that affiliation subordinates the unions to the party, making trade union leadership accountable to the party leadership, rather than to rank-

and-file members. There is also a strong belief that the unions' support is taken for granted by party leadership. Finally, some fear that political party affiliation prevents those who are not SWAPO members from joining the NUNW, and, as noted, the affiliation has been an impediment to greater trade union unity.

The deleterious consequences of party affiliation were evident most recently amid the controversy surrounding the establishment of export processing zones (EPZs). Among other things, the SWAPO government was determined that Namibia's progressive new labor legislation should not apply to the EPZs. A compromise was eventually agreed upon, but only after months of confrontation, stipulating that the Labour Act would apply to the EPZs, but the EPZs would be considered essential service areas, thus prohibiting strikes and lockouts. A number of trade unionists predicted dire consequences, noting that workers in EPZs would be forced into "wildcat, illegal strikes" that would prompt companies to lose confidence in the Namibian government. According to trade unionists, the compromise reveals the problem with affiliation: it "makes it almost impossible for the federation to vigorously oppose Government policies."[35] For the unions, the government's position on the EPZs has been a "betrayal of trust" and an example of the government's failure to consult regularly with the unions.

The student movement in Namibia has also been seriously weakened since independence, especially by political divisions. NANSO, the first national students' organization for university and secondary school students, was formed in 1984. In its early days, it played an important role in protesting the continued South African military presence in northern Namibia (especially in and around the schools) and in working with the trade unions on boycotts and stay-aways. By the time of independence, NANSO had ambitious plans for democratizing the education system in Namibia by ensuring equal access to education, enhancing teacher qualifications, improving physical infrastructure, and lowering the high student-to-teacher ratios.[36]

However, since independence was achieved, and following its decision to disaffiliate from SWAPO in 1991,[37] NANSO has been rapidly marginalized. A splinter group called "NANSO-affiliated," based in northern Namibia, was soon formed with the active assistance of SWAPO leaders. NANSO officeholders estimate that they lost half of their membership in the ensuing struggle. Observers regard the scission as "extremely serious" and as "casting doubt" on the viability of NANSO's role in democratizing education in Namibia.[38] Moreover, NANSO members speculate that the organization's struggles were anticipated by SWAPO; former NANSO leader Uhuru Dempers expressed concern in 1994 about "deliberate attempts by authorities to weaken the student movement by creating and fomenting splinter groups."[39] Today, NANSO has deteriorated to the point that a "major row" has been reported within its top echelons, most of the leadership has refused to stand for reelection, and the current president has been accused of misappropriating thousands of dollars of NANSO funds.[40]

For women, as for most workers in Namibia, independence has brought some favorable legal changes, although much remains to be accomplished.[41] However, in many ways, the women's movement also continues to suffer from lingering political divisions. This problem became most evident shortly after independence, when several women's groups attempted to form an umbrella organization for women. Disagreements about the form that this body should take quickly emerged between groups active in the women's wings of political parties and independent women's NGOs. According to two observers, "the effort fell apart primarily because of splits along party-political lines exacerbated by personal competitiveness." In the end, two different national umbrella groups emerged: a federation of women's organizations and a national organization open to individual women. Perhaps inevitably, one is believed to be allied with SWAPO, and the other with the opposition.[42]

A Department of Women's Affairs (DWA) was established in the president's office shortly after independence to facilitate relations between women and the government and to help identify priorities for action.[43] In addition, a significant number of women's organizations have been formed to pursue a variety of goals. Even so, personal and organizational competitiveness remains a serious difficulty confronting the women's movement. Other difficulties include the urban-rural divide and the large gap between educated, professional women and the majority of women who are subsistence farmers. Race and ethnicity also remain divisive factors.[44]

The historic racial divide in Namibia contributes to continued fragmentation in the business community as well. The business community remains largely white in composition, and in some respects, it is unengaged in politics. Namibian employers strongly resisted the efforts that began in the 1980s to organize them into a single national federation, and with a few important exceptions, they even refused to organize within their own sectors. In 1994, the Namibia Employers Federation was finally launched, but the still predominantly white business community faces the challenge of integrating Namibia's emergent black business sector into its ranks. One step in this direction was the formation of the Namibia National Chamber of Commerce and Industry (NNCCI) in 1990. Initially regarded as a SWAPO-supported black business organization, the NNCCI has made progress in organizationally merging the two communities.

Obstacles to Democratic Consolidation

Having discussed some of the general challenges facing democratic consolidation within the arenas of political and civil society in Namibia, this chapter will now turn to a more detailed critical analysis of these obstacles, focusing especially on political parties and the organizations of civil society.

In much recent comparative work, political parties have been identified as crucial to the processes of democratic transition and consolidation.[45] In the early 1990s, the unbanning of opposition political parties and the construction of multiparty political systems were included among the first essential steps toward democratization almost everywhere in Africa. Yet the difficulties of creating and institutionalizing viable political parties and multiparty political systems are becoming all too evident, with the problems besetting new ruling parties and opposition parties alike.[46]

In Namibia, several factors help explain SWAPO's increasing strength and the seeming inability of the opposition parties to pose a credible challenge to it. SWAPO commands the loyalty and allegiance of the majority of the Namibian people by virtue of its position as the premier nationalist organization in the prolonged struggle against South African rule. SWAPO was among the first black political organizations formed in Namibia; it was forced into exile in the early 1960s and quickly won international support. It was the only organization to engage in armed struggle, and it was one of the few parties that did not participate in the preindependence interim governments. Because of these contributions, SWAPO has been forgiven for many of its excesses while in exile. In addition, SWAPO has been the only party to secure a popular base inside Namibia among the mostly Ovambo-speaking labor force. At the same time, SWAPO has also attracted members of other ethnic groups, especially into its leadership ranks. SWAPO is also headed by a charismatic leader who is trusted by many Namibians.

Like all ruling parties, SWAPO profits from the perquisites of incumbency. These include access to state resources and, according to opposition parties, a pro-SWAPO bias in the government-controlled media. As noted, the Directorate of Elections is located in the Office of the Prime Minister, which affords SWAPO yet another advantage.

All of the opposition parties suffer from a lack of adequate financial resources.[47] A universal complaint among opposition leaders concerns the problem of insufficient funds for running an electoral campaign, let alone operating a party apparatus on a daily basis. Even the DTA, which once received generous funding from South Africa and from local Namibian donors, claims very little in the way of financial resources today. DTA leaders contend that while they once received considerable sums from the white business community in Namibia, that same community now primarily makes open contributions to the ruling party, with only occasional, under-the-table contributions to the DTA. Some provision has been made by the National Assembly for limited government funding of political parties on the basis of the share of votes obtained in the previous election, but this mechanism obviously excludes new parties and those outside of parliament.[48]

In addition to inadequate funding, opposition parties complain of insufficient links to organizations within civil society. Opposition party leaders charge that the largest civil society groups—the national church federation, the national women's federation, and the major trade union federation—are so clearly linked to SWAPO, or even formally affiliated in some cases, that connections with other parties are impossible. SWAPO affiliation also means that opposition party sympathizers are unlikely to participate in these organizations. In addition, the opposition parties argue that civil society organizations are weak, and therefore susceptible to the selective use of patronage—or even co-optation and coercion—by the government and the ruling party.

According to opposition-party leaders, some of the opposition political parties are also hindered by their association with preindependence political regimes. While SWAPO has been able to overcome its past label as a terrorist organization, some opposition parties are still treated as collaborators or stooges.

It is widely believed that ethnicity and traditional leaders continue to exert a strong influence on election outcomes in Namibia. In interviews in mid-1995, almost all opposition-party leaders asserted that ethnicity dominates electoral politics in Namibia. This trend is reinforced by past policies of ethnic segregation, including the formation of political groups along ethnic lines in the 1970s. Election data generally supports this contention, although SWAPO continues to attract the votes of a significant number of non-Ovambo speakers.[49] Since Ovambo speakers, who make up 51 percent of the population, largely support SWAPO, it will be difficult for other parties to achieve national electoral victories as long as ethnicity remains a salient factor.

Another critical indicator of the changes that are taking place in the Namibian political system is the declining importance of ideology; the once considerable ideological differences among the parties have diminished markedly since independence. The party manifestos for the 1994 election were quite similar, and the main opposition party, the DTA, claims that there is no real ideological difference between it and SWAPO, since the latter has moved rapidly toward the center in recent years. Indeed, both SWAPO and the DTA advocate liberal democracy, a free market economy, and the need for national reconciliation. Both parties also call for increased employment, foreign investment, land reform, affordable health care, and education for all. Where ideological differences can be discerned, they tend to be among the smaller, more marginal parties.

Finally, the very notion of an "opposition" continues to confound multiparty politics in Namibia. In interviews conducted in July 1995, many opposition leaders confirmed that there is no appropriate translation for the word "opposition" in many indigenous Namibian languages, but only a notion of "enemy," which has a far different connotation.[50] According to the *Namibian,* as recently as March 1997, DTA leader Mishake Muyongo "warned that democracy in Namibia was still on very shaky ground because the opposition are not seen as political opponents but as enemies of the ruling party and its supporters."[51] Without a widespread understanding and acceptance of this fundamental concept, it is hard to imagine how multiparty politics in Namibia can thrive.

If political parties are not able to play the key role in democratic consolidation in Africa that they have played elsewhere, what are the likely alternatives? For many, the organizations of civil society hold more promise for promoting a democratic alternative in Africa. As Célestin Monga notes:

> The opening up of politics in Africa has prompted a quasi-anarchic multiplication of parties. Yet in almost all countries the new leaders have almost immediately revealed their limitations. Thus, to avoid running the risk of being deprived of "their" democratization, society has had to invent alternative structures to manage and express its dissatisfaction.[52]

This embrace of "alternative structures"— whether regarded as organizations of civil society or as new social movements—also parallels similar developments elsewhere in the "democratizing" world.[53]

Many scholars recognize the real difficulties confronting the growth of vibrant civil societies in Africa, often questioning the very application of the concept to the continent.[54] What factors account for the apparent weaknesses of the institutions of political society and the organizations of civil society in Namibia? One factor would seem to be the enduring legacy of authoritarian rule, both by the South African colonial authorities and within the exiled liberation movement. It has been argued that authoritarian tendencies *within* SWAPO returned with the organization from exile in 1989. Some scholars blame the UN's 1976 designation of SWAPO as "the sole and authentic representative of the Namibian people" for its authoritarian leanings. Leys and Saul attribute such tendencies in large part to the movement's long years of exile and armed struggle. Noting the experience of liberation movements throughout southern Africa, they suggest that "the possibility exists that the very process of struggling for liberation, especially by resort to force of arms, almost inevitably generates political practices that prefigure undemocratic outcomes."[55]

In any case, there are disturbing signs of authoritarianism today.[56] SWAPO continues to show disdain for the many Namibians whose family members died while detained in its camps in Angola during the 1980s. SWAPO called upon its members to boycott a reconciliation conference held in 1998 on the detainee issue, organized by its former ally, the Council of Churches of Namibia. Following the council's insistence on holding the conference, SWAPO accused the church federation of harboring "hidden political agendas" aimed at undermining the ruling party.[57]

In addition, many leaders of the ruling party have been exceedingly harsh in their attacks on the Namibian media. In a late 1996 interview in *New Era,* President Nujoma called the press in Namibia "an enemy press" that must be denounced. Nujoma claimed that foreigners lead the press in Namibia and that the situation would only be rectified when Namibians take over.[58] Since independence, there have been a number of incidents in which the ruling party has shown a distinct lack of respect for an independent media, and members of the media have responded, in turn, with self-censorship.[59] Others, as represented by the Journalists Association of Namibia (JAN), have expressed publicly their concern at the "increasing intolerance of Namibian government officials towards the right to freedom of expression." In May 1997, JAN executive member Tom Minney called upon the government to restrain its members from launching "further unwarranted attacks on the media, educate its members in a democracy, and take urgent steps to encourage respect for the principles proclaimed in the Windhoek Declaration Promoting an Independent and Pluralistic African Press."[60]

Finally, questions about the degree of internal democracy within SWAPO, and about the increasing levels of corruption in the government, have provoked concerns about the growing arrogance of power. A December 1996 editorial in the *Namibian* noted that "tensions are building within the ruling party" as members, "although traditionally loyal and compliant, are becoming more and more concerned about the authoritarianism and top-down leadership which presently characterises the movement." Many have complained about the arbitrary decision by the president to replace the candidate chosen by the party for SWAPO secretary-general. One of the main issues to be addressed in the 1997 party congress, the editorial continued, was "the issue of democratisation within the party."[61] Meanwhile, the government has been plagued by scandals and charges of corruption regarding the purchase of presidential jets, improper farming practices among members of parliament and cabinet ministers, mismanagement and favoritism within state bureaucracies, and the misappropriation or misapplication of state funds or government property. The failure of party and government leaders to respond to such allegations and to reduce the incidence of these practices could erode Namibia's fledgling democratic political culture.

The growth of viable political parties and strong organizations of civil society is also inhibited by the limitations of the Namibian economy. While it has not experienced the hardships of many other African countries, Namibia faces significant economic hurdles in the near future. Shortly after independence, a World Bank report characterized Namibia as divided into two economies and two societies, one that was "wealthy, educated, healthy and European," and the other "poor, illiterate, malnourished and African." The division into two societies also reflects a corresponding inequality in income and access to public services, according to the report.[62] While a black middle class is rapidly emerging in Namibia, there is no doubt that the large income discrepancies will persist well into the future.

The Namibian economy remains dominated by its primary sectors. It has a variety of exploitable minerals, one of the world's richest offshore fishing grounds, and a climate that supports an extensive livestock industry (when not threatened by recurring drought).[63] The economy is fairly open, with exports averaging about 55 percent of gross domestic product (GDP). It is therefore susceptible to external factors, especially fluctuating world mineral prices. The country also has a narrow tax base and an overall shortage of skilled personnel. The subsistence agriculture sector, on which more than half of the country depends, contributes only 3 percent to GDP. Manufacturing continues to be based primarily on the processing of fish, meat, and beverages, and contributes only about 9 percent to GDP and 6 percent to employment. As discussed earlier, the government has established export processing zones with hopes of attracting increased investment in a variety of manufacturing ventures. According to the Economist Intelligence Unit, this initiative, "along with more productive use of the land, provides the main opportunity for expanding employment levels in the medium term."[64]

Between 1989 and 1994, real GDP growth averaged 3.3 percent annually, yielding an average increase in per capita income of 0.4 percent during the period. In 1996, real GDP growth averaged about 2.5 percent, although growth at about twice this rate was forecast for 1997 (following, among other things, recovery in the fishing sector). Still, there are many challenges to be overcome. First, the country's increasingly serious water shortage threatens its overall economic growth potential. Second, although the unemployment level is officially recorded as 20 percent, the true figure is thought to be 30 percent or higher. Moreover, of those considered employed, at least half work in subsistence agriculture or the informal sector and may be underemployed.[65] Finally, there are considerable constraints on industrial development in Namibia, ranging from the fragmented nature of industry to limitations on marketing, finance, and management. Some observers also identify constraints arising from regional economic relations, particularly those with South Africa.[66]

Conclusion

The enduring legacy of authoritarian rule, whether by the colonial authorities or by the exiled liberation movement, continues to stymie the growth of political parties and civil society organizations in Namibia, as the limitations of the Namibian economy further constrain the process. In some respects, then, despite the obvious cautionary lessons from around the continent, Namibia, like other newly liberalized African countries, seems poised to repeat the patterns of the past. However, there are also some indications of forces and factors that could counter this threat. For example, there is evidence that when the organizations of civil society have joined together on important policy issues, they have met with some success. When several groups convened a Land Conference in September 1994 to push for action on land issues (as an alternative to the relatively unproductive conference held by the government on this issue in 1991), and when the trade unions enlisted the assistance of NGOs to fight the government on the application of the new labor law to the export processing zones, they achieved some of their objectives. The donor and official communities in Namibia often support these organizations in their attempt to perform the various "democratic functions" of civil society. Enhancing the democratizing role of political parties remains the more formidable challenge; the only plausible scenario for countering the gradual slide toward a single-party system appears to be a division within the ruling party itself.

Notes

1. This chapter is based, in part, on research carried out in Namibia from 1991 to 1993 for my 1994 dissertation, as well as on research conducted during subsequent visits to Namibia in 1994 and 1995. I would like to acknowledge support from the University of Delaware through a General University Research grant in 1995.

2. See Weiland and Braham, eds., *Namibian Peace Process.*

3. Bauer, "Labor Movement," chap. 4.

4. Diamond, "Toward Democratic Consolidation," p. 4; Diamond cites O'Donnell and Schmitter, *Transitions,* chap. 5.

5. For a sampling of the popular conceptualizations of the democratic transition, see O'Donnell and Schmitter, *Transitions,* and any issue of *Africa Demos,* published by the Carter Center at Emory University.

6. There is less agreement among theorists about the requirements for the consolidation of democracy than for the transition to democracy. See, among others, Diamond, "Toward Democratic Consolidation"; Linz and Stepan, "Toward Consolidated Democracies"; and Beetham, "Conditions for Democratic Consolidation."

7. J. Forrest, "A Promising Start," pp. 750–751, and "Namibia," pp. 89, 96, and 99. Davidson, *Government and Opposition,* writing in 1994, is considerably less enthusiastic in his appraisal.

8. Lindeke and Wanzala, "Regional Elections," pp. 13–14.

9. Bratton, "Beyond the State," n. 26; Bratton cites Alfred Stepan, *Rethinking Military.*

10. Cliffe et al., *Transition to Independence,* p. 183; *Namibian,* December 14, 1994.

11. *Namibian,* June 2, 1997.

12. This was demonstrated, for example, in mid-1993, when President Nujoma invoked "party discipline" to justify the totally unanticipated switching of the ministers of broadcasting and information and trade and industry.

13. When the NUNW general secretary suggested that the trade union federation was considering forming its own political party to contest the 1994 elections, he was summoned to SWAPO headquarters to explain himself. According to the *Namibian* (March 16, 1994), the report of the general secretary's comments "was greeted with consternation in union, SWAPO and even state security circles."

14. Davidson, *Government and Opposition,* p. 29, makes a similar observation with regard to the fading distinction between party and government: "The domination of the mass media, the co-optation of the opposition, the intrusion of the government into the private sector of the economy, the extension of presidential powers in many areas, the assertion of the supremacy of the executive in the political sphere have led to charges of the 'erosion of the distinction between party and state.'" Davidson finds "an increasing self-identification of SWAPO as being synonymous with the nation" in speeches and others statements.

15. J. Forrest, "Namibia," p. 99, makes the same observation. He sees the weakness of opposition political parties in Namibia as contributing to an eventual weakening of the internal unity of SWAPO itself "as the perceived need for party solidarity becomes less compelling."

16. According to an editorial in the *Namibian* following the 1992 local and regional elections: "it is said, even in the ranks of SWAPO, that it is *despite* the lack of organizational leadership in the party that SWAPO won a convincing majority in the elections."

17. *Namibian,* December 18, 1992, and May 2, 1996.

18. Ibid., June 2, 1997.

19. Ibid., November 13, 1996.

20. Ibid., February 27, 1997; see also ibid., January 29, 30, and 31, 1997.

21. With the elections, regional councils and local authorities were created in Namibia to replace the ethnic-based apartheid political structures established by the interim governments. Following the recommendations of the 1990 First Delimitation Commission, Namibia was divided into 13 regions of roughly equal populations; each region is further divided into constituencies, of which there are a total of 95. The corresponding governmental structures established include 13 regional councils and dozens of local authorities; two members from each regional council represent the region in the National Council (Toetemeyer et al., *Namibia Regional Resources,* pp. 4–5).

22. J. Forrest, "Namibia," pp. 93–94.

23. Quoted in *Namibian,* August 9, 1994.

24. *Namibian,* July 17, 1995.

25. J. Forrest, "Namibia," p. 95.

26. Barkan et al., "Consolidation of Democracy," p. 24.

27. *New Era,* March 2–8, 1995.

28. Strauss, "Community Organisations," pp. 189–190.

29. Toetemeyer et al., *Namibia Regional Resources,* pp. 102–112.

30. Leys and Saul, "Introduction," p. 4. Heike Becker, *Namibian Women's Movement,* chaps. 7 and 8, while acknowledging the strides that have been made, also notes the significant struggles ahead for women's empowerment in Namibia.

31. *Namibian Worker,* January–February 1995; Peltola, *Lost May Day,* p. 281. Member unions of the NUNW include Namibia Food and Allied Workers Union, Mineworkers Union of Namibia, Namibia Public Workers Union, Metal and Allied Namibian Workers Union, Namibia Transport and Allied Workers Union, Namibia National Teachers Union, Namibia Domestic and Allied Workers Union, and Namibia Farm Workers Union. Member unions of the NPSM include South West Africa Mineworkers Union, Local Authorities Union of Namibia, Public Service

Union of Namibia, Namibian Building Workers Union, Namibia Wholesale and Retail Workers Union, and Bank Workers Union of Namibia.

32. *Namibian,* May 23, 1995.

33. *Namibian Worker,* May 1991, p. 2.

34. *Namibian,* September 27, 1993. According to Christelle Terreblanche, "Namibian Trade Unions," p. 7, journalists and observers who attended the congress "accused the congress of undemocratic procedures in this regard. The motions for disaffiliation were scantily debated and not voted on."

35. *Namibian,* May 2, 1996. According to another union member: "Because of this stumbling block [affiliation] our hands are tied and we are no longer safeguarding the interests of our members" (*Namibian,* May 17, 1996).

36. Maseko, "Namibian Student Movement," p. 128.

37. Sipho Maseko (ibid., pp. 127–128) reports the following reasons for NANSO's decision to disaffiliate: the realization that affiliation to SWAPO caused disunity among students and prevented NANSO from recruiting among students who were not SWAPO sympathizers; a concern about preventing outside control of NANSO's processes and structures (in reaction to the unexpected co-optation by SWAPO of a number of NANSO leaders); and a general desire to preserve the inner organizational democracy and autonomy of the student organization.

38. Ibid., p. 128.

39. *New Era,* July 28–August 3, 1994.

40. *Namibian,* December 18, 1996.

41. For example, the Namibian constitution explicitly forbids discrimination on the grounds of sex and essentially authorizes affirmative action for women and other disadvantaged groups. The constitution also guarantees full equality to women in marriage and its dissolution (Hubbard and Solomon, "Many Faces of Feminism," p. 171). In addition, new labor and social security laws provide important benefits to the small percentage of women in formal-sector employment.

42. Hubbard and Solomon, ibid., pp. 172–173.

43. Ibid., p. 171. Whereas some women object to the department as compartmentalizing women's concerns, others see it as a sign of the government's commitment to women.

44. Ibid., p. 182.

45. See, for example, Rueschemeyer et al., *Capitalist Development;* Haggard and Kaufman, *Political Economy;* and Mainwaring and Scully, "Introduction."

46. Julius Nyang'oro, "Critical Notes," and Julius Ihonvbere, "On the Threshold" identify many of these problems. They include a move back toward single-party rule and the emergence of authoritarian tendencies among new ruling parties, in particular, following "devastating wins at the polls"; the retention of the same institutions and structures of rule and the same people in power, despite democratic elections; a continued tendency to overpersonalize politics; a heavy reliance on foreign donors and governments for support; and a general failure to offer alternative agendas and to mobilize new constituencies. "New oppositions," meanwhile, often remain hopelessly divided.

47. This section is based, in large part, on the following interviews conducted in July 1995 in Windhoek: Katuutire Kaura, DTA vice president and member of parliament; Allen Liebenberg, UDF national treasurer and acting general secretary; Kosie Pretorius, MAG member of parliament; Moses Katjiuongua, DCN member of parliament; Uno Hengari, South West Africa National Union (SWANU) general secretary; and discussions in 1993 with the Workers' Revolutionary Party's Hewat Beukes. See also Bauer, "Re-examining Multipartyism."

48. *Namibian,* June 20, 1996.

49. Dobell, "SWAPO Sweep," p. 8.

50. Similarly, in an October 1, 1993, editorial in the *Namibian*, Gwen Lister and Chris Ndivanga note that there is no direct translation for the word "disaffiliation" in many Namibian languages, with the closest rendition being "having nothing to do with." Thus the whole notion of disaffiliation (e.g., of the unions or the student movement from SWAPO) takes on only one very strong meaning, namely, "being anti-SWAPO."

51. *Namibian*, March 6, 1997.

52. Monga, "Civil Society and Democratization," p. 365. In a similar vein, Christine Sylvester, "Whither Opposition?" p. 409, has noted the rise of "fugitive oppositions" in Zimbabwe (composed of, e.g., collective cooperatives, women factory workers, women's organizations, university students), as the ruling party has attempted to preempt the development of any alternative power centers in the country.

53. See, for example, Wignaraja, ed., *New Social Movements,* and Escobar and Alvarez, eds., *Making of Social Movements.*

54. Lewis, "Political Transition," p. 31. Peter Lewis identifies a number of formidable challenges to civil society in Africa: fragmented, weak, co-opted, disaffected, and probably undemocratic organizations; and lack of a civic orientation concerned with issues of public policy and, instead, one preoccupied with "sectional, factional and communal particularities" (ibid., pp. 51–52). Similarly, E. Gyimah-Boadi, "Civil Society," pp. 120–126, laments the fact that civil societies in Africa have not been able to ensure public accountability, to transcend ethnoregional, religious, and other cleavages, or to further economic renewal. He attributes these weaknesses to a vulnerability to repression and co-optation by the state, continued political and economic crises, material and legal constraints, low levels of institutional development, the patrimonialization of political power, and a culture of incivility following decades of authoritarian rule.

55. Leys and Saul, "Introduction," p. 5. Masipula Sithole, "Zimbabwe: In Search of Stable Democracy," p. 481, makes a similar point for Zimbabwe: "The liberation movement also left a significant mark on Zimbabwe's political culture. The commandist nature of mobilization and politicization under clandestine circumstances gave rise to the politics of intimidation and fear. Opponents were viewed in warlike terms, as enemies and, therefore, illegitimate. The culture from the liberation struggle was violent and intolerant."

56. See also Davidson, *Government and Opposition,* pp. 32-42.

57. *Namibian,* November 3 and 18, 1996. The detainee issue is one of the few problem areas identified in the U.S. State Department's 1996 report on human rights practices in Namibia (U.S. Government, 1996). According to the *Namibian*, "The report states frankly that 'SWAPO was viewed widely as having failed, once again, to deal forthrightly with the missing detainee issue'" (February 3, 1997). See also Africa Watch, *Accountability in Namibia.*

58. *New Era,* December 13, 1996.

59. Bauer, "Prospects for the Consolidation of Democracy," pp. 9–11. Most recently, SWAPO has again brazenly displayed an increasingly intolerant attitude toward others. In a number of statements, including ones made by President Nujoma and SWAPO spokesperson Alpheus Naruseb, sharp attacks were launched on gays in Namibia with vows to "uproot" homosexuality from Namibian society. The numerous statements to this effect drew criticism from several quarters, including European diplomats concerned that the expressed sentiments contravene the Namibian constitution and its protection of minorities (*Namibian*, January 30 and 31 and February 3 and 4, 1997).

60. Media Institute of Southern Africa, "Action Alert."

61. *Namibian,* December 6, 1996.

62. World Bank, *Namibia.*

63. In 1995, mining contributed about 12 percent to the gross domestic product (less than half its contribution during the 1980s), fishing about 4 percent, and commercial agriculture about 8 percent. Other sectors with large contributions include manufacturing (9 percent), wholesale and retail trade (9 percent), financial services and real estate (11 percent), and government services (28 percent) (EIU, *Namibia Country Report,* p. 5).

64. EIU, *Namibia Country Profile,* pp. 12–13.

65. EIU, *Namibia Country Report,* p. 8; ibid., *Namibia Country Profile,* p. 17.

66. Curry and Stoneman, "Problems of Industrial Development," p. 49. According to them: "Fragmentation is itself a major constraint on industrial development; growth in one subsector does not stimulate significant growth in others, but merely raises import demands. The formal sectors which exist have their main links to South Africa, for supplies and distribution arrangements."

PART 6

Conclusion

23

State, Conflict, and Democracy in Africa: The Complex Process of Renewal

Adebayo Olukoshi

Among many Africanist researchers and policymakers of different ideological hues, the last few years have witnessed the growth of profound pessimism, even outright disillusionment, about the overall prospects of the African continent. Much of this pessimism and disillusionment has been captured by the concept of "Afro-pessimism" that has gained currency since the early 1990s. The ease with which Afro-pessimism—that state of mind whereby nothing good is seen as presently or potentially coming out of Africa in the near term—has spread is quite astonishing and stands in complete contrast to the cautious hope that pervaded discussions about Africa's place in the world a few years earlier. With the rise to power of Mikhail Gorbachev in 1985, many intellectuals and politicians had pointed to the prospects for a new, brighter global order from which Africa was expected to profit considerably as the international peace dividend was distributed. However, the rapid collapse of the Soviet bloc and the Soviet Union itself, combined with a host of other factors such as the resurgence of violent ethnic nationalism, turned the table of opinion as the 1990s dawned.

Political and Economic Dimensions of "Afro-Pessimism"

The dwindling domestic economic and social fortunes of the continent, combined with a decrease in its share of global economic activity (especially trade and investment flows), a deepening debt crisis,[1] shrinking international competitiveness, declining revenue receipts, a growing refugee problem, spectacular cases of state decay and collapse,[2] and systematic violence, reinforce the feeling that the basis for hope had been (almost) exhausted, at least in the short term. This feeling was vividly captured by

Robert Kaplan in his 1994 essay on what he described as the "coming anarchy,"[3] even if several commentators shuddered at the cynical extremism and tendentiousness of his commentary and its tone. But even in otherwise respectable intellectual and policy circles, including the World Bank, few were able to resist the prognosis that Africa had become "hemmed in,"[4] with its societies sliding back to precolonial and early-colonial enclave arrangements,[5] its states undergoing a "free fall,"[6] and its people increasingly abandoned to a Hobbesian law of nature amid growing disorder. For many, the question that was posed was: can Africa survive?[7] In many respects, a significant proportion of scholarly energy during the 1990s has been devoted to seeking terminologies and concepts that were thought to best capture what has been widely seen as a season of (irretrievable) anomie and decay in Africa. It was the era of the "basket-case" thesis of Africa.

The feeling that all things are falling apart in Africa was reinforced during the early 1990s by the fact that some of the most vociferous Afro-pessimists saw very little possibility that external aid and externally imposed International Monetary Fund (IMF)/World Bank structural adjustment programs stood any chance of restoring Africa to the path of recovery. Even the appetite among foreign governments for sending in their armies to "restore" order, either unilaterally or under United Nations supervision, appeared to be in recession. Within Africa itself, "cultural" pressures were thought to be such that countries were not capable of sustaining liberal political reforms. Viewed from all possible angles, Africa appeared not only to be increasingly disengaged from the international system (rather involuntarily), but also to be abandoned by the world to its enforced isolation. Africa's "loss" was posited as Asia's "gain," as attention increasingly focused on the growing centrality of the Asia Pacific belt to the international system. Studies proliferated on how the "Asian tigers" were able, over a relatively short period of time, to transform themselves from low-income to middle- and high-income countries; pointed and partisan suggestions were made regarding the lessons that Africa could learn from them.[8]

At the same time that the raw statistics pointed to Africa's increasing "marginalization" and the spread of "aid fatigue," a parallel development—namely, the funding, curriculum, and paradigmatic crises of African studies in North America and parts of Europe—tended to reinforce the mood of Afro-pessimism in various academic and political circles. Some saw an organic interconnection between Africa's marginalization in the post–Cold War world order and the decline of African studies in the West; others felt that the problem facing African studies was much more one of inappropriate methodologies and paradigms that consistently produced one-sided interpretations of the complex processes of change on the continent. Depending on where different scholars stood in this debate, there was a tendency to express exasperation at the alleged failure of Africa to meet the challenges of the post–Cold War world by reforming along the lines prescribed by the Bretton Woods twins. The message was direct: adapt or perish. In all of this, analytic attention was focused exclusively on the internal sources of the African crisis; the role of external factors was completely downplayed or totally discounted.

The range of proposals that has been tabled purportedly to enable Africa to overcome the scourge of Afro-pessimism is legion, but two stand out in particular. The first, echoing the so-called Washington consensus, consists of a constant reiteration of the need for Africa to fully embrace the market as the only viable alternative path to recovery that is open to it. The fact that much of Africa has been implementing IMF/World Bank structural adjustment programs since the beginning of the 1980s without much to show for it is often downplayed or explained away, either through a resort to the ubiquitous concept of "neopatrimonialism" or through claims that the situation on the continent would have been far worse had the market reforms not been imposed in the first place.[9] The second proposal centers around various notions of re- and/or self-colonization, with or without a UN mandate.[10] This proposal derives from different motivations depending on who is making it. There are those who claim that recolonization is necessary because the project of "modernization" or "civilization" that was started with the onset of colonialism was abandoned hastily and in midstream by the colonial powers following the post-1945 shift in the international balance of power. Others table the proposal in the fervent belief that only external powers can stabilize the continent's violently fractious polities and prevent an implosion that would be accompanied by major humanitarian tragedies. It has also been suggested that Africa's main regional "hegemons" might lead a project of self-colonization as a means of securing peace and stability in their spheres of influence.

It is, without doubt, reflective of the cul-de-sac to which much of the fashionable academic research and policy prescriptions about Africa have led that the mainstream discourse about the future of the continent is dominated, if not by blind faith in the market, then by outright reactionary proposals for re- or self-colonization.[11] To be sure, there are many intellectuals who, reflecting on the wholesale takeover of the (economic) decisionmaking apparatuses of African countries by the Bretton Woods twins, have written with concern about the creeping onset of a "second colonialism" and/or the increasing "donorization" of several branches of government.[12] But theirs is an altogether different preoccupation from that of the advocates of re- or self-colonization, whose proposals merely appear to add an explicit political dimension to a slightly earlier intellectual trend. According to this trend, categories of modernization that were once thought to be extinct are being revived within the framework of neoliberalism and its political economy in an effort to capture the African reality, even as the twentieth century draws to a close.

Beyond Afro-Pessimism: The Struggle for Renewal

The basic underlying assumption of this chapter is that for all of the crises that have beset African countries over the last decade and a half—and these should not be diminished or glossed over—there is a neglected parallel struggle for renewal that is also unfolding on the continent, but that is not sufficiently remarked upon and supported because of the faulty analytic prisms through which attempts are made to interpret the state of the continent. This struggle is not new; the popular agitation for political reform has, in many senses, always been a constant element of Africa's political history.[13] What is new is that for the first time since independence, the local and international contexts have improved, relatively, in the post–Cold War period, allowing the bearers of the struggle for political change to organize and assert themselves more boldly and openly than in the past. This struggle is mainly underwritten by the local forces that have, historically, defined themselves as the bearers and defenders of the democratic moments in the nationalist struggle for independence and that have sought to defend the existence of autonomous political spaces for the citizenry.[14] These forces, which include diverse social categories such as workers, peasants, students, professionals, and politicians, have, with varying degrees of unity, energy, and success, been in the vanguard of the resistance to political authoritarianism, corruption, and neocolonialism.

During the Cold War years, the bearers of the local struggles for political reforms and their movements were the victims of repression, justified by the need to contain either communism or capitalist revisionism, as the case may have been. Regimes across the African continent spared no effort to prevent the associations and social movements that attempted to champion the popular aspiration for democratic governance from organizing freely. The sheer weight of the repression that was unleashed by the state against them did not, however, succeed in eliminating all resistance; it merely altered the mode and tone of the struggle. Thus, as a discernible movement, the overall resilience of the local forces for democratization has been an important factor in the open struggles for reform that have recently been played out in various parts of Africa; they were the sources of the "pressures from below" to which many governments have had to respond to since the late 1980s. If students of Africa have missed the significance of these struggles, it is partly because, for much of the period from 1960 to 1980, they were mainly preoccupied with building nation-states. Since the 1980s, that preoccupation has been replaced by the task of building markets and creating an enabling environment.

Following from the perspective developed in the preceding paragraphs, this chapter represents as much a plea for a more balanced, dialectical reflection on the African reality as for a complete shift in the prevailing conceptual and methodological approaches. These approaches have for too

long dominated the study of Africa and produced, at best, only partial interpretations of developments on the continent and, at worst, gross caricatures
that many Africans resident on the continent find difficult to recognize.
This plea has assumed a greater urgency as a wide gulf appears to be developing between African social scientists, mostly situated within Africa, and
their Africanist colleagues, mostly located outside the continent, over the
most appropriate tools for understanding the changing situation on the continent.[15] The former have expressed profound disquiet not only at the ease
with which definitive conclusions, built on weak evidence, poor understanding, and shaky methodologies, are drawn about developments in
Africa, but also about the dizzying array of terminologies, most of them of
doubtful analytic value, that are invented as quickly as they are discarded to
"explain" every twist and turn in the transitional process that is unfolding
on the continent.

The Challenge of Consolidating Democracy in Africa

Several of the chapters in this book point to different aspects of the complex process of renewal that is under way in Africa in spite of the enormous
problems that continue to affect the process and confront the continent. The
task of separating processes of renewal from those of decay is, of course,
not made easy by the fact that they are unevenly distributed in space and
time, and the rapidity with which the balance of forces is shifting calls for
considerable caution. Still, for several of the contributors, the "gains" that
have been made in the area of political reform constitute an important area
of focus. Since the late 1980s, Africa has witnessed a great deal of activity
in the political arena involving popular campaigns for reform, the convening of sovereign national conferences or constitutional assemblies, and the
abandonment, in most cases, of single-party and military rule; side by side
with the introduction or reintroduction of multiparty politics, the emergence of local nongovernmental organizations on a scale never before witnessed, the licensing of private newspapers and broadcasting organizations,
the conduct of first and repeat elections for various tiers of government,
usually under the "watchful" eyes of local and international observers, the
assertion by the public of the right to free speech and assembly in many
countries where they were once denied, and an increase, even if still insufficient, in the voices of women and the youth. It is all a far cry from the situation at the end of the 1970s, when the African political landscape was
dominated by single-party and military regimes, which mostly maintained
exclusive and tight control over the domestic sources of information and
opinion, and had scant regard for the due processes of law. Of course, the
reform process is itself incomplete in many respects, and there are still
many important missing links that need to be put in place, but at the same

time, considering the situation that prevailed before the end of the 1980s, there have been some significant changes in the political space.[16]

The Case for Democratic Constitutionalism and Against Democratie Tropicalisée

How are we to understand the changes that have occurred in the African political landscape, and how can the progress made be consolidated? These are among some of the most difficult questions that are at the heart of the ongoing debates on transitional politics in Africa. Several of the contributions in this volume have addressed different dimensions of these questions, so we need not repeat their arguments here.[17] It seems necessary, however, in the context of these debates, to emphasize a number of points for further reflection. The first of these relates to the need to distinguish between constitutionalism as such and *democratic constitutionalism*. The former, where it is overemphasized, runs the danger of, at best, getting us bogged down with *technical* minutiae that tell us little about the continuing sources of stress and strain in Africa's political space in spite of the (re)introduction of constitutional reforms; at worst, it makes us run the risk of unwittingly becoming apologists for a status quo that might be very unsatisfactory. The latter issue underlines the centrality of democratic politics to the success of the reform process in Africa and, in my view, constitutes an important element of the challenge of democratic consolidation on the continent.

I shall return more fully to the issue of democratic consolidation shortly; the really important point that I want to underline here is the necessity for students of Africa's transitional politics to pay greater attention to the democratic content of constitution making and constitutional practice, since it is perfectly possible to have authoritarian regimes that are also rooted in constitutionalism and the rule of law as such. It is not enough, when we assess political developments in Africa as part of our study of the transitional process, simply to say that the actions of governments were in accordance with the constitution and the law, since the constitution and the law can themselves easily become instruments of exclusion and oppression. It is, furthermore, important to underline this position in order to discourage the growing suggestion in some policy circles that what Africa needs is not so much democratic governance—which, it is claimed, seems at present to be unachievable, or which allegedly tends to derail economic reforms and promote fiscal "irresponsibility"—as much as "good" governance that produces "effective" and "efficient" administration for the purpose of permitting the implementation of the "rational" economic policies that are expected to restore the continent's economic fortunes.

Related to the above, in the sense that it also touches on the *qualitative* nature of the transitional process and framework, is the importance of applying standards of assessment that do not unwittingly encourage the embrace of dubious electoral and political arrangements on the grounds that, at this stage of Africa's development, this is the only outcome that can be realistically expected. Many African social scientists, reflecting on the writings of some of their Africanist colleagues, have been concerned about the ease with which, in the name of realism, assertions about Africa's political transition have been made using standards of evaluation that, elsewhere, would be completely unacceptable. This attempt to foster a notion of *democratie tropicalisée,* a tropicalized version of democracy built on lower standards of assessment—and analysis—has been vigorously rejected, and rightly so, by a host of scholars who not only insist that Africa must be judged by the highest standards possible, but also that, for better or for worse, Africa is condemned to democracy as the only viable framework within which it must seek to promote political reforms and economic development.[18]

To insist on the highest possible standards is not to call for the development of definitions of democracy and parameters for determining the existence or absence of democratic politics that correspond to no actual or known historical examples anywhere in the world. The use of ideal types that belong only to the world of those interested in mystification and fetishism is one of the biggest problems with which practitioners of African studies have long had to deal—recall here the host of ideal types that informed the debates on development and underdevelopment in Africa during the 1970s and the idealized notions of the market and its workings that have been in vogue since the early 1980s.[19] On the contrary, mine is a plea for students of Africa, fully mindful that democracy intrinsically has an element of process to it, not to attempt to wish away or excuse serious shortcomings simply on the grounds that the status quo is the only realistic thing possible at the present time. Also implicit in this critique is the need for students of Africa not to assume that the only applicable yardstick against which the African democratic project can be measured is what is loosely referred to as "Western" democracy. Quite apart from the Eurocentrism inherent in such an approach, scholars such as Claude Ake have noted that the practice of liberal democracy in much of the industrialized world is so "impoverished" as to be of limited value in the current African conjuncture.[20]

Basic Prerequisites of Democratic Consolidation

Among the range of factors that various critics have mentioned as potentially and/or actually inhibiting the consolidation of democracy in Africa are the low level of literacy on the continent, the low levels of per capita income and gross domestic product,[21] the alleged dearth of ideology,[22] the preponderance of political and professional elites of the *ancien regime* in the democratization process, the disruptive power of competing ethnicities, the supposed absence of an independent commercial class,[23] and the persistence of "neopatrimonialism" and "rent seeking"[24] in the political economies of African countries. Assuming that these explanations, alone or in combination, are valid (and there are strong grounds for questioning the explanatory power or quality of several of them), the argument here is that they still do not address what in my view remains perhaps the single most important missing factor in the debate on the prospects for democratic consolidation in Africa. This factor centers on the need to anchor democratic constitutional and political engineering to popular sovereignty in society, and it derives from the position that democracy, even in its conventional constitutional sense, cannot endure unless it is rooted in popular sovereignty.

To put it another way, the chief challenge of democratic consolidation in Africa today centers on the need to anchor representation (through electoral pluralism and universal adult suffrage), the rule of law, and the freedom of speech and association to popular participation and control in decisionmaking at all levels. This manner of posing the challenge of democratic consolidation in Africa is not altogether new, but its chief advantage rests in the possibility it offers the student of contemporary Africa to move the discourse beyond a focus on factors that are arbitrarily selected by particular authors.

The question of popular sovereignty in the democratic process broaches several other issues relevant to the consolidation of the political reform process. The first of these concerns the meaning and content of citizenship, both historically and during this transitional period in Africa.[25] In addition to the challenge of revisiting the basis for the definition of citizenship (i.e., whether it is posed in terms of the place of birth or ancestry, or the place of residence or site of labor) and citizenship rights (as they pertain to the differential meanings that they have for the urban and rural populace), it is important also to address the issue of how to reverse the erosion of what M. Roche describes as "social citizenship" on the continent.[26] The erosion of social citizenship dates back to the onset of the economic crisis on the continent, but it has been significantly accelerated by the ascendancy of neoliberalism and IMF/World Bank structural adjustment implementation since the early 1980s. The decline in social citizenship has been so severe that some African scholars have been tempted to speak of the emergence of the "irrelevant state" in their bid to draw attention to the growing irrelevance of the state to the social and welfare aspirations of the overwhelming majority of the citizenry.[27] Other scholars, like Naomi Chazan, speak of a process of "disengagement" by the citizenry from the state in the context of a gathering process of informalization.[28]

The decline of social citizenship and of the role of the state in social provisioning has, in many cases, been paralleled by the creation or revival of ethnic, communal, and religious networks and structures as individuals and groups seek alternative means of producing their own social welfare needs in a process that also challenges the postcolonial, national-territorial, secular state project of independence.[29] A key challenge of citizenship today, therefore, consists not just in the restoration of political rights and liberties, but also in the revival of the role of the state in advancing social citizenship. For, as has been pointed out by many commentators, there is a distinct danger of the legitimacy of the democratic project itself being eroded if crucial social livelihood questions are not addressed. As Thandika Mkandawire, paraphrasing sentiments that are growing across the continent, puts it, "people do not eat democracy,"[30] a point reiterated in a different context by L. Rudebeck, based on focus group discussions in Kandjanja, Guinea-Bissau, to the effect that "if no concrete improvements take place, we shall withdraw."[31]

The second issue arising from the notion of popular sovereignty in the democratization project concerns the relationship between the internal and the external in the political reform process unfolding in Africa. Among the range of questions that have been raised in this discussion, the one that bears reiterating here is what has been described as the choicelessness imposed by the international donor community on Africa's elected governments. This tendency is evident in several domains, but it appears most notably in the foreclosure of choice regarding the path to economic reform (both in terms of policy content and instruments) and in the limitation of the scope for internal policy and political debate about required economic policy mixes and their timing, phasing, and sequencing. This has meant that even as African governments have been encouraged to open up their political spaces, the scope for internal and governmental choice over economic policy has remained narrow. As a consequence, the domestic consensus and coalition building required for sustainable economic reform has been neglected and undermined, and accounting to donors has taken the place of accountability to the populace. Thus, the donor-led economic reform process has tended to erode the legitimacy of the internal democratic process through the externalization of effective economic decisionmaking.[32] Executives have been pitted against parliaments as the former attempt to keep key economic policies away from the scrutiny of the legislative arm of government, and civil society groups have also been pitted against the state as they demand public debate on key questions pertaining to the management of the national economy and the reform of social policy. It is this state of affairs that prompted Mkandawire to describe the African governments elected since the late 1980s as "choiceless democracies"[33]—a situation that must be redressed if democracy is to be successfully consolidated on the continent.

Neglected Themes in the Study of Democratic Consolidation

Three questions that have been generally neglected in the discourse on democratic consolidation, but that are crucial to the project in Africa, are the need to rehabilitate the state, the role of the military in the political reform process, and the impact of influential regional players on the direction and content of change. Regarding the state, it seems quite clear that the work of democratic renewal and consolidation cannot be fully undertaken without attention to the task of rehabilitating the state in Africa. At the beginning of the 1980s, the ruling intellectual vogue was the adoption of the zealous and decisively one-sided anti-statism of the neoliberals. Within the framework of donor structural adjustment programs, efforts were made to dismantle the African state, which, both in theory and practice, was, and to a large extent continues to be, seen as the main obstacle to growth, development, and liberty on the continent. This single-minded external attack combined with processes of internal decay to considerably weaken the state and, in many cases, rob it of an autonomous and well-anchored organizing principle. Thus, decline has gone hand in hand with drift and a worsening legitimacy deficit.

Fifteen years after the implementation of structural adjustment began in Africa, the view that the state is basically the root of all of the continent's evils is only gradually beginning to be tempered. But much of the effort to "bring the state back in" has consisted of encouraging it to create an "enabling" environment for the market and the private sector to thrive. The issue of how the state might be reconstructed to support democratization remains largely ignored. The point, therefore, that insofar as the consolidation of democracy in Africa is concerned, there can be no question of a trade-off between the state and the market still bears reiterating. The presence of effective and legitimate state structures is essential to the construction of stable and sustainable democratic systems; indeed, there is a sense in which state rehabilitation is, at this historical juncture, a central part of the African democratic project and should be more fully factored into our conceptual apparatuses. One such conceptual effort that is worth exploring and developing further consists of the notion of "developmental democracies" that was tabled before the seventh General Assembly of the Council for the Development of Social Science Research in Africa in July 1995.[34]

The second relatively neglected issue in the discourse on democratic consolidation relates to the question of the military and its response to the inauguration of political reforms that, by definition, exclude it from the direct process of governance. As Richard Joseph's chapter on Nigeria in this volume underlines, the capacity of the military to obstruct or roll back the political reform process is one that must not be underestimated. At the same time, in cases such as Mali and Malawi, the military did play an active role in enabling the political reform process by, in the former, responding to popular appeals for a national conference and, in the latter, disarming Kamuzu Banda's Young Pioneers and refusing to shoot at civilians agitating for the restoration of multiparty politics. The Malian and Malawian cases are, however, somewhat exceptional, and they do not necessarily preclude military derailment of the political reform process. This immediately raises the challenge of how to get the military to respect and uphold the constitution. At one level, the question of restoring or upgrading military professionalism in various countries has to be seen as an essential part of democratic consolidation. At another level, the entire issue of the function and organizational structure of a peacetime army is one that will also have to be debated. But beyond these, important sections of the civil population itself will need to be freed from the debilitating effects of the ideology of militarism that has sunk roots into their thinking and praxis. In many African countries, not least Nigeria, where, as Joseph notes, ethnicity plays a role in the sustenance of military autocracy, many people still have to learn that the alternative to bad civilian government is not military rule, but better civilian government. The vigilance of the democratic forces in society, linked where possible with military professionals who accept and respect the democratic framework, needs to be developed as part of this strategy. The international community, too, can assist in this by decisively sanctioning and isolating military regimes from the comity of elected governments.

A third largely neglected theme in the discourse on democratic consolidation in Africa relates to the potential and actual impact of the continent's regional hegemons on the political reform process in the regions where they are dominant. We must, of course, be aware of the limits of the regional hegemon thesis itself, not least because there are limits to what external forces can do in any given country. Intervention by a regionally influential state does not necessarily guarantee success or sustainability and, in the wrong hands, this thesis has been employed to advance the case for re- or self-colonization. But within the context of our concern with the challenges of democratic consolidation, the question of the impact of regional hegemons on the process of political reform has been brought to the fore by a number of developments across the continent. These include the intervention by South Africa, acting in concert with Botswana and Zimbabwe, to restore the elected government of Lesotho after it was toppled by the country's military; the pressures emanating from South Africa for political reforms in Swaziland; the intervention by the Economic Community of West African States and its Monitoring Group in Liberia and Sierra Leone; Nigeria's endorsement and accommodation of military putschists in The Gambia and Niger during the 1990s; and the effects on the Great Lakes area of the crippling of the Zairian state by the Mobutu kleptocracy.

At a very general and tentative level, it seems that in the parts of Africa, such as southern Africa, where the key players accept and follow a basic framework of electoral pluralism, the internal forces for political reform and constitutional government in the region enjoy a conducive environment within which to operate. Conversely, in regions of west Africa, where a key demographic and economic giant like Nigeria is under military rule, its influence and example could serve, and in many respects has served, as a source of inspiration for antidemocratic elements throughout the region, especially in the military. Though the installation of democratic governance in Nigeria does not, by itself, preclude the takeover of power by antidemocratic elements in other states in the region, such forces would at least have to contend with the adverse response of a democratic Abuja. The implication of this perspective is that democratic forces in Africa need to take more fully into account developments in other parts of the continent when formulating their strategies for initiating and sustaining political reform. Such an approach might provide regional organizations and groupings with new, meaningful mandates.

Meeting the Intellectual Challenges of the African Transition

If, as we have argued, Africa is in the throes of a process of change that has involved the formal embrace by most governments on the continent of electoral pluralism, a crucial challenge associated with scholarly efforts to understand the content, direction, and scope of the change that is under way is a willingness to revisit the analytic frames and methods by which the continent has hitherto been studied. In this connection, it is worth drawing attention to a number of limitations that have tended to weaken the quality of analysis and obscure the crucial questions that should normally engage the attention of the academic and policy communities. My starting point in this regard is the growing trend, integral to the "new" political economy, of applying the categories of economics to the quest for understanding the behavior of political actors, as well as processes and outcomes, in Africa. Such rigid dichotomizations as those made between the private and the public, the state and the market, rentier activities and market relations, the formal and the informal, the urban and the rural, and tradables and nontradables, which have underpinned much of the discourse on African economies, have been extended by political scientists and political economists to the realm of political analysis.

In the effort to apply the categories of economics to the study of African politics, what is often forgotten is that, in real-life situations on the continent, these categories interpenetrate one another in an organic relationship that is at once complementary and contradictory. Moreover, it is not as straightforward as it seems to categorize individuals and groups neatly into one slot or the other for the purpose of determining political behavior and predicting outcomes, since the distinction between these sectors is often much more blurred than is recognized. Indeed, as has been pointed out by several scholars, the sectors are quite often blended together, so that much of social, economic, and political life in Africa falls into "gray" areas.[35] Actors straddle the formal and the informal, the private and the public, the sphere of tradables and the arena of nontradables, and the state and the market.

The reality of straddling, which makes nonsense of the rigid dichotomizations on the basis of which many political economists have attempted to grasp the problems and prospects of democratic change in Africa, dates back a long time. The case for abandoning attempts to understand political life in Africa on the basis of these dichotomies has, however, never been stronger than at the present time when, by all accounts, the boundaries of informalization have been expanding rapidly, making the fashionable distinctions favored by the new political economy ever more problematic. Furthermore, the politics of straddling entails multiple modes of livelihood[36] and multiple identities that, in playing themselves out, complicate political behavior, as well as the task of understanding it. The challenge that this situation poses for students of Africa is the need to develop appropriate conceptual and methodological tools that are adequate for the task of capturing developments at a time of flux. Such tools and methods may never be able to fully capture the complexity of the situation; it will, however, be sufficient if they are the products of a painstaking effort to understand Africa on the basis of what is unfolding, rather than through preconceived notions built on methodologies that unjustifiably tend to freeze a dynamic situation and take the vitality out of politics and the activities of political actors.

While it is important for students of Africa to develop a comparative framework within which to understand the continent—indeed, there is a sense in which the future will belong to comparativists—it is equally crucial not to take this to mean that the African reality can be interpreted only through a one-sided recourse to analogies drawn from the histories of other parts of the world, especially Europe. All too often, in a bid to explicate developments in Africa, many students are tempted to go back to an earlier epoch in the history of Europe and abstract concepts from those historical phases for application to contemporary Africa. Related to this is the study of earlier experiences from other parts of the world with a view to identifying the factors that are thought to explain their successes (rarely their failures). These are then extended to the African terrain in order to argue that the absence of the factors that allegedly accounted for the success of another region explains why Africa is experiencing the difficulties it is encountering, or why the prospects for success are limited. Policy prescriptions are then derived from such accounts. It is, to say the least, an approach that is highly problematic, not only because of the ahistoricism that is involved[37] and the fact that it suggests a certain unilinear evolutionism,[38] but also because, quite often, what is described with certitude as constituting the comparative experience from which concepts are derived is, in fact, the subject of vigorous contestation among historians specializing in the study of those other regions of the world.

The African experience cannot be fully understood through its subordination, as it were, to the experiences of others. While an awareness of the experiences of others can be very useful from both a scholarly and a policy point of view, those experiences should not themselves become the implicit or explicit narratives from which the African reality is deduced. Africa needs to be studied primarily in terms of its own dynamics, which are the products of the interplay of internal and external factors. This project is one of the most important intellectual challenges confronting students of Africa at this stage in the continent's history.

Notes

1. George, *Fate Worse Than Debt.*
2. Zartman, *Collapsed States.*
3. R. Kaplan, "Coming Anarchy."
4. Callaghy, "Political Passions" and "Africa."
5. Reno, *Corruption.*
6. The notion of the "free fall" of the African state was popularized during the 1980s by World Bank officials, among them Edward Jaycox, to justify their campaign for the embrace of structural adjustment by African governments.
7. J. Whitaker, *How Can Africa Survive?*
8. World Bank, *East Asian Miracle.* For an interesting critique that also gives a detailed insight into the political maneuverings around the production of this report, see Wade, "Japan" and *Governing the Market.* It bears recalling here that during the 1960s, even up to the early 1970s, many of those who today celebrate the Asian "miracle" had written off that part of the world as a basket case, much in the same way as Africa is being written off today.
9. Mkandawire and Olukoshi, eds., *Between Liberalisation and Oppression.*
10. Mazrui, "Towards a Benign Recolonisation" and "Self-Colonisation."
11. Mafeje, "Minor Recolonisation" and "Recolonisation or Self-Colonisation"; Bangura, "Pitfalls of Recolonisation."
12. Engberg-Pedersen et al., eds., *Limits of Adjustment;* Gibbon, "Structural Adjustment and Structural Change"; Havnevik and van Arkadie, eds., *Domination or Dialogue?;* Olukoshi, "Extending the Frontiers" and "Impact of Recent Reform"; and Onimode, ed., *The IMF.*
13. Anyang' Nyong'o, ed., *Popular Struggles.*
14. Mamdani and Wamba-dia-Wamba, eds., *African Studies in Social Movements.*
15. Ibid.; Mkandawire, "African Studies"; and Zeleza, *Manufacturing African Studies.*
16. Gibbon, *Liberalized Development;* Diamond, "Prospects for Democratic Development."
17. See also Widner, ed., *Economic Change.*

18. Mkandawire, "Beyond Crisis"; Diamond, "Prospects for Democratic Development."

19. Phillips, "Concept of Development"; UNRISD, *States of Disarray.*

20. Ake, *Democracy and Development.*

21. No experience casts more serious doubt on the claim that a certain minimum income level (some put it at U.S.$1,200 per capita) is required before democracy can be consolidated than that of India, which, going by the conventional definitions, is the world's largest democracy and yet is also one of its poorer countries. See also Crawford Young's chapter in this volume (Chapter 2).

22. It is astonishing that some of those who are the most vociferous in pointing to an alleged "ideological void" in Africa today were also listed among the critics who insisted, in an earlier period, that one of Africa's main problems was an "excess" of ideology.

23. It is not at all clear why it is assumed that the existence of an "independent" commercial class will necessarily be favorable to the project of democratization when, except on the purely partisan ideological grounds organic to neoliberalism, the case is not as self-evident as it is made out to be. Various empirically rooted studies that have been carried out in different parts of Africa suggest that their organizations often demonstrate antidemocratic proclivities. See, for example, Liabes, "Entrepreneurs," on Algeria, and Olukoshi, "Bourgeois Social Movements," on Nigeria. See also Mkandawire, "Economic Policy-Making."

24. "Neopatrimonialism" and "rent seeking" are among the most abused—and ultimately limiting—concepts in the study of contemporary Africa. Elevated to the status of deus ex machina, they have been deployed to explain everything from why Africa went into crisis to why structural adjustment is not working and why democratic reforms will not endure. Surely, a concept that is capable of explaining everything ultimately explains nothing.

25. Ayoade, "States Without Citizens"; Mamdani, *Citizen and Subject;* Olukoshi, "Constitutionalism and Citizenship"; and Chapter 14 by Jeffrey Herbst in this volume.

26. Roche, *Rethinking Citizenship.*

27. Ihonvbere, "Economic Crisis."

28. Chazan, "Ghana." For a critique of the thesis of disengagement, see Gibbon et al., *Blighted Harvest.*

29. Adekanye, "Structural Adjustment"; Osaghae, *Structural Adjustment;* Olukoshi and Laakso, eds., *Challenges to the Nation-State;* and UNRISD, *States of Disarray.*

30. Mkandawire, "Economic Policy-Making," p. 43.

31. Rudebeck, "Democratisation in Africa."

32. Mkandawire, "Economic Policy-Making"; Beckman, "Empowerment or Repression?"

33. See Mkandawire, "Economic Policy-Making," as well as his Chapter 7 in this volume.

34. Mkandawire, "Beyond Crisis."

35. Cowen and Kinyanjui, "Some Problems of Class Formation"; Ng'ethe et al., "Rural Informal Sector"; Gibbon et al., eds., *Authoritarianism;* Mustapha, "Structural Adjustment"; Gibbon et al., *Blighted Harvest;* and Meagher and Yunusa, "Passing the Buck."

36. Mustapha, "Structural Adjustment."

37. Leys, "Review Essay."

38. Mamdani, "Glimpse at African Studies" and *Citizen and Subject;* Mamdani and Wamba-dia-Wamba, eds., *African Studies in Social Movements.*

ABBREVIATIONS

AAG	Affirmative Action Group
ADFL	Alliance of Democratic Forces for the Liberation of Congo-Zaire
AFL	Armed Forces of Liberia
AGP	African Governance Program
ANC	African National Congress
CDR	Coalition for the Defense of the Republic
CFA	Communauté Financière Africaine
CHRAJ	Commission on Human Rights and Administrative Justice
CODESRIA	Council for the Development of Social Science Research in Africa
CZI	Confederation of Zimbabwe Industries
DCN	Democratic Coalition of Namibia
DRC	Democratic Republic of the Congo
DTA	Democratic Turnhalle Alliance
EEC	European Economic Community
EGAT	États Généraux de l'Administration Territoriale
ELF	Eritrean Liberation Front
EPLF	Eritrean People's Liberation Front
EPM	enlarged presidential majority
EPRDF	Ethiopian People's Revolutionary Democratic Front
EPZ(s)	export processing zone(s)
ESAP	Economic Structural Adjustment Program
FAR	Armed Forces of Rwanda
FIS	Front Islamique de Salut

FPR	Front Patriotique Rwandais
FRELIMO	Front for the Liberation of Mozambique
FRODEBU	Front Démocratique Burundais
GATT	General Agreement on Tariffs and Trade
GIA	Groupe Islamique Armé
GNPC	Ghana National Petroleum Corporation
HCR	Haut Conseil de la République
IBDC	Indigenous Business Development Centre
IEA	Institute of Economic Affairs
IFI(s)	international financial institution(s)
IFP	Inkatha Freedom Party
IMF	International Monetary Fund
KANU	Kenya African National Union
LD-MPT	Ligue Démocratique-Mouvement pour le Parti du Travail
LPC	Liberia Peace Council
MDR	Democratic and Republican Movement
MLP	Mauritius Labour Party
MMD	Movement for Multiparty Democracy
MMM	Mouvement Militant Mauricien
MPLA	Popular Movement for the Liberation of Angola
MRND	Mouvement Révolutionnaire National pour le Développement
MSM	Mouvement Socialist Mauricien
NANSO	Namibian National Students Organisation
NDC	National Democratic Congress
NGO(s)	nongovernmental organization(s)
NNCCI	Namibia National Chamber of Commerce and Industry
NP	National Party
NPFL	National Patriotic Front of Liberia
NPP	New Patriotic Party
NPSM	Namibian People's Social Movement
NRM	National Resistance Movement
NUNW	National Union of Namibian Workers
OAU	Organization of African Unity
OECD	Organization for Economic Cooperation and Development
OLF	Oromo Liberation Front
PARMEHUTU/MDR	Party of the Movement for the Emancipation of Bahutu/Democratic and Republican Movement
PDG	Parti Démocratique Gabonais
PDS	Parti Démocratique Sénégalais
PDS-R	Parti Démocratique Sénégalais-Renouvellement

PFDJ	People's Front for Democracy and Justice
PIT	Parti de l'Indépendence et du Travail
PL	Liberal Party
PMSD	Parti Mauricien Social Démocrate
PNDC	Provisional National Defense Council
PRPB	Parti de la Révolution Populaire du Bénin
PS	Parti Socialiste
PSD	Social Democratic Party
PTC	Posts and Telecommunications Corporation
RENAMO	Mozambican National Resistance Movement
RPF	Rwandan Patriotic Front
RTLM	Radio-Télévision Libre des Milles Collines
SAP(s)	structural adjustment program(s)
SEDCO	Small Enterprise Development Corporation
SWAPO	South West Africa People's Organization
TPLF	Tigray People's Liberation Front
UDF	United Democratic Front
ULIMO	United Liberation Movement for Democracy in Liberia
UNCTAD	UN Conference on Trade and Development
UNIP	United National Independence Party
UNITA	National Union for the Total Independence of Angola
ZANU(PF)	Zimbabwe African National Union (Patriotic Front)
ZAPU	Zimbabwe African People's Union
ZDC	Zambia Democratic Congress

BIBLIOGRAPHY

Adam, C. 1995. "Fiscal Adjustment, Financial Liberalization, and the Dynamics of Inflation: Some Evidence from Zambia." *World Development,* vol. 23: 735–750.

Adamolekun, Ladipo. 1985. *The Fall of the Second Republic.* Ibadan, Nigeria: Spectrum.

Adedeji, Adebayo. 1994. "An Alternative for Africa." *Journal of Democracy,* vol. 5, no. 4: 119–132.

Adekanye, B. 1995. "Structural Adjustment, Democratisation, and Rising Ethnic Tensions in Africa." *Development and Change,* vol. 26, no. 2.

Adekanye, J. 'Bayo. 1997. "The Military." In Larry Diamond, Anthony Kirk-Greene, and Oyeleye Oyediran, *Transition Without End: Nigerian Politics and Civil Society Under Babanginda,* pp. 55–80. Boulder, CO: Lynne Rienner Publishers.

Adelman, Howard, and John Sorenson. 1994. "Introduction." In Howard Adelman and John Sorenson, eds., *African Refugees: Development Aid and Repatriation.* Boulder, CO: Westview Press.

Adelman, Howard, and Astri Suhrke. 1995. *Early Warning and Conflict Management: Genocide in Rwanda.* Fantoft-Bergen, Norway: Chr. Michelsen Institute.

Adesina, Jimi. 1992. "Labour Movements and Policy-Making in Africa." Working Paper 1. Dakar, Senegal: Council for the Development of Social Science Research in Africa (hereafter CODESRIA).

Adigun, O. 1989. "Nationality and Citizenship: The Legal Problematic of Transborder Ethnic Communities in Nigeria." In A. I. Asiwaju and P. O. Adeniyi, eds., *Borderlands in Africa.* Nigeria: University of Lagos Press.

Adjaho, Richard. 1992. *La Faillite du Contrôle des Finances Publiques au Bénin (1960–1990).* Porto-Novo, Benin: Editions Flamboyant.

Africa Confidential. 1996. "Nuts to the Bank." Vol. 37, no. 25 (December 13).

———. 1995. "Kume Preko—Kill Me Now." Vol. 36, no. 11 (May 26): 1–2.

Africa Demos. 1994. "Africa 1994: Ecstasy and Agony." Vol. 2, no. 3 (September).

Africa Watch. 1993. "Beyond the Rhetoric: Continuing Human Rights Abuses in Rwanda." New York: Human Rights Watch, June.

————. 1992. *Accountability in Namibia: Human Rights and the Transition to Democracy.* New York: Human Rights Watch.

Afriyie, Kwasi, and John Larvie. 1996. *Elections in Ghana, 1996: Part 1.* Accra: Electoral Commission of Ghana and the Friedreich Ebert Foundation.

Agbanglanon, Franck. 1996. "Présidentielles de l'an 2001: Adrien Houngbédji s'auto-proclame President." *Forum de la Semaine,* November 20–26.

Ainamon, Augustin. 1993. "Pouvons-nous éviter les riques d'un nettoyage ethnique?" *La Nation,* December 3.

Ake, Claude. 1998. "Globalization, Multilateralism, and the Shrinking Democratic Space." In Michael Schecter, ed., *Future Multilateralism: The Political and Social Framework.* New York: Macmillan.

————. 1996. *Democracy and Development in Africa.* Washington, DC: Brookings Institution.

————. 1993. "The Unique Case of Africa." *International Affairs,* vol. 69, no. 2: 239–244.

————. 1991. "Rethinking African Democracy." *Journal of Democracy,* vol. 2, no. 1: 32–44.

Alapini, Léa Sylvie. 1985. "Le Pouvoir et le Sacré: Le cas du Benin." Thèse du 3e cycle sociologie, Université de Paris V.

Alderfer, H. 1964. *Local Government in Developing Countries.* New York: McGraw-Hill.

Alesina, Alberto, and Roberto Perotti. 1993. "Income Distribution, Political Stability, and Investment." *NBER Working Papers.* No. 4486. Cambridge, MA: National Bureau for Economic Research.

Allen, Chris. 1989. "Benin." In Bogdan Szajkowski, ed., *Benin, the Congo, Burkina Faso: Politics, Economics, and Society.* New York: Pinter.

Almond, Gabriel. 1988. "The Return of the State." *American Political Science Review,* vol. 82, no. 3: 853–904.

Amadeo, Edward, and Tariq Banuri. 1991. "Policy, Governance, and the Conflict." In Tariq Banuri, ed., *Economic Liberalization: No Panacea.* Oxford: Clarendon Press.

Ameth, Cheikh Aliou. 1996. "Demission: Un cadre du PDS rejoint le PS." *Soleil,* August 23, p. 2.

Amin, Samir. 1973. *Neo-Colonialism in West Africa.* New York: Monthly Review Press.

Anderson, Benedict. 1983. *Imagined Communities.* London: Verso.

Anku-Tsede, E. K. D. 1996. "Defense Budgeting: Accountability and Transparency: The Experience of Ghana in the Fourth Republic, 1993–1996." Paper presented at the Conference on the Military and Civil Society in Africa, organized by the Africa Leadership Forum in Lilongwe, Malawi, September 23–25.

Anyang 'Nyong'o, P., ed. 1987. *Popular Struggles for Democracy in Africa.* London: Zed Books.

Aplogan, Jean-Luc. 1996. "Benin President Renews Oath to Include Ancestors." *Reuters,* April 6.

Armijo, Leslie Elliot. 1996. "Introduction." In Leslie Elliot Armijo, ed., *Conversations on Democratization and Economic Reform: Working Papers of the Southern California Seminar.* Los Angeles: University of Southern California.

Assevi, Akuété. 1994. "Conflits entre partis et guéguerre entre institutions." *La Nation,* May 27.

Association Rwandaise pour la Défense de la Personne et des Libertés Publiques (ADL). 1992. *Rapport sur les Droits de l'Homme au Rwanda.* Kigali, Rwanda: ADL, December.

Atchadé, Julien C. 1994. "Que dit le Projet de loi électorale?" *Forum de la Semaine,* April 13–19.

Austen, Ralph A. 1987. *African Economic History: Internal Development and External Dependency.* London: James Currey, Ltd.

Ayittey, George B. N. 1992. *Africa Betrayed.* New York: St. Martin's Press.

———. 1991. *Indigenous African Institutions.* New York: Transnational Publishers.

Ayoade, J. 1988. "States Without Citizens: An Emerging African Phenomenon." In Rothchild and Chazan, eds., *Precarious Balance.*

Azarya, Victor, and Naomi Chazan. 1987. "Disengagement from the State in Africa: Reflections on the Experience of Ghana and Guinea." *Comparative Studies in Society and History,* vol. 29, no 1: 105–131.

Babou, Youssoupha. 1996. "Commune de Mbacke: Le budget approuvé." *Sud Quotidien,* March 8, p. 3.

———. 1996. "Commune de Mbacke: Un budget en souris." *Sud Quotidien,* February 14, p. 3.

Badou, Jérome A. 1994. "Echéances électorales, 1995–1996." *La Recade,* March.

Bagde, Edmond. 1995. "Commune de Mbacke: Une gestion controversée." *Sud Quotidien,* January 12, p. 4.

Baker, Pauline H. 1984. *The Economics of Nigerian Federalism.* Washington, DC: Battelle Memorial Institute.

Bangura, Y. 1995. "The Pitfalls of Recolonisation: A Comment on the Mazrui-Mafeje Exhange." *CODESRIA Bulletin,* vol. 4.

———. 1994. "Intellectuals, Economic Reform, and Social Change: Constraint and Opportunities in the Formations of a Nigerian Technology." Dakar, Senegal: CODESRIA.

———. 1992. "Authoritarian Rule and Democracy in Africa: A Theoretical Discourse." In Gibbon et al., eds., *Authoritarianism.*

Barber, B. R. 1996. *Jihad vs. McWorld: How Globalism and Tribalism Are Reshaping the World.* New York: Ballantine Books.

Bardhan, P. 1991. "Alternative Approaches to Development Economics." In H Chenery and T. N. Srinivasan, eds., *A Handbook in Development Economics.* New York: New Holland.

Barkan, Joel. 1995. "Elections in Agrarian Societies." *Journal of Democracy,* vol. 6, no. 4: 106–116.

———. 1994. "Divergence and Convergence in Kenya and Tanzania." In Joel Barkan, ed., *Beyond Capitalism and Socialism in Kenya and Tanzania.* Boulder, CO: Lynne Rienner Publishers.

———. 1993. "Kenya: Lessons from a Flawed Election." *Journal of Democracy,* vol. 4, no. 3: 85–99.

———, ed. 1994. *Beyond Capitalism and Socialism in Kenya and Tanzania.* Boulder, CO: Lynne Rienner Publishers.

Barkan, Joel, Gretchen Bauer, and Carol Martin. 1994. "The Consolidation of Democracy in Namibia: Assessments and Recommendations." Report prepared for the Association in Rural Development (Washington, DC) and USAID (Windhoek, Namibia).

Barkan, Joel, M. L. McNutty, and M. A. O Ayeni. 1991. "Hometown Associations, Local Development, and the Emergence of Civil Society in Western Nigeria." *Journal of Modern African Studies,* vol. 29, no. 3: 457–480.

Barrington, Lowell. 1995. "The Domestic and International Consequences of Citizenship in the Soviet Successor States." *Europe-Asia Studies,* vol. 47 (July): 742.

Barry, Brian. 1995. *Justice as Impartiality.* London: Clarendon Press.

Bates, Robert H. 1994. "The Impulse to Reform in Africa." In Widner, ed., *Economic Change*, pp. 13–46.

———. 1991. "The Economics of Transition to Democracy." *Political Science and Politics*, March, pp. 24–26.

———. 1981. *Markets and States in Tropical Africa*. Berkeley and Los Angeles: University of California Press.

Bates, Robert H., and Paul Collier. 1994. "The Case of Zambia." In Robert H. Bates and Anne O. Krueger, eds., *Political and Economic Interactions in the Process of Policy Reform*, pp. 387–443. Oxford: Basil Blackwell.

Bates, Robert H., and Donald Lien. 1985. "A Note on Taxation, Development, and Representative Government." *Politics and Society*, vol. 14, no. 1: 53–70.

Bates, Robert H., Philip Brock, and Jill Tiefenthaler. 1991. "Risk and Trade Regimes: Another Exploration." *International Organization*, vol. 45, no. 1.

Bauböck, Rainer, ed. 1994. *From Aliens to Citizens: Redefining the Status of Immigrants in Europe*. Aldershot, England: Avebury.

Bauer, Gretchen. 1997. "Re-examining Multipartyism in Africa in the 1990s: With a Focus on Namibia." Revised version of paper originally presented at the Thirty-ninth Annual African Studies Association Meeting, San Francisco, November 23–26.

———. 1996. "Prospects for the Consolidation of Democracy in Namibia." Revised version of paper originally presented at the Thirty-seventh Annual African Studies Association Meeting, Toronto, November 3–6, 1994.

———. 1994. "The Labor Movement and the Prospects for Democracy in Namibia." Ph.D. diss., University of Wisconsin-Madison.

Bayart, Jean-François. 1993. *The State in Africa: The Politics of the Belly*. New York: Longman.

———. 1991. "La Problématique de la democratisation en Afrique noire." *Politique Africaine*, no. 43 (October): 5–20.

———. 1991. "Le Fiasco Français." *Le Nouvel Observateur*, May 15–21, p. 64.

Bayart, Jean-François, Stephen Eilis, and Béatrice Hibou. 1997. *La Criminalisation de l'Etat en Afrique*. Brussels: Editions Complexe.

Bearman, Jonathan. 1996. "Special Focus: African Oil and Minerals." *African Business*, June.

Beck, Linda J. 1997. "Senegal's 'Patrimonial Democrats': Incremental Reform and the Obstacles to the Consolidation of Democracy." *Canadian Journal of African Studies*, vol. 31, no. 3: 1–31.

Becker, Heike. 1995. *Namibian Women's Movement, 1980 to 1992: From Anti-Colonial Resistance to Reconstruction*. Frankfurt: Verlag fuer Interkulturelle Kommunikation.

Beckett, Paul A., and Crawford Young, eds. 1997. *Dilemmas of Democracy in Nigeria*. Rochester, NY: University of Rochester Press.

Beckman, Bjorn. 1992. "Empowerment or Repression? The World Bank and the Politics of African Adjustment." In Gibbon et al., eds., *Authoritarianism*, pp. 83–105.

Beetham, David. 1994. "Conditions for Democratic Consolidation." *Review of African Political Economy*, vol. 60: 157–172.

Bendix, Reinhard. 1964. *Nation-Building and Citizenship*. New York: John Wiley & Sons.

Bénin, République du. 1995. Loi no. 94–013 du 17 janvier 1995 portant règles générales pour les élections du Président de la République et des membres de l'Assemblée Nationale.

———. 1993. *États Généraux de l'Administration Territoriale, Cotonou, les 7, 8, 9, et 10 janvier 1993.* Cotonou: Ministère de l'Intérieur, de la Sécurité, et de l'Administration Territoriale.

———. 1990–1994. *Journal Officiel de la Republique du Bénin (hereafter JORB).* Cotonou: Office National d'Edition, de Presse, et d'Imprimerie (ONEPI).

———. 1990. *Actes des États Généraux de l'Education, Cotonou du 2 au 9 octobre 1990.* Cotonou: Ministère de l'Education Nationale.

———. 1990. *Constitution de la République du Bénin.* Porto-Novo: Imprimerie Nationale.

———, Cour Constitutionnelle. 1994. Decision DCC 31–94. *La Nation,* October 5.

———, Cour Constitutionnelle. 1994. Decision DCC 30–94. *La Nation,* September 19.

———, Cour Constitutionnelle. 1994. Avis CC–001/94. September 14. *La Nation,* September 16.

———, Cour Constitutionnelle. 1994. Decision DCC 29–94. September 9. *La Nation,* September 12.

———, Cour Constitutionnelle. 1994. Decision DCC 27–94. *La Nation,* August 26.

———, Cour Constitutionnelle. 1994. Decision DCC 16–94. May 27. *JORB,* July 1.

———, Ministère de l'Intérieur, de la Securite, et de l'Administration Territoriale. 1993. "Arrêté no. 260 portant conditions et modalites d'enregistrement des Associations."

Berman, Harold J. 1983. *Law and Revolution: The Formation of the Western Legal Tradition.* Cambridge, MA: Harvard University Press.

Bhabha, Jacqueline, and Sue Shutter. 1994. *Women's Movement: Women Under Immigration, Nationality, and Refugee Law.* Staffordshire, England: Trentham Books.

Bhattacharya, Amar, Peter J. Montiel, and Sunil Sharma. 1997. "How Can Sub-Saharan Africa Attract More Private Capital Inflows?" *Finance and Development,* vol. 34, no. 2 (June): 3–6.

Bheenkck, Rundheersing, and Morton Owen Schapiro. 1991. "The Mauritian Export Processing Zone." *Public Administration and Development,* vol. 11: 264–265.

Bienen, Henry. 1990. "The Politics of Trade Liberalization in Africa." *Economic Development and Cultural Change,* vol. 38, no. 4: 713–732.

Bienen, Henry, and Jeffrey Herbst. 1996. "The Relationship Between Political and Economic Reform in Africa." *Comparative Politics,* vol. 29, no. 1: 23–42.

Bisele, Megan. 1994. "Human Rights and Democratisation in Namibia: Some Grassroots Political Perspectives." *African Rural and Urban Studies,* vol. 1, no. 2: 49–72.

Blaise, Jean Bernard, and Jacques Mourgeon. 1970. *Lois et Décrets de Côte-d'Ivoire.* Paris: Libraries Techniques.

Blancq, B. 1994. "Congo: Corruption et Résistance au Changement." *L'Afrique Politique, 1994: Vue sure la Démocratisation a marée Basse.* Paris: Karthala.

Boahen, Adu A. 1997. "Ghana: Conflict Reoriented." In I. William Zartman, ed., *Governance as Conflict Management.* Washington, DC: Brookings Institution.

———. 1989. *The Ghanaian Sphinx: Reflections on the Contemporary History of Ghana, 1972–1987.* Accra: Academy of Arts and Sciences Press.

Boeninger, E. 1992. "Governance and Development: Issues of Governance." *Proceedings of the World Bank Annual Conference on Development Economics.* Washington, DC: World Bank, pp. 24–38.

Bond, Patrick. 1992. "Finance and Uneven Development in Zimbabwe." Unpublished Ph.D. diss., Johns Hopkins University, Baltimore.

Boone, Catherine. 1992. *Merchant Capital and the Roots of State Power in Senegal, 1930–1985*. Cambridge, England: Cambridge University Press.

Boudon, Laura E. 1997. "Burkina Faso: The 'Rectification' of the Revolution." In Clark and Gardinier, eds., *Political Reform*, pp. 127–144.

Boulaga, F. Eboussi. 1993. *Les Conférences Nationales en Afrique Noire: Une affaire a suivre*. Paris: Karthala.

Bourgi, Albert. 1997. "France-Afrique: Les Raisons d'esperer." *Jeune Afrique*, no. 1900 (June 4–7): xv.

———. 1997. "Un Yalta Africain." *Jeune Afrique*, no. 1896 (May 7–13): 8.

———. 1991. "Concubinage politique ou mariage de raison." *Jeune Afrique* (April 17–23): 20–24.

Bourgi, Albert, and Elimane Fall. 1992. "Charmes et limites de la cohabitation à la Sénégalaise." *Jeune Afrique* (March 26–April 1): 18–20.

Bowman, W. 1991. *Mauritius: Democracy and Development in the Indian Ocean*. Boulder, CO: Westview Press.

Brathier, Leon. 1994. "La Cour Constitutionnelle n'a pas donné raison à ceux qui pensaient qu'il y a violation de la Constitution" (interview with Theodore Holo). *La Nation*, August 30.

Bratton, Michael. 1995. "Testing Competing Explanations for Regime Transitions in Africa." Paper prepared for the African Studies Association meetings, Orlando, Florida, November.

———. 1994. "Civil Society and Political Transitions in Africa." In Harbeson et al., eds., *Civil Society*.

———. 1994. "Economic Crisis and Political Realignment in Zambia." In Widner, ed., *Economic Change*, pp. 101–128.

———. 1994. "Micro-Democracy? The Merger of Farmer Unions in Zimbabwe." *African Studies Review*, vol. 37, no. 1: 9–37.

———. 1992. "Zambia Starts Over." *Journal of Democracy*, vol. 3: 81–94.

———. 1989. "Beyond the State: Civil Society and Associational Life in Africa." *World Politics*, vol. 41, no. 3: 407–418.

Bratton, Michael, and Nicolas van de Walle. 1997. *Democratic Experiments in Africa: Regime Transitions in Comparative Perspective*. New York: Cambridge University Press.

———. 1994. "Neopatrimonial Regimes and Political Transitions in Africa." *World Politics*, vol. 46, no. 4: 453–489.

Bratton, Michael, and Nicolas van de Walle, with Kimberly Butler, Soo Chan Jang, Kimberly Ludwig, and Yu Wang. 1996. *Political Regimes and Regime Transitions in Africa: A Comparative Handbook*. East Lansing: Center for the Advanced Study of International Development, Michigan State University.

Bratton, Michael, and Goran Hyden, eds. 1992. *Governance and Politics in Africa*. Boulder, CO: Lynne Rienner Publishers.

Brautigam, Deborah. 1997. "Institutions, Economic Reform, and Democratic Consolidation in Mauritius." *Comparative Politics*, vol. 30, no. 1: 45–62.

———. 1996. "State Capacity and Effective Governance." In Benno Ndulu and Nicolas van de Walle, eds., *Agenda for Africa's Economic Renewal*. Washington, DC: Overseas Development Council.

———. 1994. "What Can Africa Learn from Taiwan?" *Journal of Modern African Studies*, vol. 32 (March): 111–138.

Bresser Pereira, Luiz Carlos, Jose Maria Maravell, and Adam Przeworski. 1993. *Economic Reforms in New Democracies: A Social-Democratic Approach*. Cambridge, England: Cambridge University Press.

Brewer, John. 1990. *The Sinews of Power*. Cambridge, MA: Harvard University Press.

British Broadcasting Corporation. 1996. "Network Africa Report," July 18.

Broad, Robin, and John Cavanaugh. 1988. "No More NICs." *Foreign Policy,* vol. 72: 437–464.

Brown, Douglas, and Peter Allen. 1968. *An Introduction to the Law of Uganda.* London: Sweet and Maxwell.

Bruno, Michael, and Jeffery Sachs. 1985. *Economics of Worldwide Stagflation.* Cambridge, MA: Harvard University Press.

Bruno, Michael, Martin Ravallion, and Lyn Squire. 1996. *Equity and Growth in Developing Countries.* Policy Research Working Paper No. 1563. Washington, DC: World Bank, January.

Buijtenhuijs, Rob, and Elly Rijnierse. 1993. *Democratization in Sub-Saharan Africa, 1989–1992.* Leiden, Netherlands: African Studies Center.

Buijtenhuijs, Rob, and Céeline Thiriot. 1995. *Democratization in Sub-Saharan Africa, 1992–1995.* Leiden, Netherlands: African Studies Center.

Burlamaqui, J. J. 1807. *The Principles of Natural and Political Law.* Vol 2. Translated by Thomas Nugent. Cambridge, England: Cambridge University Press.

Callaghy, Thomas M. 1995. "Civil Society, Democracy, and Economic Change in Africa: A Dissenting Opinion About Resurgent Societies." In Harbeson et al., eds., *Civil Society.*

———. 1994. "Africa: Back to the Future." *Journal of Democracy,* vol. 5, no. 4: 133–145.

———. 1993. "Political Passions and Economic Interests: Economic Reform and Political Structure in Africa." In Callaghy and Ravenhill, eds., *Hemmed In.*

———. 1990. "Lost Between Market and State: The Politics of Economic Adjustment in Ghana, Zambia, and Nigeria." In Joan Nelson, ed., *Economic Crisis and Policy Choice.* Princeton, NJ: Princeton University Press.

———. 1988. "The State and the Development of Capitalism in Africa: Regime Transitions in Comparative Perspective." In Rothchild and Chazan, eds., *Precarious Balance.*

———. 1984. *The State-Society Struggle: Zaire in Comparative Perspective.* New York: Columbia University Press.

Callaghy, Thomas M., and J. Ravenhill, eds. 1993. *Hemmed In: Responses to Africa's Economic Decline.* New York: Columbia University Press.

Campbell, Ian. 1978. "Military Withdrawal Debate in Nigeria: The Prelude to the 1975 Coup." *West African Journal of Sociology and Political Science,* vol. 1, no. 3: 316–337.

Carothers, Thomas. 1997. "The Observers Observed." *Journal of Democracy,* vol. 8, no. 3: 17–31.

———. 1991. *In Search of Democracy: U.S. Policy Toward Latin America in the Reagan Years.* Berkeley: University of California Press.

Carter Center. 1989. *Beyond Autocracy in Africa.* Atlanta, GA: Carter Center.

Case, William F. 1996. "Can the 'Halfway House' Stand? Semidemocracy and Elite Theory in Three Southeast Asian Countries." *Comparative Politics,* vol. 28, no. 4: 437–464.

Chabal, Patrick. 1992. *Power in Africa.* London: St. Martin's Press.

———, ed. 1986. *Political Domination in Africa.* Cambridge, England: Cambridge University Press.

Chabi, Maurice. 1993. *Banqueroute: Mode d'emploi un Marabout dans les Griffes de la Maffia Béninoise.* Cotonou: Editions Gazette Livres.

———. 1993. "Une Tasse de Thé qui dérange." *La Gazette du Golfe,* November 9–15.

Chalker, Linda. 1991. *Good Governance and the Aid Programme.* London: The Overseas Development Administration.

Chazan, Naomi. 1994. "Engaging the State: Associational Life in Sub-Saharan Africa." In Joel Migdal, Atul Kohli, and Vivienne Shue, eds., *State Power and Social Forces*. Cambridge, England: Cambridge University Press.

———. 1991. "Africa's Democratic Challenge." *World Policy Journal,* vol. 9, no. 2: 279–307.

———. 1988. "Ghana: Problems of Governance and the Emergence of Civil Society." In Diamond et al., eds., *Democracy in Developing Countries*.

———. 1988. "Patterns of State-Society Incorporation and Disengagement in Africa." In Rothchild and Chazan, eds., *Precarious Balance*.

———. 1982. "Ethnicity and Politics in Ghana." *Political Science Quarterly,* vol. 97: 461–485.

Chege, Michael. 1994. "The Return of Multiparty Politics." In Barkan, ed., *Beyond Capitalism and Socialism in Kenya and Tanzania*. Boulder, CO: Lynne Rienner Publishers.

Cheru, Fantu. 1996. "New Social Movements: Democratic Struggles and Human Rights in Africa." In James H. Mittelman, ed., *Globalization: Critical Reflections*. Boulder, CO: Lynne Rienner Publishers.

Chole, E., and J. Ibrahim, eds. 1995. *Democratisation Processes in Africa: Problems and Prospects*. Dakar, Senegal: CODESRIA.

Christian Science Monitor. 1996. "Benin's Ex-President Says His Loss Is a Win: Political, Economic Reforms Hold, Despite Election Outcome." August 22.

Clapham, Christopher. 1996. *Africa and the International System: The Politics of State Survival*. New York: Cambridge University Press.

———. 1988. *Transformation and Continuity in Revolutionary Ethiopia*. Cambridge, England: Cambridge University Press.

———. 1982. "Clientelism and the State." In Christopher Clapham, ed., *Private Patronage and Public Power*. New York: St. Martin's Press.

Clark, John. 1996. "Oil and Democratization in the Republic of Congo." Paper presented at the Thirty-ninth Annual African Studies Association Meeting, San Francisco, November 23–26.

Clark, John, and David Gardinier, eds. 1996. *Political Reform in Francophone Africa*. Boulder, CO: Westview Press.

Cleaver, Tessa, and Marion Wallace. 1990. *Namibian Women in War*. London: Zed Books.

Cliffe, Lionel, Ray Bush, Jenny Lindsay, Brian Mokopakgosi, Donna Pankhurst, and Baleti Tsie. 1993. *The Transition to Independence in Namibia*. Boulder, CO: Lynne Rienner Publishers.

Cnudde, Charles F., and Deane E. Neubauer. 1969. *Empirical Democratic Theory*. Chicago: Markham Publishing.

Cohen, Herman J. 1995. "Good Governance, Democracy, and 'Citizen Expectations' in Africa." *Africa Demos,* vol. 3, no. 4 (March): 5–6.

Coleman, James S. 1960. "Conclusion." In James Coleman and Gabriel Almond, eds., *The Politics of Developing Areas,* pp. 532–576. Princeton, NJ: Princeton University Press.

Collier, Paul. 1996. "Africa's External Economic Relations, 1960–1990." In Douglas Rimmer, ed., *Africa, Thirty Years On: The Record and Outlook After Thirty Years of Independence*. London: James Currey, Ltd.

———. 1991. "Living Down the Past: Redesigning Nigerian Institutions for Economic Growth." *African Affairs,* vol. 95: 325–350.

Commonwealth Observer Group. 1996. "Interim Statement by the Chairperson." Accra, Ghana: Commonwealth Observer Group, December 8.

Conaghan, Catherine. 1992. "Capitalists, Technocrats, and Politicians: Economic Policy-Making in the Central Andes." In Scott Mainwaring, Guillermo

O'Donnell, and J. Samuel Venezuela, eds., *Issues in Democratic Consolidation*. Notre Dame, IN: Notre Dame University Press.

Constitutional Commission of Eritrea. 1996. *Draft Constitution of Eritrea*. Asmara, Eritrea: The Constitutional Commission of Eritrea.

Cooper, Frederick. 1981. "Africa and the World Economy." *African Studies Review,* vol. 24, nos. 2–3 (June–September): 1–86.

Cornevin, Robert. 1981. *La République Populaire du Bénin: Des origines a nos jours*. Paris: Editions G.-P. Maisonneuve & Larose.

Couao-Zotti, Edgar. 1994. "La Cour Constitutionnelle invalide la Nomination de Yves Yehouessi: Les non-dits de la Décision." *Forum de la Semaine,* June 1–7.

Coulon, Christian. 1988. "Senegal: The Development and Fragility of Semidemocracy." In Diamond et al., eds., *Democracy in Developing Countries,* pp. 141–178.

Courade, Georges, and Luc Sindjoun. 1966. "Le Cameroun dans l'entre-deux." *Politique Africaine,* vol. 62 (June): 3–14.

Cowen, M., and K. Kinyanjui. 1997. "Some Problems of Class Formation in Kenya." Institute of Development Studies, University of Nairob. Mimeographed.

Crocker, Chester A., and Fen Osler Hampson. 1996. "Making Peace Settlements Work." *Foreign Policy,* vol. 104 (fall): 54–71.

Crossette, Barbara. 1996. "Citizenship Is a Malleable Concept." *New York Times,* August 18, p. 3.

Curry, Steve, and Colin Stoneman. 1993. "Problems of Industrial Development and Market Integration in Namibia." *Journal of Southern African Studies,* vol. 19, no. 1: 40–59.

CZI (Confederation of Zimbabwe Industries). 1991. "An Update of the Ownership Profile of Zimbabwe's Manufacturing Sector." Harare: William Bonyongwe, October.

Dahl, Robert. 1982. *Dilemmas of Pluralist Democracy*. New Haven, CT: Yale University Press.

———. 1971. *Polyarchy: Participation and Opposition*. New Haven, CT: Yale University Press.

———. 1961. *Who Governs?* London and New Haven, CT: Yale University Press.

———. 1956. *A Preface to Democratic Theory*. Chicago: University of Chicago Press.

Dar es Salaam Radio. 1980. "Comment." Quoted by British Broadcasting Corporation, *BBC Summary of World Broadcasts,* December 12, 1980.

Davenport, Michael, Adrian Hewitt, and Antonique Koning. 1994. "The Impact of the GATT Uruguay Round on ACP States." London: Overseas Development Institute.

Davidson, Alex. 1994. *Government and Opposition in Namibia: The State of Democracy Four Years After Independence*. Studies in Democracy Series, vol. 8. Uppsala: University of Uppsala.

———. 1991. *Democracy and Development in Namibia: The State of Democracy and Civil Rights, 1988–1991*. Studies in Democracy Series, vol. 2. Uppsala: University of Uppsala.

Decalo, Samuel. 1997. "Benin: First of the New Democracies." In Clark and Gardinier, eds., *Political Reform*.

———. 1990. *Coups and Army Rule in Africa*. 2nd ed. New Haven, CT: Yale University Press.

———. 1976. *Coups and Army Rule in Africa: Studies in Military Style*. New Haven, CT: Yale University Press.

Degboe, Kouassi A. 1995. *Elections et Réalités Sociologiques au Benin.* Cotonou: Intermonde Editions.

Deng, Francis N. 1995. *War of Visions: Conflict and Identities in the Sudan.* Washington, DC: Brookings Institution.

de Rham, Gérard. 1990. "Naturalisation: The Politics of Citizenship Acquisition." In Zig Layton-Henry, ed., *The Political Rights of Migrant Workers in Western Europe.* London: Sage Press.

Deutsch, Karl. 1961. "Social Mobilization and Political Development." *American Political Science Review,* vol. 55, no. 3 (September): 493–510.

de Vattel, Emmeric. 1861. *The Law of Nations.* Philadelphia: T. & J. W. Johnson.

Dia, Mamadou. 1996. *Africa's Management in the 1990s and Beyond: Reconciling Indigenous and Transplanted Institutions.* Washington, DC: World Bank.

———. 1994. "Indigenous Management Practices: Lessons for Africa's Management in the '90s." In I. Serageldin and J. Taboroff, eds., *Culture and Development in Africa,* vol. 1. Washington, DC: World Bank.

Diamond, Larry. 1996. "Is the Third Wave Over?" *Journal of Democracy,* vol. 7, no. 3: 20–37.

———. 1996. "Prospects for Democratic Development in Africa." Occasional paper for the Hoover Institution. Stanford, CA: Hoover Institution.

———. 1995. "Introduction: What Makes for Democracy?" In Larry Diamond, Juan Linz, and Seymour Martin Lipset, eds., *Politics in Developing Countries: Comparing Experiences with Democracy.* 2nd ed. Boulder, CO: Lynne Rienner Publishers.

———. 1995. "Nigeria: The Uncivic Society and the Descent into Praetorianism." In Diamond et al., eds., *Politics in Developing Countries,* pp. 417–491.

———. 1994. "Toward Democratic Consolidation." *Journal of Democracy,* vol. 5, no. 3: 4–17.

———. 1989. "Beyond Autocracy: Prospects for Democracy in Africa." Inaugural seminar of the Governance in Africa Program, Carter Center, February 17–18.

———. 1988. *Class, Ethnicity, and Democracy in Nigeria: The Failure of the First Republic.* Syracuse, NY: Syracuse University Press.

Diamond, Larry, A. Kirk-Greene, and O. Oyediran, eds. 1997. *Transition Without End: Nigerian Politics and Civil Society Under Babangida.* Boulder, CO: Lynne Rienner Publishers.

———. 1988. *Democracy in Developing Countries: Africa.* Boulder, CO: Lynne Rienner Publishers.

Diamond, Larry, Juan Linz, and Seymour Martin Lipset, eds. 1995. *Politics in Developing Countries: Comparing Experiences with Democracy.* Boulder, CO: Lynne Rienner Publishers.

Diawara, Alassane. 1997. "L'Opposition appelle: Un boycott financier." *Soleil,* January 8, p. 5.

———. 1997. "Rétrait du gouvernement élargi: La LD/MPT renvoie la question B la base." *Soleil,* January 13, p. 3.

———. 1996. "Bilan des élections locales: La LD/MPT demande une commission électorale indépendante." *Soleil,* December 13, p. 8.

———. 1996. "Bilan des élections locales: La CDP/Garab-gi crie au complot." *Soleil,* December 11, p. 7.

———. 1996. "Bilan des élections: Le PDS exprime sa grande tristesse." *Soleil,* December 9, p. 7.

———. 1996. "Consensus sur l'amélioration du Code électoral." *Soleil,* July 19, p. 3.

Diouf, Bara. 1997. "AJ/PADS tire le bilan des élections." *Soleil,* January 7, p. 3.

————. 1996. "Conférence de presse de Mê Wade: L'option des contentieux spécifiques." *Soleil,* December 5, p. 5.

Dobell, Lauren. 1995. "The SWAPO Sweep." *Southern Africa Report,* vol. 10, no. 4: 5–9.

Doner, Richard F. 1992. "Limits of State Strength: Toward an Institutional View of Economic Development." *World Politics,* March, pp. 398–431.

Dornbursch, Rudiger, and S. Edwards. 1992. "The Macroeconomics of Populism." In Rudiger Dornbursch and S. Edwards, eds., *The Macroeconomics of Populism in Latin America.* Chicago: University of Chicago Press.

Dossavi-Messy, Ephrem. 1994. "Referendum sur la loi electorale concernant les deputes? Ce qu'en disent certains elus du peuple." *La Nation,* May 5.

Dossou, Robert. 1993. "Le Bénin: Du Monolithisme a la Democratie pluraliste." In Gerard Conac, ed., *L'Afrique en Transition vers le Pluralisme politique.* Paris: Economica.

Dumont, René. 1966. *False Start in Africa,* trans. Phillis Nauts. New York: Praeger.

Easterly, William, and Ross Levine. 1996. "Africa's Growth Tragedy: Policies and Ethnic Divisions." February 1996. Mimeographed.

Easton, Peter L., L. M. Moussa, and M. Mukweso. 1995. "Meeting the Local Skill and Knowledge Requirements of Effective Decentralization: Interim Report of a Study of West African Communities." Paper presented at the Thirty-eighth Annual African Studies Association Meeting, Orlando, FL, November 3–6.

The Economist. 1996. "The World Economy: The Hitchhiker's Guide to Cybernomics," September 28.

————. 1994. "Democracy and Growth: Why Voting Is Good for You," August 27, pp. 17–19.

EIU (Economist Intelligence Unit). 1996. *Namibia Swaziland Country Profile, 1995–1996.* London: EIU.

————. 1996. *Namibia Swaziland Country Report, Fourth Quarter.* London: EIU.

————. 1993. *Quarterly Report on Mauritius and the Comoros, Fourth Quarter.* London: EIU.

————. Various years. *Mauritius: Country Report.* London: EIU.

Ekeh, Peter. 1975. "Colonialism and the Two Publics in Africa: A Theoretical Statement." *Comparative Studies in Society and History,* vol. 17, no. 1: 91–112.

Elias, T. O. 1965. "The Evolution of Law and Government in Modern Africa." In Hilda Kuper and Leo Kuper, eds., *African Law: Adoption and Development.* Berkeley: University of California Press.

Elklit, Jorgen, and Palle Svensson. 1997. "What Makes Elections Free and Fair?" *Journal of Democracy,* vol. 8, no. 3: 32–46.

Ellis, Stephen, and Janet MacGaffey. 1996. "Research on Sub-Saharan Africa's Unrecorded International Trade: Some Methodological and Conceptual Problems." *African Studies Review,* vol. 39, no. 2: 19–42.

Engberg-Pederson, P., et al., eds. 1996. *Limits of Adjustment in Africa: The Effects of Economic Liberalisation, 1986–1994.* London: James Currey, Ltd.

Enloe, Cynthia. 1980. *Ethnic Soldiers: State Sovereignty in Divided Societies.* Athens: University of Georgia Press.

Escobar, Arturo, and Sonia Alvarez, eds. 1992. *The Making of Social Movements in Latin America: Identity, Strategy, and Democracy.* Boulder, CO: Westview Press.

Esman, M. J., and N. Uphoff. 1984. *Local Institutions: Intermediaries for Rural Development.* Ithaca, NY: Cornell University Press.

Evans, Peter. 1992. "The State as Problem and Solution: Predation, Embedded

Autonomy, and Structural Change." In Stephen Haggard and Robert Kaufman, eds., *The Politics of Economic Adjustment: International Constraints, Distribution, and the State*, pp. 139–181. Princeton, NJ: Princeton University Press.

Evans, Peter, Dietrich Rueschemeyer, and Theda Skocpol. 1985. *Bringing the State Back In*. New York: Cambridge University Press.

Faes, Geraldine. 1996. "Sénégal: Le feuilleton du remaniement." *Jeune Afrique* (December 22–January 4).

Fall, Dié Maty. 1997. "Plainte du PS: la partie civile monte son dossier." *Soleil*, January 15, p. 6.

———. 1997. "Le PDS face B son avenir." *Soleil*, January 2, p. 3.

———. 1997. "AJ/PADS: 'Nous sommes le 3éme parti du Senegal,' soutient Mamdou Diop Decrois." *Soleil*, January 15, p. 6.

Fall, Elimane. 1996. "Sénégal: Le triomphe modeste du Parti Socialiste." *Jeune Afrique* (December 11–17): 24–25.

———. 1996. "Plus de peur que de mal." *Jeune Afrique* (December 4–10): 28–29.

———. 1993. "Sénégal: En attendant Wade." *Jeune Afrique* (June 17–23).

Fall, Ibrahima. 1990. "Comment la Lonase B été pillé." *Sud Hebdo*, November 15, pp. 4–5.

Fatton, Robert. 1992. *Predatory Rule: State and Civil Society in Africa*. Boulder, CO: Lynne Rienner Publishers.

Fernandez-Arias, E. 1996. "The New Wave of Private Capital Flows: Push or Pull." *Journal of Development Economics*, vol. 48: 389–418.

FIDH (Fédération Internationale des Droits de l'Homme) et al. 1993. "Rapport de la Commission Internationale d'Enquête sur les Violations des Droits de l'Homme du Rwanda depuis le 1er Octobre 1990 (7–21 Janvier 1993)." Paris: FIDH.

Fieldhouse, D. K. 1973. *Economy and Empire, 1830–1914*. London: Weidenfeld & Nicholson.

The Financial Times (London). 1996. "Foreign Direct Investment: Powerful Promoter," September 27.

———. 1996. "Sub-Saharan Africa: Silver Lining's Dark Tinge," September 27.

Finer, Samuel E. 1962. *The Man on Horseback*. New York: Praeger.

Folly, A. E. 1994. Cartoon. *Le Matin*, August 5.

Fondation Friedrich Naumann, ed. 1994. *Les Actes de la Conférence Nationale*. Cotonou, Benin: ONEPI.

Forrest, Joshua. 1994. "Namibia: The First Post Apartheid Democracy." *Journal of Democracy*, vol. 5, no. 3: 88–100.

———. 1992. "A Promising Start: The Inauguration and Consolidation of Democracy in Namibia." *World Policy Journal*, vol. 9, no. 4: 739–753.

Forrest, Tom. 1995. *Politics and Economic Development in Nigeria*. Boulder, CO: Westview Press.

Frankel, S. H. 1938. *Capital Investment in Africa*. London: Oxford University Press.

French, Howard. 1997. "France Fears Anglo-Saxons Are Usurping It in Africa." *New York Times*, April 4.

———. 1997. "New Rules in Africa: Borders Aren't Sacred." *New York Times*, October 18.

Frieden, Jeffry. 1991. "Invested Interests: The Politics of National Economic Policies in a World of Global Finance." *International Organization*, vol. 45: 425–451.

Friedman, Kajsa Ekholm, and Anne Sundberg. 1994. "Ethnic War and Ethnic

Cleansing in Brazzaville." Unpublished manuscript. University of Lund, Sweden.

Fukuyama, Francis. 1992. *The End of History and the Last Man*. London: Hamish Hamilton.

Gaidzanwa, Rudo. 1993. "Citizenship, Nationality, Gender, and Class in Southern Africa." *Alternatives,* vol. 18 (winter): 45.

Gawanas, Bience. 1993. "Legal Rights of Namibian Women and Affirmative Action: The Eradication of Gender Inequalities." *Review of African Political Economy,* vol. 56: 116–122.

Gbedji, Augustin. 1994. "Pourquoi pas un référendum." *La Nation,* May 5.

Gbesséméhlan, Victor, and Elly Riénierse. 1995. "Les Élections en milieu rural: Le cas de Ouesse." *Politique Africaine,* vol. 59 (October).

Gboyega, Alex. 1987. *Local Government and Political Values*. Lagos, Nigeria: Malthouse Press.

Geisler, Gisela. 1993. "Fair? What Has Fairness Got to Do with It? Vagaries of Election Observation and Democratic Standards." *Journal of Modern African Studies,* vol. 31: 613–637.

Gelbach, Jonah B., and Lant H. Pritchett. 1997. "When More for the Poor Is Less for the Poor: The Politics of Targeting." Unpublished draft article.

Gellner, Ernest. 1983. *Nations and Nationalism*. Ithaca, NY: Cornell University Press.

George, Susan. 1988. *A Fate Worse Than Debt*. Harmondsworth, England: Penguin.

Gereffi, Gary. 1995. "Global Production Systems and Third World Development." In Stallings, ed., *Global Change*.

Ghana: Vision 2020, the First Step: 1996–2000. 1995. Presidential report to parliament on Coordinated Program of Economic and Social Development Policies. Accra: Government Printer.

Ghosh, Bimal. 1997. "Just as Effective Aid Gets Easier, Support for It Is Dwindling." *International Herald Tribune,* May 21, p. 10.

Gibbon, P. 1996. "Structural Adjustment and Structural Change in Sub-Saharan Africa: Some Provisional Conclusions." In Gibbon and Olukoshi, eds., *Structural Adjustment.*

———. 1995. *Liberalized Development in Tanzania*. Uppsala: Scandinavian Institute of African Studies.

Gibbon, P., and A. Olukoshi, eds. 1996. *Structural Adjustment and Socio-economic Change in Sub-Saharan Africa*. Uppsala: Scandinavian Institute of African Studies.

Gibbon, P., Kjell J. Havnevik, and Kenneth Hermele. 1993. *A Blighted Harvest: The World Bank and African Agriculture in the 1980s*. Lawrenceville, NJ: Africa World Press.

Gibbon, P., Yusuf Bangura, and Arve Ofstad, eds. 1992. *Authoritarianism, Democracy, and Adjustment: The Politics of Economic Reform in Africa*. Uppsala: Scandinavian Institute of African Studies.

Gibney, Mark, ed. 1988. *Open Borders? Closed Societies? The Ethical and Political Issues*. New York: Greenwood Press.

Gilbert, Charles E. 1959. "The Framework of Administrative Accountability." *Journal of Politics,* vol. 21, no. 3: 373–407.

Glassman, Ronald M. 1995. *The Middle Class and Democracy in Socio-Historical Perspective*. Leiden, Netherlands: E. J. Brill.

Glélé, Maurice Ahahanzo. 1969. *Naissance d'un Jtat noire (L'Evolution politique et constitutionnelle du Dahomey de la colonisation a nos jours)*. Paris: R. Pichon and R. Durand-Auzias.

Golan, Daphna. 1994. *Inventing Shaka: Using History in the Construction of Zulu Nationalism.* Boulder, CO: Lynne Rienner Publishers.

Goodwin-Gill, Guy S. 1994. *Free and Fair Elections: International Law and Practice.* Geneva: Inter-Parliamentary Union.

Goudou, Cécile, and Thomas Goudou. 1994. "La Souveraineté de la Cour constitutionnelle." *Forum de la Semaine,* July 6–12, pp. 8, 10.

Government of Mauritius. 1982. *Our Economic Recovery: The Road to Job Creation.* Port-Louis: Government Printer, May 1.

Government of Tanzania. 1965. *Report of the Presidential Commission on the Establishment of a Democratic One-Party State.* Dar-es-Salaam: Government Printer.

Government of Zambia. 1995. "Summary of the Recommendations of the Mwanakatwe Constitutional Review Commission and Government Reaction to the Report." Government Paper No. 1. Lusaka: Government Printer.

Government of Zimbabwe. 1996. *Quarterly Digest of Statistics: First Quarter, 1996.* Harare: Central Statistical Office (hereafter CSO).

———. 1995. *Quarterly Digest of Statistics: Fourth Quarter, 1995.* Harare: CSO.

———. 1992. *Land Acquisition Act of 1992.* Harare: Government Printer.

———. 1992. *Census 1992: Zimbabwe National Report.* Harare: CSO.

Graham, Carol. 1994. *Safety Nets, Politics, and the Poor: Transitions to Market Economics.* Washington, DC: Brookings Institution.

Grant, Geraldine. 1983. "The State and the Formation of a Middle Class: A Chilean Example." *Latin American Perspectives,* vol. 10, nos. 1–2: 151–170.

Gray, Richard, and David Birmingham. 1970. *Pre-Colonial African Trade.* London: Oxford University Press.

Green, Reginald. 1993. "The IMF and the World Bank in Africa: How Much Learning?" In Callaghy and Ravenhill, eds., *Hemmed In.*

Greenfeld, Liah. 1992. *Nationalism: Five Roads to Modernity.* Cambridge, England: Cambridge University Press.

Grierson, John P., and Sam Moyo. 1993. "Advocacy, Enterprise Extension and Indigenous Enterprise Institution Development: A Programme of Support for the Small and Medium Enterprise Sector in Zimbabwe." Unpublished research report to the Norwegian Agency for Development Cooperation (NORAD). Harare, Zimbabwe, July 27, 1993.

Grosh, Barbara, and R. Mukandala, eds. 1994. *State Owned Enterprises in Africa.* Boulder, CO: Lynne Rienner Publishers.

Gulhati, Ravi, and Raj Nallari. 1990. *Successful Stabilization and Recovery in Mauritius.* Economic Development Institute Policy Case No. 5. Washington, DC: World Bank.

Gurr, Ted Robert, with contributions by Barbara Harff, Monty G. Marshall, and James R. Scarritt. 1993. *Minorities at Risk: A Global View of Ethnopolitical Conflicts.* Washington, DC: United States Institute of Peace Press.

Guyer, J. 1996. *African Studies in the United States: A Perspective.* Atlanta, GA: ASA Press.

Gwin, Catherine, ed. 1997. *Perspectives on Aid and Development.* Policy Essay No. 23. Washington, DC: Johns Hopkins University Press for the Overseas Development Council.

Gyimah-Boadi, E. 1996. "Civil Society in Africa." *Journal of Democracy,* vol. 7, no. 2: 118–132.

———. 1990. "Economic Recovery and Politics in the PNDC's Ghana." *Journal of Commonwealth and Comparative Politics,* vol. 28, no. 3: 228–243.

Gyimah-Boadi, E., and Nicholas van de Walle. 1996. "The Politics of Economic Renewal in Africa." In Beno Ndulu and Nicholas van de Walle, eds., *Agenda for Africa's Economic Renewal*. Washington, DC: Overseas Development Council.

Hado, Philippe. 1994. "Pouvons-nous changer au Benin?" Interview with Professor Karl August Emmanuel. *La Nation*, August 30.

Haggard, Stephan. 1995. *Developing Nations and the Politics of Global Integration*. Washington, DC: Brookings Institution.

———. 1992. "The Political Economy of Inflation and Stabilization in Middle Income Countries." In Stephan Haggard and Robert Kaufman, eds. *The Politics of Economic Adjustment: International Constraints, Distribution, and the State*, pp. 270–318. Princeton, NJ: Princeton University Press.

Haggard, Stephan, and Robert Kaufman. 1995. *The Political Economy of Democratic Transitions*. Princeton, NJ: Princeton University Press.

———. 1992. "Economic Adjustment and the Prospects for Democracy." In Haggard and Kaufman, eds., *Politics of Economic Adjustment*.

———. 1992. "The State in the Initiation and Consolidation of Market-Oriented Reform." In L. Putterman and D. Rueschemeyer, eds., *State and Market in Development: Synergy or Rivalry?* Boulder, CO: Lynne Rienner Publishers, pp. 221–243.

Haggard, Stephan, and Sylvia Maxfield. 1996. "The Political Economy of Financial Internationalization in the Developing World." *International Organization*, vol. 50, no. 1: 35–68.

Haggard, Stephan, and Steven Webb, eds. 1994. *Voting for Reform*. New York: Oxford University Press for the World Bank.

Haggblade, S. 1978. "Africanization from Below: Evolution of Cameroon's Savings Societies into Western Style Banks." *Rural Africana*, no. 2.

Hajivassiliou, V. A. 1987. "The External Debt Repayments Problems of LDCs: An Econometric Model Based on Panal Data." *Journal of Econometrics*. vol. 36, nos. 1–2: 205–230.

Hall, Peter. 1986. *Governing the Economy: The Politics of State Intervention in Britain and France*. New York: Oxford University Press.

———, ed. 1989. *The Political Power of Economic Ideas*. Princeton, NJ: Princeton University Press.

Harbeson, John. 1996. *Elections and Democratization in Post-Mengistu Ethiopia*. Washington, DC: Center for Development Information and Evaluation, Agency for International Development.

———. 1988. *The Ethiopian Transformation: The Quest for the Post-Imperial State*. Boulder, CO: Westview Press.

Harbeson, John W., Donald Rothchild, and Naomi Chazan, eds. 1994. *Civil Society and the State in Africa*. Boulder, CO: Lynne Rienner Publishers.

Hardin, Russell. 1995. *One for All: The Logic of Group Conflict*. Princeton, NJ: Princeton University Press.

Harrigan, J., Paul Mosley, and John Toye. 1991. *Aid and Power: The World Bank and Policy-Based Lending*. London: Routledge.

Harris, Nigel. 1988. "New Bourgeoisies?" *Journal of Development Studies*, vol. 24, no. 2: 237–249.

Hartzell, Caroline, and Donald Rothchild. 1997. "Political Pacts as Negotiated Agreements: Comparing Ethnic and Non-ethnic Cases." *International Negotiation*, vol. 2: 147–171.

Havnevik, K., and B. van Arkadie, eds. 1996. *Domination or Dialogue? Experiences and Prospects for African Development Cooperation*. Uppsala: Scandinavian Institute of African Studies.

Hawkins, Tony, and Michael Holman. 1994. "Survey of Mauritius." *Financial Times*, September 27.

Hayward, Fred, ed. 1987. *Elections in Independent Africa.* Boulder, CO: Westview Press.

Heilbrunn, John R. 1997. "Togo: The National Conference and Stalled Reform." In Clark and Gardinier, eds., *Political Reform,* pp. 225–245.

———. 1994. "Authority, Property, and Politics in Benin and Togo." Ph.D. diss., University of California, Los Angeles.

———. 1993. "The Social Origins of National Conferences in Benin and Togo." *Journal of Modern African Studies,* vol. 31, no. 2: 277–299.

Held, David. 1991. "Democracy and Globalization." *Alternatives: Social Transformation and Human Governance,* vol. 16, no. 2.

Heldrich, A., et al. 1995. "Persons." In Mary Ann Glendon, ed., *Persons and Family,* Vol. IV of *International Encyclopedia of Comparative Law.* Tübingen: J. C. B. Mohhr.

Herbst, Jeffrey. 1996/1997. "Responding to State Failure in Africa." *International Security,* vol. 21 (winter): 120–144.

———. 1994. "Prospects for Elite-Driven Democracy in South Africa." Paper presented at the Thirty-seventh Annual African Studies Association Meeting, Toronto. November 3–6, 1994.

———. 1992. *The Politics of Reform in Ghana, 1982–1991.* Berkeley: University of California Press.

———. 1990. "Migration, the Politics of Protest, and State Consolidation in Africa." *African Affairs,* vol. 89, no. 355: 183–203.

———. 1990. *State Politics in Zimbabwe.* Berkeley: University of California Press.

———. 1990. "The Structural Adjustment of Politics in Africa." *World Development,* vol. 18, no. 7: 949–958.

———. 1990. "War and the State in Africa." *International Security,* vol. 14, no. 4: 117–139.

Herman, Edward S., and Frank Brodhead. 1984. *Demonstration Elections.* Boston: South End Press.

Hibou, Béatrice. 1996. *L'Afrique est-elle protectionniste? Les Chemins Buissoniers de la Libéralisation Exterieure.* Paris: Karthala.

Hicks, Alexander. 1988. "Social Democratic Corporatism and Economic Growth." *Journal of Politics,* vol. 50: 677–704.

Hicks, U. K. 1961. *Local Government in Developing Countries.* London: Allen & Unwin.

Hill, Stuart, and Donald Rothchild. 1992. "The Impact of Regime on the Diffusion of Political Conflict." In Manus I. Midlarsky, ed., *The Internationalization of Communal Strife.* London: Routledge.

Hilton, Rodney H. 1973. *Bond Men Made Free: Medieval Peasant Movements and the English Rising of 1381.* London: Oxford University Press.

Himbara, David. 1994. *Kenyan Capitalists, the State, and Development.* Boulder, CO: Lynne Rienner Publishers.

Himbara, David, and David Sultan. 1994. "Reconstruction of the Uganda State and Economy: The Challenge of an International Bantustan." *Review of African Political Economy,* vol. 22, no. 63: 85–93.

Hirshman, Albert. 1977. *The Passion and the Interests.* Princeton, NJ: Princeton University Press.

Hobbes, Thomas. 1958. *Leviathan.* New York: Liberal Arts Press.

Hobsbawm, Eric. 1990. *Nations and Nationalism Since 1780.* Cambridge, England: Cambridge University Press.

Hobsbawm, Eric, and Thomas Ranger. 1983. *The Invention of Tradition.* Cambridge, England: Cambridge University Press.

Hodgkin, Thomas. 1961. *African Political Parties: An Introductory Guide.* Harmondsworth, England: Penguin.

Hoffman, Philip. 1988. "Institutions and Agriculture in Old Regime France." *Politics and Society,* vol. 16, nos. 2–3: 241–264.

Holm, John D. 1996. "Development, Democracy, and Civil Society in Botswana." In Adrian Leftwich, ed., *Democracy and Development: Theory and Practice.* Cambridge, England: Polity Press, pp. 97–113.

———. 1988. "Botswana: A Paternalistic Democracy." In Diamond et al., eds., *Democracy in Developing Countries,* pp. 179–215.

Holman, Michael, and Michela Wrong. 1996. "Ghana 1996: An African Trailblazer Begins to Falter." *Financial Times,* July 9.

Holmquist, Frank, 1995. "Stalling Political Change: Moi's Way in Kenya." *Current History,* vol. 94, no. 591: 177–181.

Holmquist, Frank, and Michael Ford. 1996. "Kenya's Post-Election Authoritarian Continuity." Unpublished manuscript.

Holo, Théodore. 1994. "A l'écoute du gouvernement: Que vaut l'idée d'une Commission électorale indépendante?" *La Nation,* July 1.

———. 1994. "Interview." *Le Matin,* May 25.

Hopkins, A. J. 1973. *An Economic History of West Africa.* New York: Columbia University Press.

Horowitz, Donald L. 1991. *A Democratic South Africa? Constitutional Engineering in a Divided Society.* Berkeley: University of California Press.

———. 1985. *Ethnic Groups in Conflict.* Berkeley: University of California Press.

Houngbédji, Adrien. 1994. "Lettre d'avis." *La Nation,* September 19.

Howe, Carolyn. 1992. *Political Ideology and Class Formation: A Study of the Middle Class.* Westport, CT: Praeger.

Hubbard, Dianne, and Colette Solomon. 1995. "The Many Faces of Feminism in Namibia." In Amrita Basu, ed., *The Challenge of Local Feminism: Women's Movements in Global Perspective.* Boulder, CO: Westview Press.

Huber, Evelyne, Dietrich Rueschemeyer, and John Stephens. 1993. "The Impact of Economic Development on Democracy." *Journal of Economic Perspectives,* vol. 7, no. 3 (summer): 71–86.

Human Rights Watch/Africa. 1996. "Zambia: Elections and Human Rights in the Third Republic." December.

Human Rights Watch Arms Project. 1994. "Arming Rwanda: The Arms Trade and Human Rights Abuses in the Rwandan War." January.

Human Rights Watch and Fédération Internationale des Ligues des Droits de l'Homme. 1996. *Zaire: Forced to Flee: Violence against the Tutsis in Zaire,* vol. 8, no. 2 (July 1996).

Huntington, Samuel P. 1997. "After Thirty Years: The Future of the Third Wave." *Journal of Democracy,* vol. 8, no. 4: 3–12.

———. 1993. "The Clash of Civilizations." *Foreign Affairs,* vol. 72, no. 3: 22–49.

———. 1991. *The Third Wave: Democratization in the Late Twentieth Century.* Norman: University of Oklahoma Press.

———. 1968. *Political Order in Changing Societies.* New Haven, CT: Yale University Press.

Hutchful, E. 1995. "Adjustment in Africa and Fifty Years of the Bretton Woods Institution: Change or Consolidation?" *Canadian Journal of Development Studies,* vol. 16.

———. 1995. "The International Dimensions of the Democratization Process." In Chole and Ibrahim, eds., *Democratization Processes.*

Hutchinson, Sharon E. 1996. *Nuer Dilemmas: Coping with Money, War, and the State*. Berkeley: University of California Press.

Hyden, Goran. 1992. "Governance and the Study of Politics." In Hyden and Bratton, eds., *Governance and Politics*.

———. 1983. *No Shortcuts to Progress: African Development Management in Perspective*. London: Heinemann.

———. 1980. *Beyond Ujamaa*. Berkeley and Los Angeles: University of California Press.

Hyden, Goran, and Michael Bratton, eds. 1992. *Governance and Politics in Africa*. Boulder, CO: Lynne Rienner Publishers.

Ibrahim, Jibrin. 1996. "Political Scientists and the Subversion of Democracy in Nigeria." Paper presented at the African Association of Political Science Conference on State and Democracy in Africa, Ibadan, Nigeria, March 1996.

IFES (International Foundation for Electoral Systems). 1997. "Supporting the Electoral Process in Ghana: Results of the 1996 Presidential and Parliamentary Elections." Washington, DC: IFES, January.

Ihonvbere, Julius. 1996. "On the Threshold of Another False Start? A Critical Evaluation of Prodemocracy Movements in Africa." *Journal of Asian and African Studies,* vol. 33, nos. 1–2: 125–142.

———. 1993. "Economic Crisis, Structural Adjustment, and Social Crisis in Nigeria." *World Development,* vol. 21, no. 1: 141–153.

IMF (International Monetary Fund). 1996. *International Capital Markets: Developments, Prospects, and Key Policy Issues*. Washington, DC: IMF.

Inter American Commission of Women. 1933. *The Nationality of Women*. Montevideo: Inter American Commission of Women.

International Parliamentary Union. 1997. "Mauritius." http://www.ipu.org. May.

Issue: A Journal of Opinion. 1993. "Focus: Toward a New African Political Order: African Perspectives on Democratization Processes, Regional Conflict Management." Vol. 21, nos. 1–2: 1–91.

———. 1991. "Focus: Challenges to and Transition from Authoritarianism in Africa." Vol. 20, no. 1: 1–64.

Jackson, Robert H. 1990. *Quasi-States: Sovereignty, International Relations, and the Third World*. Cambridge, England: Cambridge University Press.

———. 1977. *Plural Societies and New States: A Conceptual Analysis*. Berkeley: California Institute of International Studies, University of California.

Jackson, Robert H., and Carl G. Rosberg. 1982. "Why Africa's Weak States Persist: The Empirical and the Juridical in Statehood." *World Politics,* vol. 35: 1–24.

———. 1980. "Why Africa's Weak States Persist." In Atul Kohli, ed., *The State and Development,* pp. 259–282. Princeton, NJ: Princeton University Press.

Jackson, Tudor. 1986. *Law of Kenya*. Nairobi: Kenyan Literature Bureau.

Jacobson, David. 1996. *Rights Across Borders: Immigration and the Decline of Citizenship*. Baltimore: Johns Hopkins University Press.

Janowitz, Morris. 1964. *The Military in the Political Development of New Nations: An Essay in Comparative Analysis*. Chicago: University of Chicago Press.

Jenkins, Jerry, ed. 1988. *Beyond the Informal Sector*. San Francisco: ICS Press.

Johnson, Dale L. 1982. "Class Relations and the Middle Classes." In Dale L. Johnson, ed., *Class and Social Development*. Beverly Hills, CA: Sage Publications.

Johnson, John J., ed. 1962. *The Role of the Military in Underdeveloped Countries*. Princeton, NJ: Princeton University Press.

Jones, G. I. 1979. "Changing Leadership in Eastern Nigeria: Before, During, and After the Colonial Period." In N. A. Shack and P. S. Cohen, eds., *Politics in*

Leadership: A Comparative Perspective, pp. 44–64. Oxford, England: Clarendon Press.

Jones, William O. 1980. "Agricultural Trade Within Africa." In Robert H. Bates and Michael Lofchie, eds., *Agricultural Development in Africa.* New York: Praeger.

Joseph, Richard A. 1997. "Democratization Under Military Rule and Repression in Nigeria." In Beckett and Young, eds., *Dilemmas of Democracy.*

———. 1997. "Democratization in Africa After 1989: Comparative and Theoretical Perspectives." *Comparative Politics,* vol. 29, no. 3: 363–382.

———. 1996. "Nigeria: Inside the Dismal Tunnel." *Current History,* vol. 95, no. 601: 193–200.

———. 1994. "Africa 1994: Ecstasy and Agony." *Africa Demos,* vol. 3, no. 3: 1, 3.

———. 1993. "Failed States in Africa." Paper presented to the Joint Seminar on Political Development, Harvard and MIT, November.

———. 1992. "Zambia: A Model for Democratic Change." *Current History* vol. 91, no. 565 (May): 199–201.

———. 1991. "Africa: The Rebirth of Political Freedom." *Journal of Democracy,* vol. 2, no. 4: 11–24.

———. 1989. *Perestroika Without Glasnost in Africa.* Atlanta, GA: Carter Center.

———. 1987. *Democracy and Prebendal Politics in Nigeria: The Rise and Fall of the Second Republic.* New York and Cambridge, England: Cambridge University Press.

———. 1987. "Principles and Practices of Nigerian Military Government." In John W. Harbeson, ed., *The Military in African Governance,* pp. 67–92. New York: Praeger.

———. 1984. "Affluence and Underdevelopment: The Nigerian Experience." *Journal of Modern African Studies,* vol. 16, no. 2: 221–240.

———. 1981. "The Ethnic Trap: Notes on the Nigerian Campaign and Elections, 1978–79." *Issue: A Journal of Opinion,* vol. 11, nos. 1–2: 17–23.

———. 1978. *Gaullist Africa: Cameroon Under Ahmadu Ahidjo.* Enugu, Nigeria: Fourth Dimension Publishers.

———. 1976. "The Gaullist Legacy: Patterns of French Neo-Colonialism." *Review of African Political Economy,* vol. 6: 4–14.

———, ed., 1997. *African Democratic Perspectives: Evaluative Essays on Africa Demos.* Cambridge, MA: MIT Press.

———. 1997. *African Renewal: Report of a Conference on State, Conflict, and Democracy in Africa.* Cambridge, MA: MIT Press.

———. 1995. *The Democratic Challenge in Africa.* Atlanta, GA: Carter Center.

———. 1990. *African Governance in the 1990s.* Atlanta, GA: Carter Center.

———. 1989. *Beyond Autocracy in Africa.* Atlanta, GA: Carter Center.

Joseph, Richard A., Scott Taylor, and Adigun Agbaje. 1996. "Nigeria." In M. Kesselman, J. Krieger, and W. Joseph, eds., *Comparative Politics at the Crossroads,* pp. 613–690. Lexington, MA: D. C. Heath.

Kahler, Miles. 1990. "Orthodoxy and Its Alternatives: Explaining Approaches to Stabilization and Adjustment." In Joan Nelson, ed., *Economic Crisis and Policy Choice.* Princeton, NJ: Princeton University Press.

Kaldor, Mary. 1995. "European Institutions, Nation-States and Nationalism." In Daniele Archibugi and David Held, eds., *Cosmopolitan Democracy: An Agenda for a New World Order.* Cambridge, England: Polity Press.

Kapata, Dennis. 1995. "Black Empowerment." *Southern African Economist,* vol. 8, no. 2: 14–16.

Kaplan, Robert. 1994. "The Coming Anarchy: How Scarcity, Crime, Overpopulation, Tribalism, and Disease Are Rapidly Destroying the Social Fabric of Our Planet." *Atlantic Monthly,* vol. 273, no. 2: 44–65.

Kaplan, Steven Laurence. 1976. *Bread, Politics, and Political Economy in the Reign of Louis XV.* 2 vols. The Hague: Martinus Nijhoff.

Kappel, Robert. 1996. "Africa's Marginalisation in World Trade: A Result of the Uruguay Round Agreements." *Intereconomics,* January–February, pp. 33–42.

Kapstein, Ethan B. 1996. "Workers and the World Economy." *Foreign Affairs,* vol. 75, no. 3: 16–37.

Karl, Terry Lynn. 1991. "Dilemmas of Democratization in Latin America." *Comparative Politics,* vol. 23, no. 4: 1–21.

———. 1986. "Imposing Consent: Electoralism and Democratization in El Salvador." In Paul W. Drakeä and Eduardo Silva, eds., *Elections and Democratization in Latin America, 1980–1985.* La Jolla: Center for International Studies, University of California, San Diego.

Kasfir, Nelson. 1984. *State and Class in Africa.* London: Cass.

———. 1976. *The Shrinking Political Arena.* Berkeley and Los Angeles: University of California Press.

Kaspin, Deborah. 1995. "The Politics of Ethnicity in Malawi's Democratic Transition." *Journal of Modern African Studies,* vol. 33, no. 4 (December): 595–620.

Kaufmann, Chaim. 1996. "Possible and Impossible Solutions to Ethnic Civil Wars." *International Security,* vol. 20, no. 4: 136–175.

Keller, Edmond. 1988. *Revolutionary Ethiopia: From Empire to People's Republic.* Bloomington: Indiana University Press.

Kenya Broadcasting Corporation. 1991. "Kenyan Citizenship Now Open to Long-stay Tanzanian Residents." Reprinted in British Broadcasting Corporation, *BBC Summary of World Broadcasts,* April 1, 1991.

Kérékou, Matthieu. 1996. "Message du Chef de l'État sur l'État de la Nation." *Forum de la Semaine,* December 4–10.

———. 1995. *Préparer le Bénin du futur: Reflexions d'un citoyen sur le devenir du pays.* Porto-Novo: Centre Panafricaine de Prospective Sociale.

Khassay, H. M. 1994. *District Health Infrastructures: Hidden Resources.* Geneva: World Health Organization.

Kilby, Peter. 1969. *Industrialization in an Open Economy: Nigeria, 1945–1966.* Cambridge, England: Cambridge University Press.

Killick, Tony. 1978. *Development Economics in Action.* London: Heinemann.

———. 1996. "Principals, Agents, and the Limitations of BWI Conditionality." *World Economy,* vol. 19, no. 2: 211–229.

Kiser, Larry, and Elinor Ostrom. 1983. "The Three Worlds of Action: A Meta-Theoretical Synthesis of Institutional Approaches." In E. Ostrom, ed., *Strategies of Political Inquiry.* Beverly Hills, CA: Sage Publications.

Klein, Keith. 1994. "Who's Afraid of Flawed Elections?" In Emory University, Governance in Africa Program, *Democratic Challenge in Africa.* Atlanta, GA: Carter Center.

Kohli, A. 1993. "Democracy amid Economic Orthodoxy: Trends in Developing Countries." *Third World Quarterly,* vol. 14, no. 4: 671–689.

Kpatindé, Francis. 1997. "France-Afrique: Le New Deal selon Védrine." *Jeune Afrique,* nos. 1919–1920 (October 15–28).

———. 1992. "Les tares de la démocratie à la Sénégalaise." *Jeune Afrique* (July 30–August 5): pp. 22–23.

Krugmann, Harmut, Cleophas Torori, and Stephen Ngigi. 1997. "Community Water Management and Conflict Resolution: The Case of Rombo Small-scale

Irrigation Scheme, Kajiado District, Kenya." EcoPolicy Series Paper. Nairobi: African Center for Technical Studies.

Kymlicka, Will. 1995. *Multicultural Citizenship.* New York and Oxford, England: Oxford University Press.

La Nation (Benin). 1995. "Déclaration du Gouvernement," April–June.

———. 1994. "Aide-mémoire de la Mission financière française, 18–20 juillet 1994," July 28.

———. 1994. "Compte rendu des Travaux du Conseil des Ministres, 27b juillet 1994," July 28.

———. 1994. "Déclaration du Gouvernement," July 28.

Lake, David A., and Donald Rothchild. 1996. "Containing Fear: The Origins and Management of Ethnic Conflict." *International Security,* vol. 21, no. 2: 41–75.

Laloupo, Francis. 1993. "La Conférence Nationale du Benin: Un concept nouveau de changement de régime politique." *Année Africaine, 1992–93.* Bordeaux, France: Centre d'Etude d'Afrique Noire.

Landé, Carl H. 1977. "The Dyadic Basis of Clientelism." In S. W. Schmidt et al., eds., *Friends, Followers, and Factions,* pp. viii–xxxvii. Berkeley: University of California Press.

Landell-Mills, Pierre. 1992. "Governance, Cultural Change, and Empowerment." *Journal of Modern African Studies,* vol. 30, no. 4: 543–567.

Lange, Peter, and Geoffery Garrett. 1985. "The Politics of Growth: Strategic Interaction and Economic Performance in the Advanced Industrial Democracies, 1974–1980." *Journal of Politics,* vol. 47: 792–827.

Langrod, G. 1981. "Local Government and Democracy." In A. Feldman, ed., *Politics and Government of Urban Canada: Selected Readings.* 4th ed. Toronto, Canada: Methuen.

Larda, Juan Carlos. 1996. "Globalisation and the Loss of Autonomy by the Fiscal, Banking, and Monetary Authorities." *CEPAL Review,* vol. 58: 65–78.

Legum, Colin, ed. Various years. *African Contemporary Record.* London: Africana Publishing.

Lemarchand, René. 1994. *Burundi: Ethnocide as Discourse and Practice.* Washington, DC: Woodrow Wilson Center Press.

———. 1992. "Uncivil States and Civil Societies: How Illusion Became Reality." *Journal of Modern African Studies,* vol. 30, no. 2.

———. 1970. *Rwanda and Burundi.* New York: Praeger.

Levine, Donald. 1974. *Greater Ethiopia: The Evolution of a Multi-Ethnic Society.* Chicago: University of Chicago Press.

Lewis, Peter. 1996. "Economic Reform and Political Transition in Africa: The Quest for a Politics of Development." *World Politics,* vol. 49, no. 1: 92–129.

———. 1996. "From Prebendalism to Predation: The Political Economy of Decline in Nigeria." *Journal of Modern African Studies,* vol. 34, no. 1: 79–103.

———. 1994. "Economic Statism, Private Capital, and the Dilemmas of Accumulation in Nigeria." *World Development,* vol. 22, no. 3 (March): 437–451.

———. 1994. "Endgame in Nigeria: The Politics of a Failed Transition." *African Affairs,* vol. 93: 323–340.

———. 1992. "Political Transition and the Dilemma of Civil Society in Africa." *Journal of International Affairs,* vol. 46, no. 1: 31–54.

Leys, Colin. 1996. "Review Essay on J. Widner (ed.) *Economic Change and Political Liberalisation in Sub-Saharan Africa.*" *Canadian Journal of African Studies,* vol. 30, no. 2: 299–301.

———. 1994. "Theoretical Perspectives." In B. Berman and Colin Leys, eds.,

African Capitalists in African Development. Boulder, CO: Lynne Rienner Publishers.

Leys, Colin, and John Saul. 1995. "Introduction." In Colin Leys and John Saul, eds., *Namibia's Liberation Struggle: The Two-Edged Sword.* London: James Currey, Ltd.

———. 1994. "Liberation Without Democracy? The SWAPO Crisis of 1976." *Journal of Southern African Studies,* vol. 20, no. 1: 123–147.

Liabes, D. 1995. "Entrepreneurs, Privatization, and Liberalization: The Pro-Democracy Movement in Algeria." In Mamdani and Wamba-dia-Wamba, eds., *African Studies in Social Movements.*

Licklider, Roy. 1995. "The Consequences of Negotiated Settlements in Civil Wars, 1945–1993." *American Political Science Review,* vol. 89, no. 3: 681–690.

Lijphart, Arend. 1985. *Power-Sharing in South Africa.* Berkeley: Institute of International Studies, University of California Press.

———. 1977. *Democracy in Plural Societies.* Berkeley: University of California Press.

Lindbloom, Charles. 1982. "The Market as Prison." *Journal of Markets and Politics,* vol. 44, no. 2 (May): 324–336.

———. 1977. *Politics and Markets.* New York: Basic Books.

Lindeke, William, and Winnie Wanzala. 1994. "Regional Elections in Namibia: Deepening Democracy and Gender Inclusion." *Africa Today,* vol. 4, no. 13: 5–14.

Lindenberg, Marc, and Shanatayanan Devarajan. 1993. "Prescribing Strong Economic Medicine: Revisiting the Myths About Structural Adjustment, Democracy, and Economic Performances in Developing Countries." *Comparative Politics,* January, pp. 169–182.

Linz, Juan J. 1994. "Presidential or Parliamentary Democracy: Does it Make a Difference?" In Juan Linz and Arturo Valenzuela, *The Failure of Presidential Democracy,* Vol. 1. Baltimore: Johns Hopkins University Press.

Linz, Juan J., and Alfred Stepan. 1996. *Problems of Democratic Transition and Consolidation: Southern Europe, South America, and Post-Communist Europe.* Baltimore: Johns Hopkins University Press.

———. 1996. "Toward Consolidated Democracies." *Journal of Democracy,* vol. 7, no. 2: 14–33.

Lipset, Seymour Martin. 1994. "The Social Requisites of Democracy Revisited." *American Sociological Review,* vol. 59: 1–22.

———. 1966. *Political Man.* Garden City, NY: Doubleday.

———. 1959. "Some Social Requisites of Democracy: Economic Development and Political Legitimacy." *American Political Science Review,* vol. 53, no. 1.

Locke, John. 1988. *Second Treatise,* reprint. In Peter Lasslett, ed., *Two Treatises of Government.* Cambridge, England: Cambridge University Press.

Lodge, Tom. 1983. *Black Politics in South Africa Since 1945.* London: Longman.

Lofchie, Michael. 1997. "The Cycle of African Governance: A View from Political Economy." Paper prepared for the Conference on African Renewal, MIT, Cambridge, MA, March 6–9.

———. 1994. "The New Political Economy of Africa." In David E. Apter and Carl G. Rosenberg, eds., *Political Development and the New Realism in Sub-Saharan Africa.* Charlottesville: University of Virginia Press.

———. 1989. "Perestroika Without Glasnost: Reflections on Structural Adjustment." In Carter Center, *Beyond Autocracy in Africa,* pp. 119–124. Atlanta, GA: Carter Center.

Loko, Ed. 1994. "Un autre cas d'inconstitutionnalité." *Le Matin,* June 1.

————. 1994. "Atomisation de la vie politique: Derriere les milles et un partis." *Le Matin,* May 24.

Lom, Mamdou Mika. 1993. "Mbacke: Fronde contre le maire." *Sud Quotidien,* October 13, p. 3.

Longman, Timothy. 1997. "Chaos from Above: Resistance to State Reconfiguration in Rwanda." In Villalon and Huxtable, eds., *Critical Juncture.*

————. 1997. "Rwanda: Democratization and Disorder, Political Transformation, and Social Deterioration." In Clark and Gardinier, eds., *Political Reform,* pp. 287–306.

Lubeck, Paul, ed. 1987. *The African Bourgeoisie: Capitalist Development in Nigeria, Kenya, and the Ivory Coast.* Boulder, CO: Lynne Rienner Publishers.

Mabogunje, Akin. L. 1995. "The Capitalization of Money and Credit in the Development Process: The Case of Community Banking in Nigeria." *African Journal of Institutions and Development,* vol. 1, no. 2: 1–16.

MacGaffey, Janet. 1987. *Entrepreneurs and Parasites.* Cambridge, England: Cambridge University Press.

Maddison, Angus. 1989. *The World Economy in the Twentieth Century.* Paris: OECD Development Center.

Mafeje, A. 1995. "Recolonisation or Self-Colonisation and Malignant Minds in the Service of Imperialism." *CODESRIA Bulletin,* vol. 2.

Magdoff, Harry. 1969. *The Age of Imperialism: The Economics of U.S. Foreign Policy.* New York: Monthly Review Press.

Magnusson, Bruce. Forthcoming. "Democratization and Domestic Insecurity: Navigating the Transition in Benin. *Comparative Politics.*

————. 1996. "Benin: Legitimating Democracy (New Institutions and the Historical Problem of Economic Crisis)." *L'Afrique Politique, 1996 (Democratisation: Arrets sur Images).* Paris: Karthala.

Mainwaring, Scott, and Timothy Scully. 1995. "Introduction." In Scott Mainwaring and Timothy Scully, eds., *Building Democratic Institutions: Party Systems in Latin America.* Stanford, CA: Stanford University Press.

Malawi. 1966. *Malawi Citizenship Act,* para 15. In UN High Commissioner for Refugees gopher site "REFWORLD" location: gopher://iccuc2.unicc.org:70/11/unhcrcdr/legal.m/refleg.m.

Malloy, J. 1991. "Democracy, Economic Crisis, and the Problem of Governance: The Case of Bolivia." *Studies in Comparative International Development,* vol. 26.

Mamadou, Dia. 1996. *Africa's Management in the 1990s and Beyond: Reconciling Indigenous and Transplanted Institutions.* Washington, DC: World Bank.

Mamdani, M. 1996. *Citizen and Subject: Contemporary Africa and Legacy of Late Colonialism.* Princeton, NJ: Princeton University Press.

————. 1990. "A Glimpse at African Studies, Made in the USA." *CODESRIA Bulletin,* vol. 2.

Mamdani, M., and E. Wamba-dia-Wamba, eds. 1995. *African Studies in Social Movements and Democracy.* Dakar, Senegal: CODESRIA Books.

Mandaza, Ibbo. 1995. "The State and Politics in Zimbabwe." *Southern African Economic Monthly,* vol. 8, no. 6: 32.

Mandelbaum, Michael. 1996. "Foreign Policy as Social Work." *Foreign Affairs,* vol. 75, no. 1: 16–32.

"Manifesto of the Patriotic Party: Agenda for Change." 1996. Patriotic Party headquarters, Accra, Ghana, September 20. Mimeographed.

Mannick, A. R. 1979. *Mauritius: Development of a Plural Society.* Nottingham, England: Spokesman.

Manning, Patrick. 1982. *Slavery, Colonialism, and Economic Growth in Dahomey, 1640–1960*. Cambridge, England: Cambridge University Press.

Maravall, Jose Maria. 1994. "The Myth of the Authoritarian Advantage." *Journal of Democracy,* vol. 5: 18–31.

Marshall, Don D. 1996. "Understanding Late–Twentieth Century Capitalism: Reassessing the Globalization Theme." *Government and Opposition,* vol. 31, no. 2: 193–215.

Marshall, T. H. 1950. *Citizenship and Social Class*. Cambridge, England: Cambridge University Press.

Maseko, Sipho. 1995. "The Namibian Student Movement: Its Role and Effects." In Colin Leys and John Saul, eds., *Namibia's Liberation Struggle: The Two-Edged Sword*. London: James Currey, Ltd.

"Mauritius: An Island of Prosperity." 1990. *Euromoney* (Special Supplement), September 6.

Mauritius Export Development and Investment Authority. 1989. "Fact Sheet No. 4." January.

Mauritius Ministry of Finance. 1983. "Letters to the Managing Director, IMF, and to the President, World Bank." September.

Mauritius Times. 1984. "Trade Unions Express Concern over Sugar Industry and Education." April 27–May 3.

———. 1982. "Priorités du PMSD: La Zone Franche et le Tourism." May 7–13.

———. 1980. "L'Île Maurice, Quel Avenir: A. Jugnauth: 'Des Manigances Pour Un Changement Brutal.'" June 22.

———. 1980. "Social Services: How Much and How Far?" May 18.

———. 1980. "What Price Coalition?" April 27.

———. 1979. "Black Market at Its Peak! Save Democracy or Perish!" November 2.

———. 1979. "Editorial." November 2.

Maxfield, Sylvia. 1997. *Gatekeepers of Growth*. Princeton, NJ: Princeton University Press.

Mawhood, P. 1993. *Local Government in the Third World: Experiences of Decentralization in Tropical Africa*. 2nd ed. Pretoria: Africa Institute of South Africa.

Mazrui, A. 1995. "Self-Colonisation and the Search for Pax Africana: A Rejoinder." *CODESRIA Bulletin,* vol. 2.

———. 1995. "Towards a Benign Recolonisation of the Disintegrating States of Africa." *CODESRIA Bulletin,* vol. 2.

Mbembe, Achille. 1996. "The Right to Dispose." Unpublished typescript.

———. 1996. "Une Economie de Prédation: Les rapports entre la rareté matérielle et la démocratie en Afrique subsaharienne." *Foi et Dévéloppement* (Paris: Centre Lebert).

———. 1995. "Complex Transformations in Late Twentieth Century Africa." *Africa Demos,* vol. 3: 28–30.

———. 1990. "Democratization and Social Movements in Africa." *Africa Demos,* vol. 1, no. 1: 4.

———. 1990. "Le Prix de la Force." Unpublished typescript.

———. 1990. "Pouvoir, Violence, et Accumulation." *Politique Africaine,* vol. 39, no. 24: 7–24.

Mbodje, Pape Sedikh. 1996. "Le Code électoral modifié: Les conseillers ruraux plus nombreux." *Soleil,* August 6, p. 3.

McGrew, Anthony G., and Paul Lewis, eds. 1992. *Global Politics: Globalisation and the Nation-State*. Oxford, England: Polity Press.

McHenry, Dean E., Jr. 1994. *Limited Choices: The Political Struggle for Socialism in Tanzania*. Boulder, CO: Lynne Rienner Publishers.

McMahon, Edward R. 1994. "Lessons Learned." In Emory University, Governance in Africa Program, *Democratic Challenge in Africa.* Atlanta, GA: Carter Center.

Meagher, K., and M. B. Yunusa. 1996. "Passing the Buck: Structural Adjustment and the Nigerian Urban Informal Sector." Discussion Paper No. 75. Geneva: UNRISD.

Médard, Jean-François. 1982. "The Underdeveloped State in Tropical Africa: Political Clientelism or Neo-patrimonialism?" In Christopher Clapham, ed., *Private Patronage and Public Power: Political Clientelism in the Modern State.* London: Pinter.

Media Institute of Southern Africa. 1997. "Action Alert—Namibia." May 13.

Meillassoux, Claude, ed. 1971. *The Development of Indigenous Trade and Marketing in West Africa.* Oxford, England: Oxford University Press.

Melone, Stanislas, ed. 1982. *Droit des Personnes et de la Famille.* Encyclopedie Juridique de l'Afrique, Volume 6. Paris: Les Nouvelles Editions Africaines.

Migdal, Joel 1988. *Strong Societies and Weak States: State-Society Relations and State Capabilities in the Third World.* Princeton, NJ: Princeton University Press.

Miles, William F. S., and David A. Rochefort. 1991. "Nationalism versus Ethnic Identity in Sub-Saharan Africa." *American Political Science Review,* vol. 85 (June): 401.

Mills, C. Wright. 1995/1951. "The New Middle Class," parts I and II. In Arthur J. Vidich, ed., *The New Middle Classes.* New York: New York University Press.

Misser, François. 1996. "Dirty Dealings." *African Business,* June, pp. 16–18.

Mitchell, Allison. 1997. "Clinton Proposes Incentives for Free Market in Africa." *New York Times,* June 19.

Mitchell, Sidney Knox. 1951. *Taxation in Medieval England.* London and New Haven, CT: Yale University Press.

Mkandawire, Thandika. 1997. "Economic Policy-Making and the Consolidation of Democratic Institutions in Africa." In Havnevik and van Arkadie, eds., *Domination or Dialogue?*

———. 1996. "African Studies: Paradigms, Problems, and Prospects." Urbana-Champaign, IL. Mimeographed.

———. 1995. "Beyond Crisis: Towards Democratic Developmental States in Africa." Dakar, Senegal. Mimeographed.

———. 1995. "Fiscal Structure, State Contraction and Political Responses in Africa." In Thandika Mkandawire and Adebayo Olukoshi, *Between Liberalisation and Oppression: The Politics of Structural Adjustment in Africa.* Dakar, Senegal: CODESRIA.

———. 1994. "Adjustment, Political Conditionality, and Democratization in Africa." In A. Cornia and G. Helleiner, eds., *From Adjustment to Development in Africa: Conflict, Controversy, Convergence, Consensus,* pp. 155–173. London: Macmillan.

———. 1994. "The Political Economy of Privatization in Africa." In Cornia and Helleiner, eds., *From Adjustment to Development* (ibid.), pp. 192–213.

———. 1987. *The State and Agriculture in Africa.* London: CODESRIA Books.

Mkandawire, Thandika, and A. Olukoshi, eds. 1995. *Between Liberalisation and Oppression: The Politics of Structural Adjustment in Africa.* Dakar, Senegal: CODESRIA Books.

Monga, Célestin. 1996. *The Anthropology of Anger: Civil Society and Democracy in Africa.* Boulder, CO: Lynne Rienner Publishers.

———. 1995. "Civil Society and Democratization in Francophone Africa." *Journal of Modern African Studies,* vol. 33, no. 3: 359–379.

The Monitor (Zambia). 1996. "How Some Monitors Arrived at 'Not Free and Fair' Verdict." November 29–December 5.

Montecinos, Veronica. 1993. "Economic Policy Elites and Democratization." *Studies in Comparative International Development,* vol. 28: 25–53.

Moore, Barrington. 1966. *The Social Origins of Dictatorship and Democracy.* Boston: Beacon Press.

Morgenthau, Ruth Schachter. 1964. *Political Parties in French-Speaking West Africa.* Oxford, England: Clarendon Press.

Morrison, Donald George, Robert Cameron Mitchell, and John Naber Paden. 1989. *Black Africa: A Comparative Handbook,* 2nd edition. New York: Paragon House.

Mosley, Paul, Jane Harrigan, and John Toye. 1991. *Aid and Power: The World Bank and Policy Based Lending in the 1980s.* London: Routledge.

Moss, Todd, and Charles Kenny. 1997. "Africa's Emerging Stock Markets." Unpublished manuscript.

Moss, Todd, and David Williams, 1995. "Can Ghana's Economic Reform Survive the 1996 Elections?" *CSIS Africa Notes,* no. 175 (August).

Moyo, Sam. 1995. *The Land Question in Zimbabwe.* Harare: SAPES Books.

Mukonoweshuro, Eliphas G. 1991. "Containing Political Instability in a Poly-ethnic Society: The Case of Mauritius." *Ethnic and Racial Studies,* vol. 14, no. 2: 204.

Munro, J. Forbes. 1976. *Africa and the International Economy.* London: J. M. Dent & Sons.

Mustapha, A. R. 1992. "Structural Adjustment and Multiple Modes of Livelihood." In Gibbon et al., eds., *Authoritarianism.*

Muteba II, His Majesty, Kabaka of Buganda, Uganda. 1996. Speech delivered at Princeton University, NJ, February 5. Excerpts printed in "Traditional Leaders and Democracy in Africa," *West Africa,* April 15–21, 1996.

Naanen, Ben. 1995. "Oil Politics, Minority Agitation, and the Future of the Nigerian State." *African Affairs,* vol. 94: 325–344.

———. 1995. "Oil-Producing Minorities and the Restructuring of the Nigerian Federalism: The Case of the Ogoni People." *Journal of Commonwealth and Comparative Studies,* vol. 33, no. 1: 46–78.

Nash, John. 1995. "Trade Policy Reform Implementation in Sub-Saharan Africa: How Much Heat and How Much Light?" World Bank Working Paper. Washington, DC: World Bank.

Nchari, Anthony. 1990. "Cooperatives as Decentralized Socio-Economic Institutions: The Case of Cameroon." In Adamolekun et al., eds., *Decentralizing Policies,* pp. 60–102.

Ncube, Muthuli, and Colin Stoneman. 1995. "Lessons from Zimbabwe for South Africa." Unpublished article. Mimeographed. March.

"NDC 1996 Election Manifesto: Moving Ghana Forward." 1996. *Daily Graphic,* October 1.

NDI (National Democratic Institute). 1996. "Preliminary Statement by the NDI International Observer Delegation to the December 7 Elections in Ghana." Accra. December 10.

———. 1994. *Comments on the Namibian Presidential and National Assembly Elections.* Washington, DC: NDI.

Ndiaye, Ibrahima. 1996. "Défection au PDS dans la région de thiés: Le PS accueille 1255 nouveaux militants." *Soleil,* November 12, p. 8.

Nduru, Moyiga. 1996. "Anti-Asian Sentiment Slammed." Inter Press Service, May 20.

Nelson, Joan. 1993. "The Politics of Economic Transformation: Is Third World Experience Relevant for Eastern Europe?" *World Politics,* vol. 45 (April): 433–463.

Network of Domestic Election Observers. N.D. "Interim Report of Domestic Election Observers." Accra.

Neuberger, Benyamin. 1986. *National Self-Determination in Post-Colonial Africa.* Boulder, CO: Lynne Rienner Publishers.

New York Times. 1997. "Burying Mobutism" (editorial), April 13.

Ng'ethe, N., et al. 1989. "The Rural Informal Sector in Kenya: A Study of Micro-Enterprises in Nyeri, Meru, Uasin Gishu, and Siaya Districts." Institute for Development Studies (IDS) Occasional Paper No. 54. Nairobi: IDS.

Nicholas, Sheila. 1994. "The State and the Development of African Capitalism in Zimbabwe." In Colin Leys and B. Berman, eds., *African Capitalists in African Development.* Boulder, CO: Lynne Rienner Publishers.

Nikouwa, Abilee. 1994. "Contribution à la compréhension de l'imbroglio du Zou-Nord." *La Nation,* January 4.

Noor, N. A. Muhammad. 1972. *The Legal System of the Somali Democratic Republic.* Charlottesville, VA: Michie Co.

North, Douglass, and Barry Weingast. 1989. "Constitutions and Commitment: The Evolution of Institutions Governing Public Choice in Seventeenth Century England." *Journal of Economic History,* vol. 69: 803–832.

Nugent, Paul. 1995. *Big Men, Small Boys, and Politics in Ghana.* Accra: Asempa Press.

Nwajiaku, Kathryn. 1994. "The National Conferences Revisited." *Journal of Modern African Studies,* vol. 32, no. 3: 429–447.

Nwokedi, Emeka. 1995. *Politics of Democratization: Changing Authoritarian Regimes in Sub-Saharan Africa.* Münster and Hamburg, Germany: Lit Verlag.

Nyangoni, Wellington. 1978. *African Nationalism in Zimbabwe.* Lanham, MD: University Press of America.

Nyang'oro, Julius E. 1996. "Critical Notes on the Liberalization of Africa." *Journal of Asian and African Studies,* vol. 33, nos. 1–2: 112–124.

———. 1994. "Reform Politics and the Democratization Process in Africa." *African Studies Review,* vol. 37, no. 1: 133–149.

Nyang'oro, Julius E., and Timothy E. Shaw, eds. 1989. *Corporatism in Africa: Comparative Analysis and Practice.* Boulder, CO: Westview Press.

Nylander, Arthur. 1973. *The Nationality and Citizenship Laws of Nigeria.* Lagos: University of Lagos.

Oakerson, R.J. 1988. "Reciprocity: A Bottom-up View of Political Development." In Ostrom, D. Feeny, and H. Picht, eds. *Rethinking Institutional Analysis and Development.* San Francisco: International Center for Economic Growth. 141–158.

OAU (Organization of African Unity). 1996. "Statement by the Observer Group to Ghana's Presidential and Parliamentary Elections." Accra. December 8.

O'Donnell, Guillermo. 1996. "Illusions About Consolidation." *Journal of Democracy,* vol. 7, no. 2: 34–51.

———. 1996. "What Makes Democracies Endure?" *Journal of Democracy,* vol. 7, no. 1: 39–55.

———. 1994. "Delegative Democracy." *Journal of Democracy,* vol. 5, no. 1: 55–69.

O'Donnell, Guillermo, and Philippe Schmitter. 1986. *Transitions from Authoritarian Rule: Tentative Conclusions About Uncertain Democracies.* Baltimore: Johns Hopkins University Press.

Oliphant, Thomas. 1997. "An Economic Boost for Africa." *Boston Globe*, June 24, p. A15.

Olowu, Dele. 1993. "Ethical Violations in Nigeria's Public Services: Patterns, Explanations, and Remedies." In S. Rasheed and Dele Olowu, eds., *Ethics and Accountability in African Public Services,* pp. 93–118. Nairobi: ICIPE Press.

———. 1989. "Local Institutes and Development: The African Experience." *Canadian Journal of African Studies,* vol. 23, no. 2: 201–231.

———. 1988. *African Local Governments as Instruments of Economic and Social Development.* The Hague: International Union of Local Authorities.

———. 1981. *The Administration of Social Services in Nigeria: The Challenge of Local Governments.* Ile-Ife, Nigeria: University of Ife.

Olowu, Dele, and P. Smoke. 1992. "Determinants of Success in African Local Government." *Public Administration and Development,* vol. 12, no. 1: 1–17.

Olowu, Dele, B. Ayo, and B. Akande. 1991. *Local Institutions and National Development in Nigeria.* Ile-Ife, Nigeria: Obafemi Awolowo University Press.

Olukoshi. A. 1996. "Constitutionalism and Citizenship in Contemporary Africa: A Select Overview of Theoretical and Empirical Issues." Uppsala, Sweden, and Naivasha, Kenya. Mimeographed.

———. 1996. "Extending the Frontiers of Structural Adjustment Research in Africa: Some Notes on the Objectives of Phase II of the NAI SAP Research Programme." In Gibbon and Olukoshi, eds., *Structural Adjustment.*

———. 1996. "The Impact of Recent Reform Efforts on the State in Africa." In Havnevik and van Arkadie, eds., *Domination or Dialogue?*

———. 1995. "Bourgeois Social Movements and the Struggle for Democracy in Nigeria: An Enquiry into the 'Kaduna Mafia.'" In Mamdani and Wamba-dia-Wamba, eds., *African Studies in Social Movements.*

Olukoshi, A., and L. Laakso. 1995. "The Crisis of the National-State Project in Africa." In Olukoshi and Laakso, eds., *Challenges to the Nation-State.*

———, eds. 1995. *Challenges to the Nation-State in Africa.* Uppsala: Scandinavian Institute of African Studies.

Oman, Charles. 1994. *Globalization and Regionalization: The Challenge for the Developing Countries.* Paris: OECD.

Onimode, B., ed. 1989. *The IMF, the World Bank, and the African Debt.* 2 vols. London: Zed Books.

Osaghae, E. 1995. "The Ogoni Uprising: Oil Politics, Minority Agitation, and the Future of the Nigerian State." *African Affairs,* vol. 94: 325–344.

———. 1995. *Structural Adjustment and Ethnicity in Nigeria.* Uppsala: Scandinavian Institute of African Studies.

———. 1991. "Ethnic Minorities and Federalism in Nigeria." *African Affairs,* vol. 90: 237–258.

Osseni, Koubarath. 1996. "Projet de loi d'orientation portant organisation de l'Administration térritoriale de la République du Bénin. *Forum de la Semaine,* November 27–December 3.

———. 1994. "Béninoise, lève-toi et parle." *La Nation,* March 31.

Ostergaard, Tom. 1994. "The Role of the National Bourgeoisie in National Development: The Case of the Textile and Clothing Industries in Zimbabwe." In Colin Leys and B. Berman, eds., *African Capitalism in African Development.* Boulder, CO: Lynne Rienner Publishers.

Ostrom, Elinor. 1990. *Governing the Commons: The Evolution of Institutions of Collective Action.* Cambridge, England: Cambridge University Press.

Ostrom, Elinor, and V. Ostrom. 1977. "Public Goods and Public Choices." In E. S. Savas, ed., *Alternatives for Delivering Public Services: Towards Improved Performance,* pp. 7–49. Boulder, CO: Westview Press.

Othman, Shehu, and Gavin Williams. 1997. "Politics, Power, and Democracy in Nigeria." In J. Hyslop, ed., *Democratic Movements in Contemporary Africa.* London: James Currey, Ltd.

Ottaway, Marina. ed. 1997. *Democracy in Africa: The Hard Road Ahead.* Boulder, CO: Lynne Rienner Publishers.

———. 1994. *Democratization and Ethnic Nationalism: African and Eastern European Experiences.* Washington, DC: Overseas Development Council.

Ottemoeller, Daniel. 1996. "Institutionalization and Democratization: The Case of Uganda's Resistance Councils." Unpublished Ph.D. diss., Department of Political Science, University of Florida.

Owusu, Maxwell. 1983. "Chieftaincy and Constitutionalism in Ghana: The Case of the Third Republic." *Conflict and the Common Good: Studies in Third World Societies,* no. 24 (June): 29–54.

Oyovbaire, S. E. 1985. *Federalism in Nigeria.* London: Macmillan.

Pacho, Arturo G. 1980. "Political Integration Through Naturalization: A Southeast Asian Perspective." *Asia Quarterly,* vol. 4: 242–243.

Paden, John. 1997. "Nigerian Unity and the Tensions of Democracy: Geo-Cultural Zones and North-South Legacies." In Beckett and Young, eds., *Dilemmas of Democracy.*

Passell, Peter. 1997. "Economic Scene." *New York Times,* March 13.

Pastor, Manuel. 1996. "The Distributive Effects of Alternative Economic Sequences." In Leslie Elliot Armijo, ed., *Conversations About Democratization and Economic Reform: Working Papers of the Southern California Seminar,* pp. 125–130. Los Angeles: University of Southern California.

Pateman, Carole. 1970. *Participation and Democratic Theory.* Cambridge, England: Cambridge University Press.

Pearson, Scott R., Gerald C. Nelson, and J. Dirck Stryker. 1976. "Incentives and Comparative Advantage in Ghanaian Industry and Agriculture." Unpublished typescript.

Peil, Margaret. 1971. "The Expulsion of West African Aliens." *Journal of Modern African Studies,* vol. 9: 205.

Peltola, Pekka. 1995. *The Lost May Day: Namibian Workers Struggle for Independence.* Helsinki: Finnish Anthropological Society.

Pelzynski, Z. A. 1988. "Solidarity and 'The Rebirth of Civil Society' in Poland, 1976–81." In John Keane, ed., *Civil Society and the State.* New York: Verso.

Perlmutter, Amos. 1981. *Modern Authoritarianism.* London and New Haven, CT: Yale University Press.

Phillips, Anne. 1977. "The Concept of Development." *Review of African Political Economy,* no. 8 (Jan.–April): 7–20.

Pigasse, Jean-Paul. 1997. "Cherche Politique Africaine Désespérément," *Jeune Afrique,* no. 1883 (February 5–11): 28–31.

Pillar, Paul R. 1983. *Negotiating Peace: War Termination as a Bargaining Process.* Princeton, NJ: Princeton University Press.

Post, K. W. J., and Michael Vickers. 1973. *Structure and Conflict in Nigeria, 1960–1966.* London: Heinemann.

Project 2015. 1996. *Aid Dependency: Causes, Symptoms, and Remedies.* Stockholm: Swedish International Development Cooperation Agency (SIDA).

Prunier, Gérard. 1995. *The Rwanda Crisis: History of a Genocide.* New York: Columbia University Press.

Przeworski, Adam. 1995. *Sustainable Democracy.* Cambridge, England: Cambridge University Press.

———. 1991. *Democracy and the Market.* Cambridge, England: Cambridge University Press.

Przeworski, Adam, and Fernando Limongi. 1997. "Modernization: Theories and Facts." *World Politics,* vol. 49, no. 2 (January): 155–183.

———. 1993. "Political Regimes and Economic Growth." *Journal of Economic Perspectives,* vol. 7: 51–71.

Pye, Lucian. 1990. "Political Science and the Crisis of Authoritarianism." *American Political Science Review,* vol. 84, no. 1: 3–19.

Quirk, Peter J. 1996. "Macroeconomic Implications of Money Laundering." IMF Working Paper No. WP/96/66. Washington, DC: IMF.

Radio Côte d'Ivoire. 1995. "President Bédié Defends Current Electoral Law." In British Broadcasting Corporation, *BBC Summary of World Broadcasts,* August 14, 1995.

Raftopoulos, Brian. 1994. "Zimbabwe: Race and Nationalism in a Post-Colonial State." In P. Kaarsholm and J. Hyltin, eds., *Invention and Boundaries: Historical and Anthropological Approaches to the Study of Ethnicity and Nationalism.* Denmark: Roskilds University.

Raftopoulos, Brian, and Sam Moyo. 1995. "The Politics of Indigenization in Zimbabwe." *East African Social Science Review,* vol. 11, no. 2 (June): 17–33.

Ranger, Terence O. 1970. *The African Voice in Southern Rhodesia, 1898–1930.* Evanston, IL: Northwestern University Press.

Ravallion, Martin, and Shaohua Chen. 1996. "What Can Survey Data Tell Us About Recent Changes in Distribution and Poverty?" Unpublished World Bank paper. May.

Ravenhill, John, ed. 1986. *Africa in Economic Crisis.* New York: Columbia University Press.

Reno, William. 1996. "The Business of War in Liberia." *Current History,* vol. 93, no. 601 (May): 211–215.

———. 1995. *Corruption and State Politics in Sierra Leone.* Cambridge, England: Cambridge University Press.

Report 1995. New York: Oxford University Press.

Reuters. 1996. "Low Turnout of Voters in Comoro Islands Poll." December 2.

Reynolds, Andrew. 1995. "Constitutional Engineering in South Africa." *Journal of Democracy,* vol. 6, no. 2: 86–99.

Reynolds, Lloyd G. 1985. *Economic Growth in the Third World, 1850–1980.* New Haven, CT: Yale University Press.

Reyntjens, Filip. 1993. "The Proof of the Pudding Is in the Eating: The June 1993 Elections in Burundi." *Journal of Modern African Studies,* vol. 31, no. 4: 563–584.

———. 1985. *Pouvoir et droit au Rwanda: Droit public et évolution politique, 1916–1973.* Tervuren, Belgium: Musée Royal de l'Afrique Centrale.

Richey, Lisa, and Stefano Ponte. 1996. "The 1995 Tanzania Union Elections." *Review of African Political Economy,* vol. 67: 80–87.

Roberts, Andrew. 1976. *History of Zambia.* London: Heinemann.

Roberts, Matthew. 1992. *Export Processing Zones in Jamaica and Mauritius: Evolution of an Export-Oriented Development Model.* San Francisco: Mellen Research University Press.

Robinson, Pearl T. 1991. "Niger: Anatomy of a Neotraditional Corporatist State." *Comparative Politics,* vol. 24, no. 1: 1–20.

Roche, M. 1992. *Rethinking Citizenship: Welfare, Ideology, and Change in Modern Society.* London: Polity Press.

Rock, Michael T. 1994. "Transitional Democracies and the Shift to Export-Led

Industrialization: Lesssons from Thailand." *Studies in Comparative International Development,* vol. 29, no. 1: 1–18.

Rodney, Walter. 1982. *How Europe Underdeveloped Africa.* Washington, DC: Howard University Press.

Rodrik, Dani. 1996. "Labor Standards in International Trade: Do They Matter and What to Do About Them?" In Robert Z. Lawrence, Dani Rodrik, and John Whalley, *Emerging Agenda for Global Trade: High Stakes for Developing Countries.* Policy Essay No. 20. Washington, DC: Overseas Development Council.

———. 1996. "Understanding Economic Policy Reform." *Journal of Economic Literature,* vol. 34: 9–41.

Rogowski, Ronald. 1989. *Commerce and Coalition.* Princeton, NJ: Princeton University Press.

Romer, Paul M. 1992. "Two Strategies for Economic Development: Using Ideas and Producing Ideas." *Proceedings of the World Bank Annual Conference on Development Economics.* Washington, DC: World Bank, pp. 63–91.

Ronen, Dov. 1968. *Dahomey: Between Tradition and Modernity.* Ithaca, NY: Cornell University Press.

Roniger, Luis. 1994. "The Comparative Study of Clientelism and the Changing Nature of Civil Society in the Contemporary World." In Luis Roniger and A. Gunes-Ayata, eds., *Democracy, Clientelism, and Civil Society.* Boulder, CO: Lynne Rienner Publishers.

Root, Hilton. 1994. *The Fountain of Privilege.* Berkeley and Los Angeles: University of California Press.

Rosenberg, Tina. 1991. "Beyond Elections." *Foreign Policy,* no. 84.

Rosenthal, Jean Laurent. 1992. *The Fruits of Revolution: Property Rights, Litigation, and French Agriculture, 1700–1860.* Cambridge, England: Cambridge University Press.

Rothchild, Donald. 1997. *Managing Ethnic Conflict in Africa: Pressures and Incentives for Cooperation.* Washington, DC: Brookings Institution.

———. 1995. "Ethnic Bargaining and State Breakdown in Africa." *Nationalism and Ethnic Politics,* vol. 1, no. 1: 54–72.

———. 1995. "On Implementing Africa's Peace Accords: From Defection to Cooperation." *Africa Today,* vol. 42, nos. 1–2: 8–38.

———. 1994. "Structuring State-Society Relations in Africa: Toward an Enabling Political Environment." In Widner, ed., *Economic Change,* pp. 201–229.

———. 1984. "Middle Africa: Hegemonial Exchange and Resource Allocation." In A. Groth and L. Wade, eds., *Comparative Resource Allocation: Politics, Performance, and Priorities.* Vol. 13 of Sage Yearbooks in Politics and Public Policy. Beverly Hills, CA: Sage Publications.

———. 1983. "Collective Demands for Improved Distributions." In Rothchild and Olorunsola, eds., *State Versus Ethnic Claims,* pp. 172–198.

Rothchild, Donald, and Robert L. Curry Jr. 1978. *Scarcity, Choice, and Public Policy in Middle Africa.* Berkeley: University of California Press.

Rothchild, Donald, and Alexander J. Groth. 1995. "Pathological Dimensions of Domestic and International Ethnicity." *Political Science Quarterly,* vol. 110, no. 1: 69–82.

Rothchild, Donald, and Naomi Chazan, eds. 1988. *The Precarious Balance: State and Society in Africa.* Boulder, CO: Westview Press.

Rothchild, Donald, and V. Olorunsola, eds. 1983. *State Versus Ethnic Claims: African Policy Dilemmas.* Boulder, CO: Westview Press.

Royal Danish Ministry of Foreign Affairs. 1995. *Report of the Group of*

Independent Advisers on Development Cooperation Issues Between Tanzania and Its Aid Donors. Copenhagen: Ministry of Foreign Affairs, June.

Rudebeck, L. 1997. "Democratisation in Africa: Guinea-Bissau as an Illuminating Case." Lecture given at the Scandinavian Institute of African Studies, Uppsala, Sweden.

Rueschemeyer, Dietrich, E. H. Stephens, and J. D. Stephens. 1992. *Capitalist Development and Democracy.* Chicago: University of Chicago Press.

Rwanda. 1995. Fantoft-Bergen, Norway: Chr. Michelsen Institute.

Sacerdoti, E. 1994. "Letter of July 29, 1994, to Paul Dossou, Minister of Finance." *La Nation,* August 2.

Sachikonye, Lloyd. 1995. "Democracy in Zimbabwe." Paper presented at the African Association of Political Science Annual Meeting, Lagos, Nigeria, August.

Sachs, Jeffrey. 1997. "The Limits of Convergence: Nature, Nurture, and Growth." *Economist,* June 14, p. 19.

Sachs, Jeffrey, and Andrew Warner. 1995. "Economic Reform and the Process of Globalization." *Brookings Papers on Economic Activity,* vol. 1: 1–198.

Sandbrook, Richard. 1996. "Democratisation and the Implementation of Economic Reform in Africa." *Journal of International Development,* vol. 8: 21–28.

———. 1993. *The Politics of Africa's Economic Recovery.* Cambridge, England: Cambridge University Press.

———. 1985. *The Politics of Africa's Economic Stagnation.* Cambridge, England: Cambridge University Press.

Sarr, Ibrahima. 1996. "Mamadou Ndoye dénonce le plan de fraude des socialistes." *Soleil,* November 22, p. 7.

Sartori, Giovanni. 1996. *Comparative Constitutional Engineering: An Inquiry into Structures, Incentives, and Outcomes.* 2nd ed. New York: New York University Press.

———. 1987. *Democratic Theory, Revisited.* Chatham, NJ: Chatham House Publishers.

———. 1965. *Democratic Theory.* Detroit, MI: Wayne State University Press.

Sawyer, Amos. 1988. "The Putu Development Association: A Missed Opportunity." In V. Ostrom., D. Feeny, and H. Picht, eds., *Rethinking Institutional Analysis and Development,* pp. 247–278. San Francisco: International Center of Economic Growth.

Schattschneider, E. E. 1935. *Politics, Pressures, and the Tariff.* New York: Prentice Hall.

Schatz, Sayre P. 1984. "Pirate Capitalism and the Inert Economy of Nigeria." *Journal of Modern African Studies,* vol. 22, no. 1: 45–58.

Schatzberg, Michael G. 1997. "Beyond Mobutu: Kabila and the Congo." *Journal of Democracy,* vol. 8, no. 4: 70–84.

———. 1988. *The Dialectics of Oppression in Zaire.* Bloomington: Indiana University Press.

Schmidt, Vivien A. 1995. "The New World Order, Incorporated: The Rise of Business and the Decline of the Nation-State." *Daedalus,* vol. 124, no. 2: 75–106.

Schmitter, Philippe. 1992. "The Consolidation of Democracy and the Representation of Social Groups." *American Behavioral Scientist,* vol. 35: 422–449.

Schmitter, Philippe, and Terry Lynn Karl. 1991. "What Democracy Is . . . and Is Not." *Journal of Democracy,* vol. 2, no. 3: 86–87.

Schuck, Peter, and Rogers Smith. 1985. *Citizenship Without Consent: Illegal Aliens in the American Polity.* New Haven: Yale University Press.

Schumpeter, Joseph. 1962. *Capitalism, Socialism, and Democracy.* New York: Harper & Row; also published in 1942 by Allen & Unwin, London.

Seeley, Ivor. 1978. *Local Government Explained.* London: Macmillan.

Seidou, Arouna. 1994. "Faiblesse des Partis politiques au Benin: Défaut de Conviction." *Le Matin,* July 8.

———. 1994. "Le Référendum aux oubliettes." *Le Matin,* October 18.

Seligson, Mitchell A., and John A. Booth. 1996. *Elections and Democracy in Central America, Revisited.* Chapel Hill: University of North Carolina Press.

Shack, William A. 1979. "Introduction." In William A. Shack and Elliott P. Skinner, eds., *Strangers in African Societies.* Berkeley: University of California Press.

Shafer, D. Michael. 1993. "The Perverse Paradox of Peace and the Predatory State." Paper prepared for the American Political Science Association Annual Meeting, Washington, DC, September 2–5.

Sharer, Robert L., Hema R. de Zoysa, and Calvin A. MacDonald. 1995. *Uganda: Adjustment with Growth, 1987–1994.* Occasional Paper No. 121. Washington, DC: IMF.

Shephard, Anne. 1993. "Mauritius: Saving the Tiger." *Africa Report,* vol. 38, no. 2.

Sik, Ko Swan, and Teuku Moh Rhadie. 1990. "Nationality and International Law in Indonesian Perspective." In Ko Swan Sik, ed., *Nationality and International Law in Asian Perspective.* Dordrecht: Martinus Nijhoff Publishers.

Sikkink, Kathryn. 1991. *Ideas and Institutions: Developmentalism in Argentina and Brazil.* Ithaca, NY: Cornell University Press.

Simmons, Adele Smith. 1982. *Modern Mauritius: The Politics of Decolonization.* Bloomington: Indiana University Press.

Sindzingre, Alice N. 1996. "Crédibilité des États et Nouvelles Insécurités: L'Economie Politique des Réformes en Afrique." Unpublished manuscript, Paris, for the Centre National de la Recherche Scientifique.

Singh, A. 1995. "The Causes of Fast Economic Growth in East Asia." *UNCTAD Review, 1995.* Geneva: United Nations Conference on Trade and Development.

Sinnadurai, Visu. 1990. "Nationality and International Law in the Perspective of the Federation of Malaysia." In Ko Swan Sik, ed., *Nationality and International Law in Asian Perspective.* Dordrecht: Martinus Nijhoff Publishers.

Sisk, Timothy D. 1996. *Power Sharing and International Mediation in Ethnic Conflicts.* Washington, DC: Institute of Peace Press.

———. 1995. *Democratization in South Africa: The Elusive Social Contract.* Princeton, NJ: Princeton University Press.

Sithole, Masipula. 1995. "Zimbabwe: In Search of a Stable Democracy." In Diamond et al., eds., *Politics in Developing Countries.*

———. 1988. "Zimbabwe: In Search of a Stable Democracy." In Diamond et al., eds., *Democracy in Developing Countries.*

———. 1987. "State Power Consolidation in Zimbabwe: Party and Ideological Development." In Edmond J. Keller and Donald Rothchild, eds., *Afro-Marxist Regimes: Ideology and Public Policy,* pp. 85–106. Boulder, CO: Lynne Rienner Publishers.

Skalnes, Tor. 1995. *The Politics of Economic Adjustment in Zimbabwe.* New York: St. Martin's Press.

Sklar, Martin J. 1992. *The United States as a Developing Country.* Cambridge, England: Cambridge University Press.

———. 1988. *The Corporate Reconstruction of American Capitalism: The Market, the Law, and Politics.* Cambridge, England: Cambridge University Press.

Sklar, Richard L. 1996. "Towards a Theory of Developmental Democracy." In

Adrian Leftwich, ed., *Democracy and Development,* pp. 25–44. Cambridge, England: Polity Press.

———. 1993. "The African Frontier for Political Science." In Robert H. Bates, V. Y. Mudimbe, and Jean O'Barr, eds., *Africa and the Disciplines,* pp. 83–110. Chicago: University of Chicago Press.

Skocpol, Theda. 1979. *States and Social Revolutions.* Cambridge, England: Cambridge University Press.

Small, N. J. 1977. "Citizenship, Imperialism, and Independence: British Colonial Ideals and Independent African States" Part one. *Civilisations,* vol. 27.

Smith, B. C. 1996. "Sustainable Local Democracy." *Public Administration and Development,* vol. 16, no. 2: 163–178.

———. 1985. *Decentralisation: The Territorial Dimension of the State.* London: Allen & Unwin.

Smock, Audrey. 1971. *Ibo Politics: The Role of Ethnic Unions in Eastern Nigeria.* Cambridge, MA: Harvard University Press.

Soglo, Nicéphore. 1994. "Au Sujet de l'examen du projet de budget général de l'Etat." Letter No. 171-C/PR/CAB (July 26) to the President of the National Assembly. *La Nation,* July 28.

———. 1994. Speech of August 2 on Radio Bénin.

Soleil. 1997. "Bureau politique de PS: Les accusations de l'opposition . . ." January 10, pp. 1, 3.

———. 1996. "Le PS rafle la mise." November 30, p. 1.

———. 1996. "Interdiction d'une marche de l'opposition." November 29, p. 5.

———. 1996. "Idrissa Seck (PDS): 'Le governeur a été complice du PS." November 28, p. 5.

———. 1996. "Quelques idées-forces de Ousmane Tanor Dieng furent entrée au gouvernement et les projets de Me Wade." October 13, p. 7.

———. 1996. "Un autre député quitte le PDS." August 21, p. 1.

———. 1996. "Commission électorale indépendante: Non définitif du PS." July 19, p. 3.

———. 1996. "Un député démissione du PDS." July 12, p. 1.

———. 1993. "Salaire des deputés." July 15, p. 10.

Sorsa, Piritta. 1996. "Sub-Saharan African Commitments in the Uruguay Round: Myth or Reality?" *World Economy,* vol. 19, no. 3: 287–306.

Southern Africa Confidential. 1996. "Angola: Slow, Painful." Vol. 1 (April 12): 2–4.

Sovide, Valentin. 1993. "Les populations nago revendiquent le chef-lieu du Zou-Nord." *La Nation,* November 23.

Sowa, Nii. 1996. "Adjustment in Africa: Lessons from Ghana." Briefing Paper No. 3. London: Overseas Development Institute, July.

Soyinka, Wole. 1996. *The Open Sore of a Continent: A Personal Narrative of the Nigeria Crisis.* New York: New York University Press.

Sparks, Allister. 1995. *Tomorrow Is Another Country.* New York: Hill & Wang.

Stallings, Barbara, ed. 1995. *Global Change, Regional Response: The New International Context of Development.* New York: Cambridge University Press.

Stedman, Stephen John. 1996. "Negotiation and Mediation in Internal Conflict." In Michael E. Brown, ed., *The International Dimensions of Internal Conflict,* pp. 341–376. Cambridge, MA: MIT Press.

———. 1991. *Peacemaking in Civil War: International Mediation in Zimbabwe, 1974–1980.* Boulder, CO: Lynne Rienner Publishers.

———, ed. 1994. *South Africa: The Political Economy of Transformation.* Boulder, CO: Lynne Rienner Publishers.

Stedman, Stephen John, and Donald Rothchild. 1996. "Peace Operations: From

Short-Term to Long-Term Commitment." *International Peacekeeping,* vol. 3, no. 2 (summer): 17–35.

Stein, Howard, ed. 1995. *Asian Industrialization and Africa: Studies in Policy Alternatives to Structural Adjustment.* New York: St. Martin's Press.

Steinmo, Sven, Kathleen Thelen, and Frank Longstreth, eds. 1992. *Structuring Politics: Historical Institutionalism in Comparative Analysis.* New York: Cambridge University Press.

Stepan, Alfred. 1988. *Rethinking Military Politics: Brazil and the Southern Cone.* Princeton: Princeton University Press.

Strachan, Brigid. 1993. "Report on the Impact of Redressive Action Employment Policy on Redressing Racial and Gender Imbalances in the Labor Market in Zimbabwe." Harare: ARCTA Publications.

———. 1989. "Report for the Confederation of Zimbabwe Industries: Black Managerial Advancement in a Sample of CZI Member Companies." Harare: University of Zimbabwe/CASS.

Strauss, Andre. 1987. "Community Organisations in Namibia." In Gerhard Toetemeyer, Vezera Kandetu, and Wolfgang Werner, eds., *Namibia in Perspective.* Windhoek: Council of Churches of Namibia.

Stren, Richard. 1989. "Accountability in Africa." In *Strengthening Local Governments in Sub-Saharan Africa: Proceedings of Two Workshops,* pp. 121–126. Washington, DC: Economic Development Institute.

Suberu, Rotimi. 1997. "Religion and Politics: A View from the South." In Larry Diamond, Anthony Kirk-Greene, and Oyeleye Oyediran, eds., *Transition Without End: Nigerian Politics and Civil Society Under Babangida.* Boulder, CO: Lynne Rienner Publishers.

———. 1996. *Ethnic Minority Conflicts and Governance in Nigeria.* Ibadan: Spectrum Books.

———. 1995. "Federalism, Ethnicity, and Regionalism." Paper presented at the Conference on Dilemmas of Democracy, University of Wisconsin-Madison, November 10–12.

Sud Quotidien. 1993. "Salaires des deputés: Voici aussi Me Wade!" July 26, p. 2.

Summers, L. 1994. "Foreword." In Haggard and Webb, eds., *Voting for Reform.*

Sylvester, Christine. 1995. "Whither Opposition in Zimbabwe?" *Journal of Modern African Studies,* vol. 33, no. 3: 403–423.

Takaya, B. J. 1990. "'Republican Monarchies'? An Assessment of the Relevance and Roles of Traditional Rulers in Nigeria's Third Republic." Paper presented at a conference on Democratic Transition and Structural Adjustment in Nigeria, Hoover Institution, Stanford University, Palo Alto, CA, August.

Talla, M. Thierno. 1993. "Bassirou Ndao et la Lonase: Entre Détournement et faute de gestion." *Sud Quotidien,* November 12, p. 3.

Tapscott, Chris. 1994. "Land Reform in Namibia: Why Not?" *Southern African Report,* vol. 9, no. 3: 12–15.

———. 1993. "National Reconciliation, Social Equity, and Class Formation in Independent Namibia." *Journal of Southern African Studies,* vol. 19, no. 1: 29–39.

Terreblanche, Christelle. 1993. "Namibian Trade Unions in Tatters." *South,* October 29–November 2.

Tévoèdjrè, Albert. 1994. "Letter to Donors." *Le Matin,* August 3.

Thelen, Kathleen, and Sven Steinmo. 1992. "Historical Institutionalism in Comparative Analysis." In Steinmo et al., eds., *Structuring Politics,* pp. 1–32.

Tocqueville, Alexis de. 1969. *Democracy in America.* New York: Doubleday.

Toetemeyer, Gerhard, Victor Tonchi, and Andre du Pisani. 1994. *Namibia Regional Resources Manual*. Windhoek: Friedrich Ebert Foundation.

Tordoff, William. 1993. *Government and Politics in Africa*. 2nd ed. London: Macmillan and Bloomington: Indiana University Press.

Trager, Lilian. 1994. "Structural Adjustment, Hometowns, and Local Development in Nigeria." In Richard Blanton et al., eds., *Economic Analysis Beyond the Local System*. A publication of the American Society for Economic Anthropology. Lanham, MD: University Press of America.

Turner, Michael. 1994. "The Multiparty Conference on Mozambique's Draft Electoral Law: A Transition Process in Microcosm." Paper prepared for the African Studies Association meetings, Toronto, Canada, November.

UNCTAD (United Nations Conference on Trade and Development). 1996. *Trade and Development Report, 1996*. Geneva: United Nations.

United Nations. 1954. *Laws Concerning Nationality*. New York: United Nations.

United Nations Development Programme. 1996. *Human Development Indicators, 1996*. New York: Oxford University Press.

———. 1995. *Human Development Report, 1995*. New York: Oxford University Press for the UNDP.

United Nations Development Programme and the World Bank. 1993. *Mauritius: Toward the Twenty-first Century*. UNDP–World Bank Trade Extension Program, Country Report No. 12, Washington, DC, December.

UNRISD (United Nations Research Institute for Social Development). 1995. *States of Disarray: The Social Effects of Globalization*. Geneva: UNRISD.

USAID (United States Agency for International Development). 1990. *The Democracy Initiative*. Washington, DC: USAID.

U.S. Government. 1997. Human Rights Report of the Department of State.

———. 1996. Human Rights Report of the Department of State.

U.S. Institute of Peace. 1997. "Zaire's Crisis of War and Governance." Special Report. Washington, DC: USIP, April.

———. 1993. "Achieving Post-Settlement Peace in Mozambique: The Role of the International Community." Special Report. Washington, DC: USIP, May 18.

Vail, Leroy, ed. 1989. *The Creation of Tribalism in Southern Africa*. London: James Currey, Ltd.

Vance, Cyrus R., and David A. Hamburg. 1996. "Avoiding Anarchy in Burundi." *New York Times,* March 9, p. 19.

Vanderlinden, Jacques. 1971. *Introduction au Droit de L'Ethiopie Moderne*. Paris: R. Pischon.

van de Walle, Nicholas. 1996. "Globalization and African Democracy." Paper presented at the Thirty-ninth Annual Meeting of the African Studies Association, San Francisco, November 23–26.

———. 1994. "Neopatrimonialism and Democracy in Africa with an Illustration from Cameroon." In Widner, ed., *Economic Change*.

———. 1994. "Political Liberalization and Economic Policy Reform in Africa." *World Development*, vol. 22, no. 4 (April).

van de Walle, Nicholas, and Timothy Johnston. 1996. *Improving Aid to Africa*. Overseas Development Council Policy Essay No. 21. Washington, DC: Overseas Development Council.

Varshney, Ashutosh. 1995. *Democracy, Development, and the Countryside: Urban-Rural Struggles in India*. Cambridge and New York: Cambridge University Press.

———. 1993. *Beyond Urban Bias*. London: Frank Cass.

Venter, D. 1995. "The Transition to Democracy in Malawi: 1992 to 1995." *18th CODESRIA General Assembly*. Dakar, Senegal: CODESRIA, June 26–July 2.

Vernon, Raymond. 1971. *Sovereignty at Bay: The Multinational Spread of U.S. Enterprises.* New York: Penguin.

Verzaijl, J. H. W. 1972. *Nationality and other Matters Relating to Individuals,* Part V of his *International Law in Historical Perspective.* Leiden: A. W. Sitjthoff.

Videgla, Maxime. 1994. "Déclaration du gouvernement sur les lois électorales." *La Nation,* September 26.

———. 1994. "Elections législatives de '95: Quel mode de scrutin? Députés et hommes politiques se prononcent." *La Nation,* July 15.

Villalón, Leonardo, and Phil Huxtable, eds. 1997. *Critical Juncture: The African State Between Disintegration and Reconfiguration.* Boulder, CO: Lynne Rienner Publishers.

Virashawmy, Raji. 1987. "State Policies and Agriculture in Mauritius." In Thandika Mkandawire and Naceur Bourenane, eds., *The States and Agriculture in Africa,* pp. 144–157. London: CODESRIA.

Wade, Robert. 1996. "Japan, the World Bank, and the Art of Paradigm Maintenance: The East Asian Miracle in Political Perspective." *New Left Review,* vol. 217 (May-June): 3–36.

———. 1996. "Globalization and Its Limits: Reports of the Death of the National Economy Are Greatly Exaggerated." In Suzanne Berger and Ronald Dore, eds., *National Diversity and Global Capitalism.* Ithaca, NY: Cornell University Press.

———. 1990. *Governing the Market: Economic Theory and the Role of Government in East Asian Industrialization.* Princeton, NJ: Princeton University Press.

Wagner, Robert Harrison. 1993. "The Causes of Peace." In Roy Licklider, ed., *Stopping the Killing: How Civil Wars End,* pp. 235–268. New York: New York University Press.

Wall Street Journal. 1996. "On the Fringe: Fund Managers Flock to Tiny Stock Markets That Aren't Hot Yet." November 13.

Wallerstein, Immanuel. 1997. "The West and the Rest." Presidential Letter No. 6, International Sociological Association.

———. 1988. "The Bourgeoisie as Concept and Reality." *New Left Review,* vol. 167 (January–February): 91–106.

———. 1979. *The Capitalist World Economy.* Cambridge, England: Cambridge University Press.

———. 1961. *Africa: The Politics of Independence.* New York: Vintage Books.

Walter, Barbara F. 1996. "Domestic Anarchy and Civil War." Paper presented at a meeting of the International Studies Association, San Diego, CA, April 17.

Walzer, Michael. 1992. "The New Tribalism." *Dissent* (spring): 164–171.

———. 1983. *Spheres of Justice: A Defense of Pluralism and Equality.* New York: Basic Books.

Wanyande, Peter. 1988. "Democracy and the One-Party State: The African Experience." In Walter Oyungi, Atieno Odhiambo, Michael Chege, and Africa Gitonga, eds., *Democratic Theory and Practice in Africa.* London: James Currey, Ltd.

Waterbury, John. 1992. "Export-Led Growth and the Center-Right Coalition in Turkey." *Comparative Politics,* vol. 24, no. 2: 127–145.

———. 1992. "The Heart of the Matter? Public Enterprise and the Adjustment Process." In Stephen Haggard and Robert Kaufman, eds., *The Politics of Economic Adjustment: International Constraints, Distribution, and the State,* pp. 182–217. Princeton, NJ: Princeton University Press.

———. 1989. "Political Management of Economic Adjustment and Reform." In

Joan M. Nelson, ed., *Fragile Coalitions: The Politics of Economic Adjustment,* pp. 39–56. New Brunswick, NJ: Transaction Books.

Watkins, Chandra D. 1993. "Mauritius: U.S. Technology Welcomed for Export Diversification." *Business America,* April 19, p. 35.

Weaver, Tony. 1989. "The South African Defence Force in Namibia." In Jacklyn Cock and Laurie Nathan, eds., *War and Society: The Militarisation of South Africa.* Cape Town: David Philip.

———. 1987. "The War in Namibia." In Gerhard Toetemeyer, Vezera Kandetu, and Wolfgang Werner, eds., *Namibia in Perspective.* Windhoek: Council of Churches of Namibia.

Weber, Eugene. 1976. *Peasants into Frenchmen: The Modernization of Rural France, 1870–1914.* Stanford, CA: Stanford University Press.

Weiland, Heribert, and Matthew Braham, eds. 1994. *The Namibian Peace Process: Implications and Lessons for the Future.* Freiburg, Germany: Arnold Bergstraesser Institut.

Welch, Claude E. 1995. *Protecting Human Rights in Africa: Roles and Strategies of Non-Governmental Organizations.* Philadelphia: University of Pennsylvania Press.

Wellisz, Stanislaw, and Philippe Lam Shin Saw. 1993. "Mauritius." In Ronald Findlay and Stanislaw Wellisz, eds., *Five Small Open Economies,* pp. 235–243. New York: Oxford University Press for the World Bank.

West, Michael O. 1990. "African Middle Class Formation in Colonial Zimbabwe: 1890–1965." Ph.D. diss., Harvard University, Cambridge, MA.

West Africa. 1991. "Deepening Democracy?" May 6–12, p. 702.

Westebbe, Richard. 1994. "Structural Adjustment, Rent Seeking, and Liberalization in Benin." In Widner, ed., *Economic Change.*

Whitaker, C. S. 1970. *The Politics of Tradition, Continuity, and Change in Northern Nigeria, 1946–1966.* Princeton, NJ: Princeton University Press.

———, ed. 1981. *Issue: A Journal of Opinion,* vol. 11, nos. 1–2. Special Edition.

Whitaker, J. 1990. *How Can Africa Survive?* New York: Council on Foreign Relations.

Whitaker, S. 1984. "The Unfinished State of Nigeria." *Worldview,* vol. 27, no. 3.

White, Howard, and Oliver Morissey. 1997. "Tailoring Conditionality to Donor Recipient Relationships." Nottingham, England: CREDIT (Centre for Research in Economic Development and International Trade), University of Nottingham.

Whitten, Guy D., and Henry S. Bienen. n.d. "Political Violence and Leadership Lifetime Cycles." Unpublished manuscript.

Widner, Jennifer A. 1995. "States and Statelessness in Late Twentieth-Century Africa." *Daedalus,* vol. 124, no. 3: 129–154.

———, ed. 1994. *Economic Change and Political Liberalisation in Sub-Saharan Africa.* Baltimore and London: Johns Hopkins University Press.

Wignaraja, Ponna, ed. 1993. *New Social Movements in the South: Empowering the People.* London: Zed Books.

Wilson, Cédric. 1994. "Yves Yèhouéssi quitte le Gouvernement: Il est proposé à la Cour Suprême." *Tam-Tam Express,* April 18–May 1.

Wilson, Ernest J. 1997. "Globalization, Information Technology, and Conflict in the Second and Third Worlds: A Critical Review of the Literature." Manuscript for the Rockefeller Brothers Fund.

Wiseman, John A. 1990. *Democracy in Black Africa: Survival and Renewal.* New York: Paragon House.

Wood, Adrian. 1995. "How Trade Hurts the Unskilled Worker." *Journal of Economic Perspectives,* vol. 9, no. 3: 57–81.

Wood, Brian. 1988. "Trade Union Organization and the Working Class." In Colin Stoneman, ed., *Zimbabwe's Prospects*. London: Macmillan.

Woodward, Peter. 1994. "Democracy and Economy in Africa: The Optimists and the Pessimists." *Democratization*, vol. 1.

World Bank. 1997. *World Development Indicators, 1997*. Washington, DC: World Bank.

———. 1997. *Global Development Finance*. Washington, DC: World Bank.

———. 1996. *Global Economic Prospects and the Developing Countries*. Washington, DC: World Bank.

———. 1996. *World Development Report, 1996*. New York: Oxford University Press for the World Bank.

———. 1995. *African Development Indicators, 1994–95*. Washington, DC: World Bank.

———. 1995. *A Continent in Transition: Sub-Saharan Africa in the Mid–1990s*. Washington, DC: World Bank.

———. 1995. *Global Economic Prospects and the Developing Countries*. Washington, DC: World Bank.

———. 1995. *Workers in an Integrating World: World Development Report, 1995*. New York: Oxford University Press.

———. 1995. *World Development Report, 1995*. New York: Oxford University Press.

———. 1994. *Adjustment in Africa: Reforms, Results, and the Road Ahead*. Washington, DC: World Bank.

———. 1993. *The East Asian Miracle: Economic Growth and Public Policy*. Washington, DC: World Bank.

———. 1993. *World Development Report, 1993*. New York: Oxford University Press for the World Bank.

———. 1992. *Governance and Development*. Washington, DC: World Bank.

———. 1992. *Mauritius: Expanding Horizons*. Washington, DC: World Bank.

———. 1992. *World Development Report, 1992*. Washington, DC: World Bank.

———. 1991. *Namibia: Poverty Alleviation with Sustainable Growth*. Washington, DC: World Bank.

———. 1989. *Mauritius: Managing Success*. Washington, DC: World Bank.

———. 1989. *Sub-Saharan Africa: From Crisis to Sustainable Development*. Washington, DC: World Bank.

———. 1988. *World Development Report, 1988*. New York: Oxford University Press.

———. 1981. *Accelerated Development in Sub-Saharan Africa*. Washington, DC: World Bank.

———. 1964–1972. *Mauritius: Country Economic Memorandum*. Washington, DC: World Bank.

Wraith, R. E., and E. Simpkins. 1963. *Corruption in Developing Countries*. London: Allen & Unwin.

Wunsch, J. S., and Dele Olowu. 1990. *The Failure of the Centralized State: Institutions and Self-Governance in Africa*. Boulder, CO: Westview Press.

Yates, Douglas. 1997. "Oil and the Franco-American Rivalry in Africa." Paper presented at the Conference of the Groupe de Recherches sur l'Afrique Francophone, Centre d'Etude d'Afrique Noire, Bordeaux, France, May 22–24.

Yeats, Alexander J. 1990. "On the Accuracy of Economic Observations: Do Sub-Saharan Countries' Trade Statistics Mean Anything?" *World Economic Review*, vol. 2, no. 4: 135–156.

Yeats, Alexander J., Azita Amjadi, Ulrish Reincke, and Francis Ng. 1996. "Did

External Barriers Cause the Marginalization of Sub-Saharan Africa in World Trade?" World Bank Policy Research Working Paper No. 1586. Washington, DC: World Bank.

Young, Crawford. 1997. "Permanent Transition and Changing Conjuncture: Dilemmas of Democracy in Nigeria in Comparative Perspective." In Beckett and Young, eds., *Dilemmas of Democracy.*

———. 1996. "Africa: An Interim Balance Sheet." *Journal of Democracy,* vol. 7, no. 3 (July): 53–68.

———. 1994. *The African Colonial State in Comparative Perspective.* New Haven, CT: Yale University Press.

———. 1994. "Democratization in Africa: The Contradictions of a Political Imperative." In Widner, ed., *Economic Change,* pp. 230–250.

———. 1993. *The Rising Tide of Cultural Pluralism: The Nation-State at Bay?* Madison: University of Wisconsin Press.

———. 1986. "Nationalism, Ethnicity, and Class in Africa: A Retrospective." *Cahiers d' Etudes Africaines,* vol. 103, no. 26: 421–495.

———. 1982. *Ideology and Development in Africa.* New Haven, CT: Yale University Press.

———. 1979. "The State and the Small Urban Center in Africa." In Aidan Southall, ed., *Small Urban Centers in Rural Development in Africa,* pp. 313–333. Madison: African Studies Program, University of Wisconsin-Madison.

———. 1976. *The Politics of Cultural Pluralism.* Madison: University of Wisconsin Press.

———. 1970. "Decolonization in Africa." In L. H. Gann and Peter Duignan, eds., *Colonialism in Africa, 1870–1960: The History and Politics of Colonialism, 1914–1960.* Cambridge, England: Cambridge University Press.

Young, Crawford, and Thomas Turner. 1985. *The Rise and Decline of the Zairian State.* Madison: University of Wisconsin Press.

Zartman, I. William, ed. 1997. *Governance as Conflict Management.* Washington, DC: Brookings Institution.

———. 1995. *Collapsed States: The Disintegration and Restoration of Legitimate Authority.* Boulder, CO: Lynne Rienner Publishers.

———. 1989. *Ripe for Resolution: Conflict and Intervention in Africa.* Rev. ed. New York: Oxford University Press.

ZCTU (Zimbabwe Congress of Trade Unions). 1996. *Beyond ESAP: Framework for a Long-Term Development Strategy in Zimbabwe Beyond the Economic Structural Adjustment Programme (ESAP).* Harare: ZCTU.

———. 1995. "ZCTU Report on Competition Bill, 1995." June.

Zeleza, P. 1997. *Manufacturing African Studies and Crisis.* Dakar, Senegal: CODESRIA Books.

Zolberg, Aristide R. 1983. "The Formation of New States as a Refugee-Generating Process." *Annals of the American Academy of Political and Social Science,* vol. 467 (May).

Zuccarelli, François. 1988. *La vie politique sénégalaise.* Paris: Publications du CHEAM.

About the Contributors

Robert H. Bates is Easton professor of the science of government, Harvard University. He has written extensively on comparative politics and on Africa's political economy and is coeditor of *Africa and the Disciplines* and *Open Economy Politics* (1997).

Gretchen Bauer is assistant professor of political science and international relations, University of Delaware. She is the author of *Labor and Democracy in Namibia, 1971–1996* (1998).

Linda J. Beck is assistant professor of political science, Barnard College, Columbia University. Her recent publications include "Patrimonial Democrats: Incremental Reform and Obstacles to the Consolidation of Democracy in Senegal." She is currently writing a book on cultural pluralism and political reform in Senegal.

E. Gyimah-Boadi has published extensively on Ghanaian politics and contemporary democratization in Africa. He has recently been a research associate of the International Forum for Democratic Studies, Washington, D.C., and of the Institute of Economic Affairs in Ghana.

Michael Bratton is professor of political science and African studies at Michigan State University. He is coauthor of *Democratic Experiments in Africa* and coeditor of *Governance and Politics in Africa* (1992). Among other topics, his current research concerns state and civil society in South Africa.

Deborah Brautigam is associate professor, School of International

Service, American University, Washington, D.C. Her publications include "Institutions, Economic Policy, and Democratic Consolidation in Mauritius," "Governance, Economy, and Foreign Aid," and "Foreign Aid and the Export of Ideas."

John W. Harbeson is professor of political science at the Graduate School and University Center and at City College at the City University of New York. He has published extensively on the military in African politics, Ethiopian politics, and state and civil society in Africa.

Jeffrey Herbst is professor of politics and international affairs, Woodrow Wilson School, Princeton University. He has written on the politics of political and economic reform in Africa, and state failure and consolidation in Africa.

Goran Hyden is professor of political science, University of Florida. He has written on politics and development, and governance and constitutional reform in Africa. He is coeditor of a forthcoming book on "Constitution-Making in Africa: Lessons from the Second Liberation."

Richard Joseph is Asa G. Candler professor of political science, Emory University. He is a former Fellow of the Carter Center and has written on the politics of Cameroon and Nigeria and on democratization in Africa.

Timothy Longman is assistant professor of political science and African studies, Vassar College. He has written on religion and politics, and on ethnicity and ethnic violence in Rwanda, Burundi, and Congo (Zaire). He is currently writing a study of Christian churches and genocide in Rwanda.

Bruce A. Magnusson has been a visiting assistant professor of politics at Whitman College (1997–98). He completed his dissertation in 1997 on "The Politics of Democratic Regime Legitimation in Benin: Institutions, Social Policy, and Security," and is currently examining internal security in the context of democratic transitions.

Thandika Mkandawire is director of the United Nations Research Institute for Social Development (UNRISD). He formerly served as the Executive Director of the Council for the Development of Economic and Social Research in Africa (CODESRIA) and has specialized in African political economy.

Dele Olowu is professor of public administration and local government, Obafemi Awolowo University, Nigeria. He is currently a Senior Fellow at the Institute of Social Studies, The Hague, and has written extensively on public administration, African governance, and local government.

Adebayo Olukoshi is associate research professor, Nigerian Institute of International Affairs, and senior research fellow and research programme coordinator, Nordic Africa Institute, Uppsala. His recent publications include *Challenges to the Nation-State in Africa* (1996) and *The Politics of Opposition in Contemporary Africa* (1998).

Marina Ottaway is senior associate and codirector, the Democracy Project, Carnegie Endowment for International Peace, and adjunct professor of African studies, School for Advanced International Studies, Johns Hopkins University. She has written on the political evolution of southern Africa and the Horn, problems of democratic transformation in Africa, and elections in post-conflict societies.

Daniel N. Posner is assistant professor of political science, University of California, Los Angeles. His publications include "Malawi's New Dawn" and "Social Capital: Explaining Its Origins and Effects on Governmental Performance" (with Charles Boix).

Donald Rothchild is professor of political science, University of California, Davis. He is the author of *Managing Ethnic Conflict in Africa: Pressures and Incentives for Cooperation* (1997), coauthor of *Sovereignty as Responsibility: Conflict Management in Africa* (1996), and coeditor of *The International Spread of Ethnic Conflict: Fear, Diffusion, and Escalation* (1998).

Richard L. Sklar is professor emeritus of political science, University of California, Los Angeles. He has written extensively on African politics, including Nigerian politics, and on issues of class, democracy, and political economy.

Scott D. Taylor is Gwendolyn Carter Lecturer in comparative and African politics, Smith College. He conducted doctoral research in Zambia and Zimbabwe, focusing on the role of business associations in political and economic liberalization.

Nicolas van de Walle is associate professor of political science, Michigan State University. His research has focused on the dynamics of economic and political reform. He is the coauthor of *Democratic Experiments in Africa: Regime Transitions in Comparative Perspective* (1997) and is preparing a book on the politics of macroeconomic management in Africa.

Crawford Young is Rupert Emerson and H. Edwin Young professor of political science, University of Wisconsin–Madison. He has taught and conducted research in Uganda, Congo, and Senegal. Among his many publications are *The Politics of Cultural Pluralism* (1976) and *The African Colonial State in Comparative Perspective* (1994).

INDEX

ABOUT THE BOOK

This seminal volume explores the most important dimensions of state formation and erosion, social conflict, and the gains and setbacks in democratization in contemporary Africa. The result of nearly a decade of research, reflection, and collegial interaction, the collection delineates the dominant patterns of political restructuring since the upheavals of the early 1990s.

Richard Joseph is Asa G. Candler Professor of Political Science at Emory University. His numerous publications include *Democracy and Prebendal Politics in Nigeria: The Rise and Fall of the Second Republic*.